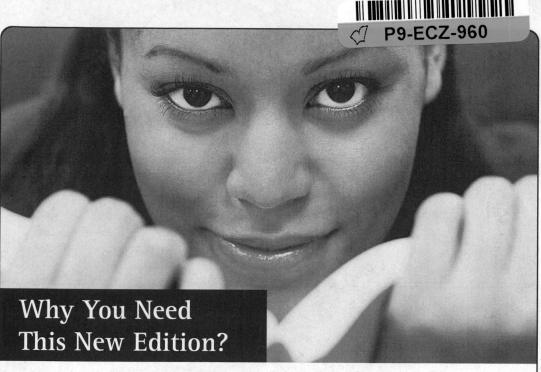

# Why You Need This New Edition?

If you are wondering why you should add this new edition of *An Introduction to Literature* to your personal library, here are ten good reasons:

**1** This book contains **works of literature from the ancient Greeks up to the present**, which is to say that it contains powerful explorations of what it means to be a human being.

**2** **New Chapter 1, "College Readiness: How to Respond to Stories, Poems, and Plays"** provides a brief guide to help you respond thoughtfully to what you have read. Among its features are examples of student annotations and checklists for responding to each genre.

**3** **A wealth of new stories** have been added including Annie Proulx's tall tale called "The Blood Bay," Ron Wallace's "Worry," Tobias Wolff's "Hunters in the Snow" and "Bullet in the Brain," and Jesse Lee Kercheval's "Carpathia."

**4** You'll find expanded coverage of the elements of fiction, **with new separate chapters on plot, character, setting, and theme.**

**5** **A new chapter on graphic fiction** includes four selections and gives guidance as to how to understand the art of pictorial story-telling.

**6** **Twenty-four poems are new to this edition** including such classics as Elizabeth Barrett Browning's "How do I love thee?" and Dylan Thomas's "Fern Hill," and also some very recent poems, such as Kay Ryan's "Turtle."

**7** **A new one-act play, Samuel Beckett's** *Krapp's Last Tape,* introduces you to the work of a great contemporary dramatist.

**8** **A new casebook on Arthur Miller's** *Death of a Salesman* gives you stimulating outside sources that you can draw on if you are required to write a research paper.

**9** **A new appendix on plagiarism provides a quiz—with answers—**so that you can test yourself and immediately (and entertainingly) see the degree to which you understand your academic responsibilities.

**10** **The appendix on documentation** reflects all of the latest MLA guidelines to ensure your documentation is up to date.

SIXTEENTH EDITION

# An Introduction to Literature

## Fiction, Poetry, and Drama

### Sylvan Barnet
*Tufts University*

### William Burto
*University of Massachusetts at Lowell*

### William E. Cain
*Wellesley College*

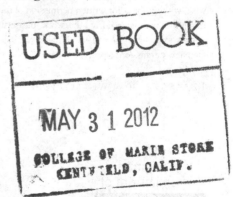

**Longman**

Boston   Columbus   Indianapolis   New York   San Francisco   Upper Saddle River
Amsterdam   Cape Town   Dubai   London   Madrid   Milan   Munich   Paris   Montreal   Toronto
Delhi   Mexico City   Sao Paulo   Sydney   Hong Kong   Seoul   Singapore   Taipei   Tokyo

Editor-in-Chief: Joseph Terry
Senior Development Editor: Katharine Glynn
Senior Supplements Editor: Donna Campion
Senior Media Producer: Stefanie Liebman
Executive Marketing Manager: Joyce Nilsen
Production Manager: Eric Jorgensen
Project Coordination, Text Design, and Electronic Page Makeup: Nesbitt Graphics, Inc.
Cover Design Manager: John Callahan
Cover Image: ©2010 C. Herscovici, London/Artists Rights Society (ARS), New York
Visual Researcher: Rona Tuccillo
Senior Manufacturing Buyer: Dennis J. Para
Printer and Binder: Quebecor World/Taunton
Cover Printer: Lehigh Phoenix

For permission to use copyrighted material, grateful acknowledgment is made to the copyright holders on pp. 1479–1492, which are hereby made part of this copyright page.

Library of Congress Cataloging-in-Publication Data

An introduction to literature : fiction, poetry, and drama / [edited by]
Sylvan Barnet, William Burto, William E. Cain. — 16th ed.
    p. cm.
Includes bibliographical references and index.
  ISBN 978-0-205-63309-8
  1. Literature—Collections.  I. Barnet, Sylvan. II. Burto, William. III. Cain, William E., 1952- IV. Title.
PN6014.I57 2010
808—dc22

                                                                    2010018274

Copyright © 2011, © 2008, © 2006 by Sylvan Barnet, William Burto, William E. Cain.

1 2 3 4 5 6 7 8 9 10—QWT—13 12 11 10

Longman is an imprint of

www.pearsonhighered.com

ISBN-13: 978-0-205-63309-8
ISBN-10: 0-205-63309-9

# CONTENTS

## PART I

# Reading, Thinking, and Writing Critically About Literature 1

## 3  The Pleasures of Reading—and of Writing Arguments About Literature    46

## 4  More About Writing About Literature: From Idea to Essay    65

**PART II**

# Fiction   97

## 15   A Collection of Short Fiction   363

**PART III**

# Poetry  539

## 16  Approaching Poetry: Responding in Writing  541

## 17  Narrative Poetry  553

## 18  Lyric Poetry  569

Contents

## 24    Students Writing About Poems    690

## 25    Poets at Work    719

PART IV

# Drama    837

## 29   How to Read a Play    839

## 30   Tragedy    905

Contents

# 31 Comedy   1112

# 32 Students Writing About Plays   1172

# 33 A Casebook on *Death of a Salesman*   1199

## 34 Seven Additional Plays   1280

## PART V

# Critical Approaches   1421

## 35 Critical Approaches: The Nature of Criticism   1422

# A Guide to MyLiteratureLab

Visit *MyLiteratureLab.com* to access a wealth of online writing and research aids. There is an abundant array of multimedia resources in MyLiteratureLab that brings literature to life by enriching the authors and selections you will study.

## Fiction

**James Baldwin**   About the Author, Bibliography, Critical Archive
*Sonny's Blues*: Longman Lecture

**Toni Cade Bambara**   About the Author
*The Lesson*: Longman Lecture

**Ambrose Bierce**   About the Author
*An Occurrence at Owl Creek Bridge*: Video Essay, Critical Essay

**T. Coraghessan Boyle**   About the Author
*Greasy Lake*: Critical Essay

**Raymond Carver**   About the Author, Bibliography, Critical Essay
*Cathedral*: Longman Lecture

**Willa Cather**   About the Author/Photos, Bibliography, Critical Archive
*Paul's Case*: Video, Audio, Critical Essay

**Anton Chekhov**   About the Author, Bibliography, Critical Archive

**Kate Chopin**   About the Author, Bibliography, Critical Archive
*Désirée's Baby*: Longman Lecture
*The Storm*: Longman Lecture, Interactive Reading, Student Paper, Critical Essay

*The Story of an Hour*: Longman Lecture

**Joseph Conrad**   About the Author
*Heart of Darkness*: Longman Lecture

**William Faulkner**   About the Author/Photos, Bibliography, Critical Archive
*Barn Burning*: Video (2), Audio (2), Critical Essay (2)
*A Rose for Emily*: Critical Essay

**F. Scott Fitzgerald**   About the Author

**Charlotte Perkins Gilman**   About the Author, Bibliography, Critical Archive
*The Yellow Wallpaper*: Critical Essay

**Nathaniel Hawthorne**   About the Author, Bibliography, Critical Archive
*Young Goodman Brown*: Longman Lecture

**Ernest Hemingway**   About the Author, Bibliography, Critical Archive
*A Clean Well-Lighted Place*: Critical Essay

**Zora Neale Hurston**
*Sweat*: Longman Lecture, Interactive Reading

**Shirley Jackson**   About the Author
*The Lottery*: Interactive Reading, Critical Essay

# Poetry

**Seamus Heaney**   About the Author
*Digging*: Longman Lecture

**Gerard Manley Hopkins**   About the Author/Photos
*Pied Beauty*: Audio, Critical Essay

**A. E. Housman**   About the Author, Bibliography, Critical Archive
*To an Athlete Dying Young*: Critical Essay

**Langston Hughes**   About the Author
*Harlem*: Audio
*The Weary Blues*: Longman Lectures

**John Keats**   About the Author/Photos, Bibliography, Critical Archive
*Bright star!*: Longman Lecture
*Ode on a Grecian Urn*: Audio, Student Paper

**X. J. Kennedy**   *For Allen Ginsburg,* Video
*In a Prominent Bar in Seacacus One Day,* Video
*Nude Descending a Staircase,* Video
*Snowflake Souffle,* Video

**Edna St. Vincent Millay**   About the Author/Photos
*Love is not all*: Audio, Longman Lecture
*What lips my lips have kissed, and where, and why*: Video, Student Paper

**Wilfred Owen**   About the Author
*Dulce et Decorum Est*: Critical Reading, Interactive Reading, Longman Lecture

**Dorothy Parker**   About the Author/Photos
*Résumé*: Video

**Sylvia Plath**   About the Author, Bibliography, Critical Archive
*Lady Lazarus*: Longman Lecture
*Metaphors*: Critical Essay, Interactive Reading

**Adrienne Rich**   About the Author, Bibliography, Critical Archive

**Edwin Arlington Robinson**   About the Author
*Richard Cory*: Longman Lecture, Critical Essay

**Theodore Roethke**   About the Author
*Root Cellar*: Interactive Reading, Critical Essay

**Mary Jo Salter**   About the Author
*Welcome to Hiroshima*: Longman Lecture

**William Shakespeare**   About the Author/Photos, Bibliography, Critical Archive
*Let me not to the marriage of true minds*: Critical Essay
*Shall I Compare Thee to a Summer's Day?*: Audio, Critical Essay (2), Student Paper
*That time of year thou mayst in me behold*: Longman Lecture, Interactive Reading

**Percy Bysshe Shelley**   About the Author
*Ozymandias*: Audio

**Wallace Stevens**   About the Author, Bibliography, Critical Archive
*Anecdote of the Jar*: Interactive Reading

**Lord Alfred Tennyson**   About the Author/Photos, Bibliography, Critical Archive

*The Splendor falls on castle walls*: Audio

**Dylan Thomas**   About the Author
*Do not go gentle into that good night*: Critical Essay

**Walt Whitman**   About the Author, Bibliography, Critical Archive
*Cavalry Crossing a Ford*: Interactive Reading

**Richard Wilbur**   About the Author
*Cold War Poetry*: Critical Essay

**William Wordsworth**   About the Author, Bibliography, Critical Archive

*Composed Upon Westminster Bridge*: Audio
*A Slumber Did My Spirit Seal*: Critical Essay
*The Wild Swans at Coole*, Audio

**William Butler Yeats**   About the Author/Photos, Bibliography, Critical Archive
*The Lake Isle of Innisfree*: Longman Lecture, Critical Essay
*Leda and the Swan*: Critical Essay
*Who Goes with Fergus?*: Interactive Reading

# Drama

**Susan Glaspell**   About the Author, Bibliography, Critical Archive
*Trifles*: Longman Lecture

**Lorraine Hansberry**   About the Author
*A Raisin in the Sun*: Longman Lecture

**David Hwang**   About the Author, Bibliography, Critical Archive

**Henrik Ibsen**   About the Author, Bibliography, Critical Archive
*A Doll's House*: Longman Lecture

**Arthur Miller**   About the Author
*Death of a Salesman*, Longman Lecture

**William Shakespeare**   About the Author/Photos, Bibliography, Critical Archive

*Hamlet*: Longman Lecture, Critical Essay, Full-length film with Olivier
*A Midsummer Night's Dream*: Longman Lecture, Critical Essay
*Othello, the Moor of Venice*: Audio, Critical Essay, Interactive Reading, Student Paper, Video, Full-length film

**Sophocles**   About the Author, Bibliography, Critical Archive
*Antigone*: Longman Lecture, Full-length film
*Oedipus the King*: Longman Lecture, Full-length film

**Tennessee Williams**   About the Author, Bibliography, Critical Archive

**August Wilson**   About the Author, Bibliography, Critical Archive
*Fences*: Longman Lecture

# Writers on Writing

Kim Addonizio
Aliki Barnstone
Jay Boyer
Andrea Hollander Budy
Janet Burroway
Ron Carlson
Rita Dove
Stephen Dunn
Bart Edelman
Albert Garcia
John Hershman
Jeff Knorr

Ruth Ellen Kocher
Craig Lesley
Valerie Miner
Stephen Minot
Todd Pierce
Alberto Ríos
Tim Schell
Virgil Suarez
Diane Thiel
C.K. Williams
Richard Yañez

# Interactive Timeline

Timeline Part 1: 20,000 B.C. to
    1600 A.D
Timeline Part 2: 1601 A.D. to
    1775 A.D.
Timeline Part 3: 1776 A.D. to
    1860 A.D.

Timeline Part 4: 1861 A.D. to
    1919 A.D.
Timeline Part 5: 1920 A.D. to
    1959 A.D.
Timeline Part 6: 1960 A.D. to
    2008 A.D.

# Literature eAnthology

Two hundred additional selections are available with this interactive eAnthology, which is organized by genre and alphabetized within each genre. In addition to providing more selections, the eAnthology is an excellent study aid: students can search, highlight, and take notes.

*An Introduction to Literature,* Sixteenth Edition, begins with four introductory chapters concerned with writing, reading, and thinking. The book then offers an anthology arranged by genre (stories, poems, plays). This genre anthology, like the introductory chapters, includes abundant material to help students to become active readers and careful, engaged writers.

# New to This Edition

- **New Chapter 1, "College Readiness: How to Respond to Stories, Poems, and Plays,"** offers a brief but thorough guide to help students respond to what they have read. Among its features are examples of student annotations and checklists for responding to each genre.
- The revised second chapter emphasizes not only **literature as a performance** in words, but also **literature as a journey** (a walk in the writer's shoes).
- **A wealth of new stories have been added** including Annie Proulx's tall tale called "The Blood Bay," Ron Wallace's "Worry," and Jesse Lee Kercheval's "Carpathia."
- In addition to Flannery O'Connor, **Tobias Wolff** is now presented in depth (four stories, and a selection of his remarks about fiction).
- The fiction section offers expanded coverage of the elements with new separate chapters on plot, character, setting, and theme.
- **A new chapter on graphic fiction** helps students to understand the art of pictorial story telling.
- **Twenty-four new poems.** We have added such favorites as Elizabeth Barrett Browning's "How do I love thee?" and Dylan Thomas's "Fern Hill," and also some very recent poems, such as Kay Ryan's "Turtle." We have also added a few older poems (for instance Stephen Duck's "On Mites") that may well be unfamiliar even to many experienced instructors.
- **A new one-act play, Samuel Beckett's *Krapp's Last Tape,*** now increases the number of short plays—plays that can be fully discussed and perhaps even performed within a single meeting—to five. The eight full-length plays continue to offer instructors a wide range of choices.

- **A new casebook on Arthur Miller's *Death of a Salesman*** includes not only Miller's well-known essay on tragedy but also a generous selection from his later remarks, as well as reviews of early and recent productions.
- **A new appendix on plagiarism provides a quiz—with answers**—so that students can test themselves and immediately (and entertainingly) see the degree to which they understand their academic responsibilities.
- **The appendix on documentation has been revised in accordance with the newest MLA guidelines.**

# About the Literature

- **Canonical works.** The book contains 70 stories, including four pieces of graphic fiction, 255 poems, and 14 plays. About a third of the selections are canonical works that for many decades—in some cases even centuries—have given readers great pleasure. Writers such as Sophocles, Shakespeare, Walt Whitman, and Emily Dickinson have stood the test of time, including the test of today's students enrolled in introductory courses in literature and composition. No editor and no instructor need apologize for asking students to read, think, and write about these authors. In "Tradition and the Individual Talent," T. S. Eliot makes the point well: "Someone said, 'The dead writers are remote from us because we know so much more than they did.' Precisely, and they are that which we know."
- **A new canon.** The remaining two-thirds of the selections are contemporary material, some of it by writers who established their reputations several decades ago (for instance, John Updike and Alice Walker), but much of it by writers who are still young (for instance, Amy Tan and Lorrie Moore). We have tried to read widely in today's writing, and we think we have found important new stories, poems, and plays worth the time of busy students and busy instructors. Again, no editor and no instructor need apologize for asking students to study and take pleasure in these authors and to see how they often return us to the authors of the past, the authors whose place in the canon is established and secure.
- **In-depth representation and critical perspectives.** We represent three fiction writers in depth—Flannery O'Connor (two stories and several of her important comments about fiction), Kate Chopin (four stories), and Tobias Wolff (four stories and important comments about fiction). Among the poets, we represent in depth Emily Dickinson (poems and letters), Robert Frost (poems and comments on poetry), and Langston Hughes (poems and comments on poetry). Of the dramatists, we give two plays by Sophocles and two by Shakespeare; we also include relevant comments by playwrights on their work—for instance, Arthur Miller

on tragedy. We think these features of the book are especially valuable and that the kinds of writing assignments we have developed—assignments that have emerged from our experiences in the classroom—will interest students and be productive for them.

- **Plays in contexts.** Several of the plays are accompanied by stimulating comments by their authors, giving students a look behind the scenes.

# Writing About Literature

Instructors know that one of the best ways to become an active reader is to read with a pencil in hand—that is, to annotate a text, to make jottings in a journal, and ultimately to draft and revise essays. We think that students, too, will find themselves saying of their experiences with literature what the philosopher Arthur C. Danto said about his experience with works of art:

> I get a lot more out of art, now that I am writing about it, than I ever did before. I think what is true of me must be true of everyone, that until one tries to write about it, the work of art remains a sort of aesthetic blur. . . . I think in a way everyone might benefit from becoming a critic in his or her own right. After seeing the work, write about it. You cannot be satisfied for very long in simply putting down what you felt. You have to go further.

—*EMBODIED MEANINGS* (1994)

To this end, we have included the following:

- **Samples of annotated pages, entries in journals, and 26 essays by students.** To prompt students to respond to the works of literature in this book and then to think and write critically about their responses, we include not only a chapter devoted to the concepts of getting ideas and revising them by means of writing (Chapter 3), but also examples of annotated pages, entries in journals, and twenty-six essays by students (some with the student's preliminary journal entries, some with our marginal comments, some with our analytic comments appended to the essays, and some with questions that ask the reader to evaluate the strengths or weaknesses of the essays).
- **Critical thinking questions.** About a third of the selections in the book are equipped with questions intended to help draw attention to matters that deserve careful thinking. Most of these questions are in effect invitations to write argumentative essays, not mere paragraphs or descriptions.
- **Material about argument.** In addition to furnishing "Your Turn" questions that raise issues for argument, our apparatus emphasizes that students, in their essays, must advance a thesis and support it

with evidence, rather than merely provide reports of their responses.

- **Critical perspectives.** A chapter on "Critical Approaches," sketch-
  ing such approaches as reader-response criticism and the New
  Historicism, will help students develop a repertoire of points of
  view.
- **Glossary.** Literary terms, defined and discussed throughout the
  text, are concisely defined in a convenient glossary at the end of
  the book, with page references to fuller discussions.
- **Manuscript form.** An appendix includes pages on the format of
  an essay—for example, margins, capitalization in a title, and so on.
- **Research and Internet resources.** An Appendix gives information about manuscript form and documenting sources in MLA style.

A complete list of available student and instructor resources begins on the
following page.

# Resources for Students and Instructors

## MYLITERATURELAB

**MyLiteratureLab** is a dynamic and comprehensive Web site that engages students as it helps to foster an understanding of literature and literary writing and research skills. The Resource area contains instructional material, multimedia tutorials, and exercises for a wide array of literature, writing, grammar, and research topics. Some of the more popular features include:

- **Longman Lectures**
  Featuring our renowned authors, including Sylvan Barnet, these engaging, illustrated audio lectures provide students with suggestions on how to read, analyze, and write about literature. Each lecture includes a reading of an influential or illustrative work, cultural/historical context for interpreting the featured author's work, and insights for writing. All the lectures are illustrated with evocative photos, pictures, and images.

- **eAnthology**
  - Two hundred additional selections are available with this Interactive eAnthology, which is organized by genre and alphabetized within each genre.
  - In addition to providing more selections, the eAnthology is an excellent study aid: students can search, highlight, and take notes.

- **Full-length films**
  - Feature-length films from Films for the Humanities and Sciences help students stay engaged with their course material.

- **Interactive Readings**
  - Interactive readings provide students with annotated readings and questions to guide analysis.

- **Gradebook**
  - You can assign pre- and post-diagnostics to help students pinpoint their needs and track their progress.
  - Export MyLiteratureLab grades to a gradebook you already use or include any that you've created in a course management system.

# PRINT SUPPLEMENTS

*Screening Shakespeare: Understanding The Plays Through Film,* Second Edition, by Michael Greer and Toby Widdicombe (Student / 0-205-63950-X)

This brief guide is an accessible introduction to Shakespeare's most popular plays on film. It provides analytical tools and suggestions for responding to films, with discussion questions and writing prompts that move from formal analysis to considerations of historical and cultural contexts.

*Evaluating a Performance,* by Michael Greenwald (Student/ 0-321-09541-3)

Designed to look like a Playbill, this is the perfect tool for the student assigned to review a local theater production. This supplement offers students a convenient place to record their evaluation of the staging, acting, costuming, set design, etc. Useful tips and suggestions of things to consider when evaluating a production are included.

*Responding to Literature: A Writer's Journal,* by Daniel Kline (Student/ 0-321-09542-1)

This spiral-bound journal provides students with their own personal space for recording their reactions to the literature they read. Guided writing prompts, suggested writing assignments, and overviews of literary terms provide students with the tools—and ideas—they need for responding to fiction, poetry, and drama.

*Analyzing Literature,* Second Edition, by Sharon James McGee (Student/ 0-321-09338-0)

This brief supplement provides critical reading strategies, writing advice, and sample student papers to help students interpret and discuss literary works in a variety of genres. Suggestions for collaborative activities and online research on literary topics are also featured, as well as numerous exercises and writing assignments.

*Glossary of Literary and Critical Terms,* by Heidi L. M. Jacobs (Student/ 0-321-12691-2)

*The Glossary of Literary and Critical Terms* is a quick, reliable and portable resource for students of Literature and Creative Writing. This easy-to-use glossary includes definitions, explanations, and examples for over 100 literary and critical terms which students commonly encounter in their reading or hear in their lectures and class discussions. In addition to basic terms related to form and genre, the glossary also includes terms and explanations related to literary history, criticism, and theory.

*Literature Timeline,* by Heidi L. M. Jacobs (Student / 0-321-14315-9)

This laminated four-page timeline provides students with a chronological overview of the major literary works throughout history. In addition, the timeline also lists major sociocultural and political events to provide students with historical and contextual insights into the impact historical events have had on writers and their works and vice versa.

*What Every Student Should Know About . . .* Series
A collection of guide books designed to help students with specific topics that are important in a number of different college courses. Instructors can package any one of these booklets with their Pearson textbook for no additional charge, or the booklets can be purchased separately.

- Avoiding Plagiarism (ISBN 0-321-44689-5)
- Citing Sources with MLA Documentation: Update Edtion (ISBN 0-205-71511-7)
- Creating Portfolios (ISBN 0-205-57250-2)
- Procrastination (ISBN 0-205-58211-7)
- Researching Online (ISBN 0-321-44531-7)
- Practicing Peer Review (ISBN 0-321-44848-0)
- Preparing Effective Oral Presentations (ISBN 0-205-50545-7)
- Study Skills (ISBN 0-321-44736-0)

*A Student's Guide to Getting Published,* by Susan Swartwout and Jim Elledge (Student/0-321-11779-4)
This clear and concise "how-to" guide takes writers of all genres through the process of publishing their work—including the considerations of submission and contracts, how to research markets, the processes of self-editing and being edited, how to produce a "well-wrought manuscript," among other useful and practical information. The manual addresses first-submission concerns as well as addressing the entire publishing process and includes practical advice from editors and publishers on what industry professionals expect from a writer.

*Journal for Creative Writing,* by Sibyl Johnston (Student/ 0-321-09540-5)
This spiral-bound journal provides students with plenty of space for writing. Helpful writing prompts and strategies are included as well as guidelines for participating in a workshop.

*A Workshop Guide for Creative Writing,* by Sibyl Johnston (Student/ 0-321-09539-1)

This laminated reference offers suggestions/tips for students to keep in mind in a workshop situation—both as a participant and presenter. Blank space is provided for students to record additional guidelines provided by their instructor.

## DICTIONARIES AND OTHER REFERENCES

*Merriam-Webster's Reader's Handbook: Your Complete Guide to Literary Terms* (Student/ 0-321-10541-9)

Includes nearly 2,000 entries including Greek and Latin terminology, descriptions for every major genre, style, and era of writing and assured authority from the combined resources of Merriam-Webster and Encyclopedia Britannica.

*The New American Webster Handy College Dictionary* (Student/ 0-451-18166-2)
This superior paperback reference text contains more than 100,000 entries, including clear and concise definitions, selected etymologies, current phrases, slang, abbreviations, and scientific terms.

**Merriam-Webster Collegiate Dictionary with CD-ROM** (ISBN 0-877-79809-5)
This new edition of America's best-selling hardcover dictionary sets the standard with: a fully revised print edition featuring more than 225,000 definitions; more than 10,000 new words and meanings; Win/Mac CD-ROM for local electronic access; free one year subscription to Collegiate Web site: www.Merriam-WebsterCollegiate.com.

*The Oxford American Desk Dictionary and Thesaurus,* Second Edition (ISBN 0-425-18068-9)
From the Oxford University Press and Berkley Publishing Group comes this one-of-a-kind reference book that combines both of the essential language tools—dictionary and thesaurus—in a single, integrated A-to-Z volume. The 1,024 page book offers more than 150,000 entries, definitions, and synonyms so you can find the right word every time, as well as appendices of valuable quick-reference information including: signs and symbols, weights and measures, presidents of the U. S., U. S. states and capitals, and more.

*The Oxford Essential Thesaurus* (ISBN 0-425-16421-7)
From Oxford University Press, renowned for quality educational and reference works, comes this concise, easy-to-use thesaurus—the essential tool for finding just the right word for every occasion. The 528-page book includes 175,000 synonyms in a simple A-to-Z format, more than 10,000 entries, extensive word choices, example sentences and phrases, and guidance on usage, punctuation, and more in exclusive "Writers Toolkit."

## PENGUIN DISCOUNT NOVEL PROGRAM

In cooperation with Penguin Group U. S. A., Longman is proud to offer a variety of Penguin paperbacks at a significant discount when packaged with any Longman title. Excellent additions to any literature course, Penguin titles give students the opportunity to explore contemporary and classical fiction and drama. The available titles include works by authors as diverse as Toni Morrison, Julia Alvarez, Mary Shelley, and Shakespeare.

To review the complete list of titles available, visit the Longman-Penguin Web site: http://www.pearsonhighered.com/penguin.

## VIDEO PROGRAM

For qualified adopters, an impressive selection of videotapes is available to enrich students' experience of literature. One video per 100 students per semester with a limit of three per semester. Contact your Pearson Longman sales consultant for more information.

## INSTRUCTOR SUPPLEMENTS

*Instructor's Manual for Barnet, An Introduction to Literature,* Sixteenth Edition (0-205-77967-0)
An instructor's manual with detailed comments and suggestions for teaching each selection is available. This important resource, prepared by the authors of this volume, also contains references to critical articles and books.

*The Longman Test Bank for Literature,* by Heidi L. M. Jacobs (Instructor / 0-321-14312-4)
This test bank features various objective questions on the major works of fiction, short fiction, poetry, and drama. A versatile and handy resource, this test bank can be used for all quizzing and testing needs.

# ACKNOWLEDGMENTS

We wish to thank the people who have helped us to write this book. For preparation of the sixteenth edition we are deeply indebted to Joe Terry, Katharine Glynn, Eric Jorgensen, and John Callahan at Longman; and to Lois Lombardo, Cathy Harlem, Stephanie Magean, Chuck Gandy, and the design team at Nesbitt Graphics, Inc. For assistance in obtaining permission to reprint copyrighted works, we have relied on Virginia Creeden.

Because their queries have caused us to think second and third thoughts, we know from our own experience the soundness of the advice we give when we tell students that they should submit their drafts to their peers and should pay serious attention to suggested changes. We hope that every author receives the kind of help that we have received.

We are grateful to reviewers of this edition and previous editions: Olga Abella, Eastern Illinois University; Michael Anzelone, Nassau Community College; Dr. Karen Aubrey, Augusta State University; Lillie Bailey, Virginia State University; Arnold J. Bradford, Northern Virginia Community College; Bob Brien, Madison Area Technical College; Carol Ann Britt, San Antonio College; Mark Brosamer, Ohlone College; Mark J. Bruhn, Regis University; Sandra Bryzek, Moraine Valley Community College; Christine Caver, The University of Texas at San Antonio; Vilma Chemers, California State University, Long Beach; Mickie Christensen, San Francisco State University; Anne Cipri, Carlow University; Philip Collington, Niagara University; Nancy Cox, Arkansas Tech University; Tracey Cummings, Lock Haven University of Pennsylvania; Corla Dawson, Missouri Western State College; Michael de Benedictis, Miami-Dade Community College; April M. Dolata, Northwestern CT Community College; Bill Dynes, University of Indianapolis; Gabriel Fagan, La Salle University; Mindy Faines, Gateway Community College; Bart Friedberg, Nassau Community College; Margaret Gardineer, Felician College; Wendy Greenstein, Long Beach City College; George V. Griffith, Chadron State College; Styron Harris, East Tennessee State University; Ruth Harrison, Arkansas Tech University; Mary Hickerson, Southwest State University; Susan Hines, LaSalle University; Kristen Isabelle, Columbia-Greene Community College; Jennifer Jett, Bakersfield College; Susan E. Jones, Palm Beach Atlantic University; Andrea Kaston Tange, Eastern Michigan University; Donald Kummings, University of Wisconsin–Parkside; Lois Leveen, University of California at Los Angeles; Elaine Lomber, Community College of the Finger Lakes; Beverly A. McCabe, John A. Logan College; Linda J. McPherson, Indiana University of

Pennsylvania; Walter S. Minot, Spring Hill College; Lyle W. Morgan, Pittsburg State University; Stacy Mulder, Davenport University; Carlene Murphy, University of Toledo; Lee Newton, Bradley University; Philip F. O'-Mara, Bridgewater College; Leland S. Person, University of Alabama at Birmingham; Trey Philpotts, Arkansas Tech University; Caroline Poor, Wharton County Junior College; Tony Procell, El Paso Community College; Elaine Razzano, Lyndon State College; Christie Rubio, American River College; Patricia Sheehy Colella, Bunker Hill Community College; Kathleen Shumate, Grossmant College; Andrew Silver, Mercer University; Diane Sims, Carlow University; Carolyn Smith Geyer, Augustana College; Barbara L. Stafford, City College of San Francisco; JoAnna Stephens Mink, Minnesota State University; Darlene Sybert, University of Missouri-Columbia; Marcia E. Tannebaum, Nichols College; David Thomson, Henderson State University; Catherine G. Thwing, Pima Community College; William Wilson, San Jose State University; Ann Woodlief, Virginia Commonwealth University; and Xiao-Ming Yang, Ocean County College; and Sue Ziefler, DeAnza College.

Our debt to those whom we have named is deep, but we are still not done with acknowledging our indebtedness. We owe much to the instructors and friends who advised us when we were preparing earlier editions: Judith Leet, Janet Frick, Ken Anderson, Floyd College; Alfred Arteaga, University of California, Berkeley; Rance Baker, San Antonio College; Lois Birky, Illinois Central College; Carol Boyd, Black Hawk College; Lois Bragg, Galludet University; Conrad Carroll, Northern Kentucky University; Robert Coltrane, Lock Haven University; Charles Darling, Greater Hartford Community College; Richard Dietrich, University of South Florida; Gail Duffy, Dean Junior College; Marilyn Edelstein, Santa Clara University; Toni Empringham, El Camino College; Craig Etchison, Glenville State College; Robert Farrell, Housatonic Community College; Elaine Fitzpatrick, Massasoit College; James E. Ford, University of Nebraska–Lincoln; Donna Galati, University of South Dakota; Marvin P. Garrett, University of Cincinnati; Francis B. Hanify, Luzerne County Community College; Blair Hemstock, Keyano College (Canada); Paul Hester, Indian Hills Community College; James L. Johnson, California State University, Fresno; Edwina Jordan, Illinois Central College; Kate Kiefer, Colorado State University; Sandra Lakey, Pennsylvania College of Technology; Wayne P. Lindquist, University of Wisconsin–Eau Claire; Cecilia G. Martyn, Montclair State College; Paul McVeigh, Northern Virginia Community College, Elizabeth Metzger, University of South Florida; William S. Nicholson, Eastern Shore Community College; Stephen O'Neill, Bucks County Community College; Richard Pepp, Massasoit Community College; Betty Jo Hicks Peters, Morehead State University; Frank Perkins, Quincy College; Barbara Pokdowka, Commonwealth College; John C. Presley, Central Virginia Community College; Patricia R. Rochester, University of Southwestern Louisiana; Betty Rhodes, Faulkner State College; Martha Saunders, West Georgia College; Allison Shumsky, Northwestern Michigan College; Isabel B. Stanley, East Tennessee State University; LaVonne Swanson, National

College; Beverly Taylor, University of North Carolina, Chapel Hill; Merle Thompson, North Virginia Community College; Cyrilla Vessey, North Virginia Community College; Mildred White, Oholone College; Margaret Whitt, University of Denver; Betty J. Williams, East Tennessee State University; Donald R. Williams, North Shore Community College; and Donnie Yeilding, Central Texas College.

Our thanks also to the many users of the earlier editions who gave us advice on how and where to make improvements: Linda Bamber, David Cavitch, Robert Cyr, Arthur Friedman, Nancy Grayson, Martha Hicks-Courant, Billie Ingram, Martha Lappen, Judy Maas, Deirdre McDonald, Patricia Meier, Ronald E. Pepin, William Roberts, Claire Seng-Niemoeller, Virginia Shine, and Charles L. Walker.

We are especially grateful for the comments and suggestions offered by the following scholars: Priscilla B. Bellair, Carroll Britch, Don Brunn, Malcolm B. Clark, William C. Clayton (a veteran of over 40 years of teaching at Nassau Community College), Terence A. Dalrymple, Franz Douskey, Gerald Duchovnay, Peter Dumanis, Estelle Easterly, Adam Fischer, Martha Flint, Robert H. Fossum, Gerald Hasham, Richard Henze, Catherine M. Hoff, Grace S. Kehrer, Nancy E. Kensicki, Linda Kraus, Juanita Laing, Vincent J. Liesenfeld, Martha McGowan, John H. Meagher III, Stuart Millner, Edward Anthony Nagel, Peter L. Neff, Robert F. Panara, Ronald E. Pepin, Jane Pierce, Robert M. Post, Kris Rapp, Mark Reynolds, John Richardson, Donald H. Sanborn, Marlene Sebeck, Frank E. Sexton, Peggy Skaggs, David Stuchler, James E. Tamer, Carol Teaff, C. Uejio, Hugh Witemeyer, Manfred Wolf, and Joseph Zaitchik.

Finally, we are also grateful for valuable suggestions made by Barbara Harman, X. J. Kennedy, Carolyn Potts, Marcia Stubbs, Helen Vendler, and Ann Chalmers Watts.

SYLVAN BARNET
WILLIAM BURTO
WILLIAM E. CAIN

We hope that you already enjoy reading literature and that *An Introduction to Literature* will help you enjoy it even more. But as you begin your course this semester with our book, we want to say a little more about why we wrote it, how we believe it can help you, and in what ways we think it can deepen and enrich your pleasure in studying literature.

Throughout the process of writing and rewriting *An Introduction to Literature* we saw ourselves as teachers, offering the kinds of suggestions and strategies that, over many years, we have offered to our students.

As you can tell from a glance at the Table of Contents, *An Introduction to Literature* includes practical advice about reading and responding to literature and writing analytical papers, advice that comes directly from our experience not only as readers and writers but also as teachers. This experience derives from classrooms, from conferences with students, and from assignments we have given, read, responded to, and graded. We have learned from our experiences and have done our best to give you the tools that will help you make yourself a more perceptive reader and a more careful, cogent writer.

Speaking of making and remaking, we are reminded of a short poem by William Butler Yeats, who was a persistent reviser of his work. (You can find three versions of his poem "Leda and the Swan" on pages 724 and 725.)

> The friends that have it I do wrong
> Whenever I remake a song,
> Should know what issue is at stake:
> It is myself that I remake.

Like Yeats, you will develop throughout your life: you will find you have new things to say, and you may even come to find that the tools you acquired in college—and that suited you for a while—are not fully adequate to the new self that you have become. We cannot claim to equip you for the rest of your life—though some of these works of literature surely will remain in your mind for years—but we do claim that, with your instructor, we are helping you develop skills that are important for your mental progress. We have in mind skills useful not merely in the course in which you are now enrolled, or other literature courses, or even courses in the humanities in general that you may take. We go further. We think that these skills in reading and writing are important for your development as an educated adult. Becoming an alert reader and an effective writer should be among the central goals of your education, and they are goals that *An Introduction to Literature* is designed to help you reach.

The skills we stress in *An Introduction to Literature* will enable you to gain confidence as a reader of literary works so that you will increase your understanding of what literature offers. You need not enjoy all authors equally. You will have your favorites—and also some authors whom you do not like much at all. There's nothing wrong with that; reading literature is very much a personal encounter. But, at the same time, the skills we highlight in *An Introduction to Literature* can help you know and explain why one author means much to you and another does not. In this respect, reading and studying literature is more than personal; as we share our responses and try to express them effectively in writing, the work that we perform becomes cooperative and communal, a type of cultural conversation among fellow students, teachers, and friends.

As you proceed through *An Introduction to Literature* and gain further experience as a reader and writer, you will start to see features of poems, stories, and plays that you had not noticed before, or that you had noticed but not really understood, or that you had understood but not, so to speak, fully experienced. You may even find yourself enjoying an author you thought you disliked and would never be able to understand. The study of literature calls for concentration, commitment, and discipline. It is work—sometimes hard, challenging work. But it is rewarding work, and we believe that it will lead you to find literature more engaging and more pleasurable.

We hope that *An Introduction to Literature* will have this effect for you. Feel free to contact us with your comments and suggestions. We are eager to know what in this book has served you well, and what we might do better. You can write to us in care of Literature Editor, Longman Publishers, 51 Madison Ave, New York, NY 10010.

SYLVAN BARNET
WILLIAM BURTO
WILLIAM E. CAIN

# An Introduction
# to Literature

# I

# Reading, Thinking, and Writing Critically About Literature

Writers of literature (as opposed to other writers, such as journalists, authors of do-it-yourself manuals, and authors of textbooks) specialize in recording their responses to life and in imagining the responses of others. They tell us how it feels to live the life they live, or the lives they know about or imagine, and by some sort of magic they set forth their responses so effectively that our own lives are expanded. Their reports, for at least a moment, become ours and cause our own pulses to beat faster. As Ezra Pound put it, "Literature is news that stays news." In Chapter 2 of this book you will read a very short story (The Parable of the Prodigal Son) that is almost two thousand years old as well as half a dozen works—stories and poems—that were written in the last fifty or so years, some by men, some by women. One of the stories in a later chapter is by Ernest Hemingway, here shown revising his work.

Good writers are good readers, careful readers: they know that they must read and reread their own drafts at least as carefully as they read published writing. They know that not until they put words down can they know what they think—and then they usually see that the thoughts are not quite good enough, that the words they put down need

1

to be revised, and revised again. Hemingway, in an interview, commented on this business of writing and revising a couple of more times:

> I always rewrite each day up to the point where I stopped. When it is all finished, naturally you go over it. You get another chance to correct and rewrite when someone else types it, and you see it in clean type. The last chance is in the proofs. You're grateful for these different chances. (*Writers at Work,* Second Series, 222)

There is a lesson here for all of us, even though our own writing probably is of a humbler sort.

What are the aims of the writers of literature? Well, one of our authors, Jamaica Kincaid, in various interviews mentions her "insistence on truth," even if—especially if—the truth is painful. It is not unusual for writers to insist that in their fictions they present truths, they tell it as it is, they wake us up, they seek to make us take off our rose-colored glasses, and to make us see and feel reality. Joseph Conrad, for example, said: "My task . . . is by the power of the written word to make you hear, to make you feel—it is, before all, to make you see."

The truth that a writer makes us see is the "news that stays news" that Ezra Pound spoke of. Here is Hemingway talking about the writer's work:

> All good books are alike in that they are truer than if they had really happened and after you are finished reading one you will feel that all that happened to you and afterwards it all belongs to you; the good and the bad, the ecstasy, the remorse, and sorrow, the people and the places and how the weather was. (*Esquire* [December 1934], 68)

The Hemingway story that we reprint, "Cat in the Rain" (page 99), deals with a young woman and a young man. It's our hunch that you will find the story true: you will believe the characters and "how the weather was," and you will also find the story highly entertaining—two qualities we hope you find in all of the works in this book.

# 1

# College Readiness:
# How to Respond to Stories,
# Poems, and Plays

My task . . . is by the power of the written word to make you hear, to make you feel—it is, before all, to make you see.

*—Joseph Conrad*

A book must be the ax that breaks the frozen sea within us.

*—Franz Kafka*

The best of all ways to make one's reading valuable is to write about it.

*—Ralph Waldo Emerson*

## Full Disclosure

First, we must admit that the title of our book, *An Introduction to Literature*, is misleading, even false. You were introduced to one kind of literature, poetry, long ago, when you heard your first lullaby.

Rock-a-bye baby, in the treetop
When the wind blows, the cradle will rock
When the bough breaks, the cradle will fall
And down will come baby, cradle and all.

Probably this or maybe another lullaby put you to sleep, as it was supposed to do, but most literature seeks to keep you awake, to deepen or heighten your experience of life. And, again years ago, you were further introduced to poetry when you heard—and soon recited—nursery rhymes and counting-out rhymes. A little later you heard and sang songs, perhaps "The Star Spangled Banner," "Swing Low, Sweet Chariot," and Robert Burns's "Auld Lang Syne" or perhaps Burns's "Coming through the Rye." (Maybe you first encountered "Coming through the Rye" in J. D. Salinger's *The Catcher in the Rye;* if so, that is yet another work that you were introduced to, a work that deepened your acquaintance with literature.)

3

When you heard your first fairy tales, maybe "Cinderella," "Hansel and Gretel," or "Snow White and the Seven Dwarfs," you were introduced to short stories—another form of literature—and somewhere along the line you were further introduced to short stories when you heard about the Parable of the Prodigal Son, or the Good Samaritan, or when you heard someone tell an Aesop fable, or even when you heard a joke. And then perhaps you graduated to telling an occasional joke, thereby becoming an interpreter or performer of one kind of popular literature.

Such was (probably) your introduction to two kinds of literature, poetry and fiction. You were introduced to a third kind, *dramatic* literature (stories presented by actors), when you first looked at television, or first went to the movies or saw a live theatrical production. Perhaps you have even performed in high school, maybe in Thornton Wilder's play, *Our Town.*

# Analyzing Literature

If our book does not in fact *introduce* you to literature, what *does* it do? We hope that it will do at least two things:

- introduce you to a *wider range* of literature than you are already familiar with, and
- introduce you to the process of *analyzing* literature.

You may perhaps regard this as Good News and Bad News—Good that you will encounter new literature, not so good (maybe even Bad) that we will be encouraging you to read analytically, critically, thoughtfully, and to write essays in the same spirit.

Why not leave well-enough alone, and just let people read in their own way, for fun? Why this business about analysis? Because some works of literature are deep, and they deserve to be read attentively, seriously, analytically. When you think about it for a moment, you will recall that *thinking* can heighten your daily experience, can increase your enjoyment. Take, for instance, attendance at spectator sports. The person who knows something about baseball surely enjoys the game more than the person who knows almost nothing and who attends the game chiefly to be in the fresh air and to eat a couple of hot dogs. Experienced viewers, for instance, find themselves thinking, "He'll probably bunt," or "Now is the time for the hit and run." Knowing the records of the players and thinking about the players in a specific context heightens—perhaps we can even say "deepens"—one's interest and one's enjoyment in the game.

Somewhat similarly, experienced readers of, say, novels by Toni Morrison, get more out of a new book by Morrison than readers who have read very few novels and who now pick up their first Morrison. Yes, of course inexperienced readers can enjoy the book, but, again, experienced readers will see more, hear more, *enjoy* more, because they know what to look for, know (so to speak) *how* to read.

A good way to learn to read analytically is to annotate a text—our next topic.

# Annotating a Text as a Way of Thinking

If you glance back to the beginning of this chapter, you will see that we quote the nineteenth-century American poet and essayist, Ralph Waldo Emerson:

> The best of all ways to make one's reading valuable is to write about it.

You probably have had the experience—whether in e-mailing a friend or in writing a paper for a course—of putting down words, and then finding, *in the act of writing,* and *only* in the act of writing, that, well,

- No, you do *not* really think what you just wrote down is quite right. A better way to put it would be to say. . . . Or you may feel, Yes, that's a step in the right direction, but
- Now that I see what I've said, I would go even further, and would add. . . .

Some of your earliest annotations of a literary text are likely to be even briefer than the jottings we have indicated. They are likely to be things like these:

- ???
- ugh
- X
- great!

Or you may find yourself putting down such things as

- this character seems to be behaving inconsistently,

or

- this setting--a forest--seems to symbolize darkness, and maybe even moral confusion,

or

- Why these terribly long sentences??? And do we need all those technical words!

Remarks such as these, the product of **close reading,** may turn out to be wrong-headed, but they are the product of a mind that is *responding* to the text, not just an eye that is mindlessly running over some print.

And of course thoughtful reading may occasionally take the form of

- underlining
- highlighting
- marking a passage with a vertical line
- circling some words, perhaps even connecting circled words with a line, thereby indicating that they have some sort of relationship

*Caution*:  If you highlight whole pages you may *not* be thinking; you probably are just expending pigment, just kidding yourself into believing that you are thinking.

What advice can we give you about annotating, beyond cautioning against mindless highlighting? The best advice we can give is this: Begin by indicating

- what you especially like—thinking about what pleases you is a pretty good first step—and also by indicating
- what you are especially puzzled by. If you don't know the meaning of a word, put a question mark in the margin, and then look up the meaning in a dictionary

# A First Assignment: Annotating
# Robert Frost's "Come In"

But here is yet another way to begin thinking about a work of literature, especially a short poem. To get our students started, we gave them as their first homework assignment a poem by Robert Frost, "Come In," accompanied by the following prose quotation drawn from a preface that Frost wrote for his short play, *A Way Out:*

> Everything written is as good as it is dramatic. . . . [A poem is] heard as sung or spoken by a person in a scene—in character, in a setting. By whom, where and when is the question. By the dreamer of a better world out in a storm in Autumn; by a lover under a window at night.

Frost says that writing is "dramatic." Presumably "dramatic" implies

- *a situation that is suspenseful,* perhaps especially because we sense
- *a conflict* (the conflict may be between two people, or between one person and his or her surroundings, or even within a single person—for instance, concerning a decision).

So we told our students that in annotating "Come In" they might want to begin by thinking about the "dramatic" situation in the poem:

- Who is speaking?
- Where?
- What conflict, if any, is implied?
- If there is a conflict, how is it resolved?

But beyond responses to these questions, the students were to jot down whatever puzzled them or interested them. Here is Frost's poem, followed by the responses of one student. Read the poem, preferably aloud, and then look at the student's annotations.

## *Come In*                                                   [1942]

As I came to the edge of the woods,
Thrush music—hark!
Now if it was dusk outside,
Inside it was dark.                                              4

Too dark in the woods for a bird
By sleight of wing
To better its perch for the night,
Though it still could sing.                                     8

The last of the light of the sun
That had died in the west
Still lived for one song more
In a thrush's breast.                                          12

Far in the pillared dark
Thrush music went—
Almost like a call to come in
To the dark and lament.                                          16

But no, I was out for stars:
I would not come in.
I meant not even if asked,
And I hadn't been.                                              20

**Please note:**
- We suggested that students read the poem (aloud at least once) and then jot down in the margins whatever responses they wished to record—their likes, dislikes, uncertainties, whatever they thought might be helpful in finding their way into the poem associations.
- We also suggested that *after* they had read the poem several times and jotted down some responses in the margins, they might at the top or bottom of the page respond to Frost's prose comment, and indicate (1) who is speaking in this poem, in what specific context, and (2) what is "dramatic" about the situation.

---

**Come In**    *Sounds like a friendly invitation*

As I came to the edge of the woods,
Thrush music—hark!    *Unusual word--old fashioned.*
Now if it was dusk outside,
Inside it was dark.                                              4

Too dark in the woods for a bird
By sleight of wing
To better its perch for the night,
Though it still could sing.                                      8

The last of the light of the sun    *light dying, but also still living in bird's song*
That had died in the west
Still lived for one song more
In a thrush's breast.                                           12

Far in the pillared dark    *Trees like pillars in a Greek temple or in a cathedral*
Thrush music went—    *Religious?*
Almost like a call to come in    *"Dark" is associated with sorrow ("lament")*
To the dark and lament.                                         16

*Very strong, emphatic!*
But no, I was out for stars:    *light, not darkness.*
I would not come in.
I meant not even if asked,
And I hadn't been.                                              20

*Sort of a joke. He realizes he had not been invited to "Come in," a sort of rejection of his own title. So--the "drama" is that he realizes his mistake. Nature did not invite him to "come in" or to "lament."*

# Thinking Critically About Responses to Literature: Arguing with Yourself

Ordinarily you will begin with a noticeable response to your reading—perhaps interest, boredom, bafflement, annoyance, shock, or pleasure. But if you are going to think critically about what you have read, you will go on to *examine* your response by checking it against the work. Revisiting the reading in the context of your response to it can help you deepen or change your response.

How can you change an instinctive emotional response? **Critical thinking** involves seeing an issue from all sides, to as great a degree as possible. As you know, in ordinary language "to criticize" usually means to find fault, but in literary studies the term does not have a negative connotation. Rather, it means "to examine carefully." (The word "criticism" comes from a Greek verb meaning "to distinguish," "to decide," "to judge.") In one respect, however, the term "critical thinking" does approach the usual meaning of "criticism," since critical thinking requires you to take a skeptical view of *your own* response. You will, so to speak, argue with yourself or seek to find fault with your initial view. That is, in an effort to improve your position you try to raise questions that a skeptical reader might raise.

Critical thinking, in short, involves examining or exploring one's own responses by questioning and testing them. Critical thinking is not so much a skill (though it does require the ability to understand a text) as it is a habit of mind, or, rather, several habits, including

- open-mindedness,
- intellectual curiosity, and
- a willingness to work.

# A Very Short Story: Fyodor Dostoevsky's "The Onion"

"The Onion" is a story within a story, almost a fable or a fairy tale told by a character within a nineteenth-century novel. (What do the words "fable" and "tale" suggest to you?)

## FYODOR DOSTOEVSKY

*A novelist of Russia's Golden Age, Fyodor Dostoevsky (1821-1881)—pronounced approximately like DAHS-tuh-yef-skee—wrote five major works:* Notes from Underground *(1864),* Crime and Punishment *(1866),* The Idiot *(1869),* The Possessed *(1871), and* The Brothers Karamazov *(1880).*

*Within* The Brothers Karamazov *(in Book 7, Chapter 3), one of the characters, Grushenka, says, rather puzzlingly, "Although I'm bad, I did give away an onion." She goes on to explain what she means: She says that when she was a child she heard a story from her cook, and she then tells the story. We give the story as she retells it.*

## The Onion

The story goes like this. Once upon a time there was a woman, and a very wicked woman she was. When she died, no one could think of a single good deed she had done. The devils caught her and pushed her into a lake of fire, but her Guardian Angel thought hard, and he remembered that she once pulled up an onion from her garden and gave it to a beggar. The angel told this to God, and God said to the angel, "Take that very same onion and hold it out to her, and let her take hold of it, and you pull, and if she gets out of the lake she can come to Paradise, but if the onion breaks, she must stay where she is."

The angel hurried to the woman, and he held out the onion. "Take hold of it and I'll pull you out." And he began pulling, and she began to get out, and when she was nearly out, other sinners in the lake saw her, and they tried to hold on to her so that they would be pulled out with her, but the woman was a wicked woman and she began to kick them away, saying "It's my onion, not yours!"

As soon as she spoke those words, the onion broke, and she fell back into the lake, and she is still there, burning to this very day. And the angel wept, and went away.

We once gave copies of this story to students at the first meeting of a course and asked them to read it and then to annotate it as a way of helping them to read it carefully. These are the annotations that one student produced.

## The Onion

The story goes like this. Once upon a time there was a woman, and a very wicked woman she was. When she died, no one could think of a single good deed she had done. The devils caught her and pushed her into a lake of fire, but her Guardian Angel thought hard, and he remembered that she once pulled up an onion from her garden and gave it to a beggar. The angel told this to God, and God said to the angel, "Take that very same onion and hold it out to her, and let her take hold of it, and you pull, and if she gets out of the lake she can come to Paradise, but if the onion breaks, she must stay where she is."

The angel hurried to the woman, and he held out the onion. "Take hold of it and I'll pull you out." And he began pulling, and she began to get out, and when she was nearly out, other sinners in the lake saw her, and they tried to hold on to her so that they would be pulled out with her, but the woman was a wicked woman and she began to kick them away, saying "It's my onion, not yours!"

As soon as she spoke those words, the onion broke, and she fell back into the lake, and she is still there, burning to this very day. And the angel wept, and went away.

*[Marginal annotations:]*

*language of a fairy tale*

*again, the world of fairy tales*

*almost child-like in the way the story is told*

*again, simple style—of a fairy tale*

*again the language of a fairy tale*

*a sort of evil version of "and they lived happily ever after."*

*Would the story be better without this sentence?*

**YOUR TURN**

1. Suppose the last sentence of the story, about the angel weeping and departing, were omitted. Would the story be better? Better in what way? More interesting? Truer? (Does it make any sense to talk about the "truth" of a story that is obviously fictional rather than historical?)

2. Suppose the onion did not break, and the story ended thus:

   > Even though she spoke these unkind words, the onion did not break, and she was rescued from the lake of fire.

   Do you think the revision is a better—more interesting, more effective—story than the original? Please explain.

3. Do you think that a nonbeliever can find this story of much interest? Please explain.

# Prompts that Stimulate Responses to Stories, Poems, and Plays: Three Checklists

We think you may find the following checklists (reprinted in expanded form later in the book) helpful as ways of getting ideas about the literature that you read, and especially helpful if you are writing about literature.

## ✔ Responding to Stories

PLOT

- ☐ Does the plot grow out of the characters, or does it depend on chance or coincidence?
- ☐ Does surprise play an important role, or does foreshadowing?
- ☐ What conflicts does the story include?
- ☐ Are certain episodes narrated out of chronological order?

CHARACTER

- ☐ Which character chiefly engages your interest?
- ☐ What purposes do minor characters serve?
- ☐ How does the author reveal character?
- ☐ Is the behavior plausible—that is, are the characters well motivated?
- ☐ If a character changes, why and how does he or she change?
- ☐ Are the characters round or flat?
- ☐ How has the author caused you to sympathize with certain characters?

| | |
|---|---|
| **POINT OF VIEW** | ☐ Who tells the story? |
| | ☐ How does the point of view help shape the theme? |
| | ☐ Does the narrator's language help you to construct a picture of the narrator's character, class, attitude, strengths, and limitations? |
| **SETTING** | ☐ Do you have a strong sense of time and place? |
| | ☐ What is the relation of the setting to the plot and characters? |
| **SYMBOLISM** | ☐ Do certain characters seem to you to stand for something in addition to themselves? |
| | ☐ If you do believe that the story has symbolic elements, do you think they are adequately integrated within the story, or do they strike you as being too obviously stuck in? |
| **STYLE** | ☐ How would you characterize the style? |
| | ☐ How has the point of view shaped or determined the style? |
| | ☐ Do you think the style is consistent? |
| | ☐ Is the title informative? |
| **THEME** | ☐ Is the title informative? |
| | ☐ Do certain passages—dialogue or description—seem to you to point especially toward the theme? |
| | ☐ Is the meaning of the story embodied in the whole story, or does it seem conveyed chiefly by certain passages of editorializing? |
| | ☐ Suppose someone asked you to state the point—the theme—of the story. Could you? |

## ✔ Responding to Poems

| | |
|---|---|
| FIRST RESPONSE | ☐ What was your response to the poem on first reading? |
| SPEAKER AND TONE | ☐ Who is the speaker? |
| | ☐ Do you think the speaker is fully aware of what he or she is saying, or does the speaker unconsciously reveal his or her personality and values? |
| | ☐ Is the speaker narrating on an earlier experience or attitude? |
| AUDIENCE | ☐ To whom is the speaker speaking? |
| STRUCTURE AND FORM | ☐ Does the poem proceed in a straightforward way, or at some point or points does the speaker reverse course, altering his or her tone or perception? |
| | ☐ Is the poem organized into sections? |
| | ☐ What is the effect on you of the form—say quatrains (stanzas of four lines) or blank verse (unrhymed lines of ten syllables of iambic pentameter)? |
| CENTER OF INTEREST AND THEME | ☐ What is the poem about? |
| | ☐ Is the theme stated explicitly (directly) or implicitly? |
| DICTION | ☐ How would you characterize the language? |
| | ☐ Do certain words have rich and relevant associations that relate to other words and help to define the speaker or the theme or both? |
| | ☐ What is the role of figurative language, if any? |
| | ☐ What do you think is to be taken figuratively or symbolically, and what literally? |
| SOUND EFFECTS | ☐ What is the role of sound effects, including repetitions of sound (for instance, alliteration) and of entire words, and shifts in versification? |
| | ☐ If there are off-rhymes (for instance, dizzy and easy, or home and come), what effect do they have on you? |
| | ☐ If there are unexpected stresses or pauses, what do they communicate about the speaker's experience? |

## ✔ Responding to Plays

PLOT AND
CONFLICT

- ☐ Does the exposition introduce elements that will be ironically fulfilled? During the exposition do you perceive things differently from the way the characters perceive them?

- ☐ Are certain happenings or situations recurrent? If so, what significance do you attach to them?

- ☐ If there is more than one plot, do the plots seem to you to be related? Is one plot clearly the main plot and another plot a sort of subplot, a minor variation on the theme?

- ☐ Do any scenes strike you as irrelevant?

- ☐ Are certain scenes so strongly foreshadowed that you anticipated them? If so, did the happenings in these scenes merely fulfill your expectations, or did they also surprise you?

- ☐ What kinds of conflict are there? One character against another, one group against another, one part of a personality against another part in the same person?

- ☐ How is the conflict resolved? By an unambiguous triumph of one side or by a triumph that is also in some degree a loss for the triumphant side? Do you find the resolution satisfying, or unsettling, or what? Why?

CHARACTER

- ☐ A dramatic character is not likely to be thoroughly realistic, a copy of someone we might know. Still, we can ask if the character is consistent and coherent. We can also ask if the character is complex or is, on the other hand, a rather simple representative of some human type.

- ☐ How is the character defined? Consider what the character says and does and what others say about him or her and do to him or her. Also consider other characters who more or less resemble the character in question, because the similarities—and the differences—may be significant.

- ☐ How trustworthy are the characters when they characterize themselves? When they characterize others?

CHARACTER
(continued)

☐ Do characters change as the play goes on, or do we simply know them better at the end?

☐ What do you make of the minor characters? Are they merely necessary to the plot, or are they foils to other characters? Or do they serve some other functions?

☐ If a character is tragic, does the tragedy seem to you to proceed from a moral flaw, from an intellectual error, from the malice of others, from sheer chance, or from some combination of these?

☐ What are the character's goals? To what degree do you sympathize with them? If a character is comic, do you laugh with or at the character?

☐ Do you think the characters are adequately motivated?

☐ Is a given character so meditative that you feel he or she is engaged less in a dialogue with others than in a dialogue with the self? If so, do you feel that this character is in large degree a spokesperson for the author, commenting not only on the world of the play but also on the outside world?

NONVERBAL
LANGUAGE

☐ If the playwright does not provide full stage directions, try to imagine for at least one scene what gestures and tones might accompany each speech. (The first scene is usually a good one to try your hand at.)

☐ What do you make of the setting? Does it help to reveal character? Do changes of scene strike you as symbolic? If so, symbolic of what?

# Converting Responses into Readable Writing

When you write about your responses, you are not just knocking off an assignment. You are writing an essay, engaging in a process that, first, will teach you, and second, will ultimately engage the interest of your readers.

After you have written your first draft, consult the following checklist. (And consult the list again, after each later draft.)

## ✔ Checklist: Readable Writing

☐ Is my title engaging?

☐ Does my introduction provide essential information (writer, work, topic, approach of essay)?

☐ Does my paper have a point, a thesis?

☐ Do I support my argument (thesis) with sufficient persuasive detail, for instance with brief quotations from the text? That is, will a reader clearly see *why* I respond as I do?

☐ Have I kept the needs of my readers in mind—for instance, have I defined unfamiliar terms? (If you keep the needs of your readers in mind, you find that you have a collaborator at your shoulder, someone who prompts you to clarify certain points.)

☐ Is the paper organized and is the organization clear to the readers?

☐ Have I set forth my views effectively and yet not talked too much about myself?

☐ Does my essay fulfill the assignment (length, scope)?

# A Story for Analysis: Kate Chopin, "The Storm"

Here is a second story for you to read critically. Notice how the student's annotations help deepen her appreciation of the story.

## KATE CHOPIN

*For a complete biographical note, see page 67. Although Kate Chopin was from St. Louis, she married a man of French descent from Louisiana and lived there for many years. Some of the characters in her stories speak a mixture of French and English, and she draws heavily on the French culture that was prevalent in coastal Louisiana at the turn of the twentieth century.*

### The Storm

[1898]

#### I

The leaves were so still that even Bibi thought it was going to rain. Bobinôt, who was accustomed to converse on terms of perfect equality with his little son, called the child's attention

*What does this detail tell us about Bobinôt?*

to certain somber clouds that were rolling with sinister intention from the west, accompanied by a sullen, threatening roar. They were at Friedheimer's store and decided to remain there till the storm had passed. They sat within the door on two empty kegs. Bibi was four years old and looked very wise.

"Mama'll be 'fraid, yes," he suggested with blinking eyes.

"She'll shut the house. Maybe she got Sylvie helpin' her this evenin'," Bobinôt responded reassuringly.

"No; she ent got Sylvie. Sylvie was helpin' her yistiday," piped Bibi.

5      Bobinôt arose and going across to the counter purchased a can of shrimps, of which Calixta was very fond. Then he returned to his perch on the keg and sat stolidly holding the can of shrimps while the storm burst. It shook the wooden store and seemed to be ripping great furrows in the distant field. Bibi laid his little hand on his father's knee and was not afraid.

## II

Calixta, at home, felt no uneasiness for their safety. She sat at a side window sewing furiously on a sewing machine. She was greatly occupied and did not notice the approaching storm. But she felt very warm and often stopped to mop her face on which the perspiration gathered in beads. She unfastened her white sacque at the throat. It began to grow dark, and suddenly realizing the situation she got up hurriedly and went about closing windows and doors.

Out on the small front gallery[1] she had hung Bobinôt's Sunday clothes to air and she hastened out to gather them before the rain fell. As she stepped outside Alcée Laballière rode in at the gate. She had not seen him very often since her marriage, and never alone. She stood there with Bobinôt's coat in her hands, and the big rain drops began to fall. Alcée rode his horse under the shelter of a side projection where the chickens had huddled and there were plows and a harrow piled up in the corner.

"May I come and wait in your gallery till the storm is over Calixta?" he asked.

"Come 'long in, M'sieur Alcée."

10      His voice and her own startled her as if from a trance, and she seized Bobinôt's vest. Alcée, mounting to the porch, grabbed the trousers and snatched Bibi's braided jacket that was about to be carried away by a sudden gust of wind. He expressed an intention to remain outside, but it was soon apparent that he might as well have been out in the open: the water beat in upon the boards in driving sheets, and he went inside, closing the door after him. It was even necessary to put something beneath the door to keep the water out.

*Why does the narrator point out that Calixta has not seen Alcée alone since her marriage? Does this statement set up any expectations about what may happen?*

*Later Alcée will, so to speak, wear Bobinôt's pants.*

---

[1]**gallery** porch or passageway along a wall, open to the air but protected by a roof supported by columns.

"My! What a rain! It's a good two years sence it rain like that," exclaimed Calixta as she rolled up a piece of bagging and Alcée helped her to thrust it beneath the crack.

She was a little fuller of figure than five years before when she married; but she had lost nothing of her vivacity. Her blue eyes still retained their melting quality; and her yellow hair, disheveled by wind and rain, kinked more stubbornly than ever about her ears and temples.

The rain beat upon the low, shingled roof with a force and clatter that threatened to break an entrance and deluge them there. They were in the dining room—the sitting room—the general utility room. Adjoining was her bed room, with Bibi's couch along side her own. The door stood open, and the room with its white, monumental bed, its closed shutters, looked dim and mysterious.

Alcée flung himself in a rocker and Calixta nervously began to gather up from the floor the lengths of a cotton sheet which she had been sewing.

15      "If this keeps up, *Dieu sait*[2] if the levees going to stan' it!" she exclaimed.

"What have you got to do with the levees?"

"I got enough to do! An' there's Bobinôt with Bibi out in that storm—if he only didn't left Friedheimer's!"

"Let us hope, Calixta, that Bobinôt got sense enough to come in out of a cyclone."

She went and stood at the window with a greatly disturbed look on her face. She wiped the frame that was clouded with moisture. It was stiflingly hot. Alcée got up and joined her at the window, looking over her shoulder. The rain was coming down in sheets obscuring the view of far-off cabins and enveloping the distant wood in a gray mist. The playing of the lightning was incessant. A bolt struck a tall chinaberry tree at the edge of the field. It filled all visible space with a blinding glare and the crash seemed to invade the very boards they stood upon.

20      Calixta put her hands to her eyes, and with a cry, staggered backward. Alcée's arm encircled her, and for an instant he drew her close and spasmodically to him.

"*Bonté!*"[3] she cried, releasing herself from his encircling arm and retreating from the window, "the house'll go next! If I only knew w'ere Bibi was!" She would not compose herself; she would not be seated. Alcée clasped her shoulders and looked into her face. The contact of her warm palpitating body when he had unthinkingly drawn her into his arms, had aroused all the old-time infatuation and desire for her flesh.

"Calixta," he said, "don't be frightened. Nothing can happen. The house is too low to be struck, with so many tall trees standing about. There! aren't you going to be quiet? say, aren't you?" He pushed her hair back from her face that was warm and steaming. Her lips were as red and moist as pomegranate seed.

---

[2]**Dieu sait** God only knows.    [3]**Bonté!** Heavens!

*Who is making this observation? The narrator? Alcée? As you continue reading this scene, think about who is relating the events, and how they are presented.*

*Consider how the storm outside mirrors the growing storm inside the house. How does Chopin use the setting to reflect the feelings of her characters?*

Her white neck and a glimpse of her full, firm bosom disturbed him powerfully. As she glanced up at him the fear in her liquid blue eyes had given place to a drowsy gleam that unconsciously betrayed a sensuous desire. He looked down into her eyes and there was nothing for him to do but gather her lips in a kiss. It reminded him of Assumption.[4]

"Do you remember—in Assumption, Calixta?" he asked in a low voice broken with passion. Oh! she remembered; for in Assumption he had kissed her and kissed and kissed her; until his senses would well nigh fail, and to save her he would resort to a desperate flight. If she was not an immaculate dove in those days, she was still inviolate; a passionate creature whose very defenselessness had made her defense, against which his honor forbade him to prevail. Now—well, now—her lips seemed in a manner free to be tasted, as well as her round, white throat and her whiter breasts.

They did not heed the crashing torrents, and the roar of the elements made her laugh as she lay in his arms. She was a revelation in that dim, mysterious chamber; as white as the couch she lay upon. Her firm, elastic flesh that was knowing for the first time its birthright, was like a creamy lily that the sun invites to contribute its breath and perfume to the undying life of the world.

25    The generous abundance of her passion, without guile or trickery, was like a white flame which penetrated and found response in depths of his own sensuous nature that had never yet been reached.

When he touched her breasts they gave themselves up in quivering ecstasy, inviting his lips. Her mouth was a fountain of delight. And when he possessed her, they seemed to swoon together at the very borderland of life's mystery.

He stayed cushioned upon her, breathless, dazed, enervated, with his heart beating like a hammer upon her. With one hand she clasped his head, her lips lightly touching his forehead. The other hand stroked with a soothing rhythm his muscular shoulders.

The growl of the thunder was distant and passing away. The rain beat softly upon the shingles, inviting them to drowsiness and sleep. But they dared not yield.

The rain was over; and the sun was turning the glistening green world into a palace of gems. Calixta, on the gallery, watched Alcée ride away. He turned and smiled at her with a beaming face; she lifted her pretty chin in the air and laughed aloud.

### III

Bobinôt and Bibi, trudging home, stopped without at the cistern to make themselves presentable.

30    "My! Bibi, w'at will yo' mama say! You ought to be ashame'. You oughtn' put on those good pants. Look at' em! An'

*The fact that Alcée and Calixta dare not yield to their drowsiness indicates that they realize they must not be caught. But do they feel they have done something wrong?*

*Instead of feeling guilty or nervous about what has just happened, Calixta laughs "aloud." Chopin does not give any signals to the reader that we should disapprove of Calixta's infidelity.*

---

[4]**Assumption** a parish (i.e., county) west of New Orleans.

that mud on yo' collar! How you got that mud on yo' collar, Bibi? I never saw such a boy!" Bibi was a picture of pathetic resignation. Bobinôt was the embodiment of serious solicitude as he strove to remove from his own person and his son's the signs of their tramp over heavy roads and through wet fields. He scraped the mud off Bibi's bare legs and feet with a stick and carefully removed all traces from his heavy brogans. Then, prepared for the worst—the meeting with an overscrupulous housewife, they entered cautiously at the back door.

Calixta was preparing supper. She had set the table and was dripping coffee at the hearth. She sprang up as they came in.

"Oh, Bobinôt! You back! My! but I was uneasy. W'ere you been during the rain? An' Bibi? he ain't wet? he ain't hurt?" She had clasped Bibi and was kissing him effusively. Bobinôt's explanations and apologies which he had been composing all along the way, died on his lips as Calixta felt him to see if he were dry, and seemed to express nothing but satisfaction at their safe return.

"I bought you some shrimps, Calixta," offered Bobinôt, hauling the can from his ample side pocket and laying it on the table.

35    "Shrimps! Oh, Bobinôt! you too good fo' anything!" and she gave him a smacking kiss on the cheek that resounded. "*J'vous résponds*,[5] we'll have a feas' tonight! umph-umph!"

Bobinôt and Bibi began to relax and enjoy themselves, and when the three seated themselves at table they laughed much and so loud that anyone might have heard them as far away as LaBallière's.

*Bobinôt had prepared himself for another "storm"--that of Calixta's reprimands. When she happily greets her husband and child, without chiding them, they relax and have a wonderful evening. It appears that the storm--the one that occurred inside the house-- has cleared the air.*

## IV

Alcée LaBallière wrote to his wife, Clarisse, that night. It was a loving letter, full of tender solicitude. He told her not to hurry back, but if she and the babies liked it at Biloxi, to stay a month longer. He was getting on nicely; and though he missed them, he was willing to bear the separation a while longer—realizing that their health and pleasure were the first things to be considered.

## V

As for Clarisse, she was charmed upon receiving her husband's letter. She and the babies were doing well. The society was agreeable; many of her old friends and acquaintances were at the bay. And the first free breath since her marriage seemed to restore the pleasant liberty of her maiden days. Devoted as she was to her husband, their conjugal life was something which she was more than willing to forgo for a while.

So the storm passed and everyone was happy.

*Why does Chopin end the story this way? What sort of moral judgment, if any, does she make on the actions of Calixta and Alcée?*

---

[5]**J'vous résponds** Take my word; let me tell you.

**YOUR TURN**

1. How would you characterize the narrator?
2. How would you characterize Calixta?
3. In Part III, do you think Calixta is insincere in her expressions of solicitation for Bobinôt? Why or why not?
4. Do you take Part IV to imply that Alcée and Calixta will continue their affair for another month? Support your answer.
5. Why does Chopin bother, in Part V, to tell us about Clarisse? And exactly what do you make of the last line of the story?
6. Is it fair to say that the story is cynical? Explain.
7. Do you think the story is immoral and, if so, ought not to be assigned in a course in literature? Explain.

# Last Words

You are in college, so you must know something, and you must have already developed methods of getting your work done, and getting it done well. Keep at it, keep thinking, keep responding—perhaps in new ways—to new experiences. Do not rely simply on the knowledge and the methods that you already have. New experiences require new responses. Remember the words of A. E. Housman, the twentieth-century poet and professor of classics:

> Knowledge is good, method is good, but one thing beyond all others is necessary; and that is to have a head, not a pumpkin on your shoulders, and brains, not pudding, in your head.

# 2

# Reading and Responding
to Literature

## What Is Literature?

Large books have been written on this subject, and large books will continue to
be written on it. But we can offer a few brief generalizations that may be useful.

First, the word "literature" can be used to refer to anything written. The Department of Agriculture will, upon request, send a correspondent "literature on
canning tomatoes." People who ask for such material expect it to be clear and informative, but they do not expect it to be interesting in itself. They do not read it
for the experience of reading it; they read it only if they are thinking about canning tomatoes.

There is, however, a sort of literature that people *do* read without expecting
a practical payoff. They read the sort of writing that is in *An Introduction to
Literature* because they expect it to hold their interest and to provide pleasure.
They may vaguely feel that it will be good for them, but they don't read it
*because* it will be good for them, any more than they dance because dancing
provides healthful exercise. Dancing may indeed be healthful, but that's not why
people dance. They dance because dancing affords a special kind of pleasure.
For similar reasons people watch athletic contests and go to concerts or to the
theater. We participate in activities such as these not because we expect some
sort of later reward but because we know that the experience of participating is
in itself rewarding. Perhaps the best explanation is that the experiences are
absorbing—which is to say they take us out of ourselves for a while—and that
(especially in the case of concerts, dance performances, and athletic contests)
they allow us to appreciate excellence, to admire achievement. Most of us can
swim or toss a ball and maybe even hit a ball, but when we go to a swimming
meet or to a ball game we see a level of performance that evokes our admiration.

## Literature as Performance

Let's begin, then, by thinking of literature as (to quote Robert Frost) "a performance in words." Here's a very short poem by Frost (1874-1963), probably
America's most famous poet.

# ROBERT FROST

### *The Span of Life*                                                        [1936]

The old dog barks backward without getting up.
I can remember when he was a pup.

Read the poem aloud once or twice, physically experiencing Frost's "performance in words." The most immediately obvious part of the performance is that Frost has written lines that rhyme. No two readers will read the lines in exactly the same way, but it is safe to say that in reading the first line most readers will put a fairly heavy stress on as many as seven or even eight syllables, whereas in reading the second line they probably will stress only three or four:

The óld dóg bárks báckward withoút gétting úp.
Í can remémber when hé was a púp.

Notice that the first line is harder to say than the second line, which more or less rolls off the tongue. Why? Because in the first line we must pause between "old" and "dog," between "backward" and "without," and between "without" and "getting"—and in fact between "back" and "ward."

And so we can say that the form (a relatively effortful hard-to-speak line followed by an easy bouncy line) is part of the content: first, a description with pauses and relatively heavy stresses of a dog that no longer has the energy or the strength to leap up, and second, a line that in a rather jingling way reports a memory of the dog as a puppy. The language, then, is highly patterned. Take a moment to read the lines again, and to enjoy the rhyme; rhyme—the repetition of a sound—is also a pattern. We can easily see what Frost meant when he said that a poem is a performance in words. The thing looks easy enough, but we know that it takes skill to make words behave properly—that is, to get the right words into the right places. Frost went into the lions' cage, did his act, and came out unharmed.

## Significance

We've been talking about Frost's skill in handling words, but we have said only a little about *what* Frost is saying. One of the things that literature does is to make us see—hear, feel, love—what the author thinks is a valuable part of the experience of living. A thousand years ago a Japanese writer, Lady Murasaki, made this point when she had one of the characters in her book talk about what motivates an author:

Again and again something in one's own life or in that around one will seem so important that one cannot bear to let it pass into oblivion. There must never come a time, the writer feels, when people do not know about this.

We can probably agree with Lady Murasaki that writers of literature try to get at something important in their experiences, emotions, or visions, and try to make the reader experience the importance. And so a writer shows us what the span of life is like, or (for instance) what it is like to be in love (plenty of room for comedy as well as tragedy here), or what it is like to be an immigrant worrying whether his or her baby will be accepted as an American. (Later in this chapter we will see Pat Mora's poem on this last topic.)

Thinking further about Frost's poem, we notice something else about the form. The first line is about a dog, but the second line is about a dog *and* a human being ("I can remember"). The speaker must be getting on, too. And although nothing is said about the dog as a symbol of human life, surely the reader, prompted by the title of the poem, makes a connection between the lifespan of a dog and that of a human being. Part of what makes the poem effective is that this point is not stated explicitly, not belabored. Readers have the pleasure of making the connection for themselves—under Frost's careful guidance.

Everyone knows that puppies are frisky and that old dogs are not—though perhaps not until we encountered this poem did we think twice about the fact that "the old dog barks backward without getting up." Or let's put it this way:

- Many people may have noticed this behavior, but
- perhaps only Frost thought (to use Lady Murasaki's words) "There must never come a time . . . when people do not know about this." And
- fortunately for all of us, Frost had the ability to put his perception into memorable words.

Part of what makes Frost's performance in words especially memorable is the relationship between the two lines. Neither line in itself is anything very special, but because of the counterpoint the whole is more than the sum of the parts. Skill in handling language, obviously, is indispensable if the writer is to produce literature. A person may know a great deal about dogs and may be a great lover of dogs, but knowledge and love are not enough equipment to write even a two-line poem about a dog (or the span of life, or both). Poems, like other kinds of literature, are produced by people who know how to delight us with verbal performances.

We can easily see that Robert Frost's "The Span of Life" is a work of literature rather than mere versification if we contrast it with another short work in rhyme:

Thirty days hath September,
April, June, and November;
All the rest have thirty-one
Excepting February alone,
Which has twenty-eight in fine,
Till leap year gives it twenty-nine.

This information is important, but it is only information. The lines rhyme, giving the work some form, but there is nothing very interesting about it, nothing insightful. (Perhaps you will want to take issue with this opinion.) The verse is true and therefore useful; it is valuable but it is not of compelling interest, probably because it only tells us facts rather than presents human experience. We all remember "Thirty days" but the lines offer neither the pleasure of an insight nor the pleasure of an interesting tune.

# Two Poems About Immigrants

Let's now think a little more about what it means to read and respond to literature. Once again we'll start with a poem by Robert Frost, but this one, titled "Immigrants," takes a little more time and effort to figure out. Frost wrote these lines for a pageant at Plymouth, Massachusetts, celebrating the three-hundredth anniversary of the arrival of the *Mayflower* from England. The *Mayflower,* a ship about 100 feet long and 25 feet wide, had a crew of about 25 and 102 passengers. The journey took 66 days.

# ROBERT FROST

## *Immigrants* [1920]

No ship of all that under sail or steam
Have gathered people to us more and more
But Pilgrim-manned the *Mayflower* in a dream
Has been her anxious convoy in to shore.

To find this poem—this performance in words—of any interest, a reader probably has to know that the *Mayflower* brought the Pilgrims to America. Second, a reader has to grasp a slightly unfamiliar construction: "No ship . . . but . . . has . . ." which means, in effect, "every ship has." (Compare: "No human being but is born of woman," which means "Every human being is born of woman.")

If, then, we **paraphrase** the poem—translate it into other words in the same language—we get something roughly along these lines:

> All of the ships (whether sailing vessels or steamships) that have collected people in increasing numbers and brought them to this country have had the *Mayflower*, with its Pilgrims, as its eager (or worried?) escort to the coast.

We have tried to make this paraphrase as accurate and as concise as possible, but for reasons that we'll explain in a moment, we have omitted giving an equivalent for Frost's "in a dream." Why, one might ask, is our paraphrase so much less interesting than the original?

We come back to Frost's idea that a work of literature is a "performance in words." The lines are metrical (stresses recur more or less regularly) and they rhyme (*steam/dream, more/shore*), which is to say Frost, like a figure-skater, has created patterns. Probably, too, the repetition, of *s* in "sail or steam" catches the ear. The words "sail" and "steam" are somewhat alike in that they are both monosyllables, they both begin with the same sound, and they both evoke images of ships. Compare "sail or steam" with "sail or oil" or "sail or engine" and you will probably agree that the original is more pleasing and more interesting.

We can't be certain about what Frost really thought of the Pilgrims and of the *Mayflower*, but we do have the poem, and that's what we are concerned with. It celebrates the anniversary, of course, but it also celebrates at least two other things: the continuing arrival of new immigrants and the close connection between the early and the later immigrants.

Persons whose ancestors came over on the *Mayflower* have a reputation for being rather sniffy about later arrivals, but Frost reminds his Yankee audience that their ancestors, the *Mayflower* passengers, were themselves immigrants. However greatly the histories and the experiences of the early immigrants differed from those of later immigrants, the experience of emigration and the hopes for a better life link the *Mayflower* passengers with more recent arrivals.

The poem says, if our paraphrase is roughly accurate, that the *Mayflower* and its passengers accompany all later immigrants. Now, what does this mean? Literally, of course, it is nonsense. The *Mayflower* and its passengers disappeared centuries ago.

### YOUR TURN

1. In our paraphrase, in an effort to avoid complexities, we did not give any equivalent for "in a dream" (line 3). The time has now come to face this

puzzle: "But Pilgrim-manned the *Mayflower* in a dream." Some read-ers take Frost to be saying that the long-deceased passengers of the *Mayflower* still dream of others following them. Other readers, how-ever, interpret the line as saying that later immigrants dream of the *Mayflower*. Now, this paraphrase, even if accurate, makes an assertion that is not strictly true, since many later immigrants probably had never even heard of the *Mayflower*. But in a larger sense the statement is true. Most later immigrants, with the terrible exception of involun-tary immigrants from Africa who were brought here in chains, dreamed of a better life, just as the *Mayflower* passengers did. Some hoped for religious freedom, some hoped to escape political oppres-sion or starvation, but again, all were seeking a better life. What do you make of line 3?

2. In our paraphrase we mentioned that "anxious" might be paraphrased either as "eager" or as "worried." (Contrast, for instance, "She was anx-ious to serve the community" and "She was anxious about the exam.") Is Frost's "anxious convoy" *eagerly* accompanying the ships with im-migrants, or is it *nervously* accompanying them, perhaps worried that these new arrivals may not be the right sort of people, or worried that the new arrivals may not be able to get on in the new country? Or does the word "anxious," which seems to modify "convoy" (here, *Mayflower*), really refer to the new immigrants, who are worried that they may not succeed? Or perhaps they are worried that America may not in fact correspond to their hopes.

    Read the poem aloud two or three times, and then think about which of these meanings—or some other meanings that you come up with—you find most rewarding. You might consider, too, whether more than one meaning can be present. Frost himself in a letter wrote that he liked to puzzle his readers a bit—to baffle them and yet (or thereby) propel them forward:

    > My poems—I should suppose everybody's poems—are all set to trip the reader head foremost into the boundless. Ever since in-fancy I have had the habit of leaving my blocks carts chairs and such like ordinaries where people would be pretty sure to fall forward over them in the dark. Forward, you understand, *and* in the dark.

    What we have been saying is this: A reader of a work of literature finds meanings in the work, but also (even when the meaning is uncertain) takes delight in the details, takes delight in the way that the work has been constructed, takes delight in (again) the performance. When we have got at what we think may be the "meaning" of a work, we do not value or hold on to the meaning only and turn away from the work itself; rather, we value even more the craftsmanship that the work displays. And we come to see that the meaning is inseparable from all of the details that go to make up the work.

3. "Pilgrim-manned" may disturb some readers. Conscious of sexist lan-guage, today we try to avoid saying things like "This shows the great-ness of man" or "Man is a rational animal" when we are speaking not about males but about all people. Does Frost's "Pilgrim-manned" strike you as slighting women? If not, why not?

4. We have already mentioned that Frost's poem cannot possibly be thought to describe involuntary immigrants. Is this a weakness in the poem? If so, how serious a weakness?

5. Frost's poem celebrates immigration and does not consider its effect on the American Indian population. The poem does not, so to speak, tell the whole truth; but no statement, however long, could tell the "whole truth" about such a complex topic. Do you agree that if the poem doesn't give us the whole truth, perhaps we get enough if it reminds us of a truth?

## PAT MORA

*Pat Mora, born in El Paso, Texas, in 1942, after graduating from Texas Western College earned a master's degree at the University of Texas at El Paso. She is best known for her poems, but she has also published books and essays on Chicano culture and is the author of many award-winning books for children. She lives in Sante Fe, New Mexico.*

## *Immigrants*                                                       [1986]

wrap their babies in the American flag,
feed them mashed hot dogs and apple pie,
name them Bill and Daisy,
buy them blonde dolls that blink blue
eyes or a football and tiny cleats                                       5
before the baby can even walk
speak to them in thick English, hallo, babee, hallo,
whisper in Spanish or Polish,
when the babies sleep, whisper
in a dark parent bed, that dark                                         10
parent fear, "Will they like
our boy, our girl, our fine american
boy, our fine american girl?"

Pat Mora's experience—that of a Mexican American woman in the United States—obviously must be very different from that of Frost, an Anglo-Saxon male and almost the official poet of the country. Further, Mora is writing in our own time, not almost a century ago. A reader expects, and finds, a very different sort of poem. We won't discuss this poem at length, but we will say that in our view she too gets at something important. Among the many things in this verbal performance that give us pleasure are these:

• The wit of making the title part of the first sentence. A reader expects the title to be relevant to the poem but does not expect it to be grammatically the first word of the poem. We like the fresh way in which the title is used.

- The aptness with which Mora has caught the immigrants' eager yet worried attempt to make their children "100% American."
- The mimicry of the immigrants talking to their children: "hallo, babee, hallo." If this mimicry came from an outsider it would be condescending and offensive, but since it is written by someone known for her concern with Mexican American culture, it probably is not offensive. It is almost affectionate.

### YOUR TURN

1. The last comment may be right, so far as it goes, but isn't it too simple? Reread the poem—preferably aloud—and then try to decide exactly what Mora's attitude is toward the immigrants. Do you think that she fully approves of their hopes? On what do you base your answer?
2. What does it mean to say that someone—a politician, for instance— "wraps himself in the American flag"? What does Mora mean when she says that immigrants "wrap their babies in the American flag"? How would you paraphrase the line?
3. After reading the poem aloud two or three times, what elements of "verbal performance"—we might say of skillful play—do you notice? Mora does not use rhyme, but she does engage in some verbal play. What examples can you point to?
4. What is your own attitude toward the efforts of some immigrants to assimilate themselves to an Anglo-American model? How does your attitude affect your reading of the poem?

# Literature as a Performance, and Literature as a Journey

You have already heard Robert Frost say that a poem is a performance in words, and we hope that our commentary on Frost's "The Span of Life" made his point clear. We showed Frost performing his act, juggling words and taming sentences. And in Pat Mora's "Immigrants" you heard performances within the performance, speeches within the overall speech of the poem. When Mora lets us hear a recent immigrant say "hallo, babee, hallo," we hear this inner performance, and when we read it, even if we read silently, in some degree we are engaging in our own performance or re-creation of the poem. And, of course, if the work is a play, it is intended to be read aloud. In short, writers expect us to walk in their shoes, to reenact their performances in words. You and millions of others at least since the seventeenth century probably performed literature in the most obvious way when, as children, you recited such a nursery rhyme as

Pat-a-cake, pat-a-cake, baker's man.
Bake me a cake as fast as you can,

where the spoken words are accompanied by hand-clapping. But even as adults, in silently reading a work of literature, we sometimes experience a degree of muscular response to the actions that the words describe.

In a moment we will return to this idea of reenacting the writer's performance, but for the moment let's turn to a related topic, literature as a journey.

When we read a particularly engrossing work, or when we see a movie, we may say to a friend that we were "carried away." Or we may speak of certain kinds of writing as "escape literature," again suggesting that the writing takes us out of our ordinary world. The following short poem by Emily Dickinson (1830–1886) uses the idea that literature carries us away. Dickinson first compares a book to a swift square-rigged ship ("frigate" in line 1), then in line 3 to swift horses ("coursers") and finally, in the next-to-last line, to a chariot, normally the vehicle of kings and warriors but also of angels (cf. "Swing low, sweet chariot,/Coming for to carry me home"). One other word in the poem may require comment: "traverse" (line 5) is a route or a journey—again a word associated with being "carried away."

## EMILY DICKINSON

### There is no frigate like a book                    [c. 1873]

There is no frigate like a book
To take us lands away,
Nor any coursers like a page
Of prancing poetry.
This traverse may the poorest take                          5
Without oppress of toll;
How frugal is the chariot
That bears a human soul!

For Dickinson, none of these swift means of transportation can carry us—we might say "transport" us—as effectively as a book can. And a book is a lot cheaper (note "frugal" in line 7) than, say, taking a cruise on a frigate.

Let's now put these two points together: (1) literature as a performance not only by the writer but also by the spectator, and (2) literature as a journey. Robert Frost put the following poem at the beginning of his collected poems. Each of the two stanzas announces that the speaker, the poet, is going to the pasture, and each stanza ends with the words "You come too." Clearly the reader is invited to journey along with the writer—that is, to enter into the writer's world.

## ROBERT FROST

### The Pasture                                             [1915]

I'm going out to clean the pasture spring;
I'll only stop to rake the leaves away
(And wait to watch the water clear, I may):
I sha'n't be gone long. You come too.                       4

I'm going out to fetch the little calf
That's standing by the mother. It's so young,
It totters when she licks it with her tongue.
I sha'n't be gone long. You come too.                       8

Even in this very short poem there is a variety of tones of voice. The first line is probably spoken matter-of-factly:

I'm going out to clean the pasture spring,

but the parenthesis in the third line,

(And wait to watch the water clear, I may)

especially because of "I may" at the end of the line, introduces an engaging tentative note. And in the last line of the first stanza ("I sha'n't be gone long. You come too") we probably hear *two* tones: "I sha'n't be gone long" is, again, matter-of-fact, but in "You come too" we hear a warm, engaging invitation, we hear affection. Frost has, so to speak, performed the role of a particular person (someone who has a chore to do) speaking in a particular situation (that is, speaking to someone whom he cherishes).

Read the poem *aloud* two or three times, and listen to the tones that you find yourself uttering during your performance. We think that when, for instance, you read about the calf being licked by its mother—

It's so young,
It totters when she licks it with her tongue—

you may hear yourself reading in a tone of amused affection, maybe tinged with wonder.

If we are right in our conjectures about the tones you will hear, we think we are also right in saying that when readers read, they are *performing* literary works. As we have already said, readers walk in the author's shoes. And in this walk—in this journey they are performing—they acquire an experience.

# A Story About a Journey

## EUDORA WELTY

*Eudora Welty (1909-2001) was born in Jackson, Mississippi. Although she earned a bachelor's degree at the University of Wisconsin and spent a year studying advertising in New York City at the Columbia University Graduate School of Business, she lived almost all of her life in Jackson.*

*In the preface to her* Collected Stories *she says:*

I have been told, both in approval and in accusation, that I seem to love all my characters. What I do in writing of any character is to try to enter into the mind, heart and skin of a human being who is not myself. Whether this happens to be a man or a woman, old or young, with skin black or white, the primary challenge lies in making the jump itself. It is the act of a writer's imagination that I set most high.

*In addition to writing stories and novels, Welty wrote a book about fiction,* The Eye of the Story *(1977), and a memoir,* One Writer's Beginnings *(1984).*

## A Worn Path                                                    [1941]

It was December—a bright frozen day in the early morning. Far out in the country there was an old Negro woman with her head tied in a red rag, coming along a path through the pinewoods. Her name was Phoenix Jackson. She was very old and small and she walked slowly in the dark pine shadows, moving a little from side to side in her steps, with the balanced heaviness and lightness of a pendulum in a grandfather clock. She carried a thin, small cane made from an umbrella, and with this she kept tapping the frozen earth in front of her. This made a grave and persistent noise in the still air, that seemed meditative like the chirping of a solitary little bird.

She wore a dark striped dress reaching down to her shoe tops, and an equally long apron of bleached sugar sacks, with a full pocket: all neat and tidy, but every time she took a step she might have fallen over her shoelaces, which dragged from her unlaced shoes. She looked straight ahead. Her eyes were blue with age. Her skin had a pattern all its own of numberless branching wrinkles and as though a whole little tree stood in the middle of her forehead, but a golden color ran underneath, and the two knobs of her cheeks were illuminated by a yellow burning under the dark. Under the red rag her hair came down on her neck in the frailest of ringlets, still black, and with an odor like copper.

Now and then there was a quivering in the thicket. Old Phoenix said, "Out of my way, all you foxes, owls, beetles, jack rabbits, coons and wild animals! . . . Keep out from under these feet, little bob-whites. . . . Keep the big wild hogs out of my path. Don't let none of those come running my direction. I got a long way." Under her small black-freckled hand her cane, limber as a buggy whip, would switch at the brush as if to rouse up any hiding things.

On she went. The woods were deep and still. The sun made the pine needles almost too bright to look at, up where the wind rocked. The cones dropped as light as feathers. Down in the hollow was the mourning dove— it was not too late for him.

5      The path ran up a hill. "Seem like there is chains about my feet, time I get this far," she said, in the voice of argument old people keep to use with themselves. "Something always take a hold of me on this hill—pleads I should stay."

After she got to the top she turned and gave a full, severe look behind her where she had come. "Up through pines," she said at length. "Now down through oaks."

Her eyes opened their widest, and she started down gently. But before she got to the bottom of the hill a bush caught her dress.

Her fingers were busy and intent, but her skirts were full and long, so that before she could pull them free in one place they were caught in another. It was not possible to allow the dress to tear. "I in the thorny bush," she said. "Thorns, you doing your appointed work. Never want to let folks pass, no sir. Old eyes thought you was a pretty little *green* bush."

Finally, trembling all over, she stood free, and after a moment dared to stoop for her cane.

10     "Sun so high!" she cried, leaning back and looking, while the thick tears went over her eyes. "The time getting all gone here."

At the foot of this hill was a place where a log was laid across the creek. "Now comes the trial," said Phoenix.

Putting her right foot out, she mounted the log and shut her eyes. Lifting her skirt, levelling her cane fiercely before her, like a festival figure in some parade, she began to march across. Then she opened her eyes and she was safe on the other side.

"I wasn't as old as I thought," she said.

15    But she sat down to rest. She spread her skirts on the bank around her and folded her hands over her knees. Up above her was a tree in a pearly cloud of mistletoe. She did not dare to close her eyes, and when a little boy brought her a plate with a slice of marble-cake on it she spoke to him. "That would be acceptable," she said. But when she went to take it there was just her own hand in the air.

So she left that tree, and had to go through a barbed-wire fence. There she had to creep and crawl, spreading her knees and stretching her fingers like a baby trying to climb the steps. But she talked loudly to herself: she could not let her dress be torn now, so late in the day, and she could not pay for having her arm or leg sawed off if she got caught fast where she was.

At last she was safe through the fence and risen up out in the clearing. Big dead trees, like black men with one arm, were standing in the purple stalks of the withered cotton field. There sat a buzzard.

"Who you watching?"

In the furrow she made her way along.

20    "Glad this not the season for bulls," she said, looking sideways, "and the good Lord made his snakes to curl up and sleep in the winter. A pleasure I don't see no two-headed snake coming around that tree, where it come once. It took a while to get by him, back in the summer."

She passed through the old cotton and went into a field of dead corn. It whispered and shook and was taller than her head. "Through the maze now," she said, for there was no path.

Then there was something tall, black, and skinny there, moving before her.

At first she took it for a man. It could have been a man dancing in the field. But she stood still and listened, and it did not make a sound. It was as silent as a ghost.

"Ghost," she said sharply, "who be you the ghost of? For I have heard of nary death close by."

25    But there was no answer—only the ragged dancing in the wind.

She shut her eyes, reached out her hand, and touched a sleeve. She found a coat and inside that an emptiness, cold as ice.

"You scarecrow," she said. Her face lighted. "I ought to be shut up for good," she said with laughter. "My senses is gone, I too old. I the oldest people I ever know. Dance, old scarecrow," she said, "while I dancing with you."

She kicked her foot over the furrow, and with mouth drawn down, shook her head once or twice in a little strutting way. Some husks blew down and whirled in streamers about her skirts.

Then she went on, parting her way from side to side with the cane, through the whispering field. At last she came to the end, to a wagon track where the silver grass blew between the red ruts. The quail were walking around like pullets, seeming all dainty and unseen.

30    "Walk pretty," she said. "This the easy place. This the easy going."

She followed the track, swaying through the quiet bare fields, through the little strings of trees silver in their dead leaves, past cabins silver from weather, with the doors and windows boarded shut, all like old women under a spell sitting there. "I walking in their sleep," she said, nodding her head vigorously.

In a ravine she went where a spring was silently flowing through a hollow log. Old Phoenix bent and drank. "Sweet-gum makes the water sweet," she said, and drank more. "Nobody know who made this well, for it was here when I was born."

The track crossed a swampy part where the moss hung as white as lace from every limb. "Sleep on, alligators, and blow your bubbles." Then the track went into the road.

Deep, deep the road went down between the high green-colored banks. Overhead the live-oaks met, and it was as dark as a cave.

35     A black dog with a lolling tongue came up out of the weeds by the ditch. She was meditating, and not ready, and when he came at her she only hit him a little with her cane. Over she went in the ditch, like a little puff of milk-weed.

Down there, her senses drifted away. A dream visited her, and she reached her hand up, but nothing reached down and gave her a pull. So she lay there and presently went to talking. "Old woman," she said to herself, "that black dog come up out of the weeds to stall you off, and now there he sitting on his fine tail, smiling at you."

A white man finally came along and found her—a hunter, a young man, with his dog on a chain.

"Well, Granny!" he laughed. "What are you doing there?"

"Lying on my back like a June-bug waiting to be turned over, mister," she said, reaching up her hand.

40     He lifted her up, gave her a swing in the air, and set her down. "Anything broken, Granny?"

"No sir, them old dead weeds is springy enough," said Phoenix, when she had got her breath. "I thank you for your trouble."

"Where do you live, Granny?" he asked, while the two dogs were growling at each other.

"Away back yonder, sir, behind the ridge. You can't even see it from here."

"On your way home?"

45     "No, sir, I going to town."

"Why, that's too far! That's as far as I walk when I come out myself, and I get something for my trouble." He patted the stuffed bag he carried, and there hung down a little closed claw. It was one of the bob-whites, with its beak hooked bitterly to show it was dead. "Now you go on home, Granny!"

"I bound to go to town, mister," said Phoenix. "The time come around."

He gave another laugh, filling the whole landscape. "I know you old colored people! Wouldn't miss going to town to see Santa Claus!"

But something held old Phoenix very still. The deep lines in her face went into a fierce and different radiation. Without warning, she had seen with her own eyes a flashing nickel fall out of the man's pocket onto the ground.

50     "How old are you, Granny?" he was saying.

"There is no telling, mister," she said, "no telling."

Then she gave a little cry and clapped her hands and said, "Git on away from here, dog! Look! Look at that dog!" She laughed as if in admiration. "He ain't scared of nobody. He a big black dog." She whispered, "Sic him!"

"Watch me get rid of that cur," said the man. "Sic him, Pete! Sic him!"

Phoenix heard the dogs fighting, and heard the man running and throwing sticks. She even heard a gunshot. But she was slowly bending forward by that time, further and further forward, the lids stretched down over her eyes, as if she were doing this in her sleep. Her chin was lowered almost to her knees. The yellow palm of her hand came out from the fold of her apron. Her fingers slid down and along the ground under the piece of money with the grace and care they would have in lifting an egg from under a sitting hen. Then she slowly straightened up, she stood erect, and the nickel was in her apron pocket. A bird flew by. Her lips moved. "God watching me the whole time. I come to stealing."

55    The man came back, and his own dog panted about them. "Well, I scared him off that time," he said, and then he laughed and lifted his gun and pointed it at Phoenix.

She stood straight and faced him.

"Doesn't the gun scare you?" he said, still pointing it.

"No, sir, I seen plenty go off closer by, in my day, and for less than what I done," she said, holding utterly still.

He smiled, and shouldered the gun. "Well, Granny," he said, "you must be a hundred years old, and scared of nothing. I'd give you a dime if I had any money with me. But you take my advice and stay home, and nothing will happen to you."

60    "I bound to go on my way, mister," said Phoenix. She inclined her head in the red rag. Then they went in different directions, but she could hear the gun shooting again and again over the hill.

She walked on. The shadows hung from the oak trees to the road like curtains. Then she smelled wood-smoke, and smelled the river, and she saw a steeple and the cabins on their steep steps. Dozens of little black children whirled around her. There ahead was Natchez shining. Bells were ringing. She walked on.

In the paved city it was Christmas time. There were red and green electric lights strung and crisscrossed everywhere, and all turned on in the daytime. Old Phoenix would have been lost if she had not distrusted her eyesight and depended on her feet to know where to take her.

She paused quietly on the sidewalk where people were passing by. A lady came along in the crowd, carrying an armful of red-, green-, and silver-wrapped presents; she gave off perfume like the red roses in hot summer, and Phoenix stopped her.

"Please, missy, will you lace up my shoe?" She held up her foot.

65    "What do you want, Grandma?"

"See my shoe," said Phoenix. "Do all right for out in the country, but wouldn't look right to go in a big building."

"Stand still then, Grandma," said the lady. She put her packages down on the sidewalk beside her and laced and tied both shoes tightly.

"Can't lace 'em with a cane," said Phoenix. "Thank you, missy. I doesn't mind asking a nice lady to tie up my shoe, when I gets out on the street."

Moving slowly and from side to side, she went into the big building and into a tower of steps, where she walked up and around and around until her feet knew to stop.

70    She entered a door, and there she saw nailed up on the wall the document that had been stamped with the gold seal and framed in the gold frame, which matched the dream that was hung up in her head.

"Here I be," she said. There was a fixed and ceremonial stiffness over her body.

"A charity case, I suppose," said an attendant who sat at the desk before her.

But Phoenix only looked above her head. There was sweat on her face, the wrinkles in her skin shone like a bright net.

"Speak up, Grandma," the woman said. "What's your name? We must have your history, you know. Have you been here before? What seems to be the trouble with you?"

75    Old Phoenix only gave a twitch to her face as if a fly were bothering her.

"Are you deaf?" cried the attendant.

But then the nurse came in.

"Oh, that's just old Aunt Phoenix," she said. "She doesn't come for herself—she has a little grandson. She makes these trips just as regular as clockwork. She lives away back off the Old Natchez Trace." She bent down. "Well, Aunt Phoenix, why don't you just take a seat? We won't keep you standing after your long trip." She pointed.

The old woman sat down, bolt upright in the chair.

80    "Now, how is the boy?" asked the nurse.

Old Phoenix did not speak.

"I said, how is the boy?"

But Phoenix only waited and stared straight ahead, her face very solemn and withdrawn into rigidity.

"Is his throat any better?" asked the nurse. "Aunt Phoenix, don't you hear me? Is your grandson's throat any better since the last time you came for the medicine?"

85    With her hands on her knees, the old woman waited, silent, erect and motionless, just as if she were in armor.

"You mustn't take up our time this way, Aunt Phoenix," the nurse said. "Tell us quickly about your grandson, and get it over. He isn't dead, is he?"

At last there came a flicker and then a flame of comprehension across her face, and she spoke.

"My grandson. It was my memory had left me. There I sat and forgot why I made my long trip."

"Forgot?" The nurse frowned. "After you came so far?"

90    Then Phoenix was like an old woman begging a dignified forgiveness for waking up frightened in the night. "I never did go to school, I was too old at the Surrender," she said in a soft voice. "I'm an old woman without an education. It was my memory fail me. My little grandson, he is just the same, and I forgot it in the coming."

"Throat never heals, does it?" said the nurse, speaking in a loud, sure voice to old Phoenix. By now she had a card with something written on it, a little list. "Yes. Swallowed lye. When was it—January—two-three years ago—"

Phoenix spoke unasked now. "No, missy, he not dead, he just the same. Every little while his throat begin to close up again, and he not able to swallow. He not get his breath. He not able to help himself. So the time come around, and I go on another trip for the soothing medicine."

"All right. The doctor said as long as you came to get it, you could have it," said the nurse. "But it's an obstinate case."

"My little grandson, he sit up there in the house all wrapped up, waiting by himself," Phoenix went on. "We is the only two left in the world. He suffer and it don't seem to put him back at all. He got a sweet look. He going to last. He wear a little patch quilt and peep out holding his mouth open like a little bird. I remembers so plain now. I not going to forget him again, no, the whole enduring time. I could tell him from all the others in creation."

95    "All right." The nurse was trying to hush her now. She brought her a bottle of medicine. "Charity," she said, making a check mark in a book.

Old Phoenix held the bottle close to her eyes and then carefully put it into her pocket.

"I thank you," she said.

"It's Christmas time, Grandma," said the attendant. "Could I give you a few pennies out of my purse?"

"Five pennies is a nickel," said Phoenix stiffly.

100    "Here's a nickel," said the attendant.

Phoenix rose carefully and held out her hand. She received the nickel and then fished the other nickel out of her pocket and laid it beside the new one. She stared at her palm closely, with her head on one side.

Then she gave a tap with her cane on the floor.

"This is what come to me to do," she said. "I going to the store and buy my child a little windmill they sells, made out of paper. He going to find it hard to believe there such a thing in the world. I'll march myself back where he waiting, holding it straight up in his hand."

She lifted her free hand, gave a little nod, turned round, and walked out of the doctor's office. Then her slow step began on the stairs, going down.

### YOUR TURN

1. If you do not know the legend of the Phoenix, look it up in a dictionary or, even better, in an encyclopedia. Then carefully reread "A Worn Path" to learn whether the story in any way connects with the legend.
2. What do you think of the hunter?
3. What would be lost if the episode (with all of its dialogue) of Phoenix falling into the ditch and being helped out of it by the hunter were omitted?
4. Is Christmas a particularly appropriate time in which to set the story? Why or why not?
5. What do you make of the title?
6. "A Worn Path" treats race relations as one of its themes. Is this theme primary, or would you say instead that it is secondary? How would the story be different in its effect if everything stayed the same except for Phoenix's race?
7. Have you ever made a difficult trip by foot? Was there a point when you were tempted to turn back? What kept you going? Do you think that your experience could be made the basis for a short story? How would you structure such a story—its beginning, middle, and end?

# Two Very Short Contemporary Short Stories

## LYDIA DAVIS

*Lydia Davis, born in 1947 in Northampton, Massachusetts, grew up in New York City and then lived for several years in France and Ireland. A professor of creative writing at the State University of New York (Albany), Davis has translated French literature and has written several books of stories;* The Collected Stories of Lydia Davis, *published in 2009, contains all of her stories to date. Among her awards is a MacArthur Fellowship.*

### Childcare                                                                 [2007]

It's his turn to take care of the baby. He is cross.
    He says, "I never get enough done."
    The baby is in a bad mood, too.
    He gives the baby a bottle of juice and sits him well back in a big armchair.
    He sits himself down in another chair and turns on the television.
    Together they watch *The Odd Couple*.

In Davis's *Varieties of Disturbance* (2007), the book from which we reprint "Childcare," the story appears in the middle of a page that is otherwise blank. The very appearance on the page is part of the performance, and it is also part of—dare we say?—the meaning. We see a largely blank page, a bare world, not much to look at, not much to make life rich. What do we know about the inhabitants of this world?

- The unnamed man (he is merely "he") is "cross," and the unnamed baby "is in a bad mood, too."
- The next thing we learn about the man is what we deduce from his statement, "I never get enough done." Ah, he is someone who wants to accomplish something. That sounds admirable.
- But he thinks the temporary job ("it's his turn") of caring for the baby interferes with his unspecified aspirations. That sounds not so nice, and we may wonder, "What sort of a guy is this who resents caring for his infant?"

The next things we learn dispose us favorably toward the man:

- "He gives the baby a bottle of juice and sits him well back in a big armchair." This business of sitting the child "well back in a big armchair" suggests that the man takes some care to make sure that the child is secure, is safely placed. We like that, we are reassured.
- The man then sits down in another chair and "turns on the television." Television? We might have thought that this man who can "never get enough done" would balance his checkbook, or read the newspaper, or answer a letter, but no, he watches television. That's not a crime, but for

a guy who complains that he "can never get enough done," it does seem a bit much.

- The final sentence is, "Together they watch *The Odd Couple*." Surely the thought crosses a reader's mind that these two are themselves an odd couple, and the reader may reasonably conclude that in some ways the man—cross, claiming that he can't get anything done—is as infantile as the baby.

It's a story told very simply, chiefly in simple sentences, "He says," "The baby is," "He gives," etc. Only twice does the author use compound sentences (simple sentences joined by a conjunction, in this case the most child-like of all conjunctions, "and," the language found in Dick and Jane children's books). Not much happens in this very simply told story, but it tells us all that we need to know about the unnamed man. And perhaps it tells us something about life, even about our own lives, for instance about the disparity between our own grand view of ourselves and the simple reality.

Now for a second very short story by Lydia Davis.

## City People
[2001]

They have moved to the country. The country is nice enough: there are quail sitting in the bushes and frogs peeping in the swamps. But they are uneasy. They quarrel more often. They cry, or she cries and he bows his head. He is pale all the time now. She wakes in a panic at night, hearing him sniffle. She wakes in a panic again, hearing a car go up the driveway. In the morning there is sunlight on their faces but mice are chattering in the walls. He hates the mice. The pump breaks. They replace the pump. They poison the mice. Their neighbor's dog barks. It barks and barks. She could poison the dog.

"We're city people," he says, "and there aren't any nice cities to live in."

**YOUR TURN**

1. What elements of "performance"—perhaps we can say Davis's "craftsmanship"—do you see in this tiny narrative?
2. We are not told *why* these people have moved from the city to the country. Is it reasonable to offer a guess? If you think a reader can plausibly guess why they moved, what, in your view, is the reason for the move?
3. Does the story give at least a tiny glimpse of some aspect of life? Please explain.

# Thinking About a Classic Story

This story, told by Jesus, is reported in the fifteenth chapter of the Gospel According to Luke. Jesus here recounts a **parable,** a short story from which a lesson is to be drawn. Luke reports that just before Jesus told the story, the Pharisees and scribes—persons whom the Gospels depict as opposed to Jesus because he sometimes found their traditions and teachings inadequate—complained that

Jesus was a man of loose morals, one who "receives sinners and eats with them." According to Luke, Jesus responded thus:

## The Parable of the Prodigal Son

And he said, "A certain man had two sons: and the younger of them said to his father, 'Father, give me the portion of goods that falleth to me.' And he divided unto them his living. And not many days after, the younger son gathered all together, and took his journey into a far country, and there wasted his substance with riotous living.

And when he had spent all, there arose a mighty famine in that land, and he began to be in want. And he went and joined himself to a citizen of that country, and he sent him into his fields to feed swine. And he would fain have filled his belly with the husks that the swine did eat: and no man gave unto him.

And when he came to himself he said, 'How many hired servants of my father's have bread enough and to spare, and I perish with hunger? I will arise and go to my father, and will say unto him, "Father, I have sinned against heaven, and before thee. And am no more worthy to be called thy son: make me as one of thy hired servants."'

And he arose, and came to his father. But when he was yet a great way off, his father saw him, and had compassion, and ran, and fell on his neck, and kissed him. And the son said unto him, 'Father, I have sinned against heaven, and in thy sight, and am no more worthy to be called thy son.' But the father said to his servants, 'Bring forth the best robe, and put it on him, and put a ring on his hand, and shoes on his feet. And bring hither the fatted calf and kill it, and let us eat, and be merry. For this my son was dead, and is alive again; he was lost, and is found.' And they began to be merry.

Now his elder son was in the field, and as he came and drew nigh to the house, he heard music and dancing. And he called one of the servants, and asked what these things meant. And he said unto him, 'Thy brother is come, and thy father hath killed the fatted calf, because he hath received him safe and sound.' And he was angry, and would not go in: therefore came his father out, and entreated him. And he answering said to his father, 'Lo, these many years do I serve thee, neither transgressed I at any time thy commandment, and yet thou never gavest me a kid, that I might make merry with my friends: but as soon as this thy son was come, which hath devoured thy living with harlots, thou has killed for him the fatted calf.' And he said unto him, 'Son, thou art ever with me, and all that I have is thine. It was meet that we should make merry, and be glad: for this thy brother was dead, and is alive again: and was lost, and is found.' " (Luke 15. 11–32, King James Version)

Now, to begin with a small point, it is not likely that any but strictly observant Jews, or Muslims (who, like these Jews, do not eat pork), can feel the disgust that Jesus's audience must have felt at the thought that the son was reduced to feeding swine and that he even envied the food that swine ate. Further, some of us may be vegetarians; if so, we are not at all delighted at the thought that the father kills the fatted calf (probably the wretched beast has been force-fed) in order to celebrate the son's return.

And some readers do not believe in God, and hence are not prepared to take the story, as many people take it, as a story whose message is that we, like God (the father in this parable is usually taken to stand for God), ought to rejoice in the restoration of the sinner. Probably, then, for all sorts of obvious reasons none of us can put ourselves back into the first century CE and hear the story exactly as Jesus's audience heard it.

Still, most of us can probably agree on what we take to be the gist of the story, and we can enjoy the skillful way in which it is told. This skill will become apparent, however, only after several readings. What are some examples of superb storytelling here, and what can a reader gain from a thoughtful reading? We begin by noting a few points:

- Although the story is customarily called "The Parable of the Prodigal Son" or "The Parable of the Lost Son," it tells of two sons, not of one. When we reread the story, we increasingly see that these brothers are compared and contrasted: the prodigal leaves his father's house for a different way of life—he thus seems lost to the father—but then he repents and returns to the father, whereas the older son, who physically remains with the father, is spiritually remote from the father, or is lost in a different way. By virtue of his self-centeredness the older son is remote from the father in feeling or spirit.
- Again, reading and rereading reveal small but telling details. For instance, when the prodigal plans to return home, he thinks of what he will say to his father. He has come to his senses and repudiated his folly, but he still does not understand his father, for we will see in a moment that the prodigal has no need of this speech. Jesus tells us that as soon as the father saw the prodigal returning, he "had compassion, and ran, and fell on his neck, and kissed him." And (another very human touch) the prodigal— although already forgiven—nevertheless cannot refrain from uttering his heartfelt but, under the circumstances, unnecessary speech of repentance.
- The elder son, learning that the merrymaking is for the returning prodigal, "was angry, and would not go in." This character is sketched only briefly, but a reader immediately recognizes the type: self-centered, unforgiving, and petulant. The older son does not realize it, but he is as distant from his father as the younger son had been. What is the father's response to this son, who is so different from the forgiving father?

> Therefore came his father out, and entreated him.

The father goes out to the dutiful son, just as he had *gone out* to the prodigal son. (What the father *does* is as important as what he *says*.) Notice, too, speaking of sons, that the older son, talking to his father, somewhat distances himself from his brother, disdainfully referring to the prodigal as "this thy son." And what is the father's response? To the elder son's "this thy son," the father replies, "this thy brother."

### YOUR TURN

This story is traditionally called the Parable of the Prodigal Son. Can a case be made for the view that it ought to be called the Parable of the Prodigal Father? Forget, if you can, the traditional title, and ask yourself if the story tells of a father who is prodigal with his property and who at the end is prodigal with his love. Explain why you accept or reject this interpretation.

# Stories True and False

The word story comes from history—the stories that historians, biographers, and journalists narrate are supposed to be true accounts of what happened. The stories of novelists and short-story writers, however, are admittedly untrue; they are fiction, things made up, imagined, manufactured. As readers, we come to a supposedly true story with expectations different from those we bring to fiction.

Consider the difference between reading a narrative in a newspaper and one in a book of short stories. If, while reading a newspaper, we come across a story of, say, a subway accident, we assume that the account is true, and we read it for the information about a relatively unusual event. Anyone hurt? What sort of people? In our neighborhood? Whose fault? When we read a book of fiction, however, we do not expect to encounter literal truths; we read novels and short stories not for facts but for pleasure and for some insight or for a sense of what an aspect of life means to the writer. Consider the following short story by Grace Paley.

## GRACE PALEY

*Grace Paley (1922–2007) was born in New York City, where she attended Hunter College and New York University, but left without a degree. While raising two children she wrote poetry and then, in the 1950s, turned to writing fiction. Paley's books include two collections of short stories,* The Little Disturbances of Man *(1959) and* Enormous Changes at the Last Minute *(1974).*

*Paley's chief subject is the life of little people struggling in the Big City. Of life she has said, "How daily life is lived is a mystery to me. You write about what's mysterious to you. What is it like? Why do people do this?" Of the short story she has said, "It can be just telling a little tale, or writing a complicated philosophical story. It can be a song, almost."*

## Samuel

[1968]

Some boys are very tough. They're afraid of nothing. They are the ones who climb a wall and take a bow at the top. Not only are they brave on the roof, but they make a lot of noise in the darkest part of the cellar where even the super hates to go. They also jiggle and hop on the platform between the locked doors of the subway cars.

Four boys are jiggling on the swaying platform. Their names are Alfred, Calvin, Samuel, and Tom. The men and the women in the cars on either side watch them. They don't like them to jiggle or jump but don't want to interfere. Of course some of the men in the cars were once brave boys like these. One of them had ridden the tail of a speeding truck from New York to Rockaway Beach without getting off, without his sore fingers losing hold. Nothing happened to him then or later. He had made a compact with other boys who preferred to watch: Starting at Eighth Avenue and Fifteenth Street, he would get to some specified place, maybe Twenty-third and the river, by hopping the tops of the moving trucks. This was hard to do when one truck turned a corner in the wrong direction and the nearest truck was a couple of feet too high. He made three or four starts before succeeding. He had gotten his idea from a film at school called *The Romance of Logging.* He had finished high school, married a good friend, was in a responsible job and going to night school.

These two men and others looked at the four boys jumping and jiggling on the platform and thought, It must be fun to ride that way, especially now the weather is nice and we're out of the tunnel and way high over the Bronx. Then they thought, These kids do seem to be acting sort of stupid. They *are* little. Then they thought of some of the brave things they had done when they were boys and jiggling didn't seem so risky.

The ladies in the car became very angry when they looked at the four boys. Most of them brought their brows together and hoped the boys could see their extreme disapproval. One of the ladies wanted to get up and say, Be careful you dumb kids, get off that platform or I'll call a cop. But three of the boys were Negroes and the fourth was something else she couldn't tell for sure. She was afraid they'd be fresh and laugh at her and embarrass her. She wasn't afraid they'd hit her, but she was afraid of embarrassment. Another lady thought, Their mothers never know where they are. It wasn't true in this particular case. Their mothers all knew that they had gone to see the missile exhibit on Fourteenth Street.

5      Out on the platform, whenever the train accelerated, the boys would raise their hands and point them up to the sky to act like rockets going off, then they rat-tat-tatted the shatterproof glass pane like machine guns, although no machine guns had been exhibited.

For some reason known only to the motorman, the train began a sudden slowdown. The lady who was afraid of embarrassment saw the boys jerk forward and backward and grab the swinging guard chains. She had her own boy at home. She stood up with determination and went to the door. She slid it open and said, "You boys will be hurt. You'll be killed. I'm going to call the conductor if you don't just go into the next car and sit down and be quiet."

Two of the boys said, "Yes'm," and acted as though they were about to go. Two of them blinked their eyes a couple of times and pressed their lips together. The train resumed its speed. The door slid shut, parting the lady and the boys. She leaned against the side door because she had to get off at the next stop.

The boys opened their eyes wide at each other and laughed. The lady blushed. The boys looked at her and laughed harder. They began to pound each other's back. Samuel laughed the hardest and pounded Alfred's back until Alfred coughed and the tears came. Alfred held tight to the chain hook. Samuel pounded him even harder when he saw the tears. He said, "Why you bawling? You a baby, huh?" and laughed. One of the men whose boyhood had been more watchful than brave became angry. He stood up straight and looked at the boys for a couple of seconds. Then he walked in a citizenly way to the end of the car, where he pulled the emergency cord. Almost at once, with a terrible hiss, the pressure of air abandoned the brakes and the wheels were caught and held.

People standing in the most secure places fell forward, then backward. Samuel had let go of his hold on the chain so he could pound Tom as well as Alfred. All the passengers in the cars whipped back and forth, but he pitched only forward and fell head first to be crushed and killed between the cars.

10      The train had stopped hard, halfway into the station, and the conductor called at once for the trainmen who knew about this kind of death and how to take the body from the wheels and brakes. There was silence except for passengers from other cars who asked, What happened! What happened! The ladies waited around wondering if he might be an only child. The men recalled other afternoons with very bad endings. The little boys stayed close to each other, leaning and touching shoulders and arms and legs.

When the policeman knocked at the door and told her about it, Samuel's mother began to scream. She screamed all day and moaned all night, though the doctors tried to quiet her with pills.

Oh, oh, she hopelessly cried. She did not know how she could ever find another boy like that one. However, she was a young woman and she became pregnant. Then for a few months she was hopeful. The child born to her was a boy. They brought him to be seen and nursed. She smiled. But immediately she saw that this baby wasn't Samuel. She and her husband together have had other children, but never again will a boy exactly like Samuel be known.

You might think about the ways in which "Samuel" differs from a newspaper story of an accident in a subway. (You might even want to write a newspaper version of the happening.) In some ways, Paley's story faintly resembles an account that might appear in a newspaper. Journalists are taught to give information about Who, What, When, Where, and Why, and Paley does provide this. Thus, the *characters* (Samuel and others) are the journalist's Who; the *plot* (the boys were jiggling on the platform, and when a man pulled the emergency cord one of them was killed) is the What; the *setting* (the subway, presumably in modern times) is the When and the Where; the *motivation* (the irritation of the man who pulls the emergency cord) is the Why.

Ask yourself questions about each of these elements, and think about how they work in Paley's story. You might also think about responses to the following questions. Your responses will teach you a good deal about what literature is and about some of the ways in which it works.

**YOUR TURN**

1. Paley wrote the story, but an unspecified person *tells* it. Describe the voice of this narrator in the first paragraph. Is the voice neutral and objective, or do you hear some sort of attitude, a point of view? If you do hear an attitude, what words or phrases in the story indicate it?

2. What do you know about the setting of "Samuel"? What can you infer about the neighborhood?

3. In the fourth paragraph we are told that "three of the boys were Negroes and the fourth was something else." Is race important in this story? Is Samuel "Negro" or "something else"? Does it matter?

4. Exactly *why* did a man walk "in a citizenly way to the end of the car, where he pulled the emergency cord"? Do you think the author blames him? What evidence can you offer to support your view? Do *you* blame him? Or do you blame the boys? Or anyone? Explain.

5. The story is called "Samuel," and it is, surely, about him. But what happens after Samuel dies? (You might want to list the events.) What else is the story about? (You might want to comment on why you believe the items in your list are important.)

6. Can you generalize about what the men think of the jigglers and about what the women think? Is Paley saying something about the sexes? About the attitudes of onlookers in a big city?

# What's Past Is Prologue

The poems and stories that you have just read cannot, of course, stand for all works of literature. For one thing, although Mora's "Immigrants" and the prose stories include some dialogue, none of these works is in dramatic form, designed for presentation on a stage. Still, these examples, as well as works of literature that you are already familiar with, will provide something of a background against which you can read the other works in this book. For instance, if you read a story that, like the parable of the prodigal son, seems strongly to imply a moral, think about how the moral is controlled by what the characters *do* as well as by what they *say,* and how one character is defined by being set against another. If you read a poem that, like Mora's "Immigrants," seems to play one tone of voice against another (for instance, the voice of the speaker of the poem against a voice quoted within the poem), think about how the voices relate to each other and how they perhaps harmonize to create a complex vision.

In short, a work of literature is not a nut to be cracked open so that a kernel of meaning can be extracted and devoured, and the rest thrown away; the whole—a performance in words—is something to be experienced and enjoyed.

We end this chapter with two short stories.

## JAMAICA KINCAID

*Jamaica Kincaid (b. 1949) was born in St. John's, Antigua, in the West Indies. She was educated at the Princess Margaret School in Antigua, and, briefly, at Westchester Community College and Franconia College. Since 1974 she has been a contributor to the* New Yorker.

*Kincaid is the author of many works of fiction and nonfiction, including* At the Bottom of the River *(1983, a collection of short pieces, including "Girl"),* Annie John *(1985, a second book recording a girl's growth, including "Columbus in Chains"),* A Small Place *(1988, a passionate essay about the destructive effects of colonialism), and* Lucy *(1990, a short novel about a young black woman who comes to the United States from the West Indies).*

## *Girl*                                                              [1978]

Wash the white clothes on Monday and put them on the stone heap; wash the color clothes on Tuesday and put them on the clothesline to dry; don't walk barehead in the hot sun; cook pumpkin fritters in very hot sweet oil; soak your little clothes right after you take them off; when buying cotton to make yourself a nice blouse, be sure that it doesn't have gum on it, because that way it won't hold up well after a wash; soak salt fish overnight before you cook it; is it true that you sing benna[1] in Sunday School? always eat your food in such a way that it won't turn someone else's stomach; on Sundays try to walk like a lady and not like the slut you are so bent on becoming; don't sing benna in Sunday School; you mustn't speak to wharf-rat boys, not even to give directions; don't eat fruits on the street—flies will follow you; *but I don't sing benna on Sundays at all and never in Sunday school;* this is how to sew on a button; this is how to make a buttonhole for the button you have just sewed on; this is how to hem a dress when you see the hem coming down and so to prevent yourself from looking like the slut I know you are so bent on becoming; this is how you iron your father's khaki pants so that they don't have a crease; this is how you grow okra—far from the house, because okra tree harbors red ants; when you are growing dasheen, make sure it gets plenty of water or else it makes your throat itch when you are eating it; this is how you sweep a corner; this is how you sweep a whole house; this is how you sweep a yard; this is how you smile to someone you don't like too much; this is how you set a table for dinner with an important guest; this is how you smile to someone you don't like at all; this is how you smile to someone you like completely; this is how you set a table for tea; this is how you set a table for dinner; this is how you set a table for lunch; this is how you set a table for breakfast; this is how to behave in the presence of men who don't know you very well, and this way they won't recognize immediately the slut I have warned you against becoming; be sure to wash every day, even if it is with your own spit; don't squat down to play marbles—you are not a boy, you know; don't pick people's flowers—you might catch something; don't throw stones at blackbirds, because it might not be a blackbird at all; this is how to make a bread pudding; this is how to make duokona;[2] this is how to make a pepper pot; this is how to make a good medicine for a cold; this is how to make a good medicine to throw away a child before it even becomes a child; this is how to catch a fish; this is how to throw back a fish you don't like, and that way something bad won't fall on you; this is how to bully a man; this is how a man bullies you; this is how to love a man, and if this doesn't work there are other ways, and if they don't work don't feel too bad about giving up; this is how to spit up in the air if you feel like it, and this is how to move quick so that it doesn't fall on you; this is how to make ends meet; always squeeze bread to make sure it's fresh; *but what if the baker won't let me feel the bread?;* you mean to say that after all you are really going to be the kind of woman who the baker won't let near the bread?

---

[1]**benna** Calypso music.    [2]**duokona** a spicy pudding made of plantains.

**YOUR TURN**

1. In a paragraph, identify the two characters whose voices we hear in this story. Explain what we know about them (their circumstances and their relationship). Cite specific evidence from the text. For example, what is the effect of the frequent repetition of "this is how"? Are there other words or phrases frequently repeated?

2. Try reading a section of "Girl" aloud in a rhythmical pattern, giving the principal and the second voices. Then reread the story, trying to incorporate this rhythm mentally into your reading. How does this rhythm contribute to the overall effect of the story? How does it compare to or contrast with speech rhythms that are familiar to you?

# 3

# The Pleasures of Reading— and of Writing Arguments About Literature

"The pleasures of reading," a student may say, are obvious, "but when it comes to talking about the 'pleasures' of writing, surely you must be kidding." Students who make this reply have on their side the authority of a good many distinguished writers. To cite only three: Edna Ferber said that writing "is a combination of ditch-digging, mountain-climbing, treadmill, and childbirth"; Ernest Hemingway is reported to have said, "There is nothing to writing. All you do is sit down at a typewriter and bleed"; and in our own day the novelist William Styron said, "Let's face it, writing is hell."

Every student and every professor understands what these writers are talking about. The bad news is that they are talking about the difficult job of getting on to paper some coherent thoughts that they think are good enough to share with a reader. But there is good news too: All writers know that the very act of writing will stimulate *better* thoughts than those that they begin with. Writers— professionals as well as students—put words on paper with the understanding that the process of writing is a way of getting better ideas, a way of improving the nearly incoherent stuff that at first drifts through our minds.

- *A Common Misapprehension:* Students often think they are writing "for the teacher." Such an assumption leads to (1) miserable attempts to guess about what this mysterious figure has in mind, and (2) writing that ultimately satisfies neither the student nor the instructor.

- *The Facts:* You are, first of all, *writing for yourself;* you are trying to clarify something. The instructor may have set the problem—let's say (to take a famous example), "Is Hamlet mad or only pretending to be?"—or the problem may be one of your own choosing, possibly even so broad and so basic as "Why don't I care for this work?" In any event, you start looking again at the text, thinking, jotting down brief notes that come to mind, then perhaps commenting on these notes, perhaps amplifying them, perhaps almost immediately seeing that even though you wrote them only a few seconds ago you no longer agree with them. Again, you are writing in order, ultimately, to explain something *to yourself.*

- *The Results:* Finally, of course, you will revise your thoughts and offer them to the instructor and perhaps to your classmates, *in an effort to help readers to see things your way.* You have listened to yourself, quarreled with yourself, taught yourself something, arrived at a place where you think you at last have some clear and coherent ideas, and now you want to teach your readers.

# The Open Secret of Good Writing

We have just said that in drafting your essay you have "quarreled with yourself." One of the great open secrets of decent writing is this: Good writers are good critics *of their own writing.* In words attributed to Truman Capote, "Writing is rewriting." When writers reread their own writing, they read in a skeptical spirit, arguing with themselves

- "Have I adequately supported this point?"
- "Have I considered all of the possible counter-evidence?"
- "Do I really want to say . . . ? Ought I to have said . . . ?"
- "Come to think of it, there aren't two reasons but three reasons why I think such-and-such,"

and so forth.

Your pleasure in writing will come chiefly from your awareness that you are *improving* your writing, getting better ideas than those that you had at the beginning. You will feel pleasure, too, in knowing that you are using words well—a pleasure of the sort we all experience when we read any work that we enjoy and admire, a work by an author who uses words skillfully. By the time you finish—although there is much to the saying that a writer doesn't finish a work, but rather just finally abandons it—you mentally say of your material, "Not at all bad." If, for instance, you are writing an analysis of a story, by the time that you abandon your essay you ought to think that you now have some neat ideas that were only half-formulated (at best) when you sat down to write your first draft.

After revising and revising again, you can reasonably feel that you have thought about an issue—for instance, about characterization in a short story—and, having argued with yourself in the process of revising your drafts, you now have come to some conclusions that you are willing to share with readers.

Let's look at a very short story, a contemporary version of a traditional Chinese story.

## EMILY WU

### *The Lesson of the Master* [2005]

In fourteenth-century China a Buddhist monk named Tung-ming, who was also a painter, was fortunate in having a merchant who supported him by buying his ink-paintings. Tung-ming excelled in his art, a very difficult art because an Asian ink painting, unlike a Western oil painting, cannot be changed as the artist works on it. Once the brush touches the paper, the ink makes its mark, and it cannot be removed. The brushstroke cannot even be widened or lengthened because a knowledgeable observer will easily detect the change, the places where the first stroke was widened or extended or whatever; the painting's lack of grace and spontaneity will be evident. Part of the beauty of ink painting is that the viewer understands the difficulty, and appreciates the skill that is evident in each line.

Tung-ming excelled in paintings of plum branches, but one day the merchant, who was a wholesaler of fish, asked him if he would paint a carp. The monk assured the merchant that he would paint the picture, and he then departed. A week passed. Then two weeks. Then three weeks, and still there was no painting. It was not that the merchant and the monk did not meet. No, they met every few days because the merchant often invited the monk to dinner. And in the past the monk sometimes invited the merchant to have a cup of tea at the temple and to discuss matters of Buddhism, but he had not invited the merchant since the conversation about the carp.

After the second week the merchant began to fret: "Have I offended Tung-ming?" he wondered. "Might he think that I don't sufficiently appreciate his paintings of plum blossoms?" And: "Is it possible that he thinks it is vulgar of me to ask for a picture of a fish because I am a fish merchant?" And: "Could it be that he thinks, because I am a specialist in fish, I will notice that in fact his picture of a carp is not very good, that he can't catch the essence of its fishiness?" Day after day, week after week, month after month the merchant tormented himself with such thoughts.

Now that months had gone by, the merchant summoned up the courage to ask Tung-ming if they might not, for a change, meet at the temple and have a cup of tea. Tung-ming agreed.

On the appointed day they met in the monk's quarters, drank tea, talked about Buddhist matters and other things, and then the merchant—having noticed that brush, ink-cake, and paper were in view—nervously broached the subject of the picture of the carp. Tung-ming ground some fresh ink from an ink-cake, dipped the brush in the ink, stood over the paper, paused for five seconds (but the pause seemed like eternity to the merchant) and then, in another five seconds, with five strokes brushed a marvelous silvery-gray carp and handed the sheet to the merchant.

The merchant was beside himself with joy. When he recovered his composure, he hesitantly asked Tung-ming why, since the task was apparently so easy, he had not produced a picture months earlier. Tung-ming walked across the room, opened the door of a cabinet, and hundreds of sheets of paper—each with a picture of a carp—streamed to the floor.

# Getting Ready to Write

We hope that this brief story gave you at least a little pleasure. When you come to write about a work of literature, it's not a bad idea to begin by thinking about *why* the work pleased you—or did not please you. In this instance, for example, you may have enjoyed the fact that

- the story has a moral (something along the lines of "Practice makes perfect"), and
- the moral is *not* stated explicitly.

Could it be that

- readers sometimes take pleasure in reading a work that offers a satisfying moral, but
- readers sometimes also take pleasure in *not* having a moral hammered home?

(We hasten to add that not all works of literature have morals; we will discuss this issue in a later chapter.)

You might have found, too, if you had been asked to write an analysis of Emily Wu's "The Lesson of the Master," that you would want to consider the following topics:

- *The title:* Although the title of a story may be the last thing the author writes, it is the first thing that the reader encounters, and it is therefore highly important. The story called "The Lesson of the Master" *might* have been called "A Very Short Story," or "Tung-ming's Fish" or "A Fishy Story" or "The Patron and the Painter" or "The Painter and the Patron" or "Easy When You Know How" or. . . . Consider the original title and the six alternate titles. Which do you think is the best? Why? Can you think of a title that is better than the original and the proposed alternatives? If so, state it and explain why you think it is better.

- *The plot:* It is probably fair to say that the ending of this small story comes as a surprise. But it is probably also fair to say that, as soon as the reader absorbs the surprise, he or she thinks, "Yes, this ending makes perfect sense. That's the way it ought to be." Some authors—notably O. Henry—are famous for their surprise endings, many of which are ingenious but seem arbitrary, unlikely, unconvincing—but on the whole serious literature does not give much weight to such surprises. This is not to say that surprise has no place in serious literature. The novelist E. M. Forster, in *Aspects of the Novel* (1927), has a shrewd comment on the importance of both fulfilling expectation and offering a slight surprise:

  > Shock, followed by the feeling, "oh, that's all right," is a sign that all is well with the plot: characters, to be real, ought to run smoothly, but a plot ought to cause surprise.

  The important point Forster is making is the "oh, that's all right." The plot causes a surprise, but upon reflection we realize that it makes sense, it is coherent, not tricky.

- *The characterization:* Suppose you were asked to characterize each of the two figures. Given this assignment, you would reread the story in preparation for jotting down (or keyboarding) some characteristics of each figure. On rereading, you might notice that although the author on several occasions takes her readers into the mind of the merchant (for example, "the merchant began to fret," "the merchant summoned up the courage to ask Tung-ming," "The merchant was beside himself with joy") but she never takes her readers into the mind of the painter. What do you make of this fact? Do you feel that you know the merchant but not the painter? Do you think the author should have told us more about the painter—for instance, more about his appearance or his mental processes?

# A Student Writes: From Jottings to a Final Draft

Here, in fact, is what one reader made out of this third topic. The assignment was to analyze, in about 250 words, the characterization in the story. We begin with the student's jottings, including his later revisions of the jottings.

> Artist (Tung-ming)
>
>    ~~historical figure? Does it matter???~~  Yes and no.
>
>    specialist (plum pictures)—but can (with practice) paint other things
>
>    says nothing; rude?? maybe just not talkative
>
>                                     strong silent type?
>
>    age? appearance? attitude toward merchant?    ←
>
> Merchant (not named)
>
>    rich (supports painter); ~~generous? may be for prestige?~~
>    ~~nothing in story about family. Maybe lonely???~~
>
>    Very worried about his request for picture. Insecure? Is the idea that
>        the merchant is of lower class than the artist? But they socialize
>        Equals?
>
>    We keep hearing the merchant worrying, but we don't hear about the
>        artist
>
>    In fact, we don't really know anything about the artist, except
>        that he is a great artist. Should we be told his thoughts?
>        Would it spoil the story if we knew he needed time to
>        practice?

The student's drafts are not available to us, but here is the final short essay, used with the student's permission.

---

Berger 1

Will Berger

Professor Cass

English 101A

30 June 2010

Less Is More: Characterization in
"The Lesson of the Master"

There are two characters in Emily Wu's short story called "The Lesson of the Master," but only one of the two does any speaking or, so far as a reader is at first concerned, any thinking. The one who does the speaking and thinking is the merchant, who is not given a name. The fact that he is not given a name is itself a part of his characterization.

He talks and he worries, but so far as the writer goes he is a nobody. On the other hand the painter is given the dignity of having a name and thus (or at least by the end of the story) the reader understands that the painter is the more important person, the person with, so to speak, a powerful identity, a powerful individuality.

We are told that "the merchant began to fret," and that he wondered if the painter thought he (the merchant) was coarse. A little later we are told that "the merchant summoned up the courage" to ask the painter if they could meet, and when the painter finally paints the picture we are told that "The merchant was beside himself with joy." In short, we understand that the merchant is a person with ordinary feelings, feelings just like our own. Meanwhile, we have heard nothing at all about the painter's thoughts or emotions or words. The painter thus remains a mystery.

What the story gives to us is not the painter's ideas or emotions but his actions, and (as usual) actions speak louder than words, or, to use another cliche, one picture is worth a thousand words. When we have finished reading the story, we understand that the painter doesn't have to talk, and readers do not have to hear about his mental processes. Wu could have written something like "The painter realized that he would have to practice for a long time," but we get no such sentences. In fact, much of the strength of the story, a reader realizes when rereading the story, is in the fact that we know so little about the painter. By the end of the story we realize that if we are to characterize him, it will be as a person who keeps his thoughts to himself and whose actions are what counts. Of course he *does* have a personality, a character. We can say he is quiet, he apparently does not express his emotions, and so forth. But when we think about him, we chiefly think of his accomplishment.

Much of the pleasure of the story undoubtedly results from the surprise ending, but unlike most stories with surprise endings, this ending is not inconsistent with what has happened earlier in the story. That is, it makes perfect sense for the painter to be able to produce a great painting of a fish—after he has had time to practice. And we are just as glad that he didn't bother to tell the merchant that he was practicing. He is a somewhat mysterious figure and perhaps that's what most great artists are. Wu tells us less about the artist than she tells us about the merchant, but in the end we see that the artist is the more interesting figure.

## The Student's Analysis Analyzed

Let's look, very briefly, at this short essay.

- **The title** is not simply "An Analysis of a Story." Rather, it is interesting ("Less Is More") and it is focused: It lets the readers know where they will be going ("Characterization"). When you write an essay, try to give it an interesting title and try to indicate the focus.
- **The opening paragraph** names the author whose work is discussed (i.e., the opening provides necessary information) and it makes an interesting assertion (the difference in the treatment of the two characters) at the very beginning. In short, it is interesting, not mere throat-clearing.
- **The second paragraph** deals with one character, the third paragraph with the other character. Conceivably the two characters could both have been discussed in one paragraph, but the division here is reasonable.
- **The final paragraph** generalizes a bit, asserting that although the artist is scarcely described he turns out to be the more interesting character. Note two other things about this final paragraph: (1) although it introduces a new point (the ending is surprising but not inconsistent), this point is closely connected to what has been said, so the paragraph does not leave the reader wondering where the writer is going, and (2) in the final sentence, the word "more" connects neatly with the title, thus helping to round off the essay. In short, the concluding paragraph is satisfying rather than boring (as a mere summary would be) or puzzling (as the introduction of a new issue might be).
- **The essay makes a point, has a thesis;** it is not a mere summary of the plot, and it is not a mere presentation of what other people have said.

# Three Poems

Probably most people would agree that one of the pleasures of literature—stories, poems, plays—is that a work of literature reveals a new world to the reader. This new world may be as strange as the world offered by a work of science fiction, or it may seem as familiar—and yet still as fresh—as the world that Robert Frost offers in "Stopping by Woods on a Snowy Evening," which ends thus:

> The woods are lovely, dark and deep,
> But I have promises to keep,
> And miles to go before I sleep,
> And miles to go before I sleep.

(If you are not already familiar with this poem, please turn to pages 755–56 and read it.)

Consider, for instance, this poem in which the writer lets us hear the thoughts of a woman who lifts weights.

# DIANE ACKERMAN

*Poet, essayist, and naturalist, Diane Ackerman was born in Washington, Illinois, in 1948. The author of many works of nonfiction and poetry, she is perhaps best known for* A Natural History of the Senses *(1990), an exploration in prose of the nature and meaning of the five senses.*

## *Pumping Iron*                                        [1985]

She doesn't want
the bunchy look
of male lifters:
torso an unyielding love-knot,
arms hard at mid-boil.                                          5
Doesn't want
the dancing bicepses
of pros.
Just to run her flesh
up the flagpole                                                10
of her body,
to pull her roaming flab
into tighter cascades,
machete a waist
through the jungle                                             15
of her hips,
a trim waist
two hands might grip
as a bouquet.

Doubtless most people who pump iron do so in order to improve their appearance, but each person has his or her own individual thoughts. Ackerman gets us into a very specific—and interesting—mind. She gives us the feel, so to speak, of the thoughts of her speaker. That's what most poems do. In Robert Frost's words, a poem embodies "the *act* of having an idea and how it feels to have an idea."

# THEODORE ROETHKE

*Theodore Roethke (1908–1963) was born in Saginaw, Michigan, and educated at the University of Michigan and Harvard. From 1947 until his death he taught at the University of Washington in Seattle, where he exerted considerable influence on the next generation of poets. Many of Roethke's best poems are lyrical memories of his childhood.*

## *My Papa's Waltz*                                      [1948]

The whiskey on your breath
Could make a small boy dizzy;
but I hung on like death:
Such waltzing was not easy.                                      4

We romped until the pans
Slid from the kitchen shelf;
My mother's countenance
Could not unfrown itself.                                    8

The hand that held my wrist
Was battered on one knuckle;
At every step you missed
My right ear scraped a buckle.                               12

You beat time on my head
With a palm caked hard by dirt,
Then waltzed me off to bed
Still clinging to your shirt.                                16

---

### YOUR TURN

1. Do the syntactical pauses vary much from stanza to stanza? Be specific. Would you say that the rhythm suggests lightness? Why?
2. Does the rhythm parallel or ironically contrast with the episode described? Was the dance a graceful waltz? Explain.
3. What would you say is the function of the stresses in lines 13–14?

## WILLIAM BUTLER YEATS

*William Butler Yeats (1865–1939) was born in Dublin, Ireland. The early Yeats was much interested in highly lyrical, romantic poetry, often drawing on Irish mythology. The later poems, from about 1910 (and especially after Yeats met Ezra Pound in 1911), are often more colloquial. Although these later poems often employ mythological references, too, one feels that the poems are more down-to-earth. He was awarded the Nobel Prize in Literature in 1923.*

*Yeats was 65 when he wrote this poem for Anne Gregory, the 19-year-old granddaughter of Lady Augusta Gregory, a woman whom Yeats had admired.*

### For Anne Gregory                                       [1930]

"Never shall a young man,
Thrown into despair
By those great honey-coloured
Ramparts at your ear
Love you for yourself alone                                 5
And not your yellow hair."

"But I can get a hair-dye
And set such colour there,
Brown, or black, or carrot,
That young men in despair                                   10
May love me for myself alone
And not my yellow hair."

"I heard an old religious man
But yesternight declare
That he had found a text to prove                                   15
That only God, my dear,
Could love you for yourself alone
And not your yellow hair."

**YOUR TURN**

1. What can you imagine Anne saying that provoked the poem?
2. In the first stanza Anne's hair is described both as "great honey-coloured ramparts" and as "yellow." Why does the speaker use these two rather different descriptions? Judging from the second stanza, how would Anne describe her hair?
3. If you did not know that Yeats was 65 when he wrote the poem, would you be able to deduce from the poem itself that the speaker of the first and third stanzas is considerably older than Anne?
4. Anne says that she wants to be loved "for myself alone." Exactly what do you think this expression means?
5. Why would "an old religious man" search until he found a text that would prove that only God could love her for herself alone? Do you think Yeats shares this view?
6. In a sentence or two characterize Yeats as he reveals himself in this poem and then characterize Anne.

# Two Stories

## KATHERINE MANSFIELD

*Katherine Mansfield (1888-1923), née Kathleen Mansfield Beauchamp, was born in New Zealand. In 1902 she went to London for schooling; in 1906 she returned to New Zealand, but dissatisfied with its provincialism, she returned to London in 1908 to become a writer. After a disastrous marriage and a love affair, she went to Germany, where she wrote stories; in 1910 she returned to London, published a book of stories in 1911, and in 1912 met and began living with the writer John Middleton Murry. In 1918, after her first husband at last divorced her, she married Murry. She died of tuberculosis in 1923, a few months after her thirty-fourth birthday.*

*Mansfield published about seventy stories, and left some others unpublished. An early admirer of Chekhov, she read his works in German translations before they were translated into English.*

### Miss Brill                                                        [1920]

Although it was so brilliantly fine—the blue sky powdered with gold and great spots of light like white wine splashed over the Jardins Publiques[1]—

---

[1]**Jardins Publiques** Public Gardens (French).

Miss Brill was glad that she had decided on her fur. The air was motionless, but when you opened your mouth there was just a faint chill, like a chill from a glass of iced water before you sip, and now and again a leaf came drifting—from nowhere, from the sky. Miss Brill put up her hand and touched her fur. Dear little thing! It was nice to feel it again. She had taken it out of its box that afternoon, shaken out the moth-powder, given it a good brush, and rubbed the life back into the dim little eyes. "What has been happening to me?" said the sad little eyes. Oh, how sweet it was to see them snap at her again from the red eiderdown! . . . But the nose, which was of some black composition, wasn't at all firm. It must have had a knock, somehow. Never mind—a little dab of black sealing-wax when the time came—when it was absolutely necessary. . . . Little rogue! Yes, she really felt like that about it. Little rogue biting its tail just by her left ear. She could have taken it off and laid it on her lap and stroked it. She felt a tingling in her hands and arms, but that came from walking, she supposed. And when she breathed, something light and sad—no, not sad, exactly—something gentle seemed to move in her bosom.

There were a number of people out this afternoon, far more than last Sunday. And the band sounded louder and gayer. That was because the Season had begun. For although the band played all year round on Sundays, out of season it was never the same. It was like some one playing with only the family to listen; it didn't care how it played if there weren't any strangers present. Wasn't the conductor wearing a new coat, too? She was sure it was new. He scraped with his foot and flapped his arms like a rooster about to crow, and the bandsmen sitting in the green rotunda blew out their cheeks and glared at the music. Now there came a little "flutey" bit—very pretty!—a little chain of bright drops. She was sure it would be repeated. It was; she lifted her head and smiled.

Only two people shared her "special" seat: a fine old man in a velvet coat, his hands clasped over a huge carved walking-stick, and a big old woman, sitting upright, with a roll of knitting on her embroidered apron. They did not speak. This was disappointing, for Miss Brill always looked forward to the conversation. She had become really quite expert, she thought, at listening as though she didn't listen, at sitting in other people's lives just for a minute while they talked round her.

She glanced, sideways, at the old couple. Perhaps they would go soon. Last Sunday, too, hadn't been as interesting as usual. An Englishman and his wife, he wearing a dreadful Panama hat and she button boots. And she'd gone on the whole time about how she ought to wear spectacles; she knew she needed them; but that it was no good getting any; they'd be sure to break and they'd never keep on. And he'd been so patient. He'd suggested everything—gold rims, the kind that curved round your ears, little pads inside the bridge. No, nothing would please her. "They'll always be sliding down my nose!" Miss Brill had wanted to shake her.

5      The old people sat on the bench, still as statues. Never mind, there was always the crowd to watch. To and fro, in front of the flower-beds and the band rotunda, the couples and groups paraded, stopped to talk, to greet, to buy a handful of flowers from the old beggar who had his tray fixed to the railings. Little children ran among them, swooping and laughing; little boys with big white silk bows under their chins, little girls, little French dolls, dressed up in velvet and lace. And sometimes a tiny staggerer came suddenly

rocking into the open from under the trees, stopped, stared, as suddenly sat down "flop," until its small high-stepping mother, like a young hen, rushed scolding to its rescue. Other people sat on the benches and green chairs, but they were nearly always the same, Sunday after Sunday, and—Miss Brill had often noticed—there was something funny about nearly all of them. They were odd, silent, nearly all old, and from the way they stared they looked as though they'd just come from dark little rooms or even—even cupboards!

Behind the rotunda the slender trees with yellow leaves down drooping, and through them just a line of sea, and beyond the blue sky with gold-veined clouds.

Tum-tum-tum tiddle-um! tiddle-um! tum tiddley-um tum ta! blew the band.

Two young girls in red came by and two young soldiers in blue met them, and they laughed and paired and went off arm-in-arm. Two peasant women with funny straw hats passed, gravely, leading beautiful smoke-colored donkeys. A cold, pale nun hurried by. A beautiful woman came along and dropped her bunch of violets, and a little boy ran after to hand them to her, and she took them and threw them away as if they'd been poisoned. Dear me! Miss Brill didn't know whether to admire that or not! And now an ermine toque[2] and a gentleman in grey met just in front of her. He was tall, stiff, dignified, and she was wearing the ermine toque she'd bought when her hair was yellow. Now everything, her hair, her face, even her eyes, was the same color as the shabby ermine, and her hand, in its cleaned glove, lifted to dab her lips, was a tiny yellowish paw. Oh, she was so pleased to see him—delighted! She rather thought they were going to meet that afternoon. She described where she'd been—everywhere, here, there, along by the sea. The day was so charming—didn't he agree? And wouldn't he, perhaps? . . . But he shook his head, lighted a cigarette, slowly breathed a great deep puff into her face, and, even while she was still talking and laughing, flicked the match away and walked on. The ermine toque was alone; she smiled more brightly than ever. But even the band seemed to know what she was feeling and played more softly, played tenderly, and the drum beat, "The Brute! The Brute!" over and over. What would she do? What was going to happen now? But as Miss Brill wondered, the ermine toque turned, raised her hand as though she'd seen some one else, much nicer, just over there, and pattered away. And the band changed again and played more quickly, more gaily than ever, and the old couple on Miss Brill's seat got up and marched away, and such a funny old man with long whiskers hobbled along in time to the music and was nearly knocked over by four girls walking abreast.

Oh, how fascinating it was! How she enjoyed it! How she loved sitting here, watching it all! It was like a play. It was exactly like a play. Who could believe the sky at the back wasn't painted? But it wasn't till a little brown dog trotted on solemn and then slowly trotted off, like a little "theatre" dog, a little dog that had been drugged, that Miss Brill discovered what it was that made it so exciting. They were all on the stage. They weren't only the audience, not only looking on; they were acting. Even she had a part and came every Sunday. No doubt somebody would have noticed if she hadn't been there; she was part of the performance after all. How strange she'd never thought of it like that before! And yet it explained why she made such a

_____

[2]**toque** a brimless, close-fitting woman's hat.

point of starting from home at just the same time each week—so as not to be late for the performance—and it also explained why she had quite a queer, shy feeling at telling her English pupils how she spent her Sunday afternoons. No wonder! Miss Brill nearly laughed out loud. She was on the stage. She thought of the old invalid gentleman to whom she read the newspaper four afternoons a week while he slept in the garden. She had got quite used to the frail head on the cotton pillow, the hollowed eyes, the open mouth and the high pinched nose. If he'd been dead she mightn't have noticed for weeks; she wouldn't have minded. But suddenly he knew he was having the paper read to him by an actress! "An actress!" The old head lifted; two points of light quivered in the old eyes. "An actress—are ye?" And Miss Brill smoothed the newspaper as though it were the manuscript of her part and said gently: "Yes, I have been an actress for a long time."

10     The band had been having a rest. Now they started again. And what they played was warm, sunny, yet there was just a faint chill—a something, what was it?—not sadness—no, not sadness—a something that made you want to sing. The tune lifted, lifted, the light shone; and it seemed to Miss Brill that in another moment all of them, all the whole company, would begin singing. The young ones, the laughing ones who were moving together, they would begin, and the men's voices, very resolute and brave, would join them. And then she too, she too, and the others on the benches—they would come in with a kind of accompaniment—something low, that scarcely rose or fell, something so beautiful—moving. . . . And Miss Brill's eyes filled with tears and she looked smiling at all the other members of the company. Yes, we understand, we understand, she thought—though what they understood she didn't know.

Just at that moment a boy and a girl came and sat down where the old couple had been. They were beautifully dressed; they were in love. The hero and heroine, of course, just arrived from his father's yacht. And still soundlessly singing, still with that trembling smile, Miss Brill prepared to listen.

"No, not now," said the girl. "Not here, I can't."

"But why? Because of that stupid old thing at the end there?" asked the boy. "Why does she come here at all—who wants her? Why doesn't she keep her silly old mug at home?"

"It's her fu-fur which is so funny," giggled the girl. "It's exactly like a fried whiting."[3]

15     "Ah, be off with you!" said the boy in an angry whisper. Then: "Tell me, my petite chère[4]—"

"No, not here," said the girl. "Not yet."

On her way home she usually bought a slice of honey-cake at the baker's. It was her Sunday treat. Sometimes there was an almond in her slice, sometimes not. It made a great difference. If there was an almond it was like carrying home a tiny present—a surprise—something that might very well not have been there. She hurried on the almond Sundays and struck the match for the kettle in quite a dashing way.

But today she passed the baker's by, climbed the stairs, went into the little dark room—her room like a cupboard—and sat down on the red eiderdown. She sat there for a long time. The box that the fur came out of was on

---

[3]**whiting** a kind of fish.    [4]**petite chère** darling.

the bed. She unclasped the necklet quickly; quickly, without looking, laid it inside. But when she put the lid on she thought she heard something crying.

1. Why do you think Mansfield did not give Miss Brill a first name?
2. What would be lost (or gained?) if the first paragraph were omitted?
3. Suppose someone said that the story is about a woman who is justly punished for her pride. What might be your response?

# TONI CADE BAMBARA

*Toni Cade Bambara (1939–1995), an African American writer, was born in New York City and grew up in black districts of the city. After studying at the University of Florence and at City College in New York, where she received a master's degree, she worked for a while as a case investigator for the New York State Welfare Department. Later she directed a recreation program for hospital patients. Once her literary reputation was established, she spent most of her time writing, though she also served as writer in residence at Spelman College in Atlanta. Perhaps the best of Bambara's books are* Gorilla, My Love *(1972), a collection of stories, and* The Salt Eaters *(1980), a novel.*

## The Lesson                                                    [1972]

Back in the days when everyone was old and stupid or young and foolish and me and Sugar were the only ones just right, this lady moved on our block with nappy hair and proper speech and no makeup. And quite naturally we laughed at her, laughed the way we did at the junk man who went about his business like he was some big-time president and his sorry-ass horse his secretary. And we kinda hated her too, hated the way we did the winos who cluttered up our parks and pissed on our handball walls and stank up our hallways and stairs so you couldn't halfway play hide-and-seek without a goddam gas mask. Miss Moore was her name. The only woman on the block with no first name. And she was black as hell, cept for her feet, which were fish-white and spooky. And she was always planning these boring-ass things for us to do, us being my cousin, mostly, who lived on the block cause we all moved North the same time and to the same apartment then spread out gradual to breathe. And our parents would yank our heads into some kinda shape and crisp up our clothes so we'd be presentable for travel with Miss Moore, who always looked like she was going to church, though she never did. Which is just one of the things the grownups talked about when they talked behind her back like a dog. But when she came calling with some sachet she'd sewed up or some gingerbread she'd made or some book, why then they'd all be too embarrassed to turn her down and we'd get handed over all spruced up. She'd been to college and said it was only right that she should take responsibility for the young ones' education, and she not even related by marriage or blood. So they'd go for it. Specially Aunt Gretchen. She was the main gofer in the family. You got some old dumb shit foolishness you want somebody to go for, you send for Aunt Gretchen. She been screwed into the go-along for so long, it's a blood-deep natural thing with her. Which is how she got saddled with me and Sugar and Junior in the first place while our mothers were in la-de-da apartment up the block having a good ole time.

So this one day Miss Moore rounds us all up at the mailbox and it's puredee hot and she's knockin herself out about arithmetic. And school suppose to let up in summer I heard, but she don't never let up. And the starch in my pinafore scratching the shit outta me and I'm really hating this nappy-head bitch and her goddam college degree. I'd much rather go to the pool or to the show where it's cool. So me and Sugar leaning on the mailbox being surly, which is a Miss Moore word. And Flyboy checking out what everybody brought for lunch. And Fat Butt already wasting his peanut-butter-and-jelly sandwich like the pig he is. And Junebug punchin on Q.T.'s arm for potato chips. And Rosie Giraffe shifting from one hip to the other waiting for somebody to step on her foot or ask her if she from Georgia so she can kick ass, preferably Mercedes'. And Miss Moore asking us do we know what money is, like we a bunch of retards. I mean real money, she say, like it's only poker chips or monopoly papers we lay on the grocer. So right away I'm tired of this and say so. And would much rather snatch Sugar and go to the Sunset and terrorize the West Indian kids and take their hair ribbons and their money too. And Miss Moore files that remark away for next week's lesson on brotherhood, I can tell. And finally I say we oughta get to the subway cause it's cooler and besides we might meet some cute boys. Sugar done swiped her mama's lipstick, so we ready.

So we heading down the street and she's boring us silly about what things cost and what our parents make and how much goes for rent and how money ain't divided up right in this country. And then she gets to the part about we all poor and live in the slums, which I don't feature. And I'm ready to speak on that, but she steps out in the street and hails two cabs just like that. Then she hustles half the crew in with her and hands me a five-dollar bill and tells me to calculate 10 percent tip for the driver. And we're off. Me and Sugar and Junebug and Flyboy hangin out the window and hollering to everybody, putting lipstick on each other cause Flyboy a faggot anyway, and making farts with our sweaty armpits. But I'm mostly trying to figure how to spend this money. But they all fascinated with the meter ticking and Junebug starts laying bets as to how much it'll read when Flyboy can't hold his breath no more. Then Sugar lays bets as to how much it'll be when we get there. So I'm stuck. Don't nobody want to go for my plan, which is to jump out at the next light and run off to the first bar-b-que we can find. Then the driver tells us to get the hell out cause we there already. And the meter reads eighty-five cents. And I'm stalling to figure out the tip and Sugar say give him a dime. And I decide he don't need it bad as I do, so later for him. But then he tries to take off with Junebug foot still in the door so we talk about his mama something ferocious. Then we check out that we on Fifth Avenue and everybody dressed up in stockings. One lady in a fur coat, hot as it is. White folks crazy.

"This is the place," Miss Moore say, presenting it to us in the voice she uses at the museum. "Let's look in the windows before we go in."

5        "Can we steal?" Sugar asks very serious like she's getting the ground rules squared away before she plays. "I beg your pardon," say Miss Moore, and

we fall out. So she leads us around the windows of the toy store and me and Sugar screamin, "This is mine, that's mine. I gotta have that, that was made for me. I was born for that," till Big Butt drowns us out.

"Hey, I'm going to buy that there."

"That there? You don't even know what it is, stupid."

"I do so," he say punchin on Rosie Giraffe. "It's a microscope."

"Whatcha gonna do with a microscope, fool?"

10     "Look at things."

"Like what, Ronald?" ask Miss Moore. And Big Butt ain't got the first notion. So here go Miss Moore gabbing about the thousands of bacteria in a drop of water and the somethinorother in a speck of blood and the million and one living things in the air around us is invisible to the naked eye. And what she say that for? Junebug go to town on that "naked" and we rolling. Then Miss Moore ask what it cost. So we all jam into the window smudgin it up and the price tag say $300. So then she ask how long'd take for Big Butt and Junebug to save up their allowances. "Too long," I say. "Yeh," adds Sugar, "outgrown it by that time." And Miss Moore say no, you never outgrow learning instruments. "Why, even medical students and interns and," blah, blah, blah. And we ready to choke Big Butt for bringing it up in the first damn place.

"This here cost four hundred eighty dollars," say Rosie Giraffe. So we pile up all over her to see what she pointin out. My eyes tell me it's a chunk of glass cracked with something heavy, and different-color inks dripped into the spits, then the whole thing put into a oven or something. But for $480 it don't make sense.

"That's a paperweight made of semi-precious stones fused together under tremendous pressure," she explains slowly, with her hands doing the mining and all the factory work.

"So what's a paperweight?" asks Rosie Giraffe.

15     "To weight paper with, dumbbell," say Flyboy, the wise man from the East.

"Not exactly," say Miss Moore, which is what she say when you warm or way off too. "It's to weigh paper down so it won't scatter and make your desk untidy." So right away me and Sugar curtsy to each other and then to Mercedes who is more the tidy type.

"We don't keep paper on top of the desk in my class," say Junebug, figuring Miss Moore crazy or lyin one.

"At home, then," she say. "Don't you have a calendar and a pencil case and a blotter and a letter-opener on your desk at home where you do your homework?" And she know damn well what our homes look like cause she nosys around in them every chance she gets.

"I don't even have a desk," say Junebug. "Do we?"

20     "No. And I don't get no homework neither," says Big Butt.

"And I don't even have a home," say Flyboy, like he do at school to keep the white folks off his back and sorry for him. Send this poor kid to camp posters, is his specialty.

"I do," says Mercedes. "I have a box of stationery on my desk and a picture of my cat. My godmother bought the stationery and the desk. There's a big rose on each sheet and the envelopes smell like roses."

"Who wants to know about your smelly-ass stationery," say Rosie Giraffe fore I can get my two cents in.

"It's important to have a work area all your own so that . . ."

25      "Will you look at this sailboat, please," say Flyboy, cuttin her off and pointin to the thing like it was his. So once again we tumble all over each other to gaze at this magnificent thing in the toy store which is just big enough to maybe sail two kittens across the pond if you strap them to the posts tight. We all start reciting the price tag like we in assembly. "Handcrafted sailboat of fiberglass at one thousand one hundred ninety-five dollars."

"Unbelievable," I hear myself say and am really stunned. I read it again for myself just in case the group recitation put me in a trance. Same thing. For some reason this pisses me off. We look at Miss Moore and she lookin at us, waiting for I dunno what.

"Who'd pay all that when you can buy a sailboat set for a quarter at Pop's, a tube of glue for a dime, and a ball of string for eight cents? It must have a motor and a whole lot else besides," I say. "My sailboat cost me about fifty cents."

"But will it take water?" say Mercedes with her smart ass.

"Took mine to Alley Pond Park once," say Flyboy. "String broke. Lost it. Pity."

30      "Sailed mine in Central Park and it keeled over and sank. Had to ask my father for another dollar."

"And you got the strap," laugh Big Butt. "The jerk didn't even have a string on it. My old man wailed on his behind."

Little Q.T. was staring hard at the sailboat and you could see he wanted it bad. But he too little and somebody'd just take it from him. So what the hell. "This boat for kids, Miss Moore?"

"Parents silly to buy something like that just to get all broke up," say Rosie Giraffe.

"That much money it should last forever," I figure.

35      "My father'd buy it for me if I wanted it."

"Your father, my ass," say Rosie Giraffe getting a chance to finally push Mercedes.

"Must be rich people shop here," say Q.T.

"You are a very bright boy," say Flyboy. "What was your first clue?" And he rap him on the head with the back of his knuckles, since Q.T. the only one he could get away with. Though Q.T. liable to come up behind you years later and get his licks in when you half expect it.

"What I want to know is," I says to Miss Moore though I never talk to her, I wouldn't give the bitch that satisfaction, "is how much a real boat costs? I figure a thousand'd get you a yacht any day."

40      "Why don't you check that out," she says, "and report back to the group?" Which really pains my ass. If you gonna mess up a perfectly good swim day least you could do is have some answers. "Let's go in," she say like she got something up her sleeve. Only she don't lead the way. So me and Sugar turn the corner to where the entrance is, but when we get there I kinda hang back. Not that I'm scared, what's there to be afraid of, just a toy store. But I feel funny, shame. But what I got to be shamed about? Got as much right to go in as anybody. But somehow I can't seem to get hold of the door, so I step away for Sugar to lead. But she hangs back too. And I look at her and she looks at me and this is ridiculous. I mean, damn, I have never ever been shy about doing nothing or going nowhere. But then Mercedes steps up and then Rosie Giraffe and Big Butt crowd in behind and shove, and next thing we all stuffed into the doorway with only Mercedes squeezing past us, smoothing

out her jumper and walking right down the aisle. Then the rest of us tumble in like a glued-together jigsaw done all wrong. And people lookin at us. And it's like the time me and Sugar crashed into the Catholic church on a dare. But once we got in there and everything so hushed and holy and the candles and the bowin and the handkerchiefs on all the drooping heads, I just couldn't go through with the plan. Which was for me to run up to the altar and do a tap dance while Sugar played the nose flute and messed around in the holy water. And Sugar kept giving me the elbow. Then later teased me so bad I tied her up in the shower and turned it on and locked her in. And she'd be there till this day if Aunt Gretchen hadn't finally figured I was lying about the boarder takin a shower.

Same thing in the store. We all walkin on tiptoe and hardly touchin the games and puzzles and things. And I watched Miss Moore who is steady watchin us like she waiting for a sign. Like Mama Drewery watches the sky and sniffs the air and takes note of just how much slant is in the bird formation. Then me and Sugar bump smack into each other, so busy gazing at the toys, 'specially the sailboat. But we don't laugh and go into our fat-lady bump-stomach routine. We just stare at that price tag. Then Sugar run a finger over the whole boat. And I'm jealous and want to hit her. Maybe not her, but I sure want to punch somebody in the mouth.

"Watcha bring us here for, Miss Moore?"

"You sound angry, Sylvia. Are you mad about something?" Givin me one of them grins like she tellin a grown-up joke that never turns out to be funny. And she's looking very closely at me like maybe she plannin to do my portrait from memory. I'm mad, but I won't give her the satisfaction. So I slouch around the store being very bored and say, "Let's go."

Me and Sugar at the back of the train watchin the tracks whizzin by large then small then gettin gobbled up in the dark. I'm thinkin about this tricky toy I saw in the store. A clown that somersaults on a bar then does chin-ups just cause you yank lightly at his leg. Cost $35. I could see me askin my mother for a $35 birthday clown. "You wanna who that costs what?" she'd say, cocking her head to the side to get a better view of the hole in my head. Thirty-five dollars could buy new bunk beds for Junior and Gretchen's boy. Thirty-five dollars and the whole household could go visit Granddaddy Nelson in the country. Thirty-five dollars would pay for the rent and the piano bill too. Who are these people that spend that much for performing clowns and $1000 for toy sailboats? What kinda work they do and how they live and how come we ain't in on it? Where we are is who we are, Miss Moore always pointin out. But it don't necessarily have to be that way, she always adds then waits for somebody to say that poor people have to wake up and demand their share of the pie and don't none of us know what kind of pie she talkin about in the first damn place. But she ain't so smart cause I still got her four dollars from the taxi and she sure ain't getting it. Messin up my day with this shit. Sugar nudges me in my pocket and winks.

Miss Moore lines us up in front of the mailbox where we started from, seem like years ago, and I got a headache for thinkin so hard. And we lean all over each other so we can hold up under the draggy-ass lecture she always finishes off with at the end before we thank her for borin us to tears. But she just looks at us like she readin tea leaves. Finally she say, "Well, what did you think of F.A.O. Schwarz?"

Rosie Giraffe mumbles, "White folks crazy."

"I'd like to go there again when I get my birthday money," says Mercedes, and we shove her out the pack so she has to lean on the mailbox by herself.

"I'd like a shower. Tiring day," say Flyboy.

Then Sugar surprises me by saying, "You know, Miss Moore, I don't think all of us here put together eat in a year what that sailboat costs." And Miss Moore lights up like somebody goosed her. "And?" she say, urging Sugar on. Only I'm standin on her foot so she don't continue.

50     "Imagine for a minute what kind of society it is in which some people can spend on a toy what it would cost to feed a family of six or seven. What do you think?"

"I think," say Sugar pushing me off her feet like she never done before, cause I whip her ass in a minute, "that this is not much of a democracy if you ask me. Equal chance to pursue happiness means an equal crack at the dough, don't it?" Miss Moore is beside herself and I am disgusted with Sugar's treachery. So I stand on her foot one more time to see if she'll shove me. She shuts up, and Miss Moore looks at me, sorrowfully I'm thinkin. And somethin weird is goin on, I can feel it in my chest.

"Anybody else learn anything today?" lookin dead at me. I walk away and Sugar has to run to catch up and don't even seem to notice when I shrug her arm off my shoulder.

"Well, we got four dollars anyway," she says.

"Uh hunh."

55     "We could go to Hascombs and get half a chocolate layer and then go to the Sunset and still have plenty of money for potato chips and ice cream sodas."

"Un hunh."

"Race you to Hascombs," she say.

We start down the block and she gets ahead which is O.K. by me cause I'm going to the West End and then over to the Drive to think this day through. She can run if she want to and even run faster. But ain't nobody gonna beat me at nuthin.

## YOUR TURN

1. What is "the lesson" that Miss Moore is trying to teach the children? How much, if any, of this lesson does Sylvia learn? Point to specific passages to support your answers.

2. Since Miss Moore intends the lesson for the children's own good, why is Sylvia so resistant to it, so impatient and exasperated?

3. Toward the end of the story, Sylvia says that she is "disgusted with Sugar's treachery." Describe their relationship. What would be missing from the story if Bambara had not included Sugar among its characters?

# 4

# More About Writing About Literature: From Idea to Essay

## Why Write Arguments About Literature?

If you have ever put exclamation points or questions marks or brief annotations ("this is ridiculous," or "great!") in the margins of your books, you are aware of the *pleasure* one gets from putting responses into writing. But people also write about literature—not only in margins of books but, let's say, in notebooks or journals and ultimately in essays—in order to clarify and account for their responses to works that interest or excite or frustrate them.

In putting words on paper you will have to take a second and a third look at what is in front of you and what is within you. Writing, then, is not only a way of expressing pleasure but also a way of *learning*. The last word about complex thoughts and feelings is never said, but when we write we hope to make at least a little progress in the difficult but rewarding job of talking about our responses. We learn, and then we hope to interest our readers because we are communicating to them our responses to something that for one reason or another is worth talking about.

This communication is, in effect, teaching. You may think that you are writing for the teacher, but that is a misconception; when you write, *you* are the teacher, offering an argument. An essay on literature is an attempt to help someone see the work as you see it. If this chapter had to be boiled down to a single sentence, that sentence would be: Because you are teaching, your essay should embody those qualities that you value in teachers—intelligence, open-mindedness, effort, a desire to offer what help one can.

## Getting Ideas: Prewriting

"All there is to writing," Robert Frost said, "is having ideas. To learn to write is to learn to have ideas." But how does one "learn to have ideas"? What can one do *before* writing? Among the activities are these: reading with a pen or pencil in hand, so that you can annotate the text; keeping a journal, in which you jot down reflections about your reading; talking with others (including your instructor) about the reading. Let's look at the first of these, annotating.

## Annotating a Text

When reading a book that you own, don't hesitate to mark it up, indicating (by highlighting or underlining or by making marginal notes) what puzzles you, what pleases or interests you, and what displeases or bores you. Later, of course, you'll want to think further about these responses, asking yourself, on reread-ing, if you still feel that way, and if not, why not, but these first responses will get you started.

One kind of annotation is a question mark in the margin, jotted down in order to indicate your uncertainty about the meaning of a word. It's a good idea to keep a *dictionary* nearby while you are reading. Of course you won't look up every word that you are unsure about—this might spoil the fun of reading—but sometimes you will sense that you need to know the precise meanings and im-plications of the writer's words in order to feel and appreciate the effects he or she is trying to create. And the more you become aware of how richly meaning-ful the words can be in a literary text, the more sensitive and self-aware you will be about the words you use in your own prose.

We have already looked at Pat Mora's short poem "Immigrants" (page 26), but here it is again, with a student's first annotations.

*unusual to use title as first word?*

### *Immigrants*

wrap their babies in the American flag,
feed them mashed hot dogs and apple pie,
name them Bill and Daisy,
buy them blonde dolls that blink blue
cycs or a football and tiny clcats
before the baby can even walk,
speak to them in thick English, hallo, babee, hallo,
whisper in Spanish or Polish
when the babies sleep, whisper
in a dark parent bed, that dark
parent fear, "Will they like
our boy, our girl, our fine american
boy, our fine american girl?"

*so what's wrong with hot dogs — and apple pie?*

*Anglo types—not Asian American or Latino types*

*Is Mora making fun of immigrants?*

*do only immigrants show a "parent fear"? Don't all parents fear for their children?*

*why not a capital letter?*

5

10

Notice that most of these annotations are questions that the student is asking herself. Asking questions is an excellent way to get yourself thinking. We will re-turn to this method shortly.

## Brainstorming to Get Ideas for Writing

Unlike annotating, which consists of making brief notes and small marks on the printed page, "brainstorming"—the free jotting down of ideas—asks that you jot down at length whatever comes to mind, without inhibition. But before we talk further about brainstorming, read the following short story.

# KATE CHOPIN

*Kate Chopin (1851-1904)—the name is pronounced in the French way, somewhat like "show pan"—was born in St. Louis, with the name Katherine O'Flaherty. Her father was an immigrant from Ireland, and her mother was descended from an old Creole family. (In the United States, a Creole is a person descended from the original French settlers in Louisiana or the original Spanish settlers in the Gulf States.) At the age of nineteen she married Oscar Chopin, a cotton broker in New Orleans. They had six children, and though Kate Chopin had contemplated a literary career, she did not turn seriously to writing until after her husband's death in 1883. Most of her fiction concerns the lives of the descendants of the French who had settled in Louisiana.*

## The Story of an Hour                                    [1894]

Knowing that Mrs. Mallard was afflicted with a heart trouble, great care was taken to break to her as gently as possible the news of her husband's death.

It was her sister Josephine who told her, in broken sentences, veiled hints that revealed in half concealing. Her husband's friend Richards was there, too, near her. It was he who had been in the newspaper office when intelligence of the railroad disaster was received, with Brently Mallard's name leading the list of "killed." He had only taken the time to assure himself of its truth by a second telegram, and had hastened to forestall any less careful, less tender friend in bearing the sad message.

She did not hear the story as many women have heard the same, with a paralyzed inability to accept its significance. She wept at once, with sudden, wild abandonment, in her sister's arms. When the storm of grief had spent itself she went away to her room alone. She would have no one follow her.

There stood, facing the open window, a comfortable, roomy armchair. Into this she sank, pressed down by a physical exhaustion that haunted her body and seemed to reach into her soul.

5    She could see in the open square before her house the tops of trees that were all aquiver with the new spring life. The delicious breath of rain was in the air. In the street below a peddler was crying his wares. The notes of a distant song which some one was singing reached her faintly, and countless sparrows were twittering in the eaves.

There were patches of blue sky showing here and there through the clouds that had met and piled one above the other in the west facing her window. She sat with her head thrown back upon the cushion of the chair quite motionless, except when a sob came up into her throat and shook her, as a child who has cried itself to sleep continues to sob in its dreams.

She was young, with a fair, calm face, whose lines bespoke repression and even a certain strength. But now there was a dull stare in her eyes, whose gaze was fixed away off yonder on one of those patches of blue sky. It was not a glance of reflection, but rather indicated a suspension of intelligent thought.

There was something coming to her and she was waiting for it, fearfully. What was it? She did not know; it was too subtle and elusive to name. But she felt it, creeping out of the sky, reaching toward her through the sounds, the scents, the color that filled the air.

Now her bosom rose and fell tumultuously. She was beginning to recognize this thing that was approaching to possess her, and she was striving to beat it back with her will—as powerless as her two white slender hands would have been.

10     When she abandoned herself a little whispered word escaped her slightly parted lips. She said it over and over under her breath: "Free, free, free!" The vacant stare and the look of terror that had followed it went from her eyes. They stayed keen and bright. Her pulses beat fast, and the coursing blood warmed and relaxed every inch of her body.

She did not stop to ask if it were not a monstrous joy that held her. A clear and exalted perception enabled her to dismiss the suggestion as trivial.

She knew that she would weep again when she saw the kind, tender hands folded in death; the face that had never looked save with love upon her, fixed and gray and dead. But she saw beyond that bitter moment a long procession of years to come that would belong to her absolutely. And she opened and spread her arms out to them in welcome.

There would be no one to live for her during those coming years; she would live for herself. There would be no powerful will bending her in that blind persistence with which men and women believe they have a right to impose a private will upon a fellow creature. A kind intention or a cruel intention made the act seem no less a crime as she looked upon it in that brief moment of illumination.

And yet she had loved him—sometimes. Often she had not. What did it matter! What could love, the unsolved mystery, count for in face of this possession of self-assertion which she suddenly recognized as the strongest impulse of her being.

15     "Free! Body and soul free!" she kept whispering.

Josephine was kneeling before the closed door with her lips to the keyhole, imploring for admission. "Louise, open the door! I beg; open the door—you will make yourself ill. What are you doing, Louise? For heaven's sake open the door."

"Go away. I am not making myself ill." No; she was drinking in a very elixir of life through that open window.

Her fancy was running riot along those days ahead of her. Spring days, and summer days, and all sorts of days that would be her own. She breathed a quick prayer that life might be long. It was only yesterday she had thought with a shudder that life might be long.

She arose at length and opened the door to her sister's importunities. There was a feverish triumph in her eyes, and she carried herself unwittingly like a goddess of Victory. She clasped her sister's waist, and together they descended the stairs. Richards stood waiting for them at the bottom.

20     Some one was opening the front door with a latchkey. It was Brently Mallard who entered, a little travel-stained, composedly carrying his gripsack and umbrella. He had been far from the scene of accident, and did not even know there had been one. He stood amazed at Josephine's piercing cry; at Richards' quick motion to screen him from the view of his wife.

But Richards was too late.

When the doctors came they said she had died of heart disease—of joy that kills.

When brainstorming, don't worry about spelling, about writing complete sentences, or about unifying your thoughts; just let one thought lead to another. Later you can review your jottings, deleting some, connecting with arrows others that are related, expanding still others, but for now you want to get going, and so there is no reason to look back. Thus you might jot down something about the title.

> Title speaks of an hour, and story covers an hour, but maybe takes five minutes to read

And then, perhaps prompted by "an hour," you might happen to add something to this effect:

> Doubt that a woman who got news of the death of her husband could move from grief to joy within an hour

Your next jotting might have little or nothing to do with this issue; it might simply say:

> Enjoyed "Hour" especially because "Hour" is so shocking

And then you might ask yourself:

> By shocking, do I mean "improbable," or what? Come to think of it, maybe it's not so improbable. A lot depends on what the marriage was like.

# Focused Freewriting

Focused, or directed, freewriting is a method related to brainstorming that some writers use to uncover ideas they may want to write about. Concentrating on one issue—for instance, a question that strikes them as worth puzzling over (What kind of person is Mrs. Mallard?)—they write at length, nonstop, for perhaps 5 or 10 minutes.

Writers who find freewriting helpful put down everything they can think of that has bearing on the one issue or question they are examining. They do not stop at this stage to evaluate the results, and they do not worry about niceties of sentence structure or of spelling. They just pour out their ideas in a steady stream of writing, drawing on whatever associations come to mind. If they pause in their writing, it is only to refer to the text, to search for more detail—perhaps a quotation—that will help them answer their question.

After the freewriting session, these writers usually go back and reread what they have written, highlighting or underlining what seems to be of value. Of course they find much that is of little or no use, but they also usually find that some strong ideas have surfaced and have received some development. At this point the writers are often able to make a scratch outline and then begin a draft.

Here is an example of one student's focused freewriting, again on Chopin's "The Story of an Hour."

> What do I know about Mrs. Mallard? Let me put everything down here I know about her or can figure out from what Kate Chopin tells me. When she finds herself alone after the death of her husband, she says, "Free! Body and

soul free!" and before that she said, "Free, free, free!" Three times. So she has suddenly perceived that she has not been free: she has been under the influence of a "powerful will." In this case it has been her husband, but she says no one, man nor woman, should impose their will on anyone else. So it's not a feminist issue— it's a power issue. No one should push anyone else around is what I guess Chopin means, force someone to do what the other person wants. I used to have a friend that did that to me all the time; he had to run everything. They say that fathers— before the women's movement—used to run things, with the father in charge of all the decisions, so maybe this is an honest reaction to having been pushed around by a husband. I think Mrs. Mallard is a believable character, even if the plot is not all that believable—all those things happening in such quick succession.

## Listing and Clustering

In your preliminary thinking you may find it useful to make lists or to jot down clusters of your ideas, insights, comments, questions. For "The Story of an Hour" you might list Mrs. Mallard's traits, or you might list the stages of her development. (Such a list is not the same as a summary of a plot. Lists help writers to see the sequence of psychological changes, helping them to offer a coherent argument about what happens.)

weeps (when she gets the news)

goes to room, alone

"pressed down by a physical exhaustion"

"dull stare"

"something coming to her"

strives to beat back "this thing"

"Free, free, free!" The "vacant stare went from her eyes"

"A clear and exalted perception"

rejects Josephine

"she was drinking in a very elixir of life"

gets up, opens door, "a feverish triumph in her eyes"

sees B, and dies

Unlike brainstorming and annotating, which let you go in all directions, listing requires that you first make a decision about what you will be listing—traits of character, images, puns, or whatever. Once you make the decision, you can then construct the list, and, with a list in front of you, you will probably see patterns that you were not fully conscious of earlier.

On the other hand, don't be unduly concerned if something does not seem to fit into a list or cluster. You can return to it, and give it more thought—maybe it will come to fit later. But you might also realize that this point needs to be placed to the side. As far as you can tell, it doesn't appear to belong in one of your lists or to link well to other points you have begun to make, and in this way you may come to realize that it is not relevant to your development of possible topics for your essay.

# Developing an Awareness of the Writer's Use of Language

In the first line of the story, Chopin notes that "Mrs. Mallard was afflicted with a heart trouble." You might want to look up "afflicted" in your dictionary. Why do you think that Chopin chose this word, as opposed to other words she might have chosen? How would the effect of the opening line be different if, for example, Chopin had written "Mrs. Mallard had a heart problem" or "Mrs. Mallard's heart was weak"?

Earlier we recommended that you keep a dictionary at hand when you read. It will help you, especially if you get into the habit of asking questions about the writer's choice of language. And this brings us to our next point.

# Asking Questions

If you feel stuck, ask yourself questions. We suggest questions for fiction on pages 265-68, for poetry on pages 690-93, and for drama on pages 1172-75. If, for instance, you are thinking about a work of fiction, you might ask yourself questions about the plot and the characters—are they believable, are they interesting, and what does it all add up to? What does the story mean *to you?* One student found it helpful to jot down the following questions:

Plot

Ending false? unconvincing? or prepared for?

Character?

Mrs. M. unfeeling? Immoral?

Mrs. M. unbelievable character?

What might her marriage have been like? Many gaps. (Can we tell what her husband was like?) "And yet she loved him—sometimes." Fickle?

Realistic?

What is "this thing that was approaching to possess her"?

Symbolism

Set on spring day = symbolic of new life?

But, again, you don't have to be as tidy as this student was. You can begin by jotting down notes and queries about what you like or dislike and about what puzzles or amuses you. Here are the jottings of another student. They are, obviously, in no particular order—the student is brainstorming, putting down whatever occurs to her—though it is equally obvious that one note sometimes led to the next:

Title nothing special. What might be better title?

Could a woman who loved her husband be so heartless?

*Is* she heartless? *Did* she love him?

What are (were) Louise's feelings about her husband?

Did she want too much? *What* did she want?

Could this story happen today? Feminist interpretation?

Sister (Josephine)—a busybody?

Tricky ending—but maybe it could be true

"And yet she loved him—sometimes. Often she had not."

Why does one love someone "sometimes"?

Irony: plot has reversal. Are characters ironic too?

These jottings will help the reader-writer to think about the story, to find a special point of interest and to develop a thoughtful argument about it.

## Keeping a Journal

A journal is not a diary, a record of what the writer did each day ("today I read Chopin's 'Hour'"); rather, a journal is a place to store some of the thoughts that you may have inscribed on a scrap of paper or in the margin of the text—for instance, your initial response to the title of a work or to the ending. It's also a place to jot down some further reflections. These reflections may include thoughts about what the work means to you or what was said in the classroom about writing in general or about specific works. You may, for instance, want to reflect on why your opinion is so different from that of another student, or you may want to apply a concept such as "character" or "irony" or "plausibility" to a story that later you may write an essay about.

You might even make an entry in the form of a letter to the author or in the form of a letter from one character to another. Similarly, you might write a dialogue between characters in two works or between two authors, or you might record an experience of your own that is comparable to something in the work.

A student who wrote about "The Story of an Hour" began with the following entry in his journal. In reading this entry, notice that one idea stimulates another. The student was, quite rightly, concerned with getting and exploring ideas, not with writing a unified paragraph.

> Apparently a "well-made" story, but seems clever rather than moving or real. Doesn't seem plausible. Mrs. M's change comes out of the blue—maybe *some* women might respond like this, but probably not most.
>
> Does literature deal with unusual people, or with usual (typical?) people? Shouldn't it deal with typical? Maybe not. (Anyway, how can I know?) Is "typical" same as "plausible"? Come to think of it, prob. not.
>
> Anyway, whether Mrs. M. is typical or not, is her change plausible, believable?
>
> Why did she change? Her husband dominated her life and controlled her action; he did "impose a private will upon a fellow creature." She calls this a crime. Why? Why not?

## Arguing a Thesis

Having raised some questions, a reader goes back to the story, hoping to read it now with increased awareness. Some of the jottings will be dead ends, but some will lead to further ideas that can be arranged in lists. What the **thesis** of the essay will be—the idea that will be asserted and supported—is still in doubt, but there is no doubt about one thing: A good essay will have a thesis, a point, an argument. You ought to be able to state your point in a **thesis sentence.**

Consider these candidates as possible thesis sentences, as assertions that can be supported in an argument:

1. Mrs. Mallard dies soon after hearing that her husband had died.

True, but scarcely a point that can be argued, or even developed. About the most the essayist can do with this sentence is to amplify it by summarizing the plot of the story, a task not worth doing. An analysis may include a sentence or two of summary, to give readers their bearings, but a summary is not an essay.

2. The story is a libel on women.

In contrast to the first statement, this one can be developed into an argument. Probably the writer will try to demonstrate that Mrs. Mallard's behavior is despicable. Whether this point can be convincingly argued is another matter; the thesis may be untenable, but it is a thesis. A second problem, however, is this: Even if the writer demonstrates that Mrs. Mallard's behavior is despicable, he or she will have to go on to demonstrate that the presentation of one despicable woman constitutes a libel on women in general. That's a pretty big order.

3. The story is clever but superficial because it is based on an unreal character.

Here, too, is a thesis, a point of view that can be argued. Whether or not this thesis is true is another matter. The writer's job will be to support it by presenting evidence. Probably the writer will have no difficulty in finding evidence that the story is "clever"; the difficulty probably will be in establishing a case that the characterization of Mrs. Mallard is "unreal." The writer will have to set forth some ideas about what makes a character real and then will have to show that Mrs. Mallard is an "unreal" (unbelievable) figure.

4. The irony of the ending is believable partly because it is consistent with earlier ironies in the story.

It happens that the student who wrote the essay printed on page 78 began by drafting an essay based on the third of these thesis topics, but as she worked on a draft she found that she couldn't support her assertion that the character was unconvincing. In fact, she came to believe that although Mrs. Mallard's joy was the reverse of what a reader might expect, several early reversals in the story helped to make Mrs. Mallard's shift from grief to joy acceptable.

# Writing a Draft

After jotting down notes and then adding more notes stimulated by rereading and further thinking, you'll probably be able to formulate a tentative thesis. At this point most writers find it useful to clear the air by glancing over their preliminary notes and by jotting down the thesis and a few especially promising notes—brief statements of what they think their key points may be. These notes may include some brief key quotations that the writer thinks will help to support the thesis.

Here are the notes (not the original brainstorming notes, but a later selection from them, with additions) and a draft (following) that makes use of them. The final version of the essay—the product produced by the process—is given on page 78.

title: Ironies in an Hour (?) An Hour of Irony (?) Kate Chopin's Irony (?)

thesis: irony at the end is prepared for by earlier ironies

chief irony: Mrs. M. dies just as she is beginning to enjoy life

smaller ironies: 1. "sad message" brings her joy

                2. Richards is "too late" at end

                3. Richards is too early at start

# Sample Draft of an Essay on Kate Chopin's "The Story of an Hour"

Now for the student's draft—not the first version, but a revised draft with some of the irrelevancies of the first draft omitted and some evidence added.

The digits within the parentheses refer to the page numbers from which the quotations are drawn, though with so short a work as "The Story of an Hour," page references are hardly necessary. Unless instructed otherwise, always provide page numbers for your quotations. This will enable your readers to quickly locate the passages to which you refer. (Detailed information about how to document a paper is given on pages 1456–67.)

---

                                               Crowe 1

Lynn Crowe

Professor O'Brian

English 102

1 June 2010

Ironies in an Hour

     After we know how the story turns out, if we reread it we find irony at the very start, as is true of many other stories. Mrs. Mallard's friends assume, mistakenly, that Mrs. Mallard was deeply in love with her husband, Brently Mallard. They take great care to tell her gently of his death. The friends mean well, and in fact they *do* well. They bring her an hour of life, an hour of freedom. They think their news is sad. Mrs. Mallard at first expresses grief when she hears the news, but soon she finds joy in it. So Richards's "sad message" (67), though sad in Richards's eyes, is in fact a happy message.

     Among the ironic details is the statement that when Mallard entered the house, Richards tried to conceal him from Mrs. Mallard, but "Richards was too late" (68). This is ironic because earlier Richards "hastened" (67) to bring his sad message; if he had at the start been "too late" (68), Brently Mallard would have arrived at home first, and Mrs. Mallard's life would not have ended an hour later but would simply have gone on as it had before. Yet another irony at the end of the story is the diagnosis of the doctors. The doctors say she died of "heart disease—of joy that kills" (68). In one sense the doctors are right: Mrs. Mallard has experienced a great joy. But of course the doctors totally misunderstood the joy that kills her.

The central irony resides not in the well-intentioned but ironic actions of Richards, nor in the unconsciously ironic words of the doctors, but in her own life. In a way she has been dead. She "sometimes" (68) loved her husband, but in a way she has been dead. Now, his apparent death brings her new life. This new life comes to her at the season of the year when "the tops of trees . . . were all aquiver with the new spring life" (67). But, ironically, her new life will last only an hour. She looks forward to "summer days" (68) but she will not see even the end of this spring day. Her years of marriage were ironic. They brought her a sort of living death instead of joy. Her new life is ironic too. It grows out of her moment of grief for her supposedly dead husband, and her vision of a new life is cut short.

Work Cited

Chopin, Kate. "The Story of an Hour." *An Introduction to Literature.*
    Ed. Sylvan Barnet, William Burto, and William E. Cain. 16th ed.
    New York: Longman, 2011. 67–68. Print.

# Revising a Draft

The draft, although thoughtful and clear, is not yet a finished essay. The student went on to improve it in many small but important ways.

First, the draft needs a good introductory paragraph, a paragraph that will let readers know where the writer will be taking them. Doubtless you know from your own experience as a reader that readers can follow an argument more easily—and with more pleasure—if early in the discussion the writer alerts them to the gist of the argument. (The title, too, can strongly suggest the thesis.) Second, some of the paragraphs could be clearer.

In revising paragraphs—or, for that matter, in revising an entire draft—writers unify, organize, clarify, and polish. Let's look at the nouns implicit in these verbs.

1.  **Unity** is achieved partly by eliminating irrelevancies. Notice that in the final version, printed on pages 78–79, the writer has deleted "as is true of many other stories" from the first sentence of the draft.
2.  **Organization** is largely a matter of arranging material into a sequence that will assist the reader to grasp the point.
3.  **Clarity** is achieved largely by providing concrete details and quotations to support generalizations and by providing helpful transitions ("for instance," "furthermore," "on the other hand," "however").
4.  **Polishing** is small-scale revision. For instance, a writer may delete unnecessary repetitions. In the second paragraph of the draft, the phrase "the doctors" appears three times, but it appears only once in the final version of the paragraph. Similarly, in polishing, a writer combines choppy sentences into longer sentences, and breaks overly long sentences into shorter ones.

Later, after producing a draft that seems close to a finished essay, writers engage in yet another activity.

5.  **Editing** concerns such things as checking the accuracy of quotations by comparing them with the original, checking a dictionary for the spelling of doubtful words, checking a handbook for doubtful punctuation—for instance, whether a comma or a semicolon is needed in a particular sentence.

## Peer Review

Your instructor may encourage (or even require) you to discuss your draft with another student or with a small group of students. That is, you may be asked to get a review from your peers. Such a procedure is helpful in several ways. First, it gives the writer a real audience, readers who can point to what pleases or puzzles them, who make suggestions, who may often disagree (with the writer or with each other), and who frequently, though not intentionally, *misread*. Though writers don't necessarily like everything they hear (they seldom hear "This is perfect. Don't change a word!"), reading and discussing their work with others almost always gives them a fresh perspective on their work, and a fresh perspective may stimulate thoughtful revision. (Having your intentions *misread* because your writing isn't clear enough can be particularly stimulating.)

The writer whose work is being reviewed is not the sole beneficiary. When students regularly serve as readers for each other, they become better readers of their own work and consequently better revisers.

When you produce a draft of your paper for peer review, it will not be in final form; the draft is an important step toward shaping the paper and bringing it to final form. But aim to do the best job possible on your draft; let your classmates respond to the best work you can do at this stage of the process.

You will have more work to do on this paper—you know that. But you don't want your classmates to be pointing out mistakes that you know are in the draft and that you could have fixed yourself.

If peer review is a part of the writing process in your course, the instructor may distribute a sheet with some suggestions and questions. An example of such a sheet is shown here.

---

QUESTIONS FOR PEER REVIEW                    ENGLISH 125A

Read each draft once, quickly. Then read it again, with the following questions in mind.

1. What is the essay's topic? Is it one of the assigned topics, or a variation from it? Does the draft show promise of fulfilling the assignment?

2. Look at the essay as a whole. What thesis (main idea) is stated or implied? If implied, try to state it in your own words.

3. Is the thesis plausible? How might the argument be strengthened?

4. Look at each paragraph separately:

   a. What is the basic point? (If it isn't clear to you, ask for clarification.)

   b. How does the paragraph relate to the essay's main idea or to the previous paragraph?

   c. Should some paragraphs be deleted? Be divided into two or more paragraphs? Be combined? Be put elsewhere? (If you outline the essay by jotting down the gist of each paragraph, you will get help in answering these questions.)

   d. Is each sentence clearly related to the sentence that precedes and to the sentence that follows?

   e. Is each paragraph adequately developed?

   f. Are there sufficient details, perhaps brief supporting quotations from the text?

5. What are the paper's chief strengths?

6. Make at least two specific suggestions that you think will assist the author to improve the paper.

# The Final Version

Here is the final version of the student's essay. The essay that was submitted to her instructor had been retyped, but here, so that you can easily see how the draft has been revised, we print the draft with the final changes written in by hand.

---

Crowe 1

Lynn Crowe

Professor O'Brian

English 102

1 June 2010

Ironies of Life in Kate Chopin's "The Story of an Hour"
~~Ironies in an Hour~~

Despite its title, Kate Chopin's "The Story of an Hour" ironically takes only a few minutes to read. In addition, the story turns out to have an ironic ending, but on rereading it one sees that the irony is not concentrated only in the outcome of the plot—Mrs. Mallard dies just when she is beginning to live—but is also present in many details.

After we know how the story turns out, if were read it we find irony at the very start. / ~~as is true of many other stories.~~ Because Mrs. Mallard's friends and her sister assume, mistakenly, that she ~~Mrs. Mallard~~ was deeply in love with her husband, Brently Mallard. / They take great care to tell her gently of his death. They ~~The friends~~ mean well, and in fact they do well. / They bring ing her an hour of life, an hour of joyous freedom. / but it is ironic that They think their news is sad. True, Mrs. Mallard at first expresses grief when she hears the news, but soon (unknown to her friends) she finds joy in it. So Richards's "sad message" (67), though sad in Richards's eyes, is in fact a happy message.

Among the small but significant ironic details is the statement near the end of the story that when Mallard entered the house, Richards tried to conceal him from Mrs. Mallard, but "Richards was too late" (68). This is ironic because ~~earlier~~ almost at the start of the story, in the second paragraph, Richards "hastened" (67) to bring his sad message; if he had at the start been "too late" (68), Brently Mallard would have arrived at home first, and Mrs. Mallard's life would not have ended an hour later but would simply have gone on as it had before. Yet another irony at the end of the story is the diagnosis of the doctors. They ~~The doctors~~ say she died of "heart disease—

Crowe 2

life would not have ended an hour later but would simply have gone on

as it had before.  Yet another irony at the end of the story is the

diagnosis of the doctors.  ~~The doctors~~ They say she died of "heart disease—

of joy that kills" (68).  In one sense ~~the doctors~~ they are right: Mrs. Mallard for the last hour

experienced a great joy.  But of course the doctors totally misunder-

stand the joy that kills her.  It is not joy at seeing her husband alive, but

her realization that the great joy she experienced during the last hour is over.

All of these ironic details add richness to the story, but

The central irony resides not in the well-intentioned but ironic

actions of Richards, nor in the unconsciously ironic words of the

doctors, but in ~~her~~ Mrs. Mallard's own life.  ~~In a way she has been dead.~~ She "some-

times" (68) loved her husband, but in a way she has been dead. a body subjected to her husband's will Now,

his apparent death brings her new life.  This new life comes to her at

the season of the year when "the tops of trees . . . were all aquiver with

the new spring life" (67). But, ironically, her new life will last only an

She is "free, free, free"—but only until her husband walks through the doorway.

hour.  She looks forward to "summer days" (68) but she will not see

even the end of this spring day.  If Her years of marriage were ironic.

bringing

~~They brought~~ her a sort of living death instead of joy.  Her new life is

not only because

ironic too.  It grows out of her moment of grief for her supposedly dead

but also because her vision of "a long progression of years"

husband, and her vision of a new life is cut short.

within an hour on a spring day.

Crowe 3

Work Cited

Chopin, Kate. "The Story of an Hour." *An Introduction to Literature*.

Ed. Sylvan Barnet, William Burto, and William E. Cain. 16th ed.

New York: Longman, 2011. 67–68. Print.

## A Brief Overview of the Final Version

Finally, as a quick review, let's look at several principles illustrated by this essay.

1. The **title of the essay** is not merely the title of the work discussed; rather, it gives the readers a clue, a small idea of the essayist's topic.
2. The **opening** or **introductory paragraph** does not begin by saying "In this story . . ." Rather, by naming the author and the title, it lets the reader know exactly what story is being discussed. It also develops the writer's thesis so readers know where they will be going.
3. The **organization** is effective. The smaller ironies are discussed in the second and third paragraphs, the central (chief) irony in the last paragraph. That is, the essay does not dwindle or become anticlimactic; rather, it builds up from the least important to the most important point.
4. Some **brief quotations** are used, both to provide evidence and to let the reader hear—even if only fleetingly—Kate Chopin's writing.
5. The essay is chiefly devoted to **analysis** (how the parts relate to each other), not to summary (a brief restatement of the happenings). The writer, properly assuming that the reader has read the work, does not tell the plot in great detail. But, aware that the reader has not memorized the story, the writer gives helpful reminders.
6. The **present tense** is used in narrating the action: "Mrs. Mallard dies"; "Mrs. Mallard's friends and her sister assume."
7. Although a **concluding paragraph** is often useful—if it does more than merely summarize what has already been clearly said—it is not essential in a short analysis. In this essay, the last sentence explains the chief irony and therefore makes an acceptable ending.

# Explication

A line-by-line commentary on what is going on in a text is an **explication** (literally, unfolding, or spreading out). Although your explication will for the most part move steadily from the beginning to the end of the selection, try to avoid writing along these lines (or, one might say, along this one line): "In line one. . . . In the second line. . . . In the third line. . . ." That is, don't hesitate to write such things as

> The poem begins. . . . In the next line. . . . The speaker immediately adds. . . . He then introduces. . . . The next stanza begins by saying. . . .

And of course you can discuss the second line before the first if that seems the best way of handling the passage.

An explication is not concerned with the writer's life or times, and it is not a paraphrase (a rewording)—though it may include paraphrase if a passage in the original seems unclear, perhaps because of an unusual word or an unfamiliar expression. On the whole, however, an explication goes beyond paraphrase, seeking to make explicit what the reader perceives as implicit in the work. To this end it calls attention, as it proceeds, to the implications of words (for instance, to their **tone**), the function of rhymes (for instance, how they may connect ideas, as in "throne" and "alone"), the development of contrasts, and any other contributions to the meaning.

Obviously you will have ideas about the merit and the meaning of a poem, and your paper will implicitly have a *thesis*—an argument, for instance this poem is very difficult, or this poem begins effectively but quickly goes downhill, or this poem is excessively sentimental. Your essay, however, is largely devoted not to making assertions of this sort but to explaining how the details make the meaning.

A good way to stimulate responses to the poem is to ask some of the questions given on pages 690-93.

Many students find that by copying the poem (by hand, or on a computer) they gain an understanding of the uses of language in a literary work. Don't photocopy the poem; the act of writing or typing it will help you to get into the piece, word by word, comma by comma. Double-space, so that you have ample room for annotations.

If you write on the computer, you can highlight key words, lines, stanzas. You can also rearrange lines and stanzas, and perhaps substitute different words for the words that the poet has selected. Some students like to make multiple printouts for contrast and comparison—the poem as the poet wrote it, the poem as the student has marked it up by using the highlighting feature of the computer program, the poem as it stands after the student has somewhat rearranged it.

A computer cannot interpret a poem or story for you. But you can employ it as a tool to deepen your own sense of how a poem is structured—why this or that word or image is crucial at this juncture, why this or that stanza or passage belongs here and could not be placed elsewhere, and so on. Your goal is to gain insight into how writers of literary texts use their artistic medium, and often a computer can be a good complement to the dictionary that you always keep nearby.

## A Sample Explication

Read this short poem (published in 1917) by the Irish poet William Butler Yeats (1865-1939). The "balloon" in the poem is a dirigible, a blimp.

## WILLIAM BUTLER YEATS

### *The Balloon of the Mind*                                    [1917]

Hands, do what you're bid:
Bring the balloon of the mind
That bellies and drags in the wind
Into its narrow shed.

A student began thinking about the poem by copying it, double-spaced. Then she jotted down her first thoughts.

*sounds abrupt*

Hands, do what you're bid:

Bring the balloon of the mind

That bellies and drags in the wind

Into its narrow shed.

*—balloon imagined by the mind? Or a mind like a balloon?*

*no real rhymes?*

*line seems to drag— it's so long!*

### Later she wrote some notes in a journal.

I'm still puzzled about the meaning of the words, "The balloon of the mind." Does "balloon of the mind" mean a balloon that belongs to the mind, sort of like "a disease of the heart"? If so, it means a balloon that the mind *has,* a balloon that the mind possesses, I guess by imagining it. Or does it mean that the mind is *like* a balloon, as when you say "he's a pig of a man," meaning he is like a pig, he is a pig? Can it mean both? What's a balloon that the mind imagines? Something like dreams of fame, wealth? Castles in Spain.

Is Yeats saying that the "hands" have to work hard to make dreams a reality? Maybe. But maybe the idea really is that the mind is *like* a balloon—hard to keep under control, floating around. Very hard to keep the mind on the job. If the mind is like a balloon, it's hard to get it into the hangar (shed).

"Bellies." Is there such a verb? In this poem it seems to mean something like "puffs out" or "flops around in the wind." Just checked *The American Heritage Dictionary*, and it says "belly" can be a verb, "to swell out," "to bulge." Well, you learn something every day.

### A later entry:

OK; I think the poem is about a writer trying to keep his balloon-like mind from floating around, trying to keep the mind under control, trying to keep it working at the job of writing something, maybe writing something with the "clarity, unity, and coherence" I keep hearing about in this course.

### Here is the student's final version of the explication.

Yeats's "Balloon of the Mind" is about writing poetry, specifically about the difficulty of getting one's floating thoughts down in lines on the page. The first line, a short, stern, heavily stressed command to the speaker's hands, perhaps implies by its severe or impatient tone that these hands will be disobedient or inept or careless if not watched closely: the poor bumbling body so often fails to achieve the goals of the mind. The bluntness of the command in the first line is emphasized by the fact that all the subsequent lines have more syllables. Furthermore, the first line is a grammatically complete sentence, whereas the thought of line 2 spills over into the next lines, implying the difficulty of fitting ideas into confining spaces, that is, of getting one's thoughts into order, especially into a coherent poem.

Lines 2 and 3 amplify the metaphor already stated in the title (the product of the mind is an airy but unwieldy balloon), and they also contain a second command, "Bring." Alliteration ties this command, "Bring," to the earlier "bid"; it also ties both of these verbs to their object, "balloon," and to the verb that most effectively describes the balloon, "bellies." In comparison with the abrupt first line of the poem, lines 2 and 3 themselves seem almost swollen, bellying and dragging, an effect aided by using adjacent unstressed syllables ("of the," "[bell]ies and," "in the") and by using an eye rhyme ("mind" and "wind") rather than an exact rhyme. And then comes the short last line: almost before we could expect it, the cumbersome balloon—here, the idea that is to be packed into the stanza—is successfully lodged in its "narrow shed."

Aside from the relatively colorless "into," the only words of more than one syllable in the poem are "balloon," "bellies," and "narrow," and all three emphasize the difficulty of the task. But after "narrow"—the word itself almost looks long and narrow, in this context like a hangar—we get the simplicity of the monosyllable "shed." The difficult job is done, the thought is safely packed away, the poem is completed—but again with an off rhyme ("bid" and "shed"), for neatness can go only so far when hands and mind and a balloon are involved.

*Note:* The reader of an explication needs to see the text, and because the explicated text is usually short, it is advisable to quote it all. (Remember, your imagined audience probably consists of your classmates; even if they have already read the work you are explicating, they have not memorized it, and so you helpfully remind them of the work by quoting it.) You can quote the entire text at the outset, or you can quote the first unit (for example, a stanza), then explicate that unit, and then quote the next unit, and so on. And if the poem or passage of prose is longer than, say, six lines, it is advisable to number every fifth line at the right for easy reference, or every fourth line if the poem is written in four-line stanzas.

# Explication as Argument

An explication unfolds or interprets a work; it is partly an exposition but it is also an *argument*, offering assertions that are supported by *reasons*. Reread the explication of "The Balloon of the Mind," and notice that the first sentence makes a claim—the poem is "about" such-and-such—and notice, too, that the subsequent assertions are supported by evidence. For instance, when the writer says that lines 2 and 3 seem to drag, she goes on to support the claim by calling attention to "adjacent unstressed syllables." She does not merely assert; she argues.

# Comparison and Contrast: A Way of Arguing

Something should be said about an essay organized around a comparison or a contrast, say, of the settings in two short stories, of two characters in a novel, or of the symbolism in two poems. (A comparison emphasizes resemblances whereas a contrast emphasizes differences, but we can use the word "comparison" to cover both kinds of writing.) Probably the student's first thought, after making some jottings, is to discuss one-half of the comparison and then go on to the second half. Instructors and textbooks (though not this one) usually condemn such an organization, arguing that the essay breaks into two parts and that the second part involves a good deal of repetition of categories set up in the first part. Usually they recommend that students organize their thoughts differently, making point-by-point comparisons. For example, in comparing *Adventures of Huckleberry Finn* with *The Catcher in the Rye,* you might organize the material like this:

1. First similarity: the narrator and his quest
   a. Huck
   b. Holden
2. Second similarity: the corrupt world surrounding the narrator
   a. society in *Huckleberry Finn*
   b. society in *Catcher*
3. First difference: degree to which the narrator fulfills his quest and escapes from society
   a. Huck's plan to "light out" to the frontier
   b. Holden's breakdown

Here is another way of organizing a comparison and contrast:

1. First point: the narrator and his quest
   a. similarities between Huck and Holden
   b. differences between Huck and Holden
2. Second point: the corrupt world
   a. similarities between the worlds in *Huck* and *Catcher*
   b. differences between the worlds in *Huck* and *Catcher*
3. Third point: degree of success
   a. similarities between Huck and Holden
   b. differences between Huck and Holden

But a comparison need not employ either of these structures. There is even the danger that an essay employing either of them may not come into focus until the essayist stands back from the seven-layer cake and announces, in the concluding paragraph, that the odd layers taste better. In your preparatory thinking, you may want to make comparisons in pairs, but you must come to some conclusions about what these add up to before writing the final version. This final version should not duplicate the thought processes; rather, it should be organized to make the point clearly and effectively. You are making a list; you are arguing a case.

   The point of the essay presumably is not to list pairs of similarities or differences, but to illuminate a work or works by making thoughtful comparisons. Although in a long essay the writer cannot postpone until page 30 a discussion of the second half of the comparison, in an essay of, say, fewer than ten pages nothing is wrong with setting forth one-half of the comparison and then, in light of it, the second half. The essay will break into two unrelated parts if the second half makes no use of the first or if it fails to modify the first half, but not if the second half looks back to the first half and calls attention to differences that the new material reveals. Learning how to write an essay with interwoven comparisons is worthwhile, but be aware that there is another, simpler and clearer way to write a comparison.

# Review: How to Write an Effective Essay

Every writer must work out his or her own writing procedures and rituals. (Hemingway liked to sharpen pencils; Robert Frost liked to do farm work before writing.) The following suggestions may provide some help.

1. **Read the work carefully.**
2. **Choose a worthwhile subject,** something that interests you and is not so big that your handling of it must be superficial. As you work, shape and narrow your topic—for example, from "The Character of Hester Prynne" to "The Effects of Alienation on Hester Prynne."
3. **Reread the work, jotting down notes of all relevant matters.** As you read, reflect on your reading and record your reflections. If you have a feeling or an idea, jot it down; don't assume that you will remember it when you get around to writing your essay. The margins of the book are a good place for initial jottings, but many people find that in the long run it is easiest to transfer these notes to $3 \times 5$ cards, writing on one side only, or to a file on your computer.
4. **Arrange and organize your thoughts into reasonable divisions,** and reject those irrelevant to your topic. If you are writing an explication, the order probably is essentially the order of the lines or of the episodes, but if you are writing an analysis you almost surely will want to rearrange your notes. If you took notes on your computer, it is best to print them out and do one of two things. (1) Either add notes on the printout (such as "put this with X" or "put this at the end of file; probably not useful") so that you can, by moving blocks of type, rearrange the sequence in your file and have something fairly well-organized to look at and think about on-screen; or (2) Cut the notes apart, reorganize them as you would index cards, and after they are in good order, go back to your file and rearrange them there.

   Whichever method you use, get the notes into order. For instance, you may wish to organize your essay from the lesser material to the greater (to avoid anticlimax) or from the simple to the complex (to ensure intelligibility). If, for instance, you are discussing the roles of three characters in a story, it may be best to build up to the one of the three that you think the most important. If you are comparing two characters it may be best to move from the most obvious contrasts to the least obvious. When you have arranged your notes into a meaningful sequence of packets, you have approximately divided your material into paragraphs, though of course two or three notes may be combined into one paragraph, or one packed note may turn into two or more paragraphs.
5. **Prepare an outline.** Most essayists find it useful to jot down some sort of outline, indicating the main idea of each paragraph and, under each main idea, supporting details that give it substance. An outline—not necessarily

anything highly formal with capital and lowercase letters and roman and arabic numerals, but merely key phrases in some sort of order—will help you to overcome the paralysis called "writer's block" that commonly afflicts professionals as well as students. A page of paper with ideas in some sort of sequence, however rough, ought to encourage you to realize that you do have something to say. And so, despite the temptation to sharpen another pencil or put a new ink cartridge into your printer or check your e-mail, the best thing to do at this point is to sit down and start writing.

If you don't feel that you can work from note cards and a rough outline, try another method: get something down on paper (or on a disk) by writing freely, sloppily, automatically, or whatever, but allowing your ideas about what the work means to you and how it conveys its meaning—rough as your ideas may be—to begin to take visible form. If you are like most people, you can't do much precise thinking until you have committed to paper at least a rough sketch of your initial ideas. Later you can push and polish your ideas into shape, perhaps even deleting all of them and starting over, but it is a lot easier to improve your ideas once you see them in front of you than it is to do the job in your head. On paper or on the screen of a computer one word leads to another; in your head one word often blocks another.

Just keep going; you may realize, as you near the end of a sentence, that you no longer believe it. OK, be glad that your first idea led you to a better one, and pick up your better one and keep going with it. What you are doing is, in a sense, by trial and error pushing your way not only toward clear expression but also toward sharper ideas and richer responses.

6. If there is time, **reread the work,** looking for additional material that strengthens or weakens your main point; take account of it in your outline or draft.

7. As soon as **your thesis (your argument) is clear to you, give your essay an informative title**—*not* simply the title of the story, poem, or play, but something that lets your reader know where you will be going.

With a thesis and title clearly in mind, **improve your draft,** checking your notes for fuller details, such as supporting quotations. If, as you work, you find that some of the points in your earlier jottings are no longer relevant, eliminate them, but make sure that the argument flows from one point to the next. As you write, your ideas will doubtless become clearer; some may prove to be poor ideas. (We rarely know exactly what our ideas are until we have them set down on paper. As the little girl said, replying to the suggestion that she should think before she spoke, "How do I know what I think until I say it?") Not until you have written a draft do you really have a strong sense of what your ideas are and how good your essay may be.

8. After a suitable interval, preferably a few days, **read the draft with a view toward revising it,** not with a view toward congratulating yourself. A revision, after all, is a re-vision, a second (and presumably sharper) view. When you revise, you will be in the company of Picasso, who said that in painting he advanced by a series of destructions. A revision—say, the substitution of a precise word for an imprecise one—is not a matter of prettifying but of thinking. As you read, correct things that disturb you (for example, awkward repetitions that bore, inflated utterances that grate), add supporting detail where the argument is undeveloped (a paragraph of only one or two sentences is usually an undeveloped paragraph), and ruthlessly delete irrelevancies however well written they may be.

But remember that a deletion probably requires some adjustment in the preceding and subsequent material.

**Use transitions** to make sure that the argument runs smoothly. The details should be relevant, the organization reasonable, the argument clear. **Check all quotations for accuracy.** Quotations are evidence, usually intended to support your assertions, and it is not nice to alter the evidence, even unintentionally. If there is time (there almost never is), put the revision aside, reread it in a day or two, and revise it again, especially with a view toward deleting wordiness and, on the other hand, supporting generalizations with evidence.

9. **Type, write, or print a clean copy,** following the principles concerning margins, pagination, footnotes, and so on set forth on pages 1452–56. If you have borrowed any ideas, be sure to give credit, usually in footnotes, to your sources. Remember that plagiarism is not limited to the unacknowledged borrowing of words; a borrowed idea, even when put into your own words, requires acknowledgment.

10. **Proofread and make corrections** as explained on page 1453. Remember that writing is a form of self-representation. Fairly or unfairly, readers will make judgments about you based on how you present yourself to them in your writing. With this in mind, proofread your work carefully, making sure that there are no misspellings, misquotations, and the like. The trick, of course, is not to feel so good about the paper that you find yourself skimming and congratulating yourself on your ideas, rather than reading word by word, with an eye for small errors.

# Additional Readings

## KATE CHOPIN

*For a biographical note, see page 67.*

### *Ripe Figs*                                                                [1893]

Maman-Nainaine said that when the figs were ripe Babette might go to visit her cousins down on the Bayou-Lafourche[1] where the sugar cane grows. Not that the ripening of figs had the least thing to do with it, but that is the way Maman-Nainaine was.

It seemed to Babette a very long time to wait; for the leaves upon the trees were tender yet, and the figs were like little hard, green marbles.

But warm rains came along and plenty of strong sunshine, and though Maman-Nainaine was as patient as the statue of la Madone,[2] and Babette as restless as a humming-bird, the first thing they both knew it was hot summertime. Every day Babette danced out to where the fig-trees were in a long line against the fence. She walked slowly beneath them, carefully peering

---

[1]**Bayou-Lafourche** a bayou in southeastern Louisiana that flows into the Gulf of Mexico.
[2]**la Madone** the Madonna.

between the gnarled, spreading branches. But each time she came disconsolate away again. What she saw there finally was something that made her sing and dance the whole long day.

When Maman-Nainaine sat down in her stately way to breakfast, the following morning, her muslin cap standing like an aureole about her white, placid face, Babette approached. She bore a dainty porcelain platter, which she set down before her godmother. It contained a dozen purple figs, fringed around with their rich, green leaves.

5      "Ah," said Maman-Nainaine arching her eyebrows, "how early the figs have ripened this year!"

"Oh," said Babette. "I think they have ripened very late."

"Babette," continued Maman-Nainaine, as she peeled the very plumpest figs with her pointed silver fruit-knife, "you will carry my love to them all down on Bayou-Lafourche. And tell your Tante[3] Frosine I shall look for her at Toussaint[4]—when the chrysanthemums are in bloom."

> **YOUR TURN**
>
> 1. Compare and contrast Maman-Nainaine and Babette.
> 2. Two questions here: What, if anything, "happens" in "Ripe Figs"? And what, in your opinion, is the story about?
> 3. What, if anything, would be lost if the last line were omitted? (If you can think of a better final line, write it, and explain why your version is preferable.)

# WILLIAM STAFFORD

*William Stafford (1914–1993) was born in Hutchinson, Kansas, and was educated at the University of Kansas and the State University of Iowa. A conscientious objector during World War II, he worked for the Brethren Service and the Church World Service. After the war he taught at several universities and then settled at Lewis and Clark College in Portland, Oregon. In addition to writing several books of poems, Stafford is the author of many books of poetry and prose, including* Down in My Heart *(1947), an account of his experiences as a conscientious objector.*

## *Traveling Through the Dark*                                      [1960]

Traveling through the dark I found a deer
dead on the edge of the Wilson River road.
It is usually best to roll them into the canyon:
the road is narrow; to swerve might make more dead.          4

By glow of the tail-light I stumbled back of the car
and stood by the heap, a doe, a recent killing;
she had stiffened already, almost cold.
I dragged her off; she was large in the belly.             8

---

[3]**Tante** aunt.    [4]**Toussaint** a bayou town in Louisiana. "La Toussaint" is the Cajun-French name for All Saints' Day, a day of religious festival and celebration.

My fingers touching her side brought me the reason—
her side was warm; her fawn lay there waiting,
alive, still, never to be born.
Beside that mountain road I hesitated.                        12

The car aimed ahead its lowered parking lights;
under the hood purred the steady engine.
I stood in the glare of the warm exhaust turning red;
around our group I could hear the wilderness listen.          16

I thought hard for us all—my only swerving—
Then pushed her over the edge into the river.

---

**YOUR TURN**

1. Look at the first sentence (the first two lines) and try to recall what your
   impression of the speaker was, based only on these two lines, or pretend that you have not read the entire poem, and characterize him
   merely on these two lines. Then take the entire poem into considera-
   tion and characterize him.
2. What do you make of the title? Do you think it is a good title for this
   poem? Explain.

# LINDA PASTAN

*Linda Pastan was born in New York City in 1932 and educated at Radcliffe
College, Simmons College, and Brandeis University. The author of many books
of poems, she has won numerous prizes and has received a grant from the
National Endowment for the Arts.*

## *Ethics*                                                   [1980]

In ethics class so many years ago
our teacher asked this question every fall:
if there were a fire in a museum
which would you save, a Rembrandt painting
or an old woman who hadn't many                               5
years left anyhow? Restless on hard chairs
caring little for pictures or old age
we'd opt one year for life, the next for art
and always half-heartedly. Sometimes
the woman borrowed my grandmother's face                      10
leaving her usual kitchen to wander
some drafty, half-imagined museum.
One year, feeling clever, I replied
Why not let the woman decide herself?
Linda, the teacher would report, eschews                      15
the burdens of responsibility.

This fall in a real museum I stand
before a real Rembrandt, old woman,
or nearly so, myself. The colors
Within this frame are darker than autumn,                    20
darker even than winter—the browns of earth,
though earth's most radiant elements burn
through the canvas. I know now that woman
and painting and season are almost one
and all beyond saving by children.                           25

### YOUR TURN

1. What, if anything, do we know about the teacher in the poem? Do you think you would like to take a course with this teacher? Why?
2. Lines 3-6 report a question that a teacher asked. Does the rest of the poem answer the question? If so, what is the answer? If not, what does the rest of the poem do?
3. Do you assume that, for this poem, the responses of younger readers (say, ages 17–22) as a group would differ from those of older readers? If so, why?

## LORNA DEE CERVANTES

*Lorna Dee Cervantes, born in San Francisco in 1954, founded a press and a poetry magazine,* Mango, *chiefly devoted to Chicano literature. In 1978 she received a fellowship from the National Endowment for the Arts, and in 1981 she published her first book of poems. "Refugee Ship," originally written in 1974, was revised for the book. We print the revised version. Cervantes is currently a professor at the University of Colorado at Boulder.*

### Refugee Ship                                            [1981]

Like wet cornstarch, I slide
past my grandmother's eyes. Bible
at her side, she removes her glasses.
The pudding thickens.

Mama raised me without language.                             5
I'm orphaned from my Spanish name.
The words are foreign, stumbling
on my tongue. I see in the mirror
my reflection: bronzed skin, black hair.

I feel I am a captive                                        10
aboard the refugee ship.
The ship that will never dock.
*El barco que nunca atraca.*°

---

**13 El barco que nunca atraca**    The ship that never docks.

**YOUR TURN**

1. What do you think the speaker means by the comparison with "wet cornstarch" in line 1? And what do you take her to mean in line 6 when she says, "I'm orphaned from my Spanish name"?
2. Judging from the poem as a whole, why does the speaker feel she is "a captive / aboard the refugee ship"? How would you characterize such feelings?
3. In an earlier version of the poem, instead of "my grandmother's eyes" Cervantes wrote "*mi abuelita's* eyes"; that is, she used the Spanish words for "my grandmother." In line 5 instead of "Mama" she wrote "*mamá*" (again, the Spanish equivalent), and in line 9 she wrote "brown skin" instead of "bronzed skin." The final line of her original version was not in Spanish but in English, a repetition of the preceding line, which ran thus: "The ship that will never dock." How does each of these changes strike you?

# JOSÉ ARMAS

*Born in 1944, José Armas has been a teacher (at the University of New Mexico and at the University of Albu-querque), publisher, critic, and community organizer. His interest in community affairs won him a fellowship, which in 1974–1975 brought him into association with the Urban Planning Department at the Massachusetts Institute of Technology. In 1980 he was awarded a writing fellowship by the National Endowment for the Arts, and he now writes a column on Hispanic affairs for* De Colores.

## El Tonto del Barrio*

Romero Estrado was called "El Cotorro"[1] because he was always whistling and singing. He made nice music even though his songs were spontaneous compositions made up of words with sounds that he liked but which seldom made any sense. But that didn't seem to bother either Romero or anyone else in the Golden Heights Centro where he lived. Not even the kids made fun of him. It just was not permitted.

Romero had a ritual that he followed almost every day. After breakfast he would get his broom and go up and down the main street of the Golden Heights Centro whistling and singing and sweeping the sidewalks for all the businesses. He would sweep in front of the Tortillería America,[2] the XXX Liquor Store, the Tres Milpas[3] bar run by Tino Gabaldon, Barelas' Barber Shop, the used furniture store owned by Goldstein, El Centro Market of the Avila family, the Model Cities Office, and Lourdes Printing Store. Then, in the

---

*El Tonto del Barrio** the barrio dummy (in the United States, a *barrio* is a Spanish-speaking community). All notes are by the editors.    [1]**El Cotorro** The Parrot.    [2]**Tortillería America** America Tortilla Factory.    [3]**Tres Milpas** Three Cornfields.

afternoons, he would come back and sit in Barelas' Barber Shop and spend the day looking at magazines and watching and waving to the passing people as he sang and composed his songs without a care in the world.

When business was slow, Barelas would let him sit in the barber's chair. Romero loved it. It was a routine that Romero kept every day except Sundays and Mondays when Barelas' Barber Shop was closed. After a period of years, people in the barrio got used to seeing Romero do his little task of sweeping the sidewalks and sitting in Barelas' Barber Shop. If he didn't show up one day someone assumed the responsibility to go to his house to see if he was ill. People would stop to say hello to Romero on the street and although he never initiated a conversation while he was sober, he always smiled and responded cheerfully to everyone. People passing the barber shop in the afternoons made it a point to wave even though they couldn't see him; they knew he was in there and was expecting some salutation.

When he was feeling real good, Romero would sweep in front of the houses on both sides of the block also. He took his job seriously and took great care to sweep cleanly, between the cracks and even between the sides of buildings. The dirt and small scraps went into the gutter. The bottles and bigger pieces of litter were put carefully in cardboard boxes, ready for the garbage man.

5      If he did it the way he wanted, the work took him the whole morning. And always cheerful—always with some song.

Only once did someone call attention to his work. Frank Avila told him in jest that Romero had forgotten to pick up an empty bottle of wine from his door. Romero was so offended and made such a commotion that it got around very quickly that no one should criticize his work. There was, in fact, no reason to.

Although it had been long acknowledged that Romero was a little "touched," he fit very well into the community. He was a respected citizen.

He could be found at the Tres Milpas Bar drinking his occasional beer in the evenings. Romero had a rivalry going with the Ranchera songs on the jukebox. He would try to outsing the songs using the same melody but inserting his own selection of random words. Sometimes, like all people, he would "bust out" and get drunk.

One could always tell when Romero was getting drunk because he would begin telling everyone that he loved them.

10     "I looov youuu," he would sing to someone and offer to compose them a song.

"Ta bueno, Romero. Ta bueno, ya bete,"[4] they would tell him.

Sometimes when he got too drunk he would crap in his pants and then Tino would make him go home.

Romero received some money from Social Security but it wasn't much. None of the merchants gave him any credit because he would always forget to pay his bills. He didn't do it on purpose, he just forgot and spent his money on something else. So instead, the businessmen preferred to do little things for him occasionally. Barelas would trim his hair when things were slow. The Tortillería America would give him menudo[5] and fresh-made tortillas at noon when he was finished with his sweeping. El Centro Market would give him the overripe fruit and broken boxes of food that no one else would buy. Although

---

[4]**Ta bueno, ya bete** OK, now go away.   [5]**menudo** tripe soup.

it was unspoken and unwritten, there was an agreement that existed between Romero and the Golden Heights Centro. Romero kept the sidewalks clean and the barrio looked after him. It was a contract that worked well for a long time.

Then, when Seferino, Barelas' oldest son, graduated from high school he went to work in the barber shop for the summer. Seferino was a conscientious and sensitive young man and it wasn't long before he took notice of Romero and came to feel sorry for him.

15      One day when Romero was in the shop Seferino decided to act.

"Mira, Romero. Yo te doy 50 centavos por cada día que me barres la banqueta. Fifty cents for every day you sweep the sidewalk for us. Qué te parece?"[6]

Romero thought about it carefully.

"Hecho! Done!" he exclaimed. He started for home right away to get his broom.

"Why did you do that for, m'ijo?"[7] asked Barelas.

20      "It don't seem right, Dad. The man works and no one pays him for his work. Everyone should get paid for what they do."

"He don't need no pay. Romero has everything he needs."

"It's not the same, Dad. How would you like to do what he does and be treated the same way? It's degrading the way he has to go around getting scraps and handouts."

"I'm not Romero. Besides you don't know about these things, m'ijo. Romero would be unhappy if his schedule was upset. Right now everyone likes him and takes care of him. He sweeps the sidewalks because he wants something to do, not because he wants money."

"I'll pay him out of my money, don't worry about it then."

25      "The money is not the point. The point is that money will not help Romero. Don't you understand that?"

"Look, Dad. Just put yourself in his place. Would you do it? Would you cut hair for nothing?"

Barelas just knew his son was putting something over on him but he didn't know how to answer. It seemed to make sense the way Seferino explained it. But it still went against his "instinct." On the other hand, Seferino had gone and finished high school. He must know something. There were few kids who had finished high school in the barrio, and fewer who had gone to college. Barelas knew them all. He noted (with some pride) that Seferino was going to be enrolled at Harvard University this year. That must count for something, he thought. Barelas himself had never gone to school. So maybe his son had something there. On the other hand . . . it upset Barelas that he wasn't able to get Seferino to see the issue. How can we be so far apart on something so simple, he thought. But he decided not to say anything else about it.

Romero came back right away and swept the front of Barelas' shop again and put what little dirt he found into the curb. He swept up the gutter, put the trash in a shoe box and threw it in a garbage can.

Seferino watched with pride as Romero went about his job and when he was finished he went outside and shook Romero's hand. Seferino told him he had done a good job. Romero beamed.

30      Manolo was coming into the shop to get his hair cut as Seferino was giving Romero his wages. He noticed Romero with his broom.

---

[6]**Qué te parece?** How does that strike you?    [7]**m'ijo** (mi hijo) my son

"What's going on?" he asked. Barelas shrugged his shoulders. "Qué tiene Romero?[8] Is he sick or something?"

"No, he's not sick," explained Seferino, who had now come inside. He told Manolo the story.

"We're going to make Romero a businessman," said Seferino. "Do you realize how much money Romero would make if everyone paid him just fifty cents a day? Like my dad says, 'Everyone should be able to keep his dignity, no matter how poor.' And he does a job, you know."

"Well, it makes sense," said Manolo.

35    "Hey, maybe I'll ask people to do that," said Seferino. "That way the poor old man could make a decent wage. Do you want to help, Manolo? You can go with me to ask people to pay him."

"Well," said Manolo as he glanced at Barelas, "I'm not too good at asking people for money."

This did not discourage Seferino. He went out and contacted all the businesses on his own, but no one else wanted to contribute. This didn't discourage Seferino either. He went on giving Romero fifty cents a day.

After a while, Seferino heard that Romero had asked for credit at the grocery store. "See, Dad. What did I tell you? Things are getting better for him already. He's becoming his own man. And look. It's only been a couple of weeks." Barelas did not reply.

But then the next week Romero did not show up to sweep any sidewalks. He was around but he didn't do any work for anybody the entire week. He walked around Golden Heights Centro in his best gray work pants and his slouch hat, looking important and making it a point to walk right past the barber shop every little while.

40    Of course, the people in the Golden Heights Centro noticed the change immediately, and since they saw Romero in the street, they knew he wasn't ill. But the change was clearly disturbing the community. They discussed him in the Tortillería America where people got together for coffee, and at the Tres Milpas Bar. Everywhere the topic of conversation was the great change that had come over Romero. Only Barelas did not talk about it.

The following week Romero came into the barber shop and asked to talk with Seferino in private. Barelas knew immediately something was wrong. Romero never initiated a conversation unless he was drunk.

They went into the back room where Barelas could not hear and then Romero informed Seferino, "I want a raise."

"What? What do you mean, a raise? You haven't been around for a week. You only worked a few weeks and now you want a raise?" Seferino was clearly angry but Romero was calm and insistent.

Romero correctly pointed out that he had been sweeping the sidewalks for a long time. Even before Seferino finished high school.

45    "I deserve a raise," he repeated after an eloquent presentation.

Seferino looked coldly at Romero. It was clearly a stand-off.

Then Seferino said, "Look, maybe we should forget the whole thing. I was just trying to help you out and look at what you do."

Romero held his ground. "I helped you out too. No one told me to do it and I did it anyway. I helped you many years."

---

[8]**Qué tiene Romero?** What's with Romero?

"Well, let's forget about the whole thing then," said Seferino.

50    "I quit then," said Romero.

"Quit?" exclaimed Seferino as he laughed at Romero.

"Quit! I quit!" said Romero as he walked out the front of the shop past Barelas, who was cutting a customer's hair.

Seferino came out shaking his head and laughing.

"Can you imagine that old guy?"

55    Barelas did not seem too amused. He felt he could have predicted that something bad like this would happen.

Romero began sweeping the sidewalks again the next day with the exception that when he came to the barber shop he would go around it and continue sweeping the rest of the sidewalks. He did this for the rest of the week. And the following Tuesday he began sweeping the sidewalk all the way up to the shop and then pushing the trash to the sidewalk in front of the barber shop. Romero then stopped coming to the barber shop in the afternoon.

The barrio buzzed with fact and rumor about Romero. Tino commented that Romero was not singing anymore. Even if someone offered to buy him a beer he wouldn't sing. Frank Avila said the neighbors were complaining because he was leaving his TV on loud the whole day and night. He still greeted people but seldom smiled. He had run up a big bill at the liquor store and when the manager stopped his credit, he caught Romero stealing bottles of whiskey. He was also getting careless about his dress. He didn't shave and clean like he used to. Women complained that he walked around in soiled pants, that he smelled bad. Even one of the little kids complained that Romero had kicked his puppy, but that seemed hard to believe.

Barelas felt terrible. He felt responsible. But he couldn't convince Seferino that what he had done was wrong. Barelas himself stopped going to the Tres Milpas Bar after work to avoid hearing about Romero. Once he came across Romero on the street and Barelas said hello but with a sense of guilt. Romero responded, avoiding Barelas' eyes and moving past him awkwardly and quickly. Romero's behavior continued to get erratic and some people started talking about having Romero committed.

"You can't do that," said Barelas when he was presented with a petition.

60    "He's flipped," said Tino, who made up part of the delegation circulating the petition. "No one likes Romero more than I do, you know that Barelas."

"But he's really crazy," said Frank Avila.

"He was crazy before. No one noticed," pleaded Barelas.

"But it was a crazy we could depend on. Now he just wants to sit on the curb and pull up the women's skirts. It's terrible. The women are going crazy. He's also running into the street stopping the traffic. You see how he is. What choice do we have?"

"It's for his own good," put in one of the workers from the Model Cities Office. Barelas dismissed them as outsiders. Seferino was there and wanted to say something but a look from Barelas stopped him.

65    "We just can't do that," insisted Barelas. "Let's wait. Maybe he's just going through a cycle. Look. We've had a full moon recently, qué no?[9] That must be it. You know how the moon affects people in his condition."

---

[9]**qué no?** right?

"I don't know," said Tino. "What if he hurts. . . ."

"He's not going to hurt anyone," cut in Barelas.

"No, Barelas. I was going to say, what if he hurts himself. He has no one at home. I'd say, let him come home with me for a while but you know how stubborn he is. You can't even talk to him any more."

"He gives everyone the finger when they try to pull him out of the traffic," said Frank Avila. "The cops have missed him, but it won't be long before they see him doing some of his antics and arrest him. Then what? Then the poor guy is in real trouble."

70    "Well, look," said Barelas. "How many names you got on the list?"

Tino responded slowly, "Well, we sort of wanted you to start off the list."

"Let's wait a while longer," said Barelas. "I just know that Romero will come around. Let's wait just a while, okay?"

No one had the heart to fight the issue and so they postponed the petition.

There was no dramatic change in Romero even though the full moon had completed its cycle. Still, no one initiated the petition again and then in the middle of August Seferino left for Cambridge to look for housing and to register early for school. Suddenly everything began to change again. One day Romero began sweeping the entire sidewalk again. His spirits began to pick up and his strange antics began to disappear.

75    At the Tortillería America the original committee met for coffee and the talk turned to Romero.

"He's going to be all right now," said a jubilant Barelas. "I guarantee it."

"Well, don't hold your breath yet," said Tino. "The full moon is coming up again."

"Yeah," said Frank Avila dejectedly.

When the next full moon was in force the group was together again drinking coffee and Tino asked, "Well, how's Romero doing?"

80    Barelas smiled and said, "Well. Singing songs like crazy."

### YOUR TURN

1. What sort of man do you think Barelas is? In your response take account of the fact that the townspeople sort of want [Barelas] "to start off the list" of petitioners seeking to commit Romero.
2. The narrator, introducing the reader to Seferino, tells us that "Seferino was a conscientious and sensitive young man." Do you agree? Why, or why not?
3. What do you make of the last line of the story?
4. Do you think this story could take place in almost any community? If you did not grow up in a barrio, could it take place in your community?

# II

# Fiction

For many readers, William Faulkner, here shown half-naked and pecking away at a type-writer, is the greatest American writer of fiction in the twentieth century. But let's begin our discussion of fiction not with this twentieth-century writer but with Lady Murasaki, a Japanese writer of the eleventh century, who in her novel, *The Tale of Genji,* has a character comment on *why* fiction-writers write. We quote the passage elsewhere in our book, but it is worth repeating:

> Again and again something in one's own life or in that around one will seem so important that one cannot bear to let it pass into oblivion. There must never come a time, the writer feels, when people do not know about this.

When Faulkner was asked how much of his writing was based on personal experience, he replied:

> I can't say. I never counted up. Because "how much" is not important. A writer needs three things, experience, observation, and imagination, any two of which, at times any one of which, can supply the lack of the others. With me, a story usually begins with a single idea or memory or mental picture. The writing of the story is simply a matter of working up to that moment, to explain why it happened or what it caused to follow. A writer is trying to create believable people in credible moving situations in the most moving way he can. Obviously he must use as one of his tools the environment which he knows. (*Writers at Work,* ed. Malcolm Cowley [1958], 133.)

All good writers draw on the life around them as well as on their own inner lives, and all good writers develop a distinctive style and vision. No one else can write a good Faulkner story, just as no one else can write a good Chekhov story, or Chopin story, or Flannery O'Connor story. The writers whom we value, the writers whose work we want to read and reread, draw on the worlds around them, telling us of their responses to highly local conditions. (Much of Faulkner's work concerns an invented Mississippi county, Yoknapatawpha.) Yet these writers make their readers value what might be thought to be remote experiences. We care about their reports of their worlds, and they help us to see our own worlds (and especially ourselves) freshly.

# 5

# Approaching Fiction:
# Responding in Writing

The next six chapters will look at specific elements, one by one, in fiction—plot, character, setting, and so on—but first let's read a brief story by Ernest Hemingway and then talk about it (and see how one student talked about it) with little or no technical language.

## ERNEST HEMINGWAY

*Ernest Hemingway (1899-1961) was born in Oak Park, Illinois. After graduating from high school in 1917 he worked on the* Kansas City Star *but left to serve as a volunteer ambulance driver in Italy, where he was wounded in action. He returned home, married, and then served as European correspondent for the* Toronto Star, *but he soon gave up journalism for fiction. In 1922 he settled in Paris, where he moved in a circle of American expatriates that included Ezra Pound, Gertrude Stein, and F. Scott Fitzgerald. It was in Paris that he wrote stories and novels about what Gertrude Stein called a "lost generation" of rootless Americans in Europe. (For Hemingway's reminiscences of the Paris years, see his posthumously published* A Moveable Feast.) *He served as a journalist during the Spanish Civil War and during World War II, but he was also something of a private soldier during World War II.*

*After World War II his reputation sank, though he was still active as a writer (for instance, he wrote* The Old Man and the Sea *in 1952). In 1954 Hemingway was awarded the Nobel Prize in Literature, but in 1961, depressed by a sense of failing power, he took his own life.*

### Cat in the Rain [1925]

There were only two Americans stopping at the hotel. They did not know any of the people they passed on the stairs on their way to and from their room. Their room was on the second floor facing the sea. It also faced the public garden and the war monument. There were big palms and green benches in the public garden. In the good weather there was always an artist with his easel. Artists liked the way the palms grew and the bright colors of the hotels facing the gardens and the sea. Italians came from a long way off to look up at the war monument. It was made of bronze and glistened in the rain. It was raining. The rain dripped from the palm trees. Water stood in pools on the gravel paths. The sea broke in a long line in the rain and slipped back down the beach to come up and break again in a long line in the rain. The motor cars were gone from the square by the war monument. Across the square in the doorway of the café a waiter stood looking out at the empty square.

The American wife stood at the window looking out. Outside right under their window a cat was crouched under one of the dripping green tables. The cat was trying to make herself so compact that she would not be dripped on.

"I'm going down and get that kitty," the American wife said.

"I'll do it," her husband offered from the bed.

5    "No, I'll get it. The poor kitty out trying to keep dry under a table."

The husband went on reading, lying propped up with the two pillows at the foot of the bed.

"Don't get wet," he said.

The wife went downstairs and the hotel owner stood up and bowed to her as she passed the office. His desk was at the far end of the office. He was an old man and very tall.

"Il piove,"[1] the wife said. She liked the hotel-keeper.

10    "Si, si, Signora, brutto tempo. It's very bad weather."

He stood behind his desk in the far end of the dim room. The wife liked him. She liked the deadly serious way he received any complaints. She liked his dignity. She liked the way he wanted to serve her. She liked the way he felt about being a hotel-keeper. She liked his old, heavy face and big hands.

Liking him she opened the door and looked out. It was raining harder. A man in a rubber cape was crossing the empty square to the café. The cat would be around to the right. Perhaps she could go along under the eaves. As she stood in the doorway an umbrella opened behind her. It was the maid who looked after their room.

"You must not get wet," she smiled, speaking Italian. Of course, the hotel-keeper had sent her.

With the maid holding the umbrella over her, she walked along the gravel path until she was under their window. The table was there, washed bright green in the rain, but the cat was gone. She was suddenly disappointed. The maid looked up at her.

15    "Ha perduto qualque cosa, Signora?"[2]

"There was a cat," said the American girl.

"A cat?"

"Si, il gatto."

"A cat?" the maid laughed. "A cat in the rain?"

20    "Yes," she said, "under the table." Then, "Oh, I wanted it so much. I wanted a kitty."

---

[1]**Il piove** It's raining (Italian).    [2]**Ha . . . Signora** Have you lost something, Madam?

When she talked English the maid's face tightened.

"Come, Signora," she said. "We must get back inside. You will be wet."

"I suppose so," said the American girl.

They went back along the gravel path and passed in the door. The maid stayed outside to close the umbrella. As the American girl passed the office, the padrone bowed from his desk. Something felt very small and tight inside the girl. The padrone made her feel very small and at the same time really important. She had a momentary feeling of being of supreme importance. She went on up the stairs. She opened the door of the room. George was on the bed, reading.

25    "Did you get the cat?" he asked, putting the book down.

"It was gone."

"Wonder where it went to," he said, resting his eyes from reading.

She sat down on the bed.

"I wanted it so much," she said. "I don't know why I wanted it so much. I wanted that poor kitty. It isn't any fun to be a poor kitty out in the rain."

30    George was reading again.

She went over and sat in front of the mirror of the dressing table looking at herself with the hand glass. She studied her profile, first one side and then the other. Then she studied the back of her head and her neck.

"Don't you think it would be a good idea if I let my hair grow out?" she asked, looking at her profile again.

George looked up and saw the back of her neck, clipped close like a boy's.

"I like it the way it is."

35    "I get so tired of it," she said. "I get so tired of looking like a boy."

George shifted his position in the bed. He hadn't looked away from her since she started to speak.

"You look pretty darn nice," he said.

She laid the mirror down on the dresser and went over to the window and looked out. It was getting dark.

"I want to pull my hair back tight and smooth and make a big knot at the back that I can feel," she said. "I want to have a kitty to sit on my lap and purr when I stroke her."

40    "Yeah?" George said from the bed.

"And I want to eat at a table with my own silver and I want candles. And I want it to be spring and I want to brush my hair out in front of a mirror and I want a kitty and I want some new clothes."

"Oh, shut up and get something to read," George said. He was reading again.

His wife was looking out of the window. It was quite dark now and still raining in the palm trees.

"Anyway, I want a cat," she said, "I want a cat. I want a cat now. If I can't have long hair or any fun, I can have a cat."

45    George was not listening. He was reading his book. His wife looked out of the window where the light had come on in the square.

Someone knocked at the door.

"Avanti,"[3] George said. He looked up from his book.

---

[3]**Avanti** Come in.

In the doorway stood the maid. She held a big tortoise-shell cat pressed tight against her and swung down against her body.

"Excuse me," she said, "the padrone asked me to bring this for the Signora."

# Responses: Annotations and Journal Entries

When you read a story—or, perhaps more accurately, when you reread a story before discussing it or writing about it—you'll find it helpful to jot an occasional note (for instance, a brief response or a question) in the margins and to underline or highlight passages that strike you as especially interesting. Here is part of the story, with a student's annotations.

The cat was trying to make herself so compact that she would not be dripped on.

"I'm going down and get that kitty," the American wife said.

"I'll do it," her husband offered from the bed. *He doesn't make a move*

"No, I'll get it. The poor kitty out trying to keep dry under a table."

The husband went on reading, lying propped up with the two pillows at the foot of the bed. *still doesn't move!*

"Don't get wet," he said. *Is he making a joke? Or maybe he just isn't even thinking about what he is saying?*

The wife went downstairs and the hotel owner stood up and bowed to her as she passed the office. His desk was at the far end of the office. He was an old man and very tall. *contrast with the husband*

"Il piove," the wife said. She liked the hotel-keeper.

"Si, si, Signora, brutto tempo. It's very bad weather."

He stood behind his desk in the far end of the dim room. The wife liked him. She liked the deadly serious way he received any complaints. She liked his dignity. She liked the way he wanted to serve her. She liked the way he felt about being a hotel-keeper. She liked his old, heavy face and big hands. *She respects him and she is pleased by the attention he shows*

Liking him she opened the door and looked out. It was raining harder. A man in a rubber cape was crossing the empty square to the café. The cat would be around to the right. *to emphasize the bad weather??*

*Everything* in a story presumably is important, but having read the story once, you are probably especially interested (or puzzled) by something, such as the relationship between two people, or the way the end of the story is connected to the beginning. On rereading, then, pen in hand, you'll find yourself noticing things that you missed or didn't find especially significant on your first reading. Now that you know the end of the story, you will read the beginning in a different way.

And of course if your instructor asks you to think about certain questions, you'll keep them in mind while you reread, and you will find ideas coming to you. In "Cat in the Rain," suppose you are asked (or you ask yourself) if the story might just as well be about a dog in the rain. Would anything be lost?

Here are a few questions that you can ask of almost any story. After scanning the questions, you will want to reread the story, pen in hand, and then jot down your responses on a sheet of paper. As you write, doubtless you will go back and reread the story or at least parts of it.

- *What happens?* In two or three sentences—say, 25 to 50 words— summarize the gist of what happens in the story.
- *What sorts of people are the chief characters?* In "Cat in the Rain" the chief characters are George, George's wife, and the innkeeper (the padrone). Jot down the traits that each seems to possess, and next to each trait briefly give some supporting evidence.
- *What especially pleased or displeased you in the story?* Devote at least a sentence or two to the end of the story. Do you find the end satisfying? Why or why not? What evidence can you offer to support an argument with someone whose response differs from yours?
- *Have you any thoughts about the title?* If so, what are they? If the story did not have a title, what would you call it?

*After* you have made your own jottings, compare them with these responses by a student. No two readers will respond in exactly the same way, but all readers can examine their responses and try to account for them, at least in part. If your responses are substantially different, how do you account for the differences?

1. *A summary.* A young wife, stopping with her husband at an Italian hotel, from her room sees a cat in the rain. She goes to get it, but it is gone, and so she returns empty-handed. A moment later the maid knocks at the door, holding a tortoise-shell cat.

2. *The characters: The woman.*

   kind-hearted (pities cat in rain)

   appreciates innkeeper's courtesy ("liked the way he wanted to serve her") and
        admires him ("She liked his dignity")

   unhappy (wants a cat, wants to change her hair, wants to eat at a table with
        her own silver)

   *The husband, George.*

   not willing to put himself out (says he'll go to garden to get cat but doesn't
        move)

   doesn't seem very interested in wife (hardly talks to her—he's reading; tells
        her to "shut up")

   but he does say he finds her attractive ("You look pretty darn nice")

   *The innkeeper.*

   serious, dignified ("She liked the deadly serious way he received any
        complaints. She liked his dignity")

   courteous, helpful (sends maid with umbrella; at end sends maid with cat)

3. *Dislikes and likes.* "Dislikes" is too strong, but I was disappointed that more didn't happen at the end. What is the husband's reaction to the cat? Or his final reaction to his wife? I mean, what does he think about his wife when the maid brings the cat? And, for that matter, what is the wife's reaction? Is she satisfied? Or does she realize that the cat can't really make her happy? Now for the *likes.* (1) I guess I did like the way it turned out; it's sort of a happy ending, I think, since she wants the cat and gets it. (2) I also especially like the innkeeper. Maybe I like him partly because the wife likes him, and if she likes him he must be nice. And he *is* nice—very helpful. And I also like the way Hemingway shows the husband. I don't mean that I like the man himself, but I like the way Hemingway shows he is such a bastard—not getting off the bed to get the cat, telling his wife to shut up and read.

Another thing about him is that the one time he says something nice about her, it's about her hair, and she isn't keen on the way her hair is. She says it makes her look "like a boy," and she is "tired" of looking like a boy. There's something wrong with this marriage. George hardly pays attention to his wife, but he wants her to look like a boy. Maybe the idea is that this macho guy wants to keep her looking like an inferior (immature) version of himself. Anyway, he certainly doesn't seem interested in letting her fulfill herself as a woman.

*I think my feelings add up to this:* I like the way Hemingway shows us the relation between the husband and wife (even though the relation is pretty bad), and I like the innkeeper. Even if the relation with the couple ends unhappily, the story has a sort of happy ending, so far as it goes, since the innkeeper does what he can to please his guest: he sends the maid, with the cat. There's really nothing more that he can do.

*More about the ending.* The more I think about it, the more I feel that the ending is as happy as it can be. George is awful. When his wife says "I want a cat and I want a cat now," Hemingway tells us "George was not listening." And then, a moment later, almost like a good fairy the maid appears and grants the wife's wish.

4. *The title.* I don't suppose that I would have called it "Cat in the Rain," but I don't know what I would have called it. Maybe "An American Couple in Italy." Or maybe "The Innkeeper." I really do think that the innkeeper is very important, even though he only has a few lines. He's very impressive—not only to the girl, but to me (and maybe to all readers), since at the end of the story we see how caring the innkeeper is.

But the more I think about Hemingway's title, the more I think that maybe it also refers to the girl. Like the "poor kitty" in the rain, the wife is in a pretty bad situation. "It isn't any fun to be a poor kitty out in the rain." Of course, the woman is indoors, but her husband generates lots of unpleasant weather. She may as well be out in the rain. She says "I want to have a kitty to sit on my lap and purr when I stroke her." This shows that she wants to be affectionate and that she also wants to have someone respond to her affection. She *is* like a cat in the rain.

Oh, I just noticed that the wife at first calls the cat "her" rather than "it." ("The cat was trying to make herself compact. . . .") Later she says "it," but at first she thinks of the cat as female—because (I think) she identifies with the cat.

The responses of this student probably include statements that you want to take issue with. Or perhaps you feel that the student did not even mention some things that you think are important. You may want to jot down some notes and raise some questions in class.

# A Sample Essay by a Student

The responses that we have quoted were written by Bill Yanagi, who later wrote an essay developing one of them. Here is the essay.

---

Yanagi 1

Bill Yanagi

Professor Lange

English 10B

20 June 2010

## Hemingway's American Wife

My title alludes not to any of the four women to whom Hemingway was married, but to "the American wife" who is twice called by this term in his short story "Cat in the Rain." We first meet her in the first sentence of the story ("There were only two Americans stopping at the hotel"), and the next time she is mentioned (apart from a reference to the wife and her husband as "they") it is as "the American wife," at the beginning of the second paragraph of the story. The term is used again at the end of the third paragraph.

She is, then, at least in the early part of this story, just an American or an American wife—someone identified only by her nationality and her marital status, but not at all by her personality, her individuality, her inner self. She first becomes something of an individual when she separates herself from her husband by leaving the hotel room and going to look for a cat that she has seen in the garden, in the rain. This act of separation, however, has not the slightest effect on her husband, who "went on reading" (100).

When she returns, without the cat, he puts down his book and speaks to her, but it is obvious that he has no interest in her, beyond as a physical object ("You look pretty darn nice"). This comment is produced when she says she is thinking of letting her hair grow out because she is "so tired of looking like a boy" (101). Why, a reader wonders, does her husband, who has paid almost no attention to her up to now, assure her that she looks "pretty darn nice"? I think it is reasonable to conclude that he *wants* her to look like someone who is not truly a woman, in particular someone who is immature. That she does not feel she has much identity is evident when she continues to talk about letting her hair grow, and she says "I want to pull my hair back tight and smooth and make a big knot at the back that I can feel" (101). Long hair is, or at least was, the traditional sign of a woman; she wants long hair, and at the same time she wants to keep it under her control by tying it in a "big knot," a knot that she can feel, a knot whose presence reminds her, because she can feel it, of her feminine nature.

She goes on to say that she wants to brush her hair "in front of a mirror." That is, she wants to *see* and to feel her femininity, since her husband apparently—so far as we can see in the story, at least—scarcely recognizes it or her. Perhaps her desire for the cat ("I want a cat") is a veiled way of saying that she wants to express her animal nature and not be simply a neglected woman who is made by her husband to look like a boy. Hemingway tells us, however, that when she looked for the cat in the garden she could not find it, a sign, I think, of her failure to break from the man. At the end of the story the maid brings her the cat, but a woman cannot just be handed a new nature and accept it, just like that. She has to find it herself, and in herself, so I think the story ends with "the American wife" still nothing more than an American wife.

Yanagi 3

Work Cited

Hemingway, Ernest. "Cat in the Rain." *An Introduction to Literature*.
    Ed. Sylvan Barnet, William Burto, and William E. Cain. 16th ed.
    New York: Longman, 2011. 99–102. Print.

A few comments and questions may be useful.

- Do you find the essay interesting? Explain your response.
- Do you find the essay well written? Explain.
- Do you find the essay convincing? Can you suggest ways of strengthening it, or do you think its argument is mistaken? Carefully reread "Cat in the Rain," taking note of passages that give further support to this student's argument, or that seem to challenge or qualify it.
- We often say that a good critical essay sends us back to the literary work with a fresh point of view. Our rereading differs from our earlier reading. Does this essay change your reading of Hemingway's story?

### YOUR TURN

1. Can we be certain that the cat at the end of the story is the cat that the woman saw in the rain? (When we first hear about the cat in the rain we are not told anything about its color, and at end of the story we are not told that the tortoiseshell cat is wet.) Does it matter if there are two cats?
2. One student argued that the cat represents the child that the girl wants to have. Do you think there is something to this idea? How might you support or refute it?
3. Consider the following passage:

    > As the American girl passed the office, the padrone bowed from his desk. Something felt very small and tight inside the girl. The padrone made her feel very small and at the same time really important. She had a momentary feeling of being of supreme importance.

    Do you think there is anything sexual here? And if so, that the passage tells us something about her relations with her husband? Support your view.
4. What do you suppose Hemingway's attitude is toward each of the three chief characters? How might you support your hunch?
5. Hemingway wrote the story in Italy, when his wife Hadley was pregnant. In a letter to F. Scott Fitzgerald he said,

    > Cat in the Rain wasn't about Hadley. . . . When I wrote that we were at Rapallo but Hadley was 4 months pregnant with Bumby. The Inn Keeper was the one at Cortina D'Ampezzo. . . . Hadley

never made a speech in her life about wanting a baby because she had been told various things by her doctor and I'd—no use going into all that. (*Letters*, p 180)

According to some biographers, the story shows that Hemingway knew his marriage was in trouble (Hemingway and Hadley divorced). Does knowing that Hemingway's marriage turned out unhappily help you to understand the story? Does it make the story more interesting? And do you think that the story tells a biographer something about Hemingway's life?

6. It is sometimes said that a good short story does two things at once: It provides a believable picture of the surface of life, and it also illuminates some moral or psychological complexity that we feel is part of the essence of human life. This dual claim may not be true, but for the moment accept it. Do you think that Hemingway's story fulfills either or both of these specifications? Support your view.

Later chapters will offer some technical vocabulary and will examine specific elements of fiction, but familiarity with technical vocabulary will not itself ensure that you will understand and enjoy fiction. There is no substitute for reading carefully, thinking about your responses, and (pen in hand) rereading the text, looking for evidence that accounts for your responses or that will lead you to different and perhaps richer responses. The essays that you will submit to your instructor are, finally, rooted in the annotations that you make in your text and the notes in which you record and explore your responses.

# 6

# Plot

Often we use the terms **story** and **plot** as if they mean the same thing, but in literary interpretation their meanings are different. "Story" comes from the same Latin word that gives us "history." What is history? Even the soberest historians have sometimes felt that, in the memorable words of a member of the profession, "History is one damned thing after another." That is, history—and a story—is just a bunch of things that happened (or that we pretend happened, as in "Once upon a time . . .") one after the other ("and they lived happily ever after"). But when an author writes a short story, he or she designs a *structure* for it, an *organization* of events.

- This is the plot—the arrangement of episodes or doings or incidents or actions or happenings or whatever we wish to call them. The plot, again, is the cunning contrivance that is an organized whole.
- If you think of another sense of "plot," a secret plan or a scheme, you are close to the literary use of the term.

Thus, in the plot of a good story, everything hangs together, just as in a good criminal plot everything is well-coordinated: The getaway car is in place, a decoy distracts the bank guard at a crucial moment, and so forth, and the whole thing coheres. (The painter Edgar Degas had something of this sort in mind when he said that it takes as much cunning to paint a picture as to commit a crime.) Or, to return to the law-abiding world, we can recall a comparison suggested by the twentieth-century English writer Ivy Compton-Burnett: "A plot is like the bones of a person. . . the support of the whole."

Perhaps the best point of departure for understanding plot is the British novelist and short-story writer E. M. Forster's definition in *Aspects of the Novel* (1927). He states that in a good plot the episodes are connected by causality:

> We have defined a story as a narrative of events arranged in their time-sequence. A plot is also a narrative of events, the emphasis falling on causality. "The king died and then the queen died" is a story. "The king died and then the queen died of grief" is a plot. The time-sequence is preserved, but the sense of causality overshadows it.

Notice how Forster goes on to develop and complicate his insight:

> Or again: "The queen died, no one knew why, until it was discovered that it was through grief at the death of the king." This is a plot with a

mystery in it, a form capable of high development. It suspends the time-sequence, it moves as far away from the story as its limitations will allow. Consider the death of the queen. If it is in a story we say: "And then?" If it is in a plot we ask: "Why?" That is the fundamental difference between these two aspects of the novel.

Thus, if "The king died, and a week later the queen was killed by a drunk driver who was driving the wrong way down a one-way street," we would have one thing after another, a story but not a plot.

Most of the time, the plot of a short story proceeds chronologically, as Forster indicates: this happened first, and this happened next, and so on to the end. There may be **foreshadowing** along the way, where the author hints at or implies a turn or twist that the story will take. We also may encounter a **flashback,** which occurs when the author returns us to an incident or episode that preceded the events being recounted in the story. For this reason it often can be useful to set out the plot on a timeline so that we can perceive its structure visually. Such a visual aid can help us to see what happens and prompt us to analyze why it happens as it does—the motives, the causes that move the plot from here to there.

Sometimes, though, an author will choose not to present the plot of a story in chronological order. We might start in the middle (*in medias res* is the Latin phrase), with, say, the death of the king, then move backward to the marriage of the king and queen, and then move forward to the death of the queen. Or the plot might begin in the middle, move backward, forward, then backward again, and so on. The novelist Joseph Conrad, author of *Heart of Darkness* (1899), has a good term for this—he calls it "sifting," moving the plot back and forth like a miner prospecting by a stream, back and forth, back and forth, sifting as the gold comes into view.

In the *Poetics* (c. 330 BCE), the Greek philosopher Aristotle examines the plot of tragic drama, not of prose fiction, but his observations also highlight plot as a structure, as a principle for the organization of a literary work. He emphasizes that the beginning, middle, and end should be unified: "The whole, the structural union of the parts [must be] such that, if any one of them is displaced or removed, the whole will be disjointed and disturbed." If the end of the plot is in some ways implicit in the beginning, and the narrative is, so to speak, the unfolding of the plot, does this mean that the reader can guess the end even at the beginning? Almost never. We can again quote E. M. Forster, who says that the incidents, the episodes, are "unexpected. This shock, followed by the feeling, 'Oh, that's all right,' is a sign that all is well with the plot: characters, to be real, ought to run smoothly, but a plot ought to cause surprise." We don't think this point can be overstated: A good plot surprises—but *not* because the author is free to write anything and everything. The plot must not only surprise but must also evoke the sense, "Oh, that's all right."

Some authors favor simple plots, whereas others prefer complex plots that require us to do careful work to figure out what happened. Even at the end, we might not be certain that we know. We then might be tempted to say that the story is confusing, and we might go so far as to say that it is badly written. But authors have their reasons for what they decide to do. The purpose of an intricate plot might be to show us that it sometimes is difficult to know what happened in a situation and why it did. The meaning and significance of this situation might be ambiguous, or indeterminate.

A short story is short: usually it focuses on a single plot. In this respect it differs from a play like Shakespeare's *King Lear,* which weaves together for comparison and contrast the main plot and the subplot—sometimes termed the primary and the secondary plots. Charles Dickens, Leo Tolstoy, and other novelists work on a wide-ranging, panoramic scale. In their books, we find multiple plots, a half-dozen or more. In Dickens's *Bleak House* (1852–1853) and in Tolstoy's *War and Peace* (1869) the authors present a number of intersecting plots. They design an elaborate structure that the author of a short story, whose space is limited, does not. A short story is perhaps closer to a lyric poem than to a novel: It usually aims at a single effect.

Authors enjoy telling stories; they take pleasure in leading us through a plot. The Canadian novelist and critic Robertson Davies (1913–1995) explains it this way:

> If you're a writer, a real writer, you're a descendant of those medieval storytellers who used to go into the square of a town and spread a little mat on the ground and sit on it and beat on a bowl and say, "if you give me a copper coin I will tell you a golden tale."

Here is a very short story told by a writer who often said he worked in the tradition of the old storyteller, sitting on a mat, that Robertson Davies speaks of.

# W. SOMERSET MAUGHAM

*W(illiam) Somerset Maugham (1874–1965), born in Paris but of English origin, grew up in England, where he was trained as a physician but never practiced medicine. Rather, he preferred to make his living as a novelist, playwright, and writer of short stories. The following story is in fact a speech uttered by a character, Death, in one of Maugham's plays,* Sheppey *(1933).*

## The Appointment in Samarra                    [1933]

*Death speaks:* There was a merchant in Baghdad who sent his servant to market to buy provisions and in a little while the servant came back, white and trembling, and said, Master, just now when I was in the marketplace I was jostled by a woman in the crowd and when I turned I saw it was Death that jostled me. She looked at me and made a threatening gesture; now, lend me your horse, and I will ride away from the city and avoid my fate. I will go to Samarra and there Death will not find me. The merchant lent him his horse, and the servant mounted it, and he dug his spurs in its flanks and as fast as the horse could gallop he went. Then the merchant went down to the marketplace and he saw me standing in the crowd and he came to me and said, Why did you make a threatening gesture to my servant when you saw him this morning? That was not a threatening gesture, I said, it was only a start of surprise. I was astonished to see him in Baghdad, for I had an appointment with him tonight in Samarra.

The plot here is everything. Neither the merchant nor the servant has any "character" in the sense of a distinctive personality. We don't know if they are young or old, stupid or wise, easily angered, oversexed, or whatever. Our interest is not in a clash of personalities shaped by differences in race or in economic class, nor is our interest in a profound relationship that goes beyond the bounds of economic class. All we know is that the servant acts reasonably, and his master is generous enough to lend the servant a horse. Our interest is not in what sort of people are these but rather in what happens next. And when we get to the end of the story, we are surprised but we don't feel that the author has tricked us by pulling an ace out of his sleeve, and we do not say the ending is improbable. On the contrary, we feel that despite the nonsense of Death speaking, it all makes sense. The end of the story is, so to speak, implicit in the beginning. The moral—the author's thesis, we might say—is not stated explicitly, and perhaps we might quibble a little about whether there really is any moral here, and, if there is, how we might state it, but the gist surely is clear: Human beings cannot elude death; it comes to us at an appointed time, whether appointed by God, or by fate, or by biology or by chance. The first thing for you, as a reader, to do when you read a short story is to enjoy it. You are not obliged to like each and every story in this chapter or in this book as a whole—all of us have our favorites—but if you approach each story with an open mind, and with some curiosity, you will find yourself engaged by and interested in most of them. You will be "caught up in the plot."

A good plot captivates and intrigues us—which, again, reminds us that the word "plot" also evokes sly maneuvering and conspiracy. When we read a story, we are something like a detective: We notice details, we wonder about their significance, we form expectations about what is going to happen next, we interpret the meaning of words and actions and the motives of the characters, and so on. Then on a second reading, or in an analytical essay, we might do even more rigorous and thorough analytical thinking about how the author crafted this plot: What is its structure? How do the pieces fit together?

# Thinking About Plot

Here are a few questions to think about:

- **The beginning:** What is the first thing that happens in the story, and in what time-period and setting?
- **The middle:** What happens next, and next, and after that? Be as specific as you can.
- What does the author do to create **suspense?**
- Does anything in the plot **surprise** you?
- Does the author present a **conflict, crisis,** or **climax** in the plot? What is the conflict? Where in the plot is the crisis? What is the climax of the plot—and its consequences? What is the **dénouement** (literally, the "unknotting") of the plot?
- Does the main **character** change a lot, or a little, or not at all as the plot unfolds?
- **The ending:** what happens as the author brings the story to its close? Is everything, or are at least some things, resolved and settled? Or not?

# MARGARET ATWOOD

*Born in 1939 in Ottawa, Canada, the poet, critic, novelist, and short-story writer Margaret Atwood now lives in Toronto. Her novels include* The Edible Woman *(1969),* Surfacing *(1972), and* The Handmaid's Tale *(1985), and more recently,* The Penelopiad *(2005) and* The Year of the Flood *(2009).*

## Happy Endings

[1983]

John and Mary meet.
What happens next?
If you want a happy ending, try A.

### A

John and Mary fall in love and get married. They both have worthwhile and remunerative jobs which they find stimulating and challenging. They buy a charming house. Real estate values go up. Eventually, when they can afford live-in help, they have two children, to whom they are devoted. The children turn out well. John and Mary have a stimulating and challenging sex life and worthwhile friends. They go on fun vacations together. They retire. They both have hobbies which they find stimulating and challenging. Eventually they die. This is the end of the story.

### B

Mary falls in love with John but John doesn't fall in love with Mary. He merely uses her body for selfish pleasure and ego gratification of a tepid kind. He comes to her apartment twice a week and she cooks him dinner, you'll notice that he doesn't even consider her worth the price of a dinner out, and after he's eaten the dinner he fucks her and after that he falls asleep, while she does the dishes so he won't think she's untidy, having all those dirty dishes lying around, and puts on fresh lipstick so she'll look good when he wakes up, but when he wakes up he doesn't even notice, he puts on his socks and his shorts and his pants and his shirt and his tie and his shoes, the reverse order from the one in which he took them off. He doesn't take off Mary's clothes, she takes them off herself, she acts as if she's dying for it every time, not because she likes sex exactly, she doesn't, but she wants John to think she does because if they do it often enough surely he'll get used to her, he'll come to depend on her and they will get married, but John goes out the door with hardly so much as a good-night and three days later he turns up at six o'clock and they do the whole thing over again.

Mary gets run-down. Crying is bad for your face, everyone knows that and so does Mary but she can't stop. People at work notice. Her friends tell her John is a rat, a pig, a dog, he isn't good enough for her, but she can't believe it. Inside John, she thinks, is another John who is much nicer. This other John will emerge like a butterfly from a cocoon, a Jack from a box, a pit from a prune, if the first John is only squeezed enough.

5      One evening John complains about the food. He has never complained about the food before. Mary is hurt.

Her friends tell her they've seen him in a restaurant with another woman, whose name is Madge. It's not even Madge that finally gets to Mary; it's the restaurant. John has never taken Mary to a restaurant. Mary collects all the sleeping pills and aspirins she can find, and takes them and half a bottle of sherry. You can see what kind of a woman she is by the fact that it's not even whiskey. She leaves a note for John. She hopes he'll discover her and get her to the hospital in time and repent and then they can get married, but this fails to happen and she dies.

John marries Madge and everything continues as in A.

## C

John, who is an older man, falls in love with Mary, and Mary, who is only twenty-two, feels sorry for him because he's worried about his hair falling out. She sleeps with him even though she's not in love with him. She met him at work. She's in love with someone called James, who is twenty-two also and not yet ready to settle down.

John on the contrary settled down long ago: this is what is bothering him. John has a steady, respectable job and is getting ahead in his field, but Mary isn't impressed by him, she's impressed by James, who has a motorcycle and a fabulous record collection. But James is often away on his motorcycle, being free. Freedom isn't the same for girls, so in the meantime Mary spends Thursday evenings with John. Thursdays are the only days John can get away.

10     John is married to a woman called Madge and they have two children, a charming house which they bought just before the real estate values went up, and hobbies which they find stimulating and challenging, when they have the time. John tells Mary how important she is to him, but of course he can't leave his wife because a commitment is a commitment. He goes on about this more than is necessary and Mary finds it boring, but older men can keep it up longer so on the whole she has a fairly good time.

One day James breezes in on his motorcycle with some top-grade California hybrid and James and Mary get higher than you'd believe possible and they climb into bed. Everything becomes very underwater, but along comes John, who has a key to Mary's apartment. He finds them stoned and entwined. He's hardly in any position to be jealous, considering Madge, but nevertheless he's overcome with despair. Finally he's middle-aged, in two years he'll be bald as an egg and he can't stand it. He purchases a handgun, saying he needs it for target practice—this is the thin part of the plot, but it can be dealt with later—and shoots the two of them and himself.

Madge, after a suitable period of mourning, marries an understanding man called Fred and everything continues as in A, but under different names.

## D

Fred and Madge have no problems. They get along exceptionally well and are good at working out any little difficulties that may arise. But their charming house is by the seashore and one day a giant tidal wave approaches. Real estate values go down. The rest of the story is about what caused the tidal wave and how they escape from it. They do, though thousands drown, but Fred and Madge are virtuous and lucky. Finally on high ground they clasp each other, wet and dripping and grateful, and continue as in A.

**E**

Yes, but Fred has a bad heart. The rest of the story is about how kind and understanding they both are until Fred dies. Then Madge devotes herself to charity work until the end of A. If you like, it can be "Madge," "cancer," "guilty and confused," and "bird watching."

**F**

15  If you think this is all too bourgeois, make John a revolutionary and Mary a counterespionage agent and see how far that gets you. Remember, this is Canada. You'll still end up with A, though in between you may get a lustful brawling saga of passionate involvement, a chronicle of our times, sort of.

You'll have to face it, the endings are the same however you slice it. Don't be deluded by any other endings, they're all fake, either deliberately fake, with malicious intent to deceive, or just motivated by excessive optimism if not by downright sentimentality.

The only authentic ending is the one provided here:

*John and Mary die. John and Mary die. John and Mary die.*

So much for endings. Beginnings are almost more fun. True connoisseurs, however, are known to favor the stretch in between, since it's the hardest to do anything with.

20  That's about all that can be said for plots, which anyway are just one thing after another, a what and a what and a what.

Now try How and Why.

### YOUR TURN

1. Did the form of Atwood's story surprise you?
2. Does this story have a plot? Does it present and develop characters?
3. Describe your response to the final paragraphs, which focus on endings and beginnings. Which, in your view, is harder for a short-story writer, the beginning or the ending?
4. Some short stories are extremely short, while others are quite long. What do you think is the right length for a short story? Why do you say that? What kinds of arguments can you use to support your claim?
5. Please compose a part G for "Happy Endings."

# KATE CHOPIN

*For a biographical note, see page 67.*

## *Désirée's Baby*                                    [1892]

As the day was pleasant, Madame Valmondé drove over to L'Abri to see Désirée and the baby.

It made her laugh to think of Désirée with a baby. Why, it seemed but yesterday that Désirée was little more than a baby herself; when Monsieur in riding through the gateway of Valmondé had found her lying asleep in the shadow of the big stone pillar.

The little one awoke in his arms and began to cry for "Dada." That was as much as she could do or say. Some people thought she might have strayed there of her own accord, for she was of the toddling age. The prevailing belief was that she had been purposely left by a party of Texans, whose canvas-covered wagon, late in the day, had crossed the ferry that Coton Maïs kept, just below the plantation. In time Madame Valmondé abandoned every speculation but the one that Désirée had been sent to her by a beneficent Providence to be the child of her affection, seeing that she was without child of the flesh. For the girl grew to be beautiful and gentle, affectionate and sincere,—the idol of Valmondé.

It was no wonder, when she stood one day against the stone pillar in whose shadow she had lain asleep, eighteen years before, that Armand Aubigny riding by and seeing her there, had fallen in love with her. That was the way all the Aubignys fell in love, as if struck by a pistol shot. The wonder was that he had not loved her before; for he had known her since his father brought him home from Paris, a boy of eight, after his mother died there. The passion that awoke in him that day, when he saw her at the gate, swept along like an avalanche, or like a prairie fire, or like anything that drives headlong over all obstacles.

5    Monsieur Valmondé grew practical and wanted things well considered: that is, the girl's obscure origin. Armand looked into her eyes and did not care. He was reminded that she was nameless. What did it matter about a name when he could give her one of the oldest and proudest in Louisiana? He ordered the *corbeille*[1] from Paris, and contained himself with what patience he could until it arrived; then they were married.

Madame Valmondé had not seen Désirée and the baby for four weeks. When she reached L'Abri she shuddered at the first sight of it, as she always did. It was a sad looking place, which for many years had not known the gentle presence of a mistress, old Monsieur Aubigny having married and buried his wife in France, and she having loved her own land too well ever to leave it. The roof came down steep and black like a cowl, reaching out beyond the wide galleries that encircled the yellow stuccoed house. Big, solemn oaks grew close to it, and their thick-leaved, far-reaching branches shadowed it like a pall. Young Aubigny's rule was a strict one, too, and under it his negroes had forgotten how to be gay, as they had been during the old master's easy-going and indulgent lifetime.

The young mother was recovering slowly, and lay full length, in her soft white muslins and laces, upon a couch. The baby was beside her, upon her arm, where he had fallen asleep, at her breast. The yellow nurse woman sat beside a window fanning herself.

Madame Valmondé bent her portly figure over Désirée and kissed her, holding her an instant tenderly in her arms. Then she turned to the child.

"This is not the baby!" she exclaimed, in startled tones. French was the language spoken at Valmondé in those days.

10    "I knew you would be astonished," laughed Désirée, "at the way he has grown. The little *cochon de lait!*[2] Look at his legs, mamma, and his hands

---

[1]**corbeille** wedding gifts from the groom to the bride.    [2]**cochon de lait** suckling pig (French).

and finger-nails,—real finger-nails. Zandrine had to cut them this morning. Isn't it true, Zandrine?"

The woman bowed her turbaned head majestically, "*Mais si*,[3] Madame."

"And the way he cries," went on Désirée, "is deafening. Armand heard him the other day as far away as La Blanche's cabin."

Madame Valmondé had never removed her eyes from the child. She lifted it and walked with it over to the window that was lightest. She scanned the baby narrowly, then looked as searchingly at Zandrine, whose face was turned to gaze across the fields.

"Yes, the child has grown, has changed;" said Madame Valmondé, slowly, as she replaced it beside its mother. "What does Armand say?"

15    Désirée's face became suffused with a glow that was happiness itself.

"Oh, Armand is the proudest father in the parish, I believe, chiefly because it is a boy, to bear his name; though he says not,—that he would have loved a girl as well. But I know it isn't true. I know he says that to please me. And mamma," she added, drawing Madame Valmondé's head down to her, and speaking in a whisper, "he hasn't punished one of them—not one of them—since baby is born. Even Négrillon, who pretended to have burnt his leg that he might rest from work—he only laughed, and said Négrillon was a great scamp. Oh, mamma, I'm so happy; it frightens me."

What Désirée said was true. Marriage, and later the birth of his son, had softened Armand Aubigny's imperious and exacting nature greatly. This was what made the gentle Désirée so happy, for she loved him desperately. When he frowned she trembled, but loved him. When he smiled, she asked no greater blessing of God. But Armand's dark, handsome face had not often been disfigured by frowns since the day he fell in love with her.

When the baby was about three months old, Désirée awoke one day to the conviction that there was something in the air menacing her peace. It was at first too subtle to grasp. It had only been a disquieting suggestion; an air of mystery among the blacks; unexpected visits from far-off neighbors who could hardly account for their coming. Then a strange, an awful change in her husband's manner, which she dared not ask him to explain. When he spoke to her, it was with averted eyes, from which the old love-light seemed to have gone out. He absented himself from home; and when there, avoided her presence and that of her child, without excuse. And the very spirit of Satan seemed suddenly to take hold of him in his dealings with the slaves. Désirée was miserable enough to die.

She sat in her room, one hot afternoon, in her *peignoir*,[4] listlessly drawing through her fingers the strands of her long, silky brown hair that hung about her shoulders. The baby, half naked, lay asleep upon her own great mahogany bed, that was like a sumptuous throne, with its satin-lined half-canopy. One of La Blanche's little quadroon boys—half naked too—stood fanning the child slowly with a fan of peacock feathers. Désirée's eyes had been fixed absently and sadly upon the baby, while she was striving to penetrate the threatening mist that she felt closing about her. She looked from her child to the boy who stood beside him, and back again; over and over. "Ah!" It was a cry that she could not help; which she was not conscious of having uttered. The blood turned like ice in her veins, and a clammy moisture gathered upon her face.

---

[3]**Mais si** Certainly (French).    [4]**peignoir** long outer garment (French).

20     She tried to speak to the little quadroon boy; but no sound would come, at first. When he heard his name uttered, he looked up, and his mistress was pointing to the door. He laid aside the great, soft fan, and obediently stole away, over the polished floor, on his bare tiptoes.

She stayed motionless, with gaze riveted upon her child, and her face the picture of fright.

Presently her husband entered the room, and without noticing her, went to a table and began to search among some papers which covered it.

"Armand," she called to him, in a voice which must have stabbed him, if he was human. But he did not notice. "Armand," she said again. Then she rose and tottered towards him. "Armand," she panted once more, clutching his arm, "look at our child. What does it mean? Tell me."

He coldly but gently loosened her fingers from about his arm and thrust the hand away from him. "Tell me what it means!" she cried despairingly.

25     "It means," he answered lightly, "that the child is not white; it means that you are not white."

A quick conception of all that this accusation meant for her nerved her with unwonted courage to deny it. "It is a lie; it is not true, I am white! Look at my hair, it is brown; and my eyes are gray, Armand, you know they are gray. And my skin is fair," seizing his wrist. "Look at my hand; whiter than yours, Armand," she laughed hysterically.

"As white as La Blanche's," he returned cruelly; and went away leaving her alone with their child.

When she could hold a pen in her hand, she sent a despairing letter to Madame Valmondé.

"My mother, they tell me I am not white. Armand has told me I am not white. For God's sake tell them it is not true. You must know it is not true. I shall die. I must die. I cannot be so unhappy, and live."

30     The answer that came was as brief:

"My own Désirée: Come home to Valmondé; back to your mother who loves you. Come with your child."

When the letter reached Désirée she went with it to her husband's study, and laid it open upon the desk before which he sat. She was like a stone image: silent, white, motionless after she placed it there.

In silence he ran his cold eyes over the written words. He said nothing. "Shall I go, Armand?" she asked in tones sharp with agonized suspense.

"Yes, go."

35     "Do you want me to go?"

"Yes, I want you to go."

He thought Almighty God had dealt cruelly and unjustly with him; and felt, somehow, that he was paying Him back in kind when he stabbed thus into his wife's soul. Moreover he no longer loved her, because of the unconscious injury she had brought upon his home and his name.

She turned away like one stunned by a blow, and walked slowly towards the door, hoping he would call her back.

"Good-by, Armand," she moaned.

40     He did not answer her. That was his last blow at fate.

Désirée went in search of her child. Zandrine was pacing the sombre gallery with it. She took the little one from the nurse's arms with no word of explanation, and descending the steps, walked away, under the live-oak branches.

It was an October afternoon; the sun was just sinking. Out in the still fields the negroes were picking cotton.

Désirée had not changed the thin white garment nor the slippers which she wore. Her hair was uncovered and the sun's rays brought a golden gleam from its brown meshes. She did not take the broad, beaten road which led to the far-off plantation of Valmondé. She walked across a deserted field, where the stubble bruised her tender feet, so delicately shod, and tore her thin gown to shreds.

She disappeared among the reeds and willows that grew thick along the banks of the deep, sluggish bayou; and she did not come back again.

45      Some weeks later there was a curious scene enacted at L'Abri. In the centre of the smoothly swept back yard was a great bonfire. Armand Aubigny sat in the wide hallway that commanded a view of the spectacle; and it was he who dealt out to a half dozen negroes the material which kept this fire ablaze.

A graceful cradle of willow, with all its dainty furbishings, was laid upon the pyre, which had already been fed with the richness of a priceless *layette*.[5] Then there were silk gowns, and velvet and satin ones added to these; laces, too, and embroideries; bonnets and gloves; for the *corbeille* had been of rare quality.

The last thing to go was a tiny bundle of letters; innocent little scribblings that Désirée had sent to him during the days of their espousal. There was the remnant of one back in the drawer from which he took them. But it was not Désirée's; it was part of an old letter from his mother to his father. He read it. She was thanking God for the blessing of her husband's love:—

> "But, above all," she wrote, "night and day, I thank the good God for having so arranged our lives that our dear Armand will never know that his mother, who adores him, belongs to the race that is cursed with the brand of slavery."

### YOUR TURN

1. Let's start with the ending. Readers find the ending powerful, but they differ in their interpretations of it. Do you think that when Armand reads the letter he learns something he had never suspected or, instead, something that he had sensed about himself all along? Find evidence in the text to support your view.

2. Describe Désirée's feelings toward Armand. Do you agree with the student who told us, "She makes him into a God"?

3. Chopin writes economically: each word counts, each phrase and sentence is significant. What is she revealing about Armand (and perhaps about the discovery he has made) when she writes, "And the very spirit of Satan seemed suddenly to take hold of him in his dealings with the slaves"?

4. Is this story primarily a character study, or is Chopin seeking to make larger points in it about race, slavery, and gender?

---

[5]**layette** collection of clothing for a newborn child.

# ALICE WALKER

*Alice Walker was born in 1944 in Eatonton, Georgia, where her parents eked out a living as sharecroppers and dairy farmers; her mother also worked as a domestic. (In a collection of essays,* In Search of Our Mothers' Gardens *[1984], Walker celebrates women who, like her mother, passed on a "respect for the possibilities [of life]—and the will to grasp them.") Walker attended Spelman College in Atlanta, and in 1965 she finished her undergraduate work at Sarah Lawrence College near New York City. She then became active in the welfare rights movement in New York and in the voter registration movement in Georgia. Later she taught writing and literature in Mississippi, at Jackson State College and Tougaloo College, and at Wellesley College, the University of Massachusetts, and Yale University.*

*Walker has written essays, poetry, and fiction. Her best-known novel,* The Color Purple *(1982), won a Pulitzer Prize and the National Book Award. She has said that her chief concern is "exploring the oppressions, the insanities, the loyalties, and the triumphs of black women."*

## *Everyday Use*                                                        [1973]

*for your grandmama*

I will wait for her in the yard that Maggie and I made so clean and wavy yesterday afternoon. A yard like this is more comfortable than most people know. It is not just a yard. It is like an extended living room. When the hard clay is swept clean as a floor and the fine sand around the edges lined with tiny, irregular grooves, anyone can come and sit and look up into the elm tree and wait for the breezes that never come inside the house.

Maggie will be nervous until after her sister goes: she will stand hopelessly in corners, homely and ashamed of the burn scars down her arms and legs, eying her sister with a mixture of envy and awe. She thinks her sister has held life always in the palm of one hand, that "no" is a word the world never learned to say to her.

You've no doubt seen those TV shows where the child who has "made it" is confronted, as a surprise, by her own mother and father, tottering in weakly from backstage. (A pleasant surprise, of course: What would they do if parent and child came on the show only to curse out and insult each other?) On TV mother and child embrace and smile into each other's faces. Sometimes the mother and father weep, the child wraps them in her arms and leans across the table to tell how she would not have made it without their help. I have seen these programs.

Sometimes I dream a dream in which Dee and I are suddenly brought together on a TV program of this sort. Out of a dark and soft-seated limousine I am ushered into a bright room filled with many people. There I meet a smiling, gray, sporty man like Johnny Carson[1] who shakes my hand

---

[1]**Johnny Carson** a popular TV comedian, best known as host of the long-running *The Tonight Show Starring Johnny Carson* (1962–1992).

and tells me what a fine girl I have. Then we are on the stage and Dee is embracing me with tears in her eyes. She pins on my dress a large orchid, even though she has told me once that she thinks orchids are tacky flowers.

5      In real life I am a large, big-boned woman with rough, man-working hands. In the winter I wear flannel nightgowns to bed and overalls during the day. I can kill and clean a hog as mercilessly as a man. My fat keeps me hot in zero weather. I can work outside all day, breaking ice to get water for washing; I can eat pork liver cooked over the open fire minutes after it comes steaming from the hog. One winter I knocked a bull calf straight in the brain between the eyes with a sledge hammer and had the meat hung up to chill before nightfall. But of course all this does not show on television. I am the way my daughter would want me to be: a hundred pounds lighter, my skin like an uncooked barley pancake. My hair glistens in the hot bright lights. Johnny Carson has much to do to keep up with my quick and witty tongue.

But that is a mistake. I know even before I wake up. Who ever knew a Johnson with a quick tongue? Who can even imagine me looking a strange white man in the eye? It seems to me I have talked to them always with one foot raised in flight, with my head turned in whichever way is farthest from them. Dee, though. She would always look anyone in the eye. Hesitation was no part of her nature.

"How do I look, Mama?" Maggie says, showing just enough of her thin body enveloped in pink skirt and red blouse for me to know she's there, almost hidden by the door.

"Come out into the yard," I say.

Have you ever seen a lame animal, perhaps a dog run over by some careless person rich enough to own a car, sidle up to someone who is ignorant enough to be kind to him? That is the way my Maggie walks. She has been like this, chin on chest, eyes on ground, feet in shuffle, ever since the fire that burned the other house to the ground.

10      Dee is lighter than Maggie, with nicer hair and a fuller figure. She's a woman now, though sometimes I forget. How long ago was it that the other house burned? Ten, twelve years? Sometimes I can still hear the flames and feel Maggie's arms sticking to me, her hair smoking and her dress falling off her in little black papery flakes. Her eyes seemed stretched open, blazed open by the flames reflected in them. And Dee. I see her standing off under the sweet gum tree she used to dig gum out of; a look of concentration on her face as she watched the last dingy gray board of the house fall in toward the red-hot brick chimney. Why don't you do a dance around the ashes? I'd wanted to ask her. She had hated the house that much.

I used to think she hated Maggie, too. But that was before we raised the money, the church and me, to send her to Augusta to school. She used to read to us without pity; forcing words, lies, other folks' habits, whole lives upon us two, sitting trapped and ignorant underneath her voice. She washed us in a river of make-believe, burned us with a lot of knowledge we didn't necessarily need to know. Pressed us to her with the serious way she read, to shove us away at just the moment, like dimwits, we seemed about to understand.

Dee wanted nice things. A yellow organdy dress to wear to her graduation from high school; black pumps to match a green suit she'd made from an old suit somebody gave me. She was determined to stare down any disaster in her efforts. Her eyelids would not flicker for minutes at a time. Often I fought off the temptation to shake her. At sixteen she had a style of her own: and knew what style was.

I never had an education myself. After second grade the school was closed down. Don't ask me why: in 1927 colored asked fewer questions than they do now. Sometimes Maggie reads to me. She stumbles along good-naturedly but can't see well. She knows she is not bright. Like good looks and money, quickness passed her by. She will marry John Thomas (who has mossy teeth in an earnest face) and then I'll be free to sit here and I guess just sing church songs to myself. Although I never was a good singer. Never could carry a tune. I was always better at a man's job. I used to love to milk till I was hooked in the side in '49. Cows are soothing and slow and don't bother you, unless you try to milk them the wrong way.

I have deliberately turned my back on the house. It is three rooms, just like the one that burned, except the roof is tin; they don't make shingle roofs any more. There are no real windows, just some holes cut in the sides, like the portholes in a ship, but not round and not square, with rawhide holding the shutters up on the outside. This house is in a pasture, too, like the other one. No doubt when Dee sees it she will want to tear it down. She wrote me once that no matter where we "choose" to live, she will manage to come see us. But she will never bring her friends. Maggie and I thought about this and Maggie asked me, "Mama, when did Dee ever *have* any friends?"

15    She had a few. Furtive boys in pink shirts hanging about on washday after school. Nervous girls who never laughed. Impressed with her they worshiped the well-turned phrase, the cute shape, the scalding humor that erupted like bubbles in lye. She read to them.

When she was courting Jimmy T she didn't have much time to pay to us, but turned all her faultfinding power on him. He *flew* to marry a cheap city girl from a family of ignorant flashy people. She hardly had time to re-compose herself.

When she comes I will meet—but there they are!

Maggie attempts to make a dash for the house, in her shuffling way, but I stay her with my hand. "Come back here," I say. And she stops and tries to dig a well in the sand with her toe.

It is hard to see them clearly through the strong sun. But even the first glimpse of leg out of the car tells me it is Dee. Her feet were always neat-looking, as if God himself had shaped them with a certain style. From the other side of the car comes a short, stocky man. Hair is all over his head a foot long and hanging from his chin like a kinky mule tail. I hear Maggie suck in her breath. "Uhnnnh," is what it sounds like. Like when you see the wriggling end of a snake just in front of your foot on the road. "Uhnnnh."

20    Dee next. A dress down to the ground, in this hot weather. A dress so loud it hurts my eyes. There are yellows and oranges enough to throw back the light of the sun. I feel my whole face warming from the heat waves it throws out. Earrings gold, too, and hanging down to her shoulders. Bracelets dangling and making noises when she moves her arm up to shake the folds of the dress out of her armpits. The dress is loose and flows, and as she walks closer, I like it. I hear Maggie go "Uhnnnh" again. It is her sister's hair. It

stands straight up like the wool on a sheep. It is black as night and around the edges are two long pigtails that rope about like small lizards disappearing behind her ears.

"Wa-su-zo-Tean-o!" she says, coming on in that gliding way the dress makes her move. The short stocky fellow with the hair to his navel is all grinning and he follows up with "Asalamalakim, my mother and sister!" He moves to hug Maggie but she falls back, right up against the back of my chair. I feel her trembling there and when I look up I see the perspiration falling off her chin.

"Don't get up," says Dee. Since I am stout it takes something of a push. You can see me trying to move a second or two before I make it. She turns, showing white heels through her sandals, and goes back to the car. Out she peeks next with a Polaroid. She stoops down quickly and lines up picture after picture of me sitting there in front of the house with Maggie cowering behind me. She never takes a shot without making sure the house is included. When a cow comes nibbling around the edge of the yard she snaps it and me and Maggie *and* the house. Then she puts the Polaroid in the back seat of the car, and comes up and kisses me on the forehead.

Meanwhile Asalamalakim is going through the motions with Maggie's hand. Maggie's hand is as limp as a fish, and probably as cold, despite the sweat, and she keeps trying to pull it back. It looks like Asalamalakim wants to shake hands but wants to do it fancy. Or maybe he don't know how people shake hands. Anyhow, he soon gives up on Maggie.

"Well," I say. "Dee."

25     "No, Mama," she says. "Not 'Dee,' Wangero Leewanika Kemanjo!"

"What happened to 'Dee'?" I wanted to know.

"She's dead," Wangero said. "I couldn't bear it any longer, being named after the people who oppress me."

"You know as well as me you was named after your aunt Dicie," I said. Dicie is my sister. She named Dee. We called her "Big Dee" after Dee was born.

"But who was *she* named after?" asked Wangero.

30     "I guess after Grandma Dee," I said.

"And who was she named after?" asked Wangero.

"Her mother," I said, and saw Wangero was getting tired. "That's about as far back as I can trace it," I said. Though, in fact, I probably could have carried it back beyond the Civil War through the branches.

"Well," said Asalamalakim, "there you are."

"Uhnnnh," I heard Maggie say.

35     "There I was not," I said, "before 'Dicie' cropped up in our family, so why should I try to trace it that far back?"

He just stood there grinning, looking down on me like somebody inspecting a Model A car. Every once in a while he and Wangero sent eye signals over my head.

"How do you pronounce this name?" I asked.

"You don't have to call me by it if you don't want to," said Wangero.

"Why shouldn't I?" I asked. "If that's what you want us to call you, we'll call you."

40     "I know it might sound awkward at first," said Wangero.

"I'll get used to it," I said. "Ream it out again."

Well, soon we got the name out of the way. Asalamalakim had a name twice as long and three times as hard. After I tripped over it two or three times he told me to just call him Hakim-a-barber. I wanted to ask him was he a barber, but I didn't really think he was, so I didn't ask.

"You must belong to those beef-cattle peoples down the road," I said. They said "Asalamalakim" when they met you, too, but they didn't shake hands. Always too busy: feeding the cattle, fixing the fences, putting up salt-lick shelters, throwing down hay. When the white folks poisoned some of the herd the men stayed up all night with rifles in their hands. I walked a mile and a half just to see the sight.

Hakim-a-barber said, "I accept some of their doctrines, but farming and raising cattle is not my style." (They didn't tell me, and I didn't ask, whether Wangero (Dee) had really gone and married him.)

45     We sat down to eat and right away he said he didn't eat collards and pork was unclean. Wangero, though, went on through the chitlins and corn bread, the greens and everything else. She talked a blue streak over the sweet potatoes. Everything delighted her. Even the fact that we still used the benches her daddy made for the table when we couldn't afford to buy chairs.

"Oh, Mama!" she cried. Then turned to Hakim-a-barber. "I never knew how lovely these benches are. You can feel the rump prints," she said, running her hands underneath her and along the bench. Then she gave a sigh and her hand closed over Grandma Dee's butter dish. "That's it!" she said. "I knew there was something I wanted to ask you if I could have." She jumped up from the table and went over in the corner where the churn stood, the milk in it clabber by now. She looked at the churn and looked at it.

"This churn top is what I need," she said. "Didn't Uncle Buddy whittle it out of a tree you all used to have?"

"Yes," I said.

"Uh huh," she said happily. "And I want the dasher, too."

50     "Uncle Buddy whittle that, too?" asked the barber.

Dee (Wangero) looked up at me.

"Aunt Dee's first husband whittled the dash," said Maggie so low you almost couldn't hear her. "His name was Henry, but they called him Stash."

"Maggie's brain is like an elephant's," Wangero said, laughing. "I can use the churn top as a centerpiece for the alcove table," she said, sliding a plate over the churn, "and I'll think of something artistic to do with the dasher."

When she finished wrapping the dasher the handle stuck out. I took it for a moment in my hands. You didn't even have to look close to see where hands pushing the dasher up and down to make butter had left a kind of sink in the wood. In fact, there were a lot of small sinks; you could see where thumbs and fingers had sunk into the wood. It was beautiful light yellow wood, from a tree that grew in the yard where Big Dee and Stash had lived.

55     After dinner Dee (Wangero) went to the trunk at the foot of my bed and started rifling through it. Maggie hung back in the kitchen over the dishpan. Out came Wangero with two quilts. They had been pieced by Grandma Dee and then Big Dee and me had hung them on the quilt frames on the front porch and quilted them. One was in the Lone Star pattern. The other was Walk Around the Mountain. In both of them were scraps of dresses Grandma Dee had worn fifty and more years ago. Bits and pieces of Grandpa Jarrell's Paisley shirts. And one teeny faded blue piece, about the size of a penny matchbox, that was from Great Grandpa Ezra's uniform that he wore in the Civil War.

Quilt made by a slave in Mississippi about 1855–1858. (Courtesy of Michigan State University Museum.)

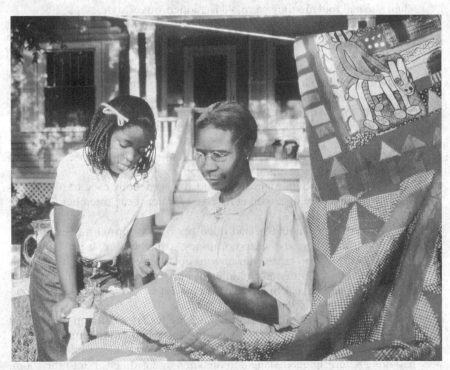

The crafting of a family heirloom.

"Mama," Wangero said sweet as a bird. "Can I have these old quilts?"

I heard something fall in the kitchen, and a minute later the kitchen door slammed.

"Why don't you take one or two of the others?" I asked. "These old things was just done by me and Big Dee from some tops your grandma pieced before she died."

"No," said Wangero. "I don't want those. They are stitched around the borders by machine."

60   "That'll make them last better," I said.

"That's not the point," said Wangero. "These are all pieces of dresses Grandma used to wear. She did all this stitching by hand. Imagine!" She held the quilts securely in her arms, stroking them.

"Some of the pieces, like those lavender ones, come from old clothes her mother handed down to her," I said, moving up to touch the quilts. Dee (Wangero) moved back just enough so that I couldn't reach the quilts. They already belonged to her.

"Imagine!" she breathed again, clutching them closely to her bosom.

"The truth is," I said, "I promised to give them quilts to Maggie, for when she marries John Thomas."

65   She gasped like a bee had stung her.

"Maggie can't appreciate these quilts!" she said. "She'd probably be backward enough to put them to everyday use."

"I reckon she would," I said. "God knows I been saving 'em for long enough with nobody using 'em. I hope she will!" I didn't want to bring up how I had offered Dee (Wangero) a quilt when she went away to college. Then she had told me they were old-fashioned, out of style.

"But they're *priceless!*" she was saying now, furiously; for she has a temper. "Maggie would put them on the bed and in five years they'd be in rags. Less than that!"

"She can always make some more," I said. "Maggie knows how to quilt."

70   Dee (Wangero) looked at me with hatred. "You just will not understand. The point is these quilts, *these* quilts!"

"Well," I said, stumped. "What would *you* do with them?"

"Hang them," she said. As if that was the only thing you *could* do with quilts.

Maggie by now was standing in the door. I could almost hear the sound her feet made as they scraped over each other.

"She can have them, Mama," she said, like somebody used to never winning anything, or having anything reserved for her. "I can 'member Grandma Dee without the quilts."

75   I looked at her hard. She had filled her bottom lip with checkerberry snuff and it gave her face a kind of dopey, hangdog look. It was Grandma Dee and Big Dee who taught her how to quilt herself. She stood there with her scarred hands hidden in the folds of her skirt. She looked at her sister with something like fear but she wasn't mad at her. This was Maggie's portion. This was the way she knew God to work.

When I looked at her like that something hit me in the top of my head and ran down to the soles of my feet. Just like when I'm in church and the spirit of God touches me and I get happy and shout. I did something I never had done before: hugged Maggie to me, then dragged her on into the room, snatched the quilts out of Miss Wangero's hands and dumped them into Maggie's lap. Maggie just sat there on my bed with her mouth open.

"Take one or two of the others," I said to Dee.

But she turned without a word and went out to Hakim-a-barber.

"You just don't understand," she said, as Maggie and I came out to the car.

80    "What don't I understand?" I wanted to know.

"Your heritage," she said. And then she turned to Maggie, kissed her, and said, "You ought to try to make something of yourself, too, Maggie. It's really a new day for us. But from the way you and Mama still live you'd never know it."

She put on some sunglasses that hid everything above the tip of her nose and her chin.

Maggie smiled; maybe at the sunglasses. But a real smile, not scared. After we watched the car dust settle I asked Maggie to bring me a dip of snuff. And then the two of us sat there just enjoying, until it was time to go in the house and go to bed.

**YOUR TURN**

1. Alice Walker wrote the story, but the story is narrated by one of the characters, Mama. How would you characterize Mama?

2. At the end of the story, Dee tells Maggie, "It's really a new day for us. But from the way you and Mama still live you'd never know it." What does Dee mean? And how do Maggie and Mama respond?"

3. In paragraph 76 the narrator says, speaking of Maggie, "When I looked at her like that something hit me in the top of my head and ran down to the soles of my feet." What "hit" Mama? That is, what does she understand at this moment that she had not understood before?

4. In "Everyday Use" why does the family conflict focus on who will possess the quilts? Why are the quilts important? What do they symbolize?

# 7

# Character

It is a bit misleading to devote separate chapters to plot and character. The novelist Henry James often stressed that the two are interdependent; a good novel or short story, he said, is an "organism," which possesses vitality and hence is lifelike because its parts form a coherent, unified whole. Using the word "incident" for almost any sort of action, large or small, James said,

> What is character but the determination of incident? What is incident but the illustration of character?

In fact, James was very clear that an "incident" need not be of the magnitude of a train wreck or even a slap in the face:

> It is an incident for a woman to stand up with her hand resting on a table and look out at you in a certain way.

That is, what we are—our personalities, our characters—are what we *do,* are the "incidents" we participate in. And "incidents" are the demonstrations of what we are, what our characters (personalities) are.

Still, just as some stories are mostly plot—the whodunit is a good example, where the reader's interest is almost entirely in what happens next rather than in the personalities—some stories are mostly character, mostly revelations of personalities.

Among the most ancient stories in Western literature are the fables of Aesop, some of which go back to the seventh century BCE. These stories also teach lessons by recounting brief incidents from which homely morals may easily be drawn, even though the stories are utterly fanciful. Among famous examples are the stories of the hare and the tortoise, the boy who cried "Wolf," the ant and the grasshopper, and a good many others that stick in the mind because of the sharply contrasted characters in sharply imagined situations. The fables just mentioned take only four or five sentences apiece, but brief as they are, Aesop told some briefer ones. Here is the briefest of all, about a female fox and a lioness.

# AESOP

*Aesop, a semi-legendary Greek storyteller, was said to have lived in the sixth century BCE, but some of the stories he told are found in Egypt, in texts that are hundreds of years older.*

## The Vixen and the Lioness

A vixen sneered at a lioness because she never bore more than one cub. "Only one," the lioness replied, "but a lion."

Just that: Nothing much happens, in the sense of a plot with comings and goings. Just a confrontation between two strongly opposed kinds of creatures: The mere confrontation of a fox and a lion brings together the ignoble and the noble. There is no setting (we are not told that "one day in June a vixen, walking down a dusty road in Nairobi, met a lioness"), but none is needed here. What there is—however briefly set forth—is characterization. The fox's baseness is effectively communicated through the verb "sneered" and through her taunt, and the lioness's nobility is even more effectively communicated through the brevity and decisiveness of her reply. This reply at first seems to agree with the fox ("Only one") and then, after a suspenseful delay provided by the words "the lioness replied," the reply is tersely and powerfully completed ("but a lion"), placing the matter firmly in a new light. Granted that the story is not much of a story, still, it is finely told, and more potent—more memorable, more lively, we might even say more real, despite its talking animals—than the mere moral: "Small-minded people confuse quantity with quality."

The fable is frankly imaginative, made-up; no one believes that foxes and lions discuss their offspring, or, for that matter, that tortoises and hares engage in races. Here is another of Aesop's animal fables, again with a striking contrast of personalities.

## The Ant and the Grasshopper

One cold winter day an ant was dragging out a grain which he had buried during the winter. A hungry grasshopper asked for a bit of the grain.
"What did you do all summer?" asked the ant.
"I was busy all summer long, singing," replied the grasshopper.
"Well," said the ant, "since you sang all summer, now dance all winter."

### YOUR TURN

1. Let's rewrite the ant's final remark, thus: "Well, since you spent the whole summer singing, I guess you'll dance now in the winter." We assume you agree that the original version is more effective. Exactly what makes the original better?

2. Grasshoppers make great leaps, whereas ants are earthbound. Write a fable in which the grasshopper represents the imaginative thinker and the ant represents the unimaginative plodder.

3. Do you think we can draw lessons from nature about how we should behave? Is a significant part of the argument (so to speak) of an Aesop

fable that it is "natural," that it shows us "nature's way"? Think of some
other fables, such as "The City Mouse and the Country Mouse" and
"The Fox and the Grapes," that draw upon the nonhuman world. (The
gist of "The Fox and the Grapes" is this: A starving fox, seeing bunches
of grapes hanging from a vine, but out of reach, went away saying,
"Those grapes aren't ripe, they're sour.")

What do such fables gain by being set in the nonhuman world? Why not just
say, "A starving man, seeing bunches of grapes that were out of reach, said 'Those
grapes aren't ripe, they're sour'"? Again, what, if anything, is gained by using talking animals? Is the moral enforced by nature?

Let's return to this matter of plot and character: Plot is character in action,
and character is the motivation for plot. This is the view that James and many
other writers have expressed. There are stories in which plot is more prominent
than character, and vice versa, but it is hard for us to imagine one without the
other. We focus both on the events of the story and on the person or persons involved in the action, the characters that are in the midst of it. A comment by
Tobias Wolff, a contemporary writer who is represented in this book with stories
and observations in fiction (pages 338–362) is relevant:

> Stories are about problems, and not the kind of problems that result
> from a safe falling out of a window, but from somebody having a choice
> and having a problem with that choice, and then the series of conse-
> quences that follow from making that choice.

Wolff clearly is very much in agreement with Henry James and E. M. Forster that
plot is the result of character in action, the result of (in Wolff's word) "choice."

One of the reasons we turn to novels and stories is for the pleasure we experience in the company of interesting characters. We know that they are not
real persons, we know that authors use their skills to imagine and invent the
characters we meet in fiction. But in a good work of fiction, we often feel
nonetheless that we are coming to know and understand a character as if he or
she were a person—someone whom we might meet in real life. This character's
words and actions, thoughts and feelings, lead us to become interested in them.
We enjoy being in their company, and this even is the case when we are reading
about a character whose actions we deplore. Why is this character like that?
What would it be like to be such a character? Characters need not be sympathetic, but they must be *interesting*. Consider the following very short story, a
story about two, no, three characters.

# RON WALLACE

*Ron Wallace, born in 1945, is the author of numerous books of poems and
stories. He is a professor of English and the codirector of the creative writing
program at the University of Wisconsin–Madison.*

### *Worry*                                                                [1996]

She worried about people; he worried about things. And between them, that
about covered it.

"What would you think of our daughter sleeping around?" she said.

"The porch steps are rotting," he replied. "Someone's going to fall
through."

They were lying in bed together, talking. They had been lying in bed together talking these twenty-five years: first, about whether to have children—she wanted to (although there was Down's Syndrome, leukemia, microcephaly, mumps); he didn't (the siding was warped; the roof was going fast)—and then, after their daughter was born, a healthy seven pounds eleven ounces ("She's not eating enough;" "The furnace is failing"), about family matters, mostly ("Her friends are hoodlums, her room is a disaster," "The brakes are squealing, the water heater's rusting out.").

5       Worry grew between them like a son, with his own small insistencies and then more pressing demands. They stroked and coddled him; they set a place for him at the table; they sent him to kindergarten, private school, and college. Because he failed at nearly everything and always returned home, they loved him. After all, he was their son.

"I've been reading her diary. She does drugs. She sleeps around."

"I just don't think I can fix them myself. Where will we find a carpenter?"

And so it went. Their daughter married her high school sweetheart, had a family, and started a health food store in a distant town. Although she recalled her childhood as fondly as anyone—how good her parents had been and how they worried for her, how old and infirm they must be growing, their house going to ruin—she rarely called or visited. She had worries of her own.

**YOUR TURN**

In our discussion of plot, in the previous chapter, we quoted E. M. Forster on plot and surprise. The episodes in a plot, Forster said, ought to be "unexpected. This shock, followed by the feeling, 'Oh, that's all right,' is a sign that all is well with the plot: characters, to be real, ought to run smoothly, but a plot ought to cause surprise." Were you surprised to hear, at the end of Wallace's story, that the daughter married her high school sweetheart, started a health food store, and recalled her childhood fondly? And were you surprised to learn that although she worried about them, "she rarely called or visited" because "she had worries of her own"? Did you experience a slight surprise as well as a sense of "Oh, that's all right"?

# Kinds of Characters

Soon in this chapter you will be making the acquaintance of characters in longer stories. Each of these stories offers its own special reward, with a vivid set of characters; each will become all the more rewarding for you when you complete your reading of this chapter and consider the stories as a group, comparing and contrasting one to the others. But before we turn to these stories, we should do some further thinking about character in general—what it is and how we might approach it as readers, interpreters, and writers of analytical essays.

In simplest terms, a character is the representation of a person in a literary work. In this chapter we are focusing on short stories, but there are characters in poems and, of course, in plays as well. The author presents a character to us through

- what the character says (dialogue),
- what the character does (actions),

- what the author explicitly tells us about the character (authorial comment), and
- what the author tells us about where the character lives (setting)—but that is a topic treated in the next chapter.

Through these techniques, the author makes a character come to life, and to many authors their characters are "alive" indeed. The English short-story writer and novelist Graham Greene noted, "I have to watch my characters crossing the room . . . . I have to see everything they do, even if I don't write it down." Deborah Moggach, a contemporary British novelist, screen writer, and author of many short stories, says this:

> Once a character has gelled it's an unmistakable sensation, like an engine starting up within one's body. From then onwards one is driven by this other person, seeing things through their eyes, shuffling round the shops as a 57-year-old man and practically feeling one has grown a beard.

In *Aspects of the Novel*, from which we have already quoted, E. M. Forster makes a distinction between **flat characters** and **round characters.** "Flat" implies a person who is two-dimensional, fairly simple, and probably unchanging: the character who we encounter at the outset is more or less the same from first appearance to last. Clearly Aesop's characters are flat: The vixen is mean-spirited, the lioness is noble, the grasshopper is imprudent, and the ant is a workaholic. "Round" characters, on the other hand, are three-dimensional, with depth and complexity. A round character is subject to change and indeed during the course of the story might change significantly. We take a special interest in round characters; we want to get to know them, and we give close attention to their words and actions—which sometimes, as in real life, can surprise us. Such characters, we could say, are dynamic, growing and progressing, moving to a new level of insight and understanding. The chief interest in such a story may be in the character's change—for instance, in the loss of innocence.

Some mention should be made of the so-called **stock character.** This term is not quite just another name for a flat character. True, stock character are highly typical or stereotypical, characters whom we recognize because we have seen others like them in other literary works, TV shows, or films. There is the damsel in distress, for example, and the absent-minded professor, the tough-as-nails army sergeant, the prostitute with a heart of gold, and so on. But good authors can give an individuality to a stock character that a flat character cannot have. We can enjoy seeing this or that variation on a stock character, especially if it is a kind of character whom we like. To say that we like the character is not to say that we need to admire him or her. (In *Seinfeld*, George Costanza is a blowhard and a loser, but there is something engaging about him. You just don't want him to be your roommate, or even to work at the desk next to yours.) It can also be interesting to observe how an author may begin with stock characters and develop and deepen them, making them more complex, giving them a distinctive personality.

When you turn to the stories that follow, and to others that are in this book, you might find it useful to keep these tips and questions in mind:

1. **Protagonist:** Is there a main character in the story, one who is the center of our interest? Note: "protagonist" derives from a Greek word for "first actor" or "first contender," from *protos* (= first) and *agonistes* (= contender).

Do not confuse *protos* with the Latin *pro,* meaning "for." Avoid using the word (not only in your essays in English classes but in your daily speech) in the sense of an advocate, as in "He was a protagonist for vegetarianism."

2. **Antagonist:** Is there a character who is in conflict with the main character? What is the nature of this conflict? How does it reveal itself in the story? *Note:* Here, the Greek word means "against the contender."

3. **Foil:** Is there a foil or are there foils in the story? That is, are there characters who bring out the qualities of the protagonist, as a sheet of gold or silver foil sets off a gem? (In *Hamlet,* Laertes and Fortinbras are foils to Hamlet: each has lost a father, and each behaves differently.)

4. **Appearance:** What does the character look like?

5. **Action:** What does each character do in the story?

6. **Dialogue:** What does each character say, and with whom (and in what ways) does the character speak? Dialogue is—though this at first sounds odd—a kind of action. As the novelist Elizabeth Bowen said, "Dialogue is what characters *do* to each other."

7. **Thoughts and feelings:** What do we learn about how the character thinks and feels—about himself or herself, other people, work, politics, and other things? That is, what is the character's inner life?

8. **Setting:** Does the locale (place and time)—nineteenth-century New England or contemporary South, for instance—help to shape the character?

9. **Point of view:** Does the author *show* or does the author *tell*—that is, does the author let us see and hear the characters in action, thereby allowing us to draw our own conclusions, or does the author tell us about them, giving us explicit guidance, perhaps even offering an explicit judgment of the character? Showing (rather than telling) is frequently termed the **objective** or the **dramatic method** of characterization.

10. **Making connections:** How is *this* character in *this* story you are studying similar to and different from the characters in other literary works you have read in this book, or have encountered in reading you have done on your own?

# WILLIAM CARLOS WILLIAMS

*William Carlos Williams (1883–1963) was the son of an English traveling salesman and a Basque-Jewish woman. The couple met in Puerto Rico and settled in Rutherford, New Jersey, where Williams was born. He spent his life there, practicing as a pediatrician and writing poems in the moments between seeing patients. In addition to many books of poetry and literary and cultural criticism, Williams also published fifty-two short stories, many of them, such as "The Use of Force," reflecting his experiences as a practicing physician.*

## *The Use of Force*                                            [1938]

They were new patients to me, all I had was the name, Olson. Please come down as soon as you can, my daughter is very sick.

When I arrived I was met by the mother, a big startled looking woman, very clean and apologetic who merely said, Is this the doctor? and let me in.

In the back, she added. You must excuse us, doctor, we have her in the kitchen where it is warm. It is very damp here sometimes.

The child was fully dressed and sitting on her father's lap near the kitchen table. He tried to get up, but I motioned for him not to bother, took off my overcoat and started to look things over. I could see that they were all very nervous, eyeing me up and down distrustfully. As often, in such cases, they weren't telling me more than they had to, it was up to me to tell them; that's why they were spending three dollars on me.

The child was fairly eating me up with her cold, steady eyes, and no expression to her face whatever. She did not move and seemed, inwardly, quiet; an unusually attractive little thing, and as strong as a heifer in appearance. But her face was flushed, she was breathing rapidly, and I realized that she had a high fever. She had magnificent blond hair, in profusion. One of those picture children often reproduced in advertising leaflets and the photogravure sections of the Sunday papers.

5      She's had a fever for three days, began the father and we don't know what it comes from. My wife has given her things, you know, like people do, but it don't do no good. And there's been a lot of sickness around. So we tho't you'd better look her over and tell us what is the matter.

As doctors often do I took a trial shot at it as a point of departure. Has she had a sore throat?

Both parents answered me together, No . . . No, she says her throat don't hurt her.

Does your throat hurt you? added the mother to the child. But the little girl's expression didn't change nor did she move her eyes from my face.

Have you looked?

10     I tried to, said the mother, but I couldn't see.

As it happens we had been having a number of cases of diphtheria in the school to which this child went during that month and we were all, quite apparently, thinking of that, though no one had as yet spoken of the thing.

Well, I said, suppose we take a look at the throat first. I smiled in my best professional manner and asking for the child's first name I said, come on, Mathilda, open your mouth and let's take a look at your throat.

Nothing doing.

Aw, come on, I coaxed, just open your mouth wide and let me take a look. Look, I said opening both hands wide, I haven't anything in my hands. Just open up and let me see.

15     Such a nice man, put in the mother. Look how kind he is to you. Come on, do what he tells you to, he won't hurt you.

At that I ground my teeth in disgust. If only they wouldn't use the word "hurt" I might be able to get somewhere. But I did not allow myself to be hurried or disturbed but speaking quietly and slowly I approached the child again.

As I moved my chair a little nearer suddenly with one catlike movement both her hands clawed instinctively for my eyes and she almost reached them too. In fact she knocked my glasses flying and they fell, though unbroken, several feet away from me on the kitchen floor.

Both the mother and father almost turned themselves inside out in embarrassment and apology. You bad girl, said the mother, taking her and shaking her by one arm. Look what you've done. The nice man . . . .

For heaven's sake, I broke in. Don't call me a nice man to her. I'm here to look at her throat on the chance that she might have diphtheria and possibly die of it. But that's nothing to her. Look here, I said to the child, we're going to look at your throat. You're old enough to understand what I'm saying. Will you open it now by yourself or shall we have to open it for you?

20   Not a move. Even her expression hadn't changed. Her breaths however were coming faster and faster. Then the battle began. I had to do it. I had to have a throat culture for her own protection. But first I told the parents that it was entirely up to them. I explained the danger but said that I would not insist on a throat examination so long as they would take the responsibility.

If you don't do what the doctor says you'll have to go to the hospital, the mother admonished her severely.

Oh yeah? I had to smile to myself. After all, I had already fallen in love with the savage brat, the parents were contemptible to me. In the ensuing struggle they grew more and more abject, crushed, exhausted while she surely rose to magnificent heights of insane fury of effort bred of her terror of me.

The father tried his best, and he was a big man but the fact that she was his daughter, his shame at her behavior and his dread of hurting her made him release her just at the critical moment several times when I had almost achieved success, till I wanted to kill him. But his dread also that she might have diphtheria made him tell me to go on, go on though he himself was almost fainting, while the mother moved back and forth behind us raising and lowering her hands in an agony of apprehension.

Put her in front of you on your lap, I ordered, and hold both her wrists.

25   But as soon as he did the child let out a scream. Don't, you're hurting me. Let go of my hands. Let them go I tell you. Then she shrieked terrifyingly, hysterically. Stop it! Stop it! You're killing me!

Do you think she can stand it, doctor! said the mother.

You get out, said the husband to his wife. Do you want her to die of diphtheria?

Come on now, hold her, I said.

Then I grasped the child's head with my left hand and tried to get the wooden tongue depressor between her teeth. She fought, with clenched teeth, desperately! But now I also had grown furious—at a child. I tried to hold myself down but I couldn't. I know how to expose a throat for inspection. And I did my best. When finally I got the wooden spatula behind the last teeth and just the point of it into the mouth cavity, she opened up for an instant but before I could see anything she came down again and gripping the wooden blade between her molars she reduced it to splinters before I could get it out again.

30   Aren't you ashamed, the mother yelled at her. Aren't you ashamed to act like that in front of the doctor?

Get me a smooth-handled spoon of some sort, I told the mother. We're going through with this. The child's mouth was already bleeding. Her tongue was cut and she was screaming in wild hysterical shrieks. Perhaps I should have desisted and come back in an hour or more. No doubt it would have been better. But I have seen at least two children lying dead in bed of neglect in such cases, and feeling that I must get a diagnosis now or never I went at it again. But the worst of it was that I too had got beyond reason. I could have torn the child apart in my own fury and enjoyed it. It was a plea-sure to attack her. My face was burning with it.

The damned little brat must be protected against her own idiocy, one says to one's self at such times. Others must be protected against her. It is social necessity. And all these things are true. But a blind fury, a feeling of adult shame, bred of a longing for muscular release are the operatives. One goes on to the end.

In a final unreasoning assault I overpowered the child's neck and jaws. I forced the heavy silver spoon back of her teeth and down her throat till she gagged. And there it was—both tonsils covered with membrane. She had fought valiantly to keep me from knowing her secret. She had been hiding that sore throat for three days at least and lying to her parents in order to es-cape just such an outcome as this.

Now truly she *was* furious. She had been on the defensive before but now she attacked. Tried to get off her father's lap and fly at me while tears of defeat blinded her eyes.

### YOUR TURN

In paragraph 16, the doctor grinds his teeth "in disgust" after the mother has called him "a nice man," and in paragraph 18 he specifi-cally tells the mother not to call him a nice man. How would you char-acterize him? Keep in mind, of course, the basic situation in which he must act.

# JAMES JOYCE

*James Joyce (1882-1941) was born into a middle-class family in Dublin, Ireland. His father drank, became increasingly irresponsible and unemployable, and the family sank in the social order. Still, Joyce received a strong classical education at excellent Jesuit schools and at University College, Dublin, where he studied modern languages. In 1902, at the age of twenty, he left Ireland so that he might spend the rest of his life writing about life in Ireland. ("The shortest way to Tara," he said, "is via Holyhead," i.e., the shortest way to the heart of Ireland is to take a ship away.) In Trieste, Zurich, and Paris he sup-ported his family in a variety of ways, sometimes teaching English in a Berlitz language school. His fifteen stories, collected under the title of* Dubliners, *were written between 1904 and 1907, but he could not get them published until 1914. Next came a highly autobiographical novel,* A Portrait of the Artist as a Young Man *(1916).* Ulysses *(1922), a long and complex novel covering eigh-teen hours in Dublin, was for some years banned by the United States Post Office, though few if any readers today find it offensive. Joyce spent most of his remaining years working on* Finnegans Wake *(1939).*

*Nine years before he succeeded in getting* Dubliners *published, Joyce described the manuscript in these terms:*

*My intention was to write a chapter of the moral history of my coun-try and I chose Dublin for the scene because that city seemed to me the centre of paralysis. . . . I have written it for the most part in a style of scrupulous meanness and with the conviction that he is a very bold man who dares to alter in the presentment, still more to deform, whatever he has seen and heard.*

## *Araby*                                                      [1905]

North Richmond Street, being blind,[1] was a quiet street except at the hour when the Christian Brothers' School set the boys free. An uninhabited house of two stories stood at the blind end, detached from its neighbors in a square ground. The other houses of the street, conscious of decent lives within them, gazed at one another with brown imperturbable faces.

The former tenant of our house, a priest, had died in the back drawing-room. Air, musty from having long been enclosed, hung in all the rooms, and the waste room behind the kitchen was littered with old useless papers. Among these I found a few paper-covered books, the pages of which were curled and damp: *The Abbot,* by Walter Scott, *The Devout Communicant* and *The Memoirs of Vidocq.*[2] I liked the last best because its leaves were yellow. The wild garden behind the house contained a central apple-tree and a few straggling bushes under one of which I found the late tenant's rusty bicycle-pump. He had been a very charitable priest; in his will he had left all his money to institutions and the furniture of his house to his sister.

When the short days of winter came dusk fell before we had well eaten our dinners. When we met in the street the houses had grown somber. The space of sky above us was the color of ever-changing violet and towards it the lamps of the street lifted their feeble lanterns. The cold air stung us and we played till our bodies glowed. Our shouts echoed in the silent street. The career of our play brought us through the dark muddy lanes behind the houses where we ran the gauntlet of the rough tribes from the cottages, to the back doors of the dark dripping gardens where odors arose from the ash-pits, to the dark odorous stables where a coachman smoothed and combed the horse or shook music from the buckled harness. When we returned to the street light from the kitchen windows had filled the area. If my uncle was seen turning the corner we hid in the shadow until we had seen him safely housed. Or if Mangan's sister came out on the doorstep to call her brother in to his tea we watched her from our shadow peer up and down the street. We waited to see whether she would remain or go in and, if she remained, we left our shadow and walked up to Mangan's steps resignedly. She was waiting for us, her figure defined by the light from the half-opened door. Her brother always teased her before he obeyed and I stood by the railings looking at her. Her dress swung as she moved her body and the soft rope of her hair tossed from side to side.

Every morning I lay on the floor in the front parlor watching her door. The blind was pulled down to within an inch of the sash so that I could not be seen. When she came out on the doorstep my heart leaped. I ran to the hall, seized my books and followed her. I kept her brown figure always in my

---

[1]**blind** a dead-end street.    [2]**The Abbot** was one of Scott's popular historical romances; **The Devout Communicant** was a Catholic religious manual; **The Memoirs of Vidocq** were the memoirs of the chief of the French detective force.

eye and, when we came near the point at which our ways diverged, I quickened my pace and passed her. This happened morning after morning. I had never spoken to her, except for a few casual words, and yet her name was like a summons to all my foolish blood.

5      Her image accompanied me even in places the most hostile to romance. On Saturday evenings when my aunt went marketing I had to go to carry some of the parcels. We walked through the flaring streets, jostled by drunken men and bargaining women, amid the curses of laborers, the shrill litanies of shop-boys who stood on guard by the barrels of pigs' cheeks, the nasal chanting of street-singers, who sang a *come-all-you* about O'Donovan Rossa,[3] or a ballad about the troubles in our native land. These noises converged in a single sensation of life for me: I imagined that I bore my chalice safely through a throng of foes. Her name sprang to my lips at moments in strange prayers and praises which I myself did not understand. My eyes were often full of tears (I could not tell why) and at times a flood from my heart seemed to pour itself out into my bosom. I thought little of the future. I did not know whether I would ever speak to her or not or, if I spoke to her, how I could tell her of my confused adoration. But my body was like a harp and her words and gestures were like fingers running upon the wires.

One evening I went into the back drawing-room in which the priest had died. It was a dark rainy evening and there was no sound in the house. Through one of the broken panes I heard the rain impinge upon the earth, the fine incessant needles of water playing in the sodden beds. Some distant lamp or lighted window gleamed below me. I was thankful that I could see so little. All my senses seemed to desire to veil themselves and, feeling that I was about to slip from them, I pressed the palms of my hands together until they trembled, murmuring: *O love! O love!* many times.

At last she spoke to me. When she addressed the first words to me I was so confused that I did not know what to answer. She asked me was I going to *Araby*. I forget whether I answered yes or no. It would be a splendid bazaar, she said; she would love to go.

—And why can't you? I asked.

While she spoke she turned a silver bracelet round and round her wrist. She could not go, she said, because there would be a retreat that week in her convent. Her brother and two other boys were fighting for their caps and I was alone at the railings. She held one of the spikes, bowing her head towards me. The light from the lamp opposite our door caught the white curve of her neck, lit up her hair that rested there and, falling, lit up the hand upon the railing. It fell over one side of her dress and caught the white border of a petticoat, just visible as she stood at ease.

10      —It's well for you, she said.

—If I go, I said, I will bring you something.

What innumerable follies laid waste my waking and sleeping thoughts after that evening! I wished to annihilate the tedious intervening days. I chafed against the work of school. At night in my bedroom and by day in the

---

[3]**come-all-you about O'Donovan Rossa** A "come-all-you" was a topical song that began "Come all you gallant Irishmen." In this case, the song is about Jeremiah O'Donovan Rossa (1831–1915), a popular Irish leader in the struggle for Irish independence from England.

classroom her image came between me and the page I strove to read. The syllables of the word *Araby* were called to me through the silence in which my soul luxuriated and cast an Eastern enchantment over me. I asked for leave to go to the bazaar on Saturday night. My aunt was surprised and hoped it was not some Freemason[4] affair. I answered few questions in class. I watched my master's face pass from amiability to sternness; he hoped I was not beginning to idle. I could not call my wandering thoughts together. I had hardly any patience with the serious work of life which, now that it stood between me and my desire, seemed to me child's play, ugly monotonous child's play.

On Saturday morning I reminded my uncle that I wished to go to the bazaar in the evening. He was fussing at the hallstand, looking for the hat-brush, and answered me curtly:

—Yes, boy, I know.

15    As he was in the hall I could not go into the front parlor and lie at the window. I left the house in bad humor and walked slowly towards the school. The air was pitilessly raw and already my heart misgave me.

When I came home to dinner my uncle had not yet been home. Still it was early. I sat staring at the clock for some time and, when its ticking began to irritate me, I left the room. I mounted the staircase and gained the upper part of the house. The high cold empty gloomy rooms liberated me and I went from room to room singing. From the front window I saw my companions playing below in the street. Their cries reached me weakened and indistinct and, leaning my forehead against the cool glass, I looked over at the dark house where she lived. I may have stood there for an hour, seeing nothing but the brown-clad figure cast by my imagination, touched discreetly by the lamplight at the curved neck, at the hand upon the railings and at the border below the dress.

When I came downstairs again I found Mrs. Mercer sitting at the fire. She was an old garrulous woman, a pawnbroker's widow, who collected used stamps for some pious purpose. I had to endure the gossip of the tea-table. The meal was prolonged beyond an hour and still my uncle did not come. Mrs. Mercer stood up to go: she was sorry she couldn't wait any longer, but it was after eight o'clock and she did not like to be out late, as the night air was bad for her. When she had gone I began to walk up and down the room, clenching my fists. My aunt said:

—I'm afraid you may put off your bazaar for this night of Our Lord.

At nine o'clock I heard my uncle's latchkey in the halldoor. I heard him talking to himself and heard the hallstand rocking when it had received the weight of his overcoat. I could interpret these signs. When he was midway through his dinner I asked him to give me the money to go to the bazaar. He had forgotten.

20    —The people are in bed and after their first sleep now, he said.

I did not smile. My aunt said to him energetically:

—Can't you give him the money and let him go? You've kept him late enough as it is.

My uncle said he was very sorry he had forgotten. He said he believed in the old saying: *All work and no play makes Jack a dull boy.* He asked me

---

[4]**Freemason** A Freemason was a member of the Free and Accepted Masons, a fraternal organization viewed with suspicion by Irish Catholics.

where I was going and, when I had told him a second time he asked me did I know *The Arab's Farewell to His Steed*.[5] When I left the kitchen he was about to recite the opening lines of the piece to my aunt.

I held a florin tightly in my hand as I strode down Buckingham Street towards the station. The sight of the streets thronged with buyers and glaring with gas recalled to me the purpose of my journey. I took my seat in a third-class carriage of a deserted train. After an intolerable delay the train moved out of the station slowly. It crept onward among ruinous houses and over the twinkling river. At Westland Row Station a crowd of people pressed to the carriage doors; but the porters moved them back, saying that it was a special train for the bazaar. I remained alone in the bare carriage. In a few minutes the train drew up beside an improvised wooden platform. I passed out on to the road and saw by the lighted dial of a clock that it was ten minutes to ten. In front of me was a large building which displayed the magical name.

25    I could not find any sixpenny entrance and, fearing that the bazaar would be closed, I passed in quickly through a turnstile, handing a shilling to a weary-looking man. I found myself in a big hall girdled at half its height by a gallery. Nearly all the stalls were closed and the greater part of the hall was in darkness. I recognised a silence like that which pervades a church after a service. I walked into the center of the bazaar timidly. A few people were gathered about the stalls which were still open. Before a curtain, over which the words *Café Chantant* were written in colored lamps, two men were counting money on a salver. I listened to the fall of the coins.

Remembering with difficulty why I had come I went over to one of the stalls and examined porcelain vases and flowered tea-sets. At the door of the stall a young lady was talking and laughing with two young gentlemen. I remarked their English accents and listened vaguely to their conversation.

—O, I never said such a thing!

—O, but you did!

—O, but I didn't!

30    —Didn't she say that?

—Yes! I heard her.

—O, there's a … fib!

Observing me the young lady came over and asked me did I wish to buy anything. The tone of her voice was not encouraging; she seemed to have spoken to me out of a sense of duty. I looked humbly at the great jars that stood like eastern guards at either side of the dark entrance to the stall and murmured:

—No, thank you.

35    The young lady changed the position of one of the vases and went back to the two young men. They began to talk of the same subject. Once or twice the young lady glanced at me over her shoulder.

I lingered before her stall, though I knew my stay was useless, to make my interest in her wares seem the more real. Then I turned away slowly

---

[5]**The Arab's Farewell to His Steed** Joyce is referring to "The Arab to His Favorite Steed," a popular sentimental poem by Caroline Norton (1808–1877).

and walked down the middle of the bazaar. I allowed the two pennies to fall against the sixpence in my pocket. I heard a voice call from one end of the gallery that the light was out. The upper part of the hall was now completely dark.

Gazing up into the darkness I saw myself as a creature driven and derided by vanity; and my eyes burned with anguish and anger.

### YOUR TURN

1. *Setting* in fiction—the time and place where the story occurs, the environment in which the characters move—will be discussed in the next chapter, but here we can make the obvious point that setting often has an influence on the characters: For instance, it may shape them or they may respond to it. What does the second paragraph of "Araby" tell us about the boy's nature?
2. Reread the story, underlining or highlighting religious images. What is the point of these images?
3. If you had to summarize the *plot* briefly, what would you say? If you briefly had to describe the personality—the character—of the protagonist, what would you say?

# RAYMOND CARVER

*Raymond Carver (1938–1988) was born in Clatskanie, a logging town in Oregon. In 1963 he graduated from Humboldt State College in northern California and then did further study at the University of Iowa.*

*His early years were not easy—he married while still in college, divorced a little later, and sometimes suffered from alcoholism. In his last years he found both personal happiness and literary success, but he died of cancer at the age of fifty.*

*As a young man he wrote poetry while working at odd jobs (janitor, deliveryman, etc.); later he turned to fiction, though he continued to write poetry. Most of his fiction is of a sort called "minimalist," narrating in a spare, understated style stories about bewildered and sometimes exhausted men and women.*

## Cathedral                                                    [1983]

This blind man, an old friend of my wife's, he was on his way to spend the night. His wife had died. So he was visiting the dead wife's relatives in Connecticut. He called my wife from his in-laws'. Arrangements were made. He would come by train, a five-hour trip, and my wife would meet him at the station. She hadn't seen him since she worked for him one summer in Seattle ten years ago. But she and the blind man had kept in touch. They made tapes and mailed them back and forth. I wasn't enthusiastic about his visit. He was no one I knew. And his being blind bothered me. My idea of blindness came from the movies. In the movies, the blind moved slowly and never laughed. Sometimes they were led by seeing-eye dogs. A blind man in my house was not something I looked forward to.

That summer in Seattle she had needed a job. She didn't have any money. The man she was going to marry at the end of the summer was in officers' training school. He didn't have any money, either. But she was in love with the guy, and he was in love with her, etc. She'd seen something in the paper: HELP WANTED—*Reading to Blind Man,* and a telephone number. She phoned and went over, was hired on the spot. She'd worked with this blind man all summer. She read stuff to him, case studies, reports, that sort of thing. She helped him organize his little office in the county social-service department. They'd become good friends, my wife and the blind man. How do I know these things? She told me. And she told me something else. On her last day in the office, the blind man asked if he could touch her face. She agreed to this. She told me he touched his fingers to every part of her face, her nose—even her neck! She never forgot it. She even tried to write a poem about it. She was always trying to write a poem. She wrote a poem or two every year, usually after something really important had happened to her.

When we first started going out together, she showed me the poem. In the poem, she recalled his fingers and the way they had moved around over her face. In the poem, she talked about what she had felt at the time, about what went through her mind when the blind man touched her nose and lips. I can remember I didn't think much of the poem. Of course, I didn't tell her that. Maybe I just don't understand poetry. I admit it's not the first thing I reach for when I pick up something to read.

Anyway, this man who'd first enjoyed her favors, the officer-to-be, he'd been her childhood sweetheart. So okay. I'm saying that at the end of the summer she let the blind man run his hands over her face, said goodbye to him, married her childhood etc., who was now a commissioned officer, and she moved away from Seattle. But they'd kept in touch, she and the blind man. She made the first contact after a year or so. She called him up one night from an Air Force base in Alabama. She wanted to talk. They talked. He asked her to send a tape and tell him about her life. She did this. She sent the tape. On the tape, she told the blind man about her husband and about their life together in the military. She told the blind man she loved her husband but she didn't like it where they lived and she didn't like it that he was part of the military-industrial thing. She told the blind man she'd written a poem and he was in it. She told him that she was writing a poem about what it was like to be an Air Force officer's wife. The poem wasn't finished yet. She was still writing it. The blind man made a tape. He sent her the tape. She made a tape. This went on for years. My wife's officer was posted to one base and then another. She sent tapes from Moody AFB, McGuire, McConnell, and finally Travis, near Sacramento, where one night she got to feeling lonely and cut off from people she kept losing in that moving-around life. She got to feeling she couldn't go it another step. She went in and swallowed all the pills and capsules in the medicine chest and washed them down with a bottle of gin. Then she got into a hot bath and passed out.

5      But instead of dying, she got sick. She threw up. Her officer—why should he have a name? he was the childhood sweetheart, and what more does he want?—came home from somewhere, found her, and called the

ambulance. In time, she put it all on a tape and sent the tape to the blind man. Over the years, she put all kinds of stuff on tapes and sent the tapes off lickety-split. Next to writing a poem every year, I think it was her chief means of recreation. On one tape, she told the blind man she'd decided to live away from her officer for a time. On another tape, she told him about her divorce. She and I began going out, and of course she told her blind man about it. She told him everything, or so it seemed to me. Once she asked me if I'd like to hear the latest tape from the blind man. This was a year ago. I was on the tape, she said. So I said okay, I'd listen to it. I got us drinks and we settled down in the living room. We made ready to listen. First she inserted the tape into the player and adjusted a couple of dials. Then she pushed a lever. The tape squeaked and someone began to talk in this loud voice. She lowered the volume. After a few minutes of harmless chitchat, I heard my own name in the mouth of this stranger, this blind man I didn't even know! And then this: "From all you've said about him, I can only conclude—" But we were interrupted, a knock at the door, something, and we didn't ever get back to the tape. Maybe it was just as well. I'd heard all I wanted to.

Now this same blind man was coming to sleep in my house.

"Maybe I could take him bowling," I said to my wife. She was at the draining board doing scalloped potatoes. She put down the knife she was us-ing and turned around.

"If you love me," she said, "you can do this for me. If you don't love me, okay. But if you had a friend, any friend, and the friend came to visit, I'd make him feel comfortable." She wiped her hands with the dish towel.

"I don't have any blind friends," I said.

10    "You don't have *any* friends," she said. "Period. Besides," she said, "god-damn it, his wife's just died! Don't you understand that? The man's lost his wife!"

I didn't answer. She'd told me a little about the blind man's wife. Her name was Beulah. Beulah! That's a name for a colored woman.

"Was his wife a Negro?" I asked.

"Are you crazy?" my wife said. "Have you just flipped or something?" She picked up a potato. I saw it hit the floor, then roll under the stove. "What's wrong with you?" she said. "Are you drunk?"

"I'm just asking," I said.

15    Right then my wife filled me in with more detail than I cared to know. I made a drink and sat at the kitchen table to listen. Pieces of the story began to fall into place.

Beulah had gone to work for the blind man the summer after my wife had stopped working for him. Pretty soon Beulah and the blind man had themselves a church wedding. It was a little wedding—who'd want to go to such a wedding in the first place?—just the two of them, plus the minister and the minister's wife. But it was a church wedding just the same. It was what Beulah had wanted, he'd said. But even then Beulah must have been carrying the cancer in her glands. After they had been inseparable for eight years—my wife's word, *inseparable*—Beulah's health went into a rapid de-cline. She died in a Seattle hospital room, the blind man sitting beside the bed and holding on to her hand. They'd married, lived and worked together, slept together—had sex, sure—and then the blind man had to bury her. All this without his having ever seen what the goddamned woman looked like. It was beyond my understanding. Hearing this, I felt sorry for the blind man for a little bit. And then I found myself thinking what a pitiful life this woman must have led. Imagine a woman who could never see herself as she was seen in the eyes of her loved one. A woman who could go on day after day and never receive the smallest compliment from her beloved. A woman whose husband could never read the expression on her face, be it misery or something better. Someone who could wear makeup or not— what difference to him? She could, if she wanted, wear green eye-shadow around one eye, a straight pin in her nostril, yellow slacks, and purple shoes, no matter. And then to slip off into death, the blind man's hand on her hand, his blind eyes streaming tears—I'm imagining now—her last thought maybe this: that he never even knew what she looked like, and she on an express to the grave. Robert was left with a small insurance policy and a half of a twenty-peso Mexican coin. The other half of the coin went into the box with her. Pathetic.

So when the time rolled around, my wife went to the depot to pick him up. With nothing to do but wait—sure, I blamed him for that—I was having a drink and watching the TV when I heard the car pull into the drive. I got up from the sofa with my drink and went to the window to have a look.

I saw my wife laughing as she parked the car. I saw her get out of the car and shut the door. She was still wearing a smile. Just amazing. She went around to the other side of the car to where the blind man was already start-ing to get out. This blind man, feature this, he was wearing a full beard! A beard on a blind man! Too much, I say. The blind man reached into the back seat and dragged out a suitcase. My wife took his arm, shut the car door, and, talking all the way, moved him down the drive and then up the steps to the front porch. I turned off the TV. I finished my drink, rinsed the glass, dried my hands. Then I went to the door.

My wife said, "I want you to meet Robert. Robert, this is my husband. I've told you all about him." She was beaming. She had this blind man by his coat sleeve.

20      The blind man let go of his suitcase and up came his hand.

I took it. He squeezed hard, held my hand, and then he let it go.

"I feel like we've already met," he boomed.

"Likewise," I said. I didn't know what else to say. Then I said, "Wel-come. I've heard a lot about you." We began to move then, a little group, from the porch into the living room, my wife guiding him by the arm. The blind man was carrying his suitcase in his other hand. My wife said things like, "To your left here, Robert. That's right. Now watch it, there's a chair. That's it. Sit down right here. This is the sofa. We just bought this sofa two weeks ago."

I started to say something about the old sofa. I'd liked that old sofa. But I didn't say anything. Then I wanted to say something else, small-talk, about the scenic ride along the Hudson. How going *to* New York, you should sit on the right-hand side of the train, and coming *from* New York, the left-hand side.

25      "Did you have a good train ride?" I said. "Which side of the train did you sit on, by the way?"

"What a question, which side!" my wife said. "What's it matter which side?" she said.

"I just asked," I said.

"Right side," the blind man said. "I hadn't been on a train in nearly forty years. Not since I was a kid. With my folks. That's been a long time. I'd nearly forgotten the sensation. I have winter in my beard now," he said. "So I've been told, anyway. Do I look distinguished, my dear?" the blind man said to my wife.

"You look distinguished, Robert," she said. "Robert," she said. "Robert, it's just so good to see you."

30     My wife finally took her eyes off the blind man and looked at me. I had the feeling she didn't like what she saw. I shrugged.

I've never met, or personally known, anyone who was blind. This blind man was late forties, a heavy-set, balding man with stooped shoulders, as if he carried a great weight there. He wore brown slacks, brown shoes, a light-brown shirt, a tie, a sports coat. Spiffy. He also had this full beard. But he didn't use a cane and he didn't wear dark glasses. I'd always thought dark glasses were a must for the blind. Fact was, I wished he had a pair. At first glance, his eyes looked like anyone else's eyes. But if you looked close, there was something different about them. Too much white in the iris, for one thing, and the pupils seemed to move around in the sockets without his knowing it or being able to stop it. Creepy. As I stared at his face, I saw the left pupil turn in toward his nose while the other made an effort to keep in one place. But it was only an effort, for that eye was on the roam without his knowing it or wanting it to be.

I said, "Let me get you a drink. What's your pleasure? We have a little of everything. It's one of our pastimes."

"Bub, I'm a Scotch man myself," he said fast enough in this big voice.

"Right," I said. Bub! "Sure you are. I knew it."

35     He let his fingers touch his suitcase, which was sitting alongside the sofa. He was taking his bearings. I didn't blame him for that.

"I'll move that up to your room," my wife said.

"No, that's fine," the blind man said loudly. "It can go up when I go up."

"A little water with the Scotch?" I said.

"Very little," he said.

40     "I knew it," I said.

He said, "Just a tad. The Irish actor, Barry Fitzgerald? I'm like that fellow. When I drink water, Fitzgerald said, I drink water. When I drink whiskey, I drink whiskey." My wife laughed. The blind man brought his hand up under his beard. He lifted his beard slowly and let it drop.

I did the drinks, three big glasses of Scotch with a splash of water in each. Then we made ourselves comfortable and talked about Robert's travels. First the long flight from the West Coast to Connecticut, we covered that. Then from Connecticut up here by train. We had another drink concerning that leg of the trip.

I remembered having read somewhere that the blind didn't smoke because, as speculation had it, they couldn't see the smoke they exhaled. I thought I knew that much and that much only about blind people. But this blind man smoked his cigarette down to the nubbin and then lit another one. This blind man filled his ashtray and my wife emptied it.

When we sat down at the table for dinner, we had another drink. My wife heaped Robert's plate with cube steak, scalloped potatoes, green beans. I buttered him up two slices of bread. I said, "Here's bread and butter for you." I swallowed some of my drink. "Now let us pray," I said, and the blind man lowered his head. My wife looked at me, her mouth agape. "Pray the phone won't ring and the food doesn't get cold," I said.

45      We dug in. We ate everything there was to eat on the table. We ate like there was no tomorrow. We didn't talk. We ate. We scarfed. We grazed that table. We were into serious eating. The blind man had right away located his foods, he knew just where everything was on his plate. I watched with ad-miration as he used his knife and fork on the meat. He'd cut two pieces of meat, fork the meat into his mouth, and then go all out for the scalloped potatoes, the beans next, and then he'd tear off a hunk of buttered bread and eat that. He'd follow this up with a big drink of milk. It didn't seem to bother him to use his fingers once in a while, either.

We finished everything, including half a strawberry pie. For a few mo-ments, we sat as if stunned. Sweat beaded on our faces. Finally, we got up from the table and left the dirty plates. We didn't look back. We took ourselves into the living room and sank into our places again. Robert and my wife sat on the sofa. I took the big chair. We had us two or three more drinks while they talked about the major things that had come to pass for them in the past ten years. For the most part, I just listened. Now and then I joined in. I didn't want him to think I'd left the room, and I didn't want her to think I was feeling left out. They talked of things that had hap-pened to them—to them!—these past ten years. I waited in vain to hear my name on my wife's sweet lips: "And then my dear husband came into my life"—something like that. But I heard nothing of the sort. More talk of Robert. Robert had done a little of everything, it seemed, a regular blind jack-of-all-trades. But most recently he and his wife had had an Amway dis-tributorship, from which, I gathered, they'd earned their living, such as it was. The blind man was also a ham radio operator. He talked in his loud voice about conversations he'd had with fellow operators in Guam, in the Philippines, in Alaska, and even in Tahiti. He said he'd have a lot of friends there if he ever wanted to go visit those places. From time to time, he'd turn his blind face toward me, put his hand under his beard, ask me some-thing. How long had I been in my present position? (Three years.) Did I like my work? (I didn't.) Was I going to stay with it? (What were the op-tions?) Finally, when I thought he was beginning to run down, I got up and turned on the TV.

My wife looked at me with irritation. She was heading toward a boil. Then she looked at the blind man and said, "Robert, do you have a TV?"

The blind man said, "My dear, I have two TVs. I have a color set and a black-and-white thing, an old relic. It's funny, but if I turn the TV on, and I'm always turning it on, I turn on the color set. It's funny, don't you think?"

I didn't know what to say to that. I had absolutely nothing to say to that. No opinion. So I watched the news program and tried to listen to what the announcer was saying.

50      "This is a color TV," the blind man said. "Don't ask me how, but I can tell."

"We traded up a while ago," I said.

The blind man had another taste of his drink. He lifted his beard, sniffed it, and let it fall. He leaned forward on the sofa. He positioned his ashtray on the coffee table, then put the lighter to his cigarette. He leaned back on the sofa and crossed his legs at the ankles.

My wife covered her mouth, and then she yawned. She stretched. She said, "I think I'll go upstairs and put on my robe. I think I'll change into something else. Robert, you make yourself comfortable," she said.

"I'm comfortable," the blind man said.

55 "I want you to feel comfortable in this house," she said.

"I am comfortable," the blind man said.

After she'd left the room, he and I listened to the weather report and then to the sports roundup. By that time, she'd been gone so long I didn't know if she was going to come back. I thought she might have gone to bed. I wished she'd come back downstairs. I didn't want to be left alone with a blind man. I asked him if he wanted another drink, and he said sure. Then I asked if he wanted to smoke some dope with me. I said I'd just rolled a number. I hadn't, but I planned to do so in about two shakes.

"I'll try some with you," he said.

"Damn right," I said. "That's the stuff."

60 I got our drinks and sat down on the sofa with him. Then I rolled us two fat numbers. I lit one and passed it. I brought it to his fingers. He took it and inhaled.

"Hold it as long as you can," I said. I could tell he didn't know the first thing.

My wife came back downstairs wearing her pink robe and her pink slippers.

"What do I smell?" she said.

"We thought we'd have us some cannabis," I said.

65 My wife gave me a savage look. Then she looked at the blind man and said, "Robert, I didn't know you smoked."

He said, "I do now, my dear. There's a first time for everything. But I don't feel anything yet."

"This stuff is pretty mellow," I said. "This stuff is mild. It's dope you can reason with," I said. "It doesn't mess you up."

"Not much it doesn't, bub," he said, and laughed.

My wife sat on the sofa between the blind man and me. I passed her the number. She took it and toked and then passed it back to me. "Which way is this going?" she said. Then she said, "I shouldn't be smoking this. I can hardly keep my eyes open as it is. That dinner did me in. I shouldn't have eaten so much."

70 "It was the strawberry pie," the blind man said. "That's what did it," he said, and he laughed his big laugh. Then he shook his head.

"There's more strawberry pie," I said.

"Do you want some more, Robert?" my wife said.

"Maybe in a little while," he said.

We gave our attention to the TV. My wife yawned again. She said, "Your bed is made up when you feel like going to bed, Robert. I know you must have had a long day. When you're ready to go to bed, say so." She pulled his arm. "Robert?"

75 He came to and said, "I've had a real nice time. This beats tapes, doesn't it?"

I said, "Coming at you," and I put the number between his fingers. He inhaled, held the smoke, and then let it go. It was like he'd been doing it since he was nine years old.

"Thanks, bub," he said. "But I think this is all for me. I think I'm beginning to feel it," he said. He held the burning roach out for my wife.

"Same here," she said. "Ditto. Me, too." She took the roach and passed it
to me. "I may just sit here for a while between you two guys with my eyes
closed. But don't let me bother you, okay? Either one of you. If it bothers
you, say so. Otherwise, I may just sit here with my eyes closed until you're
ready to go to bed," she said. "Your bed's made up, Robert, when you're
ready. It's right next to our room at the top of the stairs. We'll show you up
when you're ready. You wake me up now, you guys, if I fall asleep." She said
that and then she closed her eyes and went to sleep.

The news program ended. I got up and changed the channel. I sat back
down on the sofa. I wished my wife hadn't pooped out. Her head lay across
the back of the sofa, her mouth open. She'd turned so that her robe slipped
away from her legs, exposing a juicy thigh. I reached to draw her robe back
over her, and it was then that I glanced at the blind man. What the hell! I
flipped the robe open again.

80          "You say when you want some strawberry pie," I said.

"I will," he said.

I said, "Are you tired? Do you want me to take you up to your bed? Are
you ready to hit the hay?"

"Not yet," he said. "No, I'll stay up with you, bub. If that's all right. I'll
stay up until you're ready to turn in. We haven't had a chance to talk.
Know what I mean? I feel like me and her monopolized the evening." He
lifted his beard and he let it fall. He picked up his cigarettes and his
lighter.

"That's all right," I said. Then I said, "I'm glad for the company."

85          And I guess I was. Every night I smoked dope and stayed up as long as I
could before I fell asleep. My wife and I hardly ever went to bed at the same
time. When I did go to sleep, I had these dreams. Sometimes I'd wake up
from one of them, my heart going crazy.

Something about the church and the Middle Ages was on the TV. Not
your run-of-the-mill TV fare. I wanted to watch something else. I turned to
the other channels. But there was nothing on them, either. So I turned back
to the first channel and apologized.

"Bub, it's all right," the blind man said. "It's fine with me. Whatever you
want to watch is okay. I'm always learning something. Learning never ends.
It won't hurt me to learn something tonight. I got ears," he said.

We didn't say anything for a time. He was leaning forward with his head
turned at me, his right ear aimed in the direction of the set. Very disconcert-
ing. Now and then his eyelids drooped and then they snapped open again.
Now and then he put his fingers into his beard and tugged, like he was
thinking about something he was hearing on the television.

On the screen, a group of men wearing cowls was being set upon and
tormented by men dressed in skeleton costumes and men dressed as devils.
The men dressed as devils wore devil masks, horns, and long tails. This
pageant was part of a procession. The Englishman who was narrating the
thing said it took place in Spain once a year. I tried to explain to the blind
man what was happening.

90          "Skeletons," he said. "I know about skeletons," he said, and he nodded.

The TV showed this one cathedral. Then there was a long, slow look at another one. Finally, the picture switched to the famous one in Paris, with its flying buttresses and its spires reaching up to the clouds. The camera pulled away to show the whole of the cathedral rising above the skyline.

There were times when the Englishman who was telling the thing would shut up, would simply let the camera move around the cathedrals. Or else the camera would tour the countryside, men in fields walking behind oxen. I waited as long as I could. Then I felt I had to say something. I said, "They're showing the outside of this cathedral now. Gargoyles. Little statues carved to look like monsters. Now I guess they're in Italy. Yeah, they're in Italy. There's paintings on the walls of this one church."

"Are those fresco paintings, bub?" he asked, and he sipped from his drink.

I reached for my glass. But it was empty. I tried to remember what I could remember. "You're asking me are those frescoes?" I said. "That's a good question. I don't know."

95      The camera moved to a cathedral outside Lisbon. The differences in the Portuguese cathedral compared with the French and Italian were not that great. But they were there. Mostly the interior stuff. Then something occurred to me, and I said, "Something has occurred to me. Do you have any idea what a cathedral is? What they look like, that is? Do you follow me? If somebody says cathedral to you, do you have any notion what they're talking about? Do you know the difference between that and a Baptist church, say?"

He let the smoke dribble from his mouth. "I know they took hundreds of workers fifty or a hundred years to build," he said. "I just heard the man say that, of course. I know generations of the same families worked on a cathedral. I heard him say that, too. The men who began their life's work on them, they never lived to see the completion of their work. In that wise, bub, they're no different from the rest of us, right?" He laughed. Then his eyelids drooped again. His head nodded. He seemed to be snoozing. Maybe he was imagining himself in Portugal. The TV was showing another cathedral now. This one was in Germany. The Englishman's voice droned on. "Cathedrals," the blind man said. He sat up and rolled his head back and forth. "If you want the truth, bub, that's about all I know. What I just said. What I heard him say. But maybe you could describe one to me? I wish you'd do it. I'd like that. If you want to know, I really don't have a good idea."

I stared hard at the shot of the cathedral on the TV. How could I even begin to describe it? But say my life depended on it. Say my life was being threatened by an insane guy who said I had to do it or else.

I stared some more at the cathedral before the picture flipped off into the countryside. There was no use. I turned to the blind man and said, "To begin with, they're very tall." I was looking around the room for clues. "They reach way up. Up and up. Toward the sky. They're so big, some of them, they have to have these supports. To help hold them up, so to speak. These supports are called buttresses. They remind me of viaducts, for some reason. But maybe you don't know viaducts, either? Sometimes the cathedrals have devils and such carved into the front. Sometimes lords and ladies. Don't ask me why this is," I said.

He was nodding. The whole upper part of his body seemed to be moving back and forth.

100    "I'm not doing so good, am I?" I said.

He stopped nodding and leaned forward on the edge of the sofa. As he
listened to me, he was running his fingers through his beard. I wasn't getting through to him, I could see that. But he waited for me to go on just the
same. He nodded, like he was trying to encourage me. I tried to think what
else to say. "They're really big," I said. "They're massive. They're built of
stone. Marble, too, sometimes. In those olden days, when they built cathedrals, men wanted to be close to God. In those olden days, God was an important part of everyone's life. You could tell this from their cathedral-
building. I'm sorry," I said, "but it looks like that's the best I can do for you.
I'm just no good at it."

"That's all right, bub," the blind man said. "Hey, listen. I hope you don't mind
my asking you. Can I ask you something? Let me ask you a simple question, yes
or no. I'm just curious and there's no offense. You're my host. But let me ask
if you are in any way religious? You don't mind my asking?"

I shook my head. He couldn't see that, though. A wink is the same as a
nod to a blind man. "I guess I don't believe in it. In anything. Sometimes it's
hard. You know what I'm saying?"

"Sure, I do," he said.

105    "Right," I said.

The Englishman was still holding forth. My wife sighed in her sleep. She
drew a long breath and went on with her sleeping.

"You'll have to forgive me," I said. "But I can't tell you what a cathedral
looks like. It just isn't in me to do it. I can't do any more than I've done."

The blind man sat very still, his head down, as he listened to me.

I said, "The truth is, cathedrals don't mean anything special to me.
Nothing. Cathedrals. They're something to look at on late-night TV. That's all
they are."

110    It was then that the blind man cleared his throat. He brought something
up. He took a handkerchief from his back pocket. Then he said, "I get it, bub.
It's okay. It happens. Don't worry about it," he said. "Hey, listen to me. Will
you do me a favor? I got an idea. Why don't you find us some heavy paper?
And a pen. We'll do something. We'll draw one together. Get us a pen and
some heavy paper. Go on, bub, get the stuff," he said.

So I went upstairs. My legs felt like they didn't have any strength in
them. They felt like they did after I'd done some running. In my wife's room,
I looked around. I found some ballpoints in a little basket on her table. And
then I tried to think where to look for the kind of paper he was talking
about.

Downstairs, in the kitchen, I found a shopping bag with onion skins in
the bottom of the bag. I emptied the bag and shook it. I brought it into the
living room and sat down with it near his legs. I moved some things,
smoothed the wrinkles from the bag, spread it out on the coffee table.

The blind man got down from the sofa and sat next to me on the carpet.

He ran his fingers over the paper. He went up and down the sides of the
paper. The edges, even the edges. He fingered the corners.

115    "All right," he said. "All right, let's do her."

He found my hand, the hand with the pen. He closed his hand over my
hand. "Go ahead, bub, draw," he said. "Draw. You'll see. I'll follow along with

you. It'll be okay. Just begin now like I'm telling you. You'll see. Draw," the blind man said.

So I began. First I drew a box that looked like a house. It could have been the house I lived in. Then I put a roof on it. At either end of the roof, I drew spires. Crazy.

"Swell," he said. "Terrific. You're doing fine," he said. "Never thought anything like this could happen in your lifetime, did you, bub? Well, it's a strange life, we all know that. Go on now. Keep it up."

I put in windows with arches. I drew flying buttresses. I hung great doors. I couldn't stop. The TV station went off the air. I put down the pen and closed and opened my fingers. The blind man felt around over the paper. He moved the tips of his fingers over the paper, all over what I had drawn, and he nodded.

120    "Doing fine," the blind man said.

I took up the pen again, and he found my hand. I kept at it. I'm no artist. But I kept drawing just the same.

My wife opened up her eyes and gazed at us. She sat up on the sofa, her robe hanging open. She said, "What are you doing? Tell me, I want to know."

I didn't answer her.

The blind man said, "We're drawing a cathedral. Me and him are working on it. Press hard," he said to me. "That's right. That's good," he said. "Sure. You got it, bub, I can tell. You didn't think you could. But you can, can't you? You're cooking with gas now. You know what I'm saying? We're going to really have us something here in a minute. How's the old arm?" he said. "Put some people in there now. What's a cathedral without people?"

125    My wife said, "What's going on? Robert, what are you doing? What's going on?"

"It's all right," he said to her. "Close your eyes now," the blind man said to me.

I did it. I closed them just like he said.

"Are they closed?" he said. "Don't fudge."

"They're closed," I said.

130    "Keep them that way," he said. He said, "Don't stop now. Draw."

So we kept on with it. His fingers rode my fingers as my hand went over the paper. It was like nothing else in my life up to now.

Then he said, "I think that's it. I think you got it," he said. "Take a look. What do you think?"

But I had my eyes closed. I thought I'd keep them that way for a little longer. I thought it was something I ought to do.

"Well?" he said. "Are you looking?"

135    My eyes were still closed. I was in my house. I knew that. But I didn't feel like I was inside anything.

"It's really something," I said.

---

**YOUR TURN**

1. What was your impression of the narrator after reading the first five paragraphs?
2. Why does the narrator feel threatened by the blind man? Has he any reason to feel threatened?

3. What attitude does the narrator reveal in the following passage:

> She'd turned so that her robe had slipped away from her legs, exposing a juicy thigh. I reached to draw her robe back over her, and it was then that I glanced at the blind man. What the hell! I flipped the robe open again.

4. Why does the narrator not open his eyes at the end of the story?
5. The television program happens to be about cathedrals, but if the point is to get the narrator to draw something while the blind man's hand rests on the narrator's, the program could have been about some other topic, for example, about skyscrapers or about the Statue of Liberty. Do you think that a cathedral is a better choice, for Carver's purposes, than these other subjects? Why?
6. In what ways does Carver prepare us for the narrator's final state of mind?

CHAPTER

# 8

# Setting

Aesop's fable of the vixen and the lioness (page 129) could take place anywhere—
in a jungle or at the town dump. The particular place is of no importance; all that
matters is the meeting of the two beasts. But in some stories the setting—the
place and the time—plays so large a role that it is almost a character. Indeed,
some writers have said that their ideas for stories came from particular settings,
particular places, and particular times. Note that the setting consists not only
of the locale—for instance, Texas—but also the time—for instance, during the
Great Depression. If we take a moment or two to brainstorm examples—this is a
favorite exercise in creative writing courses—each of us can begin to imagine all
sorts of interesting settings for stories: a working-class neighborhood in a city in
the Midwest in the 1950s; a small town in Jamaica at the turn of the century; a
village in the English countryside two hundred years ago; a town on the Texas-
Mexico border in the year 2010. The settings for novels and stories are innumerable, emerging from the experiences and memories of authors, or from the curious imaginations of authors who look forward to exploring times and places
unlike any they have known themselves.

Authors of short stories usually keep the focus on a single setting—they do
not have the space to do much more than that. But not always: The action may
shift from one setting to another, as the authors use this second setting in counterpoint to the first. They might begin in one time and place, but end up in a
time and place that are significantly different.

Through the careful use of details in the setting or settings, the author also
implies the historical and political contexts, the customs and conventions and
values of the community, and the dominant issues and conflicts of the society as
a whole. Novelists, working on a bigger canvas, can do even more, but it is an ambition, a goal, for authors of short stories too. The setting is there for the character and the plot, but the character and plot are there for the setting as well—for
giving us knowledge about and insight into specific times and places, thereby enriching and deepening our human understanding. We move outside our own experience, perceiving the diverse and complex ways of life that people have lived
or are living now.

The setting may strike us as real and recognizable. On the other hand, it may
not: We may find ourselves in the midst of a time and a place far distant and different from any with which we are familiar. It may feel to us strange, exotic, alien,
even otherworldly, as we know from the settings of ghost stories and works of
science fiction—and in the settings for much popular fiction, such as the Middle

Earth where J. R. R. Tolkien locates *The Lord of the Rings* trilogy. Again, what we have known and experienced is extended and complicated: We travel to new and unusual times and strange (sometimes very strange) places. We see ourselves from a new perspective.

In this chapter, we present three short stories, Nathaniel Hawthorne's "Young Goodman Brown," which is set in Puritan New England; Charlotte Perkins Gilman's "The Yellow Wallpaper," which is set in a country estate in the late nineteenth century, where a woman is undergoing treatment for depression; and Ralph's Ellison's "Battle Royal," which is set in a rural area somewhere in the segregated American South in the late 1920s. Here are questions to keep in mind about the settings for these stories and for others in this book that you will be reading and studying:

1. What is the setting when the story begins?
2. Does the action remain in this setting throughout, or does the author move from one setting to another or others? How are these settings similar to and different from one another?
3. What does the author show us in action and tell us in description about the setting?
4. How much detail about the setting does the author give us? What kinds of details does the author draw our attention to?
5. Does the setting take on a special significance as the story progresses, per-haps becoming symbolic in its own right? Consider, for example, how an author might present New York City or London or some other great urban center—as a place of excitement, opportunity, and freedom, or as a place of anonymity, loneliness, and widespread poverty and degradation.
6. How is the main character affected, shaped, or influenced by the setting? Does the main character, in turn, cause the setting—his or her time and place—to change in any way?

# NATHANIEL HAWTHORNE

*Nathaniel Hawthorne (1804–1864) was born in Salem, Massachusetts, the son of a sea captain. Two of his ancestors were judges; one had persecuted Quakers, and another had served at the Salem witch trials. In his stories and novels Hawthorne keeps returning to the Puritan past, studying guilt, sin, and isolation.*

## Young Goodman Brown
[1835]

Young Goodman[1] Brown came forth, at sunset, into the street at Salem village; but put his head back, after crossing the threshold, to exchange a parting kiss with his young wife. And Faith, as the wife was aptly named, thrust her own pretty head into the street, letting the wind play with the pink ribbons of her cap while she called to Goodman Brown.

"Dearest heart," whispered she, softly and rather sadly, when her lips were close to his ear, "prithee put off your journey until sunrise and sleep in

---

[1]**Goodman** polite term of address for a man of humble standing.

your own bed to-night. A lone woman is troubled with such dreams and such thoughts that she's afeared of herself sometimes. Pray tarry with me this night, dear husband, of all nights in the year."

"My love and my Faith," replied young Goodman Brown, "of all nights in the year, this one night must I tarry away from thee. My journey, as thou callest it, forth and back again, must needs be done 'twixt now and sunrise. What, my sweet, pretty wife, dost thou doubt me already, and we but three months married?"

"Then God bless you!" said Faith, with the pink ribbons; "and may you find all well when you come back."

5    "Amen!" cried Goodman Brown. "Say thy prayers, dear Faith, and go to bed at dusk, and no harm will come to thee."

So they parted; and the young man pursued his way until, being about to turn the corner by the meeting-house, he looked back and saw the head of Faith still peeping after him with a melancholy air, in spite of her pink ribbons.

"Poor little Faith!" thought he, for his heart smote him. "What a wretch am I to leave her on such an errand! She talks of dreams, too. Methought as she spoke there was trouble in her face, as if a dream had warned her what work is to be done to-night. But no, no; 'twould kill her to think it. Well, she's a blessed angel on earth; and after this one night, I'll cling to her skirts and follow her to heaven."

With this excellent resolve for the future, Goodman Brown felt himself justified in making more haste on his present evil purpose. He had taken a dreary road, darkened by all the gloomiest trees of the forest, which barely stood aside to let the narrow path creep through, and closed immediately behind. It was all as lonely as could be; and there is this peculiarity in such a solitude, that the traveler knows not who may be concealed by the innumerable trunks and the thick boughs overhead; so that with lonely footsteps he may yet be passing through an unseen multitude.

"There may be a devilish Indian behind every tree," said Goodman Brown, to himself and he glanced fearfully behind him as he added, "What if the devil himself should be at my very elbow!"

10    His head being turned back, he passed a crook of the road, and, looking forward again, beheld the figure of a man, in grave and decent attire, seated at the foot of an old tree. He arose at Goodman Brown's approach and walked onward side by side with him.

"You are late, Goodman Brown," said he. "The clock of the Old South was striking as I came through Boston, and that is full fifteen minutes agone."

"Faith kept me back a while," replied the young man, with a tremor in his voice, caused by the sudden appearance of his companion, though not wholly unexpected.

It was now deep dusk in the forest, and deepest in that part of it where these two were journeying. As nearly as could be discerned, the second traveler was about fifty years old, apparently in the same rank of life as Goodman Brown, and bearing a considerable resemblance to him, though perhaps more in expression than features. Still they might have been taken for father and son. And yet, though the elder person was as simply clad as the younger, and as simple in manner too, he had an indescribable air of one who knew the world, and who would not have felt abashed at the governor's dinner table or in King William's court, were it possible that his affairs should call

him thither. But the only thing about him that could be fixed upon as remarkable was his staff, which bore the likeness of a great black snake, so curiously wrought that it might almost be seen to twist and wriggle itself like a
living serpent. This, of course, must have been an ocular deception, assisted
by the uncertain light.

"Come, Goodman Brown," cried his fellow-traveler, "this is a dull pace
for the beginning of a journey. Take my staff, if you are so soon weary."

15      "Friend," said the other, exchanging his slow pace for a full stop, "having
kept covenant by meeting thee here, it is my purpose now to return whence
I came. I have scruples touching the matter thou wot'st[2] of."

"Sayest thou so?" replied he of the serpent, smiling apart. "Let us walk
on, nevertheless, reasoning as we go; and if I convince thee not thou shalt
turn back. We are but a little way in the forest yet."

"Too far! too far!" exclaimed the goodman, unconsciously resuming his
walk. "My father never went into the woods on such an errand, nor his father before him. We have been a race of honest men and good Christians
since the days of the martyrs; and shall I be the first of the name of Brown
that ever took this path and kept—"

"Such company, thou wouldst say," observed the elder person, interpreting his pause. "Well said, Goodman Brown! I have been as well acquainted
with your family as with ever a one among the Puritans; and that's no trifle
to say. I helped your grandfather, the constable, when he lashed the Quaker
woman so smartly through the streets of Salem; and it was I that brought
your father a pitch-pine knot, kindled at my own hearth, to set fire to an
Indian village, in King Philip's war.[3] They were my good friends, both; and
many a pleasant walk have we had along this path, and returned merrily
after midnight. I would fain be friends with you for their sake."

"If it be as thou sayest," replied Goodman Brown, "I marvel they never
spoke of these matters; or, verily, I marvel not, seeing that the least rumor of
the sort would have driven them from New England. We are a people of
prayer, and good works to boot, and abide no such wickedness."

20      "Wickedness or not," said the traveler with the twisted staff, "I have a
very general acquaintance here in New England. The deacons of many a
church have drunk the communion wine with me; the selectmen of divers
towns make me their chairman; and a majority of the Great and General
Court are firm supporters of my interest. The governor and I, too—But these
are state secrets."

"Can this be so?" cried Goodman Brown, with a stare of amazement at
his undisturbed companion. "Howbeit, I have nothing to do with the governor and council; they have their own ways, and are no rule for a simple husbandman[4] like me. But, were I to go on with thee, how should I meet the eye
of that good old man, our minister, at Salem village? Oh, his voice would
make me tremble both Sabbath day and lecture day."

Thus far the elder traveler had listened with due gravity; but now burst
into a fit of irrepressible mirth, shaking himself so violently that his snake-
like staff actually seemed to wriggle in sympathy.

---

[2]**wot'st** knowest.   [3]**King Philip's war** war waged in 1675–76 by the English colonists
against the Wampanoag Indian leader Metcom, known as "King Philip."   [4]**husbandman**
farmer, or, more generally, any man of humble standing.

"Ha! ha! ha!" shouted he again and again; then composing himself, "Well, go on, Goodman Brown, go on; but, prithee, don't kill me with laughing."

"Well, then, to end the matter at once," said Goodman Brown, considerably nettled, "there is my wife, Faith. It would break her dear little heart; and I'd rather break my own."

25 "Nay, if that be the case," answered the other, "e'en go thy ways, Goodman Brown. I would not for twenty old women like the one hobbling before us that Faith should come to any harm."

As he spoke he pointed his staff at a female figure on the path, in whom Goodman Brown recognized a very pious and exemplary dame, who had taught him his catechism in youth, and was still his moral and spiritual adviser, jointly with the minister and Deacon Gookin.

"A marvel, truly, that Goody[5] Cloyse should be so far in the wilderness at nightfall," said he. "But with your leave, friend, I shall take a cut through the woods until we have left this Christian woman behind. Being a stranger to you, she might ask whom I was consorting with and whither I was going."

"Be it so," said his fellow-traveler. "Betake you the woods, and let me keep the path."

Accordingly the young man turned aside, but took care to watch his companion, who advanced softly along the road until he had come within a staff's length of the old dame. She, meanwhile, was making the best of her way, with singular speed for so aged a woman, and mumbling some indistinct words—a prayer, doubtless—as she went. The traveler put forth his staff and touched her withered neck with what seemed the serpent's tail.

30 "The devil!" screamed the pious old lady.

"Then Goody Cloyse knows her old friend?" observed the traveler, confronting her and leaning on his writhing stick.

"Ah, forsooth, and is it your worship indeed?" cried the good dame. "Yea, truly is it, and in the very image of my old gossip, Goodman Brown, the grandfather of the silly fellow that now is. But—would your worship believe it?—my broomstick hath strangely disappeared, stolen, as I suspect, by that unhanged witch, Goody Cory, and that, too, when I was all anointed with the juice of smallage and cinquefoil, and wolf's bane—"

"Mingled with fine wheat and the fat of a new-born babe," said the shape of old Goodman Brown.

"Ah, your worship knows the recipe," cried the old lady, cackling aloud. "So, as I was saying, being all ready for the meeting, and no horse to ride on, I made up my mind to foot it; for they tell me there is a nice young man to be taken into communion to-night. But now your good worship will lend me your arm, and we shall be there in a twinkling."

35 "That can hardly be," answered her friend. "I may not spare you my arm, Goody Cloyse; but here is my staff, if you will."

So saying, he threw it down at her feet, where, perhaps, it assumed life, being one of the rods which its owner had formerly lent to the Egyptian magi. Of this fact, however, Goodman Brown could not take cognizance. He had cast up his eyes in astonishment, and, looking down again, beheld neither Goody

---

[5]**Goody** contraction of Goodwife, a polite term of address for a married woman of humble standing.

Cloyse nor the serpentine staff but his fellow-traveler alone, who waited for him as calmly as if nothing had happened.

"That old woman taught me my catechism," said the young man; and there was a world of meaning in this simple comment.

They continued to walk onward, while the elder traveler exhorted his companion to make good speed and persevere in the path, discoursing so aptly that his arguments seemed rather to spring up in the bosom of his auditor than to be suggested by himself. As they went, he plucked a branch of maple to serve for a walking stick, and began to strip it of the twigs and little boughs, which were wet with evening dew. The moment his fingers touched them they became strangely withered and dried up as with a week's sunshine. Thus the pair proceeded, at a good free pace, until suddenly, in a gloomy hollow of the road, Goodman Brown sat himself down on the stump of a tree and refused to go any farther.

"Friend," said he, stubbornly, "my mind is made up. Not another step will I budge on this errand. What if a wretched old woman do choose to go to the devil when I thought she was going to heaven: is that any reason why I should quit my dear Faith and go after her?"

40      "You will think better of this by and by," said his acquaintance, composedly. "Sit here and rest yourself a while; and when you feel like moving again, there is my staff to help you along."

Without more words, he threw his companion the maple stick, and was as speedily out of sight as if he had vanished into the deepening gloom. The young man sat a few moments by the roadside, applauding himself greatly, and thinking with how clear a conscience he should meet the minister in his morning walk, nor shrink from the eye of good old Deacon Gookin. And what calm sleep would be his that very night, which was to have been spent so wickedly, but so purely and sweetly now, in the arms of Faith! Amidst these pleasant and praiseworthy meditations, Goodman Brown heard the tramp of horses along the road, and deemed it advisable to conceal himself within the verge of the forest, conscious of the guilty purpose that had brought him thither, though now so happily turned from it.

On came the hoof-tramps and the voices of the riders, two grave old voices, conversing soberly as they drew near. These mingled sounds appeared to pass along the road, within a few yards of the young man's hiding-place; but, owing doubtless to the depth of the gloom at that particular spot, neither the travelers nor their steeds were visible. Though their figures brushed the small boughs by the wayside, it could not be seen that they intercepted, even for a moment, the faint gleam from the strip of bright sky athwart which they must have passed. Goodman Brown alternately crouched and stood on tiptoe, pulling aside the branches and thrusting forth his head as far as he durst without discerning so much as a shadow. It vexed him the more, because he could have sworn, were such a thing possible, that he recognized the voices of the minister and Deacon Gookin, jogging along quietly, as they were wont to do, when bound to some ordination or ecclesiastical council. While yet within hearing, one of the riders stopped to pluck a switch.

"Of the two, reverend sir," said the voice like the deacon's, "I had rather miss an ordination dinner than to-night's meeting. They tell me that some of our community are to be here from Falmouth and beyond, and others from Connecticut and Rhode Island, besides several of the Indian powwows, who, after their fashion, know almost as much deviltry as the best of us. Moreover, there is a goodly young woman to be taken into communion."

"Mighty well, Deacon Gookin!" replied the solemn old tones of the minister. "Spur up, or we shall be late. Nothing can be done, you know, until I get on the ground."

45  The hoofs clattered again; and the voices, talking so strangely in the empty air, passed on through the forest, where no church had ever been gathered or solitary Christian prayed. Whither, then, could these holy men be journeying so deep into the heathen wilderness? Young Goodman Brown caught hold of a tree for support, being ready to sink down on the ground, faint and overburdened with the heavy sickness of his heart. He looked up to the sky, doubting whether there really was a heaven above him. Yet there was the blue arch, and the stars brightening in it.

"With heaven above and Faith below, I will yet stand firm against the devil!" cried Goodman Brown.

While he still gazed upward into the deep arch of the firmament and had lifted his hands to pray, a cloud, though no wind was stirring, hurried across the zenith and hid the brightening stars. The blue sky was still visible, except directly overhead, where this black mass of cloud was sweeping swiftly northward. Aloft in the air, as if from the depths of the cloud, came a confused and doubtful sound of voices. Once the listener fancied that he could distinguish the accents of towns-people of his own, men and women, both pious and ungodly, many of whom he had met at the communion table, and had seen others rioting at the tavern. The next moment, so indistinct were the sounds, he doubted whether he had heard aught but the murmur of the old forest, whispering without a wind. Then came a stronger swell of those familiar tones, heard daily in the sunshine at Salem village, but never until now from a cloud of night. There was one voice, of a young woman, uttering lamentations, yet with an uncertain sorrow, and entreating for some favor, which, perhaps, it would grieve her to obtain; and all the unseen multitude, both saints and sinners, seemed to encourage her onward.

"Faith!" shouted Goodman Brown, in a voice of agony and desperation; and the echoes of the forest mocked him, crying, "Faith! Faith!" as if bewildered wretches were seeking her all through the wilderness.

The cry of grief, rage, and terror was yet piercing the night, when the unhappy husband held his breath for a response. There was a scream, drowned immediately in a louder murmur of voices, fading into far-off laughter, as the dark cloud swept away, leaving the clear and silent sky above Goodman Brown. But something fluttered lightly down through the air and caught on the branch of a tree. The young man seized it, and beheld a pink ribbon.

50  "My Faith is gone!" cried he, after one stupefied moment. "There is no good on earth; and sin is but a name. Come, devil; for to thee is this world given."

And, maddened with despair, so that he laughed loud and long, did Goodman Brown grasp his staff and set forth again, at such a rate that he seemed to fly along the forest path rather than to walk or run. The road grew wilder and drearier and more faintly traced, and vanished at length, leaving him in the heart of the dark wilderness, still rushing onward with the instinct that guides mortal man to evil. The whole forest was peopled with frightful sounds—the creaking of the trees, the howling of wild beasts, and the yell of Indians; while sometimes the wind tolled like a distant church bell, and sometimes gave a broad roar around the traveler, as if all Nature were laughing him to scorn. But he was himself the chief horror of the scene, and shrank not from its other horrors.

"Ha! ha! ha!" roared Goodman Brown when the wind laughed at him. "Let us hear which will laugh loudest. Think not to frighten me with your deviltry. Come witch, come lizard, come Indian powwow, come devil himself, and here comes Goodman Brown. You may as well fear him as he fear you!"

In truth, all through the haunted forest there could be nothing more frightful than the figure of Goodman Brown. On he flew among the black pines, brandishing his staff with frenzied gestures, now giving vent to an inspiration of horrid blasphemy, and now shouting forth such laughter as set all the echoes of the forest laughing like demons around him. The fiend in his own shape is less hideous than when he rages in the breast of man. Thus sped the demoniac on his course, until, quivering among the trees, he saw a red light before him, as when the felled trunks and branches of a clearing have been set on fire, and throw up their lurid blaze against the sky, at the hour of midnight. He paused, in a lull of the tempest that had driven him onward, and heard the swell of what seemed a hymn, rolling solemnly from a distance with the weight of many voices. He knew the tune; it was a familiar one in the choir of the village meeting-house. The verse died heavily away, and was lengthened by a chorus, not of human voices, but of all the sounds of the benighted wilderness pealing in awful harmony together. Goodman Brown cried out; and his cry was lost to his own ear by its unison with the cry of the desert.

In the interval of silence he stole forward until the light glared full upon his eyes. At one extremity of an open space, hemmed in by the dark wall of the forest, arose a rock, bearing some rude, natural resemblance either to an altar or a pulpit, and surrounded by four blazing pines, their tops aflame, their stems untouched, like candles at an evening meeting. The mass of foliage that had overgrown the summit of the rock was all on fire, blazing high into the night and fitfully illuminating the whole field. Each pendent twig and leafy festoon was in a blaze. As the red light arose and fell, a numerous congregation alternately shone forth, then disappeared in shadow, and again grew, as it were, out of the darkness, peopling the heart of the solitary woods at once.

55    "A grave and dark-clad company," quoth Goodman Brown.

In truth they were such. Among them, quivering to-and-fro between gloom and splendor, appeared faces that would be seen next day at the council board of the province, and others which, Sabbath after Sabbath, looked devoutly heavenward, and benignantly over the crowded pews, from the holiest pulpits in the land. Some affirm that the lady of the governor was there. At least three were high dames well known to her, and wives of honored husbands, and widows, a great multitude, and ancient maidens, all of excellent repute, and fair young girls, who trembled lest their mothers should espy them. Either the sudden gleams of light flashing over the obscure field bedazzled Goodman Brown, or he recognized a score of the church-members of Salem village famous for their especial sanctity. Good old Deacon Gookin had arrived, and waited at the skirts of that venerable saint, his revered pastor. But, irreverently consorting with these grave, reputable, and pious people, these elders of the church, these chaste dames and dewy virgins, there were men of dissolute lives and women of spotted fame, wretches given over to all mean and filthy vice, and suspected even of horrid crimes. It was strange to see that the good shrank not from the wicked, nor were the sinners abashed by the saints. Scattered also among their pale-faced enemies were the Indian priests, or powwows, who had often scared their native forest with more hideous incantations than any known to English witchcraft.

"But, where is Faith?" thought Goodman Brown; and, as hope came into his heart, he trembled.

Another verse of the hymn arose, a slow and mournful strain, such as the pious love, but joined to words which expressed all that our nature can conceive of sin, and darkly hinted at far more. Unfathomable to mere mortals is the lore of fiends. Verse after verse was sung; and still the chorus of the desert swelled between, like the deepest tone of a mighty organ; and with the final peal of that dreadful anthem there came a sound, as if the roaring wind, the rushing streams, the howling beasts, and every other voice of the unconcerted wilderness were mingling and according with the voice of guilty man in homage to the prince of all. The four blazing pines threw up a loftier flame, and obscurely discovered shapes and visages of horror on the smoke wreaths above the impious assembly. At the same moment the fire on the rock shot redly forth and formed a glowing arch above its base, where now appeared a figure. With reverence be it spoken, the figure bore no slight similitude, both in garb and manner, to some grave divine of the New England churches.

"Bring forth the converts!" cried a voice that echoed through the field and rolled into the forest.

60 At the word, Goodman Brown stepped forth from the shadow of the trees and approached the congregation, with whom he felt a loathful brotherhood by the sympathy of all that was wicked in his heart. He could have wellnigh sworn that the shape of his own dead father beckoned him to advance, looking downward from a smoke wreath, while a woman, with dim features of despair, threw out her hand to warn him back. Was it his mother? But he had no power to retreat one step, nor to resist, even in thought, when the minister and good old Deacon Gookin seized his arms and led him to the blazing rock. Thither came also the slender form of a veiled female, led between Goody Cloyse, that pious teacher of the catechism, and Martha Carrier, who had received the devil's promise to be queen of hell. A rampant hag was she. And there stood the proselytes beneath the canopy of fire.

"Welcome, my children," said the dark figure, "to the communion of your race. Ye have found thus young your nature and your destiny. My children, look behind you!"

They turned; and flashing forth, as it were, in a sheet of flame, the fiend worshippers were seen; the smile of welcome gleamed darkly on every visage.

"There," resumed the sable form, "are all whom ye have reverenced from youth. Ye deemed them holier than yourselves, and shrank from your own sin, contrasting it with their lives of righteousness and prayerful aspirations heavenward. Yet here are they all in my worshipping assembly. This night it shall be granted you to know their secret deeds: how hoary-bearded elders of the church have whispered wanton words to the young maids of their households; how many a woman, eager for widows' weeds, has given her husband a drink at bedtime and let him sleep his last sleep in her bosom; how beardless youths have made haste to inherit their fathers' wealth; and how fair damsels—blush not, sweet ones—have dug little graves in the garden, and bidden me, the sole guest, to an infant's funeral. By the sympathy of your human hearts for sin ye shall scent out all the places—whether in church, bedchamber, street, field, or forest—where crime has been committed, and shall exult to behold the whole earth one stain of guilt, one mighty blood spot. Far more than this. It shall be yours to penetrate, in every bosom, the deep mystery of sin, the fountain of all wicked arts, and which inexhaustibly supplies more evil impulses than human power—than my power at its utmost—can make manifest in deeds. And now, my children, look upon each other."

They did so; and, by the blaze of the hell-kindled torches, the wretched man beheld his Faith, and the wife her husband, trembling before that unhallowed altar.

65    "Lo, there ye stand, my children," said the figure, in a deep and solemn tone, almost sad with its despairing awfulness, as if his once angelic nature could yet mourn for our miserable race. "Depending upon one another's hearts, ye had still hoped that virtue were not all a dream. Now are ye undeceived. Evil is the nature of mankind. Evil must be your only happiness. Welcome, again, my children, to the communion of your race."

"Welcome," repeated the fiend worshippers, in one cry of despair and triumph.

And there they stood, the only pair, as it seemed, who were yet hesitating on the verge of wickedness in this dark world. A basin was hollowed, naturally, in the rock. Did it contain water, reddened by the lurid light? or was it blood? or, perchance, a liquid flame? Herein did the shape of evil dip his hand and prepare to lay the mark of baptism upon their foreheads, that they might be partakers of the mystery of sin, more conscious of the secret guilt of others, both in deed and thought, than they could now be of their own. The husband cast one look at his pale wife, and Faith at him. What polluted wretches would the next glance show them to each other, shuddering alike at what they disclosed and what they saw!

"Faith! Faith!" cried the husband, "look up to heaven, and resist the wicked one."

Whether Faith obeyed he knew not. Hardly had he spoken when he found himself amid calm night and solitude, listening to a roar of the wind which died heavily away through the forest. He staggered against the rock, and felt it chill and damp; while a hanging twig, that had been all on fire, besprinkled his cheek with the coldest dew.

70    The next morning young Goodman Brown came slowly into the street of Salem village, staring around him like a bewildered man. The good old minister was taking a walk along the graveyard to get an appetite for breakfast and meditate his sermon, and bestowed a blessing, as he passed, on Goodman Brown. He shrank from the venerable saint as if to avoid an anathema. Old Deacon Gookin was at domestic worship, and the holy words of his prayer were heard through the open window. "What God doth the wizard pray to?" quoth Goodman Brown. Goody Cloyse, that excellent old Christian, stood in the early sunshine at her own lattice, catechizing a little girl who had brought her a pint of morning's milk. Goodman Brown snatched away the child as from the grasp of the fiend himself. Turning the corner by the

meeting-house, he spied the head of Faith, with the pink ribbons, gazing anxiously forth, and bursting into such joy at sight of him that she skipped along the street and almost kissed her husband before the whole village. But Goodman Brown looked sternly and sadly into her face, and passed on without a greeting.

Had Goodman Brown fallen asleep in the forest and only dreamed a wild dream of a witch-meeting?

Be it so, if you will; but alas! it was a dream of evil omen for young Goodman Brown. A stern, a sad, a darkly meditative, a distrustful, if not a desperate man did he become from the night of that fearful dream. On the Sabbath day, when the congregation were singing a holy psalm, he could not listen because an anthem of sin rushed loudly upon his ear and drowned all the blessed strain. When the minister spoke from the pulpit with power and fervid eloquence, and, with his hand on the open Bible, of the sacred truths of our religion, and of saint-like lives and triumphant deaths, and of future bliss or misery unutterable, then did Goodman Brown turn pale, dreading lest the roof should thunder down upon the gray blasphemer and his hearers. Often, awaking suddenly at midnight, he shrank from the bosom of Faith; and at morning or eventide, when the family knelt down at prayer, he scowled and muttered to himself, and gazed sternly at his wife, and turned away. And when he had lived long, and was borne to his grave a hoary[6] corpse, followed by Faith, an aged woman, and children and grandchildren, a goodly procession, besides neighbors not a few, they carved no hopeful verse upon his tombstone, for his dying hour was gloom.

## YOUR TURN

1. Do you take Faith to stand only for religious faith, or can she here also stand for one's faith in one's fellow human beings? Explain.
2. Hawthorne describes the second traveler as "about fifty years old, apparently in the same rank as Goodman Brown, and bearing a considerable resemblance to him." Further, "they might have been taken for father and son." What do you think Hawthorne is getting at here?
3. In the forest Brown sees (or thinks he sees) Goody Cloyse, the minister, Deacon Gookin, and others. Does he in fact meet them, or does he dream of them? Or does he encounter "figures" and "forms" (rather than real people) whom the devil conjures up in order to deceive Brown?
4. Evaluate the view that when Brown enters the dark forest he is really entering his own evil mind.
5. A Hawthorne scholar we know says that he finds this story "terrifying." Do you agree? Or would you characterize your response to it differently? Explain, making reference to passages in the text.
6. Does a person have to be a Christian in order to understand "Young Goodman Brown"? Would a Christian reader find this story reassuring or disturbing? Can a non-Christian reader understand and appreciate the story? What might he or she learn from reading it?
7. Having read and studied "Young Goodman Brown," do you find you want to read more of Hawthorne's stories? Are you very eager, a little eager, or not really? Please explain.

---

[6]**hoary** gray or white with age; very old, ancient.

8. "Young Goodman Brown" is often included in anthologies of American literature and in collections of short stories. In your view, why is this the case? Do you agree with this decision, or does it puzzle you?

# CHARLOTTE PERKINS GILMAN

*Charlotte Perkins Gilman (1860-1935), née Charlotte Perkins, was born in Hartford, Connecticut. Her father deserted the family soon after Charlotte's birth; she was brought up by her mother, who found it difficult to make ends meet. For a while Charlotte worked as an artist and teacher of art, and in 1884, when she was twenty-four, she married an artist. In 1885 she had a daughter, but soon after the birth of the girl Charlotte had a nervous breakdown. At her husband's urging she spent a month in the sanitarium of Dr. S. Weir Mitchell, a physician who specialized in treating women with nervous disorders. (Mitchell is specifically named in "The Yellow Wallpaper.") Because the treatment—isolation and total rest—nearly drove her to insanity, she fled Mitchell and her husband. In California she began a career as a lecturer and writer on feminist topics. (She also supported herself by teaching school and by keeping a boarding-house.) Among her books are* Women and Economics *(1899) and* The Man-Made World *(1911), which were revived by the feminist movement in the 1960s and 1970s. In 1900 she married a cousin, George Gilman. From all available evidence, the marriage was successful. Certainly it did not restrict her activities as a feminist. In 1935, suffering from inoperable cancer, she took her own life.*

*"The Yellow Wallpaper," written in 1892—that is, written after she had been treated by S. Weir Mitchell for her nervous breakdown—was at first interpreted either as a ghost story or as a Poe-like study of insanity. Only in recent years has it been seen as a feminist story. One might ask oneself if these interpretations are mutually exclusive.*

## *The Yellow Wallpaper*                                    [1892]

It is very seldom that mere ordinary people like John and myself secure ancestral halls for the summer.

A colonial mansion, a hereditary estate. I would say a haunted house, and reach the height of romantic felicity—but that would be asking too much of fate!

Still I will proudly declare that there is something queer about it.

Else, why should it be let so cheaply? And why have stood so long untenanted?

5      John laughs at me, of course, but one expects that in marriage.

John is practical in the extreme. He has no patience with faith, an intense horror of superstition, and he scoffs openly at any talk of things not to be felt and seen and put down in figures.

John is a physician, and *perhaps*—(I would not say it to a living soul, of course, but this is dead paper and a great relief to my mind)—*perhaps* that is one reason I do not get well faster.

You see he does not believe I am sick!

And what can one do?

10    If a physician of high standing, and one's own husband, assures friends and relatives that there is really nothing the matter with one but temporary nervous depression—a slight hysterical tendency—what is one to do?

My brother is also a physician, and also of high standing, and he says the same thing.

So I take phosphates or phosphites—whichever it is, and tonics, and journeys, and air, and exercise, and am absolutely forbidden to "work" until I am well again.

Personally, I disagree with their ideas.

Personally, I believe that congenial work, with excitement and change, would do me good.

15    But what is one to do?

I did write for a while in spite of them; but it *does* exhaust me a good deal—having to be so sly about it, or else meet with heavy opposition.

I sometimes fancy that in my condition if I had less opposition and more society and stimulus—but John says the very worst thing I can do is to think about my condition, and I confess it always makes me feel bad.

So I will let it alone and talk about the house.

The most beautiful place! It is quite alone, standing well back from the road, quite three miles from the village. It makes me think of English places that you read about, for there are hedges and walls and gates that lock, and lots of separate little houses for the gardeners and people.

20    There is a *delicious* garden! I never saw such a garden—large and shady, full of box-bordered paths, and lined with long grape-covered arbors with seats under them.

There were greenhouses, too, but they are all broken now.

There was some legal trouble, I believe, something about the heirs and coheirs; anyhow, the place has been empty for years.

That spoils my ghostliness, I am afraid, but I don't care—there is something strange about the house—I can feel it.

I even said so to John one moonlight evening, but he said what I felt was a *draught,* and shut the window.

25    I get unreasonably angry with John sometimes. I'm sure I never used to be so sensitive. I think it is due to this nervous condition.

But John says if I feel so, I shall neglect proper self-control; so I take pains to control myself—before him, at least, and that makes me very tired.

I don't like our room a bit. I wanted one downstairs that opened on the piazza and had roses all over the window, and such pretty old-fashioned chintz hangings! But John would not hear of it.

He said there was only one window and not room for two beds, and no near room for him if he took another.

He is very careful and loving, and hardly lets me stir without special direction.

30    I have a schedule prescription for each hour in the day; he takes all care from me, and so I feel basely ungrateful not to value it more.

He said we came here solely on my account, that I was to have perfect rest and all the air I could get. "Your exercise depends on your strength, my dear," said he, "and your food somewhat on your appetite; but air you can absorb all the time." So we took the nursery at the top of the house.

It is a big, airy room, the whole floor nearly, with windows that look all ways, and air and sunshine galore. It was nursery first and then playroom and gymnasium, I should judge; for the windows are barred for little children, and there are rings and things in the walls.

The paint and paper look as if a boys' school had used it. It is stripped off—the paper—in great patches all around the head of my bed, about as far as I can reach, and in a great place on the other side of the room low down. I never saw a worse paper in my life.

One of those sprawling flamboyant patterns committing every artistic sin.

35    It is dull enough to confuse the eye in following, pronounced enough to constantly irritate and provoke study, and when you follow the lame uncertain curves for a little distance they suddenly commit suicide—plunge off at outrageous angles, destroy themselves in unheard of contradictions.

The color is repellent, almost revolting; a smouldering unclean yellow, strangely faded by the slow-turning sunlight.

It is a dull yet lurid orange in some places, a sickly sulphur tint in others.

No wonder the children hated it! I should hate it myself if I had to live in this room long.

There comes John, and I must put this away,—he hates to have me write a word.

40    We have been here two weeks, and I haven't felt like writing before, since that first day.

I am sitting by the window now, up in this atrocious nursery, and there is nothing to hinder my writing as much as I please, save lack of strength.

John is away all day, and even some nights when his cases are serious.

I am glad my case is not serious!

But these nervous troubles are dreadfully depressing.

45    John does not know how much I really suffer. He knows there is no *reason* to suffer, and that satisfies him.

Of course it is only nervousness. It does weigh on me so not to do my duty in any way!

I meant to be such a help to John, such a real rest and comfort, and here I am a comparative burden already!

Nobody would believe what an effort it is to do what little I am able,—to dress and entertain, and order things.

It is fortunate Mary is so good with the baby. Such a dear baby!

50    And yet I *cannot* be with him, it makes me so nervous.

I suppose John never was nervous in his life. He laughs at me so about this wallpaper!

At first he meant to repaper the room, but afterwards he said that I was letting it get the better of me, and that nothing was worse for a nervous patient than to give way to such fancies.

He said that after the wallpaper was changed it would be the heavy bedstead, and then the barred windows, and then that gate at the head of the stairs, and so on.

"You know the place is doing you good," he said, "and really, dear, I don't care to renovate the house just for a three months' rental."

55    "Then do let us go downstairs." I said, "there are such pretty rooms there."

Then he took me in his arms and called me a blessed little goose, and said he would go down to the cellar, if I wished, and have it whitewashed into the bargain.

But he is right enough about the beds and windows and things.

It is an airy and comfortable room as any one need wish, and, of course, I would not be so silly as to make him uncomfortable just for a whim.

I'm really getting quite fond of the big room, all but that horrid paper.

60 Out of one window I can see the garden, those mysterious deep-shaded arbors, the riotous old-fashioned flowers, and bushes and gnarly trees.

Out of another I get a lovely view of the bay and a little private wharf belonging to the estate. There is a beautiful shaded lane that runs down there from the house. I always fancy I see people walking in these numerous paths and arbors, but John has cautioned me not to give way to fancy in the least. He says that with my imaginative power and habit of story-making, a nervous weakness like mine is sure to lead to all manner of excited fancies, and that I ought to use my will and good sense to check the tendency. So I try.

I think sometimes that if I were only well enough to write a little it would relieve the press of ideas and rest me.

But I find I get pretty tired when I try.

It is so discouraging not to have any advice and companionship about my work. When I get really well, John says we will ask Cousin Henry and Julia down for a long visit; but he says he would as soon put fireworks in my pillow-case as to let me have those stimulating people about now.

65 I wish I could get well faster.

But I must not think about that. This paper looks to me as if it *knew* what a vicious influence it had!

There is a recurrent spot where the pattern lolls like a broken neck and two bulbous eyes stare at you upside down.

I get positively angry with the impertinence of it and the everlastingness. Up and down and sideways they crawl, and those absurd, unblinking eyes are everywhere. There is one place where two breadths didn't match, and the eyes go all up and down the line, one a little higher than the other.

I never saw so much expression in an inanimate thing before, and we all know how much expression they have! I used to lie awake as a child and get more entertainment and terror out of blank walls and plain furniture than most children could find in a toystore.

70 I remember what a kindly wink the knobs of our big, old bureau used to have, and there was one chair that always seemed like a strong friend.

I used to feel that if any of the other things looked too fierce I could always hop into that chair and be safe.

The furniture in this room is no worse than inharmonious, however, for we had to bring it all from downstairs. I suppose when this was used as a playroom they had to take the nursery things out, and no wonder! I never saw such ravages as the children have made here.

The wallpaper, as I said before, is torn off in spots, and it sticketh closer than a brother—they must have had perseverance as well as hatred.

Then the floor is scratched and gouged and splintered, the plaster itself is dug out here and there, and this great heavy bed which is all we found in the room, looks as if it had been through the wars.

75 But I don't mind it a bit—only the paper.

There comes John's sister. Such a dear girl as she is, and so careful of me! I must not let her find me writing.

She is a perfect and enthusiastic housekeeper, and hopes for no better profession. I verily believe she thinks it is the writing which made me sick!

But I can write when she is out, and see her a long way off from these windows.

There is one that commands the road, a lovely shaded winding road, and one that just looks off over the country. A lovely country, too, full of great elms and velvet meadows.

80    This wallpaper has a kind of sub-pattern in a different shade, a particularly irritating one, for you can only see it in certain lights, and not clearly then.

But in the places where it isn't faded and where the sun is just so—I can see a strange, provoking, formless sort of figure, that seems to skulk about behind that silly and conspicuous front design.

There's sister on the stairs!

Well, the Fourth of July is over! The people are all gone and I am tired out. John thought it might do me good to see a little company, so we just had mother and Nellie and the children down for a week.

Of course I didn't do a thing. Jennie sees to everything now.

85    But it tired me all the same.

John says if I don't pick up faster he shall send me to Weir Mitchell in the fall.

But I don't want to go there at all. I had a friend who was in his hands once, and she says he is just like John and my brother, only more so!

Besides, it is such an undertaking to go so far.

I don't feel as if it was worth while to turn my hand over for anything, and I'm getting dreadfully fretful and querulous.

90    I cry at nothing, and cry most of the time.

Of course I don't when John is here, or anybody else, but when I am alone.

And I am alone a good deal just now. John is kept in town very often by serious cases, and Jennie is good and lets me alone when I want her to.

So I walk a little in the garden or down that lovely lane, sit on the porch under the roses, and lie down up here a good deal.

I'm getting really fond of the room in spite of the wallpaper. Perhaps *because* of the wallpaper.

95    It dwells in my mind so!

I lie here on this great immovable bed—it is nailed down, I believe—and follow that pattern about by the hour. It is as good as gymnastics, I assure you. I start, we'll say, at the bottom, down in the corner over there where it has not been touched, and I determine for the thousandth time that I *will* follow that pointless pattern to some sort of a conclusion.

I know a little of the principle of design, and I know this thing was not arranged on any laws of radiation, or alternation, or repetition, or symmetry, or anything else that I ever heard of.

It is repeated, of course, by the breadths, but not otherwise.

Looked at in one way each breadth stands alone, the bloated curves and flourishes—a kind of "debased Romanesque"[1] with *delirium tremens*—go waddling up and down in isolated columns of fatuity.

100    But, on the other hand, they connect diagonally, and the sprawling outlines run off in great slanting waves of optic horror, like a lot of wallowing seaweeds in full chase.

---

[1]**Romanesque** a style of architecture developed in Italy and western Europe 1000–1200, between the Roman and the Gothic styles, characterized by the use of the round arch.

The whole thing goes horizontally, too, at least it seems so, and I exhaust myself in trying to distinguish the order of its going in that direction.

They have used a horizontal breadth for a frieze, and that adds wonderfully to the confusion.

There is one end of the room where it is almost intact, and there, when the crosslights fade and the low sun shines directly upon it, I can almost fancy radiation after all,—the interminable grotesques seem to form around a common center and rush off in headlong plunges of equal distraction.

It makes me tired to follow it. I will take a nap I guess.

105     I don't know why I should write this.

I don't want to.

I don't feel able.

And I know John would think it absurd. But I *must* say what I feel and think in some way—it is such a relief.

But the effort is getting to be greater than the relief!

110     Half the time now I am awfully lazy, and lie down ever so much.

John says I mustn't lose my strength, and has me take cod liver oil and lots of tonics and things, to say nothing of ale and wine and rare meat.

Dear John! He loves me very dearly, and hates to have me sick. I tried to have a real earnest reasonable talk with him the other day, and tell him how I wish he would let me go and make a visit to Cousin Henry and Julia.

But he said I wasn't able to go, nor able to stand it after I got there; and I did not make out a very good case for myself, for I was crying before I had finished.

It is getting to be a great effort for me to think straight. Just this nervous weakness I suppose.

115     And dear John gathered me up in his arms, and just carried me upstairs and laid me on the bed, and sat by me and read to me till it tired my head.

He said I was his darling and his comfort and all he had, and that I must take care of myself for his sake, and keep well.

He says no one but myself can help me out of it, that I must use my will and self-control and not let any silly fancies run away with me.

There's one comfort, the baby is well and happy, and does not have to occupy this nursery with the horrid wallpaper.

If we had not used it, that blessed child would have! What a fortunate escape! Why, I wouldn't have a child of mine, an impressionable little thing, live in such a room for worlds.

120     I never thought of it before, but it is lucky that John kept me here after all; I can stand it so much easier than a baby, you see.

Of course I never mention it to them any more—I am too wise,—but I keep watch of it all the same.

There are things in that paper that nobody knows but me, or ever will.

Behind that outside pattern the dim shapes get clearer every day.

It is always the same shape, only very numerous.

125     And it is like a woman stooping down and creeping about behind that pattern. I don't like it a bit. I wonder—I begin to think—I wish John would take me away from here!

* * *

It is so hard to talk to John about my case, because he is so wise, and because he loves me so.

But I tried last night.

It was moonlight. The moon shines in all around just as the sun does.

I hate to see it sometimes, it creeps so slowly, and always comes in by one window or another.

130      John was asleep and I hated to waken him, so I kept still and watched the moonlight on that undulating wallpaper till I felt creepy.

The faint figure behind seemed to shake the pattern, just as if she wanted to get out.

I got up softly and went to feel and see if the paper *did* move, and when I came back John was awake.

"What is it, little girl?" he said. "Don't go walking about like that—you'll get cold."

I thought it was a good time to talk, so I told him that I really was not gaining here, and that I wished he would take me away.

135      "Why darling!" said he, "our lease will be up in three weeks, and I can't see how to leave before.

"The repairs are not done at home, and I cannot possibly leave town just now. Of course if you were in any danger, I could and would, but you really are better, dear, whether you can see it or not. I am a doctor, dear, and I know. You are gaining flesh and color, your appetite is better, I feel really much easier about you."

"I don't weigh a bit more," said I, "nor as much; and my appetite may be better in the evening when you are here, but it is worse in the morning when you are away!"

"Bless her little heart!" said he with a big hug, "she shall be as sick as she pleases! But now let's improve the shining hours by going to sleep, and talk about it in the morning!"

"And you won't go away?" I asked gloomily.

140      "Why, how can I, dear? It is only three weeks more and then we will take a nice little trip of a few days while Jennie is getting the house ready. Really dear you are better!"

"Better in body perhaps—" I began, and stopped short, for he sat up straight and looked at me with such a stern, reproachful look that I could not say another word.

"My darling," said he, "I beg of you, for my sake and for our child's sake, as well as for your own, that you will never for one instant let that idea enter your mind! There is nothing so dangerous, so fascinating, to a temperament like yours. It is a false and foolish fancy. Can you trust me as a physician when I tell you so?"

So of course I said no more on that score, and we went to sleep before long. He thought I was asleep first, but I wasn't and lay there for hours trying to decide whether that front pattern and the back pattern really did move together or separately.

On a pattern like this, by daylight, there is a lack of sequence, a defiance of law, that is a constant irritant to a normal mind.

145      The color is hideous enough, and unreliable enough, and infuriating enough, but the pattern is torturing.

You think you have mastered it, but just as you get well underway in following, it turns a back-somersault and there you are. It slaps you in the face, knocks you down, and tramples upon you. It is like a bad dream.

The outside pattern is a florid arabesque, reminding one of a fungus. If you can imagine a toadstool in joints, an interminable string of toadstools, budding and sprouting in endless convolutions—why, that is something like it.

That is, sometimes!

There is one marked peculiarity about this paper, a thing nobody seems to notice but myself, and that is that it changes as the light changes.

150   When the sun shoots in through the east window—I always watch for that first long, straight ray—it changes so quickly that I never can quite believe it.

That is why I watch it always.

By moonlight—the moon shines in all night when there is a moon—I wouldn't know it was the same paper.

At night in any kind of light, in twilight, candlelight, lamplight, and worst of all by moonlight, it becomes bars! The outside pattern I mean, and the woman behind it is as plain as can be.

I didn't realize for a long time what the thing was that showed behind, that dim sub-pattern, but now I am quite sure it is a woman.

155   By daylight she is subdued, quiet. I fancy it is the pattern that keeps her so still. It is so puzzling. It keeps me quiet by the hour.

I lie down ever so much now. John says it is good for me, and to sleep all I can.

Indeed he started the habit by making me lie down for an hour after each meal.

It is a very bad habit I am convinced, for you see I don't sleep.

And that cultivates deceit, for I don't tell them I'm awake—O no!

160   The fact is I am getting a little afraid of John.

He seems very queer sometimes, and even Jennie has an inexplicable look.

It strikes me occasionally, just as a scientific hypothesis,—that perhaps it is the paper!

I have watched John when he did not know I was looking, and come into the room suddenly on the most innocent excuses, and I've caught him several times *looking at the paper!* And Jennie too. I caught Jennie with her hand on it once.

She didn't know I was in the room, and when I asked her in a quiet, a very quiet voice, with the most restrained manner possible, what she was doing with the paper—she turned around as if she had been caught stealing, and looked quite angry—asked me why I should frighten her so!

165   Then she said that the paper stained everything it touched, that she had found yellow smooches on all my clothes and John's, and she wished we would be more careful!

Did not that sound innocent? But I know she was studying that pattern, and I am determined that nobody shall find it out but myself!

Life is very much more exciting now than it used to be. You see I have something more to expect, to look forward to, to watch. I really do eat better, and am more quiet than I was.

John is so pleased to see me improve! He laughed a little the other day, and said I seemed to be flourishing in spite of my wallpaper.

I turned it off with a laugh. I had no intention of telling him it was *because* of the wallpaper—he would make fun of me. He might even want to take me away.

170    I don't want to leave now until I have found it out. There is a week more, and I think that will be enough.

I'm feeling ever so much better! I don't sleep much at night, for it is so interesting to watch developments; but I sleep a good deal in the daytime.

In the daytime it is tiresome and perplexing.

There are always new shoots on the fungus, and new shades of yellow all over it. I cannot keep count of them, though I have tried conscientiously.

It is the strangest yellow, that wallpaper! It makes me think of all the yellow things I ever saw—not beautiful ones like buttercups, but old foul, bad yellow things.

175    But there is something else about that paper—the smell! I noticed it the moment we came into the room, but with so much air and sun it was not bad. Now we have had a week of fog and rain, and whether the windows are open or not, the smell is here.

It creeps all over the house.

I find it hovering in the dining-room, skulking in the parlor, hiding in the hall, lying in wait for me on the stairs.

It gets into my hair.

Even when I go to ride, if I turn my head suddenly and surprise it—there is that smell!

180    Such a peculiar odor, too! I have spent hours in trying to analyze it, to find what it smelled like.

It is not bad—at first, and very gentle, but quite the subtlest, most enduring odor I ever met.

In this damp weather it is awful, I wake up in the night and find it hanging over me.

It used to disturb me at first. I thought seriously of burning the house—to reach the smell.

But now I am used to it. The only thing I can think of that it is like is the *color* of the paper! A yellow smell.

185    There is a very funny mark on this wall, low down, near the mopboard. A streak that runs round the room. It goes behind every piece of furniture, except the bed, a long, straight, even *smooch,* as if it had been rubbed over and over.

I wonder how it was done and who did it, and what they did it for. Round and round and round—round and round and round—it makes me dizzy!

I really have discovered something at last.

Through watching so much at night, when it changes so, I have finally found out.

The front pattern *does* move—and no wonder! The woman behind shakes it!

190    Sometimes I think there are a great many women behind, and sometimes only one, and she crawls around fast, and her crawling shakes it all over.

Then in the very bright spots she keeps still, and in the very shady spots she just takes hold of the bars and shakes them hard.

And she is all the time trying to climb through. But nobody could climb through that pattern—it strangles so; I think that is why it has so many heads.

They get through, and then the pattern strangles them off and turns them upside down, and makes their eyes white!

If those heads were covered or taken off it would not be half so bad.

195     I think that woman gets out in the daytime!

And I'll tell you why—privately—I've seen her!

I can see her out of every one of my windows!

It is the same woman, I know, for she is always creeping, and most women do not creep by daylight.

I see her in that long shaded lane, creeping up and down. I see her in those dark grape arbors, creeping all around the garden.

200     I see her on that long road under the trees, creeping along, and when a carriage comes she hides under the blackberry vines.

I don't blame her a bit. It must be very humiliating to be caught creeping by daylight!

I always lock the door when I creep by daylight. I can't do it at night, for I know John would suspect something at once.

And John is so queer now, that I don't want to irritate him. I wish he would take another room! Besides, I don't want anybody to get that woman out at night but myself.

I often wonder if I could see her out of all the windows at once.

205     But, turn as fast as I can, I can only see out of one at one time.

And though I always see her, she *may* be able to creep faster than I can turn!

I have watched her sometimes away off in the open country, creeping as fast as a cloud shadow in a high wind.

If only that top pattern could be gotten off from the under one! I mean to try it, little by little.

I have found out another funny thing, but I shan't tell it this time! It does not do to trust people too much.

210     There are only two more days to get this paper off, and I believe John is beginning to notice. I don't like the look in his eyes.

And I heard him ask Jennie a lot of professional questions about me. She had a very good report to give.

She said I slept a good deal in the daytime.

John knows I don't sleep very well at night, for all I'm so quiet!

He asked me all sorts of questions, too, and pretended to be very loving and kind.

215     As if I couldn't see through him!

Still, I don't wonder he acts so, sleeping under this paper for three months.

It only interests me, but I feel sure John and Jennie are secretly affected by it.

Hurrah! This is the last day, but it is enough. John is to stay in town over night, and won't be out until this evening.

Jennie wanted to sleep with me—the sly thing! But I told her I should undoubtedly rest better for a night all alone.

220     That was clever, for really I wasn't alone a bit! As soon as it was moonlight and that poor thing began to crawl and shake the pattern, I got up and ran to help her.

I pulled and she shook, I shook and she pulled, and before morning we had peeled off yards of that paper.

A strip about as high as my head and half around the room.

And then when the sun came and that awful pattern began to laugh at me, I declared I would finish it to-day!

We go away to-morrow, and they are moving all the furniture down again to leave things as they were before.

225     Jennie looked at the wall in amazement, but I told her merrily that I did it out of pure spite at the vicious thing.

She laughed and said she wouldn't mind doing it herself, but I must not get tired.

How she betrayed herself that time!

But I am here, and no person touches this paper but me—not *alive!*

She tried to get me out of the room—it was too patent! But I said it was so quiet and empty and clean now that I believed I would lie down again and sleep all I could, and not to wake me even for dinner—I would call when I woke.

230     So now she is gone, and the servants are gone, and the things are gone, and there is nothing left but that great bedstead nailed down, with the canvas mattress we found on it.

We shall sleep downstairs to-night, and take the boat home to-morrow.

I quite enjoy the room, now it is bare again.

How those children did tear about here!

This bedstead is fairly gnawed!

235     But I must get to work.

I have locked the door and thrown the key down into the front path.

I don't want to go out, and I don't want to have anybody come in, till John comes.

I want to astonish him.

I've got a rope up here that even Jennie did not find. If that woman does get out, and tries to get away, I can tie her!

240     But I forgot I could not reach far without anything to stand on!

This bed will *not* move!

I tried to lift and push it until I was lame, and then I got so angry I bit off a little piece at one corner—but it hurt my teeth.

Then I peeled off all the paper I could reach standing on the floor. It sticks horribly and the pattern just enjoys it! All those strangled heads and bulbous eyes and waddling fungus growths just shriek with derision!

I am getting angry enough to do something desperate. To jump out of the window would be admirable exercise, but the bars are too strong even to try.

245     Besides I wouldn't do it. Of course not, I know well enough that a step like that is improper and might be misconstrued.

I don't like to *look* out of the windows even—there are so many of those creeping women, and they creep so fast.

I wonder if they all come out of that wallpaper as I did?

But I am securely fastened now by my well-hidden rope—you don't get *me* out in the road there!

I suppose I shall have to get back behind the pattern when it comes night, and that is hard!

250    It is so pleasant to be out in this great room and creep around as I please!

I don't want to go outside. I won't, even if Jennie asks me to.

For outside you have to creep on the ground, and everything is green instead of yellow.

But here I can creep smoothly on the floor, and my shoulder just fits in that long smooch around the wall, so I cannot lose my way.

Why there's John at the door!

255    It is no use, young man, you can't open it!

How he does call and pound!

Now he's crying for an axe.

It would be a shame to break down that beautiful door!

"John dear!" said I in the gentlest voice, "the key is down by the front steps, under a plantain leaf!"

260    That silenced him for a few moments.

Then he said—very quietly indeed, "Open the door, my darling!"

"I can't," said I. "The key is down by the front door under a plantain leaf!"

And then I said it again, several times, very gently and slowly, and said it so often that he had to go and see, and he got it of course, and came in. He stopped short by the door.

"What is the matter?" he cried. "For God's sake, what are you doing!"

265    I kept on creeping just the same, but I looked at him over my shoulder.

"I've got out at last," said I, "in spite of you and Jane. And I've pulled off most of the paper, so you can't put me back!"

Now why should that man have fainted? But he did, and right across my path by the wall, so that I had to creep over him every time!

### YOUR TURN

1. At the beginning of the story, Gilman's narrator tells us where she is. What is the setting? What do we learn about the setting as the story unfolds?

2. One scholar has said that Gilman presents a "setting within a setting"? What do you think he is referring to? Please explain.

3. How would you describe the narrator's state of mind at the start of the story? Would you agree that by the end it has changed? A lot? A little? Explain as carefully as you can, citing evidence from the text.

4. How are men presented in this story? What is your response to how they are presented?

5. Gilman's story is often included in American history courses. What does this story reveal to us about the lives of American women in the 1890s?

6. Compose a letter, written by the narrator's husband, to her parents (that is, his in-laws), in which he describes what has happened to the narrator.

# RALPH ELLISON

*Ralph Ellison (1914–1994) was born in Oklahoma City. His father died when Ellison was three, and his mother supported herself and her child by working as a domestic. A trumpeter since boyhood, after graduating from high school Ellison went to study music at Tuskegee Institute, a black college in Alabama founded by Booker T. Washington. In 1936 he dropped out of Tuskegee and went to Harlem to study music composition and the visual arts; there he met Langston Hughes and Richard Wright, who encouraged him to turn to fiction. Ellison published stories and essays, and in 1942 became the managing editor of* Negro Quarterly. *During World War II he served in the Merchant Marines. After the war he returned to writing. Acclaimed for his fiction and literary and cultural criticism, Ellison lectured and taught at various American colleges and universities, including Bard, Columbia, Rutgers, Yale, Chicago, and New York University, where he was Albert Schweitzer professor in the Humanities.*

*"Battle Royal" was first published in 1947 and slightly revised (a transitional paragraph was added at the end of the story) for the opening chapter of Ellison's novel,* Invisible Man *(1952), a book cited by* Book-Week *as "the most significant work of fiction written by an American" in the years between 1945 and 1965. In addition to publishing stories and one novel, Ellison published critical essays, which are brought together in* The Collected Essays of Ralph Ellison *(1995).*

## Battle Royal

[1947]

It goes a long way back, some twenty years. All my life I had been looking for something, and everywhere I turned someone tried to tell me what it was. I accepted their answers too, though they were often in contradiction and even self-contradictory. I was naïve. I was looking for myself and asking everyone except myself questions which I, and only I, could answer. It took me a long time and much painful boomeranging of my expectations to achieve a realization everyone else appears to have been born with: That I am nobody but myself. But first I had to discover that I am an invisible man!

And yet I am no freak of nature, nor of history. I was in the cards, other things having been equal (or unequal) eighty-five years ago. I am not ashamed of my grandparents for having been slaves. I am only ashamed of myself for having at one time been ashamed. About eighty-five years ago they were told that they were free, united with others of our country in everything pertaining to the common good, and, in everything social, separate like the fingers of the hand. And they believed it. They exulted in it. They stayed in their place, worked hard, and brought up my father to do the same. But my grandfather is the one. He was an odd old guy, my grandfather, and I am told I take after him. It was he who caused the trouble. On his deathbed he called my father to him and said, "Son, after I'm gone I want you to keep up the good fight. I never told you, but our life is a war and I have been a traitor all my born days, a spy in the enemy's country ever since I give up my gun back in the Reconstruction. Live with your head in the lion's mouth. I want you to overcome 'em with yeses, undermine 'em with grins, agree 'em to death and destruction, let 'em swoller you till they vomit or bust wide open." They thought the old man had gone out of his mind. He

Gordon Parks (1912–2006), *Ralph Ellison*. Parks, an African American photographer with an international reputation, published many books of photographs, including *Camera Portraits: The Techniques and Principles of Documentary Portraiture* (1948), where this picture appears.

had been the meekest of men. The younger children were rushed from the room, the shades drawn and the flame of the lamp turned so low that it sputtered on the wick like the old man's breathing. "Learn it to the young-uns," he whispered fiercely; then he died.

But my folks were more alarmed over his last words than over his dying. It was as though he had not died at all, his words caused so much anxiety. I was warned emphatically to forget what he had said and, indeed, this is the first time it has been mentioned outside the family circle. It had a tremendous effect upon me, however. I could never be sure of what he meant. Grandfather had been a quiet old man who never made any trouble, yet on his deathbed he had called himself a traitor and a spy, and he had spoken of his meekness as a dangerous activity. It became a constant puzzle which lay unanswered in the back of my mind. And whenever things went well for me I remembered my grandfather and felt guilty and uncomfortable. It was as though I was carrying out his advice in spite of myself. And to make it worse, everyone loved me for it. I was praised by the most lily-white men of the town. I was considered an example of desirable conduct—just as my grandfather had been. And what puzzled me was that the old man had defined it as *treachery*. When I was praised for my conduct I felt a guilt that in some way I was doing something that was really against the wishes of the white folks, that if they had understood they would have desired me to act just the opposite, that I should have been sulky and mean, and that that really would have been what they wanted, even though they were fooled and thought they wanted me to act as I did. It made me afraid that some day they would look upon me as a traitor and I would be lost. Still I was more afraid to act any other way because they didn't like that at all. The old man's words were like a curse. On my graduation day I delivered an oration in which I showed that humility was the secret, indeed, the very essence of progress.

(Not that I believed this—how could I, remembering my grandfather?—I only believed that it worked.) It was a great success. Everyone praised me and I was invited to give the speech at a gathering of the town's leading white citizens. It was a triumph for our whole community.

It was in the main ballroom of the leading hotel. When I got there I discovered that it was on the occasion of a smoker, and I was told that since I was to be there anyway I might as well take part in the battle royal to be fought by some of my schoolmates as part of the entertainment. The battle royal came first.

5    All of the town's big shots were there in their tuxedoes, wolfing down the buffet foods, drinking beer and whiskey and smoking black cigars. It was a large room with a high ceiling. Chairs were arranged in neat rows around three sides of a portable boxing ring. The fourth side was clear, revealing a gleaming space of polished floor. I had some misgivings over the battle royal, by the way. Not from a distaste for fighting, but because I didn't care too much for the other fellows who were to take part. They were tough guys who seemed to have no grandfather's curse worrying their minds. No one could mistake their toughness. And besides, I suspected that fighting a battle royal might detract from the dignity of my speech. In those pre-invisible days I visualized myself as a potential Booker T. Washington. But the other fellows didn't care too much for me either, and there were nine of them. I felt superior to them in my way, and I didn't like the manner in which we were all crowded together into the servants' elevator. Nor did they like my being there. In fact, as the warmly lighted floors flashed past the elevator we had words over the fact that I, by taking part in the fight, had knocked one of their friends out of a night's work.

We were led out of the elevator through a rococo hall into an anteroom and told to get into our fighting togs. Each of us was issued a pair of boxing gloves and ushered out into the big mirrored hall, which we entered looking cautiously about us and whispering, lest we might accidentally be heard above the noise of the room. It was foggy with cigar smoke. And already the whiskey was taking effect. I was shocked to see some of the most important men of the town quite tipsy. They were all there—bankers, lawyers, judges, doctors, fire chiefs, teachers, merchants. Even one of the more fashionable pastors. Something we could not see was going on up front. A clarinet was vibrating sensuously and the men were standing up and moving eagerly forward. We were a small tight group, clustered together, our bare upper bodies touching and shining with anticipatory sweat; while up front the big shots were becoming increasingly excited over something we still could not see. Suddenly I heard the school superintendent, who had told me to come, yell, "Bring up the shines,[1] gentlemen! Bring up the little shines!"

We were rushed up to the front of the ballroom, where it smelled even more strongly of tobacco and whiskey. Then we were pushed into place. I almost wet my pants. A set of faces, some hostile, some amused, ringed around us, and in the center, facing us, stood a magnificent blond—stark naked. There was dead silence. I felt a blast of cold air chill me. I tried to back away, but they were behind me and around me. Some of the boys stood with lowered heads, trembling. I felt a wave of irrational guilt and fear. My teeth chattered, my skin turned to goose flesh, my knees knocked. Yet I was strongly attracted and looked in spite of myself. Had the price of looking

---

[1]**shines** a racist term applied to African Americans; implying high gloss of skin color.

been blindness, I would have looked. The hair was yellow like that of a circus kewpie doll, the face heavily powdered and rouged, as though to form an abstract mask, the eyes hollow and smeared a cool blue, the color of a baboon's butt. I felt a desire to spit upon her as my eyes brushed slowly over her body. Her breasts were firm and round as the domes of East Indian temples, and I stood so close as to see the fine skin texture and beads of pearly perspiration glistening like dew around the pink and erected buds of her nipples. I wanted at one and the same time to run from the room, to sink through the floor, or go to her and cover her from my eyes and the eyes of the others with my body; to feel the soft thighs, to caress her and destroy her, to love her and murder her, to hide from her, and yet to stroke where below the small American flag tattooed upon her belly her thighs formed a capital V. I had a notion that of all in the room she saw only me with her impersonal eyes.

And then she began to dance, a slow sensuous movement; the smoke of a hundred cigars clinging to her like the thinnest of veils. She seemed like a fair bird-girl girdled in veils calling to me from the angry surface of some gray and threatening sea. I was transported. Then I became aware of the clarinet playing and the big shots yelling at us. Some threatened us if we looked and others if we did not. On my right I saw one boy faint. And now a man grabbed a silver pitcher from a table and stepped close as he dashed ice water upon him and stood him up and forced two of us to support him as his head hung and moans issued from his thick bluish lips. Another boy began to plead to go home. He was the largest of the group, wearing dark red fighting trunks much too small to conceal the erection which projected from him as though in answer to the insinuating low-registered moaning of the clarinet. He tried to hide himself with his boxing gloves.

And all the while the blonde continued dancing, smiling faintly at the big shots who watched her with fascination, and faintly smiling at our fear. I noticed a certain merchant who followed her hungrily, his lips loose and drooling. He was a large man who wore diamond studs in a shirtfront which swelled with the ample paunch underneath, and each time the blonde swayed her undulating hips he ran his hand through the thin hair of his bald head and, with his arms upheld, his posture clumsy like that of an intoxicated panda, wound his belly in a slow and obscene grind. This creature was completely hypnotized. The music had quickened. As the dancer flung herself about with a detached expression on her face, the men began reaching out to touch her. I could see their beefy fingers sink into her soft flesh. Some of the others tried to stop them and she began to move around the floor in graceful circles, as they gave chase, slipping and sliding over the polished floor. It was mad. Chairs went crashing, drinks were spilt, as they ran laughing and howling after her. They caught her just as she reached a door, raised her from the floor, and tossed her as college boys are tossed at a hazing, and above her red, fixed-smiling lips I saw the terror and disgust in her eyes, almost like my own terror and that which I saw in some of the other boys. As I watched, they tossed her twice and her soft breasts seemed to flatten against the air and her legs flung wildly as she spun. Some of the more sober ones helped her to escape. And I started off the floor, heading for the anteroom with the rest of the boys.

10    Some were still crying and in hysteria. But as we tried to leave we were stopped and ordered to get into the ring. There was nothing to do but what we were told. All ten of us climbed under the ropes and allowed ourselves

to be blindfolded with broad bands of white cloth. One of the men seemed to feel a bit sympathetic and tried to cheer us up as we stood with our backs against the ropes. Some of us tried to grin. "See that boy over there?" one of the men said. "I want you to run across at the bell and give it to him right in the belly. If you don't get him, I'm going to get you. I don't like his looks." Each of us was told the same. The blindfolds were put on. Yet even then I had been going over my speech. In my mind each word was as bright as flame. I felt the cloth pressed into place, and frowned so that it would be loosened when I relaxed.

But now I felt a sudden fit of blind terror. I was unused to darkness. It was as though I had suddenly found myself in a dark room filled with poisonous cottonmouths. I could hear the bleary voices yelling insistently for the battle royal to begin.

"Get going in there!"

"Let me at that big nigger!"

I strained to pick up the school superintendent's voice, as though to squeeze some security out of that slightly more familiar sound.

15      "Let me at those black sonsabitches!" someone yelled.

"No, Jackson, no!" another voice yelled. "Here, somebody, help me hold Jack."

"I want to get at that ginger-colored nigger. Tear him limb from limb," the first voice yelled.

I stood against the ropes trembling. For in those days I was what they called ginger-colored, and he sounded as though he might crunch me between his teeth like a crisp ginger cookie.

Quite a struggle was going on. Chairs were being kicked about and I could hear voices grunting as with a terrific effort. I wanted to see, to see more desperately than ever before. But the blindfold was as tight as a thick skin-puckering scab and when I raised my gloved hands to push the layers of white aside a voice yelled, "Oh, no, you don't, black bastard! Leave that alone!"

20      "Ring the bell before Jackson kills him a coon!" someone boomed in the sudden silence. And I heard the bell clang and the sound of the feet scuffling forward.

A glove smacked against my head. I pivoted, striking out stiffly as someone went past, and felt the jar ripple along the length of my arm to my shoulder. Then it seemed as though all nine of the boys had turned upon me at once. Blows pounded me from all sides while I struck out as best I could. So many blows landed upon me that I wondered if I were not the only blindfolded fighter in the ring, or if the man called Jackson hadn't succeeded in getting me after all.

Blindfolded, I could no longer control my motions. I had no dignity. I stumbled about like a baby or a drunken man. The smoke had become thicker and with each new blow it seemed to sear and further restrict my lungs. My saliva became like hot bitter glue. A glove connected with my head, filling my mouth with warm blood. It was everywhere. I could not tell if the moisture I felt upon my body was sweat or blood. A blow landed hard against the nape of my neck. I felt myself going over, my head hitting the floor. Streaks of blue light filled the black world behind the blindfold. I lay prone, pretending that I was knocked out, but felt myself seized by hands and yanked to my feet. "Get going, black boy! Mix it up!" My arms were like lead, my head smarting from blows. I managed to feel my way to the ropes and held on, trying to catch my breath. A glove landed in my mid-section and I went over again, feeling as though the smoke had become a knife jabbed into my guts. Pushed this way and that by the legs milling around me, I finally pulled erect and discovered that I could see the black, sweat-washed forms weaving in the smoky-blue atmosphere like drunken dancers weaving to the rapid drum-like thuds of blows.

Everyone fought hysterically. It was complete anarchy. Everybody fought everybody else. No group fought together for long. Two, three, four, fought one, then turned to fight each other, were themselves attacked. Blows landed below the belt and in the kidney, with the gloves open as well as closed, and with my eye partly opened now there was not so much terror. I moved carefully, avoiding blows, although not too many to attract attention, fighting from group to group. The boys groped about like blind, cautious crabs crouching to protect their mid-sections, their heads pulled in short against their shoulders, their arms stretched nervously before them, with their fists testing the smoke-filled air like the knobbed feelers of hypersensitive snails. In one corner I glimpsed a boy violently punching the air and heard him scream in pain as he smashed his hand against a ring post. For a second I saw him bent over holding his hand, then going down as a blow caught his unprotected head. I played one group against the other, slipping and throwing a punch then stepping out of range while pushing the others into the melee to take the blows blindly aimed at me. The smoke was agonizing and there were no rounds, no bells at three-minute intervals to relieve our exhaustion. The room spun round me, a swirl of lights, smoke, sweating bodies surrounded by tense white faces. I bled from both nose and mouth, the blood spattering upon my chest.

The men kept yelling, "Slug him, black boy! Knock his guts out!"

25      "Uppercut him! Kill him! Kill that big boy!"

Taking a fake fall, I saw a boy going down heavily beside me as though we were felled by a single blow, saw a sneaker-clad foot shoot into his groin as the two who had knocked him down stumbled upon him. I rolled out of range, feeling a twinge of nausea.

The harder we fought the more threatening the men became. And yet, I had begun to worry about my speech again. How would it go? Would they recognize my ability? What would they give me?

I was fighting automatically when suddenly I noticed that one after another of the boys was leaving the ring. I was surprised, filled with panic, as though I had been left alone with an unknown danger. Then I understood. The boys had arranged it among themselves. It was the custom for the two men left in the ring to slug it out for the winner's prize. I discovered this too late. When the bell sounded two men in tuxedoes leaped into the ring and removed the blindfold. I found myself facing Tatlock, the biggest of the gang. I felt sick at my stomach. Hardly had the bell stopped ringing in my ears than it clanged again and I saw him moving swiftly toward me. Thinking of nothing else to do I hit him smash on the nose. He kept coming, bringing the rank, sharp violence of stale sweat. His face was a black blank of a face, only his eyes alive—with hate of me and aglow with a feverish terror from what had happened to us all. I became anxious. I wanted to deliver my speech and he came at me as though he meant to beat it out of me. I smashed him again and again, taking his blows as they came. Then on a sudden impulse I struck him lightly and as we clinched, I whispered, "Fake like I knocked you out, you can have the prize."

"I'll break your behind," he whispered hoarsely.

30      "For *them?*"

"For *me,* sonofabitch!"

They were yelling for us to break it up and Tatlock spun me half around with a blow, and as a joggled camera sweeps in a reeling scene, I saw the howling red faces crouching tense beneath the cloud of blue-gray smoke. For a moment the world wavered, unraveled, flowed, then my head cleared and Tatlock bounced before me. That fluttering shadow before my eyes was his jabbing left hand. Then falling forward, my head against his damp shoulder, I whispered,

"I'll make it five dollars more."

"Go to hell!"

35      But his muscles relaxed a trifle beneath my pressure and I breathed, "Seven!"

"Give it to your ma," he said, ripping me beneath the heart.

And while I still held him I butted him and moved away. I felt myself bombarded with punches. I fought back with hopeless desperation. I wanted to deliver my speech more than anything else in the world, because I felt that only these men could judge truly my ability, and now this stupid clown was ruining my chances. I began fighting carefully now, moving in to punch him and out again with my greater speed. A lucky blow to his chin and I had him going too—until I heard a loud voice yell, "I got my money on the big boy."

Hearing this, I almost dropped my guard. I was confused: Should I try to win against the voice out there? Would not this go against my speech, and was not this a moment for humility, for nonresistance? A blow to my head as I danced about sent my right eye popping like a jack-in-the-box and settled my dilemma. The room went red as I fell. It was a dream fall, my body languid and fastidious as to where to land, until the floor became impatient and smashed up to meet me. A moment later I came to. An hypnotic voice said FIVE emphatically. And I lay there, hazily watching a dark red spot of my own blood shaping itself into a butterfly, glistening and soaking into the soiled gray world of the canvas.

When the voice drawled TEN I was lifted up and dragged to a chair. I sat dazed. My eye pained and swelled with each throb of my pounding heart and I wondered if now I would be allowed to speak. I was wringing wet, my mouth still bleeding. We were grouped along the wall now. The other boys ignored me as they congratulated Tatlock and speculated as to how much they would be paid. One boy whimpered over his smashed hand. Looking up front, I saw attendants in white jackets rolling the portable ring away and placing a small square rug in the vacant space surrounded by chairs. Perhaps, I thought, I will stand on the rug to deliver my speech.

40      Then the M.C. called to us, "Come on up here boys and get your money."

We ran forward to where the men laughed and talked in their chairs, waiting. Everyone seemed friendly now.

"There it is on the rug," the man said. I saw the rug covered with coins of all dimensions and a few crumpled bills. But what excited me, scattered here and there, were the gold pieces.

"Boys, it's all yours," the man said. "You get all you grab."

"That's right, Sambo,"[2] a blond man said, winking at me confidentially.

45      I trembled with excitement, forgetting my pain. I would get the gold and the bills, I thought. I would use both hands. I would throw my body against the boys nearest me to block them from the gold.

---

[2]**Sambo** a racist slur, deriving from Zambo, a Spanish term used to identify individuals in the Americas who are of mixed African and Amerindian ancestry.

"Get down around the rug now," the man commanded, "and don't any-one touch it until I give the signal."

"This ought to be good," I heard.

As told, we got around the square rug on our knees. Slowly the man raised his freckled hand as we followed it upward with our eyes.

I heard, "These niggers look like they're about to pray!"

50      Then, "Ready," the man said. "Go!"

I lunged for a yellow coin lying on the blue design of the carpet, touch-ing it and sending a surprised shriek to join those rising around me. I tried frantically to remove my hand but could not let go. A hot, violent force tore through my body, shaking me like a wet rat. The rug was electrified. The hair bristled up on my head as I shook myself free. My muscles jumped, my nerves jangled, writhed. But I saw that this was not stopping the other boys. Laughing in fear and embarrassment, some were holding back and scooping up the coins knocked off by the painful contortions of the others. The men roared above us as we struggled.

"Pick it up, goddamnit, pick it up!" someone called like a bass-voiced parrot. "Go on, get it!"

I crawled rapidly around the floor, picking up the coins, trying to avoid the coppers and to get greenbacks and the gold. Ignoring the shock by laughing, as I brushed the coins off quickly, I discovered that I could contain the electricity—a contradiction, but it works. Then the men began to push us onto the rug. Laughing embarrassedly, we struggled out of their hands and kept after the coins. We were all wet and slippery and hard to hold. Suddenly I saw a boy lifted into the air, glistening with sweat like a circus seal, and dropped, his wet back landing flush upon the charged rug, heard him yell and saw him literally dance upon his back, his elbows beating a frenzied tattoo upon the floor, his muscles twitching like the flesh of a horse stung by many flies. When he finally rolled off, his face was gray and no one stopped him when he ran from the floor amid booming laughter.

"Get the money," the M.C. called. "That's good hard American cash!"

55      And we snatched and grabbed, snatched and grabbed. I was careful not to come too close to the rug now, and when I felt the hot whiskey breath descend upon me like a cloud of foul air I reached out and grabbed the leg of a chair. It was occupied and I held on desperately.

"Leggo, nigger! Leggo!"

The huge face wavered down to mine as he tried to push me free. But my body was slippery and he was too drunk. It was Mr. Colcord, who owned a chain of movie houses and "entertainment palaces." Each time he grabbed me I slipped out of his hands. It became a real struggle. I feared the rug more than I did the drunk, so I held on, surprising myself for a moment by trying to topple *him* upon the rug. It was such an enormous idea that I found my-self actually carrying it out. I tried not to be obvious, yet when I grabbed his leg, trying to tumble him out of the chair, he raised up roaring with laughter, and, looking at me with soberness dead in the eye, kicked me viciously in the chest. The chair leg flew out of my hand. I felt myself going and rolled. It was as though I had rolled through a bed of hot coals. It seemed a whole century would pass before I would roll free, a century in which I was seared through the deepest levels of my body to the fearful breath within me and the breath seared and heated to the point of explosion. It'll all be over in a flash, I thought as I rolled clear. It'll all be over in a flash.

But not yet, the men on the other side were waiting, red faces swollen as though from apoplexy as they bent forward in their chairs. Seeing their fingers coming toward me I rolled away as a fumbled football rolls off the receiver's fingertips, back into the coals. That time I luckily sent the rug sliding out of place and heard the coins ringing against the floor and the boys scuffling to pick them up and the M.C. calling, "All right, boys, that's all. Go get dressed and get your money."

I was limp as a dish rag. My back felt as though it had been beaten with wires.

60        When we had dressed the M.C. came in and gave us each five dollars, except Tatlock, who got ten for being the last in the ring. Then he told us to leave. I was not to get a chance to deliver my speech, I thought. I was going out into the dim alley in despair when I was stopped and told to go back. I returned to the ballroom, where the men were pushing back their chairs and gathering in groups to talk.

The M.C. knocked on a table for quiet. "Gentlemen," he said, "we almost forgot an important part of the program. A most serious part, gentlemen. This boy was brought here to deliver a speech which he made at his gradua-tion yesterday. . . ."

"Bravo!"

"I'm told that he is the smartest boy we've got out there in Greenwood. I'm told that he knows more big words than a pocket-sized dictionary."

Much applause and laughter.

65        "So now, gentlemen, I want you to give him your attention."

There was still laughter as I faced them, my mouth dry, my eye throb-bing. I began slowly, but evidently my throat was tense, because they began shouting, "Louder! Louder!"

"We of the younger generation extol the wisdom of that great leader and educator," I shouted, "who first spoke these flaming words of wisdom: 'A ship lost at sea for many days suddenly sighted a friendly vessel. From the mast of the unfortunate vessel was seen a signal: "Water, water; we die of thirst!" The answer from the friendly vessel came back: "Cast down your bucket where you are." The captain of the distressed vessel, at last heeding the injunction, cast down his bucket, and it came up full of fresh sparkling water from the mouth of the Amazon River.' And like him I say, and in his words, 'To those of my race who depend upon bettering their condition in a foreign land, or who underestimate the importance of cultivating friendly relations with the Southern white man, who is his next-door neighbor, I would say: "Cast down your bucket where you are" — cast it down in making friends in every manly way of the people of all races by whom we are surrounded. . . .'"[3]

I spoke automatically and with such fervor that I did not realize that the men were still talking and laughing until my dry mouth, filling up with blood from the cut, almost strangled me. I coughed, wanting to stop and go to one of the tall brass, sand-filled spittoons to relieve myself, but a few of the men, especially the superintendent, were listening and I was afraid. So I gulped it down, blood, saliva and all, and continued. (What powers of endurance I had during those days! What enthusiasm! What a belief in the

---

[3]The narrator here is quoting from an important speech by the African American educator Booker T. Washington, delivered at the Atlanta Exposition in 1895, in which he expressed his willingness to accept segregation in exchange for economic advancement.

rightness of things!) I spoke even louder in spite of the pain. But still they talked and still they laughed, as though deaf with cotton in dirty ears. So I spoke with greater emotional emphasis. I closed my ears and swallowed blood until I was nauseated. The speech seemed a hundred times as long as before, but I could not leave out a single word. All had to be said, each memorized nuance considered, rendered. Nor was that all. Whenever I uttered a word of three or more syllables a group of voices would yell for me to repeat it. I used the phrase "social responsibility" and they yelled:

"What's the word you say, boy?"

70 "Social responsibility," I said.

"What?"

"Social . . ."

"Louder."

". . . responsibility."

75 "More!"

"Respon—"

"Repeat!"

"—sibility."

The room filled with the uproar of laughter until, no doubt, distracted by having to gulp down my blood, I made a mistake and yelled a phrase I had often seen denounced in newspaper editorials, heard debated in private.

80 "Social . . ."

"What?" they yelled.

". . . equality—"

The laughter hung smokelike in the sudden stillness. I opened my eyes, puzzled. Sounds of displeasure filled the room. The M.C. rushed forward. They shouted hostile phrases at me. But I did not understand.

A small dry mustached man in the front row blared out, "Say that slowly, son!"

85 "What, sir?"

"What you just said!"

"Social responsibility, sir," I said.

"You weren't being smart, were you, boy?" he said, not unkindly.

"No, sir!"

90 "You sure that about 'equality' was a mistake?"

"Oh, yes, sir," I said. "I was swallowing blood."

"Well, you had better speak more slowly so we can understand. We mean to do right by you, but you've got to know your place at all times. All right now, go on with your speech."

I was afraid. I wanted to leave but I wanted also to speak and I was afraid they'd snatch me down.

"Thank you, sir," I said, beginning where I had left off, and having them ignore me as before.

95 Yet when I finished there was a thunderous applause. I was surprised to see the superintendent come forth with a package wrapped in white tissue paper and, gesturing for quiet, address the men.

"Gentlemen, you see that I did not overpraise this boy. He makes a good speech and some day he'll lead his people in the proper paths. And I don't have to tell you that that is important in these days and times. This is a good, smart boy, and so to encourage him in the right direction, in the name of the Board of Education I wish to present him a prize in the form of this . . ."

He paused, removing the tissue paper and revealing a gleaming calfskin brief case.

"... in the form of this first-class article from Shad Whitmore's shop."

"Boy," he said, addressing me, "take this prize and keep it well. Consider it a badge of office. Prize it. Keep developing as you are and some day it will be filled with important papers that will help shape the destiny of your people."

100    I was so moved that I could hardly express my thanks. A rope of bloody saliva forming a shape like an undiscovered continent drooled upon the leather and I wiped it quickly away. I felt an importance that I had never dreamed.

"Open it and see what's inside," I was told.

My fingers a-tremble, I complied, smelling the fresh leather and finding an official-looking document inside. It was a scholarship to the state college for Negroes. My eyes filled with tears and I ran awkwardly off the floor.

I was overjoyed; I did not even mind when I discovered that the gold pieces I had scrambled for were brass pocket tokens advertising a certain make of automobile.

When I reached home everyone was excited. Next day the neighbors came to congratulate me. I even felt safe from grandfather, whose deathbed curse usually spoiled my triumphs. I stood beneath his photograph with my brief case in hand and smiled triumphantly into his stolid black peasant's face. It was a face that fascinated me. The eyes seemed to follow everywhere I went.

105    That night I dreamed I was at a circus with him and that he refused to laugh at the clowns no matter what they did. Then later he told me to open my brief case and read what was inside and I did, finding an official envelope stamped with the state seal; and inside the envelope I found another and another, endlessly, and I thought I would fall of weariness. "Them's years," he said. "Now open that one." And I did and in it I found an engraved document containing a short message in letters of gold. "Read it," my grandfather said. "Out loud."

"To Whom It May Concern," I intoned, "Keep This Nigger-Boy Running."

I awoke with the old man's laughter ringing in my ears.

(It was a dream I was to remember and dream again for many years after. But at the time I had no insight into its meaning. First I had to attend college.)

### YOUR TURN

1. Ellison's narrator says that this incident in his life took place "in the main ballroom of the leading hotel." How does he describe this setting? What are the features of it that he emphasizes?
2. Much of the action takes place within the boxing ring. How is it described? Why do you think that Ellison chose this setting for the main action?
3. Note the scene of the naked blonde woman. Why is it in the story?
4. How would you respond to someone who said, "This is a powerful story, but something like this could not happen in real life"?
5. How are white people presented in "Battle Royal"? What is your response to the way in which they are presented?
6. What is your response to the narrator overall? What kind of person is he?

# 9

# Narrative Point of View

Every story is told by someone. Mark Twain wrote *Adventures of Huckleberry Finn,* but he does not tell the story; Huck tells the story, and he begins thus:

> You don't know about me without you have read a book by the name of *The Adventures of Tom Sawyer,* but that ain't no matter. That book was made by Mr. Mark Twain, and he told the truth, mainly. There was things which he stretched, but mainly he told the truth.

Similarly, Edgar Allan Poe wrote "The Cask of Amontillado" (page 509), but the story is told by a man whose name, we learn later, is Montresor. Here is the opening:

> The thousand injuries of Fortunato I had borne as I best could, but when he ventured upon insult, I vowed revenge.

Each of these passages gives a reader a very strong sense of the narrator, that is, of the invented person who tells the story, and it turns out that the works are chiefly about the speakers. Compare those opening passages, however, with two others, which sound far more objective. The first comes from Chekhov's "Misery" (page 403):

> The twilight of evening. Big flakes of wet snow are whirling lazily about the street lamps, which have just been lighted, and lying in a thin soft layer on roofs, horses' backs, shoulders, caps. Iona Potapov, the sledge-driver, is all white like a ghost. He sits on the box without stirring, bent as double as the living body can be bent.

And another example, this one from Hawthorne's "Young Goodman Brown" (page 154):

> Young Goodman Brown came forth, at sunset, into the street at Salem village; but put his head back, after crossing the threshold, to exchange a parting kiss with his young wife. And Faith, as the wife was aptly named, thrust her own pretty head into the street, letting the wind play with the pink ribbons of her cap while she called to Goodman Brown.

In each of these two passages, a reader is scarcely aware of the personality of the narrator; our interest is almost entirely in the scene that each speaker reveals, not in the speaker's response to the scene.

The narrators of *Huckleberry Finn* and of "The Cask of Amontillado" immediately impress us with their distinctive personalities. We realize that whatever happenings they report will be colored by the special ways in which such personalities see things. But what can we say about the narrators of "Misery" and of "Young Goodman Brown"? A reader hardly notices them, at least in comparison with Huck and Montresor. We look, so to speak, not *at* these narrators, but at others (the cabman and Goodman Brown and Faith).

Of course, it is true that as we read "Misery" and "Young Goodman Brown" we are looking through the eyes of the narrators, but these narrators seem (unlike Huck and Montresor) to have 20/20 vision. This is not to say, however, that these apparently colorless narrators really are colorless or invisible. The narrator of "Misery" seems, at least if we judge from the opening sentences, to want to evoke an atmosphere. He describes the setting in some detail, whereas the narrator of "Young Goodman Brown" seems chiefly concerned with reporting the actions of people whom he sees. Moreover, if we listen carefully to Hawthorne's narrator, perhaps we can say that when he mentions that Faith was "aptly" named, he makes a judgment. Still, it is clear that the narrative voices we hear in "Misery" and "Young Goodman Brown" are relatively impartial and inconspicuous; when we hear them, we feel, for the most part, that they are talking about something objective, about something "out there." These narrative voices will produce stories very different from the narrative voices used by Twain and Poe. The voice that the writer chooses, then, will in large measure shape the story; different voices, different stories.

The narrative point of view of *Huckleberry Finn* and of "The Cask of Amontillado" (and of any other story in which a character in the story tells the story) is a **participant** (or **first-person**) point of view. The point of view of "Young Goodman Brown" (and of any other story in which a nearly invisible outsider tells the story) is a **nonparticipant** (or **third-person**) point of view.

# Participant (or First-Person) Point of View

In John Updike's "A & P" (page 191) the narrator is, like Mark Twain's Huck and Poe's Montresor, a major character. Updike has invented an adolescent boy who undergoes certain experiences and who has certain perceptions. Since the story is narrated by one of its characters, we can say that the author uses a first-person (or participant) point of view.

It happens that in Updike's "A & P" the narrator is the central character, the character whose actions—whose life, we might say—most interests the reader. But sometimes a first-person narrator tells a story that focuses on another character; the narrator still says "I" (thus the point of view is first person), but the reader feels that the story is not chiefly about this "I" but is about some other figure. For instance, the narrator may be a witness to a story about Jones, and our interest is in what happens to Jones, though we get the story of Jones filtered through, say, the eyes of Jones's friend, or brother, or cat.

When any of us tells a story (for instance, why we quit a job), our hearers may do well to take what we say with a grain of salt. After all, we are giving *our* side, our version of what happened. And so it is with first-person narrators of fiction. They may be reliable, in which case the reader can pretty much accept what they say, or they may be **unreliable narrators,** perhaps because they have an ax to grind, perhaps because they are not perceptive enough to grasp the full implications of what they report, or perhaps because they are mentally impaired, even insane. Poe's Montresor, in "The Cask of Amontillado," is so obsessed that we cannot be certain that Fortunato really did inflict a "thousand injuries" on him.

One special kind of unreliable first-person narrator (whether major or minor) is the **innocent eye:** the narrator is naive (usually a child, or a not-too-bright adult), telling what he or she sees and feels; the contrast between what the narrator perceives and what the reader understands produces an ironic effect. Such a story, in which the reader understands more than the teller himself does, is Ring Lardner's "Haircut" (1925), a story told by a garrulous barber who does not perceive that the "accident" he is describing is in fact a murder.

# Nonparticipant (or Third-Person) Points of View

In a story told from a nonparticipant (third-person) point of view, the teller of the tale is not a character in the tale. The narrator has receded from the story. If the point of view is **omniscient,** the narrator relates what he or she wishes about the thoughts as well as the deeds of the characters. The omniscient teller can at any time enter the mind of any or all of the characters; whereas the first-person narrator can only say "I was angry" or "Jones seemed angry to me," the omniscient narrator can say, "Jones was inwardly angry but gave no sign; Smith continued chatting, but he sensed Jones's anger."

Furthermore, a distinction can be made between **neutral omniscience** (the narrator recounts deeds and thoughts, but does not judge) and **editorial omniscience** (the narrator not only recounts, but also judges). The narrator in Hawthorne's "Young Goodman Brown" knows what goes on in the mind of Brown, and he comments approvingly or disapprovingly: "With this excellent resolve for the future, Goodman Brown felt himself justified in making more haste on his present evil purpose."

Because a short story can scarcely hope to effectively develop a picture of several minds, an author may prefer to limit his or her omniscience to the minds of only a few of the characters, or even to that of one of the characters; that is, the author may use **selective omniscience** as the point of view. Selective omniscience provides a focus, especially if it is limited to a single character. When thus limited, the author hovers over the shoulder of one character, seeing him or her from outside and from inside and seeing other characters only from the outside and from the impact they make on the mind of this selected receptor. In "Young Goodman Brown" the reader sees things mostly as they make their impact on the protagonist's mind.

> He could have well nigh sworn that the shape of his own dead father beckoned him to advance, looking downward from a smoke wreath, while a woman, with dim features of despair, threw out her hand to warn him back. Was it his mother? But he had no power to retreat one step, nor to resist, even in thought, when the minister and good old Deacon Gookin seized his arms and led him to the blazing rock.

When selective omniscience attempts to record mental activity ranging from consciousness to the unconscious, from clear perceptions to confused longings, point of view is sometimes labeled **stream of consciousness.** In an effort to reproduce the unending activity of the mind, some authors who use the stream-of-consciousness point of view dispense with conventional word order, punctuation, and logical transitions. The last forty-six pages in James Joyce's *Ulysses* are an unpunctuated flow of one character's thoughts.

Finally, sometimes a third-person narrator does not enter even a single mind, but records only what crosses a dispassionate eye and ear. Such a point of view is **objective** (sometimes called **the camera** or **fly-on-the-wall narrator**). The absence of editorializing and of dissection of the mind often produces the effect of a play; we see and hear the characters in action. Much of Hemingway's "Cat in the Rain" (page 99) is objective, consisting of bits of dialogue that make the story look like a play:

> "I'm going down and get that kitty," the American wife said.
> "I'll do it," her husband offered from the bed.
> "No, I'll get it. The poor kitty out trying to keep dry under a table."
> The husband went on reading, lying propped up with the two pillows at the foot of the bed.
> "Don't get wet," he said. (100)

The absence of comment on the happenings forces readers to make their own evaluations of the happenings. In the passage just quoted, when Hemingway writes "'Don't get wet,' he said," readers are probably forced to think (and to sense that Hemingway is guiding them to think) that the husband is indifferent to his wife. After all, how can she go out into the rain and not get wet? A writer can use an objective point of view, then, and still control the feelings of the reader.

# The Point of a Point of View

Generalizations about the effect of a point of view are risky, but two have already been made: that the innocent eye can achieve an ironic effect otherwise unattainable, and that an objective point of view (because we hear dialogue but get little or no comment about it) is dramatic. Three other generalizations are often made:

- that a first-person point of view lends a sense of immediacy or reality,
- that an omniscient point of view suggests human littleness, and
- that the point of view must be consistent.

To take the first of these: it is true that when Poe begins a story "The thousand injuries of Fortunato I had borne as I best could, but when he ventured upon insult, I vowed revenge," we feel that the author has gripped us by the lapels; but, on the other hand, we know that we are only reading a piece of fiction, and we do not really believe in the existence of the "I" or of Fortunato; and furthermore, when we pick up a story that begins with *any* point of view, we agree (by picking up the book) to pretend to believe the fictions we are being told. That is, all fiction—whether in the first person or not—is known to be literally false but is read with the pretense that it is true (probably because we hope to get some sort of insight, or truth). The writer must hold our attention and make us feel that the fiction is meaningful, but the use of the first-person pronoun does not of itself confer reality.

The second generalization, that an omniscient point of view can make puppets of its characters, is equally misleading; this point of view can also reveal in them a depth and complexity quite foreign to the idea of human littleness.

The third generalization, that the narrator's point of view must be consistent lest the illusion of reality be shattered, has been much preached by the followers of Henry James. But E. M. Forster has suggested, in *Aspects of the Novel,* that what is important is not consistency but "the power of the writer to bounce the reader into accepting what he says." Forster notes that in *Bleak House* Dickens uses in Chapter 1 an omniscient point of view, in Chapter 2 a selective omniscient point of view, and in Chapter 3 a first-person point of view. "Logically," Forster says, "*Bleak House* is all to pieces, but Dickens bounces us, so that we do not mind the shiftings of the viewpoint."

Perhaps the only sound generalizations possible are these:

1. Because point of view is one of the things that give form to a story, a good author chooses the point (or points) of view that he or she feels is best for the particular story.
2. The use of any other point or points of view would turn the story into a different story.

# JOHN UPDIKE

*John Updike (1932–2009) grew up in Shillington, Pennsylvania, where his father was a teacher and his mother a writer. After receiving a B.A. degree in 1954 from Harvard, where he edited the Harvard Lampoon (for which he both wrote and drew), he studied drawing at Oxford for a year, but an offer from the* New Yorker *brought him back to the United States. He was hired as a reporter for the magazine but soon began contributing poetry, essays, and fiction. In 1957 he left the* New Yorker *in order to write independently full time, though his stories and book reviews appeared regularly in it until his death.*

*In 1959 Updike published his first book of stories,* The Same Door *as well as his first novel,* The Poorhouse Fair; *the next year he published* Rabbit, Run, *a highly successful novel whose protagonist, "Rabbit" Angstrom, reappears in three later novels,* Rabbit Redux *(1971),* Rabbit Is Rich *(1981), and* Rabbit at Rest *(1990). The first and the last Rabbit books each won a Pulitzer Prize.*

*A & P*                                                    [1962]

In walks these three girls in nothing but bathing suits. I'm in the third checkout slot, with my back to the door, so I don't see them until they're over by the bread. The one that caught my eye first was the one in the plaid green two-piece. She was a chunky kid, with a good tan and a sweet broad soft-looking can with those two crescents of white just under it, where the sun never seems to hit, at the top of the backs of her legs. I stood there with my hand on a box of HiHo crackers trying to remember if I rang it up or not. I ring it up again and the customer starts giving me hell. She's one of these cash-register-watchers, a witch about fifty with rouge on her cheekbones and no eyebrows, and I know it made her day to trip me up. She'd been watching cash registers for fifty years and probably never seen a mistake before.

By the time I got her feathers smoothed and her goodies into a bag— she gives me a little snort in passing, if she'd been born at the right time they would have burned her over in Salem[1]—by the time I get her on her way the girls had circled around the bread and were coming back, without a pushcart, back my way along the counters, in the aisle between the check-outs and the Special bins. They didn't even have shoes on. There was this chunky one, with the two-piece—it was bright green and the seams on the bra were still sharp and her belly was still pretty pale so I guessed she just got it (the suit)—there was this one, with one of those chubby berry-faces, the lips all bunched together under her nose, this one, and a tall one, with black hair that hadn't quite frizzed right, and one of these sunburns right across under the eyes, and a chin that was too long—you know, the kind of girl other girls think is very "striking" and "attractive" but never quite makes it, as they very well know, which is why they like her so much—and then the third one, that wasn't quite so tall. She was the queen. She kind of led them, the other two peeking around and making their shoulders round. She didn't look around, not this queen, she just walked straight on slowly, on these long white prima-donna legs. She came down a little hard on her heels, as if she didn't walk in her bare feet that much, putting down her heels and then letting the weight move along to her toes as if she was testing the floor with every step, putting a little deliberate extra action into it. You never know for sure how girls' minds work (do you really think it's a mind in there or just a little buzz like a bee in a glass jar?) but you got the idea she had talked the other two into coming in here with her, and now she was showing them how to do it, walk slow and hold yourself straight.

She had on a kind of dirty-pink—beige maybe, I don't know—bathing suit with a little nubble all over it and, what got me, the straps were down. They were off her shoulders looped loose around the cool tops of her arms, and I guess as a result the suit had slipped a little on her, so all around the top of the cloth there was this shining rim. If it hadn't been there you wouldn't have known there could have been anything whiter than those shoulders. With the straps pushed off, there was nothing between the top of the suit and the top of her head except just *her*, this clean bare plane of the top of her chest down from the shoulder bones like a dented sheet of metal tilted in the light. I mean, it was more than pretty.

She had sort of oaky hair that the sun and salt had bleached, done up in a bun that was unravelling, and a kind of prim face. Walking into the A & P with your straps down, I suppose it's the only kind of face you *can* have. She held her head so high her neck, coming up out of those white shoulders, looked kind of stretched, but I didn't mind. The longer her neck was, the more of her there was.

5      She must have felt in the corner of her eye me and over my shoulder Stokesie in the second slot watching, but she didn't tip. Not this queen. She kept her eyes moving across the racks, and stopped, and turned so slow it

---

[1] **Salem** town in Massachusetts, where the witch trials of the 1690s occurred. Many women and men were hanged for their supposed sins and crimes; no one was burned at the stake.

made my stomach rub the inside of my apron, and buzzed to the other two, who kind of huddled against her for relief, and then they all three of them went up the cat-and-dog-food-breakfast-cereal-macaroni-rice-raisins-seasonings-spreads-spaghetti-soft-drinks-crackers-and-cookies aisle. From the third slot I look straight up this aisle to the meat counter, and I watched them all the way. The fat one with the tan sort of fumbled with the cookies, but on second thought she put the package back. The sheep pushing their carts down the aisle—the girls were walking against the usual traffic (not that we have one-way signs or anything)—were pretty hilarious. You could see them, when Queenie's white shoulders dawned on them, kind of jerk, or hop, or hiccup, but their eyes snapped back to their own baskets and on they pushed. I bet you could set off dynamite in an A & P and the people would by and large keep reaching and checking oatmeal off their lists and muttering "Let me see, there was a third thing, began with A, asparagus, no, ah, yes, applesauce!" or whatever it is they do mutter. But there was no doubt, this jiggled them. A few houseslaves in pin curlers even look around after pushing their carts past to make sure what they had seen was correct.

You know, it's one thing to have a girl in a bathing suit down on the beach, where what with the glare nobody can look at each other much anyway, and another thing in the cool of the A & P, under the fluorescent lights, against all those stacked packages, with her feet paddling along naked over our checkerboard green-and-cream rubber-tile floor.

"Oh, Daddy," Stokesie said beside me. "I feel so faint."

"Darling," I said. "Hold me tight." Stokesie's married, with two babies chalked up on his fuselage already, but as far as I can tell that's the only difference. He's twenty-two, and I was nineteen this April.

"Is it done?" he asks, the responsible married man finding his voice. I forgot to say he thinks he's going to be a manager some sunny day, maybe in 1990 when it's called the Great Alexandrov and Petrooshki Tea Company or something.

10          What he meant was, our town is five miles from a beach, with a big summer colony out on the Point, but we're right in the middle of town, and the women generally put on a shirt or shorts or something before they get out of the car into the street. And anyway these are usually women with six children and varicose veins mapping their legs and nobody, including them, could care less. As I say, we're right in the middle of town, and if you stand at our front doors you can see two banks and the Congregational church and the newspaper store and three real estate offices and about twenty-seven old freeloaders tearing up Central Street because the sewer broke again. It's not as if we're on the Cape;[2] we're north of Boston and there's people in this town haven't seen the ocean for twenty years.

The girls had reached the meat counter and were asking McMahon something. He pointed, they pointed, and they shuffled out of sight behind a pyramid of Diet Delight peaches. All that was left for us to see was old McMahon patting his mouth and looking after them sizing up their joints. Poor kids, I began to feel sorry for them, they couldn't help it.

Now here comes the sad part of the story, at least my family says it's sad, but I don't think it's so sad myself. The store's pretty empty, it being Thursday

---

[2]**Cape** Cape Cod, a peninsula in easternmost Massachusetts.

afternoon, so there was nothing much to do except lean on the register and wait for the girls to show up again. The whole store was like a pinball machine and I didn't know which tunnel they'd come out of. After a while they come around out of the far aisle, around the light bulbs, records at discount of the Caribbean Six or Tony Martin Sings or some such gunk you wonder they waste the wax on, six-packs of candy bars, and plastic toys done up in cellophane that fall apart when a kid looks at them anyway. Around they come, Queenie still leading the way, and holding a little gray jar in her hand. Slots Three through Seven are unmanned and I could see her wondering between Stokes and me, but Stokesie with his usual luck draws an old party in baggy gray pants who stumbles up with four giant cans of pineapple juice (what do these bums *do* with all that pineapple juice? I've often asked myself) so the girls come to me. Queenie puts down the jar and I take it into my fingers icy cold. Kingfish Fancy Herring Snacks in Pure Sour Cream: 49¢. Now her hands are empty, not a ring or a bracelet, bare as God made them, and I wonder where the money's coming from. Still with that prim look she lifts a folded dollar bill out of the hollow at the center of her nubbled pink top. The jar went heavy in my hand. Really, I thought that was so cute.

Then everybody's luck begins to run out. Lengel comes in from haggling with a truck full of cabbages on the lot and is about to scuttle into the door marked MANAGER behind which he hides all day when the girls touch his eye. Lengel's pretty dreary, teaches Sunday school and the rest, but he doesn't miss that much. He comes over and says, "Girls, this isn't the beach."

Queenie blushes, though maybe it's just a brush of sunburn I was noticing for the first time, now that she was so close. "My mother asked me to pick up a jar of herring snacks." Her voice kind of startled me, the way voices do when you see the people first, coming out so flat and dumb yet kind of tony, too, the way it ticked over "pick up" and "snacks." All of a sudden I slid right down her voice into her living room. Her father and the other men were standing around in ice-cream coats and bow ties and the women were in sandals picking up herring snacks on toothpicks off a big glass plate and they were all holding drinks the color of water with olives and sprigs of mint in them. When my parents have somebody over they get lemonade and if it's a real racy affair Schlitz in tall glasses with "They'll Do It Every Time" cartoons stencilled on.

15    "That's all right," Lengel said. "But this isn't the beach." His repeating this struck me as funny, as if it had just occurred to him, and he had been thinking all these years the A & P was a great big dune and he was the head lifeguard. He didn't like my smiling—as I say he doesn't miss much—but he concentrates on giving the girls that sad Sunday-school-superintendent stare.

Queenie's blush is no sunburn now, and the plump one in plaid, that I liked better from the back—a really sweet can—pipes up, "We weren't doing any shopping. We just came in for the one thing."

"That makes no difference," Lengel tells her, and I could see from the way his eyes went that he hadn't noticed she was wearing a two-piece before. "We want you decently dressed when you come in here."

"We *are* decent," Queenie says suddenly, her lower lip pushing, getting sore now that she remembers her place, a place from which the crowd that runs the A & P must look pretty crummy. Fancy Herring Snacks flashed in her very blue eyes.

"Girls, I don't want to argue with you. After this come in here with your shoulders covered. It's our policy." He turns his back. That's policy for you. Policy is what the kingpins want. What the others want is juvenile delinquency.

20  All this while, the customers had been showing up with their carts but, you know, sheep, seeing a scene, they had all bunched up on Stokesie, who shook open a paper bag as gently as peeling a peach, not wanting to miss a word. I could feel in the silence everybody getting nervous, most of all Lengel, who asks me, "Sammy, have you rung up this purchase?"

I thought and said "No" but it wasn't about that I was thinking. I go through the punches, 4, 9, GROC, TOT—it's more complicated than you think, and after you do it often enough, it begins to make a little song, that you hear words to, in my case "Hello (*bing*) there, you (*gung*) hap-py *pee*pul (*splat*)!"—the *splat* being the drawer flying out. I uncrease the bill, tenderly as you may imagine, it just having come from between the two smoothest scoops of vanilla I had ever known were there, and pass a half and a penny into her narrow pink palm, and nestle the herrings in a bag and twist its neck and hand it over, all the time thinking.

The girls, and who'd blame them, are in a hurry to get out, so I say "I quit" to Lengel quick enough for them to hear, hoping they'll stop and watch me, their unsuspected hero. They keep right on going, into the electric eye; the door flies open and they flicker across the lot to their car, Queenie and Plaid and Big Tall Goony-Goony (not that as raw material she was so bad), leaving me with Lengel and a kink in his eyebrow.

"Did you say something, Sammy?"

"I said I quit."

25  "I thought you did."

"You didn't have to embarrass them."

"It was they who were embarrassing us."

I started to say something that came out "Fiddle-de-doo." It's a saying of my grandmother's, and I know she would have been pleased.

"I don't think you know what you're saying," Lengel said.

30  "I know you don't," I said. "But I do." I pull the bow at the back of my apron and start shrugging it off my shoulders. A couple customers that had been heading for my slot begin to knock against each other, like scared pigs in a chute.

Lengel sighs and begins to look very patient and old and gray. He's been a friend of my parents for years. "Sammy, you don't want to do this to your Mom and Dad," he tells me. It's true, I don't. But it seems to me that once you begin a gesture it's fatal not to go through with it. I fold the apron, "Sammy" stitched in red on the pocket, and put it on the counter, and drop the bow tie on top of it. The bow tie is theirs, if you've ever wondered. "You'll feel this for the rest of your life," Lengel says, and I know that's true, too, but remembering how he made that pretty girl blush makes me so scrunchy inside I punch the No Sale tab and the machine whirs "pee-pul" and the drawer splats out. One advantage to this scene taking place in summer, I can follow this up with a clean exit, there's no fumbling around getting your coat and galoshes, I just saunter into the electric eye in my white shirt that my mother ironed the night before, and the door heaves itself open, and outside the sunshine is skating around on the asphalt.

I look around for my girls, but they're gone, of course. There wasn't anybody but some young married screaming with her children about some candy they didn't get by the door of a powder-blue Falcon station wagon. Looking back in the big windows, over the bags of peat moss and aluminum lawn furniture stacked on the pavement, I could see Lengel in my place in the slot, checking the sheep through. His face was dark gray and his back stiff, as if he'd just had an injection of iron, and my stomach kind of fell as I felt how hard the world was going to be to me hereafter.

**YOUR TURN**

1. In what sort of community is this A & P located? To what extent does this community resemble yours?
2. Do you think Sammy is a male chauvinist pig? Why, or why not? And if you think he is, do you find the story offensive? Again, why or why not?
3. In the last line of the story Sammy says, "I felt how hard the world was going to be to me hereafter." Do you think the world is going to be hard to Sammy? Why, or why not? And if it is hard to him, is this because of a virtue or a weakness in Sammy?
4. Write Lengel's version of the story (500–1000 words) as he might narrate it to his wife during dinner. Or write the story from Queenie's point of view.
5. In speaking of contemporary fiction Updike said:

   > I want stories to startle and engage me within the first few sentences, and in their middle to widen or deepen or sharpen my knowledge of human activity, and to end by giving me a sensation of completed statement.

   Let's assume that you share Updike's view of what a story should do. To what extent do you think "A & P" fulfills these demands? (You may want to put your response in the form of a letter to Updike.)
6. During the course of an interview published in the *Southern Review* (Spring 2002), Updike said that the original ending of "A & P" differed from the present ending. In the original, after Sammy resigns he "goes down to the beach to try to see these three girls on whose behalf he's made this sacrifice of respectability, on whose behalf he's broken with the bourgeois norm and let his parents down and Mr. Lengel down. And he doesn't see the girls, and the story ended somewhere there." Updike's editor at the *New Yorker* persuaded him that the story "ended with the resignation." Your view?

# ANONYMOUS

*The following story about King Solomon, customarily called "The Judgment of Solomon," appears in the Hebrew Bible, in the latter part of the third chapter of the book called 1 Kings or First Kings, probably written in the mid-sixth century* BCE. *The translation is from the King James Version of the Bible (1611). Two expressions in the story need clarification: (1) The woman who "overlaid" her child in her sleep rolled over on the child and suffocated it; and (2) it is said of a woman that her "bowels yearned upon her son"—that is, her heart longed for her son. (In Hebrew psychology, the bowels were thought to be the seat of emotion.)*

## *The Judgment of Solomon*

Then came there two women, that were harlots, unto the king, and stood before him. And the one woman said, "O my lord, I and this woman dwell in one house, and I was delivered of a child with her in the house. And it came to pass the third day after that I was delivered, that this woman was delivered also: and we were together; there was no stranger in the house, save we two in the house. And this woman's child died in the night; because she overlaid it. And she arose at midnight, and took my son from beside me, while thine handmaid slept, and laid it in her bosom, and laid her dead child in my bosom. And when I rose in the morning to give my child suck, behold, it was dead: but when I considered it in the morning, behold, it was not my son, which I did bear."

And the other woman said, "Nay; but the living is my son, and the dead is thy son." And this said, "No; but the dead is thy son, and the living is my son." Thus they spake before the king.

Then said the king, "The one saith, 'This is my son that liveth, and thy son is dead': and the other saith, 'Nay; but thy son is the dead, and my son is the living.'" And the king said, "Bring me a sword." And they brought a sword before the king. And the king said, "Divide the living child in two, and give half to the one, and half to the other."

Then spake the woman whose the living child was unto the king, for her bowels yearned upon her son, and she said, "O my lord, give her the living child, and in no wise slay it." But the other said, "Let it be neither mine nor thine, but divide it."

5      Then the king answered and said, "Give her the living child, and in no wise slay it: she is the mother thereof."

And all Israel heard of the judgment which the king had judged; and they feared the king, for they saw that the wisdom of God was in him to do judgment.

---

**YOUR TURN**

1. In what ways is this story like a detective story?
2. Solomon was known for his wisdom. How would you characterize his wisdom?

# KATHERINE ANNE PORTER

*Katherine Anne Porter (1890–1980) had the curious habit of inventing details in her life, but it is true that she was born in a log cabin in Indian Creek, Texas, that she was originally named Callie Russell Porter, that her mother died when she was two years old, and that Callie was brought up by her maternal grandmother in Kyle, Texas. Apparently the family was conscious of former wealth and position in Louisiana and Kentucky. She was sent to convent schools, where, in her words, she received "a strangely useless and ornamental education." At sixteen she left school, married (and soon divorced), and worked as a reporter, first in Texas and later in Denver and Chicago. She moved around a good deal, both within the United States and abroad; she lived in Mexico, Belgium, Switzerland, France, and Germany.*

*Even as a child Porter was interested in writing, but she did not publish her first story until she was thirty-three. She wrote essays and one novel* (Ship of Fools, 1962), *but she is best known for her stories. Porter's* Collected Stories *won the Pulitzer Prize and the National Book Award in 1965.*

## The Jilting of Granny Weatherall

[1929]

She flicked her wrist neatly out of Doctor Harry's pudgy careful fingers and pulled the sheet up to her chin. The brat ought to be in knee breeches. Doctoring around the country with spectacles on his nose! "Get along now, take your schoolbooks and go. There's nothing wrong with me."

Doctor Harry spread a warm paw like a cushion on her forehead where the forked green vein danced and made her eyelids twitch. "Now, now, be a good girl, and we'll have you up in no time."

"That's no way to speak to a woman nearly eighty years old just because she's down. I'd have you respect your elders, young man."

"Well, Missy, excuse me." Doctor Harry patted her cheek. "But I've got to warn you, haven't I? You're a marvel, but you must be careful or you're going to be good and sorry."

5      "Don't tell me what I'm going to be. I'm on my feet now, morally speaking. It's Cornelia. I had to go to bed to get rid of her."

Her bones felt loose, and floated around in her skin, and Doctor Harry floated like a balloon around the foot of the bed. He floated and pulled down his waistcoat and swung his glasses on a cord. "Well, stay where you are, it certainly can't hurt you."

"Get along and doctor your sick," said Granny Weatherall. "Leave a well woman alone. I'll call for you when I want you. . . . Where were you forty years ago when I pulled through milk-leg and double pneumonia? You weren't even born. Don't let Cornelia lead you on," she shouted, because Doctor Harry appeared to float up to the ceiling and out. "I pay my own bills, and I don't throw my money away on nonsense!"

She meant to wave good-by, but it was too much trouble. Her eyes closed of themselves, it was like a dark curtain drawn around the bed. The pillow rose and floated under her, pleasant as a hammock in a light wind. She listened to the leaves rustling outside the window. No, somebody was swishing newspapers: no, Cornelia and Doctor Harry were whispering together. She leaped broad awake, thinking they whispered in her ear.

"She was never like this, *never* like this!" "Well, what can we expect?" "Yes, eighty years old. . . ."

10      Well, and what if she was? She still had ears. It was like Cornelia to whisper around doors. She always kept things secret in such a public way. She was always being tactful and kind. Cornelia was dutiful; that was the trouble with her. Dutiful and good: "So good and dutiful," said Granny, "that I'd like to spank her." She saw herself spanking Cornelia and making a fine job of it.

"What'd you say, Mother?"

Granny felt her face tying up in hard knots.

"Can't a body think, I'd like to know?"

"I thought you might want something."

15        "I do. I want a lot of things. First off, go away and don't whisper."

She lay and drowsed, hoping in her sleep that the children would keep out and let her rest a minute. It had been a long day. Not that she was tired. It was always pleasant to snatch a minute now and then. There was always so much to be done, let me see: tomorrow.

Tomorrow was far away and there was nothing to trouble about. Things were finished somehow when the time came; thank God there was always a little margin over for peace: then a person could spread out the plan of life and tuck in the edges orderly. It was good to have everything clean and folded away, with the hair brushes and tonic bottles sitting straight on the white embroidered linen: the day started without fuss and the pantry shelves laid out with rows of jelly glasses and brown jugs and white stone-china jars with blue whirligigs and words painted on them: coffee, tea, sugar, ginger, cinnamon, allspice: and the bronze clock with the lion on top nicely dusted off. The dust that lion could collect in twenty-four hours! The box in the attic with all those letters tied up, well, she'd have to go through that tomorrow. All those letters—George's letters and John's letters and her letters to them both—lying around for the children to find afterwards made her uneasy. Yes, that would be tomorrow's business. No use to let them know how silly she had been once.

While she was rummaging around she found death in her mind and it felt clammy and unfamiliar. She had spent so much time preparing for death there was no need for bringing it up again. Let it take care of itself now. When she was sixty she had felt very old, finished, and went around making farewell trips to see her children and grandchildren, with a secret in her mind: This is the very last of your mother, children! Then she made her will and came down with a long fever. That was all just a notion like a lot of other things, but it was lucky too, for she had once for all got over the idea of dying for a long time. Now she couldn't be worried. She hoped she had better sense now. Her father had lived to be one hundred and two years old and had drunk a noggin of strong hot toddy on his last birthday. He told the reporters it was his daily habit, and he owed his long life to that. He had made quite a scandal and was very pleased about it. She believed she'd just plague Cornelia a little.

"Cornelia! Cornelia!" No footsteps, but a sudden hand on her cheek. "Bless you, where have you been?"

20        "Here, Mother."

"Well, Cornelia, I want a noggin of hot toddy."

"Are you cold, darling?"

"I'm chilly, Cornelia. Lying in bed stops the circulation. I must have told you that a thousand times."

Well, she could just hear Cornelia tell her husband that Mother was getting a little childish and they'd have to humor her. The thing that most annoyed her was that Cornelia thought she was deaf, dumb, and blind. Little hasty glances and tiny gestures tossed around her and over her head saying, "Don't cross her, let her have her way, she's eighty years old," and she sitting there as if she lived in a thin glass cage. Sometimes Granny almost made up her mind to pack up and move back to her own house where nobody could remind her every minute that she was old. Wait, wait, Cornelia, till your own children whisper behind your back!

25         In her day she had kept a better house and had got more work done. She wasn't too old yet for Lydia to be driving eighty miles for advice when one of the children jumped the track, and Jimmy still dropped in and talked things over: "Now, Mammy, you've a good business head, I want to know what you think of this? . . ." Old. Cornelia couldn't change the furniture around without asking. Little things, little things! They had been so sweet when they were little. Granny wished the old days were back again with the children young and everything to be done over. It had been a hard pull, but not too much for her. When she thought of all the food she had cooked, and all the clothes she had cut and sewed, and all the gardens she had made— well, the children showed it. There they were, made out of her, and they couldn't get away from that. Sometimes she wanted to see John again and point to them and say, Well, I didn't do so badly, did I? But that would have to wait. That was for tomorrow. She used to think of him as a man, but now all the children were older than their father, and he would be a child beside her if she saw him now. It seemed strange and there was something wrong in the idea. Why, he couldn't possibly recognize her. She had fenced in a hundred acres once, digging the post holes herself and clamping the wires with just a negro boy to help. That changed a woman. John would be looking for a young woman with the peaked Spanish comb in her hair and the painted fan. Digging post holes changed a woman. Riding country roads in the winter when women had their babies was another thing: sitting up nights with sick horses and sick negroes and sick children and hardly ever losing one. John, I hardly ever lost one of them! John would see that in a minute, that would be something he could understand, she wouldn't have to explain anything!

It made her feel like rolling up her sleeves and putting the whole place to rights again. No matter if Cornelia was determined to be everywhere at once, there were a great many things left undone on this place. She would start tomorrow and do them. It was good to be strong enough for everything, even if all you made melted and changed and slipped under your hands, so that by the time you finished you almost forgot what you were working for. What was it I set out to do? she asked herself intently, but she could not remember. A fog rose over the valley, she saw it marching across the creek swallowing the trees and moving up the hill like an army of ghosts. Soon it would be at the near edge of the orchard, and then it was time to go in and light the lamps. Come in, children, don't stay out in the night air.

Lighting the lamps had been beautiful. The children huddled up to her and breathed like little calves waiting at the bars in the twilight. Their eyes followed the match and watched the flame rise and settle in a blue curve, then they moved away from her. The lamp was lit, they didn't have to be scared and hang on to mother any more. Never, never, never more. God, for all my life I thank Thee. Without Thee, my God, I could never have done it. Hail, Mary, full of grace.

I want you to pick all the fruit this year and see that nothing is wasted. There's always someone who can use it. Don't let good things rot for want of using. You waste life when you waste good food. Don't let things get lost. It's bitter to lose things. Now, don't let me get to thinking, not when I am tired and taking a little nap before supper. . . .

The pillow rose about her shoulders and pressed against her heart and the memory was being squeezed out of it: oh, push down the pillow, some-body: it would smother her if she tried to hold it. Such a fresh breeze blow-ing and such a green day with no threats in it. But he had not come, just the same. What does a woman do when she has put on the white veil and set out the white cake for a man and he doesn't come? She tried to remember. No, I swear he never harmed me but in that. He never harmed me but in that . . . and what if he did? There was the day, the day, but a whirl of dark smoke rose and covered it, crept up and over into the bright field where everything was planted so carefully in orderly rows. That was hell, she knew hell when she saw it. For sixty years she had prayed against remembering him and against losing her soul in the deep pit of hell, and now the two things were mingled in one and the thought of him was a smoky cloud from hell that moved and crept in her head when she had just got rid of Doctor Harry and was trying to rest a minute. Wounded vanity, Ellen, said a sharp voice in the top of her mind. Don't let your wounded vanity get the upper hand of you. Plenty of girls get jilted. You were jilted, weren't you? Then stand up to it. Her eyelids wavered and let in streamers of blue-gray light like tissue paper over her eyes. She must get up and pull the shades down or she'd never sleep. She was in bed again and the shades were not down. How could that happen? Better turn over, hide from the light, sleeping in the light gave you nightmares. "Mother, how do you feel now?" and a stinging wet-ness on her forehead. But I don't like having my face washed in cold water!

30    Hapsy? George? Lydia? Jimmy? No, Cornelia, and her features were swollen and full of little puddles. "They're coming, darling, they'll all be here soon." Go wash your face, child, you look funny.

Instead of obeying, Cornelia knelt down and put her head on the pil-low. She seemed to be talking but there was no sound. "Well, are you tongue-tied? Whose birthday is it? Are you going to give a party?"

Cornelia's mouth moved urgently in strange shapes. "Don't do that, you bother me, daughter."

"Oh, no, Mother. Oh, no. . . ."

Nonsense. It was strange about children. They disputed your every word. "No what, Cornelia?"

35    "Here's Doctor Harry."

"I won't see that boy again. He just left five minutes ago."

"That was this morning, Mother. It's night now. Here's the nurse."

"This is Doctor Harry, Mrs. Weatherall. I never saw you look so young and happy!"

"Ah, I'll never be young again—but I'd be happy if they'd let me lie in peace and get rested."

40    She thought she spoke up loudly, but no one answered. A warm weight on her forehead, a warm bracelet on her wrist, and a breeze went on whis-pering, trying to tell her something. A shuffle of leaves in the everlasting hand of God. He blew on them and they danced and rattled. "Mother, don't mind, we're going to give you a little hypodermic." "Look here, daughter, how do ants get in this bed? I saw sugar ants yesterday." Did you send for Hapsy too?

It was Hapsy she really wanted. She had to go a long way back through a great many rooms to find Hapsy standing with a baby on her arm. She seemed to herself to be Hapsy also, and the baby on Hapsy's arm was Hapsy and himself and herself, all at once, and there was no surprise in the meeting. Then Hapsy melted from within and turned flimsy as gray gauze and the baby was a gauzy shadow, and Hapsy came up close and said, "I thought you'd never come," and looked at her very searchingly and said, "You haven't changed a bit!" They leaned forward to kiss, when Cornelia began whispering from a long way off, "Oh, is there anything you want to tell me? Is there anything I can do for you?"

Yes, she had changed her mind after sixty years and she would like to see George. I want you to find George. Find him and be sure to tell him I forgot him. I want him to know I had my husband just the same and my children and my house like any other woman. A good house too and a good husband that I loved and fine children out of him. Better than I hoped for even. Tell him I was given back everything he took away and more. Oh, no, oh, God, no, there was something else besides the house and the man and the children. Oh, surely they were not all? What was it? Something not given back. . . . Her breath crowded down under her ribs and grew into a monstrous frightening shape with cutting edges; it bored up into her head, and the agony was unbelievable: Yes, John, get the doctor now, no more talk, my time has come.

When this one was born it should be the last. The last. It should have been born first, for it was the one she had truly wanted. Everything came in good time. Nothing left out, left over. She was strong, in three days she would be as well as ever. Better. A woman needed milk in her to have her full health.

"Mother, do you hear me?"

45    "I've been telling you—"

"Mother, Father Connolly's here."

"I went to Holy Communion only last week. Tell him I'm not so sinful as all that."

"Father just wants to speak to you."

He could speak as much as he pleased. It was like him to drop in and inquire about her soul as if it were a teething baby, and then stay on for a cup of tea and a round of cards and gossip. He always had a funny story of some sort, usually about an Irishman who made his little mistakes and confessed them, and the point lay in some absurd thing he would blurt out in the confessional showing his struggles between native piety and original sin. Granny felt easy about her soul. Cornelia, where are your manners? Give Father Connolly a chair. She had her secret comfortable understanding with a few favorite saints who cleared a straight road to God for her. All as surely signed and sealed as the papers for the new Forty Acres. Forever . . . heirs and assigns forever. Since the day the wedding cake was not cut, but thrown out and wasted. The whole bottom dropped out of the world, and there she was blind and sweating with nothing under her feet and the walls falling away. His hand had caught her under the breast, she had not fallen, there was the freshly polished floor with the green rug on it, just as before. He had cursed like a sailor's parrot and said, "I'll kill him for you." Don't lay a hand on him, for my sake leave something to God. "Now, Ellen, you must believe what I tell you. . . ."

50    So there was nothing, nothing to worry about any more, except sometimes in the night one of the children screamed in a nightmare, and they

both hustled out shaking and hunting for the matches and calling, "There, wait a minute, here we are!" John, get the doctor now, Hapsy's time has come. But there was Hapsy standing by the bed in a white cap. "Cornelia, tell Hapsy to take off her cap. I can't see her plain."

Her eyes opened very wide and the room stood out like a picture she had seem somewhere. Dark colors with the shadows rising towards the ceiling in long angles. The tall black dresser gleamed with nothing on it but John's picture, enlarged from a little one, with John's eyes very black when they should have been blue. You never saw him, so how do you know how he looked? But the man insisted the copy was perfect, it was very rich and handsome. For a picture, yes, but it's not my husband. The table by the bed had a linen cover and a candle and a crucifix. The light was blue from Cornelia's silk lampshades. No sort of light at all, just frippery. You had to live forty years with kerosene lamps to appreciate honest electricity. She felt very strong and she saw Doctor Harry with a rosy nimbus around him.

"You look like a saint, Doctor Harry, and I vow that's as near as you'll ever come to it."

"She's saying something."

"I heard you, Cornelia. What's all this carrying on?"

55      "Father Connolly's saying—"

Cornelia's voice staggered and bumped like a cart in a bad road. It rounded corners and turned back again and arrived nowhere. Granny stepped up in the cart very lightly and reached for the reins, but a man sat beside her and she knew him by his hands, driving the cart. She did not look in his face, for she knew without seeing, but looked instead down the road where the trees leaned over and bowed to each other and a thousand birds were singing a Mass. She felt like singing too, but she put her hand in the bosom of her dress and pulled out a rosary, and Father Connolly murmured Latin in a very solemn voice and tickled her feet. My God, will you stop that nonsense? I'm a married woman. What if he did run away and leave me to face the priest by myself? I found another a whole world better. I wouldn't have exchanged my husband for anybody except St. Michael himself, and you may tell him that for me with a thank you in the bargain.

Light flashed on her closed eyelids, and a deep roaring shook her. Cornelia, is that lightning? I hear thunder. There's going to be a storm. Close all the windows. Call all the children in. . . . "Mother, here we are, all of us." "Is that you, Hapsy?" "Oh, no, I'm Lydia. We drove as fast as we could." Their faces drifted above her, drifted away. The rosary fell out of her hands and Lydia put it back. Jimmy tried to help, their hands fumbled together, and Granny closed two fingers around Jimmy's thumb. Beads wouldn't do, it must be something alive. She was so amazed her thoughts ran round and round. So, my dear Lord, this is my death and I wasn't even thinking about it. My children have come to see me die. But I can't, it's not time. Oh, I always hated surprises. I wanted to give Cornelia the amethyst set—Cornelia, you're to have the amethyst set, but Hapsy's to wear it when she wants, and, Doctor Harry, do shut up. Nobody sent for you. Oh, my dear Lord, do wait a minute. I meant to do something about the Forty Acres, Jimmy doesn't need it and Lydia will later on, with that worthless husband of hers. I meant to finish the altar cloth and send six bottles of wine to Sister Borgia for her dyspepsia. I want to send six bottles of wine to Sister Borgia, Father Connolly, now don't let me forget.

Cornelia's voice made short turns and tilted over and crashed. "Oh, Mother, oh, Mother, oh, Mother. . . ."

"I'm not going, Cornelia. I'm taken by surprise. I can't go."

60     You'll see Hapsy again. What about her? "I thought you'd never come." Granny made a long journey outward, looking for Hapsy. What if I don't find her? What then? Her heart sank down and down, there was no bottom to death, she couldn't come to the end of it. The blue light from Cornelia's lampshade drew into a tiny point in the center of her brain, it flickered and winked like an eye, quietly it fluttered and dwindled. Granny lay curled down within herself, amazed and watchful, staring at the point of light that was herself; her body was now only a deeper mass of shadow in an endless darkness and this darkness would curl around the light and swallow it up. God, give a sign!

For the second time there was no sign. Again no bridegroom and the priest in the house. She could not remember any other sorrow because this grief wiped them all away. Oh, no, there's nothing more cruel than this—I'll never forgive it. She stretched herself with a deep breath and blew out the light.

### YOUR TURN

1. How would you describe Granny Weatherall? In what ways does her name suit her?
2. The final paragraph begins: "For the second time there was no sign." What happened the first time? What is happening now? How are the two events linked? (The paragraph alludes to Christ's parable of the bridegroom, in Matthew 25.1–13. If you are unfamiliar with the parable, read it in the Gospel According to Matthew.)
3. What do you think happens in the last line of the story?

# ANNIE PROULX

*Annie Proulx (pronounced* proo*) was born in Norwich, Connecticut, in 1935, but her family moved frequently, not only within New England but also to North Carolina. She studied at Colby College briefly, received a bachelor's degree from the University of Vermont, and did graduate work in history at Concordia University in Quebec but abandoned the doctoral program and set out as a freelance journalist. After writing several "how to" books (such as* Sweet and Hard Cider: Making It, Using It, and Enjoying It *[1980]) and bringing up three sons, she began writing short fiction, some of it for a men's magazine. In 1988 she published her first book, a collection of nine stories,* Heart Songs and Other Stories. *Since then she has published additional novels and two collections of stories,* Close Range: Wyoming Stories *(2000)—she had moved to Wyoming in 1995—and* Bad Dirt *(2004). We reprint a story from* Close Range, *the collection that includes "Brokeback Mountain," a story that in 2005 was made into a movie.*

# *The Blood Bay*

[2000]

For Buzzy Malli[1]

The winter of 1886–87 was terrible. Every goddamn history of the high plains says so. There were great stocks of cattle on overgrazed land during the droughty summer. Early wet snow froze hard so the cattle could not break through the crust to the grass. Blizzards and freeze-eye cold followed, the gaunt bodies of cattle piling up in draws and coulees.

A young Montana cowboy, somewhat vain, had skimped on coat and mittens and put all his wages into a fine pair of handmade boots. He crossed into Wyoming Territory thinking it would be warmer, for it was south of where he was. That night he froze to death on Powder River's bitter west bank, that stream of famous dimensions and direction—an inch deep, a mile wide, and she flows uphill from Texas.

The next afternoon three cowpunchers from the Box Spring outfit near Suggs rode past his corpse, blue as a whetstone and half-buried in snow. They were savvy and salty. They wore blanket coats, woolly chaps, grease-wool scarves tied over their hats and under their bristled chins, sheepskin mitts, and two of them were fortunate enough to park their feet in good boots and heavy socks. The third, Dirt Sheets, a cross-eyed drinker of hair-oil, was all right on top but his luck was running muddy near the bottom, no socks and curl-toe boots cracked and holed.

"That can a corn beef's wearin my size boots," Sheets said and got off his horse for the first time that day. He pulled at the Montana cowboy's left boot but it was frozen on. The right one didn't come off any easier.

5          "Son of a sick steer in a snowbank," he said, "I'll cut em off and thaw em after supper." Sheets pulled out a Bowie knife and sawed through Montana's shins just above the boot tops, put the booted feet in his saddlebags, admiring the tooled leather and topstitched hearts and clubs. They rode on down the river looking for strays, found a dozen bogged in deep drifts and lost most of the daylight getting them out.

"Too late to try for the bunkhouse. Old man Grice's shack is some-wheres up along. He's bound a have dried prunes or other dainties or at least a hot stove." The temperature was dropping, so cold that spit crackled in the air and a man didn't dare to piss for fear he'd be rooted fast until spring. They agreed it must be forty below and more, the wind scything up a nice Wyoming howler.

They found the shack four miles north. Old man Grice opened the door a crack.

"Come on in, puncher or rustler, I don't care."

"We'll put our horses up. Where's the barn?"

10          "Barn. Never had one. There's a lean-to out there behind the woodpile should keep em from blowin away or maybe freezin. I got my two horses in here beside the dish cupboard. I pamper them babies somethin terrible. Sleep where you can find a space, but I'm tellin you don't bother that blood

---

[1]**Buzzy Malli** the proprietor of a bar in Arvada, Wyoming.

bay none, he will mull you up and spit you out. He's a spirited steed. Pull up a chair and have some a this son-of-a-bitch stew. And I got plenty conversation juice a wash it down. Hot biscuits just comin out a the oven."

It was a fine evening, eating, drinking, and playing cards, swapping lies, the stove kicking out heat, old man Grice's spoiled horses sighing in comfort. The only disagreeable tone to the evening from the waddies[2] point of view was the fact that their host cleaned them out, took them for three dollars and four bits. Around midnight Grice blew out the lamp and got in his bunk and the three punchers stretched out on the floor. Sheets set his trophies behind the stove, laid his head on his saddle, and went to sleep.

He woke half an hour before daylight, recalled it was his mother's birthday and if he wanted to telegraph a filial sentiment to her he would have to ride faster than chain lightning with the links snapped, for the Overland office closed at noon. He checked his grisly trophies, found them thawed and pulled the boots and socks off the originals, drew them onto his own pedal extremities. He threw the bare Montana feet and his old boots in the corner near the dish cupboard, slipped out like a falling feather, saddled his horse, and rode away. The wind was low and the fine cold air refreshed him.

Old man Grice was up with the sun grinding coffee beans and frying bacon. He glanced down at his rolled-up guests and said, "Coffee's ready." The blood bay stamped and kicked at something that looked like a man's foot. Old man Grice took a closer look.

"There's a bad start to the day," he said, "it is a man's foot and there's the other." He counted the sleeping guests. There were only two of them.

15     "Wake up, survivors, for god's sake wake up and get up."

The two punchers rolled out, stared wild-eyed at the old man who was fairly frothing, pointing at the feet on the floor behind the blood bay.

"He's ate Sheets. Ah, I knew he was a hard horse, but to eat a man whole. You savage bugger," he screamed at the blood bay and drove him out into the scorching cold. "You'll never eat human meat again. You'll sleep out with the blizzards and wolves, you hell-bound fiend." Secretly he was pleased to own a horse with the sand to eat a raw cowboy.

The leftover Box Spring riders were up and drinking coffee. They squinted at old man Grice, hitched at their gun belts.

"Ah, boys, for god's sake, it was a terrible accident. I didn't know what a brute of a animal was that blood bay. Let's keep this to ourselves. Sheets was no prize and I've got forty gold dollars says so and the three and four bits I took off a you last night. Eat your bacon, don't make no trouble. There's enough trouble in the world without no more."

20     No, they wouldn't make trouble and they put the heavy money in their saddlebags, drank a last cup of hot coffee, saddled up, and rode out into the grinning morning.

When they saw Sheets that night at the bunkhouse they nodded, congratulated him on his mother's birthday but said nothing about blood bays or forty-three dollars and four bits. The arithmetic stood comfortable.

---

[2]**Waddies** cowboys.

**YOUR TURN**

1. At what point did you first realize that you were reading a tall tale, a yarn, not a realistic short story?
2. What sorts of special pleasure—that is, pleasures different from those of the conventional short story—does the tall tale offer?
3. What, if anything, would be lost if the final paragraph of this yarn were omitted?

# 10

# Allegory and Symbolism

In Chapter 7 we looked at a fable, a short fiction that was meant to teach us: the characters clearly stood for principles of behavior, and the fictions as a whole evidently taught lessons. If you think of a fable such as "The Ant and the Grasshopper" (the ant wisely collects food during the summer in order to provide for the winter, whereas the grasshopper foolishly sings all summer and goes hungry in the winter), you can easily see that the characters may stand for something other than themselves. The ant, let's say, is the careful, foresighted person, and the grasshopper is the person who lives for the moment. Similarly, in the fable of the tortoise and the hare, the tortoise represents the person who is slow but steady, the rabbit the person who is talented but overly confident and, in the end, foolish.

A story in which each character is understood to have an equivalent is an **allegory.** Further, in an allegory, not only characters but also things (roads, forests, houses) have fairly clear equivalents. Thus, in John Bunyan's *The Pilgrim's Progress* (1678) we meet a character named Christian, who, on the road to the Celestial City, meets Giant Despair, Mr. Worldly Wiseman, and Faithful, and passes through the City of Destruction and Vanity Fair. What all of these are equivalent to is clear from their names. It is also clear that Christian's journey stands for the trials of the soul in this world. There is, so to speak, a one-to-one relationship: A = B =, and so on. If, for example, we are asked what the road represents in *The Pilgrim's Progress,* we can confidently say that it stands for the journey of life. Thus, *The Pilgrim's Progress* tells two stories, the surface story of a man making a trip, during which he meets various figures and visits various places, and a second story, understood through the first, of the trials that afflict the soul during its quest for salvation.

Modern short stories rarely have the allegory's clear system of equivalents, but we may nevertheless feel that certain characters and certain things in the story stand for more than themselves, or hint at larger meanings. We feel, that is, that they are **symbolic.** But here we must be careful. How does one know that this or that figure or place is symbolic? In Hemingway's "Cat in the Rain" (page 99), is the cat symbolic? Is the innkeeper? Is the rain? Reasonable people may differ in their answers. Again, in Chopin's "The Story of an Hour" (page 67), is the railroad accident a symbol? Is Josephine a symbol? Is the season (springtime) a symbol? And again, reasonable people may differ in their responses.

Let's assume for the moment, however, that if writers use symbols, they want readers to perceive—at least faintly—that certain characters or places or seasons or happenings have rich implications, stand for something more than what they are on the surface. How do writers help us to perceive these things? By emphasizing them—for instance, by describing them at some length, or by introducing them at times when they might not seem strictly necessary, or by calling attention to them repeatedly.

Consider, for example, Chopin's treatment of the season in which "The Story of an Hour" takes place. The story has to take place at *some* time, but Chopin does not simply say, "On a spring day," or an autumn day, and let things go at that. Rather, she tells us about the sky, the trees, the rain, the twittering sparrows—and all of this in an extremely short story where we might think there is no time for talk about the setting. After all, none of this material is strictly necessary to a story about a woman who has heard that her husband was killed in an accident, who grieves, then recovers, and then dies when he suddenly reappears.

Why, then, does Chopin give such emphasis to the season? Because, we think, she is using the season symbolically. In this story, the spring is not just a bit of detail added for realism. It is rich with suggestions of renewal, of the new life that Louise achieves for a moment. But here, a caution. We think that the spring in this story is symbolic, but this is not to say that whenever spring appears in a story, it always stands for renewal, any more than whenever winter appears it always symbolizes death. Nor does it mean that since spring recurs, Louise will be reborn. In short, in *this* story Chopin uses the season to convey specific implications.

Is the railroad accident also a symbol? Our answer is no—though we don't expect all readers to agree with us. We think that the railroad accident in "The Story of an Hour" is just a railroad accident. It's our sense that Chopin is *not* using this event to say something about (for instance) modern travel, or about industrialism. The steam-propelled railroad train could of course be used, symbolically, to say something about industrialism displacing an agrarian economy, but does Chopin give her train any such suggestion? We don't think so. Had she wished to do so, she would probably have talked about the enormous power of the train, the shriek of its whistle, the smoke pouring out of the smokestack, the intense fire burning in the engine, its indifference as it charged through the countryside, and so forth. Had she done so, the story would be a different story. Or she might have made the train a symbol of fate overriding human desires. But, again in our opinion, Chopin does not endow her train with such suggestions. She gives virtually no emphasis to the train, and so we believe it has virtually no significance for the reader.

What of Chopin's "Ripe Figs" (page 87)? Maman-Nainaine tells Babette that when the figs are ripe Babette can visit her cousins. Maman may merely be setting an arbitrary date, but as we read the story we probably feel—because of the emphasis on the *ripening* of the figs, which occurs in the spring or early summer—that the ripening of the figs in some way suggests the maturing of Babette. If we do get such ideas, we will in effect be saying that the story is not simply an anecdote about an old woman whose behavior is odd. True, the narrator of the story, after telling us of Maman-Nainaine's promise, adds, "Not that the ripening of figs had the least thing to do with it, but that is the way Maman-Nainaine was." The narrator sees nothing special—merely Maman-Nainaine's eccentricity—in the connection between the ripening of the figs and Babette's visit to her cousins. Readers, however, may see more than the narrator sees or says. They may see in Babette a young girl maturing; they may see in Maman-Nainaine an older woman who, almost collaborating with nature, helps Babette to mature.

# Symbolism and Theme

And here, as we talk about symbolism we are getting into the theme of the story. An apparently inconsequential and even puzzling action, such as is set forth in "Ripe Figs," may cast a long shadow. As Robert Frost once said,

> There is no story written that has any value at all, however straightforward it looks and free from doubleness, double entendre, that you'd value at all if it didn't have intimations of something more than itself.

The stranger, the more mysterious the story, the more likely we are to suspect some sort of significance, but even realistic stories such as Chopin's "The Storm" and "The Story of an Hour" may be rich in suggestions. This is not to say, however, that the suggestions (rather than the details of the surface) are what count. A reader does not discard the richly detailed, highly specific narrative (Mrs. Mallard learned that her husband was dead and reacted in such-and-such a way) in favor of some supposedly universal message or theme that it implies. We do not throw away the specific narrative—the memorable characters, or the interesting things that happen in the story—and move on to some "higher truth." Robert Frost went on to say, "The anecdote, the parable, the surface meaning has got to be good and got to be sufficient in itself."

Between these two extremes—on the one hand, writing that is almost all a richly detailed surface and, on the other hand, writing that has a surface so thin that we are immediately taken up with the implications or meanings—are stories in which we strongly feel both the surface happenings and their implications. In *Place in Fiction*, Eudora Welty uses an image of a china lamp to explain literature that presents an interesting surface texture filled with rich significance. When unlit, the lamp showed London; when lit, it showed the Great Fire of London. Like a painted porcelain lamp that, when illuminated, reveals an inner picture shining through the outer, the physical details in a work are illuminated from within by the author's imaginative vision. The outer painting (the literal details) presents "a continuous, shapely, pleasing, and finished surface to the eye," but this surface is not the whole. Welty happens to be talking about the novel, but her words apply equally to the short story:

> The lamp alight is the combination of internal and external, glowing at the imagination as one; and so is the good novel. . . . The good novel should be steadily alight, revealing.

Details that glow, that are themselves and are also something more than themselves, are symbols. Readers may disagree about whether in any particular story something is or is not symbolic—let's say the figs and chrysanthemums in Chopin's "Ripe Figs," or the season in "The Story of an Hour." And an ingenious reader may overcomplicate or overemphasize the symbolism of a work or may distort it by omitting some of the details and by unduly focusing on others. In many works the details glow, but the glow is so gentle and subtle that even to talk about the details is to overstate them and to understate other equally important aspects of the work.

Yet if it is false to overstate the significance of a detail, it is also false to understate a significant detail. The let's-have-no-nonsense literal reader who holds that "the figure of a man" whom Brown meets in the forest in Hawthorne's "Young Goodman Brown" is simply a man—rather than the Devil—impoverishes the story by neglecting the rich implications just as much as the symbol-hunter impoverishes "The Story of an Hour" by losing sight of Mrs. Mallard in an interpretation of the story as a symbolic comment on industrialism. To take only a single piece of evidence: the man whom Brown encounters holds a staff, "which bore the likeness of a great black snake, so curiously wrought that it might almost be seen to twist and wriggle itself like a living serpent." If we are familiar with the story of Adam and Eve, in which Satan took the form of a serpent, it is hard not to think that Hawthorne is here implying that Brown's new acquaintance is Satan. And, to speak more broadly, when reading the story we can hardly not set up opposing meanings (or at least suggestions) for the village (from which Brown sets out) and the forest (into which he enters). The village is associated with daylight, faith, and goodness; the forest with darkness, loss of faith, and evil. This is not to say that the story sets up neat categories. If you read the story, you will find that Hawthorne is careful to be ambiguous. Even in the passage quoted, about the serpent-staff, you'll notice that he does not say it twisted and wriggled, but that it "might almost be seen to twist and wriggle."

# JOHN STEINBECK

*John Steinbeck (1902–1968) was born in Salinas, California, and much of his fiction concerns this landscape and its people. As a young man he worked on ranches, farms, and road gangs, and sometimes attended Stanford University— he never graduated—but he wrote whenever he could find the time. His early efforts at writing, however, were rejected by publishers. Even when he did break into print, he did not achieve much notice for several years: a novel in 1929, a book of stories in 1932, and another novel in 1933 attracted little attention. But the publication of* Tortilla Flat *(1935), a novel about Mexican-Americans, changed all that. It was followed by other successful novels—In* Dubious Battle *(1936) and* Of Mice and Men *(1937)—and by* The Long Valley *(1938), a collection of stories that included "The Chrysanthemums." His next book,* The Grapes of Wrath *(1939), about dispossessed sharecropper migrants from the Oklahoma dustbowl, was also immensely popular and won a Pulitzer Prize. During World War II Steinbeck sent reports from battlefields in Italy and Africa. In 1962 he was awarded the Nobel Prize in Literature.*

## *The Chrysanthemums*                                              [1937]

The high grey-flannel fog of winter closed off the Salinas Valley[1] from the sky and from all the rest of the world. On every side it sat like a lid on the mountains and made of the great valley a closed pot. On the broad, level land floor the gang plows bit deep and left the black earth shining like metal where the shares had cut. On the foothill ranches across the Salinas River, the yellow stubble fields seemed to be bathed in pale cold sunshine, but there was no sunshine in the valley now in December. The thick willow scrub along the river flamed with sharp and positive yellow leaves.

---

[1]**the Salinas Valley** a fertile area in central California.

It was a time of quiet and of waiting. The air was cold and tender. A light wind blew up from the southwest so that the farmers were mildly hopeful of a good rain before long; but fog and rain do not go together.

Across the river, on Henry Allen's foothill ranch there was little work to be done, for the hay was cut and stored and the orchards were plowed up to receive the rain deeply when it should come. The cattle on the higher slopes were becoming shaggy and rough-coated.

Elisa Allen, working in her flower garden, looked down across the yard and saw Henry, her husband, talking to two men in business suits. The three of them stood by the tractor shed, each man with one foot on the side of the little Fordson.[2] They smoked cigarettes and studied the machine as they talked.

5    Elisa watched them for a moment and then went back to her work. She was thirty-five. Her face was lean and strong and her eyes were as clear as water. Her figure looked blocked and heavy in her gardening costume, a man's black hat pulled low down over her eyes, clod-hopper shoes, a figured print dress almost completely covered by a big corduroy apron with four big pockets to hold the snips, the trowel and scratcher, the seeds and the knife she worked with. She wore heavy leather gloves to protect her hands while she worked.

She was cutting down the old year's chrysanthemum stalks with a pair of short and powerful scissors. She looked down toward the men by the tractor shed now and then. Her face was eager and mature and handsome; even her work with the scissors was over-eager, over-powerful. The chrysanthemum stems seemed too small and easy for her energy.

She brushed a cloud of hair out of her eyes with the back of her glove, and left a smudge of earth on her cheek in doing it. Behind her stood the neat white farm house with red geraniums close-banked around it as high as the windows. It was a hard-swept looking little house with hard-polished windows, and a clean mud-mat on the front steps.

Elisa cast another glance toward the tractor shed. The strangers were getting into their Ford coupe. She took off a glove and put her strong fingers down into the forest of new green chrysanthemum sprouts that were growing around the old roots. She spread the leaves and looked down among the close-growing stems. No aphids were there, no sowbugs or snails or cutworms. Her terrier fingers destroyed such pests before they could get started.

Elisa started at the sound of her husband's voice. He had come near quietly, and he leaned over the wire fence that protected her flower garden from the cattle and dogs and chickens.

10    "At it again," he said. "You've got a strong new crop coming."

Elisa straightened her back and pulled on the gardening glove again. "Yes, they'll be strong this coming year." In her tone and on her face there was a little smugness.

"You've got a gift with things," Henry observed. "Some of those yellow chrysanthemums you had this year were ten inches across. I wish you'd work out in the orchard and raise some apples that big."

---

[2]**Fordson** a two-door Ford car.

Her eyes sharpened. "Maybe I could do it, too. I've a gift with things, all right. My mother had it. She could stick anything in the ground and make it grow. She said it was having planters' hands that knew how to do it."

"Well, it sure works with flowers," he said.

15    "Henry, who were those men you were talking to?"

"Why, sure, that's what I came to tell you. They were from the Western Meat Company. I sold those thirty head of three-year-old steers. Got nearly my own price, too."

"Good," she said. "Good for you."

"And I thought," he continued, "I thought how it's Saturday afternoon, and we might go into Salinas for dinner at a restaurant, and then to a picture show—to celebrate, you see."

"Good," she repeated. "Oh, yes. That will be good."

20    Henry put on his joking tone. "There's fights tonight. How'd you like to go to the fights?"

"Oh, no," she said breathlessly. "No, I wouldn't like the fights."

"Just fooling, Elisa. We'll go to a movie. Let's see. It's two now. I'm going to take Scotty and bring down those steers from the hill. It'll take us maybe two hours. We'll go in town about five and have dinner at the Cominos Hotel. Like that?"

"Of course I'll like it. It's good to eat away from home."

"All right, then. I'll go get up a couple of horses."

25    She said, "I'll have plenty of time to transplant some of these sets, I guess."

She heard her husband calling Scotty down by the barn. And a little later she saw the two men ride up the pale yellow hillside in search of the steers.

There was a little square sandy bed kept for rooting the chrysanthemums. With her trowel she turned the soil over and over, and smoothed it and patted it firm. Then she dug ten parallel trenches to receive the sets. Back at the chrysanthemum bed she pulled out the little crisp shoots, trimmed off the leaves of each one with her scissors and laid it on a small orderly pile.

A squeak of wheels and plod of hoofs came from the road. Elisa looked up. The country road ran along the dense bank of willows and cottonwoods that bordered the river, and up this road came a curious vehicle, curiously drawn. It was an old springwagon, with a round canvas top on it like the cover of a prairie schooner. It was drawn by an old bay horse and a little grey-and-white burro. A big stubble-bearded man sat between the cover flaps and drove the crawling team. Underneath the wagon, between the hind wheels, a lean and rangy mongrel dog walked sedately. Words were painted on the canvas, in clumsy, crooked letters. "Pots, pans, knives, sisors, lawn mores, Fixed." Two rows of articles, and the triumphantly definitive "Fixed" below. The black paint had run down in little sharp points beneath each letter.

Elisa, squatting on the ground, watched to see the crazy, loose-jointed wagon pass by. But it didn't pass. It turned into the farm road in front of her house, crooked old wheels skirling and squeaking. The rangy dog darted from between the wheels and ran ahead. Instantly the two ranch shepherds flew out at him. Then all three stopped, and with stiff and quivering tails, with taut straight legs, with ambassadorial dignity, they slowly circled, sniffing daintily. The caravan pulled up to Elisa's wire fence and stopped. Now the newcomer dog, feeling out-numbered, lowered his tail and retired under the wagon with raised hackles and bared teeth.

30    The man on the wagon called out, "That's a bad dog in a fight when he gets started."

Elisa laughed. "I see he is. How soon does he generally get started?"

The man caught up her laughter and echoed it heartily. "Sometimes not for weeks and weeks," he said. He climbed stiffly down, over the wheel. The horse and donkey drooped like unwatered flowers.

Elisa saw that he was a very big man. Although his hair and beard were greying, he did not look old. His worn black suit was wrinkled and spotted with grease. The laughter had disappeared from his face and eyes the moment his laughing voice ceased. His eyes were dark, and they were full of the brooding that gets in the eyes of teamsters and of sailors. The calloused hands he rested on the wire fence were cracked, and every crack was a black line. He took off his battered hat.

"I'm off my general road, ma'am," he said. "Does this dirt road cut over across the river to the Los Angeles highway?"

35    Elisa stood up and shoved the thick scissors in her apron pocket. "Well, yes, it does, but it winds around and then fords the river. I don't think your team could pull it through the sand."

He replied with some asperity. "It might surprise you what them beasts can pull through."

"When they get started?" she asked.

He smiled for a second. "Yes. When they get started."

"Well," said Elisa, "I think you'll save time if you go back to the Salinas road and pick up the highway there."

40    He drew a big finger around the chicken wire and made it sing. "I ain't in any hurry, ma'am. I go from Seattle to San Diego and back every year. Takes all my time. About six months each way. I aim to follow nice weather."

Elisa took off her gloves and stuffed them in the apron pocket with the scissors. She touched under the edge of her man's hat, searching for fugitive hairs. "That sounds like a nice kind of a way to live," she said.

He leaned confidentially over the fence. "Maybe you noticed the writing on my wagon. I mend pots and sharpen knives and scissors. You got any of them things to do?"

"Oh, no," she said quickly. "Nothing like that." Her eyes hardened with resistance.

"Scissors is the worst thing," he explained. "Most people just ruin scissors trying to sharpen 'em, but I know how. I got a special tool. It's a little bobbit kind of thing, and patented. But it sure does the trick."

45    "No. My scissors are all sharp."

"All right, then. Take a pot," he continued earnestly, "a bent pot, or a pot with a hole. I can make it like new so you don't have to buy no new ones. That's a saving for you."

"No." she said shortly. "I tell you I have nothing like that for you to do."

His face fell to an exaggerated sadness. His voice took on a whining undertone. "I ain't had a thing to do today. Maybe I won't have no supper tonight. You see I'm off my regular road. I know folks on the highway clear from Seattle to San Diego. They save their things for me to sharpen up because they know I do it so good and save them money."

"I'm sorry," Elisa said irritably. "I haven't anything for you to do."

50    His eyes left her face and fell to searching the ground. They roamed about until they came to the chrysanthemum bed where she had been working. "What's them plants, ma'am?"

The irritation and resistance melted from Elisa's face. "Oh, those are chrysanthemums, giant whites and yellows. I raise them every year, bigger than anybody around here."

"Kind of a long-stemmed flower? Looks like a quick puff of colored smoke?" he asked.

"That's it. What a nice way to describe them."

"They smell kind of nasty till you get used to them," he said.

55    "It's a good bitter smell," she retorted, "not nasty at all."

He changed his tone quickly. "I like the smell myself."

"I had ten-inch blooms this year," she said.

The man leaned farther over the fence. "Look. I know a lady down the road a piece, has got the nicest garden you ever seen. Got nearly every kind of flower but no chrysanthemums. Last time I was mending a copper-bottom washtub for her (that's a hard job but I do it good), she said to me, 'If you ever run acrost some nice chrysanthemums I wish you'd try to get me a few seeds.' That's what she told me."

Elisa's eyes grew alert and eager. "She couldn't have known much about chrysanthemums. You *can* raise them from seed, but it's much easier to root the little sprouts you see here."

60    "Oh," he said. "I s'pose I can't take none to her then."

"Why yes you can," Elisa cried. "I can put some in damp sand, and you can carry them right along with you. They'll take root in the pot if you keep them damp. And then transplant them."

"She'd sure like to have some, ma'am. You say they're nice ones?"

"Beautiful," she said. "Oh, beautiful." Her eyes shone. She tore off the battered hat and shook out her dark pretty hair. "I'll put them in a flower pot, and you can take them right with you. Come into the yard."

While the man came through the picket gate Elisa ran excitedly along the geranium-bordered path to the back of the house. And she returned carrying a big red flower pot. The gloves were forgotten now. She kneeled on the ground by the starting bed and dug up the sandy soil with her fingers and scooped it into the bright new flower pot. Then she picked up the little pile of shoots she had just prepared. With her strong fingers she pressed them into the sand and tamped around them with her knuckles. The man stood over her. "I'll tell you what to do," she said. "You remember so you can tell the lady."

65    "Yes, I'll try to remember."

"Well, look. These will take root in about a month. Then she must set them out, about a foot apart in good rich earth like this, see?" She lifted a handful of dark soil for him to look at. "They'll grow fast and tall. Now remember this: In July tell her to cut them down, about eight inches from the ground."

"Before they bloom?" he asked.

"Yes, before they bloom." Her face was tight with eagerness. "They'll grow right up again. About the last of September the buds will start."

She stopped and seemed perplexed. "It's the budding that takes the most care," she said hesitantly. "I don't know how to tell you." She looked deep into his eyes, searchingly. Her mouth opened a little, and she seemed to be listening. "I'll try to tell you," she said. "Did you ever hear of planting hands?"

70      "Can't say I have, ma'am."

"Well, I can only tell you what it feels like. It's when you're picking off the buds you don't want. Everything goes right down into your fingertips. You watch your fingers work. They do it themselves. You can feel how it is. They pick and pick the buds. They never make a mistake. They're with the plant. Do you see? Your fingers and the plant. You can feel that, right up your arm. They know. They never make a mistake. You can feel it. When you're like that you can't do anything wrong. Do you see that? Can you understand that?"

She was kneeling on the ground looking up at him. Her breast swelled passionately.

The man's eyes narrowed. He looked away self-consciously. "Maybe I know," he said. "Sometimes in the night in the wagon there—"

Elisa's voice grew husky. She broke in on him, "I've never lived as you do, but I know what you mean. When the night is dark—why, the stars are sharp-pointed, and there's quiet. Why, you rise up and up! Every pointed star gets driven into your body. It's like that. Hot and sharp and— lovely."

75      Kneeling there, her hand went out toward his legs in the greasy black trousers. Her hesitant fingers almost touched the cloth. Then her hand dropped to the ground. She crouched low like a fawning dog.

He said, "It's nice, just like you say. Only when you don't have no dinner, it ain't."

She stood up then, very straight, and her face was ashamed. She held the flower pot out to him and placed it gently in his arms. "Here. Put it in your wagon, on the seat, where you can watch it. Maybe I can find something for you to do."

At the back of the house she dug in the can pile and found two old and battered aluminum saucepans. She carried them back and gave them to him. "Here, maybe you can fix these."

His manner changed. He became professional. "Good as new I can fix them." At the back of his wagon he set a little anvil, and out of an oily tool box dug a small machine hammer. Elisa came through the gate to watch him while he pounded out the dents in the kettles. His mouth grew sure and knowing. At a difficult part of the work he sucked his under-lip.

80      "You sleep right in the wagon?" Elisa asked.

"Right in the wagon, ma'am. Rain or shine I'm dry as a cow in there."

"It must be nice," she said. "It must be very nice. I wish women could do such things."

"It ain't the right kind of life for a woman."

Her upper lip raised a little, showing her teeth. "How do you know? How can you tell?" she said.

85      "I don't know, ma'am," he protested. "Of course I don't know. Now here's your kettles done. You don't have to buy no new ones."

"How much?"

"Oh, fifty cents'll do. I keep my prices down and my work good. That's why I have all them satisfied customers up and down the highway."

Elisa brought him a fifty-cent piece from the house and dropped it in his hand. "You might be surprised to have a rival some time. I can sharpen scissors, too. And I can beat the dents out of little pots. I could show you what a woman might do."

He put his hammer back in the oily box and shoved the little anvil out of sight. "It would be a lonely life for a woman, ma'am, and a scarey life, too, with animals creeping under the wagon all night." He climbed over the singletree, steadying himself with a hand on the burro's white rump. He settled himself in the seat, picked up the lines. "Thank you kindly, ma'am," he said. "I'll do like you told me; I'll go back and catch the Salinas road."

90    "Mind," she called, "if you're long in getting there, keep the sand damp."

"Sand, ma'am? . . . Sand? Oh, sure. You mean around the chrysanthemums. Sure I will." He clucked his tongue. The beasts leaned luxuriously into their collars. The mongrel dog took his place between the back wheels. The wagon turned and crawled out the entrance road and back the way it had come, along the river.

Elisa stood in front of her wire fence watching the slow progress of the caravan. Her shoulders were straight, and her head thrown back, her eyes half-closed, so that the scene came vaguely into them. Her lips moved silently, forming the words "Good-bye—good-bye." Then she whispered, "That's a bright direction. There's a glowing there." The sound of her whisper startled her. She shook herself free and looked about to see whether anyone had been listening. Only the dogs had heard. They lifted their heads toward her from their sleeping in the dust, and then stretched out their chins and settled asleep again. Elisa turned and ran hurriedly into the house.

In the kitchen she reached behind the stove and felt the water tank. It was full of hot water from the noonday cooking. In the bathroom she tore off her soiled clothes and flung them into the corner. And then she scrubbed herself with a little block of pumice, legs and thighs, loins and chest and arms, until her skin was scratched and red. When she had dried herself she stood in front of a mirror in her bedroom and looked at her body. She tightened her stomach and threw out her chest. She turned and looked over her shoulder at her back.

After a while she began to dress, slowly. She put on her newest underclothing and her nicest stockings and the dress which was the symbol of her prettiness. She worked carefully on her hair, penciled her eyebrows and rouged her lips.

95    Before she was finished she heard the little thunder of hoofs and the shouts of Henry and his helper as they drove the red steers into the corral. She heard the gate bang shut and set herself for Henry's arrival.

His step sounded on the porch. He entered the house calling, "Elisa, where are you?"

"In my room, dressing. I'm not ready. There's hot water for your bath. Hurry up. It's getting late."

When she heard him splashing in the tub, Elisa laid his dark suit on the bed, and shirt and socks and tie beside it. She stood his polished shoes on the floor beside the bed. Then she went to the porch and sat primly and stiffly down. She looked toward the river road where the willow-line was still yellow with frosted leaves so that under the high grey fog they seemed a thin band of sunshine. This was the only color in the grey afternoon. She sat unmoving for a long time. Her eyes blinked rarely.

Henry came banging out of the door, shoving his tie inside his vest as he came. Elisa stiffened and her face grew tight. Henry stopped short and looked at her. "Why—why, Elisa. You look so nice!"

100    "Nice? You think I look nice? What do you mean by 'nice'?"

Henry blundered on. "I don't know. I mean you look different, strong and happy."

"I am strong? Yes, strong. What do you mean by 'strong'?"

He looked bewildered. "You're playing some kind of a game," he said helplessly. "It's a kind of a play. You look strong enough to break a calf over your knee, happy enough to eat it like a watermelon."

For a second she lost her rigidity. "Henry! Don't talk like that. You didn't know what you said." She grew complete again. "I'm strong," she boasted. "I never knew before how strong."

105    Henry looked down toward the tractor shed, and when he brought his eyes back to her, they were his own again. "I'll get out the car. You can put on your coat while I'm starting."

Elisa went into the house. She heard him drive to the gate and idle down his motor, and then she took a long time to put on her hat. She pulled it here and pressed it there. When Henry turned the motor off she slipped into her coat and went out.

The little roadster bounced along on the dirt road by the river, raising the birds and driving the rabbits into the brush. Two cranes flapped heavily over the willow-line and dropped into the river-bed.

Far ahead on the road Elisa saw a dark speck. She knew.

She tried not to look as they passed it, but her eyes would not obey. She whispered to herself sadly, "He might have thrown them off the road. That wouldn't have been much trouble, not very much. But he kept the pot," she explained. "He had to keep the pot. That's why he couldn't get them off the road."

110    The roadster turned a bend and she saw the caravan ahead. She swung full around toward her husband so she could not see the little covered wagon and the mismatched team as the car passed them.

In a moment it was over. The thing was done. She did not look back.

She said loudly, to be heard above the motor, "It will be good, tonight, a good dinner."

"Now you're changed again," Henry complained. He took one hand from the wheel and patted her knee. "I ought to take you in to dinner oftener. It would be good for both of us. We get so heavy out on the ranch."

"Henry," she asked, "could we have wine at dinner?"

115    "Sure we could. Say! That will be fine."

She was silent for a while; then she said, "Henry, at those prize fights, do the men hurt each other very much?"

"Sometimes a little, not often. Why?"

"Well, I've read how they break noses, and blood runs down their chests. I've read how the fighting gloves get heavy and soggy with blood."

He looked around at her. "What's the matter, Elisa? I didn't know you read things like that." He brought the car to a stop, then turned to the right over the Salinas River bridge.

120    "Do any women ever go to the fights?" she asked.

"Oh, sure, some. What's the matter, Elisa? Do you want to go? I don't think you'd like it, but I'll take you if you really want to go."

She relaxed limply in the seat. "Oh, no. No. I don't want to go. I'm sure I don't." Her face was turned away from him. "It will be enough if we can have wine. It will be plenty." She turned up her coat collar so he could not see that she was crying weakly—like an old woman.

**YOUR TURN**

1. In the first paragraph of the story, the valley, shut off by fog, is said to be "a closed pot." Is this setting significant? Would any other setting do equally well? Why, or why not?
2. What does Elisa's clothing tell us about her? By the way, do you believe that all clothing says something about the wearers? Please explain.
3. Should we make anything special out of Elisa's interest in gardening? If so, what?
4. Describe Elisa's and Henry's marriage.
5. Evaluate the view that Elisa is responsible for her troubles.

# GABRIEL GARCÍA MÁRQUEZ

*Gabriel García Márquez (b. 1928) was born in Aracataca, a small village in Colombia. After being educated in Bogota, where he studied journalism and law, he worked as a journalist in Latin America, Europe, and the United States. He began writing fiction when he was in Paris, and at twenty-seven he published his first novel,* La hojarasca *(Leaf Storm, 1955). During most of the 1960s he lived in Mexico, where he wrote film scripts and the novel that made him famous:* Cien años de soledad *(1967, translated in 1970 as* One Hundred Years of Solitude*). In 1982 García Márquez was awarded the Nobel Prize in Literature.*

*Márquez's novels include* The Autumn of the Patriarch *(1975);* Love in the Time of Cholera *(1985);* The General in his Labyrinth *(1989); and* Of Love and Demons *(1994).*

## A Very Old Man with Enormous Wings [1968]

*A Tale for Children*

*Translated by Gregory Rabassa*

On the third day of rain they had killed so many crabs inside the house that Pelayo had to cross his drenched courtyard and throw them into the sea, because the newborn child had a temperature all night and they thought it was due to the stench. The world had been sad since Tuesday. Sea and sky were a single ash-gray thing and the sands of the beach, which on March nights glimmered like powdered light, had become a stew of mud and rotten shellfish. The light was so weak at noon that when Pelayo was coming back to the house after throwing away the crabs, it was hard for him to see what it was that was moving and groaning in the rear of the courtyard. He had to go very close to see that it was an old man, a very old man, lying face down in the mud, who, in spite of his tremendous efforts, couldn't get up, impeded by his enormous wings.

Frightened by that nightmare, Pelayo ran to get Elisenda, his wife, who was putting compresses on the sick child, and he took her to the rear of the courtyard. They both looked at the fallen body with mute stupor. He was dressed like a rag-picker. There were only a few faded hairs left on his bald skull and very few teeth in his mouth, and his pitiful condition of a drenched great-grandfather had taken away any sense of grandeur he might have had. His huge buzzard wings, dirty and half-plucked, were forever entangled in the mud. They looked at him so long and so closely that Pelayo and Elisenda very soon overcame their surprise and in the end found him familiar. Then they dared speak to him, and he answered in an incomprehensible dialect with a strong sailor's voice. That was how they skipped over the inconvenience of the wings and quite intelligently concluded that he was a lonely castaway from some foreign ship wrecked by the storm. And yet, they called in a neighbor woman who knew everything about life and death to see him, and all she needed was one look to show them their mistake.

"He's an angel," she told them. "He must have been coming for the child, but the poor fellow is so old that the rain knocked him down."

On the following day everyone knew that a flesh-and-blood angel was held captive in Pelayo's house. Against the judgment of the wise neighbor woman, for whom angels in those times were the fugitive survivors of a celestial conspiracy, they did not have the heart to club him to death. Pelayo watched over him all afternoon from the kitchen, armed with his bailiff's club, and before going to bed he dragged him out of the mud and locked him up with the hens in the wire chicken coop. In the middle of the night, when the rain stopped, Pelayo and Elisenda were still killing crabs. A short time afterward the child woke up without a fever and with a desire to eat. Then they felt magnanimous and decided to put the angel on a raft with fresh water and provisions for three days and leave him to his fate on the high seas. But when they went out into the courtyard with the first light of dawn, they found the whole neighborhood in front of the chicken coop having fun with the angel, without the slightest reverence, tossing him things to eat through the openings in the wire as if he weren't a supernatural creature but a circus animal.

5    Father Gonzaga arrived before seven o'clock, alarmed at the strange news. By that time onlookers less frivolous than those at dawn had already arrived and they were making all kinds of conjectures concerning the captive's future. The simplest among them thought that he should be named mayor of the world. Others of sterner mind felt that he should be promoted to the rank of five-star general in order to win all wars. Some visionaries hoped that he could be put to stud in order to implant on earth a race of winged wise men who could take charge of the universe. But Father Gonzaga, before becoming a priest, had been a robust woodcutter. Standing by the wire, he reviewed his catechism in an instant and asked them to open the door so that he could take a close look at that pitiful man who looked more like a huge decrepit hen among the fascinated chickens. He was lying in a corner drying his open wings in the sunlight among the fruit peels and breakfast leftovers that the early risers had thrown him. Alien to the impertinences of the world, he only lifted his antiquarian eyes and murmured

something in his dialect when Father Gonzaga went into the chicken coop and said good morning to him in Latin. The parish priest had his first suspicion of an impostor when he saw that he did not understand the language of God or know how to greet His ministers. Then he noticed that seen close up he was much too human: he had an unbearable smell of the outdoors, the back side of his wings were strewn with parasites and his main feathers had been mistreated by terrestrial winds, and nothing about him measured up to the proud dignity of angels. Then he came out of the chicken coop and in a brief sermon warned the curious against the risks of being ingenuous. He reminded them that the devil had the bad habit of making use of carnival tricks in order to confuse the unwary. He argued that if wings were not the essential element in determining the difference between a hawk and an airplane, they were even less so in the recognition of angels. Nevertheless, he promised to write a letter to his bishop so that the latter would write to his primate so that the latter would write to the Supreme Pontiff in order to get the final verdict from the highest courts.

His prudence fell on sterile hearts. The news of the captive angel spread with such rapidity that after a few hours the courtyard had the bustle of a marketplace and they had to call in troops with fixed bayonets to disperse the mob that was about to knock the house down. Elisenda, her spine all twisted from sweeping up so much marketplace trash, then got the idea of fencing in the yard and charging five cents admission to see the angel.

The curious came from far away. A traveling carnival arrived with a flying acrobat who buzzed over the crowd several times, but no one paid any attention to him because his wings were not those of an angel but, rather, those of a sidereal bat. The most unfortunate invalids on earth came in search of health: a poor woman who since childhood had been counting her heartbeats and had run out of numbers; a Portuguese man who couldn't sleep because the noise of the stars disturbed him; a sleepwalker who got up at night to undo the things he had done while awake; and many others with less serious ailments. In the midst of that shipwreck disorder that made the earth tremble, Pelayo and Elisenda were happy with fatigue, for in less than a week they had crammed their rooms with money and the line of pilgrims waiting their turn to enter still reached beyond the horizon.

The angel was the only one who took no part in his own act. He spent his time trying to get comfortable in his borrowed nest, befuddled by the hellish heat of the oil lamps and sacramental candles that had been placed along the wire. At first they tried to make him eat some mothballs, which, according to the wisdom of the wise neighbor woman, were the food prescribed for angels. But he turned them down, just as he turned down the papal lunches that the penitents brought him, and they never found out whether it was because he was an angel or because he was an old man that in the end ate nothing but eggplant mush. His only supernatural virtue seemed to be patience. Especially during the first days, when the hens pecked at him, searching for the stellar parasites that proliferated in his wings, and the cripples pulled out feathers to touch their defective parts with, and even the most merciful threw stones at him, trying to get him to rise so they could see him standing. The only time they succeeded in arousing him was when they burned his side with an iron for branding steers, for he had been motionless for so many hours that they thought he was dead.

He awoke with a start, ranting in his hermetic language and with tears in his eyes, and he flapped his wings a couple of times, which brought on a whirlwind of chicken dung and lunar dust and a gale of panic that did not seem to be of this world. Although many thought that his reaction had been one not of rage but of pain, from then on they were careful not to annoy him, because the majority understood that his passivity was not that of a hero taking his ease but that of a cataclysm in repose.

Father Gonzaga held back the crowd's frivolity with formulas of maidservant inspiration while awaiting the arrival of a final judgment on the nature of the captive. But the mail from Rome showed no sense of urgency. They spent their time finding out if the prisoner had a navel, if his dialect had any connection with Aramaic, how many times he could fit on the head of a pin, or whether he wasn't just a Norwegian with wings. Those meager letters might have come and gone until the end of time if a providential event had not put an end to the priest's tribulations.

10     It so happened that during those days, among so many other carnival attractions, there arrived in town the traveling show of the woman who had been changed into a spider for having disobeyed her parents. The admission to see her was not only less than the admission to see the angel, but people were permitted to ask her all manner of questions about her absurd state and to examine her up and down so that no one would ever doubt the truth of her horror. She was a frightful tarantula the size of a ram and with the head of a sad maiden. What was most heart-rending, however, was not her outlandish shape but the sincere affliction with which she recounted the details of her misfortune. While still practically a child she had sneaked out of her parents' house to go to a dance, and while she was coming back through the woods after having danced all night without permission, a fearful thunderclap rent the sky in two and through the crack came the lightning bolt of brimstone that changed her into a spider. Her only nourishment came from the meatballs that charitable souls chose to toss into her mouth. A spectacle like that, full of so much human truth and with such a fearful lesson, was bound to defeat without even trying that of a haughty angel who scarcely deigned to look at mortals. Besides, the few miracles attributed to the angel showed a certain mental disorder, like the blind man who didn't recover his sight but grew three new teeth, or the paralytic who didn't get to walk but almost won the lottery, and the leper whose sores sprouted sunflowers. Those consolation miracles, which were more like mocking fun, had already ruined the angel's reputation when the woman who had been changed into a spider finally crushed him completely. That was how Father Gonzaga was cured forever of his insomnia and Pelayo's courtyard went back to being as empty as during the time it had rained for three days and crabs walked through the bedrooms.

The owners of the house had no reason to lament. With the money they saved they built a two-story mansion with balconies and gardens and high netting so that crabs wouldn't get in during the winter, and with iron bars on the windows so that angels couldn't get in. Pelayo also set up a rabbit warren close to town and gave up his job as bailiff for good, and Elisenda bought some satin pumps with high heels and many dresses of iridescent silk, the kind worn on Sunday by the most desirable women in those times. The chicken coop was the only thing that didn't receive any attention. If they washed it down with creolin and burned tears of myrrh inside it every so often, it was not in homage to the angel but to drive away the dungheap stench that still hung everywhere like a ghost and was turning the new house into an old one. At first, when the child learned to walk, they were careful that he not get too close to the chicken coop. But then they began to lose their fears and got used to the smell, and before the child got his second teeth he'd gone inside the chicken coop to play, where the wires were falling apart. The angel was no less stand-offish with him than with other mortals, but he tolerated the most ingenious infamies with the patience of a dog who had no illusions. They both came down with chicken pox at the same time. The doctor who took care of the child couldn't resist the temptation to listen to the angel's heart, and he found so much whistling in the heart and so many sounds in his kidneys that it seemed impossible for him to be alive. What surprised him most, however, was the logic of his wings. They seemed so natural on that completely human organism that he couldn't understand why other men didn't have them too.

When the child began school it had been some time since the sun and rain had caused the collapse of the chicken coop. The angel went dragging himself about here and there like a stray dying man. They would drive him out of the bedroom with a broom and a moment later find him in the kitchen. He seemed to be in so many places at the same time that they grew to think that he'd been duplicated, that he was reproducing himself all through the house, and the exasperated and unhinged Elisenda shouted that it was awful living in that hell full of angels. He could scarcely eat and his antiquarian eyes had also become so foggy that he went about bumping into posts. All he had left were the bare cannulae of his last feathers. Pelayo threw a blanket over him and extended him the charity of letting him sleep in the shed, and only then did they notice that he had a temperature at night, and was delirious with the tongue twisters of an old Norwegian. That was one of the few times they became alarmed, for they thought he was going to die and not even the wise neighbor woman had been able to tell them what to do with dead angels.

And yet he not only survived his worst winter, but seemed improved with the first sunny days. He remained motionless for several days in the farthest corner of the courtyard, where no one would see him, and at the beginning of December some large, stiff feathers began to grow on his wings, the feathers of a scarecrow, which looked more like another misfortune of decrepitude. But he must have known the reason for those changes, for he was quite careful that no one should notice them, that no one should hear the sea chanteys that he sometimes sang under the stars. One morning Elisenda was cutting some bunches of onions for lunch when a wind that seemed to come from the high seas blew into the kitchen. Then she went to the window and caught the angel in his first attempts at flight. They were so clumsy that his fingernails opened a furrow in the vegetable patch and he was on the point of knocking the shed down with the ungainly flapping that slipped on the light and couldn't get a grip on the air. But he did manage to gain altitude. Elisenda let out a sigh of relief, for herself and for him, when she saw him pass over the last houses, holding himself up in some way with the risky flapping of a senile vulture. She kept watching him even when she was through cutting the onions and she kept on watching until it was no longer possible for her to see him, because then he was no longer an annoyance in her life but an imaginary dot on the horizon of the sea.

**YOUR TURN**

1. The subtitle is "A Tale for Children." Do you think that the story is more suited to children than to adults? What in the story do you think children would especially like, or dislike?

2. Is the story chiefly about the inability of adults to perceive and respect the miraculous world?

3. Characterize the narrator of the story.

4. Characterize Pelayo, Elisenda, their son, and the man with wings.

5. What does it mean to say that a story is "realistic"? Could a story deal with magical events and supernatural experiences and still, somehow, be realistic? Please explain.

6. Do you enjoy stories that include elements of fantasy and magic? Are there examples that come to mind? Or do you prefer stories that are based only on the possible? Again, please give examples and reasons.

# 11

# Theme

Theme is an essential term for literary study and interpretation, but it can be confusing because we tend to use it in different, if related, senses. Sometimes "theme" may refer to the subject of a literary work, as when we note that a story treats the theme of good and evil, or has as its theme the relationship between parents and children. But sometimes "theme" may suggest the point of view—the attitude—that an author has taken toward his or her subject. It is not just that the author is dealing with the nature of good and evil, but that he or she *has something special to say about it,* a perspective on it that makes this story different from others on this same subject. Probably it is best *not* to use "theme" in this second sense but instead to use **thesis,** especially for works by authors who seem to be arguing, even preaching. An Aesop fable pretty clearly offers a thesis, but most contemporary short stories do not.

Consider the following anonymous short Japanese narrative. It is said to be literally true, but whether it really occurred or not is scarcely of any importance. It is the story, not the history, that counts.

## ANONYMOUS

### Muddy Road

Two monks, Tanzan and Ekido, were once traveling together down a muddy road. A heavy rain was still falling.

Coming around a bend, they met a lovely girl in a silk kimono and sash, unable to cross the intersection.

"Come on, girl," said Tanzan at once. Lifting her in his arms, he carried her over the mud.

Ekido did not speak again until that night when they reached a lodging temple. Then he no longer could restrain himself. "We monks don't go near females," he told Tanzan, "especially not young and lovely ones. It is dangerous. Why did you do that?"

5    "I left the girl there," said Tanzan. "Are you still carrying her?"

Do we want to say that this story *argues* that priests should not lust for women? Surely not. But we can say, reasonably, that the theme is about proper and improper responses to a potentially sexual situation. And we can admire the skill with which the story is told. After the introduction of the two characters and the setting, we quickly get the complication, the encounter with the girl. Still there is apparently no conflict, though in "Ekido did not speak again until that night" we sense an unspoken conflict, an action (or, in this case, an inaction) that must be explained, an imbalance that must be righted before we are finished. At last Ekido, no longer able to contain his thoughts, lets his indignation burst out: "We monks don't go near females . . . especially not young and lovely ones. It is dangerous. Why did you do that?" His statement and his question reveal not only his moral principles, but also his insecurity and the anger that grows from it. And now, when the conflict is out in the open, comes the brief reply that reveals Tanzan's very different character as clearly as the outburst revealed Ekido's. This reply—though we could not have predicted it—strikes us as exactly right, bringing the story to a perfect end, that is to a point at which there is no more to be said. It provides the dénouement (literally, the "unknotting"), or resolution. But, again, although we can say that the theme deals with lust, we hardly want to say that the author is arguing a thesis.

Most literary works do not offer arguments to us—not exactly at any rate. A short story is not a legal document or a case in court. But readers may sense that an author has an attitude toward his or her characters. Interviewing Tobias Wolff, a writer of novels and short stories (see page 359), Julie Orringer asked if Wolff sometimes was too "hard on the protagonists" of his stories. Wolff replied:

> It isn't so much matter of wishing to be hard on people as wishing to be truthful. If there is a moral quality to my work, I suppose it has to do with will and the exercise of choice within one's will. The choices we make tend to narrow down a myriad of opportunities to just a few, and those choices tend to reinforce themselves in whatever direction we've started to go, including the wrong direction. . . . Well, maybe it's not such a good idea to stay the course if you're headed toward the rocks. There's something to be said for changing course if you're about to drive your ship onto the shoals.

Putting aside the issue of whether writers judge their characters and thereby offer arguments, it is obviously true that good literary works often *provoke* arguments—debate and discussion about what the work means, what its theme is. In a general sense all of us might agree that the theme of Shakespeare's play *The Taming of the Shrew* is the relationship between men and women, "the battle of the sexes." But what in more precise terms is this play's theme? What is the insight into or the understanding of the relationship between men and women that Shakespeare gives us in *The Taming of the Shrew,* or that D. H. Lawrence or John Updike in a story, or John Donne or Andrew Marvell in a poem, present?

It might be best, then, to agree to use two separate terms, **subject** and **theme.** What is the subject of Ozick's story "The Shawl"? We could say that it is the unspeakable pain that the protagonist Rosa experiences when her child Magda is brutally killed in the concentration camp. What is its theme? We might propose that the theme is twofold: the extreme evil of the Holocaust and the bond—horrifically assaulted but not wholly annihilated—between mother and daughter. Ozick's writing from beginning to end gives to her treatment of the subject, and to her presentation of the theme, emotional power and depth.

Perhaps your key task as an interpreter and writer of analytical essays is for you to be as specific as you can when you describe your response to the poem, play, or novel before you. What is the theme of *this* literary work? Not another one or others, but *this* one? Fate and free will: many literary works have this theme in common, but what counts, and what makes reading and interpretation rewarding, is to perceive the distinctive way in which a given author develops this theme in a given story.

Several literary scholars have in effect said that the theme of a short story is "everything in it." What they are getting at is that in order for us to perceive the theme, we need to pay close attention to the plot, character, setting, point of view, style—all of the elements of the story as they function together. When you write an essay about the theme of a literary work, consider each of these elements and the role that it performs by itself and in relationship to the others.

Here are some additional points and questions to consider:

1. **The title:** Sometimes the title offers an insight into the story's theme.
2. **The first paragraph:** How does the story begin?
3. **The final paragraph:** How does the story end, and what is the connection between where we end and where we began in our experience of this story?
4. **Significant details:** We know that details matter: What are the most significant details in the story? Do you see a pattern or patterns among them?
5. **Conflict:** What is the major conflict presented in the story? Is there more than one?
6. **Choices:** In the beginning, middle, or conclusion of a story, the main character might make an important choice. He does something, or he says something, or else decides not to do or say something. Does this choice and its consequences help us to understand the story's theme?
7. **Change:** When the story concludes, what has changed, if anything, from the way it was at the outset? Has the main character, or other characters, changed?
8. **Responding to theme:** What have you learned from your reading and study of this story? Has it changed your thinking in any way?

Sometimes you will be asked in an assignment to do some outside reading, and in such cases you might find in an author's letters, memoirs, diary entries, interviews, and other sources a clue or two about the theme that he or she explores.

In his Preface to *The House of the Seven Gables* (1851), for example, Nathaniel Hawthorne says: "The author has provided himself with a moral—the truth, namely, that the wrongdoing of one generation lives into the successive ones." Thomas Hardy, author of *Tess of the d'Urbervilles* (1891) and *Jude the Obscure* (1895), jotted in his notebook (April 19, 1885): "The business of the poet and novelist is to show the sorriness underlying the grandest things, and the grandeur underlying the sorriest things." With these examples we can reasonably talk about the authors' *thesis* as well as about *theme* and *subject*. Flannery O'Connor, whose work we feature in this book, states in "Catholic Novelists and Their Readers" (1964): "The main concern of the fiction writer is with mystery as it is incarnated in real life."

Much of the time, though, what we are doing first is reading a story in its own terms, responding to it, thinking about it, deciding how much or little we have enjoyed and learned from it. There are points we look for, questions we ask. We then can make comparisons with other literary works in our experience inside and outside the classroom. This is how we build up and develop our literary experience and understanding.

In the pages that follow, you will find three stories: "Carpathia," "The Shawl," and "Who's Irish?" Read each one of them carefully, and ask yourself why each one is special, and also how each compares and contrasts with the other two.

# JESSE LEE KERCHEVAL

*Jesse Lee Kercheval was born in France but received her bachelor's degree from Florida State University and her master's degree (in creative writing) from the University of Iowa. The author of several books of poetry and of fiction, as well as a book about how to write fiction* (Building Fiction [1997]), *Kercheval has received numerous awards. She teaches at the University of Wisconsin–Madison. The story we include here was written in response to a challenge to write a short story consisting of no more than 300 words.*

As this story indicates, Çarpathia *was the ship that in 1912 picked up survivors from the* Titanic, *after the* Titanic *struck an iceberg and sank.*

## Carpathia

It happened on my parents' honeymoon. The fourth morning out from New York, Mother woke to find the *Carpathia* still, engines silent. She woke Father; they rushed to the deck in their nightgowns. The first thing they saw was the white of an ocean filled with ice, then they saw white boats, in groups of two or three, pulling slowly toward the *Carpathia*. My father read the name written in red across their bows—*Titanic*. The sun was shining. Here and there a deck chair floated on the calm sea. There was nothing else.

The survivors came on board in small groups. Women and children. Two sailors for each boat. The women of the *Carpathia* went to the women of the *Titanic,* wrapping them in their long warm furs. My mother left my father's side to go to them. The women went down on their knees on the deck and prayed, holding each other's children. My father stood looking at the icy water where, if he had been on the other ship, he would be.

When the *Carpathia* dropped off the survivors in New York, my parents too got off and took the train home, not talking much, the honeymoon anything but a success. At the welcome-home party, my father got drunk. When someone asked about the *Titanic,* he said, "They should have put the men in the lifeboats. Men can marry again, have new families. What's the use of all those widows and orphans?" My mother, who was standing next to him, turned her face away. She was pregnant, eighteen. She was the one drowning. But there was no one there to rescue her.

**YOUR TURN**

1. In the second paragraph, the second and third sentences have no verbs. Do you suppose verbs have been omitted simply because the author was limited to 300 words, or are these two sentences more effective than they would be if they were equipped with verbs? Explain.
2. The speaker's father offers an argument—that is, he advances a thesis. Is the story about the issue that he raises—in effect, that the traditional doctrine of "women and children first" is misguided—or is it about something else. If something else, what is it about?
3. What is the narrator's attitude toward her father? Toward her mother?
4. Please complete the following sentence: "The lesson that this story teaches is. . . ." What is your evidence for this?
5. A teacher of creative writing, commenting on this story, says, "its ending is exactly right." Do you agree? Please explain.

# CYNTHIA OZICK

*Cynthia Ozick, born in 1928 in New York of Russian Jewish parentage, graduated from New York University in 1949 with a bachelor's degree in English. In 1950 she earned a master's degree at Ohio State University, writing a thesis on "Parable in the Later Novels of Henry James." In an essay in* Art and Ardor *(1983) she says that her early worship of James caused her to worship art and to try to "live unsoiled by what we mean when we say 'Life'—relationship, family mess, distraction, exhaustion, anxiety, above all disappointment." Later, she says, she learned that the true "Lesson of the Master" was "to seek to be young while young, primitive while primitive, ungainly when ungainly—to look for crudeness and rudeness, to husband one's own stupidity or ungenius."*

*Ozick's many books include the novels* The Messiah of Stockholm *(1987),* The Puttermesser Papers *(1997), and* Heir to the Glimmering World *(2004), and* Collected Stories *(2007).*

## The Shawl
[1980]

Stella, cold, cold the coldness of hell. How they walked on the roads together, Rosa with Magda curled up between sore breasts, Magda wound up in the shawl. Sometimes Stella carried Magda. But she was jealous of Magda. A thin girl of fourteen, too small, with thin breasts of her own, Stella wanted to be wrapped in a shawl, hidden away, asleep, rocked by the march, a baby, a round infant in arms. Magda took Rosa's nipple, and Rosa never stopped walking, a walking cradle. There was not enough milk; sometimes Magda sucked air; then she screamed. Stella was ravenous. Her knees were tumors on sticks, her elbows chicken bones.

Rosa did not feel hunger; she felt light, not like someone walking but like someone in a faint, in trance, arrested in a fit, someone who is already a floating angel, alert and seeing everything, but in the air, not there, not touching the road. As if teetering on the tips of her fingernails. She looked into Magda's face through a gap in the shawl: a squirrel in a nest, safe, no one could reach her inside the little house of the shawl's windings. The face, very round, a pocket mirror of a face: but it was not Rosa's bleak complexion, dark like cholera, it was another kind of face altogether, eyes blue as air, smooth feathers of hair nearly as yellow as the Star sewn into Rosa's coat. You could think she was one of *their* babies.

Rosa, floating, dreamed of giving Magda away in one of the villages. She could leave the line for a minute and push Magda into the hands of any woman on the side of the road. But if she moved out of line they might shoot. And even if she fled the line for half a second and pushed the shawl-bundle at a stranger, would the woman take it? She might be surprised, or afraid; she might drop the shawl, and Magda would fall out and strike her head and die. The little round head. Such a good child, she gave up scream-ing, and sucked now only for the taste of the drying nipple itself. The neat grip of the tiny gums. One mite of a tooth tip sticking up in the bottom gum, how shining, an elfin tombstone of white marble gleaming there. Without complaining, Magda relinquished Rosa's teats, first the left, then the right; both were cracked, not a sniff of milk. The duct-crevice extinct, a dead vol-cano, blind eye, chill hole, so Magda took the corner of the shawl and milked it instead. She sucked and sucked, flooding the threads with wetness. The shawl's good flavor, milk of linen.

It was a magic shawl, it could nourish an infant for three days and three nights. Magda did not die, she stayed alive, although very quiet. A peculiar smell, of cinnamon and almonds, lifted out of her mouth. She held her eyes open every moment, forgetting how to blink or nap, and Rosa and some-times Stella studied their blueness. On the road they raised one burden of a leg after another and studied Magda's face. "Aryan,"[1] Stella said, in a voice grown as thin as a string; and Rosa thought how Stella gazed at Magda like a young cannibal. And the time that Stella said "Aryan," it sounded to Rosa as if Stella had really said "Let us devour her."

5      But Magda lived to walk. She lived that long, but she did not walk very well, partly because she was only fifteen months old, and partly because the spindles of her legs could not hold up her fat belly. It was fat with air, full and round. Rosa gave almost all her food to Magda, Stella gave nothing; Stella was ravenous, a growing child herself, but not growing much. Stella did not menstruate. Rosa did not menstruate. Rosa was ravenous, but also not; she learned from Magda how to drink the taste of a finger in one's mouth. They were in a place without pity, all pity was annihilated in Rosa, she looked at Stella's bones without pity. She was sure that Stella was waiting for Magda to die so she could put her teeth into the little thighs.

Rosa knew Magda was going to die very soon; she should have been dead already, but she had been buried away deep inside the magic shawl, mistaken there for the shivering mound of Rosa's breasts; Rosa clung to the shawl as if it covered only herself. No one took it away from her. Magda was mute. She never cried. Rosa hid her in the barracks, under the shawl, but she knew that one day someone would inform; or one day someone, not even Stella, would steal Magda to eat her. When Magda began to walk Rosa knew

---

[1]**Aryan** According to *The American Heritage Dictionary of the English Language,* "Aryan, a word nowadays referring to the blond-haired, blue-eyed physical ideal of Nazi Germany, originally referred to a people who looked vastly different. Its history starts with the ancient Indo-Iranians, peoples who inhabited parts of what are now Iran, Afghanistan, Pakistan and India."

that Magda was going to die very soon, something would happen. She was afraid to fall asleep; she slept with the weight of her thigh on Magda's body; she was afraid she would smother Magda under her thigh. The weight of Rosa was becoming less and less; Rosa and Stella were slowly turning into air.

Magda was quiet, but her eyes were horribly alive, like blue tigers. She watched. Sometimes she laughed—it seemed a laugh, but how could it be? Magda had never seen anyone laugh. Still, Magda laughed at her shawl when the wind blew its corners, the bad wind with pieces of black in it, that made Stella's and Rosa's eyes tear. Magda's eyes were always clear and tearless. She watched like a tiger. She guarded her shawl. No one could touch it; only Rosa could touch it. Stella was not allowed. The shawl was Magda's own baby, her pet, her little sister. She tangled herself up in it and sucked on one of the corners when she wanted to be very still.

Then Stella took the shawl away and made Magda die.

Afterward Stella said: "I was cold."

10    And afterward she was always cold, always. The cold went into her heart: Rosa saw that Stella's heart was cold. Magda flopped onward with her little pencil legs scribbling this way and that, in search of the shawl; the pencils faltered at the barracks opening, where the light began. Rosa saw and pursued. But already Magda was in the square outside the barracks, in the jolly light. It was the roll-call arena. Every morning Rosa had to conceal Magda under the shawl against a wall of the barracks and go out and stand in the arena with Stella and hundreds of others, sometimes for hours, and Magda, deserted, was quiet under the shawl, sucking on her corner. Every day Magda was silent, and so she did not die. Rosa saw that today Magda was going to die, and at the same time a fearful joy ran in Rosa's two palms, her fingers were on fire, she was astonished, febrile: Magda, in the sunlight, swaying on her pencil legs, was howling. Ever since the drying up of Rosa's nipples, ever since Magda's last scream on the road, Magda had been devoid of any syllable; Magda was a mute. Rosa believed that something had gone wrong with her vocal cords, with her windpipe, with the cave of her larynx; Magda was defective, without a voice; perhaps she was deaf; there might be something amiss with her intelligence; Magda was dumb. Even the laugh that came when the ash-stippled wind made a clown out of Magda's shawl was only the air-blown showing of her teeth. Even when the lice, head lice and body lice, crazed her so that she became as wild as one of the big rats that plundered the barracks at daybreak looking for carrion, she rubbed and scratched and kicked and bit and rolled without a whimper. But now Magda's mouth was spilling a long viscous rope of clamor.

"Maaaa—"

It was the first noise Magda had ever sent out from her throat since the drying up of Rosa's nipples.

"Maaaa . . . aaa!"

Again! Magda was wavering in the perilous sunlight of the arena, scribbling on such pitiful little bent shins. Rosa saw. She saw that Magda was grieving for the loss of her shawl, she saw that Magda was going to die. A tide of commands hammered in Rosa's nipples: Fetch, get, bring! But she did not know which to go after first, Magda or the shawl. If she jumped out into the arena to snatch Magda up, the howling would not stop, because Magda would still not have the shawl; but if she ran back into the barracks to find the shawl, and if she found it, and if she came after Magda holding it and shaking it, then she would get Magda back, Magda would put the shawl in her mouth and turn dumb again.

15      Rosa entered the dark. It was easy to discover the shawl. Stella was heaped under it, asleep in her thin bones. Rosa tore the shawl free and flew—she could fly, she was only air—into the arena. The sunheat murmured of another life, of butterflies in summer. The light was placid, mellow. On the other side of the steel fence, far away, there were green meadows speckled with dandelions and deep-colored violets; beyond them, even farther, innocent tiger lilies, tall, lifting their orange bonnets. In the barracks they spoke of "flowers," of "rain": excrement, thick turd-braids, and the slow stinking maroon waterfall that slunk down from the upper bunks, the stink mixed with a bitter fatty floating smoke that greased Rosa's skin. She stood for an instant at the margin of the arena. Sometimes the electricity inside the fence would seem to hum; even Stella said it was only an imagining, but Rosa heard real sounds in the wire: grainy sad voices. The farther she was from the fence, the more clearly the voices crowded at her. The lamenting voices strummed so convincingly, so passionately, it was impossible to suspect them of being phantoms. The voices told her to hold up the shawl, high; the voices told her to shake it, to whip with it, to unfurl it like a flag. Rosa lifted, shook, whipped, unfurled. Far off, very far, Magda leaned across her air-fed belly, reaching out with the rods of her arms. She was high up, elevated, riding someone's shoulder. But the shoulder that carried Magda was not coming toward Rosa and the shawl, it was drifting away, the speck of Magda was moving more and more into the smoky distance. Above the shoulder a helmet glinted. The light tapped the helmet and sparkled it into a goblet. Below the helmet a black body like a domino and a pair of black boots hurled themselves in the direction of the electrified fence. The electric voices began to chatter wildly. "Maamaaa, maaamaaa," they all hummed together. How far Magda was from Rosa now, across the whole square, past a dozen barracks, all the way on the other side! She was no bigger than a moth.

All at once Magda was swimming through the air. The whole of Magda traveled through loftiness. She looked like a butterfly touching a silver vine. And the moment Magda's feathered round head and her pencil legs and balloonish belly and zigzag arms splashed against the fence, the steel voices went mad in their growling, urging Rosa to run and run to the spot where Magda had fallen from her flight against the electrified fence; but of course Rosa did not obey them. She only stood, because if she ran they would shoot, and if she tried to pick up the sticks of Magda's body they would shoot, and if she let the wolf's screech ascending now through the ladder of her skeleton break out, they would shoot; so she took Magda's shawl and filled her own mouth with it, stuffed it in and stuffed it in, until she was swallowing up the wolf's screech and tasting the cinnamon and almond depth of Magda's saliva; and Rosa drank Magda's shawl until it dried.

**YOUR TURN**

1. The fourth paragraph begins, "It was a magic shawl." Why does the narrator say this? Now notice the last clause in the story: "Rosa drank Magda's shawl until it dried." Does this mean that the magic stopped working? Or that, for some reason, there was no longer a need for a magic shawl? Or what?

2. The story combines an apparently simple, matter-of-fact, realistic style with a highly figurative style. What is the effect of this combination?
3. There is very little dialogue in the story. What is the effect of the relative absence of dialogue?

# GISH JEN

*Gish Jen was born in 1955 in Yonkers, New York. The daughter of Chinese immigrants, she was named Lillian Jen by her parents. She disliked the name Lillian, and her school friends created a new name for her, derived from the name of a famous actress of the silent screen—Lillian Gish. Jen graduated from Harvard and then, in accordance with her parents' wishes, went to Stanford Business School (MBA, 1980). Jen's books include the novels* Typical American *(1991) and* Mona in the Promised Land *(1996) and a collection of stories,* Who's Irish? *(1999).*

## *Who's Irish?*                                                    [1998]

In China, people say mixed children are supposed to be smart, and definitely my granddaughter Sophie is smart. But Sophie is wild, Sophie is not like my daughter Natalie, or like me. I am work hard my whole life, and fierce besides. My husband always used to say he is afraid of me, and in our restaurant, busboys and cooks all afraid of me too. Even the gang members come for protection money, they try to talk to my husband. When I am there, they stay away. If they come by mistake, they pretend they are come to eat. They hide behind the menu, they order a lot of food. They talk about their mothers. Oh, my mother have some arthritis, need to take herbal medicine, they say. Oh, my mother getting old, her hair all white now.

I say, Your mother's hair used to be white, but since she dye it, it become black again. Why don't you go home once in a while and take a look? I tell them, Confucius[1] say a filial son knows what color his mother's hair is.

My daughter is fierce too, she is vice president in the bank now. Her new house is big enough for everybody to have their own room, including me. But Sophie take after Natalie's husband's family, their name is Shea. Irish. I always thought Irish people are like Chinese people, work so hard on the railroad, but now I know why the Chinese beat the Irish. Of course, not all Irish are like the Shea family, of course not. My daughter tell me I should not say Irish this, Irish that.

How do you like it when people say the Chinese this, the Chinese that, she say.

5      You know, the British call the Irish heathen, just like they call the Chinese, she say.

You think the Opium War[2] was bad, how would you like to live right next door to the British, she say.

---

[1] **Confucius** Chinese religious leader and philosopher (551–479 BCE).    [2] **Opium War** conflicts, 1839–1842 and 1856–1860, between China and Great Britain involving the opium trade.

And that is that. My daughter have a funny habit when she win an argument, she take a sip of something and look away, so the other person is not embarrassed. So I am not embarrassed. I do not call anybody anything either. I just happen to mention about the Shea family, an interesting fact: four brothers in the family, and not one of them work. The mother, Bess, have a job before she got sick, she was executive secretary in a big company. She is handle everything for a big shot, you would be surprised how complicated her job is, not just type this, type that. Now she is a nice woman with a clean house. But her boys, every one of them is on welfare, or so-called severance pay, or so-called disability pay. Something. They say they cannot find work, this is not the economy of the fifties, but I say, Even the black people doing better these days, some of them live so fancy, you'd be surprised. Why the Shea family have so much trouble? They are white people, they speak English. When I come to this country, I have no money and do not speak English. But my husband and I own our restaurant before he die. Free and clear, no mortgage. Of course, I understand I am just lucky, come from a country where the food is popular all over the world. I understand it is not the Shea family's fault they come from a country where everything is boiled. Still, I say.

She's right, we should broaden our horizons, say one brother, Jim, at Thanksgiving. Forget about the car business. Think about egg rolls.

Pad thai, say another brother, Mike. I'm going to make my fortune in pad thai. It's going to be the new pizza.

10      I say, You people too picky about what you sell. Selling egg rolls not good enough for you, but at least my husband and I can say, We made it. What can you say? Tell me. What can you say?

Everybody chew their tough turkey.

I especially cannot understand my daughter's husband John, who has no job but cannot take care of Sophie either. Because he is a man, he say, and that's the end of the sentence.

Plain boiled food, plain boiled thinking. Even his name is plain boiled: John. Maybe because I grew up with black bean sauce and hoisin sauce and garlic sauce, I always feel something is missing when my son-in-law talk.

But, okay: so my son-in-law can be man, I am baby-sitter. Six hours a day, same as the old sitter, crazy Amy, who quit. This is not so easy, now that I am sixty-eight, Chinese age almost seventy. Still, I try. In China, daughter take care of mother. Here it is the other way around. Mother help daughter, mother ask, Anything else I can do? Otherwise daughter complain mother is not supportive. I tell daughter, We do not have this word in Chinese, *supportive*. But my daughter too busy to listen, she has to go to meeting, she has to write memo while her husband go to the gym to be a man. My daughter say otherwise he will be depressed. Seems like all his life he has this trouble, depression.

15      No one wants to hire someone who is depressed, she say. It is important for him to keep his spirits up.

Beautiful wife, beautiful daughter, beautiful house, oven can clean itself automatically. No money left over, because only one income, but lucky enough, got the baby-sitter for free. If John lived in China, he would be very happy. But he is not happy. Even at the gym things go wrong. One day, he pull a muscle. Another day, weight room too crowded. Always something.

Until finally, hooray, he has a job. Then he feel pressure.

I need to concentrate, he say. I need to focus.

He is going to work for insurance company. Salesman job. A paycheck, he say, and at least he will wear clothes instead of gym shorts. My daughter

buy him some special candy bars from the health-food store. They say
THINK! on them, and are supposed to help John think.

20      John is a good-looking boy, you have to say that, especially now that he
shave so you can see his face.

I am an old man in a young man's game, say John.

I will need a new suit, say John.

This time I am not going to shoot myself in the foot, say John.

Good, I say.

25      She means to be supportive, my daughter say. Don't start the send her
back to China thing, because we can't.

Sophie is three years old American age, but already I see her nice Chinese side swallowed up by her wild Shea side. She looks like mostly Chinese.
Beautiful black hair, beautiful black eyes. Nose perfect size, not so flat looks
like something fell down, not so large looks like some big deal got stuck in
wrong face. Everything just right, only her skin is a brown surprise to John's
family. So brown, they say. Even John say it. She never goes in the sun, still
she is that color, he say. Brown. They say, Nothing the matter with brown.
They are just surprised. So brown. Nattie is not that brown, they say. They
say, It seems like Sophie should be a color in between Nattie and John.
Seems funny, a girl named Sophie Shea be brown. But she is brown, maybe
her name should be Sophie Brown. She never go in the sun, still she is that
color, they say. Nothing the matter with brown. They are just surprised.

The Shea family talk is like this sometimes, going around and around
like a Christmas-tree train.

Maybe John is not her father, I say one day, to stop the train. And sure
enough, train wreck. None of the brothers ever say the word *brown* to me
again.

Instead, John's mother, Bess, say, I hope you are not offended.

30      She say, I did my best on those boys. But raising four boys with no father
is no picnic.

You have a beautiful family, I say.

I'm getting old, she say.

You deserve a rest, I say. Too many boys make you old.

I never had a daughter, she say. You have a daughter.

35      I have a daughter, I say. Chinese people don't think a daughter is so
great, but you're right. I have a daughter.

I was never against the marriage, you know, she say. I never thought
John was marrying down. I always thought Nattie was just as good as white.

I was never against the marriage either, I say. I just wonder if they look
at the whole problem.

Of course you pointed out the problem, you are a mother, she say. And
now we both have a granddaughter. A little brown granddaughter, she is so
precious to me.

I laugh. A little brown granddaughter, I say. To tell you the truth, I don't
know how she came out so brown.

40      We laugh some more. These days Bess need a walker to walk. She take
so many pills, she need two glasses of water to get them all down. Her favorite TV show is about bloopers, and she love her bird feeder. All day long,
she can watch that bird feeder, like a cat.

I can't wait for her to grow up, Bess say. I could use some female company.

Too many boys, I say.

Boys are fine, she say. But they do surround you after a while.

You should take a break, come live with us, I say. Lots of girls at our house.

45    Be careful what you offer, say Bess with a wink. Where I come from, people mean for you to move in when they say a thing like that.

Nothing the matter with Sophie's outside, that's the truth. It is inside that she is like not any Chinese girl I ever see. We go to the park, and this is what she does. She stand up in the stroller. She take off all her clothes and throw them in the fountain.

Sophie! I say. Stop!

But she just laugh like a crazy person. Before I take over as baby-sitter, Sophie has that crazy-person sitter, Amy the guitar player. My daughter thought this Amy very creative—another word we do not talk about in China. In China, we talk about whether we have difficulty or no difficulty. We talk about whether life is bitter or not bitter. In America, all day long, people talk about creative. Never mind that I cannot even look at this Amy, with her shirt so short that her belly button showing. This Amy think Sophie should love her body. So when Sophie take off her diaper, Amy laugh. When Sophie run around naked, Amy say she wouldn't want to wear a diaper either. When Sophie go *shu-shu* in her lap, Amy laugh and say there are no germs in pee. When Sophie take off her shoes, Amy say bare feet is best, even the pediatrician say so. That is why Sophie now walk around with no shoes like a beggar child. Also why Sophie love to take off her clothes.

Turn around! say the boys in the park. Let's see that ass!

50    Of course, Sophie does not understand. Sophie clap her hands, I am the only one to say, No! This is not a game.

It has nothing to do with John's family, my daughter say. Amy was too permissive, that's all.

But I think if Sophie was not wild inside, she would not take off her shoes and clothes to begin with.

You never take off your clothes when you were little, I say. All my Chinese friends had babies, I never saw one of them act wild like that.

Look, my daughter say. I have a big presentation tomorrow.

55    John and my daughter agree Sophie is a problem, but they don't know what to do.

You spank her, she'll stop, I say another day.

But they say, Oh no.

In America, parents not supposed to spank the child.

It gives them low self-esteem, my daughter say. And that leads to problems later, as I happen to know.

60    My daughter never have big presentation the next day when the subject of spanking come up.

I don't want you to touch Sophie, she say. No spanking, period.

Don't tell me what to do, I say.

I'm not telling you what to do, say my daughter. I'm telling you how I feel.

I am not your servant, I say. Don't you dare talk to me like that.

65    My daughter have another funny habit when she lose an argument. She spread out all her fingers and look at them, as if she like to make sure they are still there.

My daughter is fierce like me, but she and John think it is better to explain to Sophie that clothes are a good idea. This is not so hard in the cold weather. In the warm weather, it is very hard.

Use your words, my daughter say. That's what we tell Sophie. How about if you set a good example.

As if good example mean anything to Sophie. I am so fierce, the gang members who used to come to the restaurant all afraid of me, but Sophie is not afraid.

I say, Sophie, if you take off your clothes, no snack.
70    I say, Sophie, if you take off your clothes, no lunch.
I say, Sophie, if you take off your clothes, no park.

Pretty soon we are stay home all day, and by the end of six hours she still did not have one thing to eat. You never saw a child stubborn like that.

I'm hungry! she cry when my daughter come home.

What's the matter, doesn't your grandmother feed you? My daughter laugh.
75    No! Sophie say. She doesn't feed me anything!

My daughter laugh again. Here you go, she say.

She say to John, Sophie must be growing.

Growing like a weed, I say.

Still Sophie take off her clothes, until one day I spank her. Not too hard, but she cry and cry, and when I tell her if she doesn't put her clothes back on I'll spank her again, she put her clothes back on. Then I tell her she is good girl, and give her some food to eat. The next day we go to the park and, like a nice Chinese girl, she does not take off her clothes.
80    She stop taking off her clothes, I report. Finally!

How did you do it? my daughter ask.

After twenty-eight years experience with you, I guess I learn something, I say.

It must have been a phase, John say, and his voice is suddenly like an expert.

His voice is like an expert about everything these days, now that he carry a leather briefcase, and wear shiny shoes, and can go shopping for a new car. On the company, he say. The company will pay for it, but he will be able to drive it whenever he want.
85    A free car, he say. How do you like that.

It's good to see you in the saddle again, my daughter say. Some of your family patterns are scary.

At least I don't drink, he say. He say, And I'm not the only one with scary family patterns.

That's for sure, say my daughter.

Everyone is happy. Even I am happy, because there is more trouble with Sophie, but now I think I can help her Chinese side fight against her wild side. I teach her to eat food with fork or spoon or chopsticks, she cannot just grab into the middle of a bowl of noodles. I teach her not to play with garbage cans. Sometimes I spank her, but not too often, and not too hard.
90    Still, there are problems. Sophie like to climb everything. If there is a railing, she is never next to it. Always she is on top of it. Also, Sophie like to hit the mommies of her friends. She learn this from her playground best friend, Sinbad, who is four. Sinbad wear army clothes every day and like to ambush his mommy. He is the one who dug a big hole under the play structure, a foxhole he call it, all by himself. Very hardworking. Now he wait in the foxhole with a shovel full of wet sand. When his mommy come, he throw it right at her.

Oh, it's all right, his mommy say. You can't get rid of war games, it's part of their imaginative play. All the boys go through it.

Also, he like to kick his mommy, and one day he tell Sophie to kick his mommy too.

I wish this story is not true.

Kick her, kick her! Sinbad say.

95      Sophie kick her. A little kick, as if she just so happened was swinging her little leg and didn't realize that big mommy leg was in the way. Still I spank Sophie and make Sophie say sorry, and what does the mommy say?

Really, it's all right, she say. It didn't hurt.

After that, Sophie learn she can attack mommies in the playground, and some will say, Stop, but others will say, Oh, she didn't mean it, especially if they realize Sophie will be punished.

This is how, one day, bigger trouble come. The bigger trouble start when Sophie hide in the foxhole with that shovel full of sand. She wait, and when I come look for her, she throw it at me. All over my nice clean clothes.

Did you ever see a Chinese girl act this way?

100     Sophie! I say. Come out of there, say you're sorry.

But she does not come out. Instead, she laugh. Naaah, naah-na, naaa-naaa, she say.

I am not exaggerate: millions of children in China, not one act like this.

Sophie! I say. Now! Come out now!

But she know she is in big trouble. She know if she come out, what will happen next. So she does not come out. I am sixty-eight, Chinese age almost seventy, how can I crawl under there to catch her? Impossible. So I yell, yell, yell, and what happen? Nothing. A Chinese mother would help, but American mothers, they look at you, they shake their head, they go home. And, of course, a Chinese child would give up, but not Sophie.

105     I hate you! she yell. I hate you, Meanie!

Meanie is my new name these days.

Long time this goes on, long long time. The foxhole is deep, you cannot see too much, you don't know where is the bottom. You cannot hear too much either. If she does not yell, you cannot even know she is still there or not. After a while, getting cold out, getting dark out. No one left in the playground, only us.

Sophie, I say. How did you become stubborn like this? I am go home without you now.

I try to use a stick, chase her out of there, and once or twice I hit her, but still she does not come out. So finally I leave. I go outside the gate.

110     Bye-bye! I say. I'm go home now.

But still she does not come out and does not come out. Now it is din-nertime, the sky is black. I think I should maybe go get help, but how can I leave a little girl by herself in the playground? A bad man could come. A rat could come. I go back in to see what is happen to Sophie. What if she have a shovel and is making a tunnel to escape?

Sophie! I say.

No answer.

Sophie!

115     I don't know if she is alive. I don't know if she is fall asleep down there. If she is crying, I cannot hear her.

So I take the stick and poke.

Sophie! I say. I promise I no hit you. If you come out, I give you a lol-
lipop.

No answer. By now I worried. What to do, what to do, what to do? I
poke some more, even harder, so that I am poking and poking when my
daughter and John suddenly appear.

What are you doing? What is going on? say my daughter.

120 Put down that stick! say my daughter.

You are crazy! say my daughter.

John wiggle under the structure, into the foxhole, to rescue Sophie.

She fell asleep, say John the expert. She's okay. That is one big hole.

Now Sophie is crying and crying.

125 Sophie, my daughter say, hugging her. Are you okay, peanut? Are you okay?

She's just scared, say John.

Are you okay? I say too. I don't know what happen, I say.

She's okay, say John. He is not like my daughter, full of questions. He is
full of answers until we get home and can see by the lamplight.

Will you look at her? he yell then. What the hell happened?

130 Bruises all over her brown skin, and a swollen-up eye.

You are crazy! say my daughter. Look at what you did! You are crazy!

I try very hard, I say.

How could you use a stick? I told you to use your words!

She is hard to handle, I say.

135 She's three years old! You cannot use a stick! say my daughter.

She is not like any Chinese girl I ever saw, I say.

I brush some sand off my clothes. Sophie's clothes are dirty too, but at
least she has her clothes on.

Has she done this before? ask my daughter. Has she hit you before?

She hits me all the time, Sophie say, eating ice cream.

140 Your family, say John.

Believe me, say my daughter.

A daughter I have, a beautiful daughter. I took care of her when she could
not hold her head up. I took care of her before she could argue with me,
when she was a little girl with two pigtails, one of them always crooked. I took
care of her when we have to escape from China, I took care of her when suddenly we live in a country with cars everywhere, if you are not careful your
little girl get run over. When my husband die, I promise him I will keep the
family together, even though it was just two of us, hardly a family at all.

But now my daughter take me around to look at apartments. After all, I
can cook, I can clean, there's no reason I cannot live by myself, all I need is a
telephone. Of course, she is sorry. Sometimes she cry, I am the one to say
everything will be okay. She say she have no choice, she doesn't want to end
up divorced. I say divorce is terrible, I don't know who invented this terrible
idea. Instead of live with a telephone, though, surprise, I come to live with
Bess. Imagine that. Bess make an offer and, sure enough, where she come
from, people mean for you to move in when they say things like that. A crazy
idea, go to live with someone else's family, but she like to have some female
company, not like my daughter, who does not believe in company. These
days when my daughter visit, she does not bring Sophie. Bess say we should
give Nattie time, we will see Sophie again soon. But seems like my daughter

have more presentation than ever before, every time she come she have to leave.

I have a family to support, she say, and her voice is heavy, as if soaking wet. I have a young daughter and a depressed husband and no one to turn to.

145    When she say no one to turn to, she mean me.

These days my beautiful daughter is so tired she can just sit there in a chair and fall asleep. John lost his job again, already, but still they rather hire a baby-sitter than ask me to help, even they can't afford it. Of course, the new baby-sitter is much younger, can run around. I don't know if Sophie these days is wild or not wild. She call me Meanie, but she like to kiss me too, sometimes. I remember that every time I see a child on TV. Sophie like to grab my hair, a fistful in each hand, and then kiss me smack on the nose. I never see any other child kiss that way.

The satellite TV has so many channels, more channels than I can count, including a Chinese channel from the Mainland and a Chinese channel from Taiwan, but most of the time I watch bloopers with Bess. Also, I watch the bird feeder—so many, many kinds of birds come. The Shea sons hang around all the time, asking when will I go home, but Bess tell them, Get lost.

She's a permanent resident, say Bess. She isn't going anywhere.

Then she wink at me, and switch the channel with the remote control.

150    Of course, I shouldn't say Irish this, Irish that, especially now I am become honorary Irish myself, according to Bess. Me! Who's Irish? I say, and she laugh. All the same, if I could mention one thing about some of the Irish, not all of them of course, I like to mention this: Their talk just stick. I don't know how Bess Shea learn to use her words, but sometimes I hear what she say a long time later. *Permanent resident. Not going anywhere.* Over and over I hear it, the voice of Bess.

## YOUR TURN

1. When you began this story, what was your response to the title? Did your response to it change by the time you reached the conclusion?

2. How is the title connected to the main theme of the story? What is the main theme? Please explain what it is, with reference to a key passage or passages in the text.

3. A critic has said that the voice that Gish Jen chose for her narrator is connected to the theme of the story as a whole. Do you agree? Please explain why or why not.

4. Another critic has said that this story focuses on "the war between generations." Do you agree? Does "war" strike you as the right term, or not?

5. In an interview, Gish Jen said that as a writer she finds she is keenly interested in the "different realities" of her characters. Does this apply to "Who's Irish"? Please point to evidence in the text to explain what these different realities are.

6. Did anything in this story surprise you?

# 12

# Graphic Fiction

## Letters and Pictures

Literature is, literally speaking, made out of letters ("literature," "literally," "literate," and "letters" all come from a Latin word, *littera,* "letter"). A person who can read letters is literate. Yet today we hear a good deal about "visual literacy," which means the ability to understand visual things. In short, in this usage, "literacy" is metaphoric. You cannot literally (again that word!) read a picture; you can look at it and either understand it or not understand it. For the next few minutes, in order to help prepare you to read a story that is partly told by means of pictures, we will be talking about achieving visual literacy—that is, achieving the ability to understand pictures, to "read" pictures, specifically pictures that are used as part of a way of telling stories.

The good news is that if you have spent any time at all looking at comic strips you already know a great deal about how to "read" pictures that tell stories.

- You know, for instance, that you should read the pictures and the words from left to right (if you were brought up in China or Japan, you would begin at the right and read the first column downward, then the next column, again reading downward, unless the book were a Western-style book).
- You also know that in the usual comic strip a box represents a particular scene; the next box may show the same characters, but at a later moment in time.
- You know that human actions can be conveyed by showing figures in certain postures (walking, eating, etc.) making certain gestures (pointing, making a fist).
- You know that emotions can be conveyed by facial expressions (think Smiley Face, where two dots and a curve say it all).
- You know that the setting can easily be established (a tree indicates the outdoors, the Capitol indicates Washington, D.C.).
- You know that if a heavy object is shown on the ground with the word "bang" in large thick letters next to it, a character has just dropped the object.

- You know that words that are enclosed in a circle over the character's head indicate words that the character is speaking.
- You know that a character is cursing or using dirty language when words are represented not by letters but by symbols such as @ and # and !
- You know that if the line that encloses words is scalloped, or looks something like a cloud, the words represent *thoughts* rather than utterances.

In short, you know the conventions that enable you to understand what the cartoonist/storyteller is doing, is saying, so that you can follow the story, the narrative conveyed by words and pictures. All of which says that you are already visually literate.

Nevertheless, because you may not have developed the habit of reading images closely, of taking in all the subtleties that they may offer, we will talk a bit about reading pictures.

The first thing we want to say is that although in some contexts a picture is worth a thousand words, pictures are not very good at telling *stories*. Think of any familiar story—let's say the story of Cain and Abel, or of Cinderella, or (to take an example in our text) the story of King Solomon and the two women who disputed about who was the mother of an infant. Solomon ordered a servant to bring the sword, and to divide the living child so that each woman could have half. A sword was brought, and (here we give the translated text in the Revised Standard Version of the Bible)

> then the woman whose son was alive said to the king, because her heart yearned for her son, "Oh, no my lord, give her [i.e., the other woman] the living child, and by no means slay it." But the other said, "It shall be neither mine nor yours: divide it." Then the king answered and said, "Give the living child to the first woman, and by no means slay it; she is its mother." (I Kings 3.26–27)

Striking images come to mind when reading this story—for instance, an image of two women quarreling over an infant, an image of a servant entering with a massive sword, and an image of the infant being handed over to one woman. But we think it would be impossible by images alone to tell the story, which essentially causes the reader to draw two conclusions:

- A loving mother will give up a child rather than let it die, and
- Solomon was a wise judge.

Tradition says that in the Middle Ages, when most people were illiterate, pictures such as those in stained glass windows were "the Bible of the people," and these windows did tell stories—but the stories could be understood only if the viewers were already familiar with verbal tellings. Similarly, such narratives as those told on Trajan's Column (built 113 CE), adorned with images of the Roman emperor's victories, or the Bayeux Tapestry (late eleventh century, showing the French invasion of England) show us lots of energetic figures, but to *understand* what is going on, we must already know the story.

Still, pictures can communicate meanings, and so let's now look at a picture that is accompanied by words.

# Reading an Image: A Short Story Told in One Panel

## TONY CARRILLO

*Tony Carrillo was born and raised in Tempe, Arizona. He conceived* F Minus *when he was a sophomore at Arizona State University. The strip is currently syndicated in more than a hundred newspapers.*

### *F Minus*

ONE DAY, IN A QUIET OFFICE BUILDING SOMEWHERE, A SMALL CALCULATOR SUDDENLY BECAME SELF-AWARE.

IN EIGHT SECONDS, IT PLOTTED THE EXTINCTION OF ALL MANKIND.

THEN THE BATTERY DIED.

TWO WEEKS LATER, IT WAS THROWN AWAY.

*Tony Carrillo: "F Minus" © United Feature Syndicate, Inc.*

For the moment, let's pretend that the picture didn't exist, and we were given only some text:

> One day, in a quiet office building somewhere, a small calculator suddenly became self-aware.
> In eight seconds, it plotted the extinction of all mankind.
> Then the battery died.
> Two weeks later, it was thrown away.

We don't want to make extravagant claims, but we think this is pretty good as a mini-sci-fi story. We hear much about the possibility that some day there may be machines that "think," and we hear even more about technology getting out of control and possibly destroying its creators. In the words of Elias Canetti,[1] "The planet's survival has become so uncertain that any effort, any thought that presupposes an assured future amounts to a mad gamble." So the graphic story begins with something fantastic yet something that we hear about and that we can imagine may become real:

> One day, in a quiet office building somewhere, a small calculator suddenly became self-aware.
> In eight seconds, it plotted the extinction of all mankind.

There is an engaging combination of vagueness ("One day," "somewhere") and of the highly specific ("In eight seconds"); that is, things in a leisurely

---

[1]**Elias Canetti** Bulgarian novelist (1905-1994) who won the Nobel Prize in literature in 1981.

once-upon-a-time land suddenly get down to a matter of seconds. The vague fairy-tale world of "one day" has been transformed into real time, and the "small calculator" is now a big threat. Like all good fiction, each sentence of this tiny story stimulates the reader to wonder, "What happens next?"

What does happen after the calculator "plotted the extinction of all mankind"? "Then the battery died." Well, that makes sense. We hadn't anticipated this happening, but, again, the happening that is narrated to us is plausible, and we are relieved, satisfied. In a sense the story is over—the battery is dead, so what more can be said?—but we see additional words:

Two weeks later, it was thrown away.

We think this ending is masterful. E. M. Forster's comment about a good plot, already quoted on page 110, comes to mind:

Shock, followed by the feeling, "Oh, that's all right," is a sign that all is well with plot: characters, to be real, ought to run smoothly, but a plot ought to cause surprise.

It is as if we heard a joke, laughed, and therefore thought we heard the end of the matter and then the narrator went on to top the joke, giving us an unexpected joke that builds on the first joke, a line that, after we have heard it, seems inevitable. The calculator, once an enormous menace, fails to be of even the slightest significance because—as is entirely natural, if we can speak of naturalness in connection with a mechanical device—the battery dies. The story seems to be over, there is nothing more to say. But there *is* more to say. The battery-dead calculator for two weeks is not even noticed, and then, when presumably it somehow comes to some unspecified person's attention, it is unceremoniously discarded, "thrown away." The way of all flesh.

What is convincing is not simply that A is followed by B and B is followed by C, but that there is a *logic* to the sequence, even (may we say?) a *truth* to the sequence. Notice, too, that the artist-writer does not moralize; rather, it is the reader-viewer who draws conclusions.

The theme is a great one, the humbling of the ambitious. Shakespeare, of course, often treated it—for instance, in *Richard II,* where the king meditates on his "state" (i.e., high status, exalted rank) and sees death as an "antic" (buffoon, jester) mocking even a king:

Within the hollow crown
That rounds the mortal temples of a king
Keeps Death his court and there the antic sits,
Scoffing his state and grinning at his pomp,
Allowing him a breath, a little scene,
To monarchize, be feared and kill with looks,
Infusing him with self and vain conceit,
As if this flesh which walls about our life,
Were brass impregnable, and humored thus
Comes at the last and with a little pin
Bores through his castle wall, and farewell king!
(3.2.160-70)

Or consider some lines by Shakespeare's later contemporary, James Shirley:

The glories of our blood and state
Are shadows, not substantial things;
There is no armor against fate;
Death lays his icy hand on kings:
Scepter and crown
Must tumble down,
And in the dust be equal made
With the poor crooked scythe and spade.

We are not claiming that the story about the calculator is in the same league, but we do find it memorable. We have indicated that we think the *text* of this graphic story makes a pretty good short-short story, even without the picture. Now let's examine the accompanying picture.

First of all, we think it is clever, sort of cute. The cartoonist might simply have drawn a calculator, but he cleverly—is it too much to say brilliantly?—put two eyes into the liquid crystal display, and thus animated the whole thing. The calculator *does* seem to be a person, doesn't it? So, in our view, the story becomes enriched by the image. We can call this sort of thing "graphic fiction," but, to go back to our earlier point, the truth is that the picture doesn't tell the story. It merely enriches a story that is told in words.

But our last sentence is, we admit, unfair. The image doesn't "merely" enrich the words. The picture is literally (that word again!) central to the story. If the story consisted only of text, or if all of the text were written above or below the story, the story would not be as effective. We admit it: The image is integral.

And that's our point: The best graphic fiction does not merely illustrate the verbal story; rather, the images are inseparable from the words. The story is text-and-image, not just text-adorned-with-image.

# A Second Example of Reading Images: A Story Told in Sequential Panels

Let's look now at a somewhat more complex work of graphic fiction, this one consisting of eight panels. The artist-author is Art Spiegelman. See below for a brief biography, and see page 246 for Spiegelman's work, "Nature vs. Nurture."

## ART SPIEGELMAN

*Born in Sweden in 1948, Art Spiegelman was raised in New York City. His two-part graphic story (part novel, part memoir),* Maus *(1986, 1991), based on his Polish-Jewish parents' experiences during the Holocaust, was awarded a Pulitzer Prize in 1992. A highly inventive fellow, Spiegelman not only cofounded several outlets for comic books but he also created Garbage Candy (edible candy in the shape of garbage, packaged in miniature garbage cans). In 2005* Time *magazine included Spiegelman in its list of the top 100 most influential people.*

If you were explaining the page to critters from outer space you might point out the following conventions, going panel by panel:

- Spiegelman sets the scene, in the extreme upper left, i.e. at the very beginning of the first panel, with some text in a small box. This text-box, providing the reader-viewer with background rather than with dialogue, is appropriately distinct in shape from the speech balloons.
- The little girl in the first panel is obviously happy. Her happiness is conveyed not only by the text's expressions of motherly love but also by the expression on her face. The father is also smiling.
- In the second panel the well-intentioned, politically correct father takes the doll from the girl. The girl is puzzled (the balloon says "uk" and the smile is gone from her face).
- In the third panel, the father is full of enthusiasm—his mouth is open, with a big smile—and the text conveys his enthusiasm. Additional text, "Skreeee," in different lettering (to indicate it is not human speech) comes out of the fire truck. The father has presumably pushed a button or flicked a switch so that the truck emits a sound. The girl's face and posture show puzzlement.
- The enthusiastic father (still with a big smile) seeks to show the girl how to play. His talk is (how shall we put it?) male talk, loud and aggressive ("Clang! Clang! Clang! Everybody get outa the way!").
- In the fifth panel the father, still teaching his daughter but evidently having a great time, is verging on the maniacal with his toothy grin and his "Vroom! Vroom." A viewer-reader probably thinks, "Hmmm, boys will be boys"—and may also think, seeing this father's childish enthusiasm, "You can't take the boy out of the man."
- The next panel shows the smiling—and complacent—father handing the truck to the girl, whose face conveys uncertainty.
- The bottom row begins with more uncertainty, indicated by a big question mark over the girl's head. She says nothing—there is no speech balloon—but we know that she is puzzled.
- The final panel show that the girl has covered half of the fire truck with a blanket—instead of thrusting it crazily around and making loud noises—and the father is reduced to silence. His posture—hands thrust into pockets, head slightly turned down—shows that he has given up, his attempt (the "nurture" of the title) to stifle the expression of motherly feelings (the "nature" of the title) and a balloon indicates that he is heaving a sigh of resignation. The sigh is conveyed by enclosing the word "sigh" within elongated dots, indicating he is sighing rather than *saying* "sigh."

If we were to think about the story in terms of the elements of fiction, what might we say? Well, so far as **character** (personality) goes, each of the two figures is relatively simple: The girl is just a girl—at her young age we hardly expect her to be a richly complex figure—and the father is essentially a well-meaning dad who wants his daughter to grow up free from gender stereotypes. Surely that is an admirable ambition. The **plot**—the sequence of happenings—shows his attempt to free her by offering her an alternative, a fire truck instead of a doll. He apparently is rather pleased with his efforts (the seventh panel shows him smiling when his little daughter touches the truck)—but with the final panel, reality breaks in. The girl does not career around the room shouting "Vroom," as the father did; rather, her maternal instinct manifests itself even toward the fire truck.

But this is not quite the end of the story: At the extreme right side we see the father heaving a sigh, shoulders slumped and hands in pocket: He has been forced to accept reality. Not always a bad thing, really, when you think about it. If we are asked what the **theme** of the story is—i.e., "What does the story *add up* to?" (which is very different from the plot, which is "What *happens* in the story?")—we can say that the theme concerns (as the title of the story indicates) the conflict between Nature and Nurture, or, to put it a bit differently, biology versus socialization. We most emphatically do not wish to say anything like "Spiegelman shows that human nature is unchangeable." For one thing, Spiegelman doesn't "show" us (in the sense of prove or demonstrate) anything. He just drew some pictures and wrote some words; he didn't offer anything that can be called evidence. Even if the pictures represent something that actually happened in his own family, his graphic report of his experience would not prove that other fathers will have the same experience with their daughters. Spiegelman is entertaining us, not arguing, not even preaching. Still, one feels that Spiegelman's story—the happenings that he illustrates, the doings of two figures—are plausible. One thing follows from another:

- The father sees his daughter playing with dolls, and
- being a good father, he wishes to free his daughter from stereotypical limited behavior, so
- he gives his daughter a toy that is usually associated with boys, but
- nature will have its way, and the girl turns the fire truck into an object that allows her to express her maternal instinct.
- Heaving a sigh, the father appears to recognize that his efforts have failed.

You have now instructed your Martian visitor in the language of graphic fiction. Yes, you knew it all along, and maybe the Martian did also.

## WILL EISNER

*Born in Brooklyn, New York, Will Eisner (1917-2005) drew cartoons for his high school newspaper, and after graduation studied for a year at the Art Students League of New York. He was soon publishing cartoons and comic strips, and he became an important figure in establishing the graphic novel ("sequential art") as a form of fiction. He taught at the School of Visual Arts in New York, and he published two highly informative books derived from his lectures,* Comics and Sequential Art *(1985) and* Graphic Storytelling and Visual Narrative *(1996). In* Comics and Sequential Art *Eisner includes a chapter titled "Expressive Anatomy." Among the illustrations in this chapter is "Hamlet on a Rooftop," first published in June 1981. Eisner prefaces the* Hamlet *drawings with the following remark, and then offers a running commentary on the pictures.*

### *Hamlet on a Rooftop*

#### The Body and the Face

The employment of body posture and facial expression (both having equal attention) is a major undertaking and an area of frequent failure. Properly and skillfully done, it can carry the narrative without resorting to unnecessary props or scenery. The use of expressive anatomy in the absence of words is less demanding because the latitude for the art is wider. Where the words have a depth of meaning and nuance, the task is more difficult.

This represents an example of a classic situation — that of author vs. artist. The artist must decide at the outset what his 'input' shall be; to slavishly make visual that which is in the author's mind or to embark on the raft of the author's words onto a visual sea of his own charting.

# HAMLET ON A ROOFTOP

His father is dead, mysteriously! His mother, within but a month, marries his uncle! So soon?. So soon? Can there be anything other than **SOMETHING ROTTEN** here? Can it be anything but murder!? Well, then, if murder it be all he values, indeed, his manhood cries out for retribution ....Vengeance .. to honor the filial duty his father's voice demands in the hot cauldron of his mind! Aye, to punish them, to **MURDER HIS MOTHER AND UNCLE**... as they lay in violation of his code!!! ...or perhaps something more unspeakable within him.

Yet... can he find in himself the capacity to commit so unnatural an act and in doing it forfeit the love of Ophelia, his betrothed? Wait... hold still for a moment, cling briefly to a passing raft of reason before it leaves the brain, before surrendering to the swift river of his passion, and so to be carried out into the turgid sea of violence from which there is no return.

In this experiment, Shakespeare's words are intact. The soliloquy is broken up into balloons at the artist's discretion. The intent here is to permit a meaningful fusing of word, imagery and timing. The result should provide the reader with necessary pauses.

The artist here functions as actor and in the process gives his own meaning to the lines.

A gesture signifying contemplation.

Furniture employed in intimate involvement with the actor gives the 'background' story value because it is part of the action.

Submission . . . to a ''heavy'' thought.

Here, the postures are more than a classical portrayal of emotions. This man is not the Danish Prince Hamlet! His gestures and postures are derivative of his special background. The question of how he would deliver the standard gesture for self-doubt and internal agony is the artist's real challenge!

WHETHER 'TIS NOBLER IN THE MIND TO SUFFER THE SLINGS AND ARROWS OF OUTRAGEOUS FORTUNE...

OR...

TO TAKE ARMS AGAINST A SEA OF TROUBLES, AND BY OPPOSING **END** THEM!

Bravado . . . he envisions himself as challenging the forces of troubles.

Exhaustion — beaten by the enormity of his problems

Seeking comfort he lets his body slide down along the wall

Retreat . . . into his refuge . . . sleep

The language of posture is universal and inter-changeable — the application is not.

Wishing with all his might.

Withdrawing into sleep or oblivion, he assumes an almost fetal posture.

Terror . . . in the realization of his options

AYE...
THERE'S
THE
RUB!

FOR IN THAT
SLEEP OF DEATH
— WHAT DREAMS MAY COME
WHEN WE HAVE SHUFFLED OFF
THIS MORTAL COIL
MUST GIVE US PAUSE.

Awake
again to the
thoughts
that will not
leave him!

THERE'S
THE RESPECT
THAT MAKES
CALAMITY
OF
SO LONG LIFE

Candor . . .
addressing
the unseen
manipulator
of his fate

Anger . . . now he builds his resolution

Arguing
. . . he
begins to
make a
case to but-
tress grow-
ing resolve.

Debating . . . the postures of a courtroom advocate

The use of a
long-shot, here
is meant to
reinforce
realism — and
in that way try
to deal with the
problem of
putting
Shakespeare's
language in the
mouth of such
a man.

Hesitation . . .
a recurrence
of doubt

RESOLVE!

AND ENTERPRISES OF GREAT PITCH AND MOMENT WITH THIS REGARD THEIR CURRENTS TURN AWRY AND **LOSE THE NAME OF ACTION**,!!

...SOFT YOU NOW!

ATTACK . . .
he now moves
to act upon
his resolve.

This wedding of Shake-spearean language with a modern denizen of the ghetto may not be appropriate but the exercise serves to demonstrate the potential of the medium be-cause the emotional content is so universal.

Thus far we have looked at three graphic works: A one-panel original story with a picture (Carrillo's piece, page 243, about the malevolent calculator that died and two weeks later was discarded), an eight-panel original story (Spiegelman's "Nature vs. Nurture, page 246"), and twenty-six panels, spread over ten pages (pages 249–58, devoted to a soliloquy from *Hamlet*). Now let's examine a contemporary graphic treatment of an early twentieth-century short story, Franz Kafka's "A Hunger Artist." In one obvious way the job of the illustrator of a classic text is easier than the job of the creator of an entirely original work, but in another way it is also more difficult, because the artist who illustrates a classic is in some sense putting himself or herself up against a classic writer: Reader/viewers will inevitably expect the artist to contribute something to the work, to do more than ride piggy-back on the original author.

# R. CRUMB AND DAVID ZANE MAIROWITZ

*Robert Dennis Crumb, born in Philadelphia in 1943, worked for a while in Cleveland as a designer of greeting cards, and then began drawing for underground newspapers. In 1967 he moved to San Francisco, but he now lives in France. Some of his work is strongly sexual and highly satiric, but he has also drawn* R. Crumb's Kafka *(1993), with a text by David Zane Mairowitz, illustrating several works of fiction by the writer Franz Kafka (1883–1924).*

*David Zane Mairowitz, born in New York City in 1943, emigrated in 1968 to England, where he works as a freelance writer.*

We include here the Crumb and Mairowitz version of Kafka's "A Hunger Artist," a short story found on page 438.

In June 1924, his "phantoms" saw to it — with their usual irony — that while dying of *starvation*, he would be correcting the galley-proofs of an astonishing masterwork called...

THE PERIOD OF FASTING WAS SET BY HIS IMPRESARIO AT FORTY DAYS MAXIMUM, BECAUSE AFTER THAT TIME THE PUBLIC BEGAN TO LOSE INTEREST. SO, ON THE FORTIETH DAY, WITH AN EXCITED CROWD FILLING THE ARENA AND A MILITARY BAND PLAYING, TWO YOUNG LADIES CAME TO LEAD THE HUNGER-ARTIST OUT OF HIS CAGE. WHEN THIS HAPPENED HE ALWAYS PUT UP SOME RESISTANCE... WHY STOP AFTER ONLY FORTY DAYS?!? WHY SHOULD THEY TAKE FROM HIM THE GLORY OF FASTING EVEN LONGER, OF SURPASSING EVEN HIMSELF TO REACH UNIMAGINABLE HEIGHTS, FOR HE SAW HIS ABILITY TO GO ON FASTING AS *UNLIMITED!*

THEN CAME THE FEAST, WITH THE IMPRESARIO TRYING TO SPOONFEED THE NEARLY COMATOSE HUNGER-ARTIST, ALL THE WHILE CHATTING CHEERFULLY IN ORDER TO DISTRACT ATTENTION FROM HIS CONDITION.

AFTER THAT THERE WAS EVEN A TOAST TO THE AUDIENCE, SUPPOSEDLY SUGGESTED BY THE HUNGER-ARTIST HIMSELF IN A WHISPER TO THE IMPRESARIO.

HE LIVED THIS WAY FOR MANY YEARS, HONORED BY ALL THE WORLD, YET TROUBLED IN HIS SOUL, DEEPLY FRUSTRATED THAT THEY WOULD NOT ALLOW HIS FASTING TO EXCEED FORTY DAYS. HE SPENT MOST OF HIS TIME IN A GLOOMY MOOD, AND WHEN SOME KIND-HEARTED PERSON WOULD TRY TO EXPLAIN THAT HIS DEPRESSION WAS THE RESULT OF THE FASTING, HE WOULD SOMETIMES FLY INTO A RAGE AND BEGIN RATTLING THE BARS OF HIS CAGE LIKE AN ANIMAL.

AS TIME WENT BY PEOPLE BECAME INTERESTED IN OTHER AMUSEMENTS, AND WERE REVOLTED BY PROFESSIONAL FASTING. THE HUNGER-ARTIST COULD NOT CHANGE JOBS, FANATICALLY DEVOTED TO FASTING AS HE WAS. SO, DISCHARGING THE IMPRESARIO, HE HIRED HIMSELF OUT TO A LARGE CIRCUS, WHERE HIS CAGE WAS PUT OUTSIDE, NEAR THOSE OF THE ANIMALS.

# 13

# Students Writing About Stories in Print and on the Screen

## Prompts for Writing About Fiction

The questions that follow below will help to stimulate ideas about stories. Not every question will be relevant to every story, but if after reading a story and thinking about it, you then run your eye over these pages, you will find some questions that will help you to think further about the story—in short, that will help you to get ideas, to develop a thesis that can effectively be supported with evidence.

It's best to do your thinking with a pen or pencil in hand. If some of the following questions seem to you to be especially relevant to the story you will be writing about, jot down—freely, without worrying about spelling—your initial responses, interrupting your writing only to glance again at the story when you feel the need to check the evidence you are offering in support of your thesis.

### Plot

1. Does the plot grow out of the characters, or does it depend on chance or coincidence? Did something at first strike you as irrelevant that later you perceived as relevant? Do some parts continue to strike you as irrelevant?
2. Does surprise play an important role, or does foreshadowing? If surprise is very important, can the story be read a second time with any interest? If so, what gives it this further interest?
3. What conflicts does the story include? Conflicts of one character against another? Of one character against the setting, or against society? Conflicts within a single character?
4. Are certain episodes narrated out of chronological order? If so, were you puzzled? Annoyed? On reflection, does the arrangement of episodes seem effective? Why or why not? Are certain situations repeated? If so, what do you make out of the repetitions?

### Character

1. Which character chiefly engages your interest? Why?
2. What purposes do minor characters serve? Do you find some who by their similarities and differences help to define each other or help to define the

major character? How else is a particular character defined—by his or her words, actions (including thoughts and emotions), dress, setting, narrative point of view? Do certain characters act differently in the same, or in a similar, situation?

3. How does the author reveal character? By explicit authorial (editorial) comment, for instance, or, on the other hand, by revelation through dialogue? Through depicted action? Through the actions of other characters? How are the author's methods especially suited to the whole of the story?

4. Is the behavior plausible—that is, are the characters well motivated?

5. If a character changes, why and how does he or she change? (You may want to jot down each event that influences a change.) Or did you change your attitude toward a character not because the character changes but because you came to know the character better?

6. Are the characters round or flat? Are they complex or, on the other hand, highly typical (for instance, one-dimensional representatives of a social class or age)? Are you chiefly interested in a character's psychology, or does the character strike you as standing for something, such as honesty or the arrogance of power?

7. How has the author caused you to sympathize with certain characters? How does your response—your sympathy or lack of sympathy—contribute to your judgment of the conflict?

## Point of View

1. Who tells the story? How much does the narrator know? Does the narrator strike you as reliable? What effect is gained by using this narrator?

2. How does the point of view help shape the theme? After all, the basic story of "Little Red Riding Hood"—what happens—remains unchanged whether told from the wolf's point of view or the girl's, but if we hear the story from the wolf's point of view we may feel that the story is about terrifying yet pathetic compulsive behavior; if from the girl's point of view, about terrified innocence and male violence.

3. Does the narrator's language help you to construct a picture of the narrator's character, class, attitude, strengths, and limitations? (Jot down some evidence, such as colloquial or—on the other hand—formal expressions, ironic comments, figures of speech.) How far can you trust the narrator? Why?

## Setting

1. Do you have a strong sense of the time and place? Is the story very much about, say, New England Puritanism, or race relations in the South in the late nineteenth century, or midwestern urban versus small-town life? If time and place are important, how and at what points in the story has the author conveyed this sense? If you do not strongly feel the setting, do you think the author should have made it more evident?

2. What is the relation of the setting to the plot and the characters? (For instance, do houses or rooms or their furnishings say something about their

residents?) Would anything be lost if the descriptions of the setting were deleted from the story or if the setting were changed?

## Symbolism

1. Do certain characters seem to you to stand for something in addition to themselves? Does the setting—whether a house, a farm, a landscape, a town, a period—have an extra dimension?
2. If you do believe that the story has symbolic elements, do you think they are adequately integrated within the story, or do they strike you as being too obviously stuck in?

## Style

**Style** may be defined as *how* the writer says what he or she says. It is the writer's manner of expression. The writer's choice of words, of sentence structure, and of sentence length are all aspects of style. Example: "Shut the door" and "Would you mind closing the door, please" differ substantially in style. Another example: Lincoln begins the Gettysburg Address by speaking of "Four score and seven years ago"—that is, by using language that has a biblical overtone. If he had said "Eighty-seven years ago," his style would have been different.

1. How would you characterize the style? Simple? Understated? Figurative?
2. How has the point of view shaped or determined the style?
3. Do you think that the style is consistent? If it isn't—for instance, if there are shifts from simple sentences to highly complex ones—what do you make of the shifts?

## Theme

1. Is the title informative? What does it mean or suggest? Does the meaning change after you have read the story? Does the title help you to formulate a theme? If you had written the story, what title would you use?
2. Do certain passages—dialogue or description—seem to you to point especially toward the theme? Do you find certain repetitions of words or pairs of incidents highly suggestive and helpful in directing your thoughts toward stating a theme? Flannery O'Connor, in *Mystery and Manners* (1969), says, "In good fiction, certain of the details will tend to accumulate meaning from the action of the story itself, and when that happens, they become symbolic in the way they work." Does this story work that way?
3. Is the meaning of the story embodied in the whole story, or does it seem stuck in, for example in certain passages of editorializing?
4. Suppose someone asked you to state the point—the theme—of the story. Could you? And if you could, would you say that the theme of a particular story reinforces values you hold, or does it to some degree challenge them? (It is sometimes said that the best writers are subversive, forcing readers to see something that they do not want to see.)

# Fiction into Film

Because many stories have been filmed, here we offer some comments about the nature of film, some definitions of indispensable technical terms, a few suggestions about topics, and a list of questions to consider as you begin to think about writing on a film derived from a story.

# Film as a Medium

Your first thought may be that a film (excluding cartoons, documentaries, newsreels, and so on) is rather like a play: A story is presented by means of actors. There are, however, crucial distinctions between film and drama. First, though drama uses such visual matters as gestures, tableaux effects, and scenery, the plays that we value most highly are *literature:* The word dominates, the visual component is subordinate. You need not be a film fanatic who believes that the invention of the sound track was an impediment to film in order to realize that a film is more a matter of pictures than of words. The camera usually roves, giving us crowded streets, empty skies, rainy nights, or close-ups of filled ashtrays and chipped coffee cups. A critic has aptly said that in Ingmar Bergman's *Smiles of a Summer Night* (1955) "the almost unbearably ornate crystal goblets, by their aspect and their positioning in the image, convey the oppressive luxuriousness of the diners' lives in purely and uniquely filmic terms."

In short, the speaker in a film does not usually dominate. In a play the speaker normally holds the spectator's attention, but in a film when a character speaks, the camera often gives us a **reaction shot,** focusing not on the speaker but on the face or gestures of a character who is affected by the speech, thus giving the spectator a visual interpretation of the words. In François Truffaut's *400 Blows* (1959), for example, we hear a reform school official verbally assault a boy, but we see the uncomfortable boy, not the official. Even when the camera does focus on the speaker, it is likely to offer an interpretation. An extreme example is a scene from David Lean's *Brief Encounter* (1945): A gossip is talking, and the camera gives us a close-up of her jabbering mouth, which monstrously fills the screen.

The difference between film and drama can be put another way: A film is more like a short story or a novel than it is like a play, the action being presented not directly by actors but by a narrator, in this case the camera. The camera, like a narrator telling a story from a particular point of view, *comments* on the story while telling it. Thus, a filmmaker may use out-of-focus shots or slow-motion shots to communicate the strangeness of an experience. At the end of Arthur Penn's *Bonnie and Clyde* (1968), when Clyde is riddled with bullets, because his collapse is shot in slow motion he seems endowed not only with unusual grace but also with almost superhuman powers of endurance.

Even the choice of film stock is part of the comment. A highly sensitive or "fast" film needs less light to catch an image than a "slow" film does, but it is usually grainier. Perhaps because black-and-white newsreels often used fast film, a grainy quality may suggest authenticity or realism. Robert Enrico's 1962 film of Ambrose Bierce's short story "An Occurrence at Owl Creek Bridge," a story about the hanging of a civilian farmer who is a Southern sympathizer during the Civil

War, begins with low-contrast stock that gives a rich gradation of tones from white to black, reminiscent of Civil War photographs. The director John Huston similarly chose to use black and white for his film version (1951) of Stephen Crane's *The Red Badge of Courage,* a novel about cowardice and courage in the Civil War. Different film stocks may be used within a single motion picture. In Bergman's *Wild Strawberries* (1957), for instance, Bergman uses high-contrast stock for the nightmare sequence, though elsewhere in the film the contrasts are subtle. Color film has its own methods of tone and texture control.

The medium, as everyone knows, is part of the message; Laurence Olivier made Shakespeare's *Henry V* (1944) in color but *Hamlet* (1948) in black and white because these media say different things. Similarly, although by 1971 most fiction films were being made in color, Peter Bogdanovich made *The Last Picture Show* (1971) in black and white, partly to convey a sense of the unexciting life of a small town in America in the 1950s and partly to evoke the films of the fifties.

When a film is made in color, however, the colors may be symbolic (or at least suggestive) as well as realistic. In Stanley Kubrick's *A Clockwork Orange* (1971), for example, which is based on a novel of the same title by Anthony Burgess (1962), hot colors (oranges and reds) conveying vitality and aggressiveness in the first half of the film are displaced in the second half by cool colors (blues and greens) when the emphasis turns to "clockwork"—to mechanization.

The kind of lens used also helps determine what the viewer sees. In Mike Nichols's *The Graduate* (1967), Benjamin runs toward the camera (he is trying to reach a church before his girl marries another man), but he seems to make no progress because a **telephoto lens** was used and thus his size does not increase as it normally would. The lens, that is, helps communicate Benjamin's desperate sense of frustration. Similarly, in *An Occurrence at Owl Creek Bridge,* Peyton Farquhar runs toward his wife in the foreground, but the telephoto lens makes it seem that he is making no progress. Conversely, a **wide-angle lens** makes a character approach the camera with menacing rapidity; she or he quickly looms into the foreground.

But of course filmmakers, though resembling fiction writers in offering a pervasive indirect comment, are not fiction writers any more than they are playwrights or directors of plays. The medium has its own techniques, and a filmmaker works with these techniques, not with those of a playwright or of a short-story writer.

Perhaps the most obvious way that a film may comment (as a story-writer may) on the events and characters is through the use of **voice-over:** The voice of the narrator or of an off-camera person speaks, while the visuals and other sounds (music, birds twittering, whatever) continue. Discussing the film version (1993) of a novel by Edith Wharton, *The Age of Innocence* (1920), Martin Scorsese said that he found the narrator's voice enjoyable for its satiric observations about New York society and important for an understanding of the characters, and thus he chose to present some phases of the film with a voice-over that sets the background for and interprets the action. Some reviewers criticized this decision, saying that the voice-over was imposed and artificial, as though Scorsese did not think he could trust the characters on screen to communicate their thoughts and feelings. The implication of their criticism was that Scorsese had not found visual equivalents for a fiction-writer's verbal techniques.

For the film version (1987) of James Joyce's story "The Dead" (1914), John Huston made a related, though somewhat different and perhaps more successful, choice. At the close of the story, Gabriel Conroy discovers that his wife, Gretta, has for many years harbored a deep affection for a young man who died a tragic early death. The narrator concludes by describing Gabriel's mournful feelings as he reflects on his wife, his family and friends, the past, and the approach of death (e.g., "The time had come for him to set out on his journey westward."). Huston adapted the narrator's words and gave them to Gabriel, who speaks them in a voice-over as the camera moves from one shot to the next, from inside to outside the hotel room where he and Gretta are staying. Perhaps in this way Huston avoids the distancing effect that reviewers complained about in Scorsese's film; in the case of *The Dead,* the voice speaking is that of a central character.

# Film Techniques

At this point it may be well to suspend generalizations temporarily and to look more methodically at some techniques of filmmaking. What follows is a brief grammar and dictionary of film, naming and explaining the cinematic devices that help filmmakers embody their vision in a work of art. An essay on film will discuss some of these devices, but there is no merit in mechanically trotting them all out.

## Shots

A **shot** is what is recorded between the time a camera starts and the time it stops, that is, between the director's call for "action" and the call to "cut." Perhaps the average shot is about 10 seconds (very rarely a fraction of a second, and usually not more than 15 or so seconds). The average film is about an hour and a half, with about 600 shots, but Alfred Hitchcock's *The Birds* (1963) uses 1,360 shots. Three common shots are (1) a **long shot** or **establishing shot,** showing the main object at a considerable distance from the camera and thus presenting it in relation to its general surroundings (for example, captured soldiers, seen across a prison yard, entering the yard); (2) a **medium shot,** showing the object in relation to its immediate surroundings (a couple of soldiers, from the knees up, with the yard's wall behind them); and (3) a **close-up,** showing only the main object, or, more often, only a part of it (a soldier's face or his bleeding feet).

In the outside world we can narrow our vision to the detail that interests us by moving our head and by focusing our eyes, ignoring what is not of immediate interest. The close-up is the movie director's chief way of directing our vision and of emphasizing a detail. (Another way is to focus sharply on the significant image, leaving the rest of the image in soft focus.) The close-up, a way of getting emphasis, has been heavily used in recent years, not always successfully. As the American essayist and film critic Dwight Macdonald said of John Schlesinger's *Midnight Cowboy* (1969) and *Getting Straight* (1970):

> [A] movie told in close-ups is like a comic book, or like a novel composed in punchy one-sentence paragraphs and set throughout in large caps. How refreshing is a long or middle shot, a glimpse of the real world, so lovely and so *far away,* in the midst of those interminable processions of [a] hairy ogre face.

Two excellent film versions of Shakespeare's *Henry V* nicely show the different effects that long shots and close-ups can produce. Laurence Olivier's version (1944) uses abundant long shots and, on the whole, conveys a highly pictorial, sweeping epic version of the war in which Henry was engaged. The film was made during World War II as a patriotic effort to inspire the English by showing the heroism of combat. On the other hand, Kenneth Branagh's version, made in 1989, uses lots of close-ups of soldiers with mud-splattered faces, emphasizing the grittiness of war. Olivier brought out the splendor and romance, Branagh the labor and pain, of war.

While taking a shot, the camera can move: It can swing to the right or left while its base remains fixed (a **pan shot**), up or down while fixed on its axis (a **tilt shot**), forward or backward (a **traveling shot**), or in and out and up and down fastened to a crane (a **crane shot**). The **zoom lens,** introduced in the 1950s and widespread by the middle 1960s, enables the camera to change its focus fluidly so that it can approach a detail—as a traveling shot does—while remaining fixed in place. Much will depend on the angle (high or low) from which the shots are made. If the camera is high (a **high-angle shot**), looking down on figures, it will usually dwarf them, perhaps even reduce them to crawling insects, making them vulnerable, pitiful, or contemptible. The higher the angle, the more likely it is to suggest a God's-eye view of entrapped people. If the camera is low (a **low-angle shot**), close to the ground and looking up, thereby showing figures against the sky, it will probably give them added dignity.

In F. W. Murnau's *Last Laugh* (1924), we first get low-angle shots of the self-confident doorman, communicating his grand view of himself; later, when he loses his strength and is reduced to working as a lavatory attendant, we see him from above, and he seems dwarfed. But these are not inevitable principles. A shot in Enrico's film version of Bierce's "An Occurrence at Owl Creek Bridge" shows the hangman from below, making him seem threatening. And a shot in Orson Welles's *Citizen Kane* (1941) shows Kane from above, but it does not dwarf him; rather, it shows him dominating his wife and then in effect obliterating her by casting a shadow over her. Similarly, a low-angle shot does not always add dignity: films in which children play important parts often have lots of low-angle shots showing adults as menacing giants.

In short, by its distance from the subject, its height from the ground, and its angle of elevation, the camera comments on or interprets what happens. It seems to record reality, but it offers its own version. It is only a slight exaggeration to say that the camera always lies, that is, gives a personal vision of reality.

**Slow motion** and **fast motion** also offer comments. In Kenneth Branagh's *Henry V* (1989), as in Orson Welles's *Falstaff* (1966; also titled *Chimes at Midnight*), part of the battle is filmed in slow motion; thus, the weariness of the soldiers is emphasized. In Enrico's *An Occurrence at Owl Creek Bridge,* Peyton Farquhar, imagining that he has escaped from his executioners, sees them in slow motion.

## Sequences

A group of related scenes—such as the three scenes of soldiers mentioned earlier—is a **sequence,** though a sequence is more likely to have thirty scenes than three. A sequence corresponds roughly to a chapter in a novel, the shots being sentences and the scenes being paragraphs. Within a sequence may be an **intercut,** a switch to another action that, for example, provides an ironic comment on the main action of the sequence. If intercuts are so abundant in a sequence that, in effect, two or more sequences are going at once (for example, shots of the villain about to ravish the heroine, alternating with shots of the hero riding to her rescue), we have **parallel editing** (also called a **crosscut**). In the example just given, probably the tempo would increase, the shots being progressively shorter as we get to the rescue.

Within a sequence, the **transitions** are normally made by **straight cuts**—a strip of film is spliced to another, and the result is an instantaneous transfer from one shot to the next. Usually, an audience is scarcely (if at all) conscious of transitions from, say, a long shot of a character to a medium shot of her or him, or from a close-up of a speaker to a close-up of her or his auditor. But sometimes the director wants the audience to be fully aware of the change, as an author may emphasize a change by beginning a new paragraph or, even more sharply, by beginning a new chapter. Two older, and now rather unfashionable, relatively conspicuous transitions are sometimes still used, usually between sequences rather than within a sequence. These are the **dissolve** (the shot dissolves while a new shot appears to emerge from beneath it, there being a moment when we get a superimposition of both scenes), and the **fade** (in the **fade-out** the screen grows darker until black; in the **fade-in** the screen grows lighter until the new scene is fully visible).

In effect the camera is saying, "Let us now leave X and turn to Y" or "Two weeks later." Two older methods, even less in favor today than the dissolve and the fade but used in many excellent old films and in some modern films that seek an archaic effect, are the **wipe** (a sort of windshield wiper crosses the screen, wiping off the first scene and revealing the next) and the **iris** (in an **iris-in,** the new scene first appears in the center of the previous scene and then this circle expands until it fills the screen; an **iris-out** shows the new scene first appearing around the perimeter and then the circle closes in on the previous scene). Charles Chaplin more than once ended a scene with an iris-out of the tramp walking jauntily toward the horizon. François Truffaut used iris shots in *The Wild Child* (1970), suggesting by the encircling darkness the boy's isolation from most of the world surrounding him as he concentrated on a single object before him.

## Editing

All of the transitions just discussed are examples of editing techniques. A film, no less than a poem or a play or a picture or a palace, is something made, and it is not made by simply exposing some film footage. Shots—often taken at widely separated times and places—must be appropriately joined. For example, we see a man look off to the right, and then we get a shot of what he is looking at and then a shot of his reaction. Until the shots are assembled, we don't have a film—we merely have the footage. The Russian director V. I. Pudovkin put it this way: "The film is not *shot,* but built, built up from the separate strips of celluloid that are its raw material." This building-up is the process of **editing.**

More than a story can be told, of course; something of the appropriate emotion can be communicated by juxtaposing, say, a medium-long shot of a group of impassively advancing soldiers against a close-up of a single terrified victim. Similarly, emotion can be communicated by the duration of the shots (quick shots suggest haste; prolonged shots suggest slowness) and by the lighting (progressively darker shots can suggest melancholy; progressively lighter shots can suggest hope or joy). An extremely obvious but effective example occurs in Charlie Chaplin's *Modern Times* (1936), a satire on industrialism. We see a mass of workers hurrying to their jobs, and a moment later we see a herd of sheep on the move, this shot providing a bitter comic comment on the previous shot.

The Russian theorists of film called this process of building by quick cuts **montage.** The theory held that shots, when placed together, add up to more than the sum of the parts. Montage, for them, was what made a film a work of art and not a mere replica of reality. American writers commonly use the term merely to denote quick cutting, and French writers use it merely in the sense of cutting.

All this talk about ingenious shots and their arrangement, then, assumes that the camera is a sort of pen, carefully setting forth images and thus at every point guiding the perceiver. The director (through the actors, camera technicians, cutters, and a host of others) makes an artifact, rather as a novelist makes a book or a sculptor makes a statue, and this artifact is an elaborate contraption that manipulates the spectators by telling them at every second exactly how they ought to feel.

But since the 1950s, a reaction has occurred against such artistry, a feeling that although the elaborate editing of Sergei Eisenstein and the other Russians is an aesthetic triumph, it is also a moral failure because by its insistent tricky commentary it seems to deny the inherent worth of the event in itself as it happens. Moreover, just as the nineteenth-century narrator in the novel, who continually guided the reader ("Do not fear, gentle reader, for even at this moment plans were being laid . . ."), was in the twentieth-century novel sloughed off, forcing the readers in large measure to deduce the story for themselves, so, too, some contemporary filmmakers emphasize improvisation, fully aware that the film thus made will not at every point guide or dominate the viewer.

Film affects us through sound as well as sight, and a good film usually succeeds in integrating the action with well-handled and carefully paced dialogue and keen choices of music. The long opening sequence of Francis Ford Coppola's *Apocalypse Now* (1979)—a film loosely based on Joseph Conrad's *Heart of Darkness*—unfolds to the music of the late 1960s/early 1970s rock group The Doors, as lead singer Jim Morrison sings the haunting song "The End." Later, an astonishingly vivid, breathtaking helicopter assault on a Vietnamese village takes place to the accompaniment of the German composer Richard Wagner's stirring "Ride of the Valkyries," which blasts from a speaker mounted on one of the attacking helicopters.

# Theme in Film

It is time now to point out that mastery of technique, though necessary to good filmmaking, will not in itself make a good film. A good film is not a bag of cinematic devices but the embodiment, through cinematic devices, of a vision, an underlying theme. What is this theme or vision? It is a filmmaker's perception of some aspect of existence that he or she thinks is worthy of our interest. Normally, this perception involves characters and a plot. Recent American films, relying heavily on color, rock music in surround sound, quick cutting, and the wide screen, have tended to emphasize the emotional experience and deemphasize narrative. Still, most of the best cinema—and virtually every film based on a short story—is concerned with what people do, that is, with character and plot. Character is what people are, plot is what happens, but the line between character and plot fades, for what people are is in large measure what they do, and what is done is in large measure the result of what people are.

# Comparing Filmed and Printed Stories

After seeing a film based on a novel or short story that we know, most of us are drawn to compare the two and make judgments about which one is better. If the film is not conspicuously faithful to the story, we may complain about the loss of this character or that episode; but when it is highly faithful we may find ourselves complaining, "What a disappointment! It was just like the book but it seemed so dead!" This second response is not surprising; as indicated earlier, good films use the camera creatively, and a film that is content merely to record a narrative is likely to be a dull film.

Most of the time we will conclude that the printed fiction is superior to what is shown on the screen. Yet we might do well on occasion not to emphasize which is better but, rather, to observe how entertainingly, interestingly, each works on its own. It's true that the use of voice-over may feel a bit wrong or jarring in *The Age of Innocence,* but the film is so stunning visually that the voice-over seems only a minor element in it—a distraction perhaps, but hardly a serious flaw. A similar argument could be raised about the choices made in the film versions of E. M. Forster's novel *Maurice* (published posthumously in 1971; film version 1987) and Henry James's *The Wings of the Dove* (1902; film version 1997). The frontal nudity and explicit lovemaking depicted in these films seems very far removed from the restraint and indirection of the novels themselves, in which sexual desire and activity are implied rather than shown, frequently touched on but never in graphic detail. But we could claim nonetheless that the films are in a sense true to the meanings of the novels—dramatizing encounters and themes that Forster and James, writing many decades ago, simply could not render with the fully detailed candor that is now possible.

These films, then, are not literally faithful to the novel—on the subject of sexuality, they show more, much more, than the novels do. But the changes in the films may be for the better, or at least they may strike us as understandable and defensible on the ground that they are in keeping with the expectations of a contemporary audience. The novels become revitalized—made to feel contemporary—because of the films' greater openness about daring illicit behavior.

# Getting Ready to Write

Mastery of terminology does not make anyone a perceptive film critic, but it helps writers communicate their perceptions to their readers. Probably an essay on a film will not be primarily about the use of establishing shots or of wipes or of any such matters; rather, it will be about the reasons why a particular film pleases or displeases, succeeds or fails, seems significant or insignificant, and in discussing these large matters it is sometimes necessary (or at least economical) to use the commonest technical terms. Large matters are often determined in part by such seemingly small matters as the distance of the camera from its subject or how transitions are made, and the writer may as well use the conventional terms. But it is also true that a filmmaker's technique and technology alone cannot make a first-rate film. An idea, a personal vision, a theme must be embodied in all that is flashed on the screen.

Writing an essay about a new film—one only shown in the movie theaters and not yet available for personal viewing at home—presents difficulties not encountered in writing about printed stories. If we experience film in a darkened room, we cannot easily take notes, and because the film may be shown only once, we cannot always take another look at passages that puzzle us. But

- You can take some brief notes even in the dark; it is best to amplify them as soon as light is available, while you still know what the scrawls mean.
- If you can see the film more than once, do so, and of course if the script has been published, study it.
- Draft your paper as soon as possible after your first viewing, and then see the film again, if possible.
- If you can, check hazy memories of certain scenes and techniques with fellow viewers.

# Drafting an Essay About a Film

First—but you may not discover this until you have written a draft or two—you need to have a *point,* a *thesis.* Your essay must do more than say that the film of a story is faithful to the original in points A, B, C, and D, and departs from the original in points E, F, G, and H. Your readers doubtless can see these things for themselves. Probably in your preliminary notes you will indeed want to list such things, but you will then want to go on to think about the significance of the resemblances and the differences. What do you make of them? Given the fact that film is a visual medium, is it possible that too much fidelity to a story—for instance, failure to give us interesting pictures—has turned a memorable short story into a boring movie? You will want to think about the resemblances and the differences between the story and the film, and you will want to account for them, first to yourself (probably you will have to write and revise at least one draft before you can do this). Then in your essay you will explain to your reader why you respond the way you do.

Early in the essay it is desirable to sketch enough of the plot to give readers an idea of what happens. Do not try to recount everything that happens; it can't be done, and the attempt will frustrate you and bore your readers. Once you introduce the main characters and devote a few sentences to the plot, thus giving the readers a comfortable seat, get down to the job of convincing them that you have something interesting to say about the film—that the plot is trivial, or that the hero is not really cool but cruel, or that the plot and the characters are fine achievements but the camera work is sometimes needlessly tricky, or that all is well.

Incidentally, a convenient way to give an actor's name in your essay is to put it in parentheses after the character's name or role, thus: "The detective

(Humphrey Bogart) finds a clue. . . ." Then, as you go on to talk about the film, use the names of the characters or the roles, not the names of the actors, except of course when you are talking about the actors themselves, as in "Bogart is exactly right for the part."

---

✔ **CHECKLIST:** *Getting Ideas for Writing Arguments About Film*

These questions may help to bring impressions out into the open and may with some reworking provide topics for essays.

*Preliminaries*

❑ Is the title significant? If the film's title differs from that of the published story, account for and evaluate the change.

*Literary Adaptations*

❑ Does the film slavishly follow its original and neglect the potentialities of the camera? Or does it so revel in cinematic devices that it distorts the original work? (Of course, an adaptation need not go to either extreme. Enrico's *An Occurrence at Owl Creek Bridge* is a close adaptation of Ambrose Bierce's story, and yet it is visually interesting.)

❑ Does the film do violence to the theme of the original? Is the film better than its source? Are the additions or omissions due to the medium or to a crude or faulty interpretation of the original?

*Plot and Character*

❑ How faithful is the film to the story in plot and in character? Evaluate the changes, if any.

❑ In the film version (1984) of Henry James's novel *The Bostonians* (1886), one of the protagonists, an impassioned feminist reformer, delivers a speech to an unruly crowd in a theater, which significantly changes the effect of the novel itself, where the speech is not given. What is the impact of a decision like this one (which is so at odds with the plot as the author shaped it), and what is your assessment of it? Is the film to be faulted for such a change, or does the change make good sense for the film's development of character and theme, however unfaithful it might be to the author's story?

❑ Can film deal as effectively with inner action—mental processes—as with external, physical action? In a given film, how is the inner action conveyed? By voice-over? Or by visual equivalents?

*Setting*

❑ How effectively does the film convey the setting or settings that the author chose for his or her story? Do the film's settings somehow fall short of the expressive power that they possess in the story itself?

*Editing*

❑ Does the editing—for instance, frequent sharp juxtapositions or slow panoramic shots—convey qualities that the story writer conveyed by means of sentence length or sentence structure?

❑ Are shots and sequences adequately developed, or do they seem jerky? (A shot may be jerky by being extremely brief or at an odd angle; a sequence may be jerky by using discontinuous images or fast cuts. Sometimes, of course, jerkiness may be desirable.) If such cinematic techniques as wipes, dissolves, and slow motion are used, are they meaningful and effective?

❑ Are the actors appropriately cast? Was it a mistake to cast Robert Redford as Gatsby in Jack Clayton's film version (1974) of *The Great Gatsby* (1925)? John Huston, in his film (1951) of Stephen Crane's *The Red Badge of Courage* (1894) used Audie Murphy, one of the most highly decorated and best-known heroes of World War II, as Henry Fleming, the young soldier who flees from battle but later gets a second chance to fight bravely. What is the effect of this casting?

*Symbolism*

❑ If in the story certain objects acquire symbolic meanings, are these same objects similarly used in the film? Or does the film introduce new symbols?

❑ Is the lighting in the film realistic, symbolic, or both?

*Soundtrack*

❑ Does the soundtrack offer more than realistic dialogue? Is the music appropriate and functional? (Music may, among other things, imitate natural sounds, give a sense of locale or of ethnic group, suggest states of mind, provide ironic commentary, or—by repeated melodies—help establish connections.) Are volume, tempo, and pitch—whether of music or of such sounds as the wind blowing or cars moving—used to stimulate emotions?

# Thinking About Filming Fiction

When you read a story and consider its possibilities as a film, you may want to begin thinking along these lines:

- Which story included in this book is your favorite? Do you think that this story could be made into a good film? Are there features of the story—its setting, for example—that, in your view, would work very well in a film version? Are there also features of this story that would be hard to convey in a film?

- There have been film versions (in some instances, more than one) of a number of well-known novels by English and American authors, including Jane Austen, Emily and Charlotte Brontë, Charles Dickens, Thomas Hardy, Edith Wharton, E. M. Forster, and Ernest Hemingway, to name just a few. Have you seen a film version of a novel by one of these authors, or by another author whom you admire? What was your response to the film? (*Note:* If you'd like to check on whether a novel or story has been made into a film, you can search for the title on the Web site "The Internet Movie Database" at <http://www.us.imdb.com>.)

- What does it feel like to read a really absorbing story or novel? Do you have the same feeling, or a different one, when you watch an absorbing film? Which experience appeals to you more, reading literature or seeing films?

# Seven Students Write About Short Stories

## One Student's Thoughts About Character in Poe's "The Cask of Amontillado"

If your instructor assigns a topic in advance—such as "Irony in 'The Cask of Amontillado'" or "Is Montresor Insane?"—even on your first reading of the story you will be thinking in a specific direction, looking for relevant evidence. But if a topic is not assigned, it will be up to you to find something that you think is worth talking about to your classmates. (All writers must imagine a fairly specific audience, such as the readers of *Ms.* or the readers of *Playboy*—these audiences are quite different—or the readers of the high school newspaper, or the readers of a highly technical professional journal, and so on. It's a good idea to imagine your classmates as your audience.)

You may want to begin by asking yourself (and responding in your journal) what you like or dislike in the story; or you may want to think about some of the questions mentioned, at the beginning of this chapter, on plot, character, point of view, setting, symbolism, style, and theme. Or you may have annotated some passage that puzzled you, and, on rereading, you may feel that *this* passage is what you want to talk about. In any case, after several readings of the story you will settle not only on a *topic* (for instance, symbolism) but also on a *thesis,* an argument, a point (for instance, the symbolism is for the most part effective but in two places is annoyingly obscure).

It happens that the student (Ann Geraghty) whose essay we reprint decided to write about the narrator in Poe's story, which appears on pages 509–514. The following notes are not her earliest jottings but the jottings she recorded after she had tentatively chosen her topic.

Two characters: narrator (Montresor) and his enemy,
    Fortunato
1st person narrator, so we know Fort. only through
    what M. tells us
Fortunato
    has wronged Montresor ("thousand injuries"; but
        is M. telling the truth?)
    drinks a lot ("he had been drinking much")

vain (Fort. insists he knows much more than
    Luchesi)
courteous (in the vaults, drinks to M's buried
    relatives)
foolish (?? Hard to be sure about this)
Montresor
    first parag. tells us he seeks vengeance ("I vowed revenge") for "the
        thousand injuries" he suffered from Fort. ("I would be avenged")
    of high birth
    1) he comes from a family with a motto: *Nemo me impune lacessit*
       (no one dare attack me with impunity)
    2) has coat of arms (human foot crushing serpent whose fangs are
       in heel). But what's the connection? Is the idea that he and his
       noble family are like the *foot* crushing a serpent that has bitten
       them, or on the other hand is the idea that he and family are
       like the *serpent*—if stepped on (attacked, insulted), they will
       fight back? Maybe we are supposed to think that he thinks
       *he* is like the human foot, but *we* see that he is like the
       serpent
highly educated? At least he uses hard words
    ("unredressed," "the thought of his immolation").
    (Check *"immolation"*)

*Dictionary says it is a sacrifice, a ritual killing*

cunning: knows how to work on Fortunato
    (implies that Luchesi is more highly
    regarded than F)
rich: lives in a "palazzo," and has servants
crazy:
    1) murders for vengeance
    2) enjoys hearing the sound of Fort. shaking
       chains ("that I might hearken to it with
       the more satisfaction, I ceased my labors")
    3) when he hears the screams of F., *he* screams ("I surpassed them in
       volume and in strength")
    Can we possibly sympathize with him? Can he possibly
be acting fairly? Do we judge him? Do we judge (condemn)
ourselves for liking the story? Why do I find the story interesting
instead of repulsive? Because (thesis here) his motive is good, he
thinks he is upholding family honor (in his eyes the killing is a
family duty, a sacrifice; "immolation")

## The Final Version of the Student Essay

Ann Geraghty

Professor Duff

English 102

1 March 2010

Revenge, Noble and Ignoble

Because Edgar Allan Poe's "The Cask of Amontillado" is told by a first person narrator, a man named Montresor, we cannot be sure that what the narrator tells us is true. There are some things in the story, however, that we can scarcely believe. For instance, we can accept the fact that there is a character (even though we never see him) named Luchesi, because the narrator mentions him and the other character in the story—Fortunato—also talks about him. But how sure can we be that Fortunato is the sort of man that the narrator says Fortunato is?

In the first paragraph, Montresor says that Fortunato has done him a "thousand injuries" (510). He is never specific about these, and Fortunato never says anything that we can interpret as evidence that he has injured Montresor. Further, Fortunato is courteous when he meets Montresor, which seems to suggest that he is not aware that he has injured Montresor. It seems fair to conclude, then, that Fortunato has not really injured Montresor, and that Montresor has insanely imagined that Fortunato has injured him.

What evidence is there that Montresor is insane? First, we should notice the intensity with which Montresor speaks, especially in the first paragraph. He tells us that he "vowed revenge" and that he "would be avenged" and that he would "punish with impunity" (510). He also tells us, all in the first paragraph, that he himself must not get punished for his act of vengeance ("A wrong is unredressed when retribution overtakes its redresser") and that "It is equally unredressed when the avenger fails to make himself felt as such to him who has done the wrong." There is a common saying, "Don't get mad, get even," but Montresor is going way beyond getting even, and anyway it's not certain that he was injured in the first place. He *is* getting "mad," not in the sense of "angry" but in the sense of "crazy."

If we agree that Montresor is insane, we can ask ourselves two questions about this story. First, is "The Cask of Amontillado" just a story about a mysterious madman, a story that begins and ends with a madman and does not even try to explain his madness? Second, why have people read this story for almost a hundred and fifty years? If we can answer the first question negatively, we may be able to answer the second.

I think that Montresor is insane, but his insanity is understandable, and it is even based on a concept of honor. He comes from a noble family, a family with a coat of arms (a foot is crushing a serpent that is biting the heel) and a motto (*Nemo me impune lacessit,* which means "No one dare attack me with impunity").

Fortunato may not have really injured him, but for some reason Montresor thinks he has been injured. As a nobleman who must uphold the honor of his family, Montresor acts with a degree of energy that is understandable for someone in his high position. That is, he must live up to his coat of arms, which shows a gold foot (symbolizing a nobleman) crushing a serpent. The motto in effect means that Montresor *must* take vengeance if he is to uphold his family honor. In fact, the unusual word "immolation" (510) in the second paragraph tells us a good deal about Montresor's action. To "immolate" is to "sacrifice," to perform a ritual killing. Since Montresor says his vengeance will be the "immolation" of Fortunato, we can assume that Montresor thinks that he has a duty, imposed by his noble family, to kill Fortunato. He sees himself as a priest performing a solemn sacrifice.

Interestingly, however, the *reader* can interpret the motto in a different way. The reader may see Montresor as the serpent, viciously stinging an enemy, and Fortunato as an almost innocent victim who has somehow accidentally offended (stepped on) Montresor. In reading the story we take pleasure in hearing, and seeing, a passionate nobleman performing what he thinks is a duty imposed on him by his rank. We also take pleasure in judging him accurately, that is, in seeing that his action is not really noble but is serpent-like, or base. We can thus eat our cake and have it too; we see a wicked action, a clever murder (and we enjoy seeing it), and, on the other hand, we can sit back and judge it as wicked (we see Montresor as a serpent), and therefore we can feel that we are highly moral.

Geraghty 3

Work Cited

Poe, Edgar Allan. "The Cask of Amontillado." *An Introduction to Literature*. Ed. Sylvan Barnet, William Burto, and William E. Cain. 16th ed. New York: Longman, 2011. 509–514. Print.

**YOUR TURN**

In reading this essay, you may wish to ask yourself the following questions (with an eye toward applying them also to your own writing):

1. Is the title appropriate and at least moderately interesting?
2. Does the essay have a thesis? If so, what is it?
3. Is the thesis (if there is one) adequately supported by evidence?
4. Is the organization satisfactory? Does one paragraph lead easily into the next, and is the argument presented in reasonable sequence?

# Gender Criticism: A Response to "The Judgment of Solomon"

An analytic essay might go beyond the structure of the individual work, to the relation of the work to some larger whole. For instance, we might approach "The Judgment of Solomon" (page 196) from the point of view of gender criticism (discussed in Chapter 35), which often concentrates on the ways in which women are represented. In this story, we might argue, wisdom is an attribute only of a male; women are either deceitful or emotional. Here is an essay that is an example of gender criticism. It was written by Alice McCauley, a first-year college student who tried to look at the story without preconceptions, with fresh eyes, forgetting all that she had heard about the wisdom of Solomon, or, rather, remembering it but questioning it.

**Sample Student Essay: "How Wise Was Solomon?"**

McCauley 1

Alice McCauley

Professor O'Brien

English 10lb

20 June 2010

How Wise Was Solomon?

The point of the story of Solomon, told in 1 Kings 3.16–28, is apparently to show that "the wisdom of God" was in Solomon. But if it shows something about Solomon's nature, it also shows the nature of two women. What does it show them to be? First, that neither woman is wise; wisdom is reserved for Solomon. One woman, in the obvious interpretation of the story, is a loving mother, willing to sacrifice her own happiness for the good of her child. The other woman, again in the traditional interpretation of the story, is cruel, spiteful, willing to kill the baby rather than to allow her rival to have it. Given the depiction of these two women, what is a reader to conclude about women? Women are emotional; women act on impulses—in one case, the maternal instinct and in the other case a selfish instinct ("If-I-can't-have-it-nobody-will-have-it").

That is, in this world run by men, men have all of the wisdom and women have all of the emotion. Some of this emotion is good (maternal love) and some of it is nasty (selfishness or spitefulness), but in any case women cannot (the story seems to show us) be trusted to be fair or to be wise.

And what of Solomon's justice? Solomon, by threatening to do violence with a sword, evokes the two responses from the women. It is interesting to see that his proposal evokes no exclamations of horror from members of his court. Presumably the king can do whatever he wishes. It happens that Solomon does not proceed to divide the child because the responses of the women convince him that he knows who is the true mother. But what would he have done if the women had not responded as they did? We don't know, but the fact that both women assume he really will divide the child gives us a clear sense that the women live in a world in which men rule by violence, a world in which indeed the judge might have solved the problem with the sword, just as he threatened to do.

In such a world, the woman who told Solomon to divide the child might have been daring him to act in accordance with his speech. That is, although the usual interpretation is that she is acting spitefully—this is the way her act is perceived in a world with patriarchal views—she might have been acting from a very different motive. If we look at the story through eyes opened by the Women's Movement, maybe we can see an unconventional woman who was in effect saying, "Violence is at the heart of your way of life, and you make all of the rules here. Go ahead, divide the child, if you dare; see if you can live with your decision." That is, if we free ourselves from the traditional view that Solomon is

McCauley 3

wise, we see that she bravely (and intelligently) challenges Solomon and in effect reveals the violence on which his "justice" and his "wisdom" rest. The fact that she is a harlot—a woman whose whole life is spent in subordination to men—makes her bold defiance of the powerful king especially impressive.

McCauley 4

### Work Cited

Anonymous. "The Judgment of Solomon." *An Introduction to Literature.* Ed. Sylvan Barnet, William Burto, and William E. Cain. 16th ed. New York: Longman, 2011. 196–97. Print.

### YOUR TURN

Do you find the essay convincing? Why? If you do not find it convincing, do you nevertheless find it interesting? Why?

## A Feminist Reading of James Thurber's "The Secret Life of Walter Mitty"

### Working Toward a Thesis: Journal Entries

Before reading the following entries about "The Secret Life of Walter Mitty" (pages 530–33), write some of your own. You may want to think about what (if anything) you found amusing in the story, or about whether the story is dated, or about some aspect of Mitty's character or of his wife's. But the choice is yours.

A student, Susan Levy, wrote the following entry in her journal after the story was discussed in class.

March 21. Funny, I guess, especially the business about him as a doctor performing an operation. And that "pocketa-pocketa," but I don't think that it's as hysterical as everyone else seems to think it is. And how could anyone stand being married to a man like that? In fact, it's a good thing he has her to look after him. He ought to be locked up, driving into the "Exit Only" lane, talking to himself in the street, and having those crazy daydreams. No wonder the woman in the street laughs at him.

**March 24.** He's certainly a case, and she's not nearly as bad as everyone was saying. So she tells him to put his overshoes on; well, he ought to put them on, since Thurber says there is slush in the street, and he's no kid any more. About the worst I can say of her is that she seems a little unreasonable in always wanting him to wait for her, rather than sometimes the other way around, but probably she's really telling him not to wander off, because if he ever drifts away there'll be no finding him. The joke, I guess, is that he's supposed to have these daydreams because he's henpecked, and henpecked men are supposed to be funny. Would people find the story just as funny if she had the daydreams, and he bullied her?

## Developing the Thesis: List Notes

In preparation for writing a draft, Levy reread the story and jotted down some tentative notes based on her journal and on material that she had highlighted in the text. (At this point you may want to make your own list, based on your notes.)

> Mitty helpless:   he needs her
> chains on tires
> enters Exit Only
> ~~waterbury~~
> cop tells him to get going
> fantasies
>
> wife a nag?  →causes his daydreams? Evidence?
> Makes him get to hotel first
> overshoes
> backseat driver?
>
> "Does it ever occur to you that I am sometimes thinking?" Is he thinking, or just having dreams?
>
> M. confuses Richthoven with someone called Richtman.
>
> funny—or anti-woman? would it be funny if he nagged her, and she had daydreams?

Next, Levy wrote a draft; then she revised the draft and submitted the revision (printed here) to some classmates for peer review.

## Sample Draft: "Walter Mitty Is No Joke"

Susan Levy

Professor Markus

English 102

5 April 2010

Walter Mitty Is No Joke

James Thurber's "The Secret Life of Walter Mitty" seems to be highly regarded as a comic story about a man who is so dominated by his wife that he has to escape through fantasies. In my high school course in English, everyone found Mitty's dreams and his wife's bullying funny, and everyone seems to find them funny in college, too. Everyone except me.

If we look closely at the story, we see that Mitty is a pitiful man who needs to be told what to do. The slightest glimpse of reality sets him off on a daydream, as when he passes a hospital and immediately begins to imagine that he is a famous surgeon, or when he hears a newsboy shouting a headline about a crime and he imagines himself in a courtroom. The point seems to be that his wife nags him, so he escapes into daydreams. But the fact is that she needs to keep after him because he needs someone to tell him what to do. It depends on what one considers nagging. She tells him he is driving too fast, and (given the date of the story, 1939) he probably is, since he is going 55 on a slushy or snowy road. She tells him to wear overshoes, and he probably ought to, since the weather is bad. He resents all of these orders, but he clearly is incompetent, since he delays when the traffic light turns from red to green, and he enters an "Exit Only" lane in a parking lot. We are also told that he can't put chains on tires.

In fact, he can't do anything right. All he can do is daydream, and the dreams, though they are funny, are proof of his inability to live in the real world. When his wife asks him why he didn't put the overshoes on in the store, instead of carrying them in a box, he says, "Does it ever occur to you that I am sometimes thinking?" (533). But he doesn't "think," he just daydreams. Furthermore, he can't even get things straight in his daydreams. He gets everything mixed up, confusing Richthoven with Richtman, for example.

Is "The Secret Life of Walter Mitty" really a funny story about a man who daydreams because he is henpecked? Probably it is supposed to be so, but it's also a story about a man who is lucky to have a wife who can put up with him and keep him from getting killed on the road or lost in town.

Work Cited

Thurber, James. "The Secret Life of Walter Mitty." *An Introduction to Literature*. Ed. Sylvan Barnet, William Burto, and William E. Cain. 16th ed. New York: Longman, 2011. 530–33. Print.

## Writing About Setting as Symbolic: Notes and an Essay on Kate Chopin's "The Story of an Hour"

The following essay is about Kate Chopin's "The Story of an Hour" (pages 67–68). If you have not yet read the story, take a moment now to do so.

Amy Jones, a first-year student, has kindly provided her last notes, an outline that guided her while she wrote her first draft. Not all of the notes ended up in the final version, but they were a great help in shaping the essay.

thesis: setting here not place but time-springtime title?

    Chopin and Spring

    Chopin's Spring

    Mrs. M's Spring

    Mrs. M's Symbolic Spring

    Spring in "The Story of an Hour"

    Spring Comes to Mrs. M

    Setting as Symbol

    Setting as Symbol: Spring in...

setting in "Hour"

Define Setting??? Place <u>and</u> time

    Chopin doesn't give date (or city); but in a house

spring: "the tops of the trees . . . were all aquiver with the new spring" (parag. 5)

    "sparrows were twittering in the eaves" (parag. 5)

"There were patches of blue sky showing here and there
      through the clouds" (parag. 6)
    why clouds? brightness pushing through darkness, like
joyous new life pushing aside grief???
    ~~"spring days and summer days" special significance of~~
        ~~summer??. Or just means "lots of days"?~~
        ~~etc. way of life~~
        ~~"Louise, open the door! I beg, open the door"~~
elixir (near end) medicine???
doctors say died of heart disease
End with a quotation? Or with something about life turning to death?

---

Jones 1

Amy Jones

Professor Lucas

English 222

9 March 2010

Spring Comes to Mrs. Mallard

*Title implies thesis. Opening paragraph identifies author and story; topic (setting) is introduced.*

    In reading Kate Chopin's "The Story of an Hour" a reader is hardly aware of where the story is set. We are not told the country or the city, or the period, and so (if we think about it at all) we probably assume the story is set during Chopin's own lifetime, perhaps even during the year in which she wrote it, in Chopin's own territory, although there really is nothing very specific about Louisiana in this story. Nor do we learn, at the very beginning of the story, whether the action is taking place indoors or outdoors. However, since the story begins by telling us that Mrs. Mallard's sister, Josephine, gently breaks the news of the death of Mr. Mallard, we probably assume it is taking place at Mrs. Mallard's house. This assumption is confirmed a little later, when we hear that Mrs. Mallard, once she has heard the terrible news, "went away to her room alone" (67).

*Transition ("But") leads to next point (that the season is emphasized).*

    But if Kate Chopin doesn't tell us anything about the society in which the figures in the story live, she tells us quite a bit about the time of the year during which the story takes place. The story is very short—only about two and a half pages—but Chopin finds space in which to tell us not only that the time is spring, but also that from a window in her room Mrs. Mallard could see the tops of trees that were

Jones 2

all aquiver with the new spring life. The delicious breath of
rain was in the air. In the street below a peddler was crying
his wares. The notes of distant song which someone was
singing finally reached her faintly, and countless sparrows
were twittering in the eaves. (67)

This is the fullest description of the time of year in the story, but
there are other shorter references, so we can say that the springtime is
given considerable emphasis, considering how short the story is. For
instance, the quoted paragraph is followed by a shorter paragraph that
mentions "patches of blue sky" (67), and in fact "blue sky" is mentioned
again, two paragraphs later. There is nothing especially remarkable
about the sky's being blue, and so one might wonder why Chopin
bothers to tell us that the sky is blue when she doesn't even tell us
where her story is set. And then, in the next paragraph, she tells us
more about the sky: "There was something coming to her. . . . What was
it? She did not know. . . . But she felt it, creeping out of the sky,
reaching toward her through the sounds, the scents, the color that filled
the air" (67).

Given this emphasis on the spring air, we can now see that Chopin
is contrasting two aspects of setting, the season versus the place,
springtime versus the closed room. The spring air is invading the room in
which Mrs. Mallard has locked herself. At first Mrs. Mallard resists the
mysterious invasion: "She was beginning to recognize this thing that
was approaching to possess her, and she was striving to beat it back"
(68), but, the reader comes to understand, "this thing" is the spirit of
"the new spring life" which, we learned earlier in the story, set the tops
of the trees aquiver. The trees, the swallows, and the blue sky are signs
of the spring, and the spring symbolizes life. The locked room, where
Mrs. Mallard goes to grieve, is a place of mourning, of death, but Mrs.
Mallard is a living creature, and though she sincerely grieves she cannot
shut out life.

Now it is clear why Chopin did not bother to tell us in what city,
or even in what kind of house, the action takes place. It doesn't
matter. What does matter is the feeling of new life that Mrs. Mallard
feels, and this can best be shown by relating it to springtime, a time
of new life.

*Quotation introduced as supporting evidence (set off because it is longer than four lines).*

*Brief quotations used as additional evidence.*

*Thesis is further clarified.*

*Thesis is hammered home.*

Jones 3

*Concluding paragraph furthers the argument (passage about "elixir") and also, in its final sentences, wraps up essay.*

Even though she has confined herself to her room, through the window Mrs. Mallard drinks the spring air. In Chopin's words, "She was drinking in the very elixir of life through that open window" (68). An elixir, according to *The American Heritage Dictionary*, Fourth Edition, is "a substance believed to maintain life indefinitely." This word is an effective word to describe the way Mrs. Mallard feels, as the sights and sounds of spring press upon her and give her a new sense of life. But of course although spring renews life indefinitely, each year bringing new vegetation, people do not live indefinitely. In fact Mrs. Mallard will live for less than an hour. Chopin does not make it clear to a reader whether Mrs. Mallard dies because she really has "heart trouble," as we are told in the first paragraph, or because she has lived an intense spring moment as an individual and so she cannot stand the thought of a lifetime with her husband. But what is perfectly clear is that one aspect of the setting—springtime, a season full of new life—is essential to convey to the reader a sense of Mrs. Mallard's new (and tragically brief) feelings.

Jones 4

Work Cited

*Documentation*    Chopin, Kate. "The Story of an Hour." *An Introduction to Literature*. Ed. Sylvan Barnet, William Burto, and William E. Cain. 16th ed. New York: Longman, 2011. 67–68. Print.

# Two Students Interpret Shirley Jackson's "The Lottery": Notes and Essays

Here are the preliminary notes and the final essays of two students who chose to write about the theme of Shirley Jackson's "The Lottery," which appears on pages 431–38.

Nat Komor, the first student, after reading and rereading the story jotted down the following notes as a sort of preliminary outline. Some of the notes were based on passages he had underlined. Notice that the jottings include some material specifically on the story and other material—references to the outside world—that is relevant to what the writer takes to be the theme of the story. When he reviewed his notes before starting on a first draft, Komor deleted some of them, having decided that they were not especially useful for his essay. Still, they were worth jotting down; only in retrospect can a writer clearly see which notes are useful.

Is Jackson saying that human nature is evil? Prob. no; here, people just
   follow a tradition, and don't examine it. Mr. Warner defends lottery,
   saying "There's *always* been a lottery." No real argument in defense
   of it.
We are least conscious of the things we take for granted; ~~I recall someone's~~
   ~~saying "a fish is not aware of water until it is out of it."~~
examples of blindly following society's customs
   ~~Compulsory schooling (how many people ever even remotely *think* of~~
      ~~schooling their children at home?)~~
   ~~school is 5 days a week, why not 4 or 6? Bachelor's degree is 4 years,~~
      ~~why not 3 or 5?~~
   segregation (until 1960s)
   ~~women not permitted to drive in Saudi Arabia~~
   ~~women must wear veil in Saudi Arabia~~
   eating of meat; might a vegetarian society not look with horror at our
      habit of eating meat?
   slavery (thought to be "natural" by almost all societies until
      nineteenth century)
thoughtless following of custom in "The Lottery"
   ~~exact words of ritual lost, but still necessary to address "each person~~
      ~~approaching"~~
   ~~original box gone, but present box said to be made of parts of previous~~
      ~~box~~
   lottery an established ritual: "The lottery was conducted—as were the
      square dances, the teenage club, the Halloween program—by
      Mr. Summers, who had time and energy to devote to civic
      activities." *Important*: the lottery is a civic activity, a social action,
      a *summer* (pun?) ritual.
Evil? Certainly yes, since killing an innocent, but no one in the story says
   it's evil.
   BUT Adams does say that in the north village "they're talking of giving
      up the lottery," and his wife says "Some places have already quit
      lotteries."
   Also: a girl whispers, "I hope it's not Nancy," so at least one person
      feels uneasy about the whole thing
Are these people evil? No, they seem pretty decent. They just don't much
   question what they are doing, and they do something terrible

the box
   black = death?
   made out of pieces of old box
   "faded," "splintered badly": does this
     symbolize a need for a new tradition?
the papers
   earlier, wood chips. At end, wind blows away
     slips of paper? Symbolic of life fluttering
     away? (Prob. not)
the three-legged stool
   symbolic? If so, of what?
Possible title
     The Violent Lottery
     The Irrational Lottery
     We All Participate in "The Lottery"
     The Meaning of the Lottery

A lot of the material here is good, though some of it would be more suited for an essay on symbolism, and it is chiefly this material that the writer wisely deleted in preparing to draft an essay on the theme of Jackson's story. After writing a draft and then revising it, Komor submitted the revision to a group for peer review. Ultimately, he turned in the following essay.

---

Komor 1

Nat Komor

Professor Lee

English 101B

7 March 2010

We All Participate in "The Lottery"

The townsfolk in Shirley Jackson's "The Lottery" engage in a horrible ritual. They stone an innocent person to death. It would be horrible enough if the person they stoned were guilty of some crime, and stoning was a form of capital punishment that the society practiced, but in the case of "The Lottery" the person is not guilty of any crime. Tessie Hutchinson simply has the bad luck to pick the wrong slip of paper from a box, a paper marked with a black spot.

     The people in this unnamed town every year hold a lottery to find a victim. On the whole, they seem to believe that the lottery

---

is necessary, or is natural; at least they hardly question it. True,
Mr. Adams says that in the north village "they're talking of giving up
the lottery," (435) and his wife says that "Some places have already quit
lotteries," (435) but that's about as much as one hears of anybody
questioning this institution of society. Probably most of the people in
the village would agree with Old Man Warner, who says that people who
talk about giving up the lottery are a "pack of crazy fools." He adds,
"There's *always* been a lottery," (435) and that seems to be about the
best answer that anyone can give. Of course the people don't take any
special pleasure in the lottery, and there is at least one expression of
sympathy, when a girl says, "I hope it's not Nancy." (437) On the whole,
however, the people seem to believe that the lottery must be held, and
someone has to die.

It's important to notice that the lottery is one of the "civic
activities," that is, it is part of the regular life of these people, part
(so to speak) of the air they breathe. For the most part they don't
question the lottery any more than we question compulsory education,
the length of the school year, or the eating of meat. When one thinks
about it, one might ask why the government should have the power to
compel parents to send children to school, or, for that matter, why a
child shouldn't have the right to leave school whenever he or she feels
like it. Why should children have almost no rights? People simply don't
bother to think about this issue, or about *many* others. For instance, I
can imagine that a member of a vegetarian society—say a Hindu
Brahmin society—must be horrified by the way almost all Americans
think nothing of raising animals (bringing life into the world) for the
sole purpose of eating them. We just accept these things, without
thinking, but from the view of another culture they may be horrible
customs.

What Jackson seems to be saying to her readers is this:
"Unthinkingly you follow certain conventions. These conventions seem
to you to be natural, and for the most part they are harmless, but some
of them are barbaric and destructive." That is, Jackson is telling us to
examine our lives, and to stop assuming that all of our customs are
right. Some of the beliefs we share today may, in time, come to be seen
to be as evil as slavery or murder.

Komor 3

Work Cited

Jackson, Shirley. "The Lottery." *An Introduction to Literature.*
Ed. Sylvan Barnet, William Burto, and William E. Cain. 16th ed.
New York: Longman, 2011. 431–38. Print.

Now for the notes and the essay by a second student, Anne Hearn. This writer came to a very different conclusion about the theme of "The Lottery." After reading Hearn's notes and her essay, you may want to compare the two essays. Do you find one essay more interesting than the other? More persuasive? If so, why? You may feel that even though the writers come to different conclusions, the two essays are equally interesting and equally valid.

surprise *and* shock

Shock

 violence (at end)

 *esp. shocking* because violence comes from people

  who seem normal and decent

 (only a few expressions of hesitation; Mr. and Mrs. Adams)

 Jackson claimed violence was normal *(quote passage)*

(talk of giving up lotteries)

 surprise

 we don't know, until late, what's going on;

 on rereading, we see lots of clues about what

  will happen

  Example: references to stones

Meanings?

 lottery = the draft in wartime?

 lottery = community violence? Example: War (??)

 lottery = violent U.S. society??

 "  " *any* violent custom; bad tradition?

 human nature corrupt? sinful? (Note name of Adams,

  also Graves) (other significant names: Summers,

   Warner);

  human tendency to look for a scapegoat. Is it

   true?

Jackson quoted on her meaning: "violence and

 general inhumanity" but do we have to believe

 her?

Maybe just a horror story, without "meaning" *Example of such a story?*

*Are* normal people willing to kill without great provocation?

Possible titles

> Shirley Jackson on Human Nature
> Do We All Participate in "The Lottery"?
> How Fair is Shirley Jackson's Lottery?
> Is "The Lottery" Fair?

When you read Hearn's essay, you'll notice that for a title the author settled on the last of her four tentative titles. The first title, "Shirley Jackson on Human Nature," is too broad since the essay is not on all of Jackson's work but on only one story. The second tentative title, "Do We All Participate in 'The Lottery'?" is acceptable, but it sounds a bit clumsy, so the choice apparently came down to the last two titles or to some entirely new title that the writer might discover during the process of revising her drafts.

Notice also that some points mentioned in the preliminary notes—for instance, the reference to Mr. Summers and to Mr. Warner—are omitted from the essay. And some points scarcely mentioned in the outline are emphasized in the essay. In drafting and revising the essay, the writer found that certain things weren't relevant to her point, so she dropped them and found that others required considerable amplification.

---

Hearn 1

Anne Hearn
Professor Martinez
English 101B
9 April 2010

Is "The Lottery" Fair?

Probably all readers are surprised by the ending of Shirley Jackson's "The Lottery." But the story does more than offer a surprise. It shocks, because it seems to say that people who are perfectly ordinary, just like ourselves, are capable of killing an innocent neighbor for apparently no reason at all. On rereading the story, we can see that Jackson has carefully prepared for the ending, and we can admire her skill. For instance, the second paragraph tells us that "Bobby Martin had already stuffed his pockets full of stones, and other boys soon followed his example, selecting the smoothest and roundest stones" (432). We almost feel, when we reread the story, that we should not have been surprised. But even after we see that the ending has been foreshadowed, we remain shocked by the violence, and by what the story says about human beings. But exactly what *does* it say about them? And does it say anything that strikes us as true?

If we assume that the story *does* say something about life, and is not simply a meaningless shocker, we may come up with several possible interpretations. Is Jackson saying that Americans seem peaceful and neighborly but really are quite willing to engage in violence? (Although she does not clearly set the story in an identifiable region, she clearly sets it in a small town in the United States.) Certainly newspapers every day tell us of violent acts, but the violent acts are usually of an individual (a mad killer, or a rapist) or are of nature (an earthquake, a tornado).

Of course someone might conceivably argue that this story, which is about a community, is a sort of allegory about the United States as a whole. It was written in 1948, only three years after the end of World War II, and someone might claim that it is about American willingness to use violence, that is, to go to war. Or one might even say that it is about the wartime draft, which was a sort of lottery that chose certain people whose lives were risked.

But to see the story as a reference to World War II seems very strained. Nothing in the story suggests a conscious conflict between groups, as, for instance, Jackson could have suggested if members of this town were allied against another town. And though the story certainly is set in the United States, nothing in the story calls attention to a particularly *American violence*.

Another way of thinking about "The Lottery" is to see it as a story about all human beings—not just Americans—who unthinkingly submit to destructive traditions. This interpretation can be better supported than the first interpretation. For instance, at least two people in the story briefly question the tradition of the lottery. Steve Adams says, "Over in the north village they're talking of giving up the lottery," and a moment later his wife adds, "Some places have already quit lotteries" (435). But of course the story tells us that this community does not give up the lottery; in fact, we are particularly shocked to learn, near the end, that Steve Adams is "in the front of the crowd of villagers" when they attack Tessie Hutchinson (438).

It's obvious that the story is about a terrible tradition that is accepted with relatively little objection, but we can still ask what connection the story has with our own lives. What traditions do we engage in that are so deadly? The wartime draft has already been mentioned, but even pacifists would probably grant that most of the people who engage in war are aware that war is terrible, and thus they are unlike Jackson's villagers. The story may be about the deadliness of certain traditions, but a reader is left wondering which of our traditions are represented in Jackson's lottery. Racism and sexism have had terrible effects, but it is hard to relate the lottery, which picks a victim at random, to discrimination against people of a certain color or a certain sex.

A third view, and one that I think is somewhat sounder than the first two views, is that the story is about human nature. Although most people are decent, they are also capable of terrible irrational violence. In Christian terms this is explained by original sin, a sinfulness that we have inherited from Adam. Jackson certainly allows for the possibility of some sort of Biblical interpretation, since, as we have seen, Mr. Adams is one of the leaders of the assault, and he is accompanied by Mr. Graves. The original sin of the first Adam led to death, and thus to the grave.

Shirley Jackson herself from time to time offered comments on the story. According to Judy Oppenheimer, in *Private Demons: The Life of Shirley Jackson*, when the fiction editor of the *New Yorker* asked her if "there was anything special she was trying to convey," she said, "Not really." When the editor pressed her, and asked if the story "made its point by an ironic juxtaposition of ancient superstition and modern setting," Jackson said, "Sure, that would be fine," since she didn't like to discuss her work (128). Her fullest comment, according to Oppenheimer, was given to a columnist who was writing for the *San Francisco Chronicle*:

> I suppose I hoped, by setting a particularly brutal rite in the present and in my own village, to shock the readers with a graphic demonstration of the pointless violence and general inhumanity of their own lives. (qtd. in Oppenheimer 131)

There are obvious problems with accepting this comment. First of all, as has been mentioned, Jackson offered contradictory comments on the meaning of the story. She seems not to have worried about being consistent. Second, the words she used by way of introducing her intention—"I suppose I hoped"—indicate that she herself was not entirely clear about what she had intended. Third, even if she did correctly state her intention, she may not have fulfilled it adequately.

Certainly the story shows people who seem quite decent but who with only a little hesitation participate in a barbaric ritual. Perhaps Jackson did intend to say in her story that this is what we are also like. And since the story is related to ancient rituals in which societies purify themselves by finding a scapegoat, Jackson seems to be saying that all people, no matter how normal or decent they seem, engage in violence that they think purifies them or is at least in some way necessary for their own well-being. But just because Jackson *said* something like this, and said it in a gripping story, it isn't necessarily true. Despite all of the realistic detail—for instance, Mrs. Hutchinson's desperate charge that "It isn't fair"—the final picture of life that "The Lottery" gives does not seem to me to be at all realistic, and therefore I don't think the story says anything about life. The story surprises and it shocks, like Poe's "The Fall of the House of Usher." Maybe it even shows "the pointless violence and general inhumanity" in the lives of Jackson's neighbors, but does it reflect the lives of her readers? Do apparently normal, decent people routinely engage in barbaric behavior? I'm not like these people, and I doubt that Jackson and her neighbors were like them either. "The Lottery" is a cleverly plotted story, but the more you look at it, and the more you admire the skillful foreshadowing, the more it seems to be a clever trick, and the less it seems to be related to life.

Works Cited

Jackson, Shirley. "The Lottery." *An Introduction to Literature.*
    Ed. Sylvan Barnet, William Burto, and William E. Cain. 16th ed.
    New York: Longman, 2011. 431–38. Print.
Oppenheimer, Judy. *Private Demons: The Life of Shirley Jackson.*
    New York: Putnam's, 1988. Print.

## Sample Essay with Documentation

Jean Lee
Professor McCabe
English 102
18 June 2010

Do the Pink Ribbons in Hawthorne's
"Young Goodman Brown" Have a Meaning?

In the first six paragraphs of "Young Goodman Brown," Nathaniel Hawthorne mentions three times that Faith, Brown's wife, wears a cap with pink ribbons (154). The pink ribbons are mentioned twice more in the story. The first of these later references occurs when Brown is in the forest. Having recognized Faith's voice, Brown gazes heavenward, calls to her, sees something fluttering down, seizes it, and finds that it is a "pink ribbon" (159). "My Faith is gone!" he immediately calls out. "There is no good on earth; and sin is but a name. Come devil! for to thee the world is given" (159). The next (and final) reference to the pink ribbons occurs near the end of the story. When he enters Salem village on "the next morning," Brown "spied the head of Faith, with the pink ribbons" (161), not surprising since he now sees the townspeople in their usual dress and activities.

No one can doubt that Brown's wife, named Faith, symbolizes Brown's religious faith, but many scholars have expressed some doubt about the meaning of her pink ribbons. More precisely, scholars have usually expressed doubt about someone else's interpretation of the ribbons, and then confidently offered their own. One of the first persons to comment on the pink ribbons suggested that Hawthorne himself made a mistake in giving them so much emphasis in the scene in the forest. In 1941 F. O. Matthiessen, in *American Renaissance*, quoted approximately a full page of the story, beginning with the paragraph that starts "Aloft in the air" and ending with the paragraph that begins "'My Faith is gone!' cried he, after one stupefied moment." Matthiessen praised the scene but offered one objection:

> As long as what Brown saw is left wholly in the realm of
> hallucination, Hawthorne's created illusion is compelling.
> . . . Only the literal insistence on that damaging pink

Lee 2

ribbon obtrudes the labels of a confining allegory and short-circuits the range of association. (284)

Matthiessen does not explain why he finds the ribbon more "literal" than, say, the "blue arch [of the sky] and the stars brightening in it" or the cloud that "hurried across the zenith and hid the brightening stars" (159). After all, Brown does not emerge from the forest carrying this ribbon, and the next morning compare it with the ribbons in Faith's cap. If he did, we could, like Matthiessen, complain about the author's "literal insistence on that damaging pink ribbon," but as Edward Wagenknecht has pointed out, the ribbon that flutters from the sky is no more real than anything else that Brown sees in the forest (61). If the devil can conjure up images of Brown's townspeople, surely he can also conjure up an image of a ribbon.

A few years after Matthiessen expressed reservations about the ribbon, Mark Van Doren quoted the passage about Brown's seizing the ribbon after it catches on the branch of a tree, and then commented:

> Few things in fiction are more startling, or more important, than this pink ribbon. Is it there, or is it only dreamed? If it is there, what explanation can there be save the one young Brown accepts? The Devil exists, and Faith has become one of his converts. All three answers come at once, in a texture of fact and implication which Hawthorne has woven as closely as life is woven. The ribbon may not be there, but in that case this is no ordinary dream, no nightmare. . . . which will be gone tomorrow. For Brown is changed. He thinks there is no good on earth, "and sin is but a name." (78)

What is especially interesting is Van Doren's clear implication that it doesn't matter whether Brown seizes a real ribbon or, on the other hand, only dreams that he does. What matters is that for Brown it is evidence that his wife is unholy. Probably all readers will agree with Van Doren that the encounter in the forest, real or dreamed or conjured by the devil, changes Brown.

There is no such agreement, however, about the significance of the color of the ribbon. According to E. Arthur Robinson, "Faith's pink ribbons symbolize passion" (223). Robinson compares the pink ribbon to "crimson or purple" symbols of "woman's physical nature" in other stories by Hawthorne, particularly Georgiana's flaw in "The Birthmark" and Beatrice's poisonous plant in "Rappaccini's Daughter" (224). But the connection with Goodman Brown's faith is unclear. A pink ribbon worn by Faith, if clarified by other details in the story, might serve to tell a reader what to make out of this woman—for instance, that she *really* is highly sexual, or that this faith *really* is "faith in the flesh," or some such thing—but Robinson does not offer these arguments, and the text does nothing to support them with additional details. Robinson's conclusion is that Brown comes to realize that "his father was a man like himself and his mother a woman like Faith" and that Brown glumly accepts sensuality in his wife's nature as well as in his own (222).

Robinson was not the first to argue that the pink ribbon implied passion. In 1957, six years before Robinson published his essay, Roy R. Male saw the pink ribbons as one element in "a fiery orgy of lust" (77). But given that pink suggests, if anything, innocent little baby girls, why conclude that here it suggests "lust" or even "passion"? If one wants to argue that Faith pretends to be sweet and innocent but is not, one would argue that she is hypocritical, and might even argue that the ribbons symbolize hypocrisy disguised as innocence, but there is no evidence that the ribbons symbolize sexual passion. Further, if they do symbolize Brown's wife's sexual passion, what is their connection with Brown? What do they tell us about Brown's religious faith? In the forest, he takes the pink ribbon as evidence that his wife is of the devil's party, and he therefore announces that he has lost his faith, but if the pink color is to suggest passion, Brown's loss of faith would be a loss of belief in passion—an interpretation that makes no sense in the story.

Another school of thought argues that the pink symbolizes not lust but youthful femininity, and by extension, the weakness, superficiality, or frivolity of Brown's religious beliefs. Thomas E. Connolly argues that "the ribbons seem to be symbolic of [Brown's] initial illusion . . . that his faith will lead him to heaven. The pink ribbons on a Puritan lady's cap, signs of youth, joy, and happiness, are actually entirely out of keeping with the severity of the rest of her dress . . ." (374). James W. Mathews offers a roughly similar view, arguing that "the insubstantiality of Brown's religious faith manifests itself in the pink ribbons of his wife's cap; their texture is aery and their color the pastel of infancy" (74).

Paul J. Hurley, though without commenting explicitly on the color of the ribbons, belongs to the same school:

> Goodman Brown . . . intends to get to heaven by clinging to Faith's skirts. . . . The ribbons, with their suggestions of the frivolous and ornamental, represent the ritualistic trappings of religious observance. Goodman Brown, it seems, has placed his faith and his hopes of salvation in the formal observances of religious worship rather than in the purity of his own heart and soul. (416)

Not all recent critics, of course, accept the view that the ribbons are a sign of the superficiality of Brown's faith. Edward Wagenknecht suggests that the arguments of Mathews and Hurley would be more convincing if Brown, rather than his wife, wore a ribbon (62). Against Wagenknecht's view, however, one might argue that allegory works in a different way. If in this allegory Faith stands for Brown's religious faith, then what is said about Faith—for instance what is said about her clothing—is understood to be said about Brown himself.

It seems to be a mistake to insist that the color of the ribbons is symbolic of lust, feminine passion, or insubstantial faith. None of these interpretations is traditional and therefore immediately plausible even without additional supporting detail. And no such additional detail is offered in the story to make them plausible. For instance, none of Faith's pious (or apparently pious) neighbors object to the ribbons, nor does Brown find the ribbons out of keeping with Puritan dress. Similarly, the alleged association of pink with superficiality is not traditional, and Hawthorne does not establish it by giving related details.

What, then, can we make of the ribbons? Looking at the unconvincing allegorical interpretations, perhaps the first thing to say is that we should not try to make too much of these ribbons. Perhaps the second thing to say is that the early references to the ribbons do not serve to characterize Faith as lustful, superficial, or whatever (and certainly not to characterize Brown's religious faith as marked by any of these traits) but do serve to identify Faith as a specific person—the woman who wears pink ribbons in her cap. In the forest, then, when the ribbon drifts down, Brown cannot doubt that his wife is present, is a participant in the wicked assembly. (Of course Brown may be deceived; perhaps he has dreamed the episode, or perhaps he has been duped by a show conjured up by the devil, but that's another issue.) Convinced that even Faith is a worshipper of evil, Brown loses his faith not so much in God as in his fellow creatures. "Young Goodman Brown" of course has allegorical elements, but there is no reason to insist that every detail, down to the color of the ribbons, is allegorical. Nothing is gained by insisting that the pink ribbons "mean" something. Their function is to convince Brown that his wife is in the forest, and that is enough for some ribbons to do.

On the other hand, we know that Hawthorne was a careful writer, and that in his novels and stories he is aware of the significance of details of appearance and clothing. Perhaps in "Young Goodman Brown" it is not that the pink ribbons mean one thing in particular, but, instead, that Hawthorne intends their meaning to be ambiguous. As James C. Keil has noted, the first description of Faith, with "the pink ribbons of her cap" playing in the wind, can suggest that she is either "modest or immodest," and this ambiguity, he adds, recurs "throughout the story" (37–38). If we accept Keil's interpretation, we may better understand the nature of Brown's anguish and sorrow. He becomes unsure of who Faith is—and whether she is faithful to God and to him or not. Thus the ambiguity of the pink ribbons is connected to the uncertainty that perplexes and agonizes Brown and drives him to madness. The pink ribbons do not have a single meaning, but they are nonetheless meaningful.

Lee 6

## Works Cited

Connolly, Thomas E. "Hawthorne's 'Young Goodman Brown': An Attack on Puritanic Calvinism." *American Literature* 28 (1956): 370–75. Print.

Hawthorne, Nathaniel. "Young Goodman Brown." *An Introduction to Literature.* Ed. Sylvan Barnet, William Burto, and William E. Cain. 16th ed. New York: Longman, 2011. 154–63. Print.

Hurley, Paul J. "Young Goodman Brown's 'Heart of Darkness.'" *American Literature* 37 (1966): 410–19. Print.

Keil, James C. "Hawthorne's 'Young Goodman Brown': Early Nineteenth-Century and Puritan Constructions of Gender." *New England Quarterly* 69:1 (March 1996): 33–55. Print.

Male, Roy R. *Hawthorne's Tragic Vision*. Austin: U of Texas P, 1957. Print.

Mathews, James W. "Antinomianism in 'Young Goodman Brown.'" *Studies in Short Fiction* 3 (1965): 73–75. Print.

Matthiessen, F. O. *American Renaissance: Art and Expression in the Age of Emerson and Whitman*. New York: Oxford UP, 1941. Print.

Robinson, E. Arthur. "The Vision of Goodman Brown: A Source and Interpretation." *American Literature* 35 (1963): 218–25. Print.

Van Doren, Mark. *Nathaniel Hawthorne*. New York: William Sloane, 1948. Print.

Wagenknecht, Edward. *Nathaniel Hawthorne: The Man, His Tales and Romances*. New York: Continuum, 1989. Print.

# 14

# Two Fiction Writers in Depth: Flannery O'Connor and Tobias Wolff

We read stories by authors we are unfamiliar with, just as we try new foods or play new games or listen to the music of new groups, because we want to extend our experience. But we also sometimes stay with the familiar—for pretty much the same reason, oddly. We want, so to speak, to taste more fully, to experience not something utterly unfamiliar but a variation on a favorite theme. Having read, say, one story by Poe or by Alice Walker, we want to read another, and another, because we like the sort of thing that this author does, and we find that with each succeeding story we get deeper into an interesting mind describing experiences that interest us.

We believe you'll find that each story by Flannery O'Connor and by Tobias Wolff takes on a richer significance when thought of alongside other stories and comments by the same writer.

## Flannery O'Connor: Two Stories and Comments About Writing

*Flannery O'Connor (1925-1964)—her first name was Mary but she did not use it—was born in Savannah, Georgia, but spent most of her life in Milledgeville, Georgia, where her family moved when she was twelve. She was educated in parochial schools and at the local college and then went to the Iowa Writers' Workshop, where she earned an MFA in 1946. For a few months she lived at a writers' colony in Saratoga Springs, New York, and then for a few weeks she lived in New York City, but most of her life was spent back in Milledgeville, where she wrote stories, novels, essays (posthumously published as* Mystery and Manners *in 1969), and letters (posthumously published under the title* The Habit of Being *in 1979).*

*In 1951, when she was 25, Flannery O'Connor discovered that she was a victim of lupus erythematosus, an incurable autoimmune disease that had crippled and then killed her father ten years before. She died at the age of thirty-nine. O'Connor faced her illness with stoic courage, Christian fortitude— and tough humor. Here is a glimpse, from one of her letters, of how she dealt with those who pitied her:*

> *An old lady got on the elevator behind me and as soon as I turned around she fixed me with a moist gleaming eye and said in a loud voice, "Bless you, darling!" I felt exactly like The Misfit [in "A Good Man Is Hard to Find"] and I gave her a weakly lethal look, where- upon greatly encouraged she grabbed my arm and whispered (very loud) in my ear, "Remember what they said to John at the gate, darling!" It was not my floor but I got off and I suppose the old lady was astounded at how quick I could get away on crutches. I have a one-legged friend and I asked her what they said to John at the gate. She said she reckoned they said, "The lame shall enter first." This may be because the lame will be able to knock everybody else aside with their crutches.*

*A devout Catholic, O'Connor forthrightly summarized the relation between her belief and her writing:*

> *I see from the standpoint of Christian orthodoxy. This means that for me the meaning of life is centered in our Redemption by Christ and what I see in the world I see in its relation to that.*

## A Good Man Is Hard to Find                                          [1953]

The grandmother didn't want to go to Florida. She wanted to visit some of her connections in east Tennessee and she was seizing at every chance to change Bailey's mind. Bailey was the son she lived with, her only boy. He was sitting on the edge of his chair at the table, bent over the orange sports section of the *Journal.* "Now look here, Bailey," she said, "see here, read this," and she stood with one hand on her thin hip and the other rattling the newspaper at his bald head. "Here this fellow that calls himself The Misfit is aloose from the Federal Pen and headed toward Florida and you read here what it says he did to these people. Just you read it. I wouldn't take my children in any direction with a criminal like that aloose in it. I couldn't answer to my conscience if I did."

Bailey didn't look up from his reading so she wheeled around then and faced the children's mother, a young woman in slacks, whose face was as broad and innocent as a cabbage and was tied around with a green head-kerchief that had two points on the top like rabbit's ears. She was sitting on the sofa, feeding the baby his apricots out of a jar. "The children have been to Florida before," the old lady said. "You all ought to take them somewhere else for a change so they would see different parts of the world and be broad. They never have been to east Tennessee."

The children's mother didn't seem to hear her but the eight-year-old boy, John Wesley, a stocky child with glasses, said, "If you don't want to go to Florida, why dontcha stay at home?" He and the little girl, June Star, were reading the funny papers on the floor.

"She wouldn't stay at home to be queen for a day," June Star said without raising her yellow head.

5      "Yes and what would you do if this fellow, The Misfit, caught you?" the grandmother asked.

"I'd smack his face," John Wesley said.

"She wouldn't stay at home for a million bucks," June Star said. "Afraid she'd miss something. She has to go everywhere we go."

"All right, Miss," the grandmother said. "Just remember that the next time you want me to curl your hair."

June Star said her hair was naturally curly.

10     The next morning the grandmother was the first one in the car, ready to go. She had her big black valise that looked like the head of a hippopotamus in one corner, and underneath it she was hiding a basket with Pitty Sing, the cat, in it. She didn't intend for the cat to be left alone in the house for three days because he would miss her too much and she was afraid he might brush against one of the gas burners and accidentally asphyxiate himself. Her son, Bailey, didn't like to arrive at a motel with a cat.

She sat in the middle of the back seat with John Wesley and June Star on either side of her. Bailey and the children's mother and the baby sat in front and they left Atlanta at eight forty-five with the mileage on the car at 55890. The grandmother wrote this down because she thought it would be interesting to say how many miles they had been when they got back. It took them twenty minutes to reach the outskirts of the city.

The old lady settled herself comfortably, removing her white cotton gloves and putting them up with her purse on the shelf in front of the back window. The children's mother still had on slacks and still had her head tied up in a green kerchief, but the grandmother had on a navy blue straw sailor hat with a bunch of white violets on the brim and a navy blue dress with a small white dot in the print. Her collars and cuffs were white organdy trimmed with lace and at her neckline she had pinned a purple spray of cloth violets containing a sachet. In case of an accident, anyone seeing her dead on the highway would know at once that she was a lady.

She said she thought it was going to be a good day for driving, neither too hot nor too cold, and she cautioned Bailey that the speed limit was fifty-five miles an hour and that the patrolmen hid themselves behind bill-boards and small clumps of trees and sped out after you before you had a chance to slow down. She pointed out interesting details of the scenery: Stone Mountain; the blue granite that in some places came up to both sides of the highway; the brilliant red clay banks slightly streaked with purple; and the various crops that made rows of green lace-work on the ground. The trees were full of silver-white sunlight and the meanest of them sparkled. The children were reading comic magazines and their mother had gone back to sleep.

"Let's go through Georgia fast so we won't have to look at it much," John Wesley said.

15     "If I were a little boy," said the grandmother, "I wouldn't talk about my native state that way. Tennessee has the mountains and Georgia has the hills."

"Tennessee is just a hillbilly dumping ground," John Wesley said, "and Georgia is a lousy state too."

"You said it," June Star said.

2

*the grandmother*

~~Of course she~~ was the first one ready to load up the next morning at six

o'clock. She had Baby Brother's bucking bronco ~~that~~ and ~~horsxxbxn~~ what she

called her "~~whee~~" and Pitty Sing, the cat, ~~xx those~~ *got the* packed in the car before

Boatwrite had a chance to ~~getxanythingzxbxexinx~~ ~~come out of the door with the~~

rest of the luggage. ~~out of the hall.~~ They got off at seven-thirty, Boatwrite

and ~~Baby~~ the children's mother in the front and Granny, John Wesley, Baby Brother,

Little Sister Mary Ann, Pitty Sing, and the bucking bronco in the back.

"Why the hell did you bring that goddam rocking horse?" Boatwrite asked

because as soon as ~~the car began to move,~~ *they were out of the city + on the smooth highway* Baby Brother began to squall to get

on the bucking bronco. "He can't get on that thing in this car and that's final,"

his father who was a stern man said.

"Can we open the lunch now?" Little Sister ~~Maryxxxxx~~ asked. "It'll shut

Baby Brother up. Mamma, can we open up the lunch?"

"No," their grandmother said. *It's only eight-thirty*

Their mother was ~~xxxxx~~ reading SCREEN MOTHERS AND THEIR CHILDREN. "Yeah,

sure," she said. without looking up. She was all dressed up today. She had on

a purple silk dress and a hat and ~~gxxxxxxxxx~~ a choker of pink beads and a new

pocket book, and high heel pumps. *her red*

"Let's go through Georgia quick so we won't have to look at it much," John

Wesley said. "~~I seen enough of it myself.~~"

"You should see Tennessee," his grandmother said. "Now there is a *beautiful* state."

"Like hell," John Wesley said. "That's just a hillbilly dumping ground."

"Ha," his mother said, and nudged Boatwrite. "Didjer hear that?" *She was* *no* *from Arkansas.*

They ate their lunch and got along fine ~~after that~~ for a while until Pitty

Sing who had been asleep jumped into the front of the car and caused Boatwrite

to swerve to the right into a ditch. Pitty Sing was a large grey-striped cat

with a yellow hind leg and a ~~x~~ *big* soiled white face. Granny thought that she

was the only person in the world that he really loved but he had never ~~really~~ *the truth was*

looked ~~xxxfxxxxpxxxxhxxxfxxx~~ ~~any~~ farther *up* than her middle and he didn't even

like other cats. He jumped snarling into the front seat and Boatwrite's shoulders

Draft page from Flannery O'Connor's "A Good Man Is Hard to Find."

"In my time," said the grandmother, folding her thin veined fingers, "children were more respectful of their native states and their parents and everything else. People did right then. Oh look at the cute little pickaninny!" she said and pointed to a Negro child standing in the door of a shack. "Wouldn't that make a picture, now?" she asked and they all turned and looked at the little Negro out of the back window. He waved.

"He didn't have any britches on," June Star said.

20   "He probably didn't have any," the grandmother explained. "Little niggers in the country don't have things like we do. If I could paint, I'd paint that picture," she said.

The children exchanged comic books.

The grandmother offered to hold the baby and the children's mother passed him over the front seat to her. She set him on her knee and bounced him and told him about the things they were passing. She rolled her eyes and screwed up her mouth and stuck her leathery thin face into his smooth bland one. Occasionally he gave her a faraway smile. They passed a large cotton field with five or six graves fenced in the middle of it, like a small island. "Look at the graveyard!" the grandmother said, pointing it out. "That was the old family burying ground. That belonged to the plantation."

"Where's the plantation?" John Wesley asked.

"Gone With the Wind," said the grandmother. "Ha. Ha."

25    When the children finished all the comic books they had brought, they opened the lunch and ate it. The grandmother ate a peanut butter sandwich and an olive and would not let the children throw the box and the paper napkins out the window. When there was nothing else to do they played a game by choosing a cloud and making the other two guess what shape it suggested. John Wesley took one the shape of a cow and June Star guessed a cow and John Wesley said, no, an automobile, and June Star said he didn't play fair, and they began to slap each other over the grandmother.

The grandmother said she would tell them a story if they would keep quiet. When she told a story, she rolled her eyes and waved her head and was very dramatic. She said once when she was a maiden lady she had been courted by a Mr. Edgar Atkins Teagarden from Jasper, Georgia. She said he was a very good-looking man and a gentleman and that he brought her a watermelon every Saturday afternoon with his initials cut in it, E. A. T. Well, one Saturday, she said, Mr. Teagarden brought the watermelon and there was nobody at home and he left it on the front porch and returned in his buggy to Jasper, but she never got the watermelon, she said, because a nigger boy ate it when he saw the initials, E.A.T.! This story tickled John Wesley's funny bone and he giggled and giggled but June Star didn't think it was any good. She said she wouldn't marry a man that just brought her a watermelon on Saturday. The grandmother said she would have done well to marry Mr. Teagarden because he was a gentleman and had bought Coca-Cola stock when it first came out and that he had died only a few years ago, a very wealthy man.

They stopped at The Tower for barbecued sandwiches. The Tower was a part stucco and part wood filling station and dance hall set in a clearing outside of Timothy. A fat man named Red Sammy Butts ran it and there were signs stuck here and there on the building and for miles up and down the highway saying, TRY RED SAMMY'S FAMOUS BARBECUE. NONE LIKE FAMOUS RED SAMMY'S! RED SAM! THE FAT BOY WITH THE HAPPY LAUGH. A VETERAN! RED SAMMY'S YOUR MAN!

Red Sammy was lying on the bare ground outside The Tower with his head under a truck while a gray monkey about a foot high, chained to a small chinaberry tree, chattered nearby. The monkey sprang back into the tree and got on the highest limb as soon as he saw the children jump out of the car and run toward him.

Inside, The Tower was a long dark room with a counter at one end and tables at the other and dancing space in the middle. They all sat down at a board table next to the nickelodeon and Red Sam's wife, a tall burnt-brown woman with hair and eyes lighter than her skin, came and took their order. The children's mother put a dime in the machine and played "The Tennessee

Waltz," and the grandmother said that tune always made her want to dance. She asked Bailey if he would like to dance but he only glared at her. He didn't have a naturally sunny disposition like she did and trips made him nervous. The grandmother's brown eyes were very bright. She swayed her head from side to side and pretended she was dancing in her chair. June Star said play something she could tap to so the children's mother put in another dime and played a fast number and June Star stepped out onto the dance floor and did her tap routine.

30      "Ain't she cute?" Red Sam's wife said, leaning over the counter. "Would you like to come be my little girl?"

"No, I certainly wouldn't," June Star said. "I wouldn't live in a broken-down place like this for a million bucks!" and she ran back to the table.

"Ain't she cute?" the woman repeated, stretching her mouth politely.

"Arn't you ashamed?" hissed the grandmother.

Red Sam came in and told his wife to quit lounging on the counter and hurry with these people's order. His khaki trousers reached just to his hip bones and his stomach hung over them like a sack of meal swaying under his shirt. He came over and sat down at a table nearby and let out a combination sigh and yodel. "You can't win," he said. "You can't win," and he wiped his sweating red face off with a gray handkerchief. "These days you don't know who to trust," he said. "Ain't that the truth?"

35      "People are certainly not nice like they used to be," said the grandmother.

"Two fellers come in here last week," Red Sammy said, "driving a Chrysler. It was a old beat-up car but it was a good one and these boys looked all right to me. Said they worked at the mill and you know I let them fellers charge the gas they bought? Now why did I do that?"

"Because you're a good man!" the grandmother said at once.

"Yes'm, I suppose so," Red Sam said as if he were struck with this answer.

His wife brought the orders, carrying the five plates all at once without a tray, two in each hand and one balanced on her arm. "It isn't a soul in this green world of God's that you can trust," she said. "And I don't count nobody out of that, not nobody," she repeated, looking at Red Sammy.

40      "Did you read about that criminal, The Misfit, that's escaped?" asked the grandmother.

"I wouldn't be a bit surprised if he didn't attact this place right here," said the woman. "If he hears about it being here, I wouldn't be none surprised to see him. If he hears it's two cent in the cash register, I wouldn't be a tall surprised if he . . ."

"That'll do," Red Sam said. "Go bring these people their Co'-Colas," and the woman went off to get the rest of the order.

"A good man is hard to find," Red Sammy said. "Everything is getting terrible. I remember the day you could go off and leave your screen door unlatched. Not no more."

He and the grandmother discussed better times. The old lady said that in her opinion Europe was entirely to blame for the way things were now. She said the way Europe acted you would think we were made of money and Red Sam said it was no use talking about it, she was exactly right. The children ran outside into the white sunlight and looked at the monkey in the lacy chinaberry tree. He was busy catching fleas on himself and biting each one carefully between his teeth as if it were a delicacy.

45      They drove off again into the hot afternoon. The grandmother took cat naps and woke up every few minutes with her own snoring. Outside of Toombsboro she woke up and recalled an old plantation that she had visited in this neighborhood once when she was a young lady. She said the house had six white columns across the front and that there was an avenue of oaks leading up to it and two little wooden trellis arbors on either side in front where you sat down with your suitor after a stroll in the garden. She recalled exactly which road to turn off to get to it. She knew that Bailey would not be willing to lose any time looking at an old house, but the more she talked about it, the more she wanted to see it once again and find out if the little twin arbors were still standing. "There was a secret panel in this house," she said craftily, not telling the truth but wishing that she were, "and the story went that all the family silver was hidden in it when Sherman came through but it was never found ..."

"Hey!" John Wesley said. "Let's go see it! We'll find it! We'll poke all the woodwork and find it! Who lives there? Where do you turn off at? Hey Pop, can't we turn off there?"

"We never have seen a house with a secret panel!" June Star shrieked. "Let's go to the house with the secret panel! Hey Pop, can't we go see the house with the secret panel!"

"It's not far from here, I know," the grandmother said. "It wouldn't take over twenty minutes."

Bailey was looking straight ahead. His jaw was as rigid as a horseshoe. "No," he said.

50      The children began to yell and scream that they wanted to see the house with the secret panel. John Wesley kicked the back of the front seat and June Star hung over her mother's shoulder and whined desperately into her ear that they never had any fun even on their vacation, that they could never do what THEY wanted to do. The baby began to scream and John Wesley kicked the back of the seat so hard that his father could feel the blows in his kidney.

"All right!" he shouted and drew the car to a stop at the side of the road. "Will you all shut up? Will you all just shut up for one second? If you don't shut up, we won't go anywhere."

"It would be very educational for them," the grandmother murmured.

"All right," Bailey said, "but get this: this is the only time we're going to stop for anything like this: this is the one and only time."

"The dirt road that you have to turn down is about a mile back," the grandmother directed. "I marked it when we passed."

55      "A dirt road," Bailey groaned.

After they had turned around and were headed toward the dirt road, the grandmother recalled other points about the house, the beautiful glass over the front doorway and the candle-lamp in the hall. John Wesley said that the secret panel was probably in the fireplace.

"You can't go inside this house," Bailey said. "You don't know who lives there."

"While you all talk to the people in front, I'll run around behind and get in a window," John Wesley suggested.

"We'll all stay in the car," his mother said.

60      They turned onto the dirt road and the car raced roughly along in a swirl of pink dust. The grandmother recalled the times when there were no paved roads and thirty miles was a day's journey. The dirt road was hilly and

there were sudden washes in it and sharp curves on dangerous embankments. All at once they would be on a hill, looking down over the blue tops of trees for miles around, then the next minute, they would be in a red depression with the dust-coated trees looking down on them.

"This place had better turn up in a minute," Bailey said, "or I'm going to turn around."

The road looked as if no one had traveled on it in months.

"It's not much farther," the grandmother said and just as she said it, a horrible thought came to her. The thought was so embarrassing that she turned red in the face and her eyes dilated and her feet jumped up, upsetting her valise in the corner. The instant the valise moved, the newspaper top she had over the basket under it rose with a snarl and Pitty Sing, the cat, sprang onto Bailey's shoulder.

The children were thrown to the floor and their mother, clutching the baby, was thrown out the door onto the ground; the old lady was thrown into the front seat. The car turned over once and landed right-side-up in a gulch off the side of the road. Bailey remained in the driver's seat with the cat—gray-striped with a broad white face and an orange nose—clinging to his neck like a caterpillar.

65     As soon as the children saw they could move their arms and legs, they scrambled out of the car, shouting, "We've had an ACCIDENT!" The grandmother was curled up under the dashboard, hoping she was injured so that Bailey's wrath would not come down on her all at once. The horrible thought she had had before the accident was that the house she had remembered so vividly was not in Georgia but in Tennessee.

Bailey removed the cat from his neck with both hands and flung it out the window against the side of a pine tree. Then he got out of the car and started looking for the children's mother. She was sitting against the side of the red gutted ditch, holding the screaming baby, but she only had a cut down her face and a broken shoulder. "We've had an ACCIDENT!" the children screamed in a frenzy of delight.

"But nobody's killed," June Star said with disappointment as the grandmother limped out of the car, her hat still pinned to her head but the broken front brim standing up at a jaunty angle and the violet spray hanging off the side. They all sat down in the ditch, except the children, to recover from the shock. They were all shaking.

"Maybe a car will come along," said the children's mother hoarsely.

"I believe I have injured an organ," said the grandmother, pressing her side, but no one answered her. Bailey's teeth were clattering. He had on a yellow sport shirt with bright blue parrots designed in it and his face was as yellow as the shirt. The grandmother decided that she would not mention that the house was in Tennessee.

70     The road was about ten feet above and they could see only the tops of the trees on the other side of it. Behind the ditch they were sitting in there were more woods, tall and dark and deep. In a few minutes they saw a car some distance away on top of a hill, coming slowly as if the occupants were watching them. The grandmother stood up and waved both arms dramatically to attract their attention. The car continued to come on slowly, disappeared around a bend and appeared again, moving even slower, on top of the hill they had gone over. It was a big black battered hearse-like automobile. There were three men in it.

It came to a stop just over them and for some minutes, the driver looked down with a steady expressionless gaze to where they were sitting, and didn't speak. Then he turned his head and muttered something to the other two and they got out. One was a fat boy in black trousers and a red sweat shirt with a silver stallion embossed on the front of it. He moved around on the right side of them and stood staring, his mouth partly open in a kind of loose grin. The other had on khaki pants and a blue striped coat and a gray hat pulled down very low, hiding most of his face. He came around slowly on the left side. Neither spoke.

The driver got out of the car and stood by the side of it, looking down at them. He was an older man than the other two. His hair was just beginning to gray and he wore silver-rimmed spectacles that gave him a scholarly look. He had a long creased face and didn't have on any shirt or undershirt. He had on blue jeans that were too tight for him and was holding a black hat and a gun. The two boys also had guns.

"We've had an ACCIDENT!" the children screamed.

The grandmother had the peculiar feeling that the bespectacled man was someone she knew. His face was as familiar to her as if she had known him all her life but she could not recall who he was. He moved away from the car and began to come down the embankment, placing his feet carefully so that he wouldn't slip. He had on tan and white shoes and no socks, and his ankles were red and thin. "Good afternoon," he said. "I see you all had you a little spill."

75      "We turned over twice!" said the grandmother.

"Oncet," he corrected. "We seen it happen. Try their car and see will it run, Hiram," he said quietly to the boy with the gray hat.

"What you got that gun for?" John Wesley asked. "Whatcha gonna do with that gun?"

"Lady," the man said to the children's mother, "would you mind calling them children to sit down by you? Children make me nervous. I want all you all to sit down right together there where you're at."

"What are you telling US what to do for?" June Star asked.

80      Behind them the line of woods gaped like a dark open mouth. "Come here," said their mother.

"Look here now," Bailey began suddenly, "we're in a predicament! We're in . . ."

The grandmother shrieked. She scrambled to her feet and stood staring. "You're The Misfit!" she said. "I recognized you at once!"

"Yes'm," the man said, smiling slightly as if he were pleased in spite of himself to be known, "but it would have been better for all of you, lady, if you hadn't of reckernized me."

Bailey turned his head sharply and said something to his mother that shocked even the children. The old lady began to cry and The Misfit reddened.

85      "Lady," he said, "don't you get upset. Sometimes a man says things he don't mean. I don't reckon he meant to talk to you thataway."

"You wouldn't shoot a lady, would you?" the grandmother said and removed a clean handkerchief from her cuff and began to slap at her eyes with it.

The Misfit pointed the toe of his shoe into the ground and made a little hole and then covered it up again. "I would hate to have to," he said.

"Listen," the grandmother almost screamed, "I know you're a good man. You don't look a bit like you have common blood. I know you must come from nice people!"

"Yes mam," he said, "finest people in the world." When he smiled he showed a row of strong white teeth. "God never made a finer woman than my mother and my daddy's heart was pure gold," he said. The boy with the red sweat shirt had come around behind them and was standing with his gun at his hip. The Misfit squatted down on the ground. "Watch them children, Bobby Lee," he said. "You know they make me nervous." He looked at the six of them huddled together in front of him and he seemed to be embarrassed as if he couldn't think of anything to say. "Ain't a cloud in the sky," he remarked, looking up at it. "Don't see no sun but don't see no cloud neither."

90    "Yes, it's a beautiful day," said the grandmother. "Listen," she said, "you shouldn't call yourself The Misfit because I know you're a good man at heart. I can just look at you and tell."

"Hush!" Bailey yelled. "Hush! Everybody shut up and let me handle this!" He was squatting in the position of a runner about to sprint forward but he didn't move.

"I pre-chate that, lady," The Misfit said and drew a little circle in the ground with the butt of his gun.

"It'll take a half a hour to fix this here car," Hiram called, looking over the raised hood of it.

"Well, first you and Bobby Lee get him and that little boy to step over yonder with you," The Misfit said, pointing to Bailey and John Wesley. "The boys want to ast you something," he said to Bailey. "Would you mind stepping back in them woods there with them?"

95    "Listen," Bailey began, "we're in a terrible predicament! Nobody realizes what this is," and his voice cracked. His eyes were as blue and intense as the parrots in his shirt and he remained perfectly still.

The grandmother reached up to adjust her hat brim as if she were going to the woods with him but it came off in her hand. She stood staring at it and after a second she let it fall on the ground. Hiram pulled Bailey up by the arm as if he were assisting an old man. John Wesley caught hold of his father's hand and Bobby Lee followed. They went off toward the woods and just as they reached the dark edge, Bailey turned and supporting himself against a gray naked pine trunk, he shouted, "I'll be back in a minute, Mamma, wait on me!"

"Come back this instant!" his mother shrilled but they all disappeared into the woods.

"Bailey Boy!" the grandmother called in a tragic voice but she found she was looking at The Misfit squatting on the ground in front of her. "I just know you're a good man," she said desperately. "You're not a bit common!"

"Nome, I ain't a good man," The Misfit said after a second as if he had considered her statement carefully, "but I ain't the worst in the world neither. My daddy said I was a different breed of dog from my brothers and sisters. 'You know,' Daddy said, 'It's some that can live their whole life out without asking about it and it's others has to know why it is, and this boy is one of the latters. He's going to be into everything!'" He put on his black hat and looked up suddenly and then away deep into the woods as if he were embarrassed again. "I'm sorry I don't have on a shirt before you ladies," he said, hunching his shoulders slightly. "We buried our clothes that we had on when we escaped and we're just making do until we can get better. We borrowed these from some folks we met," he explained.

100 "That's perfectly all right," the grandmother said. "Maybe Bailey has an extra shirt in his suitcase."

"I'll look and see terrectly," The Misfit said.

"Where are they taking him?" the children's mother screamed.

"Daddy was a card himself," The Misfit said. "You couldn't put anything over on him. He never got in trouble with the Authorities though. Just had the knack of handling them."

"You could be honest too if you'd only try," said the grandmother. "Think how wonderful it would be to settle down and live a comfortable life and not have to think about somebody chasing you all the time."

105 The Misfit kept scratching in the ground with the butt of his gun as if he were thinking about it. "Yes'm, somebody is always after you," he murmured.

The grandmother noticed how thin his shoulder blades were just behind his hat because she was standing up looking down on him. "Do you ever pray?" she asked.

He shook his head. All she saw was the black hat wiggle between his shoulder blades. "Nome," he said.

There was a pistol shot from the woods, followed closely by another. Then silence. The old lady's head jerked around. She could hear the wind move through the tree tops like a long satisfied insuck of breath. "Bailey Boy!" she called.

"I was a gospel singer for a while," The Misfit said. "I been most everything. Been in the arm service, both land and sea, at home and abroad, been twict married, been an undertaker, been with the railroads, plowed Mother Earth, been in a tornado, seen a man burnt alive oncet," and he looked up at the children's mother and the little girl who were sitting close together, their faces white and their eyes glassy; "I even seen a woman flogged," he said.

110 "Pray, pray," the grandmother began, "pray, pray . . ."

"I never was a bad boy that I remember of," The Misfit said in an almost dreamy voice, "but somewheres along the line I done something wrong and got sent to the penitentiary. I was buried alive," and he looked up and held her attention to him by a steady stare.

"That's when you should have started to pray," she said. "What did you do to get sent up to the penitentiary that first time?"

"Turn to the right, it was a wall," The Misfit said, looking up again at the cloudless sky. "Turn to the left, it was a wall. Look up it was a ceiling, look down it was a floor. I forget what I done, lady. I set there and set there, trying to remember what it was I done and I ain't recalled it to this day. Oncet in a while, I would think it was coming to me, but it never come."

"Maybe they put you in by mistake," the old lady said vaguely.

115 "Nome," he said. "It wasn't no mistake. They had the papers on me."

"You must have stolen something," she said.

The Misfit sneered slightly. "Nobody had nothing I wanted," he said. "It was a head-doctor at the penitentiary said what I had done was kill my daddy but I known that for a lie. My daddy died in nineteen ought nineteen of the epidemic flu and I never had a thing to do with it. He was buried in the Mount Hopewell Baptist churchyard and you can go there and see for yourself."

"If you would pray," the old lady said, "Jesus would help you."

"That's right," The Misfit said.

120    "Well then, why don't you pray?" she asked trembling with delight suddenly.

"I don't want no hep," he said. "I'm doing all right by myself."

Bobby Lee and Hiram came ambling back from the woods. Bobby Lee was dragging a yellow shirt with bright blue parrots in it.

"Thow me that shirt, Bobby Lee," The Misfit said. The shirt came flying at him and landed on his shoulder and he put it on. The grandmother couldn't name what the shirt reminded her of. "No, lady," The Misfit said while he was buttoning it up, "I found out the crime don't matter. You can do one thing or you can do another, kill a man or take a tire off his car, because sooner or later you're going to forget what it was you done and just be punished for it."

The children's mother had begun to make heaving noises as if she couldn't get her breath. "Lady," he asked, "would you and that little girl like to step off yonder with Bobby Lee and Hiram and join your husband?"

125    "Yes, thank you," the mother said faintly. Her left arm dangled helplessly and she was holding the baby, who had gone to sleep, in the other. "Hep that lady up, Hiram," The Misfit said as she struggled to climb out of the ditch, "and Bobby Lee, you hold onto that little girl's hand."

"I don't want to hold hands with him," June Star said. "He reminds me of a pig."

The fat boy blushed and laughed and caught her by the arm and pulled her off into the woods after Hiram and her mother.

Alone with The Misfit, the grandmother found that she had lost her voice. There was not a cloud in the sky nor any sun. There was nothing around her but woods. She wanted to tell him that he must pray. She opened and closed her mouth several times before anything came out. Finally she found herself saying, "Jesus. Jesus," meaning, Jesus will help you, but the way she was saying it, it sounded as if she might be cursing.

"Yes'm," The Misfit said as if he agreed. "Jesus thown everything off balance. It was the same case with Him as with me except He hadn't committed any crime and they could prove I had committed one because they had the papers on me. Of course," he said, "they never shown me my papers. That's why I sign myself now. I said long ago, you get you a signature and sign everything you do and keep a copy of it. Then you'll know what you done and you can hold up the crime to the punishment and see do they match and in the end you'll have something to prove you ain't been treated right. I call myself The Misfit," he said, "because I can't make what all I done wrong fit what all I gone through in punishment."

130    There was a piercing scream from the woods, followed closely by a pistol report. "Does it seem right to you, lady, that one is punished a heap and another ain't punished at all?"

"Jesus!" the old lady cried. "You've got good blood! I know you wouldn't shoot a lady! I know you come from nice people! Pray! Jesus, you ought not to shoot a lady. I'll give you all the money I've got!"

"Lady," The Misfit said, looking beyond her far into the woods, "there never was a body that give the undertaker a tip."

There were two more pistol reports and the grandmother raised her head like a parched old turkey hen crying for water and called, "Bailey Boy, Bailey Boy!" as if her heart would break.

"Jesus was the only One that ever raised the dead," The Misfit continued, "and He shouldn't have done it. He thown everything off balance. If He did what He said, then it's nothing for you to do but thow away everything and follow Him, and if He didn't, then it's nothing for you to do but enjoy the few minutes you got left the best way you can—by killing somebody or burning down his house or doing some other meanness to him. No pleasure but meanness," he said and his voice had become almost a snarl.

135    "Maybe He didn't raise the dead," the old lady mumbled, not knowing what she was saying and feeling so dizzy that she sank down in the ditch with her legs twisted under her.

"I wasn't there so I can't say He didn't," The Misfit said. "I wisht I had of been there," he said, hitting the ground with his fist. "It ain't right I wasn't there because if I had of been there I would of known. Listen lady," he said in a high voice, "if I had of been there I would of known and I wouldn't be like I am now." His voice seemed about to crack and the grandmother's head cleared for an instant. She saw the man's face twisted close to her own as if he were going to cry and she murmured, "Why you're one of my babies. You're one of my own children!" She reached out and touched him on the shoulder. The Misfit sprang back as if a snake had bitten him and shot her three times through the chest. Then he put his gun down on the ground and took off his glasses and began to clean them.

Hiram and Bobby Lee returned from the woods and stood over the ditch, looking down at the grandmother who half sat and half lay in a puddle of blood with her legs crossed under her like a child's and her face smiling up at the cloudless sky.

Without his glasses, The Misfit's eyes were red-rimmed and pale and defenseless-looking. "Take her off and thow her where you thown the others," he said, picking up the cat that was rubbing itself against his leg.

"She was a talker, wasn't she?" Bobby Lee said, sliding down the ditch with a yodel.

140    "She would of been a good woman," The Misfit said, "if it had been somebody there to shoot her every minute of her life."

"Some fun!" Bobby Lee said.

"Shut up, Bobby Lee," The Misfit said. "It's no real pleasure in life."

### YOUR TURN

1. Explain the significance of the title.
2. Interpret and evaluate The Misfit's comment on the grandmother: "She would of been a good woman if it had been somebody there to shoot her every minute of her life."
3. O'Connor reported that once, when she read aloud "A Good Man Is Hard to Find," a member of the audience said that "it was a shame someone with so much talent should look upon life as a horror show." Two questions: What evidence of O'Connor's "talent" do you see in the story, and does the story suggest that O'Connor looked on life as a horror show?
4. What are the values of the members of the family?

5. As we noted earlier, Flannery O'Connor, a Roman Catholic, said, "I see from the standpoint of Christian orthodoxy. This means that for me the meaning of life is centered in our Redemption by Christ and what I see in the world I see in relation to that." In the light of this statement, and drawing on "A Good Man Is Hard to Find," explain what O'Connor saw in the world.

## Revelation
[1964]

The doctor's waiting room, which was very small, was almost full when the Turpins entered and Mrs. Turpin, who was very large, made it look even smaller by her presence. She stood looming at the head of the magazine table set in the center of it, a living demonstration that the room was inadequate and ridiculous. Her little bright black eyes took in all the patients as she sized up the seating situation. There was one vacant chair and a place on the sofa occupied by a blond child in a dirty blue romper who should have been told to move over and make room for the lady. He was five or six, but Mrs. Turpin saw at once that no one was going to tell him to move over. He was slumped down in the seat, his arms idle at his sides and his eyes idle in his head; his nose ran unchecked.

Mrs. Turpin put a firm hand on Claud's shoulder and said in a voice that included anyone who wanted to listen, "Claud, you sit in that chair there," and gave him a push down into the vacant one. Claud was florid and bald and sturdy, somewhat shorter than Mrs. Turpin, but he sat down as if he were accustomed to doing what she told him to.

Mrs. Turpin remained standing. The only man in the room besides Claud was a lean stringy old fellow with a rusty hand spread out on each knee, whose eyes were closed as if he were asleep or dead or pretending to be so as not to get up and offer her his seat. Her gaze settled agreeably on a well-dressed grey-haired lady whose eyes met hers and whose expression said: if that child belonged to me, he would have some manners and move over—there's plenty of room there for you and him too.

Claud looked up with a sigh and made as if to rise.

5    "Sit down," Mrs. Turpin said. "You know you're not supposed to stand on that leg. He has an ulcer on his leg," she explained.

Claud lifted his foot onto the magazine table and rolled his trouser leg up to reveal a purple swelling on a plump marble-white calf.

"My!" the pleasant lady said. "How did you do that?"

"A cow kicked him," Mrs. Turpin said.

"Goodness!" said the lady.

10    Claud rolled his trouser leg down.

"Maybe the little boy would move over," the lady suggested, but the child did not stir.

"Somebody will be leaving in a minute," Mrs. Turpin said. She could not understand why a doctor—with as much money as they made charging five dollars a day to just stick their head in the hospital door and look at you—couldn't afford a decent-sized waiting room. This one was hardly bigger than a garage. The table was cluttered with limp-looking magazines and at one end of it there was a big green glass ash tray full of cigaret butts and cotton wads with little blood spots on them. If she had had anything to do with the running of the place, that would have been emptied every so often. There were no chairs against the wall at the head of the room. It had a rectangular-shaped panel in it that permitted a view of the office where the nurse came and went and the secretary listened to the radio. A plastic fern in a gold pot sat in the opening and trailed its fronds down almost to the floor. The radio was softly playing gospel music.

Just then the inner door opened and a nurse with the highest stack of yellow hair Mrs. Turpin had ever seen put her face in the crack and called for the next patient. The woman sitting beside Claud grasped the two arms of her chair and hoisted herself up; she pulled her dress free from her legs and lumbered through the door where the nurse had disappeared.

Mrs. Turpin eased into the vacant chair, which held her tight as a corset. "I wish I could reduce," she said, and rolled her eyes and gave a comic sigh.

15     "Oh, *you* aren't fat," the stylish lady said.

"Ooooo I am too," Mrs. Turpin said. "Claud he eats all he wants to and never weighs over one hundred and seventy-five pounds, but me I just look at something good to eat and I gain some weight," and her stomach and shoulders shook with laughter. "You can eat all you want to, can't you, Claud?" she asked, turning to him.

Claud only grinned.

"Well, as long as you have such a good disposition," the stylish lady said, "I don't think it makes a bit of difference what size you are. You just can't beat a good disposition."

Next to her was a fat girl of eighteen or nineteen, scowling into a thick blue book which Mrs. Turpin saw was entitled *Human Development*. The girl raised her head and directed her scowl at Mrs. Turpin as if she did not like her looks. She appeared annoyed that anyone should speak while she tried to read. The poor girl's face was blue with acne and Mrs. Turpin thought how pitiful it was to have a face like that at that age. She gave the girl a friendly smile but the girl only scowled the harder. Mrs. Turpin herself was fat but she had always had good skin, and, though she was forty-seven years old, there was not a wrinkle in her face except around her eyes from laughing too much.

20     Next to the ugly girl was the child, still in exactly the same position, and next to him was a thin leathery old woman in a cotton print dress. She and Claud had three sacks of chicken feed in their pump house that was in the same print. She had seen from the first that the child belonged with the old woman. She could tell by the way they sat—kind of vacant and white-trashy, as if they would sit there until Doomsday if nobody called and told them to get up. And at right angles but next to the well-dressed pleasant lady was a lank-faced woman who was certainly the child's mother. She had on a yellow sweat shirt and wine-colored slacks, both gritty-looking, and the rims of her lips were stained with snuff. Her dirty yellow hair was tied behind with a little piece of red paper ribbon. Worse than niggers any day, Mrs. Turpin thought.

The gospel hymn playing was, "When I looked up and He looked down," and Mrs. Turpin, who knew it, supplied the last line mentally, "And wona these days I know I'll we-eara crown."

Without appearing to, Mrs. Turpin always noticed people's feet. The well-dressed lady had on red and grey suede shoes to match her dress. Mrs. Turpin had on her good black patent leather pumps. The ugly girl had on

Girl Scout shoes and heavy socks. The old woman had on tennis shoes and the white-trashy mother had on what appeared to be bedroom slippers, black straw with gold braid threaded through them—exactly what you would have expected her to have on.

Sometimes at night when she couldn't go to sleep, Mrs. Turpin would occupy herself with the question of who she would have chosen to be if she couldn't have been herself. If Jesus had said to her before he made her, "There's only two places available for you. You can either be a nigger or white-trash," what would she have said? "Please, Jesus, please," she would have said, "just let me wait until there's another place available," and he would have said, "No, you have to go right now and I have only those two places so make up your mind." She would have wiggled and squirmed and begged and pleaded but it would have been no use and finally she would have said, "All right, make me a nigger then—but that don't mean a trashy one." And he would have made her a neat clean respectable Negro woman, herself but black.

Next to the child's mother was a red-headed youngish woman, reading one of the magazines and working a piece of chewing gum, hell for leather, as Claud would say. Mrs. Turpin could not see the woman's feet. She was not white-trash, just common. Sometimes Mrs. Turpin occupied herself at night naming the classes of people. On the bottom of the heap were most colored people, not the kind she would have been if she had been one, but most of them; then next to them—not above, just away from—were the white-trash; then above them were the homeowners, and above them the home-and-land owners, to which she and Claud belonged. Above she and Claud were people with a lot of money and much bigger houses and much more land. But here the complexity of it would begin to bear in on her, for some of the people with a lot of money were common and ought to be below she and Claud and some of the people who had good blood had lost their money and had to rent and then there were colored people who owned their homes and land as well. There was a colored dentist in town who had two red Lincolns and a swimming pool and a farm with registered white-face cattle on it. Usually by the time she had fallen asleep all the classes of people were moiling and roiling around in her head, and she would dream they were all crammed in together in a box car, being ridden off to be put in a gas oven.

25      "That's a beautiful clock," she said and nodded to her right. It was a big wall clock, the face encased in a brass sunburst.

"Yes, it's very pretty," the stylish lady said agreeably. "And right on the dot too," she added, glancing at her watch.

The ugly girl beside her cast an eye upward at the clock, smirked, then looked directly at Mrs. Turpin and smirked again. Then she returned her eyes to her book. She was obviously the lady's daughter because, although they didn't look anything alike as to disposition, they both had the same shape of face and the same blue eyes. On the lady they sparkled pleasantly but in the girl's seared face they appeared alternately to smolder and to blaze.

What if Jesus had said, "All right, you can be white-trash or a nigger or ugly"!

Mrs. Turpin felt an awful pity for the girl, though she thought it was one thing to be ugly and another to act ugly.

30      The woman with the snuff-stained lips turned around in her chair and looked up at the clock. Then she turned back and appeared to look a little to

the side of Mrs. Turpin. There was a cast in one of her eyes. "You want to know wher you can get you one of themther clocks?" she asked in a loud voice.

"No, I already have a nice clock," Mrs. Turpin said. Once somebody like her got a leg in the conversation, she would be all over it.

"You can get you one with green stamps," the woman said. "That's most likely wher he got hisn. Save you up enough, you can get you most anythang. I got me some joo'ry."

Ought to have got you a wash rag and some soap, Mrs. Turpin thought.

"I get contour sheets with mine," the pleasant lady said.

35        The daughter slammed her book shut. She looked straight in front of her, directly through Mrs. Turpin and on through the yellow curtain and the plate glass window which made the wall behind her. The girl's eyes seemed lit all of a sudden with a peculiar light, an unnatural light like night road signs give. Mrs. Turpin turned her head to see if there was anything going on outside that she should see, but she could not see anything. Figures passing cast only a pale shadow through the curtain. There was no reason the girl should single her out for her ugly looks.

"Miss Finley," the nurse said, cracking the door. The gum-chewing woman got up and passed in front of her and Claud and went into the office. She had on red high-heeled shoes.

Directly across the table, the ugly girl's eyes were fixed on Mrs. Turpin as if she had some very special reason for disliking her.

"This is wonderful weather, isn't it?" the girl's mother said.

"It's good weather for cotton if you can get the niggers to pick it," Mrs. Turpin said, "but niggers don't want to pick cotton any more. You can't get the white folks to pick it and now you can't get the niggers—because they got to be right up there with the white folks."

40        "They gonna *try* anyways," the white-trash woman said, leaning forward.

"Do you have one of those cotton-picking machines?" the pleasant lady asked.

"No," Mrs. Turpin said, "they leave half the cotton in the field. We don't have much cotton anyway. If you want to make it farming now, you have to have a little of everything. We got a couple of acres of cotton and a few hogs and chickens and just enough white-face that Claud can look after them himself."

"One thang I don't want," the white-trash woman said, wiping her mouth with the back of her hand. "Hogs. Nasty stinking things, a-gruntin and a-rootin all over the place."

Mrs. Turpin gave her the merest edge of her attention. "Our hogs are not dirty and they don't stink," she said. "They're cleaner than some children I've seen. Their feet never touch the ground. We have a pig-parlor— that's where you raise them on concrete," she explained to the pleasant lady, "and Claud scoots them down with the hose every afternoon and washes off the floor." Cleaner by far than that child right there, she thought. Poor nasty little thing. He had not moved except to put the thumb of his dirty hand into his mouth.

45        The woman turned her face away from Mrs. Turpin. "I know I wouldn't scoot down no hog with no hose," she said to the wall.

You wouldn't have no hog to scoot down, Mrs. Turpin said to herself.

"A-gruntin and a-rootin and a-groanin," the woman muttered.

"We got a little of everything," Mrs. Turpin said to the pleasant lady. "It's no use in having more than you can handle yourself with help like it is. We found enough niggers to pick our cotton this year but Claud he has to go after them and take them home again in the evening. They can't walk that half a mile. No they can't. I tell you," she said and laughed merrily, "I sure am tired of buttering up niggers, but you got to love em if you want em to work for you. When they come in the morning, I run out and I say, 'Hi yawl this morning?' and when Claud drives them off to the field I just wave to beat the band and they just wave back." And she waved her hand rapidly to illustrate.

"Like you read out of the same book," the lady said, showing she understood perfectly.

50   "Child, yes," Mrs. Turpin said. "And when they come in from the field, I run out with a bucket of icewater. That's the way it's going to be from now on," she said. "You may as well face it."

"One thang I know," the white-trash woman said. "Two thangs I ain't going to do: love no niggers or scoot down no hog with no hose." And she let out a bark of contempt.

The look that Mrs. Turpin and the pleasant lady exchanged indicated they both understood that you had to *have* certain things before you could *know* certain things. But every time Mrs. Turpin exchanged a look with the lady, she was aware that the ugly girl's peculiar eyes were still on her, and she had trouble bringing her attention back to the conversation.

"When you got something," she said, "you got to look after it." And when you ain't got a thing but breath and britches, she added to herself, you can afford to come to town every morning and just sit on the Court House coping and spit.

A grotesque revolving shadow passed across the curtain behind her and was thrown palely on the opposite wall. Then a bicycle clattered down against the outside of the building. The door opened and a colored boy glided in with a tray from the drug store. It had two large red and white paper cups on it with tops on them. He was a tall, very black boy in discolored white pants and a green nylon shirt. He was chewing gum slowly, as if to music. He set the tray down in the office opening next to the fern and stuck his head through to look for the secretary. She was not in there. He rested his arms on the ledge and waited, his narrow bottom stuck out, swaying slowly to the left and right. He raised a hand over his head and scratched the base of his skull.

55   "You see that button there, boy?" Mrs. Turpin said. "You can punch that and she'll come. She's probably in the back somewhere."

"Is that right?" the boy said agreeably, as if he had never seen the button before. He leaned to the right and put his finger on it. "She sometime out," he said and twisted around to face his audience, his elbows behind him on the counter. The nurse appeared and he twisted back again. She handed him a dollar and he rooted in his pocket and made the change and counted it out to her. She gave him fifteen cents for a tip and he went out with the empty tray. The heavy door swung to slowly and closed at length with the sound of suction. For a moment no one spoke.

"They ought to send all them niggers back to Africa," the white-trash woman said. "That's wher they come from in the first place."

"Oh, I couldn't do without my good colored friends," the pleasant lady said.

"There's a heap of things worse than a nigger," Mrs. Turpin agreed. "It's all kinds of them just like it's all kinds of us."

60 "Yes, and it takes all kinds to make the world go round," the lady said in her musical voice.

As she said it, the raw-complexioned girl snapped her teeth together. Her lower lip turned downwards and inside out, revealing the pale pink inside of her mouth. After a second it rolled back up. It was the ugliest face Mrs. Turpin had ever seen anyone make and for a moment she was certain that the girl had made it at her. She was looking at her as if she had known and disliked her all her life—all of Mrs. Turpin's life, it seemed too, not just all the girl's life. Why, girl, I don't even know you, Mrs. Turpin said silently.

She forced her attention back to the discussion. "It wouldn't be practical to send them back to Africa," she said. "They wouldn't want to go. They got it too good here."

"Wouldn't be what they wanted—if I had anythang to do with it," the woman said.

"It wouldn't be a way in the world you could get all the niggers back over there," Mrs. Turpin said. "They'd be hiding out and lying down and turning sick on you and wailing and hollering and raring and pitching. It wouldn't be a way in the world to get them over there."

65 "They got over here," the trashy woman said. "Get back like they got over."

"It wasn't so many of them then," Mrs. Turpin explained.

The woman looked at Mrs. Turpin as if here was an idiot indeed but Mrs. Turpin was not bothered by the look, considering where it came from.

"Nooo," she said, "they're going to stay here where they can go to New York and marry white folks and improve their color. That's what they all want to do, every one of them, improve their color."

"You know what comes of that, don't you?" Claud asked.

70 "No, Claud, what?" Mrs. Turpin said.

Claud's eyes twinkled. "White-faced niggers," he said with never a smile.

Everybody in the office laughed except the white-trash and the ugly girl. The girl gripped the book in her lap with white fingers. The trashy woman looked around her from face to face as if she thought they were all idiots. The old woman in the feed sack dress continued to gaze expressionless across the floor at the high-top shoes of the man opposite her, the one who had been pretending to be asleep when the Turpins came in. He was laughing heartily, his hands still spread out on his knees. The child had fallen to the side and was lying now almost face down in the old woman's lap.

While they recovered from their laughter, the nasal chorus on the radio kept the room from silence.

*"You go to blank blank*
*And I'll go to mine*
*But we'll all blank along*
*To-geth-ther,*
*And all along the blank*
*We'll hep eachother out*
*Smile-ling in any kind of*
*Weath-ther!"*

Mrs. Turpin didn't catch every word but she caught enough to agree with the spirit of the song and it turned her thoughts sober. To help anybody out that needed it was her philosophy of life. She never spared herself when she found somebody in need, whether they were white or black, trash or decent. And of all she had to be thankful for, she was most thankful that this was so. If Jesus had said, "You can be high society and have all the money you want and be thin and svelte-like, but you can't be a good woman with it," she would have had to say, "Well don't make me that then. Make me a good woman and it don't matter what else, how fat or how ugly or how poor!" Her heart rose. He had not made her a nigger or white-trash or ugly! He had made her herself and given her a little of everything. Jesus, thank you! she said. Thank you thank you thank you! Whenever she counted her blessings she felt as buoyant as if she weighed one hundred and twenty-five pounds instead of one hundred and eighty.

75      "What's wrong with your little boy?" the pleasant lady asked the white-trashy woman.

"He has a ulcer," the woman said proudly. "He ain't give me a minute's peace since he was born. Him and her are just alike," she said, nodding at the old woman, who was running her leathery fingers through the child's pale hair. "Look like I can't get nothing down them two but Co' Cola and candy."

That's all you try to get down em, Mrs. Turpin said to herself. Too lazy to light the fire. There was nothing you could tell her about people like them that she didn't know already. And it was not just that they didn't have anything. Because if you gave them everything, in two weeks it would all be broken or filthy or they would have chopped it up for lightwood. She knew all this from her own experience. Help them you must, but help them you couldn't.

All at once the ugly girl turned her lips inside out again. Her eyes were fixed like two drills on Mrs. Turpin. This time there was no mistaking that there was something urgent behind them.

Girl, Mrs. Turpin exclaimed silently, I haven't done a thing to you! The girl might be confusing her with somebody else. There was no need to sit by and let herself be intimidated. "You must be in college," she said boldly, looking directly at the girl. "I see you reading a book there."

80      The girl continued to stare and pointedly did not answer.

Her mother blushed at this rudeness. "The lady asked you a question, Mary Grace," she said under her breath.

"I have ears," Mary Grace said.

The poor mother blushed again. "Mary Grace goes to Wellesley College,"[1] she explained. She twisted one of the buttons on her dress. "In Massachusetts," she added with a grimace. "And in the summer she just keeps right on studying. Just reads all the time, a real book worm. She's done real well at Wellesley; she's taking English and Math and History and Psychology and Social Studies," she rattled on, "and I think it's too much. I think she ought to get out and have fun."

The girl looked as if she would like to hurl them all through the plate glass window.

85      "Way up north," Mrs. Turpin murmured and thought, well, it hasn't done much for her manners.

---

[1]**Wellesley College** a distinguished women's college.

"I'd almost rather to have him sick," the white-trash woman said, wrenching the attention back to herself. "He's so mean when he ain't. Look like some children just take natural to meanness. It's some gets bad when they get sick but he was the opposite. Took sick and turned good. He don't give me no trouble now. It's me waitin to see the doctor," she said.

If I was going to send anybody back to Africa, Mrs. Turpin thought, it would be your kind, woman. "Yes, indeed," she said aloud, but looking up at the ceiling, "it's a heap of things worse than a nigger." And dirtier than a hog, she added to herself.

"I think people with bad dispositions are more to be pitied than anyone on earth," the pleasant lady said in a voice that was decidedly thin.

"I thank the Lord he has blessed me with a good one," Mrs. Turpin said. "The day has never dawned that I couldn't find something to laugh at."

90      "Not since she married me anyways," Claud said with a comical straight face.

Everybody laughed except the girl and the white-trash.

Mrs. Turpin's stomach shook. "He's such a caution," she said, "that I can't help but laugh at him."

The girl made a loud ugly noise through her teeth.

Her mother's mouth grew thin and tight. "I think the worst thing in the world," she said, "is an ungrateful person. To have everything and not appreciate it. I know a girl," she said, "who has parents who would give her anything, a little brother who loves her dearly, who is getting a good education, who wears the best clothes, but who can never say a kind word to anyone, who never smiles, who just criticizes and complains all day long."

95      "Is she too old to paddle?" Claud asked.

The girl's face was almost purple.

"Yes," the lady said. "I'm afraid there's nothing to do but leave her to her folly. Some day she'll wake up and it'll be too late."

"It never hurt anyone to smile," Mrs. Turpin said. "It just makes you feel better all over."

"Of course," the lady said sadly, "but there are just some people you can't tell anything to. They can't take criticism."

100     "If it's one thing I am," Mrs. Turpin said with feeling, "it's grateful. When I think who all I could have been besides myself and what all I got, a little of everything, and a good disposition besides, I just feel like shouting, 'Thank you, Jesus, for making everything the way it is!' It could have been different!" For one thing, somebody else could have got Claud. At the thought of this, she was flooded with gratitude and a terrible pang of joy ran through her. "Oh thank you, Jesus, Jesus, thank you!" she cried aloud.

The book struck her directly over her left eye. It struck almost at the same instant that she realized the girl was about to hurl it. Before she could utter a sound, the raw face came crashing across the table toward her, howling. The girl's fingers sank like clamps into the soft flesh of her neck. She heard the mother cry out and Claud shout, "Whoa!" There was an instant when she was certain that she was about to be in an earthquake.

All at once her vision narrowed and she saw everything as if it were happening in a small room far away, or as if she were looking at it through the wrong end of a telescope. Claud's face crumpled and fell out of sight. The nurse ran in, then out, then in again. Then the gangling figure of the doctor rushed out of the inner door. Magazines flew this way and that as the table turned over. The girl fell with a thud and Mrs. Turpin's vision suddenly reversed itself and she saw everything large instead of small. The eyes of the white-trashy woman were staring hugely at the floor. There the girl, held down on one side by the nurse and on the other by her mother, was wrenching and turning in their grasp. The doctor was kneeling astride her, trying to hold her arm down. He managed after a second to sink a long needle into it.

Mrs. Turpin felt entirely hollow except for her heart which swung from side to side as if it were agitated in a great empty drum of flesh.

"Somebody that's not busy call for the ambulance," the doctor said in the off-hand voice young doctors adopt for terrible occasions.

105    Mrs. Turpin could not have moved a finger. The old man who had been sitting next to her skipped nimbly into the office and made the call, for the secretary still seemed to be gone.

"Claud!" Mrs. Turpin called.

He was not in his chair. She knew she must jump up and find him but she felt like some one trying to catch a train in a dream, when everything moves in slow motion and the faster you try to run the slower you go.

"Here I am," a suffocated voice, very unlike Claud's, said.

He was doubled up in the corner on the floor, pale as paper, holding his leg. She wanted to get up and go to him but she could not move. Instead, her gaze was drawn slowly downward to the churning face on the floor, which she could see over the doctor's shoulder.

110    The girl's eyes stopped rolling and focused on her. They seemed a much lighter blue than before, as if a door that had been tightly closed behind them was now open to admit light and air.

Mrs. Turpin's head cleared and her power of motion returned. She leaned forward until she was looking directly into the fierce brilliant eyes. There was no doubt in her mind that the girl did know her, knew her in some intense and personal way, beyond time and place and condition. "What you got to say to me?" she asked hoarsely and held her breath, waiting, as for a revelation.

The girl raised her head. Her gaze locked with Mrs. Turpin's. "Go back to hell where you came from, you old wart hog," she whispered. Her voice was low but clear. Her eyes burned for a moment as if she saw with pleasure that her message had struck its target.

Mrs. Turpin sank back in her chair.

After a moment the girl's eyes closed and she turned her head wearily to the side.

115    The doctor rose and handed the nurse the empty syringe. He leaned over and put both hands for a moment on the mother's shoulders, which were shaking. She was sitting on the floor, her lips pressed together, holding Mary Grace's hand in her lap. The girl's fingers were gripped like a baby's around her thumb. "Go on to the hospital," he said. "I'll call and make the arrangements."

"Now let's see that neck," he said in a jovial voice to Mrs. Turpin. He began to inspect her neck with his first two fingers. Two little moon-shaped lines like pink fish bones were indented over her windpipe. There was the beginning of an angry red swelling above her eye. His fingers passed over this also.

"Lea' me be," she said thickly and shook him off. "See about Claud. She kicked him."

"I'll see about him in a minute," he said and felt her pulse. He was a thin gray-haired man, given to pleasantries. "Go home and have yourself a vacation the rest of the day," he said and patted her on the shoulder.

Quit your pattin me, Mrs. Turpin growled to herself.

120    "And put an ice pack over that eye," he said. Then he went and squatted down beside Claud and looked at his leg. After a moment he pulled him up and Claud limped after him into the office.

Until the ambulance came, the only sounds in the room were the tremulous moans of the girl's mother, who continued to sit on the floor. The white-trash woman did not take her eyes off the girl. Mrs. Turpin looked straight ahead at nothing. Presently the ambulance drew up, a long dark shadow, behind the curtain. The attendants came in and set the stretcher down beside the girl and lifted her expertly onto it and carried her out. The nurse helped the mother gather up her things. The shadow of the ambulance moved silently away and the nurse came back in the office.

"That there girl is going to be a lunatic, ain't she?" the white-trash woman asked the nurse, but the nurse kept on to the back and never answered her.

"Yes, she's going to be a lunatic," the white-trash woman said to the rest of them.

"Po' critter," the old woman murmured. The child's face was still in her lap. His eyes looked idly out over her knees. He had not moved during the disturbance except to draw one leg up under him.

125    "I thank Gawd," the white-trash woman said fervently, "I ain't a lunatic."

Claud came limping out and the Turpins went home.

As their pick-up truck turned into their own dirt road and made the crest of the hill, Mrs. Turpin gripped the window ledge and looked out suspiciously. The land sloped gracefully down through a field dotted with lavender weeds and at the start of the rise their small yellow frame house, with its little flower beds spread out around it like a fancy apron, sat primly in its accustomed place between two giant hickory trees. She would not have been startled to see a burnt wound between two blackened chimneys.

Neither of them felt like eating so they put on their house clothes and lowered the shade in the bedroom and lay down, Claud with his leg on a pillow and herself with a damp washcloth over her eye. The instant she was flat on her back, the image of a razor-backed hog with warts on its face and horns coming out behind its ears snorted into her head. She moaned, a low quiet moan.

"I am not," she said tearfully, "a wart hog. From hell." But the denial had no force. The girl's eyes and her words, even the tone of her voice, low but clear, directed only to her, brooked no repudiation. She had been singled out for the message, though there was trash in the room to whom it might justly have been applied. The full force of this fact struck her only now. There was a woman there who was neglecting her own child but she had been overlooked. The message had been given to Ruby Turpin, a respectable, hardworking, church-going woman. The tears dried. Her eyes began to burn instead with wrath.

130    She rose on her elbow and the washcloth fell into her hand. Claud was lying on his back, snoring. She wanted to tell him what the girl had said. At

the same time she did not wish to put the image of herself as a wart hog from hell into his mind.

"Hey, Claud," she muttered and pushed his shoulder.

Claud opened one pale baby blue eye.

She looked into it warily. He did not think about anything. He just went his way.

"Wha, whasit?" he said and closed his eye again.

135    "Nothing," she said. "Does your leg pain you?"

"Hurts like hell," Claud said.

"It'll quit terreckly," she said and lay back down. In a moment Claud was snoring again. For the rest of the afternoon they lay there. Claud slept. She scowled at the ceiling. Occasionally she raised her fist and made a small stabbing motion over her chest as if she was defending her innocence to invisible guests who were the comforters of Job, reasonable-seeming but wrong.

About five-thirty Claud stirred. "Got to go after those niggers," he sighed, not moving.

She was looking straight up as if there were unintelligible handwriting on the ceiling. The protuberance over her eye had turned a greenish-blue. "Listen here," she said.

140    "What?"

"Kiss me."

Claud leaned over and kissed her loudly on the mouth. He pinched her side and their hands interlocked. Her expression of ferocious concentration did not change. Claud got up, groaning and growling, and limped off. She continued to study the ceiling.

She did not get up until she heard the pick-up truck coming back with the Negroes. Then she rose and thrust her feet in her brown oxfords, which she did not bother to lace, and stumped out onto the back porch and got her red plastic bucket. She emptied a tray of ice cubes into it and filled it half full of water and went out into the back yard. Every afternoon after Claud brought the hands in, one of the boys helped him put out hay and the rest waited in the back of the truck until he was ready to take them home. The truck was parked in the shade under one of the hickory trees.

"Hi yawl this evening?" Mrs. Turpin asked grimly, appearing with the bucket and the dipper. There were three women and a boy in the truck.

145    "Us doin nicely," the oldest woman said. "Hi you doin?" and her gaze stuck immediately on the dark lump on Mrs. Turpin's forehead. "You done fell down, ain't you?" she asked in a solicitous voice. The old woman was dark and almost toothless. She had on an old felt hat of Claud's set back on her head. The other two women were younger and lighter and they both had new bright green sun hats. One of them had hers on her head; the other had taken hers off and the boy was grinning beneath it.

Mrs. Turpin set the bucket down on the floor of the truck. "Yawl hep yourselves," she said. She looked around to make sure Claud had gone. "No. I didn't fall down," she said, folding her arms. "It was something worse than that."

"Ain't nothing bad happen to you!" the old woman said. She said it as if they all knew Mrs. Turpin was protected in some special way by Divine Providence. "You just had you a little fall."

"We were in town at the doctor's office for where the cow kicked Mr. Turpin," Mrs. Turpin said in a flat tone that indicated they could leave off their foolishness. "And there was this girl there. A big fat girl with her face all broke out. I could look at that girl and tell she was peculiar but I couldn't tell how. And me and her mama were just talking and going along and all of a sudden WHAM! She throws this big book she reading at me and . . ."

"Naw!" the old woman cried out.

150     "And then she jumps over the table and commences to choke me."

"Naw!" they all exclaimed, "naw!"

"Hi come she do that?" the old woman asked. "What ail her?"

Mrs. Turpin only glared in front of her.

"Somethin ail her," the old woman said.

155     "They carried her off in an ambulance," Mrs. Turpin continued, "but before she went she was rolling on the floor and they were trying to hold her down to give her a shot and she said something to me." She paused. "You know what she said to me?"

"What she say?" they asked.

"She said," Mrs. Turpin began, and stopped, her face very dark and heavy. The sun was getting whiter and whiter, blanching the sky overhead so that the leaves of the hickory tree were black in the face of it. She could not bring forth the words. "Something real ugly," she muttered.

"She sho shouldn't said nothin ugly to you," the old woman said. "You so sweet. You the sweetest lady I know."

"She pretty too," the one with the hat on said.

160     "And stout," the other one said. "I never knowed no sweeter white lady."

"That's the truth befo' Jesus," the old woman said. "Amen! You des as sweet and pretty as you can be."

Mrs. Turpin knew just exactly how much Negro flattery was worth and it added to her rage. "She said," she began again and finished this time with a fierce rush of breath, "that I was an old wart hog from hell."

There was an astounded silence.

"Where she at?" the youngest woman cried in a piercing voice.

165     "Lemme see her. I'll kill her!"

"I'll kill her with you!" the other one cried.

"She b'long in the sylum," the old woman said emphatically. "You the sweetest white lady I know."

"She pretty too," the other two said. "Stout as she can be and sweet. Jesus satisfied with her!"

"Deed he is," the old woman declared.

170     Idiots! Mrs. Turpin growled to herself. You could never say anything intelligent to a nigger. You could talk at them but not with them. "Yawl ain't drunk your water," she said shortly. "Leave the bucket in the truck when you're finished with it. I got more to do than just stand around and pass the time of day," and she moved off and into the house.

She stood for a moment in the middle of the kitchen. The dark protuberance over her eye looked like a miniature tornado cloud which might any moment sweep across the horizon of her brow. Her lower lip protruded dangerously. She squared her massive shoulders. Then she marched into the front of the house and out the side door and started down the road to the pig parlor. She had the look of a woman going single-handed, weaponless, into battle.

The sun was a deep yellow now like a harvest moon and was riding westward very fast over the far tree line as if it meant to reach the hogs before she did. The road was rutted and she kicked several good-sized stones out of her path as she strode along. The pig parlor was on a little knoll at the end of a lane that ran off from the side of the barn. It was a square of concrete as large as a small room, with a board fence about four feet high around it. The concrete floor sloped slightly so that the hog wash could drain off into a trench where it was carried to the field for fertilizer. Claud was standing on the outside, on the edge of the concrete, hanging onto the top board, hosing down the floor inside. The hose was connected to the faucet of a water trough nearby.

Mrs. Turpin climbed up beside him and glowered down at the hogs inside. There were seven long-snouted bristly shoats in it—tan with liver-colored spots—and an old sow a few weeks off from farrowing. She was lying on her side grunting. The shoats were running about shaking themselves like idiot children, their little slit pig eyes searching the floor for anything left. She had read that pigs were the most intelligent animal. She doubted it. They were supposed to be smarter than dogs. There had even been a pig astronaut. He had performed his assignment perfectly but died of a heart attack afterwards because they left him in his electric suit, sitting upright throughout his examination when naturally a hog should be on all fours.

A-gruntin and a-rootin and a-groanin.

175    "Gimme that hose," she said, yanking it away from Claud. "Go on and carry them niggers home and then get off that leg."

"You look like you might have swallowed a mad dog," Claud observed, but he got down and limped off. He paid no attention to her humors.

Until he was out of earshot, Mrs. Turpin stood on the side of the pen, holding the hose and pointing the stream of water at the hind quarter of any shoat that looked as if it might try to lie down. When he had had time to get over the hill, she turned her head slightly and her wrathful eyes scanned the path. He was nowhere in sight. She turned back again and seemed to gather herself up. Her shoulders rose and she drew in her breath.

"What do you send me a message like that for?" she said in a low fierce voice, barely above a whisper but with the force of a shout in its concentrated fury. "How am I a hog and me both? How am I saved and from hell too?" Her free fist was knotted and with the other she gripped the hose, blindly pointing the stream of water in and out of the eye of the old sow whose outraged squeal she did not hear.

The pig parlor commanded a view of the back pasture where their twenty beef cows were gathered around the hay-bales Claud and the boy had put out. The freshly cut pasture sloped down to the highway. Across it was their cotton field and beyond that a dark green dusty wood which they owned as well. The sun was behind the wood, very red, looking over the paling of trees like a farmer inspecting his own hogs.

180    "Why me?" she rumbled. "It's no trash around here, black or white, that I haven't given to. And break my back to the bone every day working. And do for the church."

She appeared to be the right size woman to command the arena before her. "How am I a hog?" she demanded. "Exactly how am I like them?" and she jabbed the stream of water at the shoats. "There was plenty of trash there. It didn't have to be me."

"If you like trash better, go get yourself some trash then," she railed. "You could have made me trash. Or a nigger. If trash is what you wanted why didn't you make me trash?" She shook her fist with the hose in it and a watery snake appeared momentarily in the air. "I could quit working and take it easy and be filthy," she growled. "Lounge about the sidewalks all day drinking root beer. Dip snuff and spit in every puddle and have it all over my face. I could be nasty.

"Or you could have made me a nigger. It's too late for me to be a nigger," she said with deep sarcasm, "but I could act like one. Lay down in the middle of the road and stop traffic. Roll on the ground."

In the deepening light everything was taking on a mysterious hue. The pasture was growing a peculiar glassy green and the streak of highway had turned lavender. She braced herself for a final assault and this time her voice rolled out over the pasture. "Go on," she yelled, "call me a hog! Call me a hog again. From hell. Call me a wart hog from hell. Put that bottom rail on top. There'll still be a top and bottom!"

185        A garbled echo returned to her.

A final surge of fury shook her and she roared, "Who do you think you are?"

The color of everything, field and crimson sky, burned for a moment with a transparent intensity. The question carried over the pasture and across the highway and the cotton field and returned to her clearly like an answer from beyond the wood.

She opened her mouth but no sound came out of it.

A tiny truck, Claud's, appeared on the highway, heading rapidly out of sight. Its gears scraped thinly. It looked like a child's toy. At any moment a bigger truck might smash into it and scatter Claud's and the niggers' brains all over the road.

190        Mrs. Turpin stood there, her gaze fixed on the highway, all her muscles rigid, until in five or six minutes the truck reappeared, returning. She waited until it had had time to turn into their own road. Then like a monumental statue coming to life, she bent her head slowly and gazed, as if through the very heart of mystery, down into the pig parlor at the hogs. They had settled all in one corner around the old sow who was grunting softly. A red glow suffused them. They appeared to pant with a secret life.

Until the sun slipped finally behind the tree line, Mrs. Turpin remained there with her gaze bent to them as if she were absorbing some abysmal life-giving knowledge. At last she lifted her head. There was only a purple streak in the sky, cutting through a field of crimson and leading, like an extension of the highway, into the descending dusk. She raised her hands from the side of the pen in a gesture hieratic and profound. A visionary light settled in her eyes. She saw the streak as a vast swinging bridge extending upward from the earth through a field of living fire. Upon it a vast horde of souls were rumbling toward heaven. There were whole companies of white-trash, clean for the first time in their lives, and bands of black niggers in white robes, and battalions of freaks and lunatics shouting and clapping and leaping like frogs. And bringing up the end of the procession was a tribe of people whom she recognized at once as those who, like herself and Claud, had always had a little of everything and the God-given wit to use it right. She leaned forward to observe them closer. They were marching behind the others with great dignity, accountable as they had always been for good order and common sense and respectable behavior. They alone were on key. Yet she could see by their shocked and altered faces that even their virtues were being burned away. She lowered her hands and gripped the rail of the hog pen, her eyes small but fixed unblinkingly on what lay ahead. In a moment the vision faded but she remained where she was, immobile.

At length she got down and turned off the faucet and made her slow way on the darkening path to the house. In the woods around her the invisible cricket choruses had struck up, but what she heard were the voices of the souls climbing upward into the starry field and shouting hallelujah.

### YOUR TURN

1. Why does Mary Grace attack Mrs. Turpin?
2. Characterize Mrs. Turpin before her revelation. Did your attitude toward her change at the end of the story?
3. The two chief settings are a doctor's waiting room and a "pig parlor." Can these settings reasonably be called "symbolic"? If so, symbolic of what?
4. When Mrs. Turpin goes toward the pig parlor, she has "the look of a woman going single-handed, weaponless, into battle." Once there, she dismisses Claud, uses the hose as a weapon against the pigs, and talks to herself "in a low fierce voice." What is she battling, besides the pigs?

# On Fiction: Remarks from O'Connor's Essays and Letters

## From "The Fiction Writer and His Country"                    [1957]

In the greatest fiction, the writer's moral sense coincides with his dramatic sense, and I see no way for it to do this unless his moral judgment is part of the very act of seeing, and he is free to use it. I have heard it said that belief in Christian dogma is a hindrance to the writer, but I myself have found nothing further from the truth. Actually, it frees the storyteller to observe. It is not a set of rules which fixes what he sees in the world. It affects his writing primarily by guaranteeing his respect for mystery. . . .

When I look at stories I have written I find that they are, for the most part, about people who are poor, who are afflicted in both mind and body, who have little—or at best a distorted—sense of spiritual purpose, and whose actions do not apparently give the reader a great assurance of the joy of life.

Yet how is this? For I am no disbeliever in spiritual purpose and no vague believer. I see from the standpoint of Christian orthodoxy. This means that for me the meaning of life is centered in our Redemption by Christ and that what I see in the world I see in its relation to that. . . .

The novelist with Christian concerns will find in modern life distortions which are repugnant to him, and his problem will be to make these appear as distortions to an audience which is used to seeing them as natural; and he may well be forced to take ever more violent means to get his vision across to this hostile audience. When you can assume that your audience holds the same beliefs you do, you can relax a little and use more normal ways of talking to it;

when you have to assume that it does not, then you have to make your vision apparent by shock—to the hard of hearing you shout, and for the almost blind you draw large and startling figures.

## From "Some Aspects of the Grotesque in Southern Fiction" [1960]

If the writer believes that our life is and will remain essentially mysterious, if he looks upon us as beings existing in a created order to whose laws we freely respond, then what he sees on the surface will be of interest to him only as he can go through it into an experience of mystery itself. His kind of fiction will always be pushing its own limits outward toward the limits of mystery, because for this kind of writer, the meaning of a story does not begin except at a depth where the adequate motivation and the adequate psychology and the various determinations have been exhausted. Such a writer will be interested in what we don't understand rather than in what we do. He will be interested in possibility rather than in probability. He will be interested in characters who are forced out to meet evil and grace and who act on a trust beyond themselves—whether they know very clearly what it is they act upon or not. To the modern mind, this kind of character, and his creator, are typical Don Quixotes, tilting at what is not there.

## From "The Nature and Aim of Fiction" [Date Unknown]

The novel works by a slower accumulation of detail than the short story does. The short story requires more drastic procedures than the novel because more has to be accomplished in less space. The details have to carry more immediate weight. In good fiction, certain of the details will tend to accumulate meaning from the story itself, and when this happens, they become symbolic in their action.

Now the word *symbol* scares a good many people off, just as the word *art* does. They seem to feel that a symbol is some mysterious thing put in arbitrarily by the writer to frighten the common reader—sort of a literary Masonic grip that is only for the initiated. They seem to think that it is a way of saying something that you aren't actually saying, and so if they can be got to read a reputedly symbolic work at all, they approach it as if it were a problem in algebra. Find *x*. And when they do find or think they find this abstraction, *x*, then they go off with an elaborate sense of satisfaction and the notion that they have "understood" the story. Many students confuse the *process* of understanding a thing with understanding it.

I think that for the fiction writer himself, symbols are something he uses simply as a matter of course. You might say that these are details that, while having their essential place in the literal level of the story, operate in depth as well as on the surface, increasing the story in every direction. . . .

People have a habit of saying, "What is the theme of your story?" and they expect you to give them a statement: "The theme of my story is the economic pressure of the machine on the middle class"—or some such absurdity. And when they've got a statement like that, they go off happy and feel it is no longer necessary to read the story.

Some people have the notion that you read the story and then climb out of it into the meaning, but for the fiction writer himself the whole story is the meaning, because it is an experience, not an abstraction.

## From "Writing Short Stories"    [Date Unknown]

Being short does not mean being slight. A short story should be long in depth and should give us an experience of meaning. . . .

Meaning is what keeps the short story from being short. I prefer to talk about the meaning in a story rather than the theme of a story. People talk about the theme of a story as if the theme were like the string that a sack of chicken feed is tied with. They think that if you can pick out the theme, the way you pick the right thread in the chicken-feed sack, you can rip the story open and feed the chickens. But this is not the way meaning works in fiction.

When you can state the theme of a story, when you can separate it from the story itself, then you can be sure the story is not a very good one. The meaning of a story has to be embodied in it, has to be made concrete in it. A story is a way to say something that can't be said any other way, and it takes every word in the story to say what the meaning is. You tell a story because a statement would be inadequate. When anybody asks what a story is about, the only proper thing is to tell him to read the story. The meaning of fiction is not abstract meaning but experienced meaning, and the purpose of making statements about the meaning of a story is only to help you to experience that meaning more fully.

## "A Reasonable Use of the Unreasonable"    [1957]

Last fall I received a letter from a student who said she would be "graciously appreciative" if I would tell her "just what enlightenment" I expected her to get from each of my stories. I suspect she had a paper to write. I wrote her back to forget about the enlightenment and just try to enjoy them. I knew that was the most unsatisfactory answer I could have given because, of course, she didn't want to enjoy them, she just wanted to figure them out.

In most English classes the short story has become a kind of literary specimen to be dissected. Every time a story of mine appears in a Freshman anthology, I have a vision of it, with its little organs laid open, like a frog in a bottle.

I realize that a certain amount of this what-is-the-significance has to go on, but I think something has gone wrong in the process when, for so many students, the story becomes simply a problem to be solved, something which you evaporate to get Instant Enlightenment.

A story really isn't any good unless it successfully resists paraphrase, unless it hangs on and expands in the mind. Properly, you analyze to enjoy, but it's equally true that to analyze with any discrimination, you have to have enjoyed already, and I think that the best reason to hear a story read is that it should stimulate that primary enjoyment.

I don't have any pretensions to being an Aeschylus or Sophocles and providing you in this story with a cathartic experience out of your mythic background, though this story I'm going to read certainly calls up a good deal of the South's mythic background, and it should elicit from you a degree of pity and terror, even though its way of being serious is a comic one. I do think, though, that like the Greeks you should know what is going to happen in this story so that any element of suspense in it will be transferred from its surface to its interior.

I would be most happy if you had already read it, happier still if you knew it well, but since experience has taught me to keep my expectations along these lines modest, I'll tell you that this is the story of a family of six which, on its way driving to Florida, gets wiped out by an escaped convict who calls himself The Misfit. The family is made up of the Grandmother and her son, Bailey, and his children, John Wesley and June Star and the baby, and there is also the cat and the children's mother. The cat is named Pitty Sing, and the Grandmother is taking him with them, hidden in a basket.

Now I think it behooves me to try to establish with you the basis on which reason operates in this story. Much of my fiction takes its character from a reasonable use of the unreasonable, though the reasonableness of my use of it may not always be apparent. The assumptions that underlie this use of it, however, are those of the central Christian mysteries. These are assumptions to which a large part of the modern audience takes exception. About this I can only say that there are perhaps other ways than my own in which this story could be read, but none other by which it could have been written. Belief, in my own case anyway, is the engine that makes perception operate.

The heroine of this story, the Grandmother, is in the most significant position life offers the Christian. She is facing death. And to all appearances she, like the rest of us, is not too well prepared for it. She would like to see the event postponed. Indefinitely.

I've talked to a number of teachers who use this story in class and who tell their students that the Grandmother is evil, that in fact, she's a witch, even down to the cat. One of these teachers told me that his students, and particularly his Southern students, resisted this interpretation with a certain bemused vigor, and he didn't understand why. I had to tell him that they resisted it because they all had grandmothers or great-aunts just like her at home, and they knew, from personal experience, that the old lady lacked comprehension, but that she had a good heart. The Southerner is usually tolerant of those weaknesses that proceed from innocence, and he knows that a taste for self-preservation can be readily combined with the missionary spirit.

This same teacher was telling his students that morally The Misfit was several cuts above the Grandmother. He had a really sentimental attachment to The Misfit. But then a prophet gone wrong is almost always more interesting than your grandmother, and you have to let people take their pleasures where they find them.

It is true that the old lady is a hypocritical old soul; her wits are no match for The Misfit's, nor is her capacity for grace equal to his; yet I think the unprejudiced reader will feel that the Grandmother has a special kind of triumph in this story which instinctively we do not allow to someone altogether bad.

I often ask myself what makes a story work, and what makes it hold up as a story, and I have decided that it is probably some action, some gesture of a character that is unlike any other in the story, one which indicates where the real heart of the story lies. This would have to be an action or a gesture which was both totally right and totally unexpected; it would have to be one that was both in character and beyond character; it would have to suggest both the world and eternity. The action or gesture I'm talking about would have to be on the anagogical level, that is, the level which has to do with the Divine life and our participation in it. It would be a gesture that transcended any neat allegory that might have been intended or any pat moral categories a reader could make. It would be a gesture which somehow made contact with mystery.

There is a point in this story where such a gesture occurs. The Grandmother is at last alone, facing The Misfit. Her head clears for an instant and she realizes, even in her limited way, that she is responsible for the man before her and joined to him by ties of kinship which have their roots deep in the mystery she has been merely prattling about so far. And at this point, she does the right thing, she makes the right gesture.

I find that students are often puzzled by what she says and does here, but I think myself that if I took out this gesture and what she says with it, I would have no story. What was left would not be worth your attention. Our age not only does not have a very sharp eye for the almost imperceptible intrusions of grace, it no longer has much feeling for the nature of the violences which precede and follow them. The devil's greatest wile, Baudelaire has said, is to convince us that he does not exist.

I suppose the reasons for the use of so much violence in modern fiction will differ with each writer who uses it, but in my own stories I have found that violence is strangely capable of returning my characters to reality and preparing them to accept their moment of grace. Their heads are so hard that almost nothing else will do the work. This idea, that reality is something to which we must be returned at considerable cost, is one which is seldom understood by the casual reader, but it is one which is implicit in the Christian view of the world.

I don't want to equate The Misfit with the devil. I prefer to think that, however unlikely this may seem, the old lady's gesture, like the mustard-seed, will grow to be a great crow-filled tree in The Misfit's heart, and will be enough of a pain to him there to turn him into the prophet he was meant to become. But that's another story.

This story has been called grotesque, but I prefer to call it literal. A good story is literal in the same sense that a child's drawing is literal. When a child draws, he doesn't intend to distort but to set down exactly what he sees, and as his gaze is direct, he sees the lines that create motion. Now the lines of motion that interest the writer are usually invisible. They are lines of spiritual motion. And in this story you should be on the lookout for such things as the action of grace in the Grandmother's soul, and not for the dead bodies.

We hear many complaints about the prevalence of violence in modern fiction, and it is always assumed that this violence is a bad thing and meant to be an end in itself. With the serious writer, violence is never an end in itself. It is the extreme situation that best reveals what we are essentially, and I believe these are times when writers are more interested in what we are essentially than in the tenor of our daily lives. Violence is a force which can be used for good or evil, and among other things taken by it is the kingdom of heaven. But regardless of what can be taken by it, the man in the violent situation reveals those qualities least dispensable in his personality, those qualities which are all he will have to take into eternity with him; and since the characters in this story are all on the verge of eternity, it is appropriate to think of what they take with them. In any case, I hope that if you consider these points in connection with the story, you will come to see it as something more than an account of a family murdered on the way to Florida.

## On Interpreting "A Good Man is Hard to Find"

*A professor of English had sent O'Connor the following letter:*

"I am writing as spokesman for three members of our department and some ninety university students in three classes who for a week now have been discussing your story 'A Good Man Is Hard to Find.' We have debated at length several possible interpretations, none of which fully satisfies us. In general we believe that the appearance of The Misfit is not 'real' in the same sense that the incidents of the first half of the story are real. Bailey, we believe, imagines the appearance of The Misfit, whose activities have been called to his attention on the night before the trip and again during the stopover at the roadside restaurant. Bailey, we further believe, identifies himself with The Misfit and so plays two roles in the imaginary last half of the story. But we cannot, after great effort, determine the point at which reality fades into illusion or reverie. Does the accident literally occur, or is it a part of Bailey's dream? Please believe me when I say we are not seeking an easy way out of our difficulty. We admire your story and have examined it with great care, but we are convinced that we are missing something important which you intended for us to grasp. We will all be very grateful if you comment on the interpretation which I have outlined above and if you will give us further comments about your intention in writing 'A Good Man Is Hard to Find.'"

*She replied:*

28 March 61

*(To a Professor of English)*

The interpretation of your ninety students and three teachers is fantastic and about as far from my intentions as it could get to be. If it were a legitimate interpretation, the story would be little more than a trick and its interest would be simply for abnormal psychology. I am not interested in abnormal psychology.

There is a change of tension from the first part of the story to the second where The Misfit enters, but this is no lessening of reality. This story is, of course, not meant to be realistic in the sense that it portrays the everyday doings of people in Georgia. It is stylized and its conventions are comic even though its meaning is serious.

Bailey's only importance is as the Grandmother's boy and the driver of the car. It is the Grandmother who first recognizes The Misfit and who is most concerned with him throughout. The story is a duel of sorts between

the Grandmother and her superficial beliefs and The Misfit's more profoundly felt involvement with Christ's action which set the world off balance for him.

The meaning of a story should go on expanding for the reader the more
he thinks about it, but meaning cannot be captured in an interpretation. If
teachers are in the habit of approaching a story as if it were a research
problem for which any answer is believable so long as it is not obvious, then
I think students will never learn to enjoy fiction. Too much interpretation is
certainly worse than too little, and where feeling for a story is absent, theory
will not supply it.

My tone is not meant to be obnoxious. I am in a state of shock.

# Tobias Wolff: Four Stories, Comments About Writing, and an Essay by a Student

*Tobias Wolff was born in Birmingham, Alabama, in 1945,
but he was raised in the state of Washington. He served in
the army between 1964 and 1968, including a tour of
duty in Vietnam. He graduated from Oxford University in
1972 and then studied creative writing at Stanford. Wolff's
first two books were* In the Garden of North American
Martyrs *(1981) and* Back in the World *(1985), collections of
short stories that both received good reviews. He achieved
greater success and acclaim with the publication of* The
Boy's Life *(1989), a memoir of his teenage years. He also
has written a memoir of his military service,* In Pharaoh's
Army *(1994). The author of many short stories and two novels, his recent publications include* Our Story Begins: New and Selected Stories *(2008). From 1980
to 1997, Wolff taught courses in English and in creative writing at Syracuse
University, and, since then, he has taught at Stanford, where he is the Ward W.
and Priscilla B. Woods Professor in the School of Humanities and Sciences.*

*In an essay in the* London Review of Books, *on Wolff's work, the critic Wyatt
Mason comments:* "Typically, his protagonists face an acute moral dilemma, unable to reconcile what they know to be true with what they feel to be true. Duplicity is their great failing, and Wolff's main theme." *The novelist and essayist
Robert Stone, focusing on Wolff's achievement as a writer of short stories, states:*

> *The work of Tobias Wolff provides a blend of satisfactions not always
> available in combination. Wolff is both subtle and passionate. He
> often appears as a wry but sympathetic observer of the disappoint-
> ments and petty strategies that define obscure unexamined lives. Yet,
> his true subject is nothing less than the world, how it goes. (*Times
> Literary Supplement, *15 November 1996)*

## Hunters in the Snow                                                    [1982]

Tub had been waiting for an hour in the falling snow. He paced the sidewalk
to keep warm and stuck his head out over the curb whenever he saw lights

approaching. The fall of snow thickened. Tub stood below the overhang of a building. Across the road the clouds whitened just above the rooftops, and the whiteness seeped up through the sky. He shifted the rifle strap to his other shoulder.

A truck slid around the corner, horn blaring, rear end sashaying. Tub moved to the sidewalk and held up his hand. The truck jumped the curb and kept coming, half on the street and half on the sidewalk. It wasn't slowing down at all. Tub stood for a moment, still holding up his hand, then jumped back. His rifle slipped off his shoulder, clattering on the ice, and a sandwich fell out of his pocket. The truck went careening past him and stopped at the end of the block.

Tub picked up his sandwich and slung the rifle and walked down to the truck. The driver was bent against the steering wheel, slapping his knees and drumming his feet on the floorboards. He looked like a cartoon of a person laughing. "Tub, you ought to see yourself," he said. "You look just like a beach ball with a hat on. Doesn't he, Frank?"

The man beside him smiled and looked off.

5    "You almost ran me down," Tub said. "You could've killed me."

"Come on, Tub," said the man beside the driver. "Be mellow. Kenny was just messing around." He opened the door and slid over to the middle of the seat.

Tub took the bolt out of his rifle and climbed in beside him. "My feet are frozen," he said. "If you meant ten o'clock, why didn't you *say* ten o'clock?"

"Tub, you haven't done anything but complain since we got here," said the man in the middle. "If you want to piss and moan all day you might as well go home and bitch at your kids. Take your pick." When Tub didn't say anything, he turned to the driver. "Okay, Kenny, let's hit the road."

Some juvenile delinquents had heaved a brick through the windshield on the driver's side, so the cold and snow funneled right into the cab. The heater didn't work. They covered themselves with a couple of blankets Kenny had brought along and pulled down the flaps on their caps. Tub tried to keep his hands warm by rubbing them under the blanket, but Frank made him stop.

10    They left Spokane and drove deep into the country, running along black lines of fences. The snow let up, but still there was no edge to the land where it met the sky. Nothing moved in the chalky fields. The cold bleached their faces and made the stubble stand out on their cheeks and along their upper lips. They stopped twice for coffee before they got to the woods where Kenny wanted to hunt.

Tub was for trying someplace different; two years in a row they'd been up and down this land and hadn't seen a thing. Frank didn't care one way or the other, he just wanted to get out of the goddamned truck. "Feel that," he said, slamming the door. He spread his feet and closed his eyes and leaned his head back and breathed deeply. "Tune in on that energy."

"Another thing," Kenny said. "This is open land. Most of the land around here is posted."

"I'm cold," Tub said.

Frank breathed out. "Stop bitching, Tub. Get centered."

"I wasn't bitching."

15    "Centered," Kenny said. "Next thing you'll be wearing a nightgown, Frank. Selling flowers out at the airport."

"Kenny," Frank said, "you talk too much."

"Okay," Kenny said. "I won't say a word. Like I won't say anything about a certain babysitter."

"What babysitter?" Tub asked.

20      "That's between us," Frank said, looking at Kenny.

Kenny laughed.

"You're asking for it," Frank said.

"Asking for what?"

"Hey," Tub said, "are we hunting or what?"

25      They started off across the field. Tub had trouble getting through the fences. Frank and Kenny could have helped him; they could've lifted up the top wire and stepped on the bottom wire, but they didn't. They stood and watched him. There were a lot of fences, and Tub was puffing when they reached the woods.

They hunted for two hours and saw no deer, no tracks, no sign. Finally they stopped by the creek to eat. Kenny had several slices of pizza and a couple of candy bars; Frank had a sandwich, an apple, two carrots, and a square of chocolate; Tub ate one hard-boiled egg and a stick of celery.

"You ask me how I want to die today," Kenny said, "I'll tell you burn me at the stake." He turned to Tub. "You still on that diet?" He winked at Frank.

"What do you think? You think I like hard-boiled eggs?"

"All I can say is, it's the first diet I ever heard of where you gained weight from it."

30      "Who said I gained weight?"

"Oh, pardon me. I take it back. You're just wasting away before my very eyes. Isn't he, Frank?"

Frank had his fingers fanned out on the stump where he'd laid his food. His knuckles were hairy. He wore a heavy wedding band and on his right pinkie another gold ring with a flat face and an "F" in what looked like diamonds. "Tub," he said, "you haven't seen your own balls in ten years."

Kenny doubled over laughing. He took off his hat and slapped his leg with it.

"What am I supposed to do?" Tub said. "It's my glands."

35      They left the woods and hunted along the creek. Frank and Kenny worked one bank and Tub worked the other, moving upstream. The snow was light but the drifts were deep and hard to move through. Wherever Tub looked the surface was smooth, undisturbed, and after a time he lost interest. He stopped looking for tracks and just tried to keep up with Frank and Kenny on the other side. A moment came when he realized he hadn't seen them in a long time. The breeze was moving from him to them; when it stilled he could sometimes hear Kenny laughing—nothing more. He quickened his pace, breasting the drifts, fighting away the snow. He heard his heart and felt the flush on his face but never once stopped.

Tub caught up with Frank and Kenny at a bend of the creek. They were standing on a log that stretched from their bank to his. Ice had backed up behind the log. Frozen reeds stuck out.

"See anything?" Frank asked.

Tub shook his head.

There wasn't much daylight left and they decided to head back toward the road. Frank and Kenny crossed the log and they all started downstream, using the trail Tub had broken. Before they'd gone very far Kenny stopped. "Look at that," he said, and pointed to some tracks going from the creek back into the woods. Tub's footprints crossed right over them. There on the bank, plain as day, were several mounds of deer shit. "What do you think that is, Tub?" Kenny kicked at it. "Walnuts on vanilla icing?"

"I guess I didn't notice."

Kenny looked at Frank.

"I was lost."

"You were lost. Big deal."

40    They followed the tracks into the woods. The deer had gone over a fence half buried in drifting snow. A no-hunting sign was nailed to the top of one of the posts. Kenny wanted to go after him but Frank said no way, the people out here didn't mess around. He thought maybe the farmer who owned the land would let them use it if they asked. Kenny wasn't so sure. Anyway, he figured that by the time they walked to the truck and drove up the road and doubled back it would be almost dark.

"Relax," Frank said. "You can't hurry nature. If we're meant to get that deer, we'll get it. If we're not, we won't."

They started back toward the truck. This part of the woods was mainly pine. The snow was shaded and had a glaze on it. It held up Kenny and Frank but Tub kept falling through. As he kicked forward, the edge of the crust bruised his shins. Kenny and Frank pulled ahead of him, to where he couldn't even hear their voices anymore. He sat down on a stump and wiped his face. He ate both his sandwiches and half the cookies, taking his own sweet time. It was dead quiet.

When Tub crossed the last fence into the road the truck started moving. He had to run for it and just managed to grab hold of the tailgate and hoist himself into the bed. He lay there, panting. Kenny looked out the rear window and grinned. Tub crawled into the lee of the cab to get out of the freezing wind. He pulled his earflaps low and pushed his chin into the collar of his coat. Someone rapped on the window but Tub wouldn't turn around.

He and Frank waited outside while Kenny went into the farmhouse to ask permission. The house was old and paint was curling off the sides. The smoke streamed westward off the top of the chimney, fanning away into a thin gray plume. Above the ridge of the hills another ridge of blue clouds was rising.

45    "You've got a short memory," Tub said.

"What?" Frank said. He had been staring off.

"I used to stick up for you."

"Okay, so you used to stick up for me. What's eating you?"

"You shouldn't have just left me back there like that."

50    "You're a grown-up, Tub. You can take care of yourself. Anyway, if you think you're the only person with problems I can tell you that you're not."

"Is something bothering you, Frank?"

Frank kicked at a branch poking out of the snow. "Never mind," he said.

"What did Kenny mean about the babysitter?"

"Kenny talks too much," Frank said.

55    Kenny came out of the farmhouse and gave the thumbs-up and they began walking back toward the woods. As they passed the barn a large black hound with a grizzled snout ran out and barked at them. Every time he

barked he slid backward a bit, like a cannon recoiling. Kenny got down on all fours and snarled and barked back at him, and the dog slunk away into the barn, looking over his shoulder and peeing a little as he went.

"That's an old-timer," Frank said. "A real graybeard. Fifteen years if he's a day."

"Too old," Kenny said.

Past the barn they cut off through the fields. The land was unfenced and the crust was freezing up thick, so they made good time. They kept to the edge of the field until they picked up the tracks again and followed them into the woods, farther and farther back toward the hills. The trees started to blur with the shadows, and the wind rose and needled their faces with the crystals it swept off the glaze. Finally they lost the tracks.

Kenny swore and threw down his hat. "This is the worst day of hunting I ever had, bar none." He picked up his hat and brushed off the snow. "This will be the first season since I was fifteen I haven't got my deer."

60    "It isn't the deer," Frank said. "It's the hunting. There are all these forces out here and you just have to go with them."

"You go with them," Kenny said. "I came out here to get me a deer, not listen to a bunch of hippie bullshit. And if it hadn't been for Dimples here I would have too."

"That's enough," Frank said.

"And you—you're so busy thinking about that little jailbait of yours you wouldn't know a deer if you saw one."

"Drop dead," Frank said, and turned away.

65    Kenny and Tub followed him back across the fields. When they were coming up to the barn Kenny stopped and pointed. "I hate that post," he said. He raised his rifle and fired. It sounded like a dry branch cracking. The post splintered along its right side, up toward the top. "There," Kenny said. "It's dead."

"Knock it off," Frank said, walking ahead.

Kenny looked at Tub. He smiled. "I hate that tree," he said, and fired again. Tub hurried to catch up with Frank. He started to speak but just then the dog ran out of the barn and barked at them. "Easy, boy," Frank said.

"I hate that dog." Kenny was behind them.

"That's enough," Frank said. "You put that gun down."

70    Kenny fired. The bullet went in between the dog's eyes. He sank right down into the snow, his legs splayed out on each side, his yellow eyes open and staring. Except for the blood he looked like a small bearskin rug. The blood ran down the dog's muzzle into the snow.

They all looked at the dog lying there.

"What did he ever do to you?" Tub asked. "He was just barking."

Kenny turned to Tub. "I hate you."

Tub shot from the waist. Kenny jerked backward against the fence and buckled to his knees. He knelt there with his hands pressed across his stomach. "Look," he said. His hands were covered with blood. In the dusk his blood was more blue than red. It seemed to belong to the shadows. It didn't seem out of place. Kenny eased himself onto his back. He sighed several times, deeply. "You shot me," he said.

75    "I had to," Tub said. He knelt beside Kenny. "Oh God," he said. "Frank. Frank."

Frank hadn't moved since Kenny killed the dog.

"Frank!" Tub shouted.

"I was just kidding around," Kenny said. "It was a joke. Oh!" he said, and arched his back suddenly. "Oh!" he said again, and dug his heels into the snow and pushed himself along on his head. Then he stopped and lay there, rocking back and forth on his heels and head like a wrestler doing warm-up exercises.

"Kenny," Frank said. He bent down and put his gloved hand on Kenny's brow. "You shot him," he said to Tub.

80    "He made me," Tub said.

"No, no, no," Kenny said.

Tub was weeping from the eyes and nostrils. His whole face was wet. Frank closed his eyes, then looked down at Kenny again. "Where does it hurt?"

"Everywhere," Kenny said, "just everywhere."

"Oh God," Tub said.

85    "I mean, where did it go in?" Frank said.

"Here." Kenny pointed at the wound in his stomach. It was welling slowly with blood.

"You're lucky," Frank said. "It's on the left side. It missed your appendix. If it had hit your appendix you'd really be in the soup." He turned and threw up onto the snow, holding his sides as if to keep warm.

"Are you all right?" Tub said.

"There's some aspirin in the truck," Kenny said.

90    "I'm all right," Frank said.

"For me," Kenny said.

"We'd better call an ambulance," Tub said.

"Jesus," Frank said. "What are we going to say?"

"Exactly what happened," Tub said. "He was going to shoot me but I shot him first."

95    "No sir!" Kenny said. "I wasn't either!"

Frank patted Kenny on the arm. "Easy does it, partner." He stood. "Let's go."

Tub picked up Kenny's rifle as they walked down toward the farmhouse. "No sense leaving this around," he said. "Kenny might get ideas."

"I can tell you one thing," Frank said. "You've really done it this time. This definitely takes the cake."

They had to knock on the door twice before it was opened by a thin man with lank hair. The room behind him was filled with smoke. He squinted at them. "You get anything?" he asked.

100    "No," Frank said.

"I knew you wouldn't. That's what I told the other fellow."

"We've had an accident."

The man looked past Frank and Tub into the gloom. "Shoot your friend, did you?"

Frank nodded.

105    "I did," Tub said.

"I suppose you want to use the phone."

"If it's okay."

The man in the doorway looked behind him, then stepped back. Frank and Tub followed him into the house. There was a woman sitting by the stove in the middle of the room. The stove was smoking badly. She looked up and then down again at the child asleep in her lap. Her face was white and damp; strands of hair were pasted across her forehead. Tub warmed his hands over the stove while Frank went into the kitchen to call. The man who'd let them in stood at the window, his hands in his pockets.

"My friend shot your dog," Tub said.

110    The man nodded without turning around. "I should have done it myself. I just couldn't."

"He loved that dog so much," the woman said. The child squirmed and she rocked it.

"You asked him to?" Tub said. "You asked him to shoot your dog?"

"He was old and sick. Couldn't chew his food anymore. I should have done it myself."

"You couldn't have," the woman said. "Never in a million years."

115    The man shrugged.

Frank came out of the kitchen. "We'll have to take him ourselves. The nearest hospital is fifty miles from here and all their ambulances are out already."

The woman knew a shortcut but the directions were complicated and Tub had to write them down. The man told them where they could find some boards to carry Kenny on. He didn't have a flashlight but said he'd turn the porch light on.

It was dark outside. The clouds were low and heavy and the wind blew in shrill gusts. There was a screen loose on the house and it banged slowly and then quickly as the wind rose again. Frank went for the boards while Tub looked for Kenny, who was not where they had left him. Tub found him farther up the drive, lying on his stomach. "You okay?" Tub said.

"It hurts."

120    "Frank says it missed your appendix."

"I already had my appendix out."

"All right," Frank said, coming up to them. "We'll have you in a nice warm bed before you can say Jack Robinson." He put the two boards on Kenny's right side.

"Just as long as I don't have one of those male nurses," Kenny said.

"Ha ha," Frank said. "That's the spirit. Ready, set, *over you go*," and he rolled Kenny onto the boards. Kenny screamed and kicked his legs in the air. When he quieted down Frank and Tub lifted the boards and carried him down the drive. Tub had the back end, and with the snow blowing into his face he had trouble with his footing. Also he was tired and the man inside had forgotten to turn the porch light on. Just past the house Tub slipped and threw out his hands to catch himself. The boards fell and Kenny tumbled out and rolled to the bottom of the drive, yelling the whole way down. He came to rest against the right front wheel of the truck.

125    "You fat moron," Frank said. "You aren't good for diddly."

Tub grabbed Frank by the collar and backed him hard up against the fence. Frank tried to pull his hands away but Tub shook him and snapped his head back and forth and finally Frank gave up.

"What do you know about fat," Tub said. "What do you know about glands." As he spoke he kept shaking Frank. "What do you know about me."

"All right," Frank said.

"No more," Tub said.

130       "All right."

"No more talking to me like that. No more watching. No more laughing."

"Okay, Tub. I promise."

Tub let go of Frank and turned away. His arms hung straight at his sides.

"I'm sorry, Tub." Frank touched him on the shoulder. "I'll be down at the truck."

135       Tub stood by the fence for a while and then got the rifles off the porch. Frank had rolled Kenny back onto the boards and they lifted him into the bed of the truck. Frank spread the seat blankets over him. "Warm enough?" he asked.

Kenny nodded.

"Okay. Now how does reverse work on this thing?"

"All the way to the left and up." Kenny sat up as Frank started forward to the cab. "Frank!"

"What?"

140       "If it sticks don't force it."

The truck started right away. "One thing," Frank said, "you've got to hand it to the Japanese. A very ancient, very spiritual culture and they can still make a hell of a truck." He glanced over at Tub. "Look, I'm sorry. I didn't know you felt like that, honest to God I didn't. You should've said something."

"I did."

"When? Name one time."

"A couple hours ago."

145       "I guess I wasn't paying attention."

"That's true, Frank," Tub said. "You don't pay attention very much."

"Tub," Frank said, "what happened back there, I should've been more sympathetic. I realize that. You were going through a lot. I just want you to know it wasn't your fault. He was asking for it."

"You think so?"

"Absolutely. It was him or you. I would've done the same thing in your shoes, no question."

150       The wind was blowing into their faces. The snow was a moving white wall in front of their lights; it swirled into the cab through the hole in the windshield and settled on them. Tub clapped his hands and shifted around to stay warm, but it didn't work.

"I'm going to have to stop," Frank said. "I can't feel my fingers."

Up ahead they saw some lights off the road. It was a tavern. In the parking lot there were several jeeps and trucks. A couple of them had deer strapped across their hoods. Frank parked and they went back to Kenny. "How you doing, partner?" Frank said.

"I'm cold."

"Well, don't feel like the Lone Ranger. It's worse inside, take my word for it. You should get that windshield fixed."

155       "Look," Tub said, "he threw the blankets off." They were lying in a heap against the tailgate.

"Now look, Kenny," Frank said, "it's no use whining about being cold if you're not going to try and keep warm. You've got to do your share." He spread the blankets over Kenny and tucked them in at the corners.

"They blew off."

"Hold on to 'em, then."

"Why are we stopping, Frank?"

160    "Because if me and Tub don't get warmed up we're going to freeze solid and then where will you be?" He punched Kenny lightly in the arm. "So just hold your horses."

The bar was full of men in colored jackets, mostly orange. The waitress brought coffee. "Just what the doctor ordered," Frank said, cradling the steaming cup in his hand. "Tub, I've been thinking. What you said about me not paying attention, that's true."

"It's okay."

"No. I really had that coming. I guess I've just been a little too interested in old number one. I've had a lot on my mind. Not that that's any excuse."

"Forget it, Frank. I sort of lost my temper back there. I guess we're both a little on edge."

165    Frank shook his head. "It isn't just that."

"You want to talk about it?"

"Just between us, Tub?"

"Sure, Frank. Just between us."

"Tub, I think I'm going to be leaving Nancy."

170    "Oh, Frank. Oh, Frank." Tub sat back and shook his head.

Frank reached out and laid his hand on Tub's arm. "Tub, have you ever been really in love?"

"Well—"

"I mean *really* in love." He squeezed Tub's wrist. "With your whole being."

"I don't know. When you put it like that, I don't know."

175    "Then you haven't. Nothing against you, but you'd know it if you had." Frank let go of Tub's arm. "This isn't just some bit of fluff I'm talking about."

"Who is she, Frank?"

Frank paused. He looked into his empty cup. "Roxanne Brewer."

"Cliff Brewer's kid? The babysitter?"

"You can't just put people into categories like that, Tub. That's why the whole system is wrong. And that's why this country's going to hell in a rowboat."

180    Tub shook his head. "But she can't be more than—"

"Sixteen. She'll be seventeen in May." Frank smiled. "May fourth, three twenty-seven p.m. Hell, Tub, a hundred years ago she'd have been an old maid by that age. Juliet was only thirteen."

"Juliet? Juliet Miller? Jesus, Frank, she doesn't even have breasts. She's still collecting frogs."

"Not Juliet Miller. The *real* Juliet. Tub, don't you see how you're dividing people up into categories? He's an executive, she's a secretary, he's a truck driver, she's sixteen years old. Tub, this so-called babysitter, this so-called sixteen-year-old, has more in her little finger than most of us have in our entire bodies. I can tell you this little lady is something special."

"I know the kids like her."

185    "She's opened up whole worlds to me that I never knew were there."

"What does Nancy think about all this?"

"She doesn't know."

"You haven't told her?"

"Not yet. It's not so easy. She's been damned good to me all these years. Then there's the kids to consider." The brightness in Frank's eyes trembled and he wiped quickly at them with the back of his hand. "I guess you think I'm a complete bastard."

190    "No, Frank. I don't think that."

"Well, you *ought* to."

"Frank, when you've got a friend it means you've always got someone on your side, no matter what. That's how I feel about it, anyway."

"You mean that, Tub?"

"Sure I do."

195    "You don't know how good it feels to hear you say that."

Kenny had tried to get out of the truck. He was jackknifed over the tailgate, his head hanging above the bumper. They lifted him back into the bed and covered him again. He was sweating and his teeth chattered. "It hurts, Frank."

"It wouldn't hurt so much if you just stayed put. Now we're going to the hospital. Got that? Say it—'I'm going to the hospital.'"

"I'm going to the hospital."

"Again."

200    "I'm going to the hospital."

"Now just keep saying that to yourself and before you know it we'll be there."

After they had gone a few miles Tub turned to Frank. "I just pulled a real boner," he said.

"What's that?"

"I left the directions on the table back there."

205    "That's okay. I remember them pretty well."

The snowfall lightened and the clouds began to roll back off the fields, but it was no warmer, and after a time both Frank and Tub were bitten through and shaking. Frank almost didn't make it around a curve, and they decided to stop at the next roadhouse.

There was an automatic hand dryer in the bathroom and they took turns standing in front of it, opening their jackets and shirts and letting the jet of hot air blow across their faces and chests.

"You know," Tub said, "what you told me back there, I appreciate it. Trusting me."

Frank opened and closed his fingers in front of the nozzle. "The way I look at it, Tub, no man is an island. You've got to trust someone."

210    "Frank?"

Frank waited.

"When I said that about my glands, that wasn't true. The truth is I just shovel it in. Day and night. In the shower. On the freeway." He turned and let the air play over his back. "I've even got stuff in the paper-towel machine at work."

"There's nothing wrong with your glands at all?" Frank had taken his boots and socks off. He held first his right foot, then his left, up to the nozzle.

"No. There never was."

215    "Does Alice know?" The machine went off and Frank started lacing up his boots.

"Nobody knows. That's the worst of it, Frank. Not the being fat—I never got any big kick out of being thin—but the lying. Having to lead a double life like a spy or a hit man. I understand those guys, I know what they go through. Always having to think about what you say and do. Always feeling like people are watching you, trying to catch you at something. Never able to just be yourself. Like when I make a big deal about only having an orange for breakfast and then scarf all the way to work. Oreos, Mars bars, Twinkies. Sugar Babies. Snickers." Tub glanced at Frank and looked quickly away. "Pretty disgusting, isn't it?"

"Tub. Tub." Frank shook his head. "Come on." He took Tub's arm and led him into the restaurant half of the bar. "My friend is hungry," he told the waitress. "Bring four orders of pancakes, plenty of butter and syrup."

"Frank—"

"Sit down."

220    When the dishes came Frank carved out slabs of butter and just laid them on the pancakes. Then he emptied the bottle of syrup, moving it back and forth over the plates. He leaned forward on his elbows and rested his chin in one hand. "Go on, Tub."

Tub ate several mouthfuls, then started to wipe his lips. Frank took the napkin away from him. "No wiping," he said. Tub kept at it. The syrup covered his chin; it dripped to a point like a goatee. "Weigh in, Tub," Frank said, pushing another fork across the table. "Get down to business." Tub took the fork in his left hand and lowered his head and started really chowing down. "Clean your plate," Frank said when the pancakes were gone, and Tub lifted each of the four plates and licked it clean. He sat back, trying to catch his breath.

"Beautiful," Frank said. "Are you full?"

"I'm full," Tub said. "I've never been so full."

Kenny's blankets were bunched up against the tailgate again.

225    "They must've blown off," Tub said.

"They're not doing him any good," Frank said. "We might as well get some use out of them."

Kenny mumbled. Tub bent over him. "What? Speak up."

"I'm going to the hospital," Kenny said.

"Attaboy," Frank said.

230    The blankets helped. The wind still got their faces and Frank's hands, but it was much better. The fresh snow on the road and the trees sparkled under the beam of the headlight. Squares of light from farmhouse windows fell onto the blue snow in the fields.

"Frank," Tub said after a time, "you know that farmer? He told Kenny to kill his dog."

"You're kidding!" Frank leaned forward, considering. "That Kenny. What a card." He laughed, and so did Tub.

Tub smiled out the back window. Kenny lay with his arms folded over his stomach, moving his lips at the stars. Right overhead was the Big Dipper, and behind, hanging between Kenny's feet in the direction of the hospital, was the North Star, polestar, Help to Sailors. As the truck twisted through the gentle hills the star went back and forth between Kenny's boots, staying always in his sight. "I'm going to the hospital," Kenny said. But he was wrong. They had taken a different turn a long way back.

## Say Yes

[1985]

They were doing the dishes, his wife washing while he dried. He'd washed the night before. Unlike most men he knew, he really pitched in on the housework. A few months earlier he'd overheard a friend of his wife's congratulate her on having such a considerate husband, and he thought, *I try.* Helping out with the dishes was one way of showing how considerate he was.

They talked about different things and somehow got on the subject of whether white people should marry black people. He said that all things considered, he thought it was a bad idea.

"Why?" she asked.

Sometimes his wife got this look where she pinched her brows together and bit her lower lip and stared down at something. When he saw her like this he knew he should keep his mouth shut, but he never did. Actually it made him talk more. She had that look now.

5    "Why?" she asked again, and stood there with her hand inside a bowl, not washing it but just holding it above the water.

"Listen," he said, "I went to school with blacks and I've worked with blacks and lived on the same street with blacks and we've always gotten along just fine. I don't need you coming along now and implying that I'm a racist."

"I didn't imply anything," she said, and began washing the bowl again, turning it around in her hand as though she were shaping it. "I just don't see what's wrong with a white person marrying a black person, that's all."

"They don't come from the same culture as we do. Listen to them sometime—they even have their own language. That's okay with me, I *like* hearing them talk"—he did; for some reason it always lifted his mood—"but it's different. A person from their culture and a person from our culture could never really *know* each other."

"Like you know me?" his wife asked.

10    "Yes. Like I know you."

"But if they love each other," she said. She was washing faster now, not looking at him.

*Oh boy,* he thought. He said, "Don't take my word for it. Look at the statistics. Most of those marriages break up."

"Statistics." She was piling dishes on the drainboard at a terrific rate, just swiping at them with the cloth. Many of them were greasy, and he could see flecks of food between the tines of the forks. "All right," she said, "what about foreigners? I suppose you think the same thing about two foreigners getting married."

"Yes," he said, "as a matter of fact I do. How can you understand someone who comes from a completely different background?"

15    "Different," said his wife. "Not the same, like us."

"Yes, different," he snapped, angry with her for resorting to this trick of repeating his words so they sounded crass, or hypocritical. "These are dirty," he said, and dumped all the silverware back into the sink.

The water had gone flat and gray. She stared down at it, her lips pressed tight together, then plunged her hands under the surface. "Oh!" she cried, and jumped back. She took her right hand by the wrist and held it up. Her thumb was bleeding.

"Ann, don't move," he said. "Stay right there." He ran upstairs to the bathroom and rummaged in the medicine chest for alcohol, cotton, and a Band-Aid. When he came back down she was leaning against the refrigerator with her eyes closed, still holding her hand by the wrist. He took the hand and dabbed at her thumb with the cotton. The bleeding had stopped. He squeezed it to see how deep the wound was and a single drop of blood welled up, trembling and bright, and fell to the floor. Over the thumb she stared at him accusingly. "It's shallow," he said. "Tomorrow you won't even know it's there." He hoped that she appreciated how quickly he'd come to her aid. He had acted out of concern for her, with no thought of getting anything in return, but now the thought occurred to him that it would be a nice gesture on her part not to start up that conversation again, as he was tired of it. "I'll finish up here," he said. "You go and relax."

"That's okay," she said. "I'll dry."

20    He began to wash the silverware again, giving a lot of attention to the forks.

"So," she said, "you wouldn't have married me if I'd been black."

"For Christ's sake, Ann!"

"Well, that's what you said, didn't you?"

"No, I did not. The whole question is ridiculous. If you had been black we probably wouldn't even have met. You would've had your friends and I would've had mine. The only black girl I ever really knew was my partner in the debating club, and I was already going out with you by then."

25    "But if we had met, and I'd been black?"

"Then you probably would have been going out with a black guy." He picked up the rinsing nozzle and sprayed the silverware. The water was so hot that the metal darkened to pale blue, then turned silver again.

"Let's say I wasn't," she said. "Let's say I'm black and unattached and we meet and fall in love."

He glanced over at her. She was watching him, and her eyes were bright. "Look," he said, taking a reasonable tone, "this is stupid. If you were black you wouldn't be you." As he said this he realized it was absolutely true. There was no possible argument against the fact that she would not be herself if she were black. So he said it again: "If you were black you wouldn't be you."

"I know," she said, "but let's just say."

30    He took a deep breath. He had won the argument but still felt cornered. "Say what?" he asked.

"That I'm black, but still me, and we fall in love. Will you marry me?"

He thought about it.

"Well?" she said, and stepped close to him. Her eyes were even brighter. "Will you marry me?"

"I'm thinking," he said.

35    "You won't, I can tell. You're going to say no."

"Let's not move too fast on this," he said. "There are lots of things to consider. We don't want to do something we might regret for the rest of our lives."

"No more considering. Yes or no."

"Since you put it that way—"

"Yes or no."

40          "Jesus, Ann. All right—no."

"Thank you," she said, and walked from the kitchen into the living room. A moment later he heard her turning the pages of a magazine. He knew she was too angry to be actually reading it, but she wasn't snapping through the pages like he would've done; she turned them slowly, as if she were studying every word. She was demonstrating her indifference to him, and it had the effect he knew she'd intended. It hurt him.

He had no choice but to demonstrate his indifference to her. Quietly, thoroughly, he washed the rest of the dishes. Then he dried them and put them away. He wiped the counters and the stove and scoured the linoleum where the drop of blood had fallen. While he was at it, he decided, he might as well mop the whole floor. When he was done the kitchen looked new, just as it had when they were first shown the house, before they had ever lived here.

He picked up the garbage pail and went outside. The night was clear and he could see a few stars to the west, where the lights of the town didn't blur them out. On El Camino the traffic was steady and light, peaceful as a river. He felt ashamed that he'd let his wife get him into a fight. In another thirty years or so they both would be dead. What would all that stuff matter then? He thought of the years they had spent together and how close they were and how well they knew each other, and his throat tightened so that he could hardly breathe. His face and neck began to tingle. Warmth flooded his chest. He stood there for a while, enjoying these sensations, then picked up the pail and went out the back gate.

The two mutts from down the street had pulled over the garbage can again. One of them was rolling around on his back and the other had something in its mouth. When they saw him coming they trotted away with short, mincing steps. Normally he would've tossed a rock or two after them, but this time he let them go.

45          The house was dark when he came back inside. She was in the bathroom. He stood outside the door and called her name. He heard bottles clinking, but she didn't answer him. "Ann, I'm really sorry," he said. "I'll make it up to you, I promise."

"How?" she asked.

He wasn't expecting this. But from a sound in her voice, a level and definite note that was strange to him, he knew he had to come up with the right answer. He leaned against the door. "I'll marry you," he whispered.

"We'll see," she said. "Go on to bed. I'll be out in a minute."

He undressed and got under the covers. Finally he heard the bathroom door open and close.

50          "Turn off the light," she said from the hallway.

"What?"

"Turn off the light."

He reached over and pulled the chain on the bedside lamp. The room went dark. "All right," he said. He lay there, but nothing happened. "All right," he said again. Then he heard a movement across the room. He sat up but couldn't see a thing. The room was silent. His heart pounded as it had on their first night together, as it still did when he woke at a noise in the darkness and waited to hear it again—the sound of someone moving through the house, a stranger.

## *Powder*                                          [1992]

Just before Christmas my father took me skiing at Mount Baker. He'd had to fight for the privilege of my company, because my mother was still angry with him for sneaking me into a nightclub during his last visit, to see Thelonius Monk.

He wouldn't give up. He promised, hand on heart, to take good care of me and have me home for dinner on Christmas Eve, and she relented. But as we were checking out of the lodge that morning it began to snow, and in this snow he observed some quality that made it necessary for us to get in one last run. We got in several last runs. He was indifferent to my fretting. Snow whirled around us in bitter, blinding squalls, hissing like sand, and still we skied. As the lift bore us to the peak yet again, my father looked at his watch and said:"Criminey. This'll have to be a fast one."

By now I couldn't see the trail. There was no point in trying. I stuck to him like white on rice and did what he did and somehow made it to the bottom without sailing off a cliff. We returned our skis and my father put chains on the Austin-Healy while I swayed from foot to foot, clapping my mittens and wishing I were home. I could see everything. The green tablecloth, the plates with the holly pattern, the red candles waiting to be lit.

We passed a diner on our way out. "You want some soup?" my father asked. I shook my head. "Buck up," he said. "I'll get you there. Right, doctor?"

5          I was supposed to say, "Right, doctor," but I didn't say anything.

A state trooper waved us down outside the resort. A pair of sawhorses were blocking the road. The trooper came up to our car and bent down to my father's window. His face was bleached by the cold. Snowflakes clung to his eyebrows and to the fur trim of his jacket and cap.

"Don't tell me," my father said.

The trooper told him. The road was closed. It might get cleared, it might not. Storm took everyone by surprise. So much, so fast. Hard to get people moving. Christmas Eve. What can you do?

My father said:"Look. We're talking about four, five inches. I've taken this car through worse than that."

10         The trooper straightened up, boots creaking. His face was out of sight but I could hear him. "The road is closed."

My father sat with both hands on the wheel, rubbing the wood with his thumbs. He looked at the barricade for a long time. He seemed to be trying to master the idea of it. Then he thanked the trooper, and with a weird, old-maidy show of caution turned the car around. "Your mother will never forgive me for this," he said.

"We should have left before," I said. "Doctor."

He didn't speak to me again until we were both in a booth at the diner, waiting for our burgers. "She won't forgive me," he said. "Do you understand? Never."

"I guess," I said, but no guesswork was required; she wouldn't forgive him.

15         "I can't let that happen." He bent toward me. "I'll tell you what I want. I want us to be all together again. Is that what you want?"

"Yes, sir."

He bumped my chin with his knuckles. "That's all I needed to hear."

When we finished eating he went to the pay phone in the back of the diner, then joined me in the booth again. I figured he'd called my mother, but he didn't give a report. He sipped at his coffee and stared out the window at the empty road. "Come on, come on," he said. A little while later he said, "Come on!" When the trooper's car went past, lights flashing, he got up and dropped some money on the check. "O.K. Vámonos."

The wind had died. The snow was falling straight down, less of it now; lighter. We drove away from the resort, right up to the barricade. "Move it," my father told me. When I looked at him he said, "What are you waiting for?" I got out and dragged one of the sawhorses aside, then put it back after he drove through. He pushed the door open for me. "Now you're an accomplice," he said. "We go down together." He put the car into gear and gave me a look. "Joke, doctor."

20      "Funny, doctor."

Down the first long stretch I watched the road behind us, to see if the trooper was on our tail. The barricade vanished. Then there was nothing but snow: snow on the road, snow kicking up from the chains, snow on the trees, snow in the sky; and our trail in the snow. I faced around and had a shock. The lie of the road behind us had been marked by our own tracks, but there were no tracks ahead of us. My father was breaking virgin snow between a line of tall trees. He was humming "Stars Fell on Alabama." I felt snow brush along the floorboards under my feet. To keep my hands from shaking, I clamped them between my knees.

My father grunted in a thoughtful way and said, "Don't ever try this yourself."

"I won't."

"That's what you say now, but someday you'll get your license and then you'll think you can do anything. Only you won't be able to do this. You need, I don't know—a certain instinct."

25      "Maybe I have it."

"You don't. You have your strong points, but not . . . this. I only mention it, because I don't want you to get the idea this is something just anybody can do. I'm a great driver. That's not a virtue, O.K.? It's just a fact, and one you should be aware of. Of course you have to give the old heap some credit, too—there aren't many cars I'd try this with. Listen!"

I listened. I heard the slap of the chains, the stiff, jerky rasps of the wipers, the purr of the engine. It really did purr. The car was almost new. My father couldn't afford it, and kept promising to sell it, but here it was.

I said, "Where do you think that policeman went to?"

"Are you warm enough?" He reached over and cranked up the blower. Then he turned off the wipers. We didn't need them. The clouds had brightened. A few sparse, feathery flakes drifted into our slipstream and were swept away. We left the trees and entered a broad field of snow that ran level for a while and then tilted sharply downward. Orange stakes had been planted at intervals in two parallel lines and my father steered a course between them, though they were far enough apart to leave considerable doubt in my mind as to where exactly the road lay. He was humming again, doing little scat riffs around the melody.

30      "O.K. then. What are my strong points?"

"Don't get me started," he said. "It'd take all day."

"Oh, right. Name one."

"Easy. You always think ahead."

True. I always thought ahead. I was a boy who kept his clothes on numbered hangers to insure proper rotation. I bothered my teachers for homework assignments far ahead of their due dates so I could make up schedules.

I thought ahead, and that was why I knew that there would be other troopers waiting for us at the end of our ride, if we got there. What I did not know was that my father would wheedle and plead his way past them—he didn't sing "O Tannenbaum" but just about—and get me home for dinner, buying a little more time before my mother decided to make the split final. I knew we'd get caught; I was resigned to it. And maybe for this reason I stopped moping and began to enjoy myself.

35      Why not? This was one for the books. Like being in a speedboat, but better. You can't go downhill in a boat. And it was all ours. And it kept coming, the laden trees, the unbroken surface of snow, the sudden white vistas. Here and there I saw hints of the road, ditches, fences, stakes, but not so many that I could have found my way. But then I didn't have to. My father was driving. My father in his 48th year, rumpled, kind, bankrupt of honor, flushed with certainty. He was a great driver. All persuasion, no coercion. Such subtlety at the wheel, such tactful pedalwork. I actually trusted him. And the best was yet to come—the switchbacks and hairpins. Impossible to describe. Except maybe to say this: If you haven't driven fresh powder, you haven't driven.

## Bullet in the Brain                                        [1995]

Anders couldn't get to the bank until just before it closed, so of course the line was endless and he got stuck behind two women whose loud, stupid conversation put him in a murderous temper. He was never in the best of tempers anyway, Anders—a book critic known for the weary, elegant savagery with which he dispatched almost everything he reviewed.

With the line still doubled around the rope, one of the tellers stuck a POSITION CLOSED sign in her window and walked to the back of the bank, where she leaned against a desk and began to pass the time with a man shuffling papers. The women in front of Anders broke off their conversation and watched the teller with hatred. "Oh, that's nice," one of them said. She turned to Anders and added, confident of his accord, "One of those little human touches that keep us coming back for more."

Anders had conceived his own towering hatred of the teller, but he immediately turned it on the presumptuous crybaby in front of him. "Damned unfair," he said. "Tragic, really. If they're not chopping off the wrong leg or bombing your ancestral village, they're closing their positions."

She stood her ground. "I didn't say it was tragic," she said. "I just think it's a pretty lousy way to treat your customers."

5      "Unforgivable," Anders said. "Heaven will take note."

She sucked in her cheeks but stared past him and said nothing. Anders saw that her friend was looking in the same direction. And then the tellers stopped what they were doing, the other customers slowly turned, and silence came over the bank. Two men wearing black ski masks and blue business suits were standing to the side of the door. One of them had a pistol pressed against the guard's neck. The guard's eyes were closed, and his lips were moving. The other man had a sawed-off shotgun. "Keep your big mouth shut!" the man with the pistol said, though no one had spoken a word. "One of you tellers hits the alarm, you're all dead meat."

"Oh, bravo," Anders said. "'*Dead meat.*'" He turned to the woman in front of him. "Great script, eh? The stern, brass-knuckled poetry of the dangerous classes."

She looked at him with drowning eyes.

The man with the shotgun pushed the guard to his knees. He handed the shotgun to his partner and yanked the guard's wrists up behind his back and locked them together with a pair of handcuffs. He toppled him onto the floor with a kick between the shoulder blades, then took his shotgun back and went over to the security gate at the end of the counter. He was short and heavy and moved with peculiar slowness. "Buzz him in," his partner said. The man with the shotgun opened the gate and sauntered along the line of tellers; handing each of them a plastic bag. When he came to the empty position he looked over at the man with the pistol, who said, "Whose slot is that?"

10    Anders watched the teller. She put her hand to her throat and turned to the man she'd been talking to. He nodded. "Mine," she said.

"Then get your ugly ass in gear and fill that bag."

"There you go," Anders said to the woman in-front of him. "Justice is done."

"Hey! Bright boy! Did I tell you to talk?"

"No," Anders said.

15    "Then shut your trap."

"Did you hear that?" Anders said, " 'Bright boy.' Right out of *The Killers*." [1]

"Please, be quiet," the woman said.

"Hey, you deaf or what?" The man with the pistol walked over to Anders and poked the weapon into his gut. "You think I'm playing games?"

"No," Anders said, but the barrel tickled like a stiff finger and he had to fight back the titters. He did this by making himself stare into the man's eyes, which were clearly visible behind the holes in the mask: pale blue and rawly red-rimmed. The man's left eyelid kept twitching. He breathed out a piercing, ammoniac smell that shocked Anders more than anything that had happened, and he was beginning to develop a sense of unease when the man prodded him again with the pistol.

20    "You like me, bright boy?" he said. "You want to suck my dick?"

"No," Anders said.

"Then stop looking at me."

Anders fixed his gaze on the man's shiny wing-tip shoes.

"Not down there. Up there." He stuck the pistol under Anders's chin and pushed it upward until he was looking at the ceiling.

25    Anders had never paid much attention to that part of the bank, a pompous old building with marble floors and counters and gilt scroll-work over the tellers' cages. The domed ceiling had been decorated with mythological figures whose fleshy, toga-draped ugliness Anders had taken in at a glance many years earlier and afterward declined to notice. Now he had no choice but to scrutinize the painter's work. It was even worse than he remembered, and all of it executed with the utmost gravity. The artist had a few tricks up his sleeve and used them again and again—a certain rosy blush on the underside of the clouds, a coy backward glance on the faces of the cupids and fauns. The ceiling was crowded with various dramas, but the one that caught Anders's eye was Zeus and Europa—portrayed, in this rendition, as a bull ogling a cow from behind a haystack. To make the cow sexy, the painter had canted her hips suggestively and

[1] **Bright boy . . . The killers** a gunman in Ernest Hemingway's short story "The Killers" (1927) uses this term.

given her long, droopy eyelashes through which she gazed back at the bull with sultry welcome. The bull wore a smirk and his eyebrows were arched. If there'd been a caption bubbling out of his mouth, it would have said HUBBA HUBBA.

"What's so funny, bright boy?"

"Nothing."

30    "You think I'm comical? You think I'm some kind of clown?"

"No."

"You think you can fuck with me?"

"No."

"Fuck with me again, you're history. *Capiche*?"[2]

Anders burst out laughing. He covered his mouth with both hands and said, "I'm sorry, I'm sorry," then snorted helplessly through his fingers and said, "*Capiche*—oh, God, *capiche*," and at that the man with the pistol raised the pistol and shot Anders right in the head.

The bullet smashed Anders's skull and plowed through his brain and exited behind his right ear, scattering shards of bone into the cerebral cortex, the corpus callosum, back toward the basal ganglia, and down into the thalamus. But before all this occurred, the first appearance of the bullet in the cerebrum set off a crackling chain of ion transports and neurotransmissions. Because of their peculiar origin these traced a peculiar pattern, flukishly calling to life a summer afternoon some forty years past, and long since lost to memory. After striking the cranium, the bullet was moving at nine hundred feet per second, a pathetically sluggish, glacial pace compared with the synaptic lightning that flashed around it. Once in the brain, that is, the bullet came under the mediation of brain time, which gave Anders plenty of leisure to contemplate the scene that, in a phrase he would have abhorred, "passed before his eyes."

35    It is worth noting what Anders did not remember, given what he did recall. He did not remember his first lover, Sherry, or what he had most madly loved about her, before it came to irritate him—her unembarrassed carnality, and especially the cordial way she had with his unit, which she called Mr. Mole, as in *Uh-oh, looks like Mr. Mole wants to play.* Anders did not remember his wife, whom he had also loved before she exhausted him with her predictability, or his daughter, now a sullen professor of economics at Dartmouth. He did not remember standing just outside his daughter's door as she lectured her bear about his naughtiness and described the appalling punishments Paws would receive unless he changed his ways. He did not remember a single line of the hundreds of poems he had committed to memory in his youth so he could give himself the shivers at will—not "Silent, upon a peak in Darien," or "My God, I heard this day," or "All my pretty ones? Did you say all? O hell-kite! All?"[3] None of these did he remember; not one. Anders did not remember his dying mother saying of his father. "I should have stabbed him in his sleep."

---

[2]**Capiche?** Get it? (from the Italian verb, capire, "to understand").    [3]**He did not remember . . . O hell-kite! All?"** The first quotation ("Silent . . . Darien") is from John Keats's "On First Looking into Chapman's Homer" (see page 622); the second ("My God") is from George Herbert's poem called "Man" (early seventeenth century); the third quotation ("All . . . All?") is from Shakespeare's *Macbeth*, 4.3.217, when Macduff learns that Macbeth has killed Macduff's children.

He did not remember Professor Josephs telling his class how Athenian prisoners in Sicily had been released if they could recite Aeschylus,[4] and then reciting Aeschylus himself, right there, in the Greek. Anders did not remember how his eyes had burned at those sounds. He did not remember the surprise of seeing a college classmate's name on the dust jacket of a novel not long after they graduated, or the respect he had felt after reading the book. He did not remember the pleasure of giving respect.

Nor did Anders remember seeing a woman leap to her death from the building opposite his own just days after his daughter was born. He did not remember shouting. "Lord have mercy!" He did not remember deliberately crashing his father's car into a tree, or having his ribs kicked in by three policemen at an antiwar rally, or waking himself up with laughter. He did not remember when he began to regard the heap of books on his desk with boredom and dread, or when he grew angry at writers for writing them. He did not remember when everything began to remind him of something else.

This is what he remembered. Heat. A baseball field. Yellow grass, the whir of insects, himself leaning against a tree as the boys of the neighborhood gather for a pickup game. He looks on as the others argue the relative genius of Mantle and Mays. They have been worrying this subject all summer, and it has become tedious to Anders: an oppression, like the heat.

Then the last two boys arrive, Coyle and a cousin of his from Mississippi. Anders has never met Coyle's cousin before and will never see him again. He says hi with the rest but takes no further notice of him until they've chosen sides and someone asks the cousin what position he wants to play. "Shortstop," the boy says. "Short's the best position they is." Anders turns and looks at him. He wants to hear Coyle's cousin repeat what he's just said, though he knows better than to ask. The others will think he's being a jerk, ragging the kid for his grammar. But that isn't it, not at all—it's that Anders is strangely roused, elated, by those final two words, their pure unexpectedness and their music. He takes the field in a trance, repeating them to himself.

40    The bullet is already in the brain; it won't be outrun forever, or charmed to a halt. In the end it will do its work and leave the troubled skull behind, dragging its comet's tail of memory and hope and talent and love into the marble hall of commerce. That can't be helped. But for now Anders can still make time. Time for the shadows to lengthen on the grass, time for the tethered dog to bark at the flying ball, time for the boy in right field to smack his sweat-blackened mitt and softly chant, *They is, they is, they is.*

---

[4]**Aeschylus** Wolff seems to have made a mistake: Tradition says that some Athenian prisoners in Sicily earned a reprieve by reciting verses from the Greek dramatist Euripides (not, as Wolff says, Aeschylus).

**YOUR TURN**

1. How would you characterize the Anders whom we see in the first part of "Bullet in the Brain" (i.e., up to the place where Wolff indicates a break)? How would you characterize the youthful Anders, the Anders whom we see in the second part of the story?
2. The second part itself can be thought of as having two parts—first, What Anders *did not* remember and second, What Anders *did* remember.

Suppose these two parts (of the second part) had been reversed. What would the story gain or lose?

3. Suppose Wolff showed you the manuscript and said he had not yet chosen a title but he was thinking of the following possibilities, given here in alphabetic order: "Anders," "The Bank Robbery," "Brain Works," "Bullet in the Brain," "Memories, " "Shortstop," "They Is." In an argumentative essay of about 500 words, set forth your choice. You may want to devote approximately equal space to your examination of each candidate, or you may want to (for instance) quickly dispose of the two or three that you think are obviously poor choices—but you will have to explain, briefly why you think they are obviously poor choices—and then spend more time on the remaining (serious) candidates. In any case, please remember that you are writing an argument. *Optional variation:* In your essay you may want to reject all of these candidates and offer a title of your own invention.

# Tobias Wolff on Novels and Short Stories

## On Stories and Poems

**INTERVIEWER:** Your stories remind me of poems, actually.

**WOLFF:** Good. I believe that the short story is as different a form from the novel as poetry is, and the best stories seem to me to be perhaps closer in spirit to poetry than to novels. They have to be; there just can't be any kind of relaxation of the narrative. Everything has to be pulling weight in a short story for it to be really of the first order. And you can't do that with a novel. A novel invites digression and a little relaxation of the grip because a reader can't endure being held that tightly in hand for so long a time.

—From interview, *Salon,* December 1996. Web. 22 Jan, 2010. www.salon.com.

## On Stories and Novels

**INTERVIEWER:** How do the processes of working on a short story or novel or memoir differ from one another, for you? Is there any difference once you've actually sat down and begun to work?

**WOLFF:** In the process itself, no, not really. The great thing about writing a short story is that you know the damn thing's going to end—no time soon, perhaps, but you can see the horizon. But then you're also thinking, Oh no, when I get there I'm going to have to call another world into existence. The beauty of working in a longer form is that, though you can't always see the horizon, and usually don't, you are returning to the same world day after day, enriching it and deepening it. But there's always the anxiety—My God, I haven't finished anything in years. Will I ever do this or will lightning strike me dead before I finish, and will all this time and work be wasted? I have great admiration for people who spend ten, fifteen, twenty years on a single piece of work, the courage and fortitude it takes to do that.

—From "The Art of Fiction," Interview by Jack Livings. *Paris Review* 171. 183 (Fall 2004). Print.

## On Judging Characters

**ORRINGER:** Do you think that the tendency to be hard on yourself in your memoirs translates to the tendency to be hard on the protagonists of your fictional narratives?

**WOLFF:** I hope not. I do write, as indeed most writers do, about things that have gone wrong. There's not much of a story if things have gone right. Stories are about problems, and not the kinds of problems that result from a safe falling out of a window, but from somebody having a choice and having a problem with that choice, and then the series of consequences that follow from making that choice. To portray that honestly is to show the way people parse out their choices, and self-interest naturally comes into play. It isn't so much a matter of wishing to be hard on people as wishing to be truthful. If there's a moral quality to my work, I suppose it has to do with will and the exercise of choice within one's will. The choices we make tend to narrow down a myriad of opportunities to just a few, and those choices tend to reinforce themselves in whatever direction we've started to go, including the wrong direction. Our present government[1] likes to lecture us on the virtue of *staying the course*. Well, maybe it's not such a good idea to stay the course if you're headed toward the rocks. There's something to be said for changing course if you're about to drive your ship onto the shoals.

—From interview by Julie Orringer, *Believer Magazine*, June 2004.
Web. 22 Jan. 2010. www.believermag.com.

## On Ambiguity

Wolff discussed the importance of leaving some ambiguity in each story he writes, in response to an audience member/teacher who asked about the details Wolff used, and their symbolism. "Otherwise,'" he said, "it would just be another Op-Ed piece."

—From Adam Daum, "Tobias Wolff Speaks About Perfection and His New Collection of Short Stories," *Bay Area Intellect*, 30 April 2008. Web. 22 Jan. 2010. www.bayareaintellect.com.

## On Economy in Writing

**INTERVIEWER:** More important than irony to you seems to be economy. You strategically parse out details to create mood and character, such as a character pouring "a long stream of sugar into her coffee." Are you ever nervous that you've pared it too much?

**WOLFF:** If I repeat something, it'll spoil the effect I'm after. When I finish a story and it feels starved or I find I've cut too much into the bone, I can always go back and add flesh afterwards.

**INTERVIEWER:** You have a lot of faith in your readers to pay attention, don't you?

**WOLFF:** Short story readers tend to be a self-screening group, but, yes, I've been pretty lucky in my readers. The best writing is writing that trusts the reader.

—From "In Conversation with Tobias Wolff," Interview by Daniel Asa Rose.
*Washington Post*, 13 April, 2008. Print.

---

[1] **present government** the administration of George W. Bush, with reference to the war in Iraq.

## On the Elements of a Good Story

**TAVIS:** What for you, since you teach this and since you write rather well yourself, what are the elements? I'm not looking so much for an example, although I'm happy to take it. I'm not looking so much for an example as I am for the elements of what you think makes for a good or a great short story.

**WOLFF:** Well, that's a good question. I suppose the first thing is that it be of compelling interest to the reader in some way, that the reader should feel that even though the character may come from a different country, different ethnicity, different faith, that what is at stake for the character in a short story is somehow at stake for you too, that that shared humanity is somehow made—that the reader is made to feel that with the character.

So what is consequential to the people in the story is consequential for you as the reader. That, I think, is what you're after in the novel as well as the short story. From then on, I think, you know, all bets are off. How you do that is up to each writer, but that's the essential.

**TAVIS:** That's a good answer. I like that. That said, how would you describe the new and selected stories in this text?

**WOLFF:** Well, I hope that, in some way or other, they all, each in its own way, advance that sense of particular humanity and the various moral and spiritual crises that all of us undergo, that somehow they're tracked in these stories. Our tendency to duplicity, to self-interest, to putting conditions on our love, to posing, all those sorts of things that we, in ways large and small, find ourselves doing.

The short story, I think, is a very good form for that. It kind of catches those moments beautifully. In a novel, in a more sustained narrative, you need more colors, you know, more facets, but a short story is very good at catching that thing, you know, seen almost out of the corner of the eye in your own nature. So I find dramatic form for these things and that's how these stories took their shape.

—From interview by Tavis Smiley, "A Conversation with Tobias Wolff." 2 May 2008. Web. 22 Jan. 2010. www.pbs.org.

# Student Essay About Gender Conflict in "Say Yes"

A student, Bob Williams, was assigned in a literature course to write a short essay about "gender conflict" in Tobias Wolff's story "Say Yes." After reading the story carefully, he noted some impressions in his journal:

> I'm not sure how I am supposed to feel about the husband. Sometimes he seems to be basically a good guy who loves his wife even though they are having problems. But then sometimes he seems to be the problem himself, in this scene just itching for a fight. But she's no prize either.
>
> I can't figure out why Wolff has included the conversation about interracial marriages. Why did he pick this subject for the couple to fight about?

Here is the final version of the essay that Bob wrote about "Say Yes." Notice how he keyed it to the opening paragraph of the story.

Williams 1

Bob Williams
Professor Jacobs
Literature 100
1 June 2010

He's the Problem: The Husband in "Say Yes"

Tobias Wolff's insights into "gender conflict" are evident in the first paragraph of his story. He starts by showing the couple doing something together—"they were washing the dishes"—but then in the next phrase he indicates that they performed separate tasks—"his wife washing while he dried." It seems like a small point, but in its own way I think this sentence is already revealing the emotional divide between the husband and the wife, and is foreshadowing the angry argument to come.

The next sentences seem to portray the husband in a positive light. He helped with the dishes the night before, and that time *he* washed, so it seems that this couple shares the domestic chores each night. Wolff appears, then, to be bringing them back together a bit after separating them, through their different activities, in the first sentence of the story. This husband is a good, sensitive person who doesn't expect his wife to handle all of the messy chores in the kitchen.

But maybe Wolff wants us to realize that the husband is taken with himself—that not only does he help his wife with the chores, but also likes to compliment himself, as though he were doing her a favor. He likes to think of himself as better than other husbands; when Wolff writes how the husband "pitches in," I can hear the husband saying these words to himself as evidence of what a decent, down-to-earth guy he is. I notice that the husband also enjoys hearing other people compliment him: "he'd overheard a friend of his wife's congratulate her on having such a considerate husband." Is Wolff's main point that the husband *is* considerate, or that he is a little too proud of himself?

When Wolff writes in the final sentence of this paragraph that "helping out with the dishes was a way he had of showing how considerate he was," he makes clear how we are to respond to the husband. What matters to the husband is not what he feels toward his wife, but, instead, *showing* what he feels. He wants to prove to the world that unlike other men, he treats his wife as an equal; he won't take advantage of her or insist that because she is the wife, she ought

Williams 2

to do the household duties. From one point of view, this sounds appealing.
But Wolff's aim is to make the reader understand the difference between
doing something for its own sake and doing something for the purpose
of self-approval. For this husband, washing the dishes is just another
opportunity for feeling pleased with himself.

Williams 3

Work Cited

Wolff, Tobias, "Say Yes." *An Introduction to Literature*. Sylvan Barnet,
    William Burto, and William E. Cain. 16th ed. Ed. New York:
    Longman, 2011. 349–51. Print.

## The Analysis Briefly Analyzed

- The student pays close attention to Wolff's language in the opening paragraph. Do you agree with his interpretations—for example, his explanation of the meaning of "showing how considerate he was"?
- Do you think it is effective to focus the entire paper on this single opening paragraph? Should the student have included references to later
  passages, or does his point not require them?
- The student several times uses italics to give extra emphasis to a word. Is
  this a good idea?
- In his journal, the student said that he didn't know how to make sense of
  the subject of interracial marriages that takes up so much of the story, and
  this no doubt explains why his essay makes no mention of it. Is this a wise
  or a risky strategy? Explain.
- Notice, too, that the student wrote in his journal that the wife's "no prize
  either." Should he have addressed this issue in his essay? Can you find evidence in the text that might support such a claim?

# A Collection of Short Fiction

The stories of Cain and Abel, Ruth, Samson, and Joseph in the Hebrew Bible and the parables of Jesus in the New Testament are sufficient evidence that brief narratives existed in ancient times. The short tales in Boccaccio's *Decameron* and Chaucer's *Canterbury Tales* (the latter an amazing variety of narrative poems ranging from bawdy stories to legends of saints) are medieval examples of the ancient form. But, speaking generally, short narratives before the nineteenth century were either didactic pieces, with the narrative existing for the sake of a moral point, or they were "curious and striking" tales (to use Somerset Maugham's words for his favorite kind of story) recounted in order to entertain.

The contemporary short story is rather different from both of these genres, which can be called the **parable** and the **anecdote.** Like the parable, the contemporary short story has a point, a meaning; but, unlike the parable, it has a richness of surface as well as depth, so that it is interesting whether or not the reader goes on to ponder "the meaning." Like the anecdote, the short story relates a happening, but whereas the happening in the anecdote is curious and is the center of interest, the happening in the contemporary story often is less interesting in itself than as a manifestation of a character's state of mind. A good short story usually has a psychological interest that an anecdote lacks.

The anecdotal story is what "story" means for most readers. It is an interesting happening or series of happenings, usually with a somewhat surprising ending. The anecdotal story, however, is quite different from most of the contemporary short stories in this book. The anecdote is good entertainment, and good entertainment should not be lightly dismissed. But it has two elements within it that prevent it (unless it is something in addition to an anecdote) from taking a high place among the world's literature. First, it cannot be reread with increasing or even continued pleasure. Even when it is well told, once we know the happening we may lose patience with the telling. Second, effective anecdotes are often highly implausible. Now, implausible anecdotes alleged to be true have a special impact by virtue of their alleged truth: They make us say to ourselves, "Truth is stranger than fiction." But the invented anecdote lacks this power; its unlikely coincidence, its unconvincing ironic situation, its surprise ending, are both untrue and unbelievable. It is entertaining but it is usually not especially meaningful.

The short story of the last hundred and fifty years is not an anecdote and is not an abbreviated novel. If it were the latter, *Reader's Digest* condensations of novels would be short stories. But they are not; they are only eviscerated novels. Novelists usually cover a long period of time, presenting not only a few individuals but also something of a society. They often tell of the development of several many-sided figures. In contrast, short-story writers, having only a few pages, usually focus on a single figure in a single episode, revealing a character rather than recording its development.

Whereas the novel is narrative, the contemporary short story often seems less narrative than lyric or dramatic: In the short story we have a sense of a present mood or personality revealed, rather than the sense of a history reported. The revelation in a story is presented through incidents, of course, but the interest commonly resides in the character revealed through the incidents, rather than in the incidents themselves. Little "happens," in the sense that there is little rushing from place to place. What does "happen" is usually a mental reaction to an experience, and the mental reaction, rather than the external experience, is the heart of the story. In older narratives the plot usually involves a conflict that is resolved, bringing about a change in the protagonist's condition; in contemporary stories the plot usually is designed to reveal a protagonist's state of mind. This deemphasis of overt actions results in a kinship with the lyric and the drama.

One way of looking at the matter is to distinguish between literature of *resolution* and literature of *revelation*—that is, between

1. literature that resolves a plot (literature that stimulates us to ask, "And what happened next?" and that finally leaves us with a settled state of affairs), and
2. literature that reveals a condition (literature that causes us to say, "Ah, now I understand how these people feel").

Two great writers of the later nineteenth century can be taken as representatives of the two kinds: Guy de Maupassant (1850–1893), who usually put the emphasis on resolution, and Anton Chekhov (1860–1904), who usually focused on revelation. Maupassant's tightly plotted stories move to a decisive end, ordinarily marked by a great change in fortune (usually to the characters' disadvantage). Chekhov's stories, on the other hand, seem loosely plotted and may end with the characters pretty much in the condition they were in at the start, but *we* see them more clearly, even if *they* have not achieved any self-knowledge.

A slightly different way of putting the matter is this: Much of the best short fiction from Chekhov onward is less concerned with *what happens* than it is with how a character (often the narrator) *feels* about the happenings. Thus the emphasis is not on external action but on inner action, feeling. Perhaps one can say that the reader is left with a mood rather than with an awareness of a decisive happening.

The distinction between a story of resolution and a story of revelation will probably be clear enough if you are familiar with stories by Maupassant and Chekhov, but of course the distinction should not be overemphasized. These are poles; most stories exist somewhere in between, closer to one pole or the other, but not utterly apart from the more remote pole. Consider again "The Parable of the Prodigal Son," in Chapter 2. Insofar as the story stimulates responses such as "The son left, *and then what happened? Did he prosper?*" it is a story of resolution. Insofar as it makes increasingly evident the unchanging love of the father, it is a story of revelation.

The de-emphasis on narrative in the contemporary short story is not an in-vention of the twentieth-century mind. It goes back at least to three important American writers of the early nineteenth century—Washington Irving, Nathaniel Hawthorne, and Edgar Allan Poe. In 1824 Irving wrote:

> I fancy much of what I value myself upon in writing, escapes the obser-vation of the great mass of my readers: who are intent more upon the story than the way in which it is told. For my part I consider a story merely as a frame on which to stretch my materials. It is the play of thought, and sentiments and language; the weaving in of characters, lightly yet expressively delineated; the familiar and faithful exhibition of scenes in common life; and the half-concealed vein of humor that is often playing through the whole—these are among what I aim at, and upon which I felicitate myself in proportion as I think I succeed.

Hawthorne and Poe may seem stranger than Irving as forebears of the contem-porary short story: Both are known for their fantastic narratives (and, in addition, Poe is known as the inventor of the detective story, a genre in which there is strong interest in curious happenings). But because Hawthorne's fantastic narra-tives are, as he said, highly allegorical, the reader's interest is pushed beyond the narrative to the moral significance. Poe's "arabesques," as he called his fanciful tales (in distinction from his detective tales of "ratiocination"), are aimed at re-vealing and arousing unusual mental states. The weird happenings and person-ages are symbolic representations of the mind or soul. In "The Cask of Amontil-lado," for instance, perhaps the chief interest is not in what happens but rather in the representation of an almost universal fear of being buried alive. But, it must be noted, in both Hawthorne and Poe we usually get what is commonly called the tale rather than the short story: We get short prose fiction dealing with the strange rather than the usual.

A paragraph from Poe's review (1842) of Hawthorne's *Twice-Told Tales*, though more useful in revealing Poe's theory of fiction than Hawthorne's, illu-minates something of the kinship between the contemporary short story and the best short fictions of the earlier nineteenth century. In the review Poe has been explaining that because "unity of effect or impression" is essential, a tale (Poe doubtless uses "tale" to mean short fiction in general, rather than the spe-cial type just discussed) that can be read at a single sitting has an advantage over the novel.

> A skillful artist has constructed a tale. He has not fashioned his thoughts to accommodate his incidents, but having deliberately conceived a cer-tain single effect to be wrought, he then invents such incidents, he then combines such events, and discusses them in such tone as may best serve him in establishing this preconceived effect. If his very first sen-tence tends not to be outbringing of this effect, then in his very first step has he committed a blunder. In the whole composition there should be no word written of which the tendency, direct or indirect, is not to the one pre-established design. And by such means, with such care and skill a picture is at length painted which leaves in the mind of him who contemplates it with a kindred art, a sense of the fullest satisfaction. The idea of the tale, its thesis, has been presented unblem-ished, because undisturbed—an end absolutely demanded, yet, in the novel, altogether unattainable.

Nothing that we have said should be construed as suggesting that short fiction from the mid-nineteenth century to the present is necessarily better than older short narratives. The object of these comments has been less to evaluate than to call attention to the characteristics dominating short fiction of the last century and a half. Not that all of this fiction is of a piece; the stories in this book demonstrate something of its variety. Readers who do not like one story need not despair; they need only (in the words of an early writer of great short fiction) "turne over the leef and chese another tale."

# JAMES BALDWIN

*A prolific essayist, playwright, novelist, and lecturer, James Baldwin (1924–1987) is one of the foremost African American authors of the twentieth century. He was born in Harlem, the son of an unwed mother. After graduation from high school, Baldwin worked briefly in New York City and New Jersey. In 1944 he moved to Greenwich Village, where he wrote his first essays and book reviews, and began to work on the writing of fiction.*

*From the 1940s to the end of his life Baldwin traveled widely, spending long periods in France, Switzerland, and Turkey. His novels include* Go Tell It on the Mountain *(1953)* and Giovanni's Room *(1956), but many find his nonfiction, especially* Notes of a Native Son *(1955),* Nobody Knows My Name *(1961), and* The Fire Next Time *(1963), even more compelling. His story "Sonny's Blues" was first published in 1957 and later was included in the collection* Going to Meet the Man *(1965).*

## Sonny's Blues                                          [1948]

I read about it in the paper, in the subway, on my way to work. I read it, and I couldn't believe it, and I read it again. Then perhaps I just stared at it, at the newsprint spelling out his name, spelling out the story. I stared at it in the swinging lights of the subway car, and in the faces and bodies of the people, and in my own face, trapped in the darkness which roared outside.

It was not to be believed and I kept telling myself that, as I walked from the subway station to the high school. And at the same time I couldn't doubt it. I was scared, scared for Sonny. He became real to me again. A great block of ice got settled in my belly and kept melting there slowly all day long, while I taught my classes algebra. It was a special kind of ice. It kept melting, sending trickles of ice water all up and down my veins, but it never got less. Sometimes it hardened and seemed to expand until I felt my guts were going to come spilling out or that I was going to choke or scream. This would always be at a moment when I was remembering some specific thing Sonny had once said or done.

When he was about as old as the boys in my classes his face had been bright and open, there was a lot of copper in it; and he'd had wonderfully direct brown eyes, and great gentleness and privacy. I wondered what he looked like now. He had been picked up, the evening before, in a raid on an apartment downtown, for peddling and using heroin.

I couldn't believe it: but what I mean by that is that I couldn't find any room for it anywhere inside me. I had kept it outside me for a long time. I hadn't wanted to know. I had had suspicions, but I didn't name them, I kept putting them away. I told myself that Sonny was wild, but he wasn't crazy. And he'd always been a good boy, he hadn't ever turned hard or evil or disrespectful, the way kids can, so quick, so quick, especially in Harlem. I didn't want to believe that I'd ever see my brother going down, coming to nothing, all that light in his face gone out, in the condition I'd already seen so many others. Yet it had happened and here I was, talking about algebra to a lot of boys who might, every one of them for all I knew, be popping off needles every time they went to the head.[1] Maybe it did more for them than algebra could.

5      I was sure that the first time Sonny had ever had horse,[2] he couldn't have been much older than these boys were now. These boys, now, were living as we'd been living then, they were growing up with a rush and their heads bumped abruptly against the low ceiling of their actual possibilities. They were filled with rage. All they really knew were two darknesses, the darkness of their lives, which was now closing in on them, and the darkness of the movies, which had blinded them to that other darkness, and in which they now, vindictively, dreamed, at once more together than they were at any other time, and more alone.

When the last bell rang, the last class ended, I let out my breath. It seemed I'd been holding it for all that time. My clothes were wet—I may have looked as though I'd been sitting in a steam bath, all dressed up, all afternoon. I sat alone in the classroom a long time. I listened to the boys outside, downstairs, shouting and cursing and laughing. Their laughter struck me for perhaps the first time. It was not the joyous laughter which—God knows why—one associates with children. It was mocking and insular, its intent was to denigrate. It was disenchanted, and in this, also, lay the authority of their curses. Perhaps I was listening to them because I was thinking about my brother and in them I heard my brother. And myself.

One boy was whistling a tune, at once very complicated and very simple, it seemed to be pouring out of him as though he were a bird, and it sounded very cool and moving through all that harsh, bright air, only just holding its own through all those other sounds.

I stood up and walked over to the window and looked down into the courtyard. It was the beginning of the spring and the sap was rising in the boys. A teacher passed through them every now and again, quickly, as though he or she couldn't wait to get out of that courtyard, to get those boys out of their sight and off their minds. I started collecting my stuff. I thought I'd better get home and talk to Isabel.

The courtyard was almost deserted by the time I got downstairs. I saw this boy standing in the shadow of a doorway, looking just like Sonny. I almost called his name. Then I saw that it wasn't Sonny, but somebody we used to know, a boy from around our block. He'd been Sonny's friend. He'd never been mine, having been too young for me, and, anyway, I'd never liked him. And now, even though he was a grown-up man, he still hung around that block, still spent hours on the street corners, was always high and raggy.

---

[1] **head** toilet.    [2] **horse** heroin.

I used to run into him from time to time and he'd often work around to asking me for a quarter or fifty cents. He always had some real good excuse, too, and I always gave it to him. I don't know why.

10 But now, abruptly, I hated him. I couldn't stand the way he looked at me, partly like a dog, partly like a cunning child. I wanted to ask him what the hell he was doing in the school courtyard.

He sort of shuffled over to me, and he said, "I see you got the papers. So you already know about it."

"You mean about Sonny? Yes, I already know about it. How come they didn't get you?"

He grinned. It made him repulsive and it also brought to mind what he'd looked like as a kid. "I wasn't there. I stay away from them people."

"Good for you." I offered him a cigarette and I watched him through the smoke. "You come all the way down here just to tell me about Sonny?"

15 "That's right." He was sort of shaking his head and his eyes looked strange, as though they were about to cross. The bright sun deadened his damp dark brown skin and it made his eyes look yellow and showed up the dirt in his kinked hair. He smelled funky.[3] I moved a little away from him and I said, "Well, thanks. But I already know about it and I got to get home."

"I'll walk you a little ways," he said. We started walking. There were a couple of kids still loitering in the courtyard and one of them said goodnight to me and looked strangely at the boy beside me.

"What're you going to do?" he asked me. "I mean, about Sonny?"

"Look. I haven't seen Sonny for over a year, I'm not sure I'm going to do anything. Anyway, what the hell *can* I do?"

"That's right," he said quickly, "ain't nothing you can do. Can't much help old Sonny no more, I guess."

20 It was what I was thinking and so it seemed to me he had no right to say it.

"I'm surprised at Sonny, though," he went on—he had a funny way of talking, he looked straight ahead as though he were talking to himself— "I thought Sonny was a smart boy, I thought he was too smart to get hung."

"I guess he thought so too," I said sharply, "and that's how he got hung. And how about you? You're pretty goddamn smart, I bet."

Then he looked directly at me, just for a minute. "I ain't smart," he said. "If I was smart, I'd have reached for a pistol a long time ago."

"Look. Don't tell *me* your sad story, if it was up to me, I'd give you one." Then I felt guilty—guilty, probably, for never having supposed that the poor bastard *had* a story of his own, much less a sad one, and I asked, quickly, "What's going to happen to him now?"

25 He didn't answer this. He was off by himself some place.

"Funny thing," he said, and from his tone we might have been discussing the quickest way to get to Brooklyn, "when I saw the papers this morning, the first thing I asked myself was if I had anything to do with it. I felt sort of responsible."

I began to listen more carefully. The subway station was on the corner, just before us, and I stopped. He stopped, too. We were in front of a bar and

---

[3]**funky** smelly.

he ducked slightly, peering in, but whoever he was looking for didn't seem to be there. The juke box was blasting away with something black and bouncy and I half watched the barmaid as she danced her way from the juke box to her place behind the bar. And I watched her face as she laughingly responded to something someone said to her, still keeping time to the music. When she smiled one saw the little girl, one sensed the doomed, still-struggling woman beneath the battered face of the semi-whore.

"I never *give* Sonny nothing," the boy said finally, "but a long time ago I come to school high and Sonny asked me how it felt." He paused, I couldn't bear to watch him, I watched the barmaid, and I listened to the music which seemed to be causing the pavement to shake. "I told him it felt great." The music stopped, the barmaid paused and watched the juke box until the music began again. "It did."

All this was carrying me some place I didn't want to go. I certainly didn't want to know how it felt. It filled everything, the people, the houses, the music, the dark, quicksilver barmaid, with menace; and this menace was their reality.

30       "What's going to happen to him now?" I asked again.

"They'll send him away some place and they'll try to cure him." He shook his head. "Maybe he'll even think he's kicked the habit. Then they'll let him loose"—he gestured, throwing his cigarette into the gutter. "That's all."

"What do you mean, that's *all?*"

But I knew what he meant.

"I *mean,* that's *all.*" He turned his head and looked at me, pulling down the corners of his mouth. "Don't you know what I mean?" he asked, softly.

35       "How the hell *would* I know what you mean?" I almost whispered it, I don't know why.

"That's right," he said to the air, "how would *he* know what I mean?" He turned toward me again, patient and calm, and yet I somehow felt him shaking, shaking as though he were going to fall apart. I felt that ice in my guts again, the dread I'd felt all afternoon; and again I watched the barmaid, moving about the bar, washing glasses, and singing. "Listen. They'll let him out and then it'll just start all over again. That's what I mean."

"You mean—they'll let him out. And then he'll just start working his way back in again. You mean he'll never kick the habit. Is that what you mean?"

"That's right," he said, cheerfully. "*You* see what I mean."

"Tell me," I said at last, "why does he want to die? He must want to die, he's killing himself, why does he want to die?"

40       He looked at me in surprise. He licked his lips. "He don't want to die. He wants to live. Don't nobody want to die, ever."

Then I wanted to ask him—too many things. He could not have answered, or if he had, I could not have borne the answers. I started walking. "Well, I guess it's none of my business."

"It's going to be rough on old Sonny," he said. We reached the subway station. "This is your station?" he asked. I nodded. I took one step down. "Damn!" he said, suddenly. I looked up at him. He grinned again. "Damn it if I didn't leave all my money home. You ain't got a dollar on you, have you? Just for a couple of days, is all."

All at once something inside gave and threatened to come pouring out of me. I didn't hate him any more. I felt that in another moment I'd start crying like a child.

"Sure," I said. "Don't sweat." I looked in my wallet and didn't have a dollar, I only had a five. "Here," I said. "That hold you?"

45    He didn't look at it—he didn't want to look at it. A terrible, closed look came over his face, as though he were keeping the number on the bill a secret from him and me. "Thanks," he said, and now he was dying to see me go. "Don't worry about Sonny. Maybe I'll write him or something."

"Sure," I said. "You do that. So long."

"Be seeing you," he said. I went on down the steps.

And I didn't write Sonny or send him anything for a long time. When I finally did, it was just after my little girl died, and he wrote me back a letter which made me feel like a bastard.

Here's what he said:

Dear brother,

You don't know how much I needed to hear from you. I wanted to write you many a time but I dug how much I must have hurt you and so I didn't write. But now I feel like a man who's been trying to climb up out of some deep, real deep and funky hole and just saw the sun up there, outside. I got to get outside.

I can't tell you much about how I got here. I mean I don't know how to tell you. I guess I was afraid of something or I was trying to escape from something and you know I have never been very strong in the head (smile). I'm glad Mama and Daddy are dead and can't see what's happened to their son and I swear if I'd known what I was doing I would never have hurt you so, you and a lot of other fine people who were nice to me and who believed in me.

I don't want you to think it had anything to do with me being a musician. It's more than that. Or maybe less than that. I can't get anything straight in my head down here and I try not to think about what's going to happen to me when I get outside again. Sometime I think I'm going to flip and *never* get outside and sometime I think I'll come straight back. I tell you one thing, though, I'd rather blow my brains out than go through this again. But that's what they all say, so they tell me. If I tell you when I'm coming to New York and if you could meet me, I sure would appreciate it. Give my love to Isabel and the kids and I was sure sorry to hear about little Grace. I wish I could be like Mama and say the Lord's will be done, but I don't know it seems to me that trouble is the one thing that never does get stopped and I don't know what good it does to blame it on the Lord. But maybe it does some good if you believe it.

Your brother,
Sonny

50    Then I kept in constant touch with him and I sent him whatever I could and I went to meet him when he came back to New York. When I saw him many things I thought I had forgotten came flooding back to me. This was because I had begun, finally, to wonder about Sonny, about the life that Sonny lived inside. This life, whatever it was, had made him older and thinner and it had deepened the distant stillness in which he had always moved. He looked very unlike my baby brother. Yet, when he smiled, when we shook hands, the baby brother I'd never known looked out from the depths of his private life, like an animal waiting to be coaxed into the light.

"How you been keeping?" he asked me.

"All right. And you?"

"Just fine." He was smiling all over his face. "It's good to see you again."

"It's good to see you."

55   The seven years' difference in our ages lay between us like a chasm: I wondered if these years would ever operate between us as a bridge. I was remembering, and it made it hard to catch my breath, that I had been there when he was born; and I had heard the first words he had ever spoken. When he started to walk, he walked from our mother straight to me. I caught him just before he fell when he took the first steps he ever took in this world.

"How's Isabel?"

"Just fine. She's dying to see you."

"And the boys?"

"They're fine, too. They're anxious to see their uncle."

60   "Oh, come on. You know they don't remember me."

"Are you kidding? Of course they remember you."

He grinned again. We got into a taxi. We had a lot to say to each other, far too much to know how to begin.

As the taxi began to move, I asked, "You still want to go to India?"

He laughed. "You still remember that. Hell, no. This place is Indian enough for me."

65   "It used to belong to them," I said.

And he laughed again. "They damn sure knew what they were doing when they got rid of it."

Years ago, when he was around fourteen, he'd been all hipped on the idea of going to India. He read books about people sitting on rocks, naked, in all kinds of weather, but mostly bad, naturally, and walking barefoot through hot coals and arriving at wisdom. I used to say that it sounded to me as though they were getting away from wisdom as fast as they could. I think he sort of looked down on me for that.

"Do you mind," he asked, "if we have the driver drive alongside the park? On the west side—I haven't seen the city in so long."

"Of course not," I said. I was afraid that I might sound as though I were humoring him, but I hoped he wouldn't take it that way.

70   So we drove along, between the green of the park and the stony, lifeless elegance of hotels and apartment buildings, toward the vivid, killing streets of our childhood. These streets hadn't changed, though housing projects jutted up out of them now like rocks in the middle of a boiling sea. Most of the houses in which we had grown up had vanished, as had the stores from which we had stolen, the basements in which we had first tried sex, the rooftops from which we had hurled tin cans and bricks. But houses exactly like the houses of our past yet dominated the landscape, boys exactly like the boys we once had been found themselves smothering in these houses, came down into the streets for light and air and found themselves encircled by disaster. Some escaped the trap, most didn't. Those who got out always left something of themselves behind, as some animals amputate a leg and leave it in the trap. It might be said, perhaps, that I had escaped, after all, I was a school teacher; or that Sonny had, he hadn't lived in Harlem for years. Yet, as the cab moved uptown through streets which seemed, with a rush, to darken with dark people, and as I covertly studied Sonny's face, it came to

me that what we both were seeking through our separate cab windows was that part of ourselves which had been left behind. It's always at the hour of trouble and confrontation that the missing member aches.

We hit 110th Street and started rolling up Lenox Avenue. And I'd known this avenue all my life, but it seemed to me again, as it had seemed on the day I'd first heard about Sonny's trouble, filled with a hidden menace which was its very breath of life.

"We almost there," said Sonny.

"Almost." We were both too nervous to say anything more.

We live in a housing project. It hasn't been up long. A few days after it was up it seemed uninhabitably new, now, of course, it's already rundown. It looks like a parody of the good, clean, faceless life—God knows the people who live in it do their best to make it a parody. The beat-looking grass lying around isn't enough to make their lives green, the hedges will never hold out the streets, and they know it. The big windows fool no one, they aren't big enough to make space out of no space. They don't bother with the windows, they watch the TV screen instead. The playground is most popular with the children who don't play at jacks, or skip rope, or roller skate, or swing, and they can be found in it after dark. We moved in partly because it's not too far from where I teach, and partly for the kids; but it's really just like the houses in which Sonny and I grew up. The same things happen, they'll have the same things to remember. The moment Sonny and I started into the house I had the feeling that I was simply bringing him back into the danger he had almost died trying to escape.

75    Sonny has never been talkative. So I don't know why I was sure he'd be dying to talk to me when supper was over the first night. Everything went fine, the oldest boy remembered him, and the youngest boy liked him, and Sonny had remembered to bring something for each of them; and Isabel, who is really much nicer than I am, more open and giving, had gone to a lot of trouble about dinner and was genuinely glad to see him. And she's always been able to tease Sonny in a way that I haven't. It was nice to see her face so vivid again and to hear her laugh and watch her make Sonny laugh. She wasn't, or, anyway, she didn't seem to be, at all uneasy or embarrassed. She chatted as though there were no subject which had to be avoided and she got Sonny past his first, faint stiffness. And thank God she was there, for I was filled with that icy dread again. Everything I did seemed awkward to me, and everything I said sounded freighted with hidden meaning. I was trying to remember everything I'd heard about dope addiction and I couldn't help watching Sonny for signs. I wasn't doing it out of malice. I was trying to find out something about my brother. I was dying to hear him tell me he was safe.

"Safe!" my father grunted, whenever Mama suggested trying to move to a neighborhood which might be safer for children. "Safe, hell! Ain't no place safe for kids, nor nobody."

He always went on like this, but he wasn't, ever, really as bad as he sounded, not even on weekends, when he got drunk. As a matter of fact, he was always on the lookout for "something a little better," but he died before he found it. He died suddenly, during a drunken weekend in the middle of the war, when Sonny was fifteen. He and Sonny hadn't ever got on too well. And this was partly because Sonny was the apple of his father's eye. It was because he loved Sonny so much and was frightened for him, that he was always fighting with him. It doesn't do any good to fight with Sonny. Sonny just moves back, inside himself, where he can't be reached. But the principal reason that they never hit it off is that they were so much alike. Daddy was big and rough and loud-talking, just the opposite of Sonny, but they both had—that same privacy.

Mama tried to tell me something about this, just after Daddy died. I was home on leave from the army.

This was the last time I ever saw my mother alive. Just the same, this picture gets all mixed up in my mind with pictures I had of her when she was younger. The way I always see her is the way she used to be on a Sunday afternoon, say, when the old folks were talking after the big Sunday dinner. I always see her wearing pale blue. She'd be sitting on the sofa. And my father would be sitting in the easy chair, not far from her. And the living room would be full of church folks and relatives. There they sit, in chairs all around the living room, and the night is creeping up outside, but nobody knows it yet. You can see the darkness growing against the windowpanes and you hear the street noises every now and again, or maybe the jangling beat of a tambourine from one of the churches close by, but it's real quiet in the room. For a moment nobody's talking, but every face looks darkening, like the sky outside. And my mother rocks a little from the waist, and my father's eyes are closed. Everyone is looking at something a child can't see. For a minute they've forgotten the children. Maybe a kid is lying on the rug, half asleep. Maybe somebody's got a kid in his lap and is absent-mindedly stroking the kid's head. Maybe there's a kid, quiet and big-eyed, curled up in a big chair in the corner. The silence, the darkness coming, and the darkness in the faces frighten the child obscurely. He hopes that the hand which strokes his forehead will never stop—will never die. He hopes that there will never come a time when the old folks won't be sitting around the living room, talking about where they've come from, and what they've seen, and what's happened to them and their kinfolk.

80    But something deep and watchful in the child knows that this is bound to end, is already ending. In a moment someone will get up and turn on the light. Then the old folks will remember the children and they won't talk any more that day. And when light fills the room, the child is filled with darkness. He knows that every time this happens he's moved just a little closer to that darkness outside. The darkness outside is what the old folks have been talking about. It's what they've come from. It's what they endure. The child knows that they won't talk any more because if he knows too much about what's happened to *them,* he'll know too much too soon, about what's going to happen to *him.*

The last time I talked to my mother, I remember I was restless. I wanted to get out and see Isabel. We weren't married then and we had a lot to straighten out between us.

There Mama sat, in black, by the window. She was humming an old church song, *Lord, you brought me from a long ways off.* Sonny was out somewhere. Mama kept watching the streets.

"I don't know," she said, "if I'll ever see you again, after you go off from here. But I hope you'll remember the things I tried to teach you."

"Don't talk like that," I said, and smiled. "You'll be here a long time yet."

85    She smiled, too, but she said nothing. She was quiet for a long time. And I said, "Mama, don't you worry about nothing. I'll be writing all the time, and you be getting the checks. . . ."

"I want to talk to you about your brother," she said, suddenly. "If any-thing happens to me he ain't going to have nobody to look out for him."

"Mama," I said, "ain't nothing going to happen to you *or* Sonny. Sonny's all right. He's a good boy and he's got good sense."

"It ain't a question of his being a good boy," Mama said, "nor of his hav-ing good sense. It ain't only the bad ones, nor yet the dumb ones that gets sucked under." She stopped, looking at me. "Your Daddy once had a brother," she said, and she smiled in a way that made me feel she was in pain. "You didn't never know that, did you?"

"No," I said, "I never knew that," and I watched her face.

90    "Oh, yes," she said, "your Daddy had a brother." She looked out of the window again. "I know you never saw your Daddy cry. But *I* did—many a time, through all these years."

I asked her, "What happened to his brother? How come nobody's ever talked about him?"

This was the first time I ever saw my mother look old.

"His brother got killed," she said, "when he was just a little younger than you are now. I knew him. He was a fine boy. He was maybe a little full of the devil, but he didn't mean nobody no harm."

Then she stopped and the room was silent, exactly as it had sometimes been on those Sunday afternoons. Mama kept looking out into the streets.

95    "He used to have a job in the mill," she said, "and, like all young folks, he just liked to perform on Saturday nights. Saturday nights, him and your father would drift around to different places, go to dances and things like that, or just sit around with people they knew, and your father's brother would sing, he had a fine voice, and play along with himself on his guitar. Well, this par-ticular Saturday night, him and your father was coming home from some place, and they were both a little drunk and there was a moon that night, it was bright like day. Your father's brother was feeling kind of good, and he was whistling to himself, and he had his guitar slung over his shoulder. They was coming down a hill and beneath them was a road that turned off from the highway. Well, your father's brother, being always kind of frisky, decided to run down this hill, and he did, with that guitar banging and clang-ing behind him, and he ran across the road, and he was making water be-hind a tree. And your father was sort of amused at him and he was still com-ing down the hill, kind of slow. Then he heard a car motor and that same minute his brother stepped from behind the tree, into the road, in the moon-light. And he started to cross the road. And your father started to run down the hill, he says he don't know why. This car was full of white men. They was all drunk, and when they seen your father's brother they let out a great whoop and holler and they aimed the car straight at him. They was having fun, they just wanted to scare him, the way they do sometimes, you know. But they was drunk. And I guess the boy, being drunk, too, and scared, kind of lost his head. By the time he jumped it was too late. Your father says he heard his brother scream when the car rolled over him, and he heard the wood of that guitar when it give, and he heard them strings go flying, and he heard them white men shouting, and the car kept on a-going and it ain't stopped till this day. And, time your father got down the hill, his brother weren't nothing but blood and pulp."

Tears were gleaming on my mother's face. There wasn't anything I could say.

"He never mentioned it," she said, "because I never let him mention it before you children. Your Daddy was like a crazy man that night and for many a night thereafter. He says he never in his life seen anything as dark as that road after the lights of that car had gone away. Weren't nothing, weren't nobody on that road, just your Daddy and his brother and that busted guitar. Oh, yes. Your Daddy never did really get right again. Till the day he died he weren't sure but that every white man he saw was the man that killed his brother."

She stopped and took out her handkerchief and dried her eyes and looked at me.

"I ain't telling you all this," she said, "to make you scared or bitter or to make you hate nobody. I'm telling you this because you got a brother. And the world ain't changed."

100    I guess I didn't want to believe this. I guess she saw this in my face. She turned away from me, toward the window again, searching those streets.

"But I praise my Redeemer," she said at last, "that He called your Daddy home before me. I ain't saying it to throw no flowers at myself, but, I declare, it keeps me from feeling too cast down to know I helped your father get safely through this world. Your father always acted like he was the roughest, strongest man on earth. And everybody took him to be like that. But if he hadn't had me there—to see his tears!"

She was crying again. Still, I couldn't move. I said, "Lord, Lord, Mama, I didn't know it was like that."

"Oh, honey," she said, "there's a lot that you don't know. But you are going to find out." She stood up from the window and came over to me. "You got to hold on to your brother," she said, "and don't let him fall, no matter what it looks like is happening to him and no matter how evil you gets with him. You going to be evil with him many a time. But don't you forget what I told you, you hear?"

"I won't forget," I said. "Don't you worry, I won't forget. I won't let nothing happen to Sonny."

105    My mother smiled as though she were amused at something she saw in my face. Then, "You may not be able to stop nothing from happening. But you got to let him know you's *there*."

Two days later I was married, and then I was gone. And I had a lot of things on my mind and I pretty well forgot my promise to Mama until I got shipped home on a special furlough for her funeral.

And, after the funeral, with just Sonny and me alone in the empty kitchen, I tried to find out something about him.

"What do you want to do?" I asked him.

"I'm going to be a musician," he said.

110    For he had graduated, in the time I had been away, from dancing to the juke box to finding out who was playing what, and what they were doing with it, and he had bought himself a set of drums.

"You mean, you want to be a drummer?" I somehow had the feeling that being a drummer might be all right for other people but not for my brother Sonny.

"I don't think," he said, looking at me very gravely, "that I'll ever be a good drummer. But I think I can play a piano."

I frowned. I'd never played the role of the older brother quite so seriously before, had scarcely ever, in fact, *asked* Sonny a damn thing. I sensed myself in the presence of something I didn't really know how to handle, didn't understand. So I made my frown a little deeper as I asked: "What kind of musician do you want to be?"

He grinned. "How many kinds do you think there are?"

115     "Be *serious*," I said.

He laughed, throwing his head back, and then looked at me. "I *am* serious."

"Well, then, for Christ's sake, stop kidding around and answer a serious question. I mean, do you want to be a concert pianist, you want to play classical music and all that; or—or what?" Long before I finished he was laughing again. "For Christ's *sake*, Sonny!"

He sobered, but with difficulty. "I'm sorry. But you sound so—*scared!*" and he was off again.

"Well, you may think it's funny now, baby, but it's not going to be so funny when you have to make your living at it, let me tell you *that*." I was furious because I knew he was laughing at me and I didn't know why.

120     "*No*," he said, very sober now, and afraid, perhaps, that he'd hurt me, "I don't want to be a classical pianist. That isn't what interests me. I mean"— he paused, looking hard at me, as though his eyes would help me to understand, and then gestured helplessly, as though perhaps his hand would help—"I mean, I'll have a lot of studying to do, and I'll have to study *everything*, but, I mean, I want to play *with*—jazz musicians." He stopped. "I want to play jazz," he said.

Well, the word had never before sounded as heavy, as real, as it sounded that afternoon in Sonny's mouth. I just looked at him and I was probably frowning a real frown by this time. I simply couldn't see why on earth he'd want to spend his time hanging around nightclubs, clowning around on bandstands, while people pushed each other around a dance floor. It seemed—beneath him, somehow. I had never thought about it before, had never been forced to, but I suppose I had always put jazz musicians in a class with what Daddy called "good-time people."

"Are you *serious?*"

"Hell, *yes*, I'm serious."

He looked more helpless than ever, and annoyed, and deeply hurt.

125     I suggested, helpfully: "You mean—like Louis Armstrong?"

His face closed as though I'd struck him. "No. I'm not talking about none of that old-time, down home crap."

"Well, look, Sonny, I'm sorry, don't get mad. I just don't altogether get it, that's all. Name somebody—you know, a jazz musician you admire."

"Bird."[4]

"Who?"

130     "Bird! Charlie Parker! Don't they teach you nothing in the goddamn army?"

I lit a cigarette. I was surprised and then a little amused to discover that I was trembling. "I've been out of touch," I said. "You'll have to be patient with me. Now. Who's this Parker character?"

"He's just one of the greatest jazz musicians alive," said Sonny, sullenly, his hands in his pockets, his back to me. "Maybe *the* greatest," he added, bitterly, "that's probably why *you* never heard of him."

---

[4]**Bird** Charlie "Bird" Parker (1920–1955), saxophonist and jazz innovator for whom the Birdland ballroom in New York City is named.

"All right," I said, "I'm ignorant. I'm sorry. I'll go out and buy all the cat's records right away, all right?"

"It don't," said Sonny, with dignity, "make any difference to me. I don't care what you listen to. Don't do me no favors."

135     I was beginning to realize that I'd never seen him so upset before. With another part of my mind I was thinking that this would probably turn out to be one of those things kids go through and that I shouldn't make it seem important by pushing it too hard. Still, I didn't think it would do any harm to ask: "Doesn't all this take a lot of time? Can you make a living at it?"

He turned back to me and half leaned, half sat, on the kitchen table. "Everything takes time," he said, "and—well, yes, sure, I can make a living at it. But what I don't seem to be able to make you understand is that it's the only thing I want to do."

"Well, Sonny," I said, gently, "you know people can't always do exactly what they *want* to do—"

"*No*, I don't know that," said Sonny, surprising me. "I think people *ought* to do what they want to do, what else are they alive for?"

"You getting to be a big boy," I said desperately, "it's time you started thinking about your future."

140     "I'm thinking about my future," said Sonny, grimly. "I think about it all the time."

I gave up. I decided, if he didn't change his mind, that we could always talk about it later. "In the meantime," I said, "you got to finish school." We had already decided that he'd have to move in with Isabel and her folks. I knew this wasn't the ideal arrangement because Isabel's folks are inclined to be dicty[5] and they hadn't especially wanted Isabel to marry me. But I didn't know what else to do. "And we have to get you fixed up at Isabel's."

There was a long silence. He moved from the kitchen table to the window. "That's a terrible idea. You know it yourself."

"Do you have a *better* idea?"

He just walked up and down the kitchen for a minute. He was as tall as I was. He had started to shave. I suddenly had the feeling that I didn't know him at all.

145     He stopped at the kitchen table and picked up my cigarettes. Looking at me with a kind of mocking, amused defiance, he put one between his lips. "You mind?"

"You smoking already?"

He lit the cigarette and nodded, watching me through the smoke. "I just wanted to see if I'd have the courage to smoke in front of you." He grinned and blew a great cloud of smoke to the ceiling. "It was easy." He looked at my face. "Come on, now. I bet you was smoking at my age, tell the truth."

I didn't say anything but the truth was on my face, and he laughed. But now there was something very strained in his laugh. "Sure. And I bet that ain't all you was doing."

He was frightening me a little. "Cut the crap," I said. "We already decided that you was going to go and live at Isabel's. Now what's got into you all of a sudden?"

---

[5]**dicty** dictatorial, bossy, and snobbish.

150    "*You* decided it," he pointed out. "I didn't decide nothing." He stopped
in front of me, leaning against the stove, arms loosely folded. "Look, brother.
I don't want to stay in Harlem no more, I really don't." He was very earnest. He
looked at me, then over toward the kitchen window. There was something in
his eyes I'd never seen before, some thoughtfulness, some worry all his own.
He rubbed the muscle of one arm. "It's time I was getting out of here."

"Where do you want to *go,* Sonny?"

"I want to join the army. Or the navy, I don't care. If I say I'm old
enough, they'll believe me."

Then I got mad. It was because I was so scared. "You must be crazy. You
goddamn fool, what the hell do you want to go and join the *army* for?"

"I just told you. To get out of Harlem."

155    "Sonny, you haven't even finished *school.* And if you really want to be a
musician, how do you expect to study if you're in the *army?*"

He looked at me, trapped, and in anguish. "There's ways. I might be able to
work out some kind of deal. Anyway, I'll have the G.I. Bill when I come out."

"*If* you come out." We stared at each other. "Sonny, please. Be reasonable.
I know the setup is far from perfect. But we got to do the best we can."

"I ain't learning nothing in school," he said. "Even when I go." He turned
away from me and opened the window and threw his cigarette out into the
narrow alley. I watched his back. "At least, I ain't learning nothing you'd want
me to learn." He slammed the window so hard I thought the glass would fly
out, and turned back to me. "And I'm sick of the stink of these garbage cans!"

"Sonny," I said, "I know how you feel. But if you don't finish school
now, you're going to be sorry later that you didn't." I grabbed him by the
shoulders. "And you only got another year. It ain't so bad. And I'll come back
and I swear I'll help you do *whatever* you want to do. Just try to put up with
it till I come back. Will you please do that? For me?"

160    He didn't answer and he wouldn't look at me.

"Sonny. You hear me?"

He pulled away. "I hear you. But you never hear anything *I* say."

I didn't know what to say to that. He looked out of the window and
then back at me. "OK," he said, and sighed. "I'll try."

Then I said, trying to cheer him up a little, "They got a piano at Isabel's.
You can practice on it."

165    And as a matter of fact, it did cheer him up for a minute. "That's right,"
he said to himself. "I forgot that." His face relaxed a little. But the worry, the
thoughtfulness, played on it still, the way shadows play on a face which is
staring into the fire.

But I thought I'd never hear the end of that piano. At first, Isabel would
write me, saying how nice it was that Sonny was so serious about his music
and how, as soon as he came in from school, or wherever he had been when
he was supposed to be at school, he went straight to that piano and stayed
there until suppertime. And, after supper, he went back to that piano and
stayed there until everybody went to bed. He was at the piano all day Saturday and all day Sunday. Then he bought a record player and started playing
records. He'd play one record over and over again, all day long sometimes,
and he'd improvise along with it on the piano. Or he'd play one section of
the record, one chord, one change, one progression, then he'd do it on the
piano. Then back to the record. Then back to the piano.

Well, I really don't know how they stood it. Isabel finally confessed that it wasn't like living with a person at all, it was like living with sound. And the sound didn't make any sense to her, didn't make any sense to any of them—naturally. They began, in a way, to be afflicted by this presence that was living in their home. It was as though Sonny were some sort of god, or monster. He moved in an atmosphere which wasn't like theirs at all. They fed him and he ate, he washed himself, he walked in and out of their door; he certainly wasn't nasty or unpleasant or rude, Sonny isn't any of those things; but it was as though he were all wrapped up in some cloud, some fire, some vision all his own; and there wasn't any way to reach him.

At the same time, he wasn't really a man yet, he was still a child, and they had to watch out for him in all kinds of ways. They certainly couldn't throw him out. Neither did they dare to make a great scene about that piano because even they dimly sensed, as I sensed, from so many thousands of miles away, that Sonny was at that piano playing for his life.

But he hadn't been going to school. One day a letter came from the school board and Isabel's mother got it—there had, apparently, been other letters but Sonny had torn them up. This day, when Sonny came in, Isabel's mother showed him the letter and asked where he'd been spending his time. And she finally got it out of him that he'd been down in Greenwich Village, with musicians and other characters, in a white girl's apartment. And this scared her and she started to scream at him and what came up, once she began—though she denies it to this day—was what sacrifices they were making to give Sonny a decent home and how little he appreciated it.

170     Sonny didn't play the piano that day. By evening, Isabel's mother had calmed down but then there was the old man to deal with, and Isabel herself. Isabel says she did her best to be calm but she broke down and started crying. She says she just watched Sonny's face. She could tell, by watching him, what was happening with him. And what was happening was that they penetrated his cloud, they had reached him. Even if their fingers had been a thousand times more gentle than human fingers ever are, he could hardly help feeling that they had stripped him naked and were spitting on that nakedness. For he also had to see that his presence, that music, which was life or death to him, had been torture for them and that they had endured it, not at all for his sake, but only for mine. And Sonny couldn't take that. He can take it a little better today than he could then but he's still not very good at it and, frankly, I don't know anybody who is.

The silence of the next few days must have been louder than the sound of all the music ever played since time began. One morning, before she went to work, Isabel was in his room for something and she suddenly realized that all of his records were gone. And she knew for certain that he was gone. And he was. He went as far as the navy would carry him. He finally sent me a postcard from some place in Greece and that was the first I knew that Sonny was still alive. I didn't see him any more until we were both back in New York and the war had long been over.

He was a man by then, of course, but I wasn't willing to see it. He came by the house from time to time, but we fought almost every time we met. I didn't like the way he carried himself, loose and dreamlike all the time, and I didn't like his friends, and his music seemed to be merely an excuse for the life he led. It sounded just that weird and disordered.

Then we had a fight, a pretty awful fight, and I didn't see him for months. By and by I looked him up, where he was living, in a furnished room in the Village, and I tried to make it up. But there were lots of other people in the room and Sonny just lay on his bed, and he wouldn't come downstairs with me, and he treated these other people as though they were his family and I weren't. So I got mad and then he got mad, and then I told him that he might just as well be dead as live the way he was living. Then he stood up and he told me not to worry about him any more in life, that he *was* dead as far as I was concerned. Then he pushed me to the door and the other people looked on as though nothing were happening, and he slammed the door behind me. I stood in the hallway, staring at the door. I heard somebody laugh in the room and then the tears came to my eyes. I started down the steps, whistling to keep from crying, I kept whistling to myself, *You going to need me, baby, one of these cold, rainy days.*

I read about Sonny's trouble in the spring. Little Grace died in the fall. She was a beautiful little girl. But she only lived a little over two years. She died of polio and she suffered. She had a slight fever for a couple of days, but it didn't seem like anything and we just kept her in bed. And we would certainly have called the doctor, but the fever dropped, she seemed to be all right. So we thought it had just been a cold. Then, one day, she was up, playing, Isabel was in the kitchen fixing lunch for the two boys when they'd come in from school, and she heard Grace fall down in the living room. When you have a lot of children you don't always start running when one of them falls, unless they start screaming or something. And, this time, Gracie was quiet. Yet, Isabel says that when she heard that *thump* and then that silence, something happened to her to make her afraid. And she ran to the living room and there was little Grace on the floor, all twisted up, and the reason she hadn't screamed was that she couldn't get her breath. And when she did scream, it was the worst sound, Isabel says, that she'd ever heard in all her life, and she still hears it sometimes in her dreams. Isabel will sometimes wake me up with a low, moaning, strangling sound and I have to be quick to awaken her and hold her to me and where Isabel is weeping against me seems a mortal wound.

175    I think I may have written Sonny the very day that little Grace was buried. I was sitting in the living room in the dark, by myself, and I suddenly thought of Sonny. My trouble made his real.

One Saturday afternoon, when Sonny had been living with us, or anyway, been in our house, for nearly two weeks, I found myself wandering aimlessly about the living room, drinking from a can of beer, and trying to work up courage to search Sonny's room. He was out, he was usually out whenever I was home, and Isabel had taken the children to see their grandparents. Suddenly I was standing still in front of the living room window, watching Seventh Avenue. The idea of searching Sonny's room made me still. I scarcely dared to admit to myself what I'd be searching for. I didn't know what I'd do if I found it. Or if I didn't.

On the sidewalk across from me, near the entrance to a barbecue joint, some people were holding an old-fashioned revival meeting. The barbecue cook, wearing a dirty white apron, his conked[6] hair reddish and metallic in the

---

[6]**conked** straightened and greased

pale sun, and a cigarette between his lips, stood in the doorway, watching them. Kids and older people paused in their errands and stood there, along with some older men and a couple of very tough-looking women who watched everything that happened on the avenue, as though they owned it, or were maybe owned by it. Well, they were watching this, too. The revival was being carried on by three sisters in black, and a brother. All they had were their voices and their Bibles and a tambourine. The brother was testifying and while he testified two of the sisters stood together, seeming to say, amen, and the third sister walked around with the tambourine outstretched and a couple of people dropped coins into it. Then the brother's testimony ended and the sister who had been taking up the collection dumped the coins into her palm and transferred them to the pocket of her long black robe. Then she raised both hands, striking the tambourine against the air, and then against one hand, and she started to sing. And the two other sisters and the brother joined in.

It was strange, suddenly, to watch, though I had been seeing these meetings all my life. So, of course, had everybody else down there. Yet, they paused and watched and listened and I stood still at the window. *"'Tis the old ship of Zion,"* they sang, and the sister with the tambourine kept a steady, jangling beat, *"it has rescued many a thousand!"* Not a soul under the sound of their voices was hearing this song for the first time, not one of them had been rescued. Nor had they seen much in the way of rescue work being done around them. Neither did they especially believe in the holiness of the three sisters and the brother, they knew too much about them, knew where they lived, and how. The woman with the tambourine, whose voice dominated the air, whose face was bright with joy, was divided by very little from the woman who stood watching her, a cigarette between her heavy, chapped lips, her hair a cuckoo's nest, her face scarred and swollen from many beatings, and her black eyes glittering like coal. Perhaps they both knew this, which was why, when, as rarely, they addressed each other, they addressed each other as Sister. As the singing filled the air the watching, listening faces underwent a change, the eyes focusing on something within; the music seemed to soothe a poison out of them; and time seemed, nearly, to fall away from the sullen, belligerent, battered faces, as though they were fleeing back to their first condition, while dreaming of their last. The barbecue cook half shook his head and smiled, and dropped his cigarette and disappeared into his joint. A man fumbled in his pockets for change and stood holding it in his hand impatiently, as though he had just remembered a pressing appointment further up the avenue. He looked furious. Then I saw Sonny, standing on the edge of the crowd. He was carrying a wide, flat notebook with a green cover, and it made him look, from where I was standing, almost like a schoolboy. The coppery sun brought out the copper in his skin, he was very faintly smiling, standing very still. Then the singing stopped, the tambourine turned into a collection plate again. The furious man dropped in his coins and vanished, so did a couple of the women, and Sonny dropped some change in the plate, looking directly at the woman with a little smile. He started across the avenue, toward the house. He has a slow, loping walk, something like the way Harlem hipsters walk, only he's imposed on this his own half-beat. I had never really noticed it before.

I stayed at the window, both relieved and apprehensive. As Sonny disappeared from my sight, they began singing again. And they were still singing when his key turned in the lock.

180     "Hey," he said.

"Hey, yourself. You want some beer?"

"No. Well, maybe." But he came up to the window and stood beside me, looking out. "What a warm voice," he said.

They were singing *If I could only hear my mother pray again!*

"Yes," I said, "and she can sure beat that tambourine."

185     "But what a terrible song," he said, and laughed. He dropped his notebook on the sofa and disappeared into the kitchen. "Where's Isabel and the kids?"

"I think they went to see their grandparents. You hungry?"

"No." He came back into the living room with his can of beer. "You want to come some place with me tonight?"

I sensed, I don't know how, that I couldn't possibly say no. "Sure. Where?"

He sat down on the sofa and picked up his notebook and started leafing through it. "I'm going to sit in with some fellows in a joint in the Village."

190     "You mean, you're going to play, tonight?"

"That's right." He took a swallow of his beer and moved back to the window. He gave me a sidelong look. "If you can stand it."

"I'll try," I said.

He smiled to himself and we both watched as the meeting across the way broke up. The three sisters and the brother, heads bowed, were singing *God be with you till we meet again.* The faces around them were very quiet. Then the song ended. The small crowd dispersed. We watched the three women and the lone man walk slowly up the avenue.

"When she was singing before," said Sonny, abruptly, "her voice reminded me for a minute of what heroin feels like sometimes—when it's in your veins. It makes you feel sort of warm and cool at the same time. And distant. And—and sure." He sipped his beer, very deliberately not looking at me. I watched his face. "It makes you feel—in control. Sometimes you've got to have that feeling."

195     "Do you?" I sat down slowly in the easy chair.

"Sometimes." He went to the sofa and picked up his notebook again. "Some people do."

"In order," I asked, "to play?" And my voice was very ugly, full of contempt and anger.

"Well"—he looked at me with great, troubled eyes, as though, in fact, he hoped his eyes would tell me things he could never otherwise say—"they *think* so. And *if* they think so—!"

"And what do *you* think?" I asked.

200     He sat on the sofa and put his can of beer on the floor. "I don't know," he said, and I couldn't be sure if he were answering my question or pursuing his thoughts. His face didn't tell me. "It's not so much to *play.* It's to *stand* it, to be able to make it at all. On any level." He frowned and smiled: "In order to keep from shaking to pieces."

"But these friends of yours," I said, "they seem to shake themselves to pieces pretty goddamn fast."

"Maybe." He played with the notebook. And something told me that I should curb my tongue, that Sonny was doing his best to talk, that I should listen. "But of course you only know the ones that've gone to pieces. Some don't—or at least they haven't *yet* and that's just about all *any* of us can say."

He paused. "And then there are some who just live, really, in hell, and they know it and they see what's happening and they go right on. I don't know." He sighed, dropped the notebook, folded his arms. "Some guys, you can tell from the way they play, they on something *all* the time. And you can see that, well, it makes something real for them. But of course," he picked up his beer from the floor and sipped it and put the can down again, "they *want* to, too, you've got to see that. Even some of them that say they don't—*some*, not all."

"And what about you?" I asked—I couldn't help it. "What about you? Do *you* want to?"

He stood up and walked to the window and I remained silent for a long time. Then he sighed. "Me," he said. Then: "While I was downstairs before, on my way here, listening to that woman sing, it struck me all of a sudden how much suffering she must have had to go through—to sing like that. It's *repulsive* to think you have to suffer that much."

205      I said: "But there's no way not to suffer—is there, Sonny?"

"I believe not," he said and smiled, "but that's never stopped anyone from trying." He looked at me. "Has it?" I realized, with this mocking look, that there stood between us, forever, beyond the power of time or forgiveness, the fact that I had held silence—so long!—when he had needed human speech to help him. He turned back to the window. "No, there's no way not to suffer. But you try all kinds of ways to keep from drowning in it, to keep on top of it, and to make it seem—well, like *you*. Like you did something, all right, and now you're suffering for it. You know?" I said nothing. "Well you know," he said, impatiently, "why *do* people suffer? Maybe it's better to do something to give it a reason, *any* reason."

"But we just agreed," I said, "that there's no way not to suffer. Isn't it better, then, just to—take it?"

"But nobody just takes it," Sonny cried, "that's what I'm telling you! *Everybody* tries not to. You're just hung up on the *way* some people try—it's not *your* way!"

The hair on my face began to itch, my face felt wet. "That's not true," I said, "that's not true. I don't give a damn what other people do, I don't even care how they suffer. I just care how *you* suffer." And he looked at me. "Please believe me," I said, "I don't want to see you—die—trying not to suffer."

210      "I won't," he said flatly, "die trying not to suffer. At least, not any faster than anybody else."

"But there's no need," I said, trying to laugh, "is there? in killing yourself."

I wanted to say more, but I couldn't. I wanted to talk about will power and how life could be—well, beautiful. I wanted to say that it was all within; but was it? or, rather, wasn't that exactly the trouble? And I wanted to promise that I would never fail him again. But it would all have sounded—empty words and lies.

So I made the promise to myself and prayed that I would keep it.

"It's terrible sometimes, inside," he said, "that's what's the trouble. You walk these streets, black and funky and cold, and there's not really a living ass to talk to, and there's nothing shaking, and there's no way of getting it out—that storm inside. You can't talk it and you can't make love with it, and when you finally try to get with it and play it, you realize *nobody's* listening. So *you've* got to listen. You got to find a way to listen."

215    And then he walked away from the window and sat on the sofa again, as though all the wind had suddenly been knocked out of him. "Sometimes you'll do *anything* to play, even cut your mother's throat." He laughed and looked at me. "Or your brother's." Then he sobered. "Or your own." Then: "Don't worry. I'm all right now and I think I'll *be* all right. But I can't forget—where I've been. I don't mean just the physical place I've been, I mean where I've *been*. And *what* I've been."

"What have you been, Sonny?" I asked.

He smiled—but sat sideways on the sofa, his elbow resting on the back, his fingers playing with his mouth and chin, not looking at me. "I've been something I didn't recognize, didn't know I could be. Didn't know anybody could be." He stopped, looking inward, looking helplessly young, looking old. "I'm not talking about it now because I feel *guilty* or anything like that—maybe it would be better if I did, I don't know. Anyway, I can't really talk about it. Not to you, not to anybody," and now he turned and faced me. "Sometimes, you know, and it was actually when I was most *out* of the world, I felt that I was in it, that I was *with* it, really, and I could play or I didn't really have to *play*, it just came out of me, it was there. And I don't know how I played, thinking about it now, but I know I did awful things, those times, sometimes, to people. Or it wasn't that I *did* anything to them—it was that they weren't real." He picked up the beer can; it was empty; he rolled it between his palms: "And other times—well, I needed a fix, I needed to find a place to lean, I needed to clear a space to *listen*—and I couldn't find it, and I—went crazy, I did terrible things to *me*, I was terrible *for* me." He began pressing the beer can between his hands, I watched the metal begin to give. It glittered, as he played with it like a knife, and I was afraid he would cut himself, but I said nothing. "Oh well. I can never tell you. I was all by myself at the bottom of something, stinking and sweating and crying and shaking, and I smelled it, you know? *my* stink, and I thought I'd die if I couldn't get away from it and yet, all the same, I knew that everything I was doing was just locking me in with it. And I didn't know," he paused, still flattening the beer can, "I didn't know, I still *don't* know, something kept telling me that maybe it was good to smell your own stink, but I didn't think that *that* was what I'd been trying to do—and— who can stand it?" and he abruptly dropped the ruined beer can, looking at me with a small, still smile, and then rose, walking to the window as though it were the lodestone rock. I watched his face, he watched the avenue. "I couldn't tell you when Mama died—but the reason I wanted to leave Harlem so bad was to get away from drugs. And then, when I ran away, that's what I was running from—really. When I came back, nothing had changed, *I* hadn't changed, I was just—older." And he stopped, drumming with his fingers on the windowpane. The sun had vanished, soon darkness would fall. I watched his face. "It can come again," he said, almost as though speaking to himself. Then he turned to me. "It can come again," he repeated. "I just want you to know that."

"All right," I said, at last. "So it can come again. All right."

He smiled, but the smile was sorrowful. "I had to try to tell you," he said.

220    "Yes," I said. "I understand that."

"You're my brother," he said, looking straight at me, and not smiling at all.

"Yes," I repeated, "yes. I understand that."

He turned back to the window, looking out. "All that hatred down there," he said, "all that hatred and misery and love. It's a wonder it doesn't blow the avenue apart."

We went to the only nightclub on a short, dark street, downtown. We squeezed through the narrow, chattering, jampacked bar to the entrance of the big room, where the bandstand was. And we stood there for a moment, for the lights were very dim in this room and we couldn't see. Then, "Hello, boy," said the voice and an enormous black man, much older than Sonny or myself, erupted out of all that atmospheric lighting and put an arm around Sonny's shoulder. "I been sitting right here," he said, "waiting for you."

225      He had a big voice, too, and heads in the darkness turned toward us.

Sonny grinned and pulled a little away, and said, "Creole, this is my brother. I told you about him."

Creole shook my hand. "I'm glad to meet you, son," he said, and it was clear that he was glad to meet me *there,* for Sonny's sake. And he smiled, "You got a real musician in *your* family," and he took his arm from Sonny's shoulder and slapped him, lightly, affectionately, with the back of his hand.

"Well. Now I've heard it all," said a voice behind us. This was another musician, and a friend of Sonny's, a coal-black, cheerful-looking man, built close to the ground. He immediately began confiding to me, at the top of his lungs, the most terrible things about Sonny, his teeth gleaming like a lighthouse and his laugh coming up out of him like the beginning of an earthquake. And it turned out that everyone at the bar knew Sonny, or almost everyone; some were musicians, working there, or nearby, or not working, some were simply hangers-on, and some were there to hear Sonny play. I was introduced to all of them and they were all very polite to me. Yet, it was clear that, for them, I was only Sonny's brother. Here, I was in Sonny's world. Or, rather: his kingdom. Here, it was not even a question that his veins bore royal blood.

They were going to play soon and Creole installed me, by myself, at a table in a dark corner. Then I watched them, Creole, and the little black man, and Sonny, and the others, while they horsed around, standing just below the bandstand. The light from the bandstand spilled just a little short of them and, watching them laughing and gesturing and moving about, I had the feeling that they, nevertheless, were being most careful not to step into that circle of light too suddenly: that if they moved into the light too suddenly, without thinking, they would perish in flame. Then, while I watched, one of them, the small black man, moved into the light and crossed the bandstand and started fooling around with his drums. Then—being funny and being, also, extremely ceremonious—Creole took Sonny by the arm and led him to the piano. A woman's voice called Sonny's name and a few hands started clapping. And Sonny, also being funny and being ceremonious, and so touched, I think, that he could have cried, but neither hiding it nor showing it, riding it like a man, grinned, and put both hands to his heart and bowed from the waist.

230      Creole then went to the bass fiddle and a lean, very bright-skinned brown man jumped up on the bandstand and picked up his horn. So there they were, and the atmosphere on the bandstand and in the room began to change and tighten. Someone stepped up to the microphone and announced them. Then there were all kinds of murmurs. Some people at the bar shushed

others. The waitress ran around, frantically getting in the last orders, guys and chicks got closer to each other, and the lights on the bandstand, on the quartet, turned to a kind of indigo. Then they all looked different there. Creole looked about him for the last time, as though he were making certain that all his chickens were in the coop, and then he—jumped and struck the fiddle. And there they were.

All I know about music is that not many people ever really hear it. And even then, on the rare occasions when something opens within, and the music enters, what we mainly hear, or hear corroborated, are personal, private, vanishing evocations. But the man who creates the music is hearing something else, is dealing with the roar rising from the void and imposing order on it as it hits the air. What is evoked in him, then, is of another order, more terrible because it has no words, and triumphant, too, for that same reason. And his triumph, when he triumphs, is ours. I just watched Sonny's face. His face was troubled, he was working hard, but he wasn't with it. And I had the feeling that, in a way, everyone on the bandstand was waiting for him, both waiting for him and pushing him along. But as I began to watch Creole, I realized that it was Creole who held them all back. He had them on a short rein. Up there, keeping the beat with his whole body, wailing on the fiddle, with his eyes half closed, he was listening to everything, but he was listening to Sonny. He was having a dialogue with Sonny. He wanted Sonny to leave the shoreline and strike out for the deep water. He was Sonny's witness that deep water and drowning were not the same thing— he had been there, and he knew. And he wanted Sonny to know. He was waiting for Sonny to do the things on the keys which would let Creole know that Sonny was in the water.

And, while Creole listened, Sonny moved, deep within, exactly like someone in torment. I had never before thought of how awful the relationship must be between the musician and his instrument. He has to fill it, this instrument, with the breath of life, his own. He has to make it do what he wants it to do. And a piano is just a piano. It's made out of so much wood and wires and little hammers and big ones, and ivory. While there's only so much you can do with it, the only way to find this out is to try; and try and make it do everything.

And Sonny hadn't been near a piano for over a year. And he wasn't on much better terms with his life, not the life that stretched before him. He and the piano stammered, started one way, got scared, stopped; started another way, panicked, marked time, started again; then seemed to have found a direction, panicked again, got stuck. And the face I saw on Sonny I'd never seen before. Everything had been burned out of it, and, at the same time, things usually hidden were being burned in, by the fire and fury of the battle which was occurring in him up there.

Yet, watching Creole's face as they neared the end of the first set, I had the feeling that something had happened, something I hadn't heard. Then they finished, there was scattered applause, and then, without an instant's warning, Creole started into something else, it was almost sardonic, it was *Am I Blue*. And, as though he commanded, Sonny began to play. Something began to happen. And Creole let out the reins. The dry, low, black man said something awful on the drums, Creole answered, and the drums talked back. Then the horn insisted, sweet and high, slightly detached perhaps, and Creole listened, commenting now and then, dry, and driving, beautiful and calm and old. Then they all came together again, and Sonny was part of the family again. I could tell this from his face. He seemed to have found, right there beneath his fingers, a damn brand-new piano. It seemed that he couldn't get over it. Then, for a while, just being happy with Sonny, they seemed to be agreeing with him that brand-new pianos certainly were a gas.

235        Then Creole stepped forward to remind them that what they were playing was the blues. He hit something in all of them, he hit something in me, myself, and the music tightened and deepened, apprehension began to beat the air. Creole began to tell us what the blues were all about. They were not about anything very new. He and his boys up there were keeping it new, at the risk of ruin, destruction, madness, and death, in order to find new ways to make us listen. For, while the tale of how we suffer, and how we are delighted, and how we may triumph is never new, it always must be heard. There isn't any other tale to tell, it's the only light we've got in all this darkness.

And this tale, according to that face, that body, those strong hands on those strings, has another aspect in every country, and a new depth in every generation. Listen, Creole seemed to be saying, listen. Now these are Sonny's blues. He made the little black man on the drums know it, and the bright, brown man on the horn. Creole wasn't trying any longer to get Sonny in the water. He was wishing him Godspeed. Then he stepped back, very slowly, filling the air with the immense suggestion that Sonny speak for himself.

Then they all gathered around Sonny and Sonny played. Every now and again one of them seemed to say, amen. Sonny's fingers filled the air with life, his life. But that life contained so many others. And Sonny went all the way back, he really began with the spare, flat statement of the opening phrase of the song. Then he began to make it his. It was very beautiful because it wasn't hurried and it was no longer a lament. I seemed to hear with what burning he had made it his, with what burning we had yet to make it ours, how we could cease lamenting. Freedom lurked around us and I understood, at last, that he could help us to be free if we would listen, that he would never be free until we did. Yet, there was no battle in his face now, I heard what he had gone through, and would continue to go through until he came to rest in earth. He had made it his: that long line, of which we knew only Mama and Daddy. And he was giving it back, as everything must be given back, so that, passing through death, it can live forever. I saw my mother's face again, and felt, for the first time, how the stones of the road she had walked on must have bruised her feet. I saw the moonlit road where my father's brother died. And it brought something else back to me, and carried me past it. I saw my little girl again and felt Isabel's tears again, and I felt my own tears begin to rise. And I was yet aware that this was only a moment, that the world waited outside, as hungry as a tiger, and that trouble stretched above us, longer than the sky.

Then it was over. Creole and Sonny let out their breath, both soaking wet, and grinning. There was a lot of applause and some of it was real. In the dark, the girl came by and I asked her to take drinks to the bandstand. There was a long pause, while they talked up there in the indigo light and after awhile I saw the girl put a Scotch and milk on top of the piano for Sonny. He didn't seem to notice it, but just before they started playing again, he sipped from it and looked toward me, and nodded. Then he put it back on top of the piano. For me, then, as they began to play again, it glowed and shook above my brother's head like the very cup of trembling.[7]

---

[7]**cup of trembling** an allusion to Isaiah 51.22:"Thus saith thy Lord the Lord, and thy God that pleadeth the cause of his people, Behold, I have taken out of thine hand the cup of trembling, even the dregs of the cup of my fury; thou shalt no more drink it again."

# JORGE LUIS BORGES

*Jorge Luis Borges (1899-1986), one of the first writers in Spanish to achieve an international reputation, was born in Buenos Aires. His paternal grandfather was English, and Borges learned English before he learned Spanish. When his family went to Geneva before World War I, he became fluent in German and French. After the war the family spent two years in Spain, in 1921 Borges returned to Argentina, and in 1925 he published his first book, a collection of poems. In 1938 he accepted a post as a municipal librarian in Buenos Aires, but in 1946—by which time Borges's fiction had won him an international reputation—the dictator Juan Perón removed him from the post. In 1955, after Perón was deposed, Borges—already blind from a congenital disease— was made the director of the National Library of Buenos Aires, and in 1956 he was appointed Professor of English at the University of Buenos Aires.*

*Borges, widely regarded as the greatest contemporary writer in Spanish, is known for his poetry, literary criticism, and especially his highly innovative and immensely influential short fiction. For him, stories are not representations of the surface of life but are re-creations of the cultural myths that human beings have devised.*

## *The Gospel According to Mark*                              [1970]

These events took place at La Colorada ranch, in the southern part of the township of Junín, during the last days of March, 1928. The protagonist was a medical student named Baltasar Espinosa. We may describe him, for now, as one of the common run of young men from Buenos Aires, with nothing more noteworthy about him than an almost unlimited kindness and a capacity for public speaking that had earned him several prizes at the English school in Ramos Mejía. He did not like arguing, and preferred having his listener rather than himself in the right. Although he was fascinated by the probabilities of chance in any game he played, he was a bad player because it gave him no pleasure to win. His wide intelligence was undirected; at the age of thirty-three, he still lacked credit for graduation, by one course—the course to which he was most drawn. His father, who was a freethinker (like all the gentlemen of his day), had introduced him to the lessons of Herbert Spencer,[1] but his mother, before his leaving on a trip for Montevideo, once asked him to say the Lord's Prayer[2] and make the sign of the cross every night. Through the years, he had never gone back on that promise.

---

[1]**Herbert Spencer** British philosopher and sociologist (1820-1903).     [2]**the Lord's Prayer** the prayer Jesus taught to his disciples (Matthew 6.9-13).

Espinosa was not lacking in spirit; one day, with more indifference than anger, he had exchanged two or three punches with a group of fellow-students who were trying to force him to take part in a university demonstration. Owing to an acquiescent nature, he was full of opinions, or habits of mind, that were questionable: Argentina mattered less to him than a fear that in other parts of the world people might think of us as Indians; he worshiped France but despised the French; he thought little of Americans but approved the fact that there were tall buildings, like theirs, in Buenos Aires; he believed the gauchos of the plains to be better riders than those of hill or mountain country. When his cousin Daniel invited him to spend the summer months out at La Colorada, he said yes at once—not because he was really fond of the country, but more out of his natural complacency and also because it was easier to say yes than to dream up reasons for saying no.

The ranch's main house was big and slightly run-down; the quarters of the foreman, whose name was Gutre, were close by. The Gutres were three: the father, an unusually uncouth son, and a daughter of uncertain paternity. They were tall, strong, and bony, and had hair that was on the reddish side and faces that showed traces of Indian blood. They were barely articulate. The foreman's wife had died years before.

There in the country, Espinosa began learning things he never knew, or even suspected—for example, that you do not gallop a horse when approaching settlements, and that you never go out riding except for some special purpose. In time, he was to come to tell the birds apart by their calls.

After a few days, Daniel had to leave for Buenos Aires to close a deal on some cattle. At most, this bit of business might take him a week. Espinosa, who was already somewhat weary of hearing about his cousin's incessant luck with women and his tireless interest in the minute details of men's fashion, preferred staying on at the ranch with his textbooks. But the heat was unbearable, and even the night brought no relief. One morning at daybreak, thunder woke him. Outside, the wind was rocking the Australian pines. Listening to the first heavy drops of rain, Espinosa thanked God. All at once, cold air rolled in. That afternoon, the Salado overflowed its banks.

The next day, looking out over the flooded fields from the gallery of the main house, Baltasar Espinosa thought that the stock metaphor comparing the pampas to the sea was not altogether false—at least, not that morning—though W. H. Hudson[3] had remarked that the sea seems wider because we view it from a ship's deck and not from a horse or from eye level.

The rain did not let up. The Gutres, helped or hindered by Espinosa, the town dweller, rescued a good part of the livestock, but many animals were drowned. There were four roads leading to La Colorada; all of them were under water. On the third day, when a leak threatened the foreman's house, Espinosa gave the Gutres a room near the tool shed, at the back of the main house. This drew them all closer; they ate together in the big dining room. Conversation turned out to be difficult. The Gutres, who knew so much about country things, were hard put to it to explain them.

[3]**W. H. Hudson** William Henry Hudson (1841–1922), born of American parents in Argentina, went to England in 1869 and spent most of the rest of his life there. Several of his books are about Argentina.

One night, Espinosa asked them if people still remembered the Indian raids from back when the frontier command was located there in Junín. They told him yes, but they would have given the same answer to a question about the beheading of Charles I. Espinosa recalled his father's saying that almost every case of longevity that was cited in the country was really a case of bad memory or of a dim notion of dates. Gauchos are apt to be ignorant of the year of their birth or of the name of the man who begot them.

In the whole house, there was apparently no other reading matter than a set of the *Farm Journal,* a handbook of veterinary medicine, a deluxe edition of the Uruguayan epic *Tabaré,* a *History of Shorthorn Cattle in Argentina,* a number of erotic or detective stories, and a recent novel called *Don Segundo Sombra.* Espinosa, trying in some way to bridge the inevitable after-dinner gap, read a couple of chapters of this novel to the Gutres, none of whom could read or write. Unfortunately, the foreman had been a cattle drover, and the doings of the hero, another cattle drover, failed to whet his interest. He said that the work was light, that drovers always traveled with a pack horse that carried everything they needed, and that, had he not been a drover, he would never have seen such far-flung places as the Laguna de Gómez, the town of Bragado, and the spread of the Núñez family in Chacabuco. There was a guitar in the kitchen; the ranch hands, before the time of the events I am describing, used to sit around in a circle. Someone would tune the instrument without ever getting around to playing it. This was known as a guitarfest.

10    Espinosa, who had grown a beard, began dallying in front of the mirror to study his new face, and he smiled to think how, back in Buenos Aires, he would bore his friends by telling them the story of the Salado flood. Strangely enough, he missed places he never frequented and never would: a corner of Cabrera Street on which there was a mailbox; one of the cement lions of a gateway on Jujuy Street, a few blocks from the Plaza del Once; an old barroom with a tiled floor, whose exact whereabouts he was unsure of. As for his brothers and his father, they would already have learned from Daniel that he was isolated—etymologically, the word was perfect—by the floodwaters.

Exploring the house, still hemmed in by the watery waste, Espinosa came across an English Bible. Among the blank pages at the end, the Guthries—such was their original name—had left a handwritten record of their lineage. They were natives of Inverness;[4] had reached the New World, no doubt as common laborers, in the early part of the nineteenth century; and had intermarried with Indians. The chronicle broke off sometime during the eighteen-seventies, when they no longer knew how to write. After a few generations, they had forgotten English; their Spanish, at the time Espinosa knew them, gave them trouble. They lacked any religious faith, but there survived in their blood, like faint tracks, the rigid fanaticism of the Calvinists and the superstitions of the pampas Indians. Espinosa later told them of his find, but they barely took notice.

Leafing through the volume, his fingers opened it at the beginning of the Gospel according to St. Mark. As an exercise in translation, and maybe to find out whether the Gutres understood any of it, Espinosa decided to begin reading them that text after their evening meal. It surprised him that they listened attentively, absorbed. Maybe the gold letters on the cover lent the

---

[4]**Inverness** a county in northwest Scotland.

book authority. It's still there in their blood, Espinosa thought. It also occurred to him that the generations of men, throughout recorded time, have always told and retold two stories—that of a lost ship which searches the Mediterranean seas for a dearly loved island, and that of a god who is crucified on Golgotha.[5] Remembering his lessons in elocution from his schooldays in Ramos Mejía, Espinosa got to his feet when he came to the parables.

The Gutres took to bolting their barbecued meat and their canned sardines so as not to delay the Gospel. A pet lamb that the girl adorned with a small blue ribbon had injured itself on a strand of barbed wire. To stop the bleeding, the three had wanted to apply a cobweb to the wound, but Espinosa treated the animal with some pills. The gratitude that this treatment awakened in them took him aback. (Not trusting the Gutres at first, he'd hidden away in one of his books the two hundred and forty pesos he had brought with him.) Now, with the owner of the place away, Espinosa took over and gave timid orders, which were immediately obeyed. The Gutres, as if lost without him, liked following him from room to room and along the gallery that ran around the house. While he read to them, he noticed that they were secretly stealing the crumbs he had dropped on the table. One evening, he caught them unawares, talking about him respectfully, in very few words.

Having finished the Gospel according to St. Mark, he wanted to read another of the three Gospels that remained, but the father asked him to repeat the one he had just read, so that they could understand it better. Espinosa felt that they were like children, to whom repetition is more pleasing than variations or novelty. That night—this is not to be wondered at—he dreamed of the Flood; the hammer blows of the building of the Ark woke him up, and he thought that perhaps they were thunder. In fact, the rain, which had let up, started again. The cold was bitter. The Gutres had told him that the storm had damaged the roof of the tool shed, and that they would show it to him after the beams were fixed. No longer a stranger now, he was treated by them with special attention, almost to the point of spoiling him. None of them liked coffee, but for him there was always a small cup into which they heaped sugar.

15      The second storm had broken out on a Tuesday. Thursday night, Espinosa was awakened by a soft knock at his door, which—just in case—he always kept locked. He got out of bed and opened it; there was the girl. In the dark he could hardly make her out, but by her footsteps he could tell she was barefoot, and moments later, in bed, that she must have come all the way from the other end of the house naked. She did not embrace him or speak a single word; she lay beside him, trembling. It was the first time she had known a man. When she left, she did not kiss him; Espinosa realized that he didn't even know her name. For some reason that he did not want to pry into, he made up his mind that upon returning to Buenos Aires he would tell no one about what had taken place.

The next day began like the previous ones, except that the father spoke to Espinosa and asked him if Christ had let Himself be killed so as to save all

---

[5]**two stories . . . Golgotha** the first story is Homer's *Odyssey*, in which Homer tells of the wanderings of Odysseus; the second story is of Jesus's crucifixion at Golgotha, "Place of the Skull" (the Semitic name for Calvary).

other men on earth. Espinosa, who was a freethinker but who felt committed to what he had read to the Gutres, answered, "Yes, to save everyone from Hell."

Gutre then asked, "What's Hell?"

"A place under the ground where souls burn and burn."

"And the Roman soldiers who hammered in the nails—were they saved, too?"

20    "Yes," said Espinosa, whose theology was rather dim.

All along, he was afraid that the foreman might ask him about what had gone on the night before with his daughter. After lunch, they asked him to read the last chapters over again.

Espinosa slept a long nap that afternoon. It was a light sleep, disturbed by persistent hammering and by vague premonitions. Toward evening, he got up and went out onto the gallery. He said, as if thinking aloud, "The waters have dropped. It won't be long now."

"It won't be long now," Gutre repeated, like an echo.

The three had been following him. Bowing their knees to the stone pavement, they asked his blessing. Then they mocked at him, spat on him, and shoved him toward the back part of the house. The girl wept. Espinosa understood what awaited him on the other side of the door. When they opened it, he saw a patch of sky. A bird sang out. A goldfinch,[6] he thought. The shed was without a roof; they had pulled down the beams to make the cross.

---

[6]**goldfinch** in art the infant Jesus is often shown holding a goldfinch. Legend says that at Calvary a goldfinch drew a thorn from Christ's brow.

# OSCAR CASARES

*Oscar Casares, born (1964) and raised in Brownsville, Texas, is a graduate of the Iowa Writers' Workshop. Casares, who teaches creative writing at the University of Texas in Austin, has published widely and received numerous prizes, including the James Michener Award. We reprint a story from his collection,* Brownsville Stories *(2003).*

## *Yolanda*                                                    [2003]

When I can't sleep at night I think of Yolanda Castro. She was a woman who lived next door to us one summer when I was growing up. I've never told Maggie about her because it's not something she'd appreciate knowing. Trust me. Tonight, like most nights, she fell asleep before I was even done brushing my teeth. And now all I can hear are little snores. Sometimes she even talks to herself, shouts out other people's names, and then in the morning says she can't remember any of it. Either way, I let her go on sleeping. She's over on her side of the bed. It's right where she ought to be. This thing with Yolanda doesn't really concern her.

I was only twelve years old when Frank and Yolanda Castro moved into the beige house with green trim. Frank pulled up on our street in a U-Haul he'd driven all the way from California to Texas. I remember it being a different neighborhood back then. Everybody knew everybody, and people left their doors unlocked at night. You didn't worry about people stealing shit you didn't lock up. I'm talking about more than twenty years ago now. I'm talking about before some drunk spent all afternoon in one of the cantinas on Fourteenth Street, then drove his car straight into the Rivas front yard and ran over the Baby Jesus that was still lying in the manger because Lonny Rivas was too flojo[1] to put it away a month after Christmas, and then the guy tried to run, but fell down, asleep, in our yard, and when the cops were handcuffing him all he could say was *ma-ri-juan-a,* which even then, at the age of fifteen, I knew wasn't a good thing to say when you were being arrested. This was before Pete Zuniga was riding his brand-new ten-speed from Western Auto and, next to the Friendship Garden, saw a white dude who'd been knifed a couple of dozen times and was floating in the green water of the resaca.[2] Before some crazy woman hired a curandera[3] to put a spell on her daughter's ex-boyfriend, which really meant hiring a couple of hit men from Matamoros to do a drive-by. Before the cops ever had to show up at El Disco de Oro Tortillería. Like holding up a 7-Eleven was getting old, right? You know, when you could sit at the Brownsville Coffee Shop #1 and not worry about getting it in the back while you ate your menudo.[4] When you didn't have to put an alarm *and* the Club on your car so it wouldn't end up in Reynosa. Before my father had to put iron bars on the windows and doors because some future convict from the junior high was always breaking into the house. And before my father had to put a fence in the front because, in his words, I'm sick and tired of all those damn dogs making poo in my yard. I guess what I'm trying to say is, things were different back then.

Frank Castro was an older man, in his fifties by that point, and Yolanda couldn't have been more than thirty, if that. My mother got along with Yolanda okay and even helped her get a job at the HEB store where she had worked since before I was born. You could say that was where the problems started, because Frank Castro didn't want his wife working at HEB, or any other place for that matter. You have no business being in that grocery store, I heard him yell one night when I was trying to fall asleep. I could hear almost everything Frank yelled that summer. Our houses were only a few yards apart, and my window was the closest to the action. My father's bougainvilleas were the dividing line between the two properties. I heard Yolanda beg Frank to please let her take the job. I heard Frank yell something in Spanish about how no woman in his family had ever worked behind a cosmetics counter, selling lipstick. I heard her promise she'd only work part-time, and she'd quit if they ever scheduled her on nights or weekends. I heard her tell him how much she loved him and how she'd never take a job that would keep them apart. Francisco, tú eres mi vida,[5] she said to him. I heard him get real quiet. Then I heard Frank and Yolanda Castro making love. I didn't know what making love sounded like back then, but I can tell you now that's what it was.

If you saw what Yolanda looked like, you might not have blamed Frank for not wanting her to leave the house. It also wouldn't have been a big mystery to you how she went into the store applying for a job in the meat department and ended up getting one in cosmetics. The only girl I'd ever seen that even

---

[1]**flojo** weak-willed.   [2]**resaca** dry streambed.   [3]**curandera** midwife.   [4]**menudo** tripe soup.   [5]**tú . . . vida** you are my life.

came close to being as beautiful as Yolanda was in a *Playboy* I found under my parents' bed the summer before. The girl in the magazine had the same long black hair, light brown skin, and green eyes that Yolanda did, only she was sitting bareback on an Appaloosa.

5        The thing I remember most about Frank was his huge forearms. They were like Popeye's, except with a lot more black and gray hair mixed in. But the hair on his arms was just the beginning. There wasn't a time I saw the guy that he didn't look like he could've used a good shave. And it didn't help that his thick eyebrows were connected into one long eyebrow that stretched across the bottom of his forehead like a piece of electrical tape. He was average size, but he looked short and squatty when he stood next to Yolanda. Frank was a mechanic at the airport and, according to my father, probably made good money. I was with my father the first time he met Frank. He always made it a point to meet any new neighbors and then come back to the house and give a full report to my mother, who would later meet the neighbors herself and say he was exaggerating about how shifty so-and-so's eyes were or how rich he thought another neighbor might be because he had one of those new foreign cars in the driveway, un carro extranjero,[6] a Toyota or a Honda. Frank was beginning to mow his front yard when we walked up. My father introduced me as his boy, and I shook our neighbor's sweaty hand. I've lived thirty-six years on this earth and never shaken hands with a bear, but I have a good idea that it wouldn't be much different from shaking Frank Castro's hand. Even his fingers needed a haircut. Frank stood there answering a couple of my father's questions about whether he liked the neighborhood (he liked it) and how long he had lived in California before moving back to Texas (ten years—he held up both hands to show us exactly how many). Suddenly, my father nodded and said we had to go. He turned around and walked off, then looked over his shoulder and yelled at me to hurry up. This whole time, Frank had not shut off his mower. My father was forced to stand there and shout over the sound of the engine. The report on Frank wasn't pretty when we got back to the house. From that point on, my father would only refer to him as El Burro.

It wasn't just my father. Nobody liked Frank. He had this thing about his yard where he didn't want anybody getting near it. We found this out one day when Lonny and I were throwing the football around in the street. Lonny was showing off and he threw the ball over my head, way over, and it landed in Frank's yard. When I was getting the ball, Frank opened the front door and yelled something about it being private property. Then he went over, turned on the hose, and started watering his yard and half the street in front of his yard. He did this every afternoon from that day on. The hose with a spray gun in his right hand, and a Schlitz tallboy in his left. Lonny thought we should steal the hose when Frank wasn't home, or maybe poke a few holes in it, just to teach the fucker a lesson. One Saturday morning we even saw him turn the hose on some Jehovahs who were walking up the street towards his house. A skinny man wearing a tie and short-sleeve shirt kept trying to give him a pamphlet, but Frank wasn't listening.

My mother gave Yolanda a ride to work every day. In the afternoons, Yolanda got off work early enough to be waiting for Frank to pull up in his

---

[6]**carro extranjero** foreign car.

car and drive her back to the house. My mother told us at home that Yolanda
had asked Frank to teach her how to drive when they first got married but
that Frank had said she was his princesa now and any place she needed to
go, he'd take her. One morning, when both my mother and Yolanda had the
day off, my mother asked her if she wanted to learn how to drive. They
drove out by the port, and my mother pulled over so Yolanda could take the
wheel. I was hanging out at the Jiffy-Mart, down the street, when I saw
Yolanda driving my mother's car. Yolanda honked the horn, and they both
waved at me as they turned the corner.

That night—like a lot of nights that summer—I listened to Frank and
Yolanda Castro. What they said went something like this:

"I can show you."

10   "I don't wanna see."

"Why not?"

"Because you have *no* business driving a car around town."

"But this way you don't have to pick me up every day. You can come
straight home, and I'll be here already, waiting."

"I don't care. I'm talking about you learning to drive."

15   "Frank, it's nothing."

"You don't even have a car. What do you want with a license?"

"I can buy one."

"With what?"

"I've been getting bonuses. The companies gives us a little extra if we
sell more of their makeup."

20   "Is that right?"

"It isn't that much, Frank."

"And then?"

"Well, maybe I can buy a used one."

"It's because of that store."

25   "What's wrong with the store?"

"It's putting ideas in your head."

"Frank, what ideas?"

"Ideas! Is there some place I haven't taken you?"

"No."

30   "Well, then?"

"Francisco."

"Don't 'Francisco' me."

"Baby . . . "

"¡Qué no!"[7]

35   They were beginning to remind me of one of my mother's novellas,
which she was probably watching in the living room at that very moment.
Things like that usually made me want to laugh—and I did a little, into my
pillow, but it was only because I couldn't believe I was actually hearing it,
and I could see Frank Castro pounding me into the ground with his big forearms if he ever found out.

"No! I said."

"I'm not Trini."

"I never said . . . "

---

[7]**¡Qué no!** Why not?

"Then stop treating me like her. ¿No sabes qué tanto te quiero, Francisco?"[8]

40      It got quiet for a while after that. Then there was the sound of something hitting the floor, the sound of two bodies dropping on a bed with springs that had seen better days (and nights), the sound of Yolanda saying, *Ay, Diosito,*[9] over and over and over again—just like my tía[10] Hilda did the day her son, my cousin Rudy, almost drowned in the swimming pool at the Civic Center—then the sound of the bed springs making their own crazy music, and the sound of what I imagine a bear is like when he's trying to make little bears.

Yolanda kept getting a ride to work with my mother, and Frank kept bringing her home in the afternoons. My mother had offered to drive Yolanda to the DPS office and let her borrow our car for the driving part of the test, but Yolanda said she'd changed her mind and didn't want to talk about it. I heard my mother telling my father what she'd said, and they agreed it probably had something to do with Frank. El Burro, my father let out when they didn't have anything else to say.

It was the Fourth of July when I got sick that summer. I remember my mother wouldn't let me go outside with Lonny. He kept yelling at me from the street that night to stop being a baby and come out of the house so I could pop some firecrackers. We'd been talking all week about shooting some bottle rockets in the direction of Frank's house. It didn't feel like anything at first, just a fever, but the next morning we knew it was the chicken pox. My mother had to miss a few days of work, staying home with me until I got over the worst part. After that, Yolanda volunteered to come look in on me when she wasn't working. But I told my mother I didn't want her coming over when I still looked like those dead people in that *Night of the Living Dead* movie. My mother said Yolanda would understand I was sick, and if she didn't, that's what I'd get for watching those kinds of movies. So for about a week she came over in the mornings and we watched *The Price Is Right* together. Yolanda was great at guessing the prices of things, and she said it was from working in a grocery store and having a good memory. I told her I thought she should go on the show. She laughed and said she probably wouldn't win anything, since she'd be too nervous. What I meant to say was that she should go on the show and be one of the girls who stands next to the car, smiling. She was prettier than any of them, but I never told her that, because I got embarrassed whenever I thought about saying it.

If Yolanda came over in the afternoon, we'd watch *General Hospital* together. She said she'd been watching it for years. There wasn't anything else on at that hour, so I didn't really care. Once, she brought over some lime sherbert, and we played Chinese checkers in my room until she had to get home to Frank Castro. Each time she left she'd reach down and give me a little kiss on the cheek, and each time her hair smelled like a different fruit. Sometimes like a pear, sometimes like a strawberry, sometimes like an apple. The strawberry was my favorite.

---

[8]**¿No . . . Francisco?** Don't you know how much I love you, Francisco?    [9]*Ay, Diosito* Oh, God.    [10]**tía** aunt.

* * *

This was about the time when Frank said that from now on, he would take Yolanda to work in the morning—no matter how out of the way it was for him, or the fact that he and my mother were always pulling out of the driveway at the same time. A week or two went by, and then my mother told my father that Frank had started showing up at the store in the middle of the day, usually during his lunch hour, but sometimes also at two or three in the afternoon. He wouldn't talk to Yolanda, but instead just hung out by the magazine rack, pretending to read a wrestling magazine. Yolanda tried to ignore him. My mother said she had talked to her in the break room, but Yolanda kept saying it was nothing, that Frank's hours had changed at the airport.

45     There was one Saturday when he was off from work, and as usual, he spent it in his front yard, sitting in a green lawn chair, drinking tallboys. He had turned on the sprinkler and was watching his grass and half the street get a good watering. Lonny and I were throwing the football around. Frank sat in that stupid chair all afternoon. He only went in to grab another beer and, I guess, take a piss. Each time he got up and turned around, we shot him the finger.

That night, I heard Frank's voice loud and clear. He wanted answers. Something about a phone number. Something about a customer he'd seen Yolanda talking to a couple of days earlier. Did she think he was blind? What the hell was so funny when the two of them were talking? How many times? he wanted to know. ¡Desgraciado![11] Where? Goddammit! he wanted to know. What game show? ¡El sanavabiche! Something shattered against the wall and then a few seconds later Yolanda screamed. I sat up. I didn't know if I could form words if I had to. What the hell were you doing listening anyway? they would ask me. There was another scream and then the sound of the back door slamming. I looked out my window and saw Frank Castro chase Yolanda into their backyard. She was wearing a nightgown that came down to her knees. Frank had on the same khakis and muscle shirt he'd worn that afternoon. He only ran a few feet down from the back steps before his head hit the clothesline, and he fell to the ground, hard. Yolanda didn't turn to look back and ran around the right side of their house. I thought she'd gone back inside to call the police. Then I heard footsteps and a tapping on my window. It was Yolanda whispering, Open it, open it.

I didn't say anything for a long time. Yolanda had climbed in and let down the blinds. We were lying on the bed, facing the window. She was behind me, holding me tight. I finally asked her if she wanted a glass of water or some Kool-Aid. I made it myself, I told her. It's the orange kind, I said. I didn't know what else to talk about. She said no, and then she told me to be quiet. I kept thinking, This has to be a dream and any minute now my mother's going to walk in and tell me the barbacoa[12] is sitting on the table and to come eat because we're going to eleven o'clock mass and don't even think about putting on those blue jeans with the patches in the knees ¿me entiendes?[13] But that wasn't happening, and something told me then that no matter what happened after tonight, this was something I'd never forget. There would always be a time *before* Yolanda crawled into my bed and a

---

[11]**Desgraciado** disgraceful.    [12]**barbacoa** baked lamb or goat.    [13]**me entiendes** do you understand me?

time *after*. As she held me, I could feel her heart beating. Then I felt her chiches[14] pressed against my back. And even though I couldn't see them, I knew they were perfect like the rest of her. I knew that they'd fit right in the palms of my hands, if only I had enough guts to turn around. Just turn around, that's all I had to do. I thought back to when she was tapping on the window, and I was sure she wasn't wearing a bra. I was sure there was nothing but Yolanda underneath her nightgown. I could have sworn I'd seen even more. I'd been close to a woman's body before. But this wasn't like when my tía Gloria came into town and couldn't believe how much I'd grown, and then she squeezed me so hard my head got lost in her huge and heavily perfumed chiches. And it wasn't anything like the Sears catalog where the girls had a tiny rose at the top of their panties. No, this was Yolanda and she was in my bed, pressed up against my back, like it was the only place in the world for us to be.

I could go on and tell you the rest of the details—how I never turned around and always regretted it, how we stayed there and listened to Frank crying in his backyard, how Lonny's dad finally called the cops on his ass, how Yolanda had a cousin pick her up the next morning, how she ended up leaving Frank for a man who worked for one of the shampoo companies, how it didn't matter because she'd also been seeing an assistant manager and would be having his baby soon enough, and how it really didn't matter because the assistant manager was already married and wasn't about to leave his wife and kids, and how, actually, none of it mattered because she'd been taking money out of the register and was about to be caught—but that's not the part of the story I like to remember.

In that bed of mine, the one with the Dallas Cowboy pillows and covers, Yolanda and I were safe. We were safe from Frank Castro and safe from anybody else that might try to hurt us. And it was safe for me to fall asleep in Yolanda's arms, with her warm, beautiful body pressed against mine, and dream that we were riding off to some faraway place on an Appaloosa.

---

[14]**chiches** breasts.

# DIANA CHANG

*Diana Chang (1934–2009), the author of several novels and books of poems, taught creative writing at Barnard College. Chang identified herself as an American writer whose background was mostly Chinese.*

## *The Oriental Contingent*                                                    [1989]

Connie couldn't remember whose party it was, whose house. She had an impression of kerosene lamps on brown wicker tables, of shapes talking in doorways. It was summer, almost the only time Connie has run into her since, too, and someone was saying, "You must know Lisa Mallory."

"I don't think so."

"She's here. You must know her."

Later in the evening, it was someone else who introduced her to a figure perched on the balustrade of the steps leading to the lawn where more shapes milled. In stretching out a hand to shake Connie's, the figure almost fell off sideways. Connie had pushed her back upright onto her perch and, peering, took in the fact that Lisa Mallory had a Chinese face. For a long instant, she felt nonplussed, and was rendered speechless.

5      But Lisa Mallory was filling the silence. "Well, now, Connie Sung," she said, not enthusiastically but with a kind of sophisticated interest, "I'm not in music myself, but Paul Wu's my cousin. Guilt by association!" She laughed. "No-tone music, I call his. He studied with John Cage, Varese, and so forth."

Surprised that Lisa knew she was a violinist, Connie murmured something friendly, wondering if she should simply ask outright, "I'm sure I should know, but what do you do?" but she hesitated, taking in her appearance instead, while Lisa went on with, "It's world class composing. Nothing's wrong with the level. But it's hard going for the layman, believe me."

Lisa Mallory wore a one-of-a-kind kimono dress, but it didn't make her look Japanese at all, and her hair was drawn back tightly in a braid which stood out from close to the top of her head horizontally. You could probably lift her off her feet by grasping it, like the handle of a pot.

"You should give a concert here, Connie," she said, using her first name right away, Connie noticed, like any American. "Lots of culturati around." Even when she wasn't actually speaking, she pursued her own line of thought actively and seemed to find herself mildly amusing.

"I'm new to the area," Connie said, deprecatingly. "I've just been a weekend guest, actually, till a month ago."

10     "It's easy to be part of it. Nothing to it. I should know. You'll see."

"I wish it weren't so dark," Connie found herself saying, waving her hand in front of her eyes as if the night were a veil to brush aside. She recognized in herself that intense need to see, to see into fellow Orientals, to fathom them. So far, Lisa Mallory had not given her enough clues, and the darkness itself seemed to be interfering.

Lisa dropped off her perch. "It's important to be true to oneself," she said. "Keep the modern stuff out of your repertory. Be romantic. Don't look like that! You're best at the romantics. Anyhow, take it from me. I know. And *I* like what I like."

Released by her outspokenness, Connie laughed and asked, "I'm sure I should know, but what is it that you do?" She was certain Lisa would say something like, "I'm with a public relations firm." "I'm in city services."

But she replied, "What do all Chinese excel at?" Not as if she'd asked a rhetorical question, she waited, then answered herself. "Well, aren't we all physicists, musicians, architects, or in software?"

15     At that point a voice broke in, followed by a large body which put his arms around both women, "The Oriental contingent! I've got to break this up."

Turning, Lisa kissed him roundly, and said over her shoulder to Connie, "I'll take him away before he tells us we look alike!"

They melted into the steps below, and Connie, feeling put off balance and somehow slow-witted, was left to think over her new acquaintance.

"Hello, Lisa Mallory," Connie Sung always said on the infrequent occasions when they ran into one another. She always said "Hello, Lisa Mallory," with a shyness she did not understand in herself. It was strange, but they had no mutual friends except for Paul Wu, and Connie had not seen him in ages.

Connie had no one of whom to ask her questions. But sometime soon, she'd be told Lisa's maiden name. Sometime she'd simply call her Lisa. Sometime what Lisa did with her life would be answered.

Three, four years passed, with their running into one another at receptions and openings, and still Lisa Mallory remained an enigma. Mildly amused herself, Connie wondered if other people, as well, found her inscrutable. But none of her American friends (though, of course, Lisa and she were Americans, too, she had to remind herself), none of the Caucasian friends seemed curious about backgrounds. In their accepting way, they did not wonder about Lisa's background, or about Connie's or Paul Wu's. Perhaps they assumed they were all cut from the same cloth. But to Connie, the Orientals she met were unread books, books she never had the right occasion or time to fully pursue.

20     She didn't even see the humor in her situation—it was such an issue with her. The fact was she felt less, much less, sure of herself when she was with real Chinese.

As she was realizing this, the truth suddenly dawned on her. Lisa Mallory never referred to her own background because it was more Chinese than Connie's, and therefore a higher order. She was tact incarnate. All along, she had been going out of her way not to embarrass Connie. Yes, yes. Her assurance was definitely uppercrust (perhaps her father had been in the diplomatic service), and her offhand didacticness, her lack of self-doubt, was indeed characteristically Chinese-Chinese. Connie was not only impressed by these traits, but also put on the defensive because of them.

Connie let out a sigh—a sigh that follows the solution to a nagging problem . . . Lisa's mysteriousness. But now Connie knew only too clearly that her own background made her decidedly inferior. Her father was a second-generation gynecologist who spoke hardly any Chinese. Yes, inferior and totally without recourse.

Of course, at one of the gatherings, Connie met Bill Mallory, too. He was simply American, maybe Catholic, possibly lapsed. She was not put off balance by him at all. But most of the time he was away on business, and Lisa cropped up at functions as single as Connie.

Then one day, Lisa had a man in tow—wiry and tall, he looked Chinese from the Shantung area, or perhaps from Beijing, and his styled hair made him appear vaguely artistic.

25     "Connie, I'd like you to meet Eric Li. He got out at the beginning of the _détente,_ went to Berkeley, and is assimilating a mile-a-minute," Lisa said, with her usual irony. "Bill found him and is grooming him, though he came with his own charisma."

Eric waved her remark aside. "Lisa has missed her calling. She was born to be in PR," he said, with an accent.

"Is that what she does?" Connie put in at once, looking only at him. "Is that her profession?"

"You don't know?" he asked, with surprise.

Though she was greeting someone else, Lisa turned and answered, "I'm a fabrics tycoon, I think I can say without immodesty." She moved away and continued her conversation with the other friend.

30     Behind his hand, he said, playfully, as though letting Connie in on a secret, "Factories in Hongkong and Taipei, and now he's—Bill, that is—is exploring them on the mainland."

"With her fabulous contacts over there!" Connie exclaimed, now seeing it all. "Of course, what a wonderful business combination they must make."

Eric was about to utter something, but stopped, and said flatly, "I have all the mainland contacts, even though I was only twenty when I left, but my parents . . ."

"How interesting," Connie murmured lamely. "I see," preoccupied as she was with trying to put two and two together.

Lisa was back and said without an introduction, continuing her line of thought, "You two look good together, if I have to say so myself. Why don't you ask him to one of your concerts? And you, Eric, you're in America now, so don't stand on ceremony, or you'll be out in left field." She walked away with someone for another drink.

35     Looking uncomfortable, but recovering himself with a smile, Eric said, "Lisa makes me feel more Chinese than I am becoming—it is her directness, I suspect. In China, we'd say she is too much like a man."

At which Connie found herself saying, "She makes me feel *less* Chinese."

"Less!"

"Less Chinese than she is."

"That is not possible," Eric said, with a shade of contempt—for whom? Lisa or Connie? He barely suppressed a laugh, cold as Chinese laughter could be.

40     Connie blurted out, "I'm a failed Chinese. Yes, and it's to you that I need to say it." She paused and repeated emphatically, "I am a failed Chinese." Her heart was beating quicker, but she was glad to have got that out, a confession and a definition that might begin to free her. "Do you know you make me feel that, too? You've been here only about ten years, right?"

"Right, and I'm thirty-one."

"You know what I think? I think it's harder for a Chinese to do two things."

At that moment, an American moved in closer, looking pleased somehow to be with them.

She continued, "It's harder for us to become American than, say, for a German, and it's also harder not to remain residually Chinese, even if you are third generation."

45     Eric said blandly, "Don't take yourself so seriously. You can't help being an American product."

Trying to be comforting, the American interjected with, "The young lady is not a product, an object. She is a human being, and there is no difference among peoples that I can see."

"I judge myself both as a Chinese and as an American," Connie said.

"You worry too much," Eric said, impatiently. Then he looked around and though she wasn't in sight, he lowered his voice. "She is what she is. I know what she is. But she avoids going to Hong Kong. She avoids it."

Connie felt turned around. "Avoids it?"

50     "Bill's in Beijing right now. She's here. How come?"

"I don't know," Connie replied, as though an answer had been required of her.

"She makes up many excuses, reasons. Ask her. Ask her yourself," he said, pointedly.

"Oh, I couldn't do that. By the way, I'm going on a concert tour next year in three cities—Shanghai, Beijing, and Nanking," Connie said. "It'll be my first time in China."

"Really! You must be very talented to be touring at your age," he said, genuinely interested for the first time. Because she was going to China, or because she now came across as an over-achiever, even though Chinese American?

55    "I'm just about your age," she said, realizing then that maybe Lisa Mallory had left them alone purposely.

"You could both pass as teenagers!" the American exclaimed.

Two months later, she ran into Lisa again. As usual, Lisa began in the middle of her own thought. "Did he call?"

"Who? Oh. No, no."

"Well, it's true he's been in China the last three weeks with Bill. They'll be back this weekend."

60    Connie saw her opportunity. "Are you planning to go to China yourself?"

For the first time, Lisa seemed at a loss for words. She raised her shoulders, then let them drop. Too airily, she said, "You know, there's always Paris. I can't bear not to go to Paris, if I'm to take a trip."

"But you're Chinese. You *have* been to China, you came from China originally, didn't you?"

"I could go to Paris twice a year, I love it so," Lisa said. "And then there's London, Florence, Venice."

"But—but your business contacts?"

65    "*My* contacts? Bill, he's the businessman who makes the contacts. Always has. I take care of the New York office, which is a considerable job. We have a staff of eighty-five."

Connie said, "I told Eric I'll be giving a tour in China. I'm taking Chinese lessons right now."

Lisa Mallory laughed, "Save your time. They'll still be disdainful over there. See, *they* don't care," and she waved her hand at the crowd. "Some of them have been born in Buffalo, too! It's the Chinese you can't fool. They know you're not the genuine article—you and I."

Her face was suddenly heightened in color, and she was breathing as if ready to flee from something. "Yes, you heard right. I was born in Buffalo."

"You were!" Connie exclaimed before she could control her amazement.

70    "Well, what about you?" Lisa retorted. She was actually shaking and trying to hide it by making sudden gestures.

"Westchester."

"But your parents at least were Chinese."

"Well, so were, so are, yours!"

"I was adopted by Americans. My full name is Lisa Warren Mallory."

75    Incredulous, Connie said, "I'm more Chinese than you!"

"Who isn't?" She laughed, unhappily. "Having Chinese parents makes all the difference. We're worlds apart."

"And all the time I thought . . . never mind what I thought."

"You have it over me. It's written all over you. I could tell even in the dark that night."

"Oh, Lisa," Connie said to comfort her, "none of this matters to anybody except us. Really and truly. They're too busy with their own problems."

80    "The only time I feel Chinese is when I'm embarrassed I'm not more Chinese—which is a totally Chinese reflex I'd give anything to be rid of!"

"I know what you mean."

"And as for Eric looking down his nose at me, he's knocking himself out to be so American, *but as a secure Chinese!* What's so genuine about that article?"

Both of them struck their heads laughing, but their eyes were not merry.

"Say it again," Connie asked of her, "say it again that my being more Chinese is written all over me."

85      "Consider it said," Lisa said. "My natural mother happened to be there at the time—I can't help being born in Buffalo."

"I know, I know," Connie said with feeling. "If only you had had some say in the matter."

"It's only Orientals who haunt me!" Lisa stamped her foot. "Only them!"

"I'm so sorry," Connie Sung said, for all of them. "It's all so turned around."

"So I'm made in America, so there!" Lisa Mallory declared, making a sniffing sound, and seemed to be recovering her *sangfroid*.

90      Connie felt tired—as if she'd traveled—but a lot had been settled on the way.

# ANTON CHEKHOV

*Anton Chekhov (1860–1904) was born in Russia, the son of a shopkeeper. While a medical student at Moscow University, Chekhov wrote stories, sketches, and reviews to help support his family and to finance his education. In 1884 he received his medical degree, began to practice medicine, published his first book of stories, and suffered the first of a series of hemorrhages from tuberculosis. In his remaining twenty years, in addition to writing several hundred stories, he wrote plays, half a dozen of which have established themselves as classics. He died from tuberculosis at the age of forty-four.*

## Misery                                                                [1886]

*Translated by Constance Garnett*

*"To Whom Shall I Tell My Grief?"*

The twilight of evening. Big flakes of wet snow are whirling lazily about the street lamps, which have just been lighted, and lying in a thin soft layer on roofs, horses' backs, shoulders, caps. Iona Potapov, the sledgedriver, is all white like a ghost. He sits on the box without stirring, bent as double as the living body can be bent. If a regular snowdrift fell on him it seems as though even then he would not think it necessary to shake it off. . . . His little mare is white and motionless too. Her stillness, the angularity of her lines, and the stick-like straightness of her legs make her look like a halfpenny gingerbread horse. She is probably lost in thought. Anyone who has been torn away from the plough, from the familiar gray landscapes, and cast into this slough, full of monstrous lights, of unceasing uproar and hurrying people, is bound to think.

It is a long time since Iona and his nag have budged. They came out of the yard before dinner-time and not a single fare yet. But now the shades of evening are falling on the town. The pale light of the street lamps changes to a vivid color, and the bustle of the street grows noisier.

"Sledge to Vyborgskaya!" Iona hears. "Sledge!"

Iona starts, and through his snow-plastered eyelashes sees an officer in a military overcoat with a hood over his head.

5      "To Vyborgskaya," repeats the officer. "Are you asleep? To Vyborgskaya!"

In token of assent Iona gives a tug at the reins which sends cakes of snow flying from the horse's back and shoulders. The officer gets into the sledge. The sledge-driver clicks to the horse, cranes his neck like a swan, rises in his seat, and more from habit than necessity brandishes his whip. The mare cranes her neck, too, crooks her stick-like legs, and hesitatingly sets off. . . .

"Where are you shoving, you devil?" Iona immediately hears shouts from the dark mass shifting to and fro before him. "Where the devil are you going? Keep to the r-right!"

"You don't know how to drive! Keep to the right," says the officer angrily.

A coachman driving a carriage swears at him; a pedestrian crossing the road and brushing the horse's nose with his shoulder looks at him angrily and shakes the snow off his sleeve. Iona fidgets on the box as though he were sitting on thorns, jerks his elbows, and turns his eyes about like one possessed, as though he did not know where he was or why he was there.

10      "What rascals they all are!" says the officer jocosely. "They are simply doing their best to run up against you or fall under the horse's feet. They must be doing it on purpose."

Iona looks at his fare and moves his lips. . . . Apparently he means to say something, but nothing comes out but a sniff.

"What?" inquires the officer.

Iona gives a wry smile, and straining his throat, brings out huskily: "My son . . . , er . . . my son died this week, sir."

"H'm! What did he die of?"

15      Iona turns his whole body round to his fare, and says:

"Who can tell! It must have been from fever. . . . He lay three days in the hospital and then he died. . . . God's will."

"Turn round, you devil!" comes out of the darkness. "Have you gone cracked, you old dog? Look where you are going!"

"Drive on! drive on! . . ." says the officer. "We shan't get there till tomorrow going on like this. Hurry up!"

The sledge-driver cranes his neck again, rises in his seat, and with heavy grace swings his whip. Several times he looks round at the officer, but the latter keeps his eyes shut and is apparently disinclined to listen. Putting his fare down at Vyborgskaya, Iona stops by a restaurant, and again sits huddled up on the box. . . . Again the wet snow paints him and his horse white. One hour passes, and then another. . . .

20      Three young men, two tall and thin, one short and hunchbacked, come up, railing at each other and loudly stamping on the pavement with their galoshes.

"Cabby, to the Police Bridge!" the hunchback cries in a cracked voice. "The three of us, . . . twenty kopecks!"

Iona tugs at the reins and clicks to his horse. Twenty kopecks is not a fair price, but he has no thoughts for that. Whether it is a rouble or whether it is five kopecks does not matter to him now so long as he has a fare. . . . The three young men, shoving each other and using bad language, go up to the sledge, and all three try to sit down at once. The question remains to be settled: Which are to sit down and which one is to stand? After a long alter-cation, ill-temper, and abuse, they come to the conclusion that the hunch-back must stand because he is the shortest.

"Well, drive on," says the hunchback in his cracked voice, settling him-self and breathing down Iona's neck. "Cut along! What a cap you've got, my friend! You wouldn't find a worse one in all Petersburg. . . ."

"He-he! . . . he-he! . . ." laughs Iona. "It's nothing to boast of!"

25 "Well, then, nothing to boast of, drive on! Are you going to drive like this all the way? Eh? Shall I give you one in the neck?"

"My head aches," says one of the tall ones. "At the Dukmasovs' yesterday Vaska and I drank four bottles of brandy between us."

"I can't make out why you talk such stuff," says the other tall one an-grily. "You lie like a brute."

"Strike me dead, it's the truth! . . ."

"It's about as true as that a louse coughs."

30 "He-he!" grins Iona. "Me-er-ry gentlemen!"

"Tfoo! the devil take you!" cries the hunchback indignantly. "Will you get on, you old plague, or won't you? Is that the way to drive? Give her one with the whip. Hang it all, give it her well."

Iona feels behind his back the jolting person and quivering voice of the hunchback. He hears abuse addressed to him, he sees people, and the feel-ing of loneliness begins little by little to be less heavy on his heart. The hunchback swears at him, till he chokes over some elaborately whimsical string of epithets and is overpowered by his cough. His tall companions begin talking of a certain Nadyezhda Petrovna. Iona looks round at them. Waiting till there is a brief pause, he looks round once more and says:

"This week. . . er . . . my . . . er . . . son died!"

"We shall all die, . . ." says the hunchback with a sigh, wiping his lips after coughing. "Come, drive on! drive on! My friends, I simply cannot stand crawling like this! When will he get us there?"

35 "Well, you give him a little encouragement . . . one in the neck!"

"Do you hear, you old plague? I'll make you smart. If one stands on cere-mony with fellows like you one may as well walk. Do you hear, you old dragon? Or don't you care a hang what we say?"

And Iona hears rather than feels a slap on the back of his neck.

"He-he! . . ." he laughs. "Merry gentlemen . . . God give you health!"

"Cabman, are you married?" asks one of the tall ones.

40 "I? He-he! Me-er-ry gentlemen. The only wife for me now is the damp earth. . . . He-ho-ho! . . . The grave that is! . . . Here my son's dead and I am alive. . . . It's a strange thing, death has come in at the wrong door. . . . Instead of coming for me it went for my son. . . ."

And Iona turns round to tell them how his son died, but at that point the hunchback gives a faint sigh and announces that, thank God! they have arrived at last. After taking his twenty kopecks, Iona gazes for a long while after the revelers, who disappear into a dark entry. Again he is alone and again there is silence for him. . . . The misery which has been for a brief space eased comes back again and tears his heart more cruelly than ever. With a look of anxiety and suffering Iona's eyes stray restlessly among the crowds moving to and fro on both sides of the street: can he not find among those thousands someone who will listen to him? But the crowds flit by heedless of him and his misery. . . . His misery is immense, beyond all bounds. If Iona's heart were to burst and his misery to flow out, it would flood the whole world, it seems, but yet it is not seen. It has found a hiding-place in such an insignificant shell that one would not have found it with a candle by daylight. . . .

Iona sees a house-porter with a parcel and makes up his mind to address him.

"What time will it be, friend?" he asks.

"Going on for ten. . . . Why have you stopped here? Drive on!"

45    Iona drives a few paces away, bends himself double, and gives himself up to his misery. He feels it is no good to appeal to people. But before five minutes have passed he draws himself up, shakes his head as though he feels a sharp pain, and tugs at the reins. . . . He can bear it no longer.

"Back to the yard!" he thinks. "To the yard!"

And his little mare, as though she knew his thoughts, falls to trotting. An hour and a half later Iona is sitting by a big dirty stove. On the stove, on the floor, and on the benches are people snoring. The air is full of smells and stuffiness. Iona looks at the sleeping figures, scratches himself, and regrets that he has come home so early. . . .

"I have not earned enough to pay for the oats, even," he thinks. "That's why I am so miserable. A man who knows how to do his work, . . . who has had enough to eat, and whose horse has had enough to eat, is always at ease. . . ."

In one of the corners a young cabman gets up, clears his throat sleepily, and makes for the waterbucket.

50    "Want a drink?" Iona asks him.

"Seems so."

"May it do you good. . . . But my son is dead, mate. . . . Do you hear? This week in the hospital. . . . It's queer business. . . ."

Iona looks to see the effect produced by his words, but he sees nothing. The young man has covered his head over and is already asleep. The old man sighs and scratches himself. . . . Just as the young man had been thirsty for water, he thirsts for speech. His son will soon have been dead a week, and he has not really talked to anybody yet. . . . He wants to talk of it properly, with deliberation. . . . He wants to tell how his son was taken ill, how he suffered, what he said before he died, how he died. . . . He wants to describe the funeral, and how he went to the hospital to get his son's clothes. He still has his daughter Anisya in the country. . . . And he wants to talk about her too. . . . Yes, he has plenty to talk about now. His listener ought to sigh and exclaim and lament. . . . It would be even better to talk to women. Though they are silly creatures, they blubber at the first word.

"Let's go out and have a look at the mare," Iona thinks. "There is always time for sleep. . . . You'll have sleep enough, no fear. . . ."

55    He puts on his coat and goes into the stables where his mare is standing. He thinks about oats, about hay, about the weather. . . . He cannot think about his son when he is alone. . . . To talk about him with someone is possible, but to think of him and picture him is insufferable anguish. . . .

"Are you munching?" Iona asks his mare, seeing her shining eyes. "There, munch away, munch away. . . . Since we have not earned enough for oats, we will eat hay. . . . Yes, . . . I have grown too old to drive. . . . My son ought to be driving, not I. . . . He was a real coachman. . . . He ought to have lived. . . ."

Iona is silent for a while, and then he goes on:

"That's how it is, old girl. . . . Kuzma Ionitch is gone. . . . He said good-by to me. . . . He went and died for no reason. . . . Now, suppose you had a little colt, and you were mother to that little colt. . . . And all at once that same little colt went and died. . . . You'd be sorry, wouldn't you?. . ."

The little mare munches, listens, and breathes on her master's hands. Iona is carried away and tells her all about it.

# WILLIAM FAULKNER

*William Faulkner (1897–1962) was brought up in Oxford, Mississippi. His great-grandfather had been a Civil War hero, and his father was treasurer of the University of Mississippi in Oxford; the family was no longer rich, but it was still respected. In 1918 he enrolled in the Royal Canadian Air Force, though he never saw overseas service. After the war he returned to Mississippi and went to the university for two years. He then moved to New Orleans, where he became friendly with Sherwood Anderson, who was already an established writer. Faulkner's major novels include* The Sound and the Fury *(1929),* As I Lay Dying *(1930), and* Light in August *(1932). Even after he had established himself as a major novelist with* The Sound and the Fury *(1929), he had to do some work in Hollywood in order to make ends meet. In 1950 he was awarded the Nobel Prize in Literature*

## Barn Burning                    [1939]

The store in which the Justice of the Peace's court was sitting smelled of cheese. The boy, crouched on his nail keg at the back of the crowded room, knew he smelled cheese, and more: from where he sat he could see the ranked shelves close-packed with the solid, squat, dynamic shapes of tin cans whose labels his stomach read, not from the lettering which mean nothing to his mind but from the scarlet devils and the silver curve of fish— this, the cheese which he knew he smelled and the hermetic meat which his intestines believed he smelled coming in intermittent gusts momentary and brief between the other constant one, the smell and sense just a little of fear because mostly of despair and grief, the old fierce pull of blood. He could not see the table where the Justice sat and before which his father and his father's enemy (*our enemy* he thought in that despair; *ourn! mine and hisn both! He's my father!*) stood, but he could hear them, the two of them, that is, because his father had said no word yet:

"But what proof have you, Mr. Harris?"

"I told you. The hog got into my corn. I caught it up and sent it back to him. He had no fence that would hold it. I told him so, warned him. The next time I put the hog in my pen. When he came to get it I gave him enough wire to patch up his pen. The next time I put the hog up and kept it. I rode down to his house and saw the wire I gave him still rolled on to the spool in his yard. I told him he could have the hog when he paid me a dollar pound fee. That evening a nigger came with the dollar and got the hog. He was a strange nigger. He said, 'He say to tell you wood and hay kin burn.' I said, 'What?' 'That whut he say to tell you,' the nigger said. 'Wood and hay kin burn.' That night my barn burned. I got the stock out but I lost the barn."

"Where is the nigger? Have you got him?"

5      "He was a strange nigger, I tell you. I don't know what became of him."

"But that's not proof. Don't you see that's not proof?"

"Get that boy up here. He knows." For a moment the boy thought too that the man meant his older brother until Harris said, "Not him. The little one. The boy," and, crouching, small for his age, small and wiry like his father, in patched and faded jeans even too small for him, with straight, uncombed, brown hair and eyes gray and wild as storm scud, he saw the men between himself and the table part and become a lane of grim faces, at the end of which he saw the Justice, a shabby, collarless, graying man in spectacles, beckoning him. He felt no floor under his bare feet; he seemed to walk beneath the palpable weight of the grim turning faces. His father, stiff in his black Sunday coat donned not for the trial but for the moving, did not even look at him. *He aims for me to lie,* he thought, again with that frantic grief and despair. *And I will have to do hit.*

"What's your name, boy?" the Justice said.

"Colonel Sartoris Snopes," the boy whispered.

10     "Hey?" the Justice said. "Talk louder. Colonel Sartoris? I reckon anybody named for Colonel Sartoris in this country can't help but tell the truth, can they?" The boy said nothing. *Enemy! Enemy!* he thought; for a moment he could not even see, could not see that the Justice's face was kindly nor discern that his voice was troubled when he spoke to the man named Harris: "Do you want me to question this boy?" But he could hear, and during those subsequent long seconds while there was absolutely no sound in the crowded little room save that of quiet and intent breathing it was as if he had swung outward at the end of a grape vine, over a ravine, and at the top of the swing had been caught in a prolonged instant of mesmerized gravity, weightless in time.

"No!" Harris said violently, explosively. "Damnation! Send him out of here!" Now time, the fluid world, rushed beneath him again, the voices coming to him again through the smell of cheese and sealed meat, the fear and despair and the old grief of blood:

"This case is closed. I can't find against you, Snopes, but I can give you advice. Leave this country and don't come back to it."

His father spoke for the first time, his voice cold and harsh, level, without emphasis: "I aim to. I don't figure to stay in a country among people who . . ." he said something unprintable and vile, addressed to no one.

"That'll do," the Justice said. "Take your wagon and get out of this country before dark. Case dismissed."

15     His father turned, and he followed the stiff black coat, the wiry figure walking a little stiffly from where a Confederate provost's man's musket ball had taken him in the heel on a stolen horse thirty years ago, followed the two backs now, since his older brother had appeared from somewhere in

the crowd, no taller than the father but thicker, chewing tobacco steadily, between the two lines of grim-faced men and out of the store and across the worn gallery and down the sagging steps and among the dogs and half-grown boys in the mild May dust, where as he passed a voice hissed: "Barn burner!"

Again he could not see, whirling; there was a face in a red haze, moonlike, bigger than the full moon, the owner of it half again his size, he leaping in the red haze toward the face, feeling no blow, feeling no shock when his head struck the earth, scrabbling up and leaping again, feeling no blow this time either and tasting no blood, scrabbling up to see the other boy in full flight and himself already leaping into pursuit as his father's hand jerked him back, the harsh, cold voice speaking above him: "Go get in the wagon."

It stood in a grove of locusts and mulberries across the road. His two hulking sisters in their Sunday dresses and his mother and her sister in calico and sunbonnets were already in it, sitting on and among the sorry residue of the dozen and more movings which even the boy could remember—the battered stove, the broken beds and chairs, the clock inlaid with mother-of-pearl, which would not run, stopped at some fourteen minutes past two o'clock of a dead and forgotten day and time, which had been his mother's dowry. She was crying, though when she saw him she drew her sleeve across her face and began to descend from the wagon. "Get back," the father said.

"He's hurt. I got to get some water and wash his . . ."

20      "Get back in the wagon," his father said. He got in too, over the tail-gate. His father mounted to the seat where the older brother already sat and struck the gaunt mules two savage blows with the peeled willow, but without heat. It was not even sadistic; it was exactly that same quality which in later years would cause his descendants to over-run the engine before putting a motor car into motion, striking and reining back in the same movement. The wagon went on, the store with its quiet crowd of grimly watching men dropped behind; a curve in the road hid it. *Forever* he thought. *Maybe he's done satisfied now, now that he has . . .* stopping himself, not to say it aloud even to himself. His mother's hand touched his shoulder.

"Does hit hurt?" she said.

"Naw," he said. "Hit don't hurt. Lemme be."

"Can't you wipe some of the blood off before hit dries?"

"I'll wash to-night," he said. "Lemme be, I tell you."

25      The wagon went on. He did not know where they were going. None of them ever did or ever asked, because it was always somewhere, always a house of sorts waiting for them a day or two days or even three days away. Likely his father had already arranged to make a crop on another farm before he . . . . Again he had to stop himself. He (the father) always did. There was something about his wolflike independence and even courage when the advantage was at least neutral which impressed strangers, as if they got from his latent ravening ferocity not so much a sense of dependability as a feeling that his ferocious conviction in the rightness of his own actions would be of advantage to all whose interest lay with his.

That night they camped, in a grove of oaks and beeches where a spring ran. The nights were still cool and they had a fire against it, of a rail lifted from a nearby fence and cut into lengths—a small fire, neat, niggard almost, a shrewd fire; such fires were his father's habit and custom always, even in freezing weather. Older, the boy might have remarked this and wondered why not a big one; why should not a man who had not only seen the waste and extravagance of war, but who had in his blood an inherent voracious prodigality with material not his own, have burned everything in sight? Then he might have gone a step farther and thought that that was the reason: that niggard blaze was the living fruit of nights passed during those four years in the woods hiding from all men, blue or gray, with his strings of horses (captured horses, he called them). And older still, he might have divined the true reason: that the element of fire spoke to some deep mainspring of his father's being, as the element of steel or of powder spoke to other men, as the one weapon for the preservation of integrity, else breath were not worth the breathing, and hence to be regarded with respect and used with discretion.

But he did not think this now and he had seen those same niggard blazes all his life. He merely ate his supper beside it and was already half asleep over his iron plate when his father called him, and once more he followed the stiff back, the stiff and ruthless limp, up the slope and on to the starlit road where, turning, he could see his father against the stars but without face or depth—a shape black, flat, and bloodless as though cut from tin in the iron folds of the frockcoat which had not been made for him, the voice harsh like tin and without heat like tin:

"You were fixing to tell them. You would have told him." He didn't answer. His father struck him with the flat of his hand on the side of the head, hard but without heat, exactly as he had struck the two mules at the store, exactly as he would strike either of them with any stick in order to kill a horse fly, his voice still without heat or anger: "You're getting to be a man. You got to learn. You got to learn to stick to your own blood or you ain't going to have any blood to stick to you. Do you think either of them, any man there this morning, would? Don't you know all they wanted was a chance to get at me because they knew I had them beat? Eh?" Later, twenty years later, he was to tell himself, "If I had said they wanted only truth, justice, he would have hit me again." But now he said nothing. He was not crying. He just stood there. "Answer me," his father said.

"Yes," he whispered. His father turned.

30      "Get on to bed. We'll be there to-morrow."

Tomorrow they were there. In the early afternoon the wagon stopped before a paintless two-room house identical almost with the dozen others it had stopped before even in the boy's ten years, and again, as on the other dozen occasions, his mother and aunt got down and began to unload the wagon, although his two sisters and his father and brother had not moved.

"Likely hit ain't fitten for hawgs," one of the sisters said.

"Nevertheless, fit it will and you'll hog it and like it," his father said. "Get out of them chairs and help your Ma unload."

The two sisters got down, big, bovine, in a flutter of cheap ribbons; one of them drew from the jumbled wagon bed a battered lantern, the other a worn broom. His father handed the reins to the older son and began to climb stiffly over the wheel. "When they get unloaded, take the team to the barn and feed them." Then he said, and at first the boy thought he was still speaking to his brother: "Come with me."

35      "Me?" he said.

"Yes," his father said. "You."

"Abner," his mother said. His father paused and looked back—the harsh level stare beneath the shaggy, graying, irascible brows.

"I reckon I'll have a word with the man that aims to begin tomorrow owning me body and soul for the next eight months."

They went back up the road. A week ago—or before last night, that is—he would have asked where they were going, but not now. His father had struck him before last night but never before had he paused afterward to explain why; it was as if the blow and the following calm, outrageous voice still rang, repercussed, divulging nothing to him save the terrible handicap of being young, the light weight of his few years, just heavy enough to prevent his soaring free of the world as it seemed to be ordered but not heavy enough to keep him footed solid in it, to resist it and try to change the course of its events.

40     Presently he could see the grove of oaks and cedars and the other flowering trees and shrubs where the house would be, though not the house yet. They walked beside a fence massed with honeysuckle and Cherokee roses and came to a gate swinging open between two brick pillars, and now, beyond a sweep of drive, he saw the house for the first time and at that instant he forgot his father and the terror and despair both, and even when he remembered his father again (who had not stopped) the terror and despair did not return. Because, for all the twelve movings, they had sojourned until now in a poor country, a land of small farms and fields and houses, and he had never seen a house like this before. *Hit's big as a courthouse* he thought quietly, with a surge of peace and joy whose reason he could not have thought into words, being too young for that: *They are safe from him. People whose lives are a part of this peace and dignity are beyond his touch, he no more to them than a buzzing wasp: capable of stinging for a little moment but that's all; the spell of this peace and dignity rendering even the barns and stable and cribs which belong to it impervious to the puny flames he might contrive* . . . this, the peace and joy, ebbing for an instant as he looked again at the stiff black back, the stiff and implacable limp of the figure which was not dwarfed by the house, for the reason that it had never looked big anywhere and which now, against the serene columned backdrop, had more than ever that impervious quality of something cut ruthlessly from tin, depthless, as though, sidewise to the sun, it would cast no shadow. Watching him, the boy remarked the absolutely undeviating course which his father held and saw the stiff foot come squarely down in a pile of fresh droppings where a horse had stood in the drive and which his father could have avoided by a simple change of stride. But it ebbed only for a moment, though he could not have thought this into words either, walking on in the spell of the house, which he could even want but without envy, without sorrow, certainly never with that ravening and jealous rage which unknown to him walked in the ironlike black coat before him: *Maybe he will feel it too. Maybe it will even change him now from what maybe he couldn't help but be.*

They crossed the portico. Now he could hear his father's stiff foot as it came down on the boards with clocklike finality, a sound out of all proportion to the displacement of the body it bore and which was not dwarfed either by the white door before it, as though it had attained to a sort of vicious and ravening minimum not to be dwarfed by anything—the flat, wide, black hat, the formal coat of broadcloth which had once been black but which had now that friction-glazed greenish cast of the bodies of old house flies, the lifted sleeve which was too large, the lifted hand like a curled claw. The door opened so promptly that the boy knew the Negro must have been watching them all the time, an old man with neat grizzled hair, in a linen jacket, who stood barring the door with his body, saying, "Wipe yo foots, white man, fo you come in here. Major ain't home nohow."

"Get out of my way, nigger," his father said, without heat too, flinging the door back and the Negro also and entering, his hat still on his head. And now the boy saw the prints of the stiff foot on the doorjamb and saw them appear on the pale rug behind the machinelike deliberation of the foot which seemed to bear (or transmit) twice the weight which the body compassed. The Negro was shouting "Miss Lula! Miss Lula!" somewhere behind them, then the boy, deluged as though by a warm wave by a suave turn of carpeted stair and a pendant glitter of chandeliers and a mute gleam of gold frames, heard the swift feet and saw her too, a lady—perhaps he had never seen her like before either—in a gray, smooth gown with lace at the throat and an apron tied at the waist and the sleeves turned back, wiping cake or biscuit dough from her hands with a towel as she came up the hall, looking not at his father at all but at the tracks on the blond rug with an expression of incredulous amazement.

"I tried," the Negro cried. "I tole him to . . ."

"Will you please go away?" she said in a shaking voice. "Major de Spain is not at home. Will you please go away?"

45        His father had not spoken again. He did not speak again. He did not even look at her. He just stood stiff in the center of the rug, in his hat, the shaggy iron-gray brows twitching slightly above the pebble-colored eyes as he appeared to examine the house with brief deliberation. Then with the same deliberation he turned; the boy watched him pivot on the good leg and saw the stiff foot drag round the arc of the turning, leaving a final long and fading smear. His father never looked at it, he never once looked down at the rug. The Negro held the door. It closed behind them, upon the hysteric and indistinguishable woman-wail. His father stopped at the top of the steps and scraped his boot clean on the edge of it. At the gate he stopped again. He stood for a moment, planted stiffly on the stiff foot, looking back at the house. "Pretty and white, ain't it?" he said. "That's sweat. Nigger sweat. Maybe it ain't white enough yet to suit him. Maybe he wants to mix some white sweat with it."

Two hours later the boy was chopping wood behind the house within which his mother and aunt and the two sisters (the mother and aunt, not the two girls, he knew that; even at this distance and muffled by walls the flat loud voices of the two girls emanated an incorrigible idle inertia) were setting up the stove to prepare a meal, when he heard the hooves and saw the linen-clad man on a fine sorrel mare, whom he recognized even before he saw the rolled rug in front of the Negro youth following on a fat bay carriage horse—a suffused, angry face vanishing, still at full gallop, behind the corner of the house where his father and brother were sitting in the two tilted chairs; and a moment later, almost before he could have put the axe down, he heard the hooves again and watched the sorrel mare go back out of the yard, already galloping again. Then his father began to shout one of the sisters' names, who presently emerged backward from the kitchen door dragging the rolled rug along the ground by one end while the other sister walked behind it.

"If you ain't going to tote, go on and set up the wash pot," the first said.

"You, Sarty!" the second shouted. "Set up the wash pot!" His father appeared at the door, framed against that shabbiness, as he had been against that other bland perfection, impervious to either, the mother's anxious face at his shoulder.

"Go on," the father said. "Pick it up." The two sisters stooped, broad, lethargic; stooping, they presented an incredible expanse of pale cloth and a flutter of tawdry ribbons.

50 "If I thought enough of a rug to have to git hit all the way from France I wouldn't keep hit where folks coming in would have to tromp on hit," the first said. They raised the rug.

"Abner," the mother said. "Let me do it."

"You go back and git dinner," his father said. "I'll tend to this."

From the woodpile through the rest of the afternoon the boy watched them, the rug spread flat in the dust beside the bubbling washpot, the two sisters stooping over it with that profound and lethargic reluctance, while the father stood over them in turn, implacable and grim, driving them though never raising his voice again. He could smell the harsh homemade lye they were using; he saw his mother come to the door once and look toward them with an expression not anxious now but very like despair; he saw his father turn, and he fell to with the axe and saw from the corner of his eye his father raise from the ground a flattish fragment of field stone and examine it and return to the pot, and this time his mother actually spoke: "Abner. Abner. Please don't. Please, Abner."

Then he was done too. It was dusk; the whippoorwills had already begun. He could smell coffee from the room where they would presently eat the cold food remaining from the mid-afternoon meal, though when he entered the house he realized they were having coffee again probably because there was a fire on the hearth, before which the rug now lay spread over the backs of the two chairs. The tracks of his father's foot were gone. Where they had been were now long, water-cloudy scoriations resembling the sporadic course of a Liliputian mowing machine.

55 It still hung there while they ate the cold food and then went to bed, scattered without order or claim up and down the two rooms, his mother in one bed, where his father would later lie, the older brother in the other, himself, the aunt, and the two sisters on pallets on the floor. But his father was not in bed yet. The last thing the boy remembered was the depthless, harsh silhouette of the hat and coat bending over the rug and it seemed to him that he had not even closed his eyes when the silhouette was standing over him, the fire almost dead behind it, the stiff foot prodding him awake. "Catch up the mule," his father said.

When he returned with the mule his father was standing in the back door, the rolled rug over his shoulder. "Ain't you going to ride?" he said.

"No. Give me your foot."

He bent his knee into his father's hand, the wiry, surprising power flowed smoothly, rising, he rising with it, on to the mule's bare back (they had owned a saddle once; the boy could remember it though not when or where) and with the same effortlessness his father swung the rug up in front of him. Now in the starlight they retraced the afternoon's path, up the dusty road rife with honeysuckle, through the gate and up the black tunnel of the drive to the lightless house, where he sat on the mule and felt the rough warp of the rug drag across his thighs and vanish.

"Don't you want me to help?" he whispered. His father did not answer and now he heard again that stiff foot striking the hollow portico with that wooden and clocklike deliberation, that outrageous overstatement of the weight it carried. The rug, hunched, not flung (the boy could tell that even in the darkness) from his father's shoulder struck the angle of wall and floor with a sound unbelievably loud, thunderous, then the foot again, unhurried and enormous; a light came on in the house and the boy sat, tense, breathing steadily and quietly and just a little fast, though the foot itself did not increase its beat at all, descending the steps now; now the boy could see him.

60     "Don't you want to ride now?" he whispered. "We kin both ride now," the light within the house altering now, flaring up and sinking. *He's coming down the stairs now,* he thought. He had already ridden the mule up beside the horse block; presently his father was up behind him and he doubled the reins over and slashed the mule across the neck, but before the animal could begin to trot the hard, thin arm came round him, the hard, knotted hand jerking the mule back to a walk.

In the first red rays of the sun they were in the lot, putting plow gear on the mules. This time the sorrel mare was in the lot before he heard it at all, the rider collarless and even bareheaded, trembling, speaking in a shaking voice as the woman in the house had done, his father merely looking up once before stooping again to the hame he was buckling, so that the man on the mare spoke to his stooping back:

"You must realize you have ruined that rug. Wasn't there anybody here, any of your women . . ." he ceased, shaking, the boy watching him, the older brother leaning now in the stable door, chewing, blinking slowly and steadily at nothing apparently. "It cost a hundred dollars. But you never had a hundred dollars. You never will. So I'm going to charge you twenty bushels of corn against your crop. I'll add it in your contract and when you come to the commissary you can sign it. That won't keep Mrs. de Spain quiet but maybe it will teach you to wipe your feet off before you enter her house again."

Then he was gone. The boy looked at his father, who still had not spoken or even looked up again, who was now adjusting the logger-head in the hame.

"Pap," he said. His father looked at him—the inscrutable face, the shaggy brows beneath which the gray eyes glinted coldly. Suddenly the boy went toward him, fast, stopping as suddenly. "You done the best you could!" he cried. "If he wanted hit done different why didn't he wait and tell you how? He won't git no twenty bushels! He won't git none! We'll gether hit and hide hit! I kin watch . . . "

65     "Did you put the cutter back in that straight stock like I told you?"

"No, sir," he said.

"Then go do it."

That was Wednesday. During the rest of that week he worked steadily, at what was within his scope and some which was beyond it, with an industry that did not need to be driven nor even commanded twice; he had this from his mother, with the difference that some at least of what he did he liked to do, such as splitting wood with the half-size axe which his mother and aunt had earned, or saved money somehow, to present him with at Christmas. In company with the two older women (and on one afternoon, even one of the sisters), he built pens for the shoat and the cow which were a part of his father's contract with the landlord, and one afternoon, his father being absent, gone somewhere on one of the mules, he went to the field.

They were running a middle buster now, his brother holding the plow straight while he handled the reins, and walking beside the straining mule, the rich black soil shearing cool and damp against his bare ankles, he thought *Maybe this is the end of it. Maybe even that twenty bushels that seems hard to have to pay for just a rug will be a cheap price for him to stop forever and always from being what he used to be;* thinking, dreaming now, so that his brother had to speak sharply to him to mind the mule: *Maybe he even won't collect the twenty bushels. Maybe it will all add up and balance and vanish—corn, rug, fire; the terror and grief, the being pulled two ways like between two teams of horses—gone, done with for ever and ever.*

70    Then it was Saturday; he looked up from beneath the mule he was harnessing and saw his father in the black coat and hat. "Not that," his father said. "The wagon gear." And then, two hours later, sitting in the wagon bed behind his father and brother on the seat, the wagon accomplished a final curve, and he saw the weathered paintless store with its tattered tobacco- and patent-medicine posters and the tethered wagons and saddle animals below the gallery. He mounted the gnawed steps behind his father and brother, and there again was the lane of quiet, watching faces for the three of them to walk through. He saw the man in spectacles sitting at the plank table and he did not need to be told this was a Justice of the Peace; he sent one glare of fierce, exultant, partisan defiance at the man in collar and cravat now, whom he had seen but twice before in his life, and that on a galloping horse, who now wore on his face an expression not of rage but of amazed unbelief which the boy could not have known was at the incredible circumstance of being sued by one of his own tenants, and came and stood against his father and cried at the Justice: "He ain't done it! He ain't burnt . . ."

"Go back to the wagon," his father said.

"Burnt?" the Justice said. "Do I understand this rug was burned too?"

"Does anybody here claim it was?" his father said. "Go back to the wagon." But he did not, he merely retreated to the rear of the room, crowded as that other had been, but not to sit down this time, instead, to stand pressing among the motionless bodies, listening to the voices:

"And you claim twenty bushels of corn is too high for the damage you did to the rug?"

75    "He brought the rug to me and said he wanted the tracks washed out of it. I washed the tracks out and took the rug back to him."

"But you didn't carry the rug back to him in the same condition it was in before you made the tracks on it."

His father did not answer, and now for perhaps half a minute there was no sound at all save that of breathing, the faint, steady suspiration of complete and intent listening.

"You decline to answer that, Mr. Snopes?" Again his father did not answer. "I'm going to find against you, Mr. Snopes. I'm going to find that you were responsible for the injury to Major de Spain's rug and hold you liable for it. But twenty bushels of corn seems a little high for a man in your circumstances to have to pay. Major de Spain claims it costs a hundred dollars. October corn will be worth about fifty cents. I figure that if Major de Spain can stand a ninety-five-dollar loss on something he paid cash for, you can stand a five-dollar loss you haven't earned yet. I hold you in damages to Major de Spain to the amount of ten bushels of corn over and above your contract with him, to be paid to him out of your crop at gathering time. Court adjourned."

It had taken no time hardly, the morning was but half begun. He thought they would return home and perhaps back to the field, since they were late, far behind all other farmers. But instead his father passed on behind the wagon, merely indicating with his hand for the older brother to follow with it, and crossed the road toward the blacksmith shop opposite, pressing on after his father, overtaking him, speaking, whispering up at the harsh, calm face beneath the weathered hat: "He won't git no ten bushels neither. He won't git one. We'll . . ." until his father glanced for an instant down at him, the face absolutely calm, the grizzled eyebrows tangled above the cold eyes, the voice almost pleasant, almost gentle:

80        "You think so? Well, we'll wait till October anyway."

The matter of the wagon—the setting of a spoke or two and the tightening of the tires—did not take long either, the business of the tires accomplished by driving the wagon into the spring branch behind the shop and letting it stand there, the mules nuzzling into the water from time to time, and the boy on the seat with the idle reins, looking up the slope and through the sooty tunnel of the shed where the slow hammer rang and where his father sat on an upended cypress bolt, easily, either talking or listening, still sitting there when the boy brought the dripping wagon up out of the branch and halted it before the door.

"Take them on to the shade and hitch," his father said. He did so and returned. His father and the smith and a third man squatting on his heels inside the door were talking, about crops and animals; the boy, squatting too in the ammoniac dust and hoof-parings and scales of rust, heard his father tell a long and unhurried story out of the time before the birth of the older brother even when he had been a professional horsetrader. And then his father came up beside him where he stood before a tattered last year's circus poster on the other side of the store, gazing rapt and quiet at the scarlet horses, the incredible poisings and convolutions of tulle and tights and the painted leers of comedians, and said, "It's time to eat."

But not at home. Squatting beside his brother against the front wall, he watched his father emerge from the store and produce from a paper sack a segment of cheese and divide it carefully and deliberately into three with his pocket knife and produce crackers from the same sack. They all three squatted on the gallery and ate, slowly, without talking; then in the store again, they drank from a tin dipper tepid water smelling of the cedar bucket and of living beech trees. And still they did not go home. It was a horse lot this time, a tall rail fence upon and along which men stood and sat and out of which one by one horses were led, to be walked and trotted and then cantered back and forth along the road while the slow swapping and buying went on and the sun began to slant westward, they—the three of them— watching and listening, the older brother with his muddy eyes and his steady, inevitable tobacco, the father commenting now and then on certain of the animals, to no one in particular.

It was after sundown when they reached home. They ate supper by lamplight, then, sitting on the doorstep, the boy watched the night fully accomplish, listening to the whippoorwills and the frogs, when he heard his mother's voice: "Abner! No! No! Oh, God. Oh, God. Abner!" and he rose, whirled, and saw the altered light through the door where a candle stub now burned in a bottle neck on the table and his father, still in the hat and coat, at once formal and burlesque as though dressed carefully for some shabby and ceremonial violence, emptying the reservoir of the lamp back into the five-gallon kerosene can from which it had been filled, while the mother tugged at his arm until he shifted the lamp to the other hand and flung her back, not savagely or viciously, just hard, into the wall, her hands flung out against the wall for balance, her mouth open and in her face the same quality of hopeless despair as had been in her voice. Then his father saw him standing in the door.

85     "Go to the barn and get that can of oil we were oiling the wagon with," he said. The boy did not move. Then he could speak.

"What . . ." he cried. "What are you . . ."

"Go get that oil," his father said. "Go."

Then he was moving, running, outside the house, toward the stable: this the old habit, the old blood which he had not been permitted to choose for himself, which had been bequeathed him willy nilly and which had run for so long (and who knew where, battening on what of outrage and savagery and lust) before it came to him. *I could keep on,* he thought. *I could run on and on and never look back, never need to see his face again. Only I can't. I can't,* the rusted can in his hand now, the liquid sploshing in it as he ran back to the house and into it, into the sound of his mother's weeping in the next room, and handed the can to his father.

"Ain't you going to even send a nigger?" he cried. "At least you sent a nigger before!"

90     This time his father didn't strike him. The hand came even faster than the blow had, the same hand which had set the can on the table with almost excruciating care flashing from the can toward him too quick for him to follow it, gripping him by the back of his shirt and on to tiptoe before he had seen it quit the can, the face stooping at him in breathless and frozen ferocity, the cold, dead voice speaking over him to the older brother who leaned against the table, chewing with that steady, curious, sidewise motion of cows:

"Empty the can into the big one and go on. I'll catch up with you."

"Better tie him up to the bedpost," the brother said.

"Do like I told you," the father said. Then the boy was moving, his bunched shirt and the hard, bony hand between his shoulderblades, his toes just touching the floor, across the room and into the other one, past the sisters sitting with spread heavy thighs in the two chairs over the cold hearth, and to where his mother and aunt sat side by side on the bed, the aunt's arms about his mother's shoulders.

"Hold him," the father said. The aunt made a startled movement. "Not you," the father said. "Lennie. Take hold of him. I want to see you do it." His mother took him by the wrist. "You'll hold him better than that. If he gets loose don't you know what he is going to do? He will go up yonder." He jerked his head toward the road. "Maybe I'd better tie him."

95     "I'll hold him," his mother whispered.

"See you do then." Then his father was gone, the stiff foot heavy and measured upon the boards, ceasing at last.

Then he began to struggle. His mother caught him in both arms, he jerking and wrenching at them. He would be stronger in the end, he knew that. But he had no time to wait for it. "Lemme go!" he cried. "I don't want to have to hit you!"

"Let him go!" the aunt said. "If he don't go, before God, I am going up there myself!"

"Don't you see I can't?" his mother cried. "Sarty! Sarty! No! No! Help me, Lizzie!"

100    Then he was free. His aunt grasped at him but it was too late. He whirled, running, his mother stumbled forward on to her knees behind him, crying to the nearer sister: "Catch him, Net! Catch him!" But that was too late too, the sister (the sisters were twins, born at the same time, yet either of them now gave the impression of being, encompassing as much living meat and volume and weight as any other two of the family) not yet having begun to rise from the chair, her head, face, alone merely turned, presenting to him in the flying instant an astonishing expanse of young female features untroubled by any surprise even, wearing only an expression of bovine interest. Then he was out of the room, out of the house, in the mild dust of the starlit road and the heavy rifeness of honeysuckle, the pale ribbon unspooling with terrific slowness under his running feet, reaching the gate at last and turning in, running, his heart and lungs drumming, on up the drive toward the lighted house, the lighted door. He did not knock, he burst in, sobbing for breath, incapable for the moment of speech; he saw the astonished face of the Negro in the linen jacket without knowing when the Negro had appeared.

"De Spain!" he cried, panted. "Where's . . ." then he saw the white man too emerging from a white door down the hall. "Barn!" he cried. "Barn!"

"What?" the white man said. "Barn?"

"Yes!" the boy cried. "Barn!"

"Catch him!" the white man shouted.

105    But it was too late this time too. The Negro grasped his shirt, but the entire sleeve, rotten with washing, carried away, and he was out that door too and in the drive again, and had actually never ceased to run even while he was screaming into the white man's face.

Behind him the white man was shouting, "My horse! Fetch my horse!" and he thought for an instant of cutting across the park and climbing the fence into the road, but he did not know the park nor how high the vine-massed fence might be and he dared not risk it. So he ran on down the drive, blood and breath roaring; presently he was in the road again though he could not see it. He could not hear either: the galloping mare was almost upon him before he heard her, and even then he held his course, as if the very urgency of his wild grief and need must in a moment more find him wings, waiting until the ultimate instant to hurl himself aside and into the weed-choked roadside ditch as the horse thundered past and on, for an instant in furious silhouette against the stars, the tranquil early summer night sky which, even before the shape of the horse and rider vanished, strained abruptly and violently upward: a long, swirling roar incredible and soundless, blotting the stars, and he springing up and into the road again, running again, knowing it was too late yet still running even after he heard the shot and, an instant later, two shots, pausing now without knowing he had ceased to run, crying "Pap! Pap!", running again before he knew he had begun to run, stumbling, tripping over something and scrabbling up again without ceasing to run, looking backward over his shoulder at the glare as he got up, running on among the invisible trees, panting, sobbing, "Father! Father!"

At midnight he was sitting on the crest of a hill. He did not know it was midnight and he did not know how far he had come. But there was no glare behind him now and he sat now, his back toward what he had called home for four days anyhow, his face toward the dark woods which he would enter when breath was strong again, small, shaking steadily in the chill darkness, hugging himself into the remainder of his thin, rotten shirt, the grief and despair now no longer terror and fear but just grief and despair. *Father. My father,* he thought. "He was brave!" He cried suddenly, aloud but not loud, no more than a whisper: "He was! He was in the war! He was in Colonel Sartoris' cav'ry!" not knowing that his father had gone to that war a private in the fine old European sense, wearing no uniform, admitting the authority of and giving fidelity to no man or army or flag, going to war as Malbrouck himself did: for booty—it meant nothing and less than nothing to him if it were enemy booty or his own.

The slow constellations wheeled on. It would be dawn and then sun-up after a while and he would be hungry. But that would be tomorrow and now he was only cold, and walking would cure that. His breathing was easier now and he decided to get up and go on, and then he found that he had been asleep because he knew it was almost dawn, the night almost over. He could tell that from the whippoorwills. They were everywhere now among the dark trees below him, constant and inflectioned and ceaseless, so that, as the instant for giving over to the day birds drew nearer and nearer, there was no interval at all between them. He got up. He was a little stiff, but walking would cure that too as it would the cold, and soon there would be the sun. He went on down the hill, toward the dark woods within which the liquid silver voices of the birds called unceasing—the rapid and urgent beating of the urgent and quiring heart of the late spring night. He did not look back.

# WILLIAM FAULKNER

*For a biographical note, see page 407.*
*The illustrations, by Weldon Barley (1905-1945) were published when the story was first printed in a magazine called* Forum *in 1930.*

## A Rose for Emily

### I

When Miss Emily Grierson died, our whole town went to her funeral: the men through a sort of respectful affection for a fallen monument, the women mostly out of curiosity to see the inside of her house, which no one save an old Negro manservant—a combined gardener and cook—had seen in at least ten years.

It was a big, squarish, frame house that had once been white, decorated with cupolas and spires and scrolled balconies in the heavily lightsome style of the seventies, set on what had once been our most select street. But garages and cotton gins had encroached and obliterated even the august names of that neighborhood; only Miss Emily's house was left, lifting its stubborn and coquettish decay above the cotton wagons and the gasoline pumps—an eyesore among eyesores. And now Miss Emily had gone to join the representatives of those august names where they lay in the cedar-bemused cemetery among the ranked and anonymous graves of Union and Confederate soldiers who fell at the battle of Jefferson.

Alive, Miss Emily had been a tradition, a duty, and a care; a sort of hereditary obligation upon the town, dating from that day in 1894 when Colonel Sartoris, the mayor—he who fathered the edict that no Negro woman should appear on the streets without an apron—remitted her taxes, the dispensation dating from the death of her father on into perpetuity. Not that Miss Emily would have accepted charity. Colonel Sartoris invented an involved tale to the effect that Miss Emily's father had loaned money to the town, which the town, as a matter of business, preferred this way of repaying. Only a man of Colonel Sartoris' generation and thought could have invented it, and only a woman could have believed it.

When the next generation, with its more modern ideas, became mayors and aldermen, this arrangement created some little dissatisfaction. On the first of the year they mailed her a tax notice. February came, and there was no reply. They wrote her a formal letter, asking her to call at the sheriff's office at her convenience. A week later the mayor wrote her himself, offering to call or to send his car for her, and received in reply a note on paper of an archaic shape, in a thin, flowing calligraphy in faded ink, to the effect that she no longer went out at all. The tax notice was also enclosed, without comment.

5    They called a special meeting of the Board of Aldermen. A deputation waited upon her, knocked at the door through which no visitor had passed since she ceased giving china-painting lessons eight or ten years earlier. They were admitted by the old Negro into a dim hall from which a stairway mounted into still more shadow. It smelled of dust and disuse—a close, dank smell. The Negro led them into the parlor. It was furnished in heavy, leather-covered furniture. When the Negro opened the blinds of one window, they could see that the leather was cracked; and when they sat down, a faint dust rose sluggishly about their thighs, spinning with slow motes in the single sun-ray. On a tarnished gilt easel before the fireplace stood a crayon portrait of Miss Emily's father.

They rose when she entered—a small, fat woman in black, with a thin gold chain descending to her waist and vanishing into her belt, leaning on an ebony cane with a tarnished gold head. Her skeleton was small and spare; perhaps that was why what would have been merely plumpness in another was obesity in her. She looked bloated, like a body long submerged in motionless water, and of that pallid hue. Her eyes, lost in the fatty ridges of her face, looked like two small pieces of coal pressed into a lump of dough as they moved from one face to another while the visitors stated their errand.

She did not ask them to sit. She just stood in the door and listened quietly until the spokesman came to a stumbling halt. Then they could hear the invisible watch ticking at the end of the gold chain.

Her voice was dry and cold. "I have no taxes in Jefferson. Colonel Sartoris explained it to me. Perhaps one of you can gain access to the city records and satisfy yourselves."

"But we have. We are the city authorities, Miss Emily. Didn't you get a notice from the sheriff, signed by him?"

10      "I received a paper, yes," Miss Emily said. "Perhaps he considers himself the sheriff. . . . I have no taxes in Jefferson."

"But there is nothing on the books to show that, you see. We must go by the—"

"See Colonel Sartoris. I have no taxes in Jefferson."

"But, Miss Emily—"

"See Colonel Sartoris." (Colonel Sartoris had been dead almost ten years.) "I have no taxes in Jefferson. Tobe!" The Negro appeared. "Show these gentlemen out."

## II

15      So she vanquished them, horse and foot, just as she had vanquished their fathers thirty years before about the smell. That was two years after her father's death and a short time after her sweetheart—the one we believed would marry her—had deserted her. After her father's death she went out very little; after her sweetheart went away, people hardly saw her at all. A few of the ladies had the temerity to call, but were not received, and the only sign of life about the place was the Negro man—a young man then—going in and out with a market basket.

"Just as if a man—any man—could keep a kitchen properly," the ladies said; so they were not surprised when the smell developed. It was another link between the gross, teeming world and the high and mighty Griersons.

A neighbor, a woman, complained to the mayor, Judge Stevens, eighty years old.

"But what will you have me do about it, madam?" he said.

"Why, send her word to stop it," the woman said. "Isn't there a law?"

20      "I'm sure that won't be necessary," Judge Stevens said. "It's probably just a snake or a rat that nigger of hers killed in the yard. I'll speak to him about it."

The next day he received two more complaints, one from a man who came in diffident deprecation. "We really must do something about it, Judge. I'd be the last one in the world to bother Miss Emily, but we've got to do something." That night the Board of Aldermen met—three graybeards and one younger man, a member of the rising generation.

"It's simple enough," he said. "Send her word to have her place cleaned up. Give her a certain time to do it in, and if she don't . . ."

"Dammit, sir," Judge Stevens said, "will you accuse a lady to her face of smelling bad?"

So the next night, after midnight, four men crossed Miss Emily's lawn and slunk about the house like burglars, sniffing along the base of the brick-work and at the cellar openings while one of them performed a regular sowing motion with his hand out of a sack slung from his shoulder. They broke open the cellar door and sprinkled lime there, and in all the out-buildings. As they recrossed the lawn, a window that had been dark was lighted and Miss Emily sat in it, the light behind her, and her upright torso motionlesss as that of an idol. They crept quietly across the lawn and into the shadow of the locusts that lined the street. After a week or two the smell went away.

25      That was when people had begun to feel really sorry for her. People in our town, remembering how old lady Wyatt, her great-aunt, had gone com-pletely crazy at last, believed that the Griersons held themselves a little too high for what they really were. None of the young men were quite good enough for Miss Emily and such. We had long thought of them as a tableau, Miss Emily a slender figure in white in the background, her father a sprad-dled silhouette in the foreground, his back to her and clutching a horse-whip, the two of them framed by the back-flung front door. So when she got to be thirty and was still single, we were not pleased exactly, but vindicated; even with insanity in the family she wouldn't have turned down all of her chances if they had really materialized.

When her father died, it got about that the house was all that was left to her; and in a way, people were glad. At last they could pity Miss Emily. Being left alone, and a pauper, she had become humanized. Now she too would know the old thrill and the old despair of a penny more or less.

The day after his death all the ladies prepared to call at the house and offer condolence and aid, as is our custom. Miss Emily met them at the door, dressed as usual and with no trace of grief on her face. She told them that her father was not dead. She did that for three days, with the ministers call-ing on her, and the doctors, trying to persuade her to let them dispose of the body. Just as they were about to resort to law and force, she broke down, and they buried her father quickly.

We did not say she was crazy then. We believed she had to do that. We remembered all the young men her father had driven away, and we knew that with nothing left, she would have to cling to that which had robbed her, as people will.

So we were not surprised when Homer Barron—the streets had been finished some time since—was gone. We were a little disappointed that there was not a public blowing-off, but we believed that he had gone on to prepare for Miss Emily's coming, or to give her a chance to get rid of the cousins. (By that time it was a cabal, and we were all Miss Emily's allies to help circumvent the cousins.) Sure enough, after another week they departed. And, as we had expected all along, within three days Homer Barron was back in town. A neighbor saw the Negro man admit him at the kitchen door at dusk one evening.

And that was the last we saw of Homer Barron. And of Miss Emily for some time. The Negro man went in and out with the market basket, but the front door remained closed. Now and then we would see her at a window for a moment, as the men did that night when they sprinkled the lime, but for almost six months she did not appear on the streets. Then we knew that this was to be expected too; as if that quality of her father which had thwarted her woman's life so many times had been too virulent and too furious to die.

When we next saw Miss Emily, she had grown fat and her hair was turning gray. During the next few years it grew grayer and grayer until it attained an even pepper-and-salt iron gray, when it ceased turning. Up to the day of her death at seventy-four it was still that vigorous iron-gray, like the hair of an active man.

From that time on her front door remained closed, save for a period of six or seven years, when she was about forty, during which she gave lessons in china-painting. She fitted up a studio in one of the downstairs rooms, where the daughters and grand-daughters of Colonel Sartoris' contemporaries were sent to her with the same regularity and in the same spirit that they were sent to church on Sundays with a twenty-five cent piece for the collection plate. Meanwhile her taxes had been remitted.

50    Then the newer generation became the backbone and the spirit of the town, and the painting pupils grew up and fell away and did not send their children to her with boxes of color and tedious brushes and pictures cut from the ladies' magazines. The front door closed upon the last one and remained closed for good. When the town got free postal delivery, Miss Emily alone refused to let them fasten the metal numbers above her door and attach a mailbox to it. She would not listen to them.

Daily, monthly, yearly we watched the Negro grow grayer and more stooped, going in and out with the market basket. Each December we sent her a tax notice, which would be returned by the post office a week later, unclaimed. Now and then we would see her in one of the downstairs windows—she had evidently shut up the top floor of the house—like the carven torso of an idol in a niche, looking or not looking at us, we could never tell which. Thus she passed from generation to generation—dear, inescapable, impervious, tranquil, and perverse.

And so she died. Fell ill in the house filled with dust and shadows, with only a doddering Negro man to wait on her. We did not even know she was sick; we had long since given up trying to get any information from the Negro. He talked to no one, probably not even to her, for his voice had grown harsh and rusty, as if from disuse.

She died in one of the downstairs rooms, in a heavy walnut bed with a curtain, her gray head propped on a pillow yellow and moldy with age and lack of sunlight.

## V

The Negro met the first of the ladies at the front door and let them in, with their hushed, sibilant voices and their quick, curious glances, and then he disappeared. He walked right through the house and out the back and was not seen again.

55      The two female cousins came at once. They held the funeral on the second day, with the town coming to look at Miss Emily beneath a mass of bought flowers, with the crayon face of her father musing profoundly above the bier and the ladies sibilant and macabre; and the very old men—some in their brushed Confederate uniforms—on the porch and the lawn, talking of Miss Emily as if she had been a contemporary of theirs, believing that they had danced with her and courted her perhaps, confusing time with its mathematical progression, as the old do, to whom all the past is not a diminishing road but, instead, a huge meadow which no winter ever quite touches, divided from the now by the narrow bottle-neck of the most recent decade of years.

Already we knew that there was one room in that region above stairs which no one had seen in forty years, and which would have to be forced. They waited until Miss Emily was decently in the ground before they opened it.

The violence of breaking down the door seemed to fill this room with pervading dust. A thin, acrid pall as of the tomb seemed to lie everywhere upon this room decked and furnished as for a bridal: upon the valance curtains of faded rose color, upon the rose-shaded lights, upon the dressing table, upon the delicate array of crystal and the man's toilet things backed with tarnished silver, silver so tarnished that the monogram was obscured. Among them lay a collar and tie, as if they had just been removed, which, lifted, left upon the surface a pale crescent in the dust. Upon a chair hung the suit, carefully folded; beneath it the two mute shoes and the discarded socks.

The man himself lay in the bed.

For a long while we just stood there, looking down at the profound and fleshless grin. The body had apparently once lain in the attitude of an embrace, but now the long sleep that outlasts love, that conquers even the grimace of love, had cuckolded him. What was left of him, rotted beneath what was left of the nightshirt, had become inextricable from the bed in which he lay; and upon him and upon the pillow beside him lay that even coating of the patient and biding dust.

60    Then we noticed that in the second pillow was the indentation of a head. One of us lifted something from it, and leaning forward, that faint and invisible dust dry and acrid in the nostrils, we saw a long strand of iron-gray hair.

# AMY HEMPEL

*Born in Chicago in 1951, Amy Hempel published her first collection of stories in 1985. The* New York Times *called her* Collected Stories *(2006) one of the ten best books of the year. The winner of numerous awards for writing, Hempel, currently teaching fiction at Harvard University, has taught at Brooklyn College, the New School, Bennington College, and Princeton University.*

## *Today Will Be a Quiet Day*                                        [1986]

"I think it's the other way around," the boy said. "I think if the quake hit now the *bridge* would collapse and the *ramps* would be left."

He looked at his sister with satisfaction.

"You are just trying to scare your sister," the father said. "You know that is not true."

"No, really," the boy insisted, "and I heard birds in the middle of the night. Isn't that a warning?"

5    The girl gave her brother a toxic look and ate a handful of Raisinets. The three of them were stalled in traffic on the Golden Gate Bridge.

That morning, before waking his children, the father had canceled their music lessons and decided to make a day of it. He wanted to know how they were, is all. Just—how were they. He thought his kids were as self-contained as one of those dogs you sometimes see carrying home its own leash. But you could read things wrong.

Could you ever.

The boy had a friend who jumped from a floor of Langley Porter. The friend had been there for two weeks, mostly playing Ping-Pong. All the friend said the day the boy visited and lost every game was never play Ping-Pong with a mental patient because it's all we do and we'll kill you. That night the friend had cut the red belt he wore in two and left the other half on his bed. That was this time last year when the boy was twelve years old.

You think you're safe, the father thought, but it's thinking you're invisible because you closed your eyes.

10    This day they were headed for Petaluma—the chicken, egg, and arm-wrestling capital of the nation—for lunch. The father had offered to take them to the men's arm-wrestling semifinals. But it was said that arm wrestling wasn't so interesting since the new safety precautions, that hardly anyone broke an arm or a wrist anymore. The best anyone could hope to see would be dislocation, so they said they would rather go to Pete's. Pete's was a gas station turned into a place to eat. The hamburgers there were named after cars, and the gas pumps in front still pumped gas.

"Can I have one?" the boy asked, meaning the Raisinets.

"No," his sister said.

"Can I have two?"

"Neither of you should be eating candy before lunch," the father said. He said it with the good sport of a father who enjoys his kids and gets a kick out of saying Dad things.

15    "You mean dinner," said the girl. "It will be dinner before we get to Pete's."

Only the northbound lanes were stopped. Southbound traffic flashed past at the normal speed.

"Check it out," the boy said from the back seat. "Did you see the bumper sticker on that Porsche? 'If you don't like the way I drive, stay off the sidewalk.'"

He spoke directly to his sister. "I've just solved my Christmas shopping."

"I got the highest score in my class in Driver's Ed," she said.

20    "I thought I would let your sister drive home today," the father said.

From the back seat came sirens, screams for help, and then a dirge.

The girl spoke to her father in a voice rich with complicity. "Don't people make you want to give up?"

"Don't the two of you know any jokes? I haven't laughed all day," the father said.

"Did I tell you the guillotine joke?" the girl said.

25    "He hasn't laughed all day, so you must've," her brother said.

The girl gave her brother a look you could iron clothes with. Then her gaze dropped down. "Oh-oh," she said, "Johnny's out of jail."

Her brother zipped his pants back up. He said, "Tell the joke."

"Two Frenchmen and a Belgian were about to be beheaded," the girl began. "The first Frenchman was led to the block and blindfolded. The executioner let the blade go. But it stopped a quarter inch above the Frenchman's neck. So he was allowed to go free, and ran off shouting, 'C'est un miracle! C'est un miracle!'"

"It's a miracle," the father said.

30 "Then the second Frenchman was led to the block, and same thing—the blade stopped just before cutting off his head. So *he* got to go free, and ran off shouting, 'C'est un miracle!'

"Finally the Belgian was led to the block. But before they could blindfold him, he looked up, pointed to the top of the guillotine, and cried, 'Voilà la difficulté!'"

She doubled over.

"Maybe I would be wetting *my* pants if I knew what that meant," the boy said.

"You can't explain after the punch line," the girl said, "and have it still be funny."

35 "There's the problem," said the father.

The waitress handed out menus to the party of three seated in the corner booth of what used to be the lube bay. She told them the specialty of the day was Moroccan chicken.

"That's what I want," the boy said. "Morerotten chicken."

But he changed his order to a Studeburger and fries after his father and sister had ordered.

"So," the father said, "who misses music lessons?"

40 "I'm serious about what I asked you last week," the girl said. "About switching to piano? My teacher says a real flutist only breathes with the stomach, and I can't."

"The real reason she wants to change," said the boy, "is her waist will get two inches bigger when she learns to stomach-breathe. That's what *else* her teacher said."

The boy buttered a piece of sourdough bread and flipped a chunk of cold butter onto his sister's sleeve.

"Jeezo-beezo," the girl said, "why don't they skip the knife and fork and just set his place with a slingshot!"

"Who will ever adopt you if you don't mind your manners?" the father said. "Maybe we could try a little quiet today."

45 "You sound like your tombstone," the girl said. "Remember what you wanted it to say?"

Her brother joined in with his mouth full: "Today will be a quiet day."

"Because it never is with us around," the boy said.

"You guys," said the father.

The waitress brought plates. The father passed sugar to the boy and salt to the girl without being asked. He watched the girl shake out salt onto the fries.

50 "If I had a sore throat, I would gargle with those," he said.

"Looks like she's trying to melt a driveway," the boy offered.

The father watched his children eat. They ate fast. They called it Hoovering. He finished while they sucked at straws in empty drinks.

"Funny," he said thoughtfully, "I'm not hungry anymore."

Every meal ended this way. It was his benediction, one of the Dad things they expected him to say.

55 "That reminds me," the girl said. "Did you feed Rocky before we left?"

"Uh-uh," her brother said. "I fed him yesterday."

"*I* fed him yesterday!" the girl said.

"Okay, we'll compromise," the boy said. "We won't feed the cat today."

"I'd say you are out of bounds on that one," the father said.

60    He meant you could not tease her about animals. Once, during dinner, that cat ran into the dining room shot from guns. He ran around the table at top speed, then spun out on the parquet floor into a leg of the table. He fell over onto his side and made short coughing sounds. "Isn't he smart?" the girl had crooned, kneeling beside him. "He knows he's hurt."

For years, her father had to say that the animals seen on shoulders of roads were napping.

"He never would have not fed Homer," she said to her father.

"Homer was a dog," the boy said. "If I forgot to feed him, he could just go into the hills and bite a deer."

"Or a Campfire Girl selling mints at the front door," their father reminded them.

65    "Homer," the girl sighed. "I hope he likes chasing sheep on that ranch in the mountains."

The boy looked at her, incredulous.

"You *believed* that? You actually *believed* that?"

In her head, a clumsy magician yanked the cloth and the dishes all crashed to the floor. She took air into her lungs until they filled, and then she filled her stomach, too.

"I thought she knew," the boy said.

70    The dog was five years ago.

"The girl's parents insisted," the father said. "It's the law in California."

"Then I hate California," she said. "I hate its guts."

The boy said he would wait for them in the car, and left the table.

"What would help?" the father asked.

75    "For Homer to be alive," she said.

"What would help?"

"Nothing."

"Help."

She pinched a trail of salt on her plate.

80    "A ride," she said. "I'll drive."

The girl started the car and screamed, "Goddammit."

With the power off, the boy had tuned in the Spanish station. Mariachis exploded on ignition.

"Dammit isn't God's last name," the boy said, quoting another bumper sticker.

"Don't people make you want to give up?" the father said.

85    "No talking," the girl said to the rearview mirror, and put the car in gear.

She drove for hours. Through groves of eucalyptus with their damp peeling bark, past acacia bushes with yellow flowers pulsing off their stems. She cut over to the coast route and the stony gray-green tones of Inverness.

"What you'd call scenic," the boy tried.

Otherwise they were quiet.

No one said anything else until the sky started to close, and then it was the boy again, asking shouldn't they be going home.

90       "No, no," the father said, and made a show of looking out the window, up at the sky and back at his watch. "No," he said, "keep driving—it's getting earlier."

But the sky spilled rain, and the girl headed south toward the bridge. She turned on the headlights and the dashboard lit up green. She read off the odometer on the way home: "Twenty-six thousand, three hundred eighty three and eight-tenths miles."

"Today?" the boy said.

The boy got to Rocky first. "Let's play the cat," he said, and carried the Siamese to the upright piano. He sat on the bench holding the cat in his lap and pressed its paws to the keys. Rocky played "Born Free." He tried to twist away.

"Come on, Rocky, ten more minutes and we'll break."

95       "Give him to me," the girl said.

She puckered up and gave the cat a five-lipper.

"Bring the Rock upstairs," the father called. "Bring sleeping bags, too."

Pretty soon three sleeping bags formed a triangle in the master bedroom. The father was the hypotenuse. The girl asked him to brush out her hair, which he did while the boy ate a tangerine, peeling it up close to his face, inhaling the mist. Then he held each segment to the light to find seeds. In his lap, cat paws fluttered like dreaming eyes.

"What are you thinking?" the father asked.

100       "Me?" the girl said. "Fifty-seven T-bird, white with red interior, convertible. I drive it to Texas and wear skirts with rick-rack. I'm changing my name to Ruby," she said, "or else Easy."

The father considered her dream of a checkered future.

"Early ripe, early rot," he warned.

A wet wind slammed the window in its warped sash, and the boy jumped. "I hate rain," he said. "I hate its guts."

105       The father got up and closed the window tighter against the storm. "It's a real frog-choker," he said.

In darkness, lying still, it was no less camp-like than if they had been under the stars, singing to a stone-ringed fire burned down to embers.

They had already said good-night some minutes earlier when the boy and girl heard their father's voice in the dark.

"Kids, I just remembered—I have some good news and some bad news. Which do you want first?"

It was his daughter who spoke. "Let's get it over with," she said. "Let's get the bad news over with."

110       The father smiled. They are all right, he decided. My kids are as right as this rain. He smiled at the exact spots he knew their heads were turned to his, and doubted he would ever feel—not better, but *more* than he did now.

"I lied," he said. "There is no bad news."

# SHIRLEY JACKSON

*Shirley Jackson (1919–1965) was born in San Francisco and went to college in New York, first at the University of Rochester and then at Syracuse University. Although one of her stories was published in* The Best American Short

Stories 1944, *she did not receive national attention until 1948 when the* New Yorker *published "The Lottery." The magazine later reported that none of its earlier publications had produced so strong a response.*

*In 1962 she experienced a breakdown and was unable to write, but she recovered and worked on a new novel. Before completing the book, however, she died of cardiac arrest at the age of forty-six. The book was published posthumously under the title* Come Along with Me.

*Two of her books,* Life Among the Savages *(1953) and* Raising Demons *(1957), are engaging self-portraits of a harried mother in a house full of children. But what seems amusing also has its dark underside. After her breakdown Jackson said, "I think all my books laid end to end would be one long documentary of anxiety."*

*Her husband, Stanley Edgar Hyman (her college classmate and later a professor of English), said of Jackson, "If she used the resources of supernatural terror, it was to provide metaphors for the all-too-real terrors of the natural."*

## The Lottery

[1948]

The morning of June 27th was clear and sunny, with the fresh warmth of a full-summer day; the flowers were blossoming profusely and the grass was richly green. The people of the village began to gather in the square, between the post office and the bank, around ten o'clock; in some towns there were so many people that the lottery took two days and had to be started on June 26th, but in this village, where there were only about three hundred people, the whole lottery took less than two hours, so it could begin at ten o'clock in the morning and still be through in time to allow the villagers to get home for noon dinner.

The children assembled first, of course. School was recently over for the summer, and the feeling of liberty sat uneasily on most of them; they tended to gather together quietly for a while before they broke into boisterous play, and their talk was still of the classroom and the teacher, of books and reprimands. Bobby Martin had already stuffed his pockets full of stones, and the other boys soon followed his example, selecting the smoothest and roundest stones; Bobby and Harry Jones and Dickie Delacroix—the villagers pronounced this name "Dellacroy"—eventually made a great pile of stones in one corner of the square and guarded it against the raids of the other boys. The girls stood aside, talking among themselves, looking over their shoulders at the boys, and the very small children rolled in the dust or clung to the hands of their older brothers or sisters.

Soon the men began to gather, surveying their own children, speaking of planting and rain, tractors and taxes. They stood together, away from the pile of stones in the corner, and their jokes were quiet and they smiled rather than laughed. The women, wearing faded house dresses and sweaters, came shortly after their menfolk. They greeted one another and exchanged bits of gossip as they went to join their husbands. Soon the women, standing by their husbands, began to call to their children, and the children came reluctantly, having to be called four or five times. Bobby Martin ducked under his mother's grasping hand and ran, laughing, back to the pile of stones. His father spoke up sharply, and Bobby came quickly, and took his place between his father and his oldest brother.

The lottery was conducted—as were the square dances, the teenage club, the Halloween program—by Mr. Summers, who had time and energy to devote to civic activities. He was a roundfaced, jovial man and he ran the coal business, and people were sorry for him, because he had no children and his wife was a scold. When he arrived in the square, carrying the black wooden box, there was a murmur of conversation among the villagers and he waved and called, "Little late today, folks." The postmaster, Mr. Graves, followed him, carrying a three-legged stool, and the stool was put in the center of the square and Mr. Summers set the black box down on it. The villagers kept their distance, leaving a space between themselves and the stool, and when Mr. Summers said, "Some of you fellows want to give me a hand?" there was a hesitation before two men, Mr. Martin and his oldest son, Baxter, came forward to hold the box steady on the stool while Mr. Summers stirred up the papers inside it.

5       The original paraphernalia for the lottery had been lost long ago, and the black box now resting on the stool had been put into use even before Old Man Warner, the oldest man in town, was born. Mr. Summers spoke frequently to the villagers about making a new box, but no one liked to upset even as much tradition as was represented by the black box. There was a story that the present box had been made with some pieces of the box that had preceded it, the one that had been constructed when the first people settled down to make a village here. Every year, after the lottery, Mr. Summers began talking again about a new box, but every year the subject was allowed to fade off without anything's being done. The black box grew shabbier each year; by now it was no longer completely black but splintered badly along one side to show the original wood color, and in some places faded or stained.

Mr. Martin and his oldest son, Baxter, held the black box securely on the stool until Mr. Summers had stirred the papers thoroughly with his hand. Because so much of the ritual had been forgotten or discarded, Mr. Summers had been successful in having slips of paper substituted for the chips of wood that had been used for generations. Chips of wood, Mr. Summers had argued, had been all very well when the village was tiny, but now that the population was more than three hundred and likely to keep on growing, it was necessary to use something that would fit more easily into the black box. The night before the lottery, Mr. Summers and Mr. Graves made up the slips of paper and put them in the box, and it was then taken to the safe of Mr. Summers's coal company and locked up until Mr. Summers was ready to take it to the square next morning. The rest of the year, the box was put away, sometimes one place, sometimes another; it had spent one year in Mr. Graves's barn and another year underfoot in the post office, and sometimes it was set on a shelf in the Martin grocery and left there.

There was a great deal of fussing to be done before Mr. Summers declared the lottery open. There were lists to make up—of heads of families, heads of households in each family, members of each household in each family. There was the proper swearing-in of Mr. Summers by the postmaster, as the official of the lottery; at one time, some people remembered, there had been a recital of some sort, performed by the official of the lottery, a perfunctory, tuneless chant that had been rattled off duly each year; some people believed that the official of the lottery used to stand just so when he said or sang it, others believed that he was supposed to walk among the people, but years and years ago this part of the ritual had been allowed to lapse. There had been, also, a ritual salute, which the official of the lottery had had to use in addressing each person who came up to draw from the box, but this also had changed with time, until now it was felt necessary only for the official to speak to each person approaching. Mr. Summers was very good at all this; in his clean white shirt and blue jeans, with one hand resting carelessly on the black box, he seemed very proper and important as he talked interminably to Mr. Graves and the Martins.

Just as Mr. Summers left off talking and turned to the assembled villagers, Mrs. Hutchinson came hurriedly along the path to the square, her sweater thrown over her shoulders, and slid into place in the back of the crowd. "Clean forgot what day it was," she said to Mrs. Delacroix, who stood next to her, and they both laughed softly. "Thought my old man was out back stacking wood," Mrs. Hutchinson went on, "and then I looked out the window and the kids were gone, and then I remembered it was the twenty-seventh and came a-running." She dried her hands on her apron, and Mrs. Delacroix said, "You're in time, though. They're still talking away up there."

Mrs. Hutchinson craned her neck to see through the crowd and found her husband and children standing near the front. She tapped Mrs. Delacroix on the arm as a farewell and began to make her way through the crowd. The people separated good-humoredly to let her through, two or three people said, in voices just loud enough to be heard across the crowd, "Here comes your Missus, Hutchinson," and "Bill, she made it after all." Mrs. Hutchinson reached her husband, and Mr. Summers, who had been waiting, said cheerfully, "Thought we were going to have to get on without you, Tessie." Mrs. Hutchinson said, grinning, "Wouldn't have me leave m'dishes in the sink, now would you, Joe?," and soft laughter ran through the crowd as the people stirred back into position after Mrs. Hutchinson's arrival.

10    "Well, now," Mr. Summers said soberly, "guess we better get started, get this over with, so's we can go back to work. Anybody ain't here?"

"Dunbar," several people said. "Dunbar, Dunbar."

Mr. Summers consulted his list. "Clyde Dunbar," he said. "That's right. He's broke his leg, hasn't he? Who's drawing for him?"

"Me, I guess," a woman said, and Mr. Summers turned to look at her. "Wife draws for her husband," Mr. Summers said. "Don't you have a grown boy to do it for you, Janey?" Although Mr. Summers and everyone else in the village knew the answer perfectly well, it was the business of the official of the lottery to ask such questions formally. Mr. Summers waited with an expression of polite interest while Mrs. Dunbar answered.

"Horace's not but sixteen yet," Mrs. Dunbar said regretfully. "Guess I gotta fill in for the old man this year."

15    "Right," Mr. Summers said. He made a note on the list he was holding. Then he asked, "Watson boy drawing this year?"

A tall boy in the crowd raised his hand. "Here," he said. "I'm drawing for m'mother and me." He blinked his eyes nervously and ducked his head as several voices in the crowd said things like "Good fellow, Jack," and "Glad to see your mother's got a man to do it."

"Well," Mr. Summers said, "guess that's everyone. Old Man Warner make it?"

"Here," a voice said, and Mr. Summers nodded.

A sudden hush fell on the crowd as Mr. Summers cleared his throat and looked at the list. "All ready?" he called. "Now, I'll read the names—heads of families first—and the men come up and take a paper out of the box. Keep the paper folded in your hand without looking at it until everyone has had a turn. Everything clear?"

20    The people had done it so many times that they only half listened to the directions; most of them were quiet, wetting their lips, not looking around. Then Mr. Summers raised one hand high and said, "Adams." A man disengaged himself from the crowd and came forward. "Hi, Steve," Mr. Summers said, and Mr. Adams said, "Hi, Joe." They grinned at one another humorlessly and nervously. Then Mr. Adams reached into the black box and took out a folded paper. He held it firmly by one corner as he turned and went hastily back to his place in the crowd, where he stood a little apart from his family, not looking down at his hand.

"Allen," Mr. Summers said. "Anderson. . . . Bentham."

"Seems like there's no time at all between lotteries any more," Mrs. Delacroix said to Mrs. Graves in the back row. "Seems like we got through with the last one only last week."

"Time sure goes fast," Mrs. Graves said.

"Clark. . . . Delacroix."

25    "There goes my old man," Mrs. Delacroix said. She held her breath while her husband went forward.

"Dunbar," Mr. Summers said, and Mrs. Dunbar went steadily to the box while one of the women said, "Go on, Janey," and another said, "There she goes."

"We're next," Mrs. Graves said. She watched while Mr. Graves came around from the side of the box, greeted Mr. Summers gravely, and selected a slip of paper from the box. By now, all through the crowd there were men holding the small folded papers in their large hands, turning them over and over nervously. Mrs. Dunbar and her two sons stood together, Mrs. Dunbar holding the slip of paper.

"Harburt. . . . Hutchinson."

"Get up there, Bill," Mrs. Hutchinson said, and the people near her laughed.

30    "Jones."

"They do say," Mr. Adams said to Old Man Warner, who stood next to him, "that over in the north village they're talking of giving up the lottery."

Old Man Warner snorted. "Pack of crazy fools," he said. "Listening to the young folks, nothing's good enough for *them*. Next thing you know, they'll be wanting to go back to living in caves, nobody work any more, live *that* way for a while. Used to be a saying about 'Lottery in June, corn be heavy soon.' First thing you know, we'd all be eating stewed chickweed and acorns. There's *always* been a lottery," he added petulantly. "Bad enough to see young Joe Summers up there joking with everybody."

"Some places have already quit lotteries," Mrs. Adams said.

"Nothing but trouble in *that*," Old Man Warner said stoutly. "Pack of young fools."

35    "Martin." And Bobby Martin watched his father go forward. "Overdyke. . . . Percy."

"I wish they'd hurry," Mrs. Dunbar said to her older son. "I wish they'd hurry."

"They're almost through," her son said.

"You get ready to run tell Dad," Mrs. Dunbar said.

Mr. Summers called his own name and then stepped forward precisely and selected a slip from the box. Then he called, "Warner."

40        "Seventy-seventh year I been in the lottery," Old Man Warner said as he
went through the crowd. "Seventy-seventh time."

"Watson." The tall boy came awkwardly through the crowd. Someone
said, "Don't be nervous, Jack," and Mr. Summers said, "Take your time, son."

"Zanini."

After that, there was a long pause, a breathless pause, until Mr. Summers,
holding his slip of paper in the air, said, "All right, fellows." For a minute, no
one moved, and then all of the slips of paper were opened. Suddenly, all
women began to speak at once, saying, "Who is it?" "Who's got it?" "Is it the
Dunbars?" "Is it the Watsons?" Then the voices began to say, "It's Hutchinson.
It's Bill." "Bill Hutchinson's got it."

"Go tell your father," Mrs. Dunbar said to her older son.

45        People began to look around to see the Hutchinsons. Bill Hutchinson
was standing quiet, staring down at the paper in his hand. Suddenly, Tessie
Hutchinson shouted to Mr. Summers, "You didn't give him time enough to
take any paper he wanted. I saw you. It wasn't fair!"

"Be a good sport, Tessie," Mrs. Delacroix called, and Mrs. Graves said, "All
of us took the same chance."

"Shut up, Tessie," Bill Hutchinson said.

"Well, everyone," Mr. Summers said, "That was done pretty fast, and now
we've got to be hurrying a little more to get done in time." He consulted his
next list. "Bill," he said, "you draw for the Hutchinson family. You got any
other households in the Hutchinsons?"

"There's Don and Eva," Mrs. Hutchinson yelled. "Make *them* take their
chance!"

50        "Daughters draw with their husbands' families, Tessie," Mr. Summers said
gently. "You know that as well as anyone else."

"It wasn't fair," Tessie said.

"I guess not, Joe," Bill Hutchinson said regretfully. "My daughter draws
with her husband's family, that's only fair. And I've got no other family except the kids."

"Then, as far as drawing for families is concerned, it's you," Mr. Summers
said in explanation, "and as far as drawing for households is concerned,
that's you, too. Right?"

"Right," Bill Hutchinson said.

55        "How many kids, Bill?" Mr. Summers asked formally.

"Three," Bill Hutchinson said. "There's Bill, Jr., and Nancy, and little Dave.
And Tessie and me."

"All right, then," Mr. Summers said. "Harry, you got their tickets back?"

Mr. Graves nodded and held up the slips of paper. "Put them in the box,
then," Mr. Summers directed. "Take Bill's and put it in."

"I think we ought to start over," Mrs. Hutchinson said, as quietly as she
could. "I tell you it wasn't *fair*. You didn't give him time enough to choose.
*Everybody* saw that."

60        Mr. Graves had selected the five slips and put them in the box, and he
dropped all the papers but those onto the ground, where the breeze caught
them and lifted them off.

"Listen, everybody," Mrs. Hutchinson was saying to the people around
her.

"Ready, Bill?" Mr. Summers asked, and Bill Hutchinson, with one quick
glance around at his wife and children, nodded.

"Remember," Mr. Summers said, "take the slips and keep them folded until each person has taken one. Harry, you help little Dave." Mr. Graves took the hand of the little boy, who came willingly with him up to the box. "Take a paper out of the box, Davy," Mr. Summers said. Davy put his hand into the box and laughed. "Take just *one* paper," Mr. Summers said. "Harry, you hold it for him." Mr. Graves took the child's hand and removed the folded paper from the tight fist and held it while little Dave stood next to him and looked up at him wonderingly.

"Nancy next," Mr. Summers said. Nancy was twelve, and her school friends breathed heavily as she went forward, switching her skirt, and took a slip daintily from the box. "Bill, Jr.," Mr. Summers said, and Billy, his face red and his feet overlarge, nearly knocked the box over as he got a paper out. "Tessie," Mr. Summers said. She hesitated for a minute, looking around defiantly, and then set her lips and went up to the box. She snatched a paper out and held it behind her.

65    "Bill," Mr. Summers said, and Bill Hutchinson reached into the box and felt around, bringing his hand out at last with the slip of paper in it.

The crowd was quiet. A girl whispered, "I hope it's not Nancy," and the sound of the whisper reached the edges of the crowd.

"It's not the way it used to be," Old Man Warner said clearly. "People ain't the way they used to be."

"All right," Mr. Summers said. "Open the papers. Harry, you open little Dave's."

Mr. Graves opened the slip of paper and there was a general sigh through the crowd as he held it up and everyone could see that it was blank. Nancy and Bill, Jr., opened theirs at the same time, and both beamed and laughed, turning around to the crowd and holding their slips of paper above their heads.

70    "Tessie," Mr. Summers said. There was a pause, and then Mr. Summers looked at Bill Hutchinson, and Bill unfolded his paper and showed it. It was blank.

"It's Tessie," Mr. Summers said, and his voice was hushed. "Show us her paper, Bill."

Bill Hutchinson went over to his wife and forced the slip of paper out of her hand. It had a black spot on it, the black spot Mr. Summers had made the night before with the heavy pencil in the coal-company office. Bill Hutchinson held it up, and there was a stir in the crowd.

"All right, folks," Mr. Summers said, "let's finish quickly."

Although the villagers had forgotten the ritual and lost the original black box, they still remembered to use stones. The pile of stones the boys had made earlier was ready; there were stones on the ground with the blowing scraps of paper that had come out of the box. Mrs. Delacroix selected a stone so large she had to pick it up with both hands and turned to Mrs. Dunbar. "Come on," she said. "Hurry up."

75    Mrs. Dunbar had small stones in both hands, and she said, gasping for breath, "I can't run at all. You'll have to go ahead and I'll catch up with you."

The children had stones already, and someone gave little Davy Hutchinson a few pebbles.

Tessie Hutchinson was in the center of a cleared space by now, and she held her hands out desperately as the villagers moved in on her. "It isn't fair," she said. A stone hit her on the side of the head.

Old Man Warner was saying, "Come on, come on, everyone." Steve Adams was in the front of the crowd of villagers, with Mrs. Graves beside him.

"It isn't fair, it isn't right," Mrs. Hutchinson screamed, and then they were upon her.

# FRANZ KAFKA

*Franz Kafka (1883–1924) was born in Prague, Austria-Hungary, the son of German-speaking middle-class Jewish parents. Trained in law, he worked from 1907 to 1922 in an insurance company sponsored by the government. In 1923 he moved to Berlin to concentrate on becoming a writer, but he suffered from poor health and during his brief literary career he published only a few stories, including "A Hunger Artist" (1914).*

*Through the agency of his friend Max Brod, a number of works by Kafka were published posthumously, including* The Trial *(1925, trans. 1937),* The Castle *(1926, trans. 1937), and* Amerika *(1927, trans. 1938). Among twentieth-century authors, Kafka's accounts of alienation and anxiety, of bewildered, isolated individuals trapped by law and bureaucracy, are unparalleled in their power and pain. In the words of the poet-critic W. H. Auden, writing in the late 1950s, "Had one to name the author who comes nearest to bearing the same kind of relation to our age as Dante, Shakespeare, and Goethe bore to theirs, Kafka is the first one would think of."*

*See the graphic story version of "A Hunger Artist" by R. Crumb and David Zane Mairowitz in Chapter 12, page 259.*

## *A Hunger Artist*                                                    [1924]

*Translated by Edwin and Willa Muir*

During these last decades the interest in professional fasting has markedly diminished. It used to pay very well to stage such great performances under one's own management, but today that is quite impossible. We live in a different world now. At one time the whole town took a lively interest in the hunger artist; from day to day of his fast the excitement mounted; everybody wanted to see him at least once a day; there were people who bought season tickets for the last few days and sat from morning till night in front of his small barred cage; even in the nighttime there were visiting hours, when the whole effect was heightened by torch flares; on fine days the cage was set out in the open air, and then it was the children's special treat to see the hunger artist; for their elders he was often just a joke that happened to be in fashion, but the children stood open-mouthed, holding each other's hands for greater security, marveling at him as he sat there pallid in black tights, with his ribs sticking out so prominently, not even on a seat but down among straw on the ground, sometimes giving a courteous nod, answering questions with a constrained smile, or perhaps stretching an arm through the bars so that one might feel how thin it was, and then again withdrawing deep into himself, paying no attention to anyone or anything, not even to the all-important striking of the clock that was the only piece of furniture in his cage, but merely staring into vacancy with half-shut eyes, now and then taking a sip from a tiny glass of water to moisten his lips.

Besides casual onlookers there were also relays of permanent watchers selected by the public, usually butchers, strangely enough, and it was their task to watch the hunger artist day and night, three of them at a time, in case he should have some secret recourse to nourishment. This was nothing but a formality, instituted to reassure the masses, for the initiates knew well enough that during his fast the artist would never in any circumstances, not even under forcible compulsion, swallow the smallest morsel of food; the honor of his profession forbade it. Not every watcher, of course, was capable of understanding this, there were often groups of night watchers who were very lax in carrying out their duties and deliberately huddled together in a retired corner to play cards with great absorption, obviously intending to give the hunger artist the chance of a little refreshment, which they supposed he could draw from some private hoard. Nothing annoyed the artist more than such watchers; they made him miserable; they made his fast seem unendurable; sometimes he mastered his feebleness sufficiently to sing during their watch for as long as he could keep going, to show them how unjust their suspicions were. But that was of little use; they only wondered at his cleverness in being able to fill his mouth even while singing. Much more to his taste were the watchers who sat close up to the bars, who were not content with the dim night lighting of the hall but focused him in the full glare of the electric pocket torch given them by the impresario. The harsh light did not trouble him at all, in any case he could never sleep properly, and he could always drowse a little, whatever the light, at any hour, even when the hall was thronged with noisy onlookers. He was quite happy at the prospect of spending a sleepless night with such watchers; he was ready to exchange jokes with them, to tell them stories out of his nomadic life, anything at all to keep them awake and demonstrate to them again that he had no eatables in his cage and that he was fasting as not one of them could fast. But his happiest moment was when the morning came and an enormous breakfast was brought them, at his expense, on which they flung themselves with the keen appetite of healthy men after a weary night of wakefulness. Of course there were people who argued that this breakfast was an unfair attempt to bribe the watchers, but that was going rather too far, and when they were invited to take on a night's vigil without a breakfast, merely for the sake of the cause, they made themselves scarce, although they stuck stubbornly to their suspicions.

Such suspicions, anyhow, were a necessary accompaniment to the profession of fasting. No one could possibly watch the hunger artist continuously, day and night, and so no one could produce first-hand evidence that the fast had really been rigorous and continuous; only the artist himself could know that, he was therefore bound to be the sole completely satisfied spectator of his own fast. Yet for other reasons he was never satisfied; it was not perhaps mere fasting that had brought him to such skeleton thinness that many people had regretfully to keep away from his exhibitions, because the sight of him was too much for them, perhaps it was dissatisfaction with himself that had worn him down. For he alone knew, what no other initiate knew, how easy it was to fast. It was the easiest thing in the world. He made no secret of this, yet people did not believe him; at the best they set him down as modest; most of them, however, thought he was out for publicity or else was some kind of cheat who found it easy to fast because he had discovered a way of making it easy, and then had the impudence to admit the fact, more or less. He had to put up with all that, and in the course of time had got used to it, but his inner dissatisfaction always rankled, and never yet, after any term of fasting—this must be granted to his credit—had he left the cage of his own free will. The longest period of fasting was fixed by his impresario at forty days, beyond that term he was not allowed to go, not even in great cities, and there was good reason for it, too. Experience had proved that for about forty days the interest of the public could be stimulated by a steadily increasing pressure of advertisement, but after that the town began to lose interest, sympathetic support began notably to fall off; there were of course local variations as between one town and another or one country and another, but as a general rule forty days marked the limit. So on the fortieth day the flower-bedecked cage was opened, enthusiastic spectators filled the hall, a military band played, two doctors entered the cage to measure the results of the fast, which were announced through a megaphone, and finally two young ladies appeared, blissful at having been selected for the honor, to help the hunger artist down the few steps leading to a small table on which was spread a carefully chosen invalid repast. And at this very moment the artist always turned stubborn. True, he would entrust his bony arms to the outstretched helping hands of the ladies bending over him, but stand up he would not. Why stop fasting at this particular moment, after forty days of it? He had held out for a long time, an illimitably long time; why stop now, when he was in his best fasting form, or rather, not yet quite in his best fasting form? Why should he be cheated of the fame he would get for fasting longer, for being not only the record hunger artist of all time, which presumably he was already, but for beating his own record by a performance beyond human imagination, since he felt that there were no limits to his capacity for fasting? His public pretended to admire him so much, why should it have so little patience with him; if he could endure fasting longer, why shouldn't the public endure it? Besides, he was tired, he was comfortable sitting in the straw, and now he was supposed to lift himself to his full height and go down to a meal the very thought of which gave him a nausea that only the presence of the ladies kept him from betraying, and even that with an effort. And he looked up into the eyes of the ladies who were apparently so friendly and in reality so cruel, and shook his head, which felt too heavy on its strengthless neck. But then there happened yet again what always happened. The impresario came forward, without a word—for the band made speech impossible—lifted his arms in the air above the artist, as if inviting Heaven to look down upon its creature here in the straw, this suffering martyr, which indeed he was, although in quite another sense; grasped him around the emaciated waist, with exaggerated caution, so that the frail condition he was in might be appreciated; and committed him to the care of the blenching ladies, not without secretly giving him a shaking so that his legs and body tottered and swayed. The artist now submitted completely; his head lolled on his breast as if it had landed there by chance; his body was hollowed out; his legs in a spasm of self-preservation clung close to each other at the knees, yet scraped on the ground as if it were not really solid ground, as if they were only trying to find solid ground; and the whole weight of his body, a featherweight after all, relapsed onto one of the ladies, who, looking around for help and panting a little—this post of honor was not at all what she had expected it to be—first stretched her neck as far as she could to keep her face at least free from contact with the artist, then finding this impossible, and her more fortunate companion not coming to her aid but merely holding extended in her own trembling hand the little bunch of knucklebones that was the artist's, to the great delight of the spectators burst into tears and had to be replaced by an attendant who had long been stationed in readiness. Then came the food, a little of which the impresario managed to get between the artist's lips, while he sat in a kind of half-fainting trance, to the accompaniment of cheerful patter designed to distract the public's attention from the artist's condition; after that, a toast was drunk to the public, supposedly prompted by a whisper from the artist in the impresario's ear; the band confirmed it with a mighty flourish, the spectators melted away, and no one had any cause to be dissatisfied with the proceedings, no one except the hunger artist himself, he only, as always.

So he lived for many years, with small regular intervals of recuperation, in visible glory, honored by the world, yet in spite of that troubled in spirit, and all the more troubled because no one would take his trouble seriously. What comfort could he possibly need? What more could he possibly wish for? And if some good-natured person, feeling sorry for him, tried to console him by pointing out that his melancholy was probably caused by fasting, it could happen, especially when he had been fasting for some time, that he reacted with an outburst of fury and to the general alarm began to shake the bars of his cage like a wild animal. Yet the impresario had a way of punishing these outbreaks which he rather enjoyed putting into operation. He would apologize publicly for the artist's behavior, which was only to be excused, he admitted, because of the irritability caused by fasting; a condition hardly to be understood by well-fed people; then by natural transition he went on to mention the artist's equally incomprehensible boast that he could fast for much longer than he was doing; he praised the high ambition, the good will, the great self-denial undoubtedly implicit in such a statement; and then quite simply countered it by bringing out photographs, which were also on sale to the public, showing the artist on the fortieth day of a fast lying in bed almost dead from exhaustion. This perversion of the truth, familiar to the artist though it was, always unnerved him afresh and proved too much for him. What was a consequence of the premature ending of his fast was here presented as the cause of it! To fight against this lack of understanding, against a whole world of non-understanding, was impossible. Time and again in good faith he stood by the bars listening to the impresario, but as soon as the photographs appeared he always let go and sank with a groan back onto his straw, and the reassured public could once more come close and gaze at him.

5     A few years later when the witnesses of such scenes called them to mind, they often failed to understand themselves at all. For meanwhile the aforementioned change in public interest had set in; it seemed to happen almost overnight; there may have been profound causes for it, but who was going to bother about that; at any rate the pampered hunger artist suddenly found himself deserted one fine day by the amusement seekers, who went streaming past him to other more favored attractions. For the last time the impresario hurried him over half Europe to discover whether the old interest might still survive here and there; all in vain; everywhere, as if by secret agreement, a positive revulsion from professional fasting was in evidence. Of course it could not really have sprung up so suddenly as all that, and many premonitory symptoms which had not been sufficiently remarked or suppressed during the rush and glitter of success now came retrospectively to

mind, but it was now too late to take any countermeasures. Fasting would surely come into fashion again at some future date, yet that was no comfort for those living in the present. What, then, was the hunger artist to do? He had been applauded by thousands in his time and could hardly come down to showing himself in a street booth at village fairs, and as for adopting another profession, he was not only too old for that but too fanatically devoted to fasting. So he took leave of the impresario, his partner in an unparalleled career, and hired himself to a large circus; in order to spare his own feelings he avoided reading the conditions of his contract.

A large circus with its enormous traffic in replacing and recruiting men, animals and apparatus can always find a use for people at any time, even for a hunger artist, provided of course that he does not ask too much, and in this particular case anyhow it was not only the artist who was taken on but his famous and long-known name as well; indeed considering the peculiar nature of his performance, which was not impaired by advancing age, it could not be objected that here was an artist past his prime, no longer at the height of his professional skill, seeking a refuge in some quiet corner of a circus; on the contrary, the hunger artist averred that he could fast as well as ever, which was entirely credible; he even alleged that if he were allowed to fast as he liked, and this was at once promised him without more ado, he could astound the world by establishing a record never yet achieved, a statement which certainly provoked a smile among the other professionals, since it left out of account the change in public opinion, which the hunger artist in his zeal conveniently forgot.

He had not, however, actually lost his sense of the real situation and took it as a matter of course that he and his cage should be stationed, not in the middle of the ring as a main attraction, but outside, near the animal cages, on a site that was after all easily accessible. Large and gaily painted placards made a frame for the cage and announced what was to be seen inside it. When the public came thronging out in the intervals to see the animals, they could hardly avoid passing the hunger artist's cage and stopping there for a moment, perhaps they might even have stayed longer had not those pressing behind them in the narrow gangway, who did not understand why they should be held up on their way toward the excitements of the menagerie, made it impossible for anyone to stand gazing quietly for any length of time. And that was the reason why the hunger artist, who had of course been looking forward to these visiting hours as the main achievement of his life, began instead to shrink from them. At first he could hardly wait for the intervals; it was exhilarating to watch the crowds come streaming his way, until only too soon—not even the most obstinate self-deception, clung to almost consciously, could hold out against the fact—the conviction was borne in upon him that these people, most of them, to judge from their actions, again and again, without exception, were all on their way to the menagerie. And the first sight of them from the distance remained the best. For when they reached his cage he was at once deafened by the storm of shouting and abuse that arose from the two contending factions, which renewed themselves continuously, of those who wanted to stop and stare at him—he soon began to dislike them more than the others—not out of real interest but only out of obstinate self-assertiveness, and those who wanted to go straight on to the animals. When the first great rush was past, the stragglers came along, and these, whom nothing could have prevented from stopping to look at him as long as they had breath, raced past with long strides, hardly even glancing at him, in their haste to get to the menagerie in time. And all too rarely did it happen that he had a stroke of luck, when some father of a family fetched up before him with his children, pointed a finger at the hunger artist, and explained at length what the phenomenon meant, telling stories of earlier years when he himself had watched similar but much more thrilling performances, and the children, still rather uncomprehending, since neither inside nor outside school had they been sufficiently prepared for this lesson—what did they care about fasting?—yet showed by the brightness of their intent eyes that new and better times might be coming. Perhaps, said the hunger artist to himself many a time, things would be a little better if his cage were set not quite so near the menagerie. That made it too easy for people to make their choice, to say nothing of what he suffered from the stench of the menagerie, the animals' restlessness by night, the carrying past of raw lumps of flesh for the beasts of prey, the roaring at feeding times, which depressed him continually. But he did not dare to lodge a complaint with the management; after all, he had the animals to thank for the troops of people who passed his cage, among whom there might always be one here and there to take an interest in him, and who could tell where they might seclude him if he called attention to his existence and thereby to the fact that, strictly speaking, he was only an impediment on the way to the menagerie.

A small impediment, to be sure, one that grew steadily less. People grew familiar with the strange idea that they could be expected, in times like these, to take an interest in a hunger artist, and with this familiarity the verdict went out against him. He might fast as much as he could, and he did so; but nothing could save him now, people passed him by. Just try to explain to anyone the art of fasting! Anyone who has no feeling for it cannot be made to understand it. The fine placards grew dirty and illegible, they were torn down; the little notice board telling the number of fast days achieved, which at first was changed carefully every day, had long stayed at the same figure, for after the first few weeks even this small task seemed pointless to the staff; and so the artist simply fasted on and on, as he had once dreamed of doing, and it was no trouble to him, just as he had always foretold, but no one counted the days, no one, not even the artist himself, knew what records he was already breaking, and his heart grew heavy. And when once in a while some leisurely passer-by stopped, made merry over the old figure on the board, and spoke of swindling, that was in its way the stupidest lie ever invented by indifference and inborn malice, since it was not the hunger artist who was cheating, he was working honestly, but the world was cheating him of his reward.

Many more days went by, however, and that too came to an end. An overseer's eye fell on the cage one day and he asked the attendants why this perfectly good cage should be left standing there unused with dirty straw inside it; nobody knew, until one man, helped out by the notice board, remembered about the hunger artist. They poked into the straw with sticks and found him in it. "Are you still fasting?" asked the overseer, "when on earth do you mean to stop?" "Forgive me, everybody," whispered the hunger artist; only the overseer, who had his ear to the bars, understood him. "Of course," said the overseer, and tapped his forehead with a finger to let the attendants know what state the man was in, "we forgive you." "I always wanted you to admire my fasting," said the hunger artist. "We do admire it," said the overseer, affably. "But you shouldn't admire it," said the hunger artist. "Well then we don't admire it," said the overseer, "but why shouldn't we admire it?" "Because I have to fast, I can't help it," said the hunger artist. "What a fellow you are," said the overseer, "and why can't you help it?" "Because," said the hunger artist, lifting his head a little and speaking, with his lips pursed, as if for a kiss, right into the overseer's ear, so that no syllable might be lost, "because I couldn't find the food I liked. If I had found it, believe me, I should have made no fuss and stuffed myself like you or anyone else." These were his last words, but in his dimming eyes remained the firm though no longer proud persuasion that he was still continuing to fast.

10         "Well, clear this out now!" said the overseer, and they buried the hunger artist, straw and all. Into the cage they put a young panther. Even the most insensitive felt it refreshing to see this wild creature leaping around the cage that had so long been dreary. The panther was all right. The food he liked was brought him without hesitation by the attendants; he seemed not even to miss his freedom; his noble body, furnished almost to the bursting point with all that it needed, seemed to carry freedom around with it too; somewhere in his jaws it seemed to lurk; and the joy of life streamed with such ardent passion from his throat that for the onlookers it was not easy to stand the shock of it. But they braced themselves, crowded around the cage, and did not want ever to move away.

# BOBBIE ANN MASON

*Bobbie Ann Mason, born in 1940 in rural western Kentucky is a graduate of the University of Kentucky, where she is writer in residence. She received a master's degree from the State University of New York at Binghamton, and a PhD from the University of Connecticut, writing a dissertation on a novel by Vladimir Nabokov. Between graduate degrees she worked for various magazines, including* T.V. Star Parade. *In 1974 she published her first book—the dissertation on Nabokov—and in 1975 she published her second,* The Girl Sleuth: A Guide to the Bobbsey Twins, Nancy Drew and Their Sisters. *She is, however, most widely known for her fiction, which usually deals with blue-collar people in rural Kentucky.*

*I write [she says in an interview published in* Boca Raton News, *January 9, 1983] about people trapped in circumstances. . . . I identify with people who are ambivalent about their situation. And I guess in my stories, I'm in a way imagining myself as I would have felt if I had not gotten away and gotten a different perspective on things—if, for example, I had gotten pregnant in high school and had to marry a truck driver as the woman did in my story "Shiloh."*

## *Shiloh*                                                          [1982]

Leroy Moffitt's wife, Norma Jean, is working on her pectorals. She lifts three-pound dumbbells to warm up, then progresses to a twenty-pound barbell. Standing with her legs apart, she reminds Leroy of Wonder Woman.

"I'd give anything if I could just get these muscles to where they're real hard," says Norma Jean. "Feel this arm. It's not as hard as the other one."

"That's cause you're right-handed," says Leroy, dodging as she swings the barbell in an arc.

"Do you think so?"

5      "Sure."

Leroy is a truckdriver. He injured his leg in a highway accident four months ago, and his physical therapy, which involves weights and a pulley, prompted Norma Jean to try building herself up. Now she is attending a body-building class. Leroy has been collecting temporary disability since his tractor-trailer jackknifed in Missouri, badly twisting his left leg in its socket. He has a steel pin in his hip. He will probably not be able to drive his rig again. It sits in the backyard, like a gigantic bird that has flown home to roost. Leroy has been home in Kentucky for three months, and his leg is almost healed, but the accident frightened him and he does not want to drive any more long hauls. He is not sure what to do next. In the meantime, he makes things from craft kits. He started by building a miniature log cabin from notched Popsicle sticks. He varnished it and placed it on the TV set, where it remains. It reminds him of a rustic Nativity scene. Then he tried string art (sailing ships on black velvet), a macramé owl kit, a snaptogether B-17 Flying Fortress, and a lamp made out of a model truck, with a light fixture screwed in the top of the cab. At first the kits were diversions, something to kill time, but now he is thinking about building a full-scale log house from a kit. It would be considerably cheaper than building a regular house, and besides, Leroy has grown to appreciate how things are put together. He has begun to realize that in all the years he was on the road he never took time to examine anything. He was always flying past scenery.

"They won't let you build a log cabin in any of the new subdivisions," Norma Jean tells him.

"They will if I tell them it's for you," he says, teasing her. Ever since they were married, he has promised Norma Jean he would build her a new home one day. They have always rented, and the house they live in is small and nondescript. It does not even feel like a home, Leroy realizes now.

Norma Jean works at the Rexall drugstore, and she has acquired an amazing amount of information about cosmetics. When she explains to Leroy the three stages of complexion care, involving creams, toners, and moisturizers, he thinks happily of other petroleum products—axle grease, diesel fuel. This is a connection between him and Norma Jean. Since he has been home, he has felt unusually tender about his wife and guilty over his long absences. But he can't tell what she feels about him. Norma Jean has never complained about his traveling; she has never made hurt remarks, like calling his truck a "widow-maker." He is reasonably certain she has been faithful to him, but he wishes she would celebrate his permanent home-coming more happily. Norma Jean is often startled to find Leroy at home, and he thinks she seems a little disappointed about it. Perhaps he reminds her too much of the early days of their marriage, before he went on the road. They had a child who died as an infant, years ago. They never speak about their memories of Randy, which have almost faded, but now that Leroy is home all the time, they sometimes feel awkward around each other, and Leroy wonders if one of them should mention the child. He has the feeling that they are waking up out of a dream together—that they must create a new marriage, start afresh. They are lucky they are still married. Leroy has read that for most people losing a child destroys the marriage—or else he heard this on *Donahue*.[1] He can't always remember where he learns things anymore.

10    At Christmas, Leroy bought an electric organ for Norma Jean. She used to play the piano when she was in high school. "It don't leave you," she told him once. "It's like riding a bicycle."

The new instrument had so many keys and buttons that she was bewildered by it at first. She touched the keys tentatively, pushed some buttons, then pecked out "Chopsticks." It came out in an amplified fox-trot rhythm, with marimba sounds.

"It's an orchestra!" she cried.

The organ had a pecan-look finish and eighteen preset chords, with optional flute, violin, trumpet, clarinet, and banjo accompaniments. Norma Jean mastered the organ almost immediately. At first she played Christmas songs. Then she bought *The Sixties Songbook* and learned every tune in it, adding variations to each with the rows of brightly colored buttons.

"I didn't like these old songs back then," she said. "But I have this crazy feeling I missed something."

15    "You didn't miss a thing," said Leroy.

Leroy likes to lie on the couch and smoke a joint and listen to Norma Jean play "Can't Take My Eyes Off You" and "I'll Be Back." He is back again. After fifteen years on the road, he is finally settling down with the woman he loves. She is still pretty. Her skin is flawless. Her frosted curls resemble pencil trimmings.

Now that Leroy has come home to stay, he notices how much the town has changed. Subdivisions are spreading across western Kentucky like an oil slick. The sign at the edge of town says "Pop: 11,500"—only seven hundred more than it said twenty years before. Leroy can't figure out who is living in all the new houses. The farmers who used to gather around the courthouse square on Saturday afternoons to play checkers and spit tobacco juice have gone. It has been years since Leroy has thought about the farmers, and they have disappeared without his noticing.

Leroy meets a kid named Stevie Hamilton in the parking lot at the new shopping center. While they pretend to be strangers meeting over a stalled car, Stevie tosses an ounce of marijuana under the front seat of Leroy's car. Stevie is wearing orange jogging shoes and a T-shirt that says CHATTAHOOCHEE SUPER-RAT. His father is a prominent doctor who lives in one of the expensive subdivisions in a new white-columned brick house that looks like a funeral parlor. In the phone book under his name there is a separate number, with the listing "Teenagers."

"Where do you get this stuff?" asks Leroy. "From your pappy?"

20    "That's for me to know and you to find out," Stevie says. He is slit-eyed and skinny.

"What else you got?"

"What you interested in?"

"Nothing special. Just wondered."

---

[1]**Donahue** The Phil Donahue Show, a popular television program, 1972–1991.

Leroy used to take speed on the road. Now he has to go slowly. He needs to be mellow. He leans back against the car and says, "I'm aiming to build me a log house, soon as I get time. My wife, though, I don't think she likes the idea."

25    "Well, let me know when you want me again," Stevie says. He has a cigarette in his cupped palm, as though sheltering it from the wind. He takes a long drag, then stomps it on the asphalt and slouches away.

Stevie's father was two years ahead of Leroy in high school. Leroy is thirty-four. He married Norma Jean when they were both eighteen, and their child Randy was born a few months later, but he died at the age of four months and three days. He would be about Stevie's age now. Norma Jean and Leroy were at the drive-in, watching a double feature (*Dr. Strangelove* and *Lover Come Back*), and the baby was sleeping in the back seat. When the first movie ended, the baby was dead. It was the sudden infant death syndrome. Leroy remembers handing Randy to a nurse at the emergency room, as though he were offering her a large doll as a present. A dead baby feels like a sack of flour. "It just happens sometimes," said the doctor, in what Leroy always recalls as a nonchalant tone. Leroy can hardly remember the child anymore, but he still sees vividly a scene from *Dr. Strangelove* in which the President of the United States was talking in a folksy voice on the hot line to the Soviet premier about the bomber accidentally headed toward Russia. He was in the War Room, and the world map was lit up. Leroy remembers Norma Jean standing catatonically beside him in the hospital and himself thinking: Who is this strange girl? He had forgotten who she was. Now scientists are saying that crib death is caused by a virus. Nobody knows anything, Leroy thinks. The answers are always changing.

When Leroy gets home from the shopping center, Norma Jean's mother, Mabel Beasley, is there. Until this year, Leroy has not realized how much time she spends with Norma Jean. When she visits, she inspects the closets and then the plants, informing Norma Jean when a plant is droopy or yellow. Mabel calls the plants "flowers," although there are never any blooms. She also notices if Norma Jean's laundry is piling up. Mabel is a short, overweight woman whose tight, brown-dyed curls look more like a wig than the actual wig she sometimes wears. Today she has brought Norma Jean an off-white dust ruffle she made for the bed; Mabel works in a custom-upholstery shop.

"This is the tenth one I made this year," Mabel says. "I got started and couldn't stop."

"It's real pretty," says Norma Jean.

30    "Now we can hide things under the bed," says Leroy, who gets along with his mother-in-law primarily by joking with her. Mabel has never really forgiven him for disgracing her by getting Norma Jean pregnant. When the baby died, she said that fate was mocking her.

"What's that thing?" Mabel says to Leroy in a loud voice, pointing to a tangle of yarn on a piece of canvas.

Leroy holds it up for Mabel to see. "It's my needlepoint," he explains. "This is a *Star Trek* pillow cover."

"That's what a woman would do," says Mabel. "Great day in the morning!"

"All the big football players on TV do it," he says.

35    "Why, Leroy, you're always trying to fool me. I don't believe you for one minute. You don't know what to do with yourself—that's the whole trouble. Sewing!"

"I'm aiming to build us a log house," says Leroy. "Soon as my plans come."

"Like *heck* you are," says Norma Jean. She takes Leroy's needlepoint and shoves it into a drawer. "You have to find a job first. Nobody can afford to build now anyway."

Mabel straightens her girdle and says. "I still think before you get tied down y'all ought to take a little run to Shiloh."

"One of these days, Mama," Norma Jean says impatiently.

40    Mabel is talking about Shiloh, Tennessee. For the past few years, she has been urging Leroy and Norma Jean to visit the Civil War battleground there. Mabel went there on her honeymoon—the only real trip she ever took. Her husband died of a perforated ulcer when Norma Jean was ten, but Mabel, who was accepted into the United Daughters of the Confederacy in 1975, is still preoccupied with going back to Shiloh.

"I've been to kingdom come and back in that truck out yonder," Leroy says to Mabel, "but we never yet set foot in that battleground. Ain't that something? How did I miss it?"

"It's not even that far," Mabel says.

After Mabel leaves, Norma Jean reads to Leroy from a list she has made. "Things you could do," she announces. "You could get a job as a guard at Union Carbide, where they'd let you set on a stool. You could get on at the lumberyard. You could do a little carpenter work, if you want to build so bad. You could—"

"I can't do something where I'd have to stand up all day."

45    "You ought to try standing up all day behind a cosmetics counter. It's amazing that I have strong feet, coming from two parents that never had strong feet at all." At the moment Norma Jean is holding on to the kitchen counter, raising her knees one at a time as she talks. She is wearing two-pound ankle weights.

"Don't worry," says Leroy. "I'll do something."

"You could truck calves to slaughter for somebody. You wouldn't have to drive any big old truck for that."

"I'm going to build you this house," says Leroy. "I want to make you a real home."

"I don't want to live in any log cabin."

50    "It's not a cabin. It's a house."

"I don't care. It looks like a cabin."

"You and me together could lift those logs. It's just like lifting weights."

Norma Jean doesn't answer. Under her breath, she is counting. Now she is marching through the kitchen. She is doing goose steps.

Before his accident, when Leroy came home he used to stay in the house with Norma Jean, watching TV in bed and playing cards. She would cook fried chicken, picnic ham, chocolate pie—all his favorites. Now he is home alone much of the time. In the mornings, Norma Jean disappears, leaving a cooling place in the bed. She eats a cereal called Body Buddies, and she leaves the bowl on the table, with the soggy tan balls floating in a milk puddle. He sees things about Norma Jean that he never realized before. When she chops onions, she stares off into a corner, as if she can't bear to look. She puts on her house slippers almost precisely at nine o'clock every evening and nudges her jogging shoes under the couch. She saves bread heels for the birds. Leroy watches the birds at the feeder. He notices the peculiar way goldfinches fly past the window. They close their wings, then fall, then spread their wings to catch and lift themselves. He wonders if they close their eyes when they fall. Norma Jean closes her eyes when they are in bed. She wants the lights turned out. Even then, he is sure she closes her eyes.

55 He goes for long drives around town. He tends to drive a car rather carelessly. Power steering and an automatic shift make a car feel so small and inconsequential that his body is hardly involved in the driving process. His injured leg stretches out comfortably. Once or twice he has almost hit something, but even the prospect of an accident seems minor in a car. He cruises the new subdivisions, feeling like a criminal rehearsing for a robbery. Norma Jean is probably right about a log house being inappropriate here in the new subdivision. All the houses look grand and complicated. They depress him.

One day when Leroy comes home from a drive he finds Norma Jean in tears. She is in the kitchen making a potato and mushroom-soup casserole, with grated cheese topping. She is crying because her mother caught her smoking.

"I didn't hear her coming. I was standing here puffing away pretty as you please," Norma Jean says, wiping her eyes.

"I knew it would happen sooner or later," says Leroy, putting his arm around her.

"She don't know the meaning of the word 'knock,'" says Norma Jean. "It's a wonder she hadn't caught me years ago."

60 "Think of it this way," Leroy says. "What if she caught me with a joint?"

"You better not let her!" Norma Jean shrieks. "I'm warning you, Leroy Moffitt!"

"I'm just kidding. Here, play me a tune. That'll help you relax."

Norma Jean puts the casserole in the oven and sets the timer. Then she plays a ragtime tune, with horns and banjo, as Leroy lights up a joint and lies on the couch, laughing to himself about Mabel's catching him at it. He thinks of Stevie Hamilton—a doctor's son pushing grass. Everything is funny. The whole town seems crazy and small. He is reminded of Virgil Mathis, a boastful policeman Leroy used to shoot pool with. Virgil recently led a drug bust in a back room at a bowling alley, where he seized ten thousand dollars' worth of marijuana. The newspaper had a picture of him holding up the bags of grass and grinning widely. Right now, Leroy can imagine Virgil breaking down the door and arresting him with a lungful of smoke. Virgil would probably have been alerted to the scene because of all the racket Norma Jean is making. Now she sounds like a hard-rock band. Norma Jean is terrific. When she switches to a Latin-rhythm version of "Sunshine Superman," Leroy hums along. Norma Jean's foot goes up and down, up and down.

"Well, what do you think?" Leroy says, when Norma Jean pauses to search through her music.

65 "What do I think about what?"

His mind has gone blank. Then he says, "I'll sell my rig and build us a house." That wasn't what he wanted to say. He wanted to know what she thought—what she *really* thought—about them.

"Don't start in on that again," says Norma Jean. She begins playing "Who'll Be the Next in Line?"

Leroy used to tell hitchhikers his whole life story—about his travels, his hometown, the baby. He would end with a question: "Well, what do you think?" It was just a rhetorical question. In time, he had the feeling that he'd been telling the same story over and over to the same hitchhikers. He quit talking to hitchhikers when he realized how his voice sounded—whining and self-pitying, like some teenage-tragedy song. Now Leroy has the sudden impulse to tell Norma Jean about himself, as if he had just met her. They have known each other so long they have forgotten a lot about each other. They could become reacquainted. But when the oven timer goes off and she runs to the kitchen, he forgets why he wants to do this.

The next day, Mabel drops by. It is Saturday and Norma Jean is cleaning. Leroy is studying the plans of his log house, which have finally come in the mail. He has them spread out on the table—big sheets of stiff blue paper, with diagrams and numbers printed in white. While Norma Jean runs the vacuum, Mabel drinks coffee. She sets her coffee cup on a blueprint.

70    "I'm just waiting for time to pass," she says to Leroy, drumming her fingers on the table.

As soon as Norma Jean switches off the vacuum, Mabel says in a loud voice, "Did you hear about the datsun dog that killed the baby?"

Norma Jean says, "The word is 'dachshund.'"

"They put the dog on trial. It chewed the baby's legs off. The mother was in the next room all the time." She raises her voice. "They thought it was neglect."

Norma Jean is holding her ears. Leroy manages to open the refrigerator and get some Diet Pepsi to offer Mabel. Mabel still has some coffee and she waves away the Pepsi.

75    "Datsuns are like that," Mabel says. "They're jealous dogs. They'll tear a place to pieces if you don't keep an eye on them."

"You better watch out what you're saying, Mabel," says Leroy.

"Well, facts is facts."

Leroy looks out the window at his rig. It is like a huge piece of furniture gathering dust in the backyard. Pretty soon it will be an antique. He hears the vacuum cleaner. Norma Jean seems to be cleaning the living room rug again.

Later, she says to Leroy, "She just said that about the baby because she caught me smoking. She's trying to pay me back."

80    "What are you talking about?" Leroy says, nervously shuffling blueprints.

"You know good and well," Norma Jean says. She is sitting in a kitchen chair with her feet up and her arms wrapped around her knees. She looks small and helpless. She says, "The very idea, her bringing up a subject like that! Saying it was neglect."

"She didn't mean that," Leroy says.

"She might not have *thought* she meant it. She always says things like that. You don't know how she goes on."

"But she didn't really mean it. She was just talking."

85    Leroy opens a king-sized bottle of beer and pours it into two glasses dividing it carefully. He hands a glass to Norma Jean and she takes it from him mechanically. For a long time, they sit by the kitchen window watching the birds at the feeder.

Something is happening. Norma Jean is going to night school. She has graduated from her six-week body-building course and now she is taking an adult-education course in composition at Paducah Community College. She spends her evenings outlining paragraphs.

"First, you have a topic sentence," she explains to Leroy. "Then you divide it up. Your secondary topic has to be connected to your primary topic."

To Leroy, this sounds intimidating. "I never was any good in English," he says.

"It makes a lot of sense."

90 "What are you doing this for, anyhow?"

She shrugs. "It's something to do." She stands up and lifts her dumbbells a few times.

"Driving a rig, nobody cared about my English."

"I'm not criticizing your English."

Norma Jean used to say, "If I lose ten minutes' sleep, I just drag all day." Now she stays up late, writing compositions. She got a B on her first paper— a how-to theme on soup-based casseroles. Recently Norma Jean has been cooking unusual foods—tacos, lasagna, Bombay chicken. She doesn't play the organ anymore, though her second paper was called "Why Music Is Important to Me." She sits at the kitchen table, concentrating on her outlines, while Leroy plays with his log house plans, practicing with a set of Lincoln Logs. The thought of getting a truckload of notched, numbered logs scares him, and he wants to be prepared. As he and Norma Jean work together at the kitchen table, Leroy has the hopeful thought that they are sharing something, but he knows he is a fool to think this. Norma Jean is miles away. He knows he is going to lose her. Like Mabel, he is just waiting for time to pass.

95 One day, Mabel is there before Norma Jean gets home from work, and Leroy finds himself confiding in her. Mabel, he realizes, must know Norma Jean better than he does.

"I don't know what's got into that girl," Mabel says. "She used to go to bed with the chickens. Now you say she's up all hours. Plus her a-smoking. I like to died."

"I want to make her this beautiful home," Leroy says, indicating the Lincoln Logs. "I don't think she even wants it. Maybe she was happier with me gone."

"She don't know what to make of you, coming home like this."

"Is that it?"

100 Mabel takes the roof off his Lincoln Log cabin. "You couldn't get *me* in a log cabin," she says. "I was raised in one. It's no picnic, let me tell you."

"They're different now," says Leroy.

"I tell you what," Mabel says, smiling oddly at Leroy.

"What?"

"Take her on down to Shiloh. Y'all need to get out together, stir a little. Her brain's all balled up over them books."

105 Leroy can see traces of Norma Jean's features in her mother's face. Mabel's worn face has the texture of crinkled cotton, but suddenly she looks pretty. It occurs to Leroy that Mabel has been hinting all along that she wants them to take her with them to Shiloh.

"Let's all go to Shiloh," he says. "You and me and her. Come Sunday."

Mabel throws up her hand in protest. "Oh, no, not me. Young folks want to be by theirselves."

When Norma Jean comes in with groceries, Leroy says excitedly. "Your mama here's been dying to go to Shiloh for thirty-five years. It's about time we went, don't you think?"

"I'm not going to butt in on anybody's second honeymoon," Mabel says.

110    "Who's going on a honeymoon, for Christ's sake?" Norma Jean says loudly.

"I never raised no daughter of mine to talk that-a-way," Mabel says.

"You ain't seen nothing yet," says Norma Jean. She starts putting away boxes and cans, slamming cabinet doors.

"There's a log cabin at Shiloh," Mabel says. "It was there during the battle. There's bullet holes in it."

"When are you going to *shut up* about Shiloh, Mama?" asks Norma Jean.

115    "I always thought Shiloh was the prettiest place, so full of history," Mabel goes on. "I just hoped y'all could see it once before I die, so you could tell me about it." Later, she whispers to Leroy. "You do what I said. A little change is what she needs."

"Your name means 'the king,'" Norma Jean says to Leroy that evening. He is trying to get her to go to Shiloh, and she is reading a book about another century.

"Well, I reckon I ought to be right proud."

"I guess so."

"Am I still king around here?"

120    Norma Jean flexes her biceps and feels them for hardness. "I'm not fooling around with anybody, if that's what you mean," she says.

"Would you tell me if you were?"

"I don't know."

"What does *your* name mean?"

"It was Marilyn Monroe's real name."

125    "No kidding!"

"Norma comes from the Normans. They were invaders," she says. She closes her book and looks hard at Leroy. "I'll go to Shiloh with you if you'll stop staring at me."

On Sunday, Norma Jean packs a picnic and they go to Shiloh. To Leroy's relief Mabel says she does not want to come with them. Norma Jean drives, and Leroy, sitting beside her, feels like some boring hitchhiker she has picked up. He tries some conversation, but she answers him in monosyllables. At Shiloh, she drives aimlessly through the park, past bluffs and trails and steep ravines. Shiloh is an immense place, and Leroy cannot see it as a battleground. It is not what he expected. He thought it would look like a golf course. Monuments are everywhere, showing through the thick clusters of trees. Norma Jean passes the log cabin Mabel mentioned. It is surrounded by tourists looking for bullet holes.

"That's not the kind of log house I've got in mind," says Leroy apologetically.

"I know *that*."

130    "This is a pretty place. Your mama was right."

"It's O.K.," says Norma Jean. "Well, we've seen it. I hope she's satisfied."

They burst out laughing together.

At the park museum, a movie on Shiloh is shown every half hour, but they decide that they don't want to see it. They buy a souvenir Confederate flag for Mabel, and then they find a picnic spot near the cemetery. Norma Jean has brought a picnic cooler, with pimento sandwiches, soft drinks, and

Yodels. Leroy eats a sandwich and then smokes a joint, hiding it behind the picnic cooler. Norma Jean has quit smoking altogether. She is picking cake crumbs from the cellophane wrapper, like a fussy bird.

Leroy says, "So the boys in gray ended up in Corinth. The Union soldiers zapped 'em finally. April 7, 1862."

135　　They both know that he doesn't know any history. He is just talking about some of the historical plaques they have read. He feels awkward, like a boy on a date with an older girl. They are still just making conversation.

"Corinth is where Mama eloped to," says Norma Jean.

They sit in silence and stare at the cemetery for the Union dead and, beyond, at a tall cluster of trees. Campers are parked nearby, bumper to bumper, and small children in bright clothing are cavorting and squealing. Norma Jean wads up the cake wrapper and squeezes it tightly in her hand. Without looking at Leroy, she says, "I want to leave you."

Leroy takes a bottle of Coke out of the cooler and flips off the cap. He holds the bottle poised near his mouth but cannot remember to take a drink. Finally he says, "No, you don't."

"Yes, I do."

140　　"I won't let you."

"You can't stop me."

"Don't do me that way."

Leroy knows Norma Jean will have her own way. "Didn't I promise to be home from now on?" he says.

"In some ways, a woman prefers a man who wanders," says Norma Jean. "That sounds crazy, I know."

145　　"You're not crazy." Leroy remembers to drink from his Coke. Then he says, "Yes, you *are* crazy. You and me could start all over again. Right back at the beginning."

"We *have* started all over again," says Norma Jean. "And this is how it turned out."

"What did I do wrong?"

"Nothing."

"Is this one of those women's lib things?" Leroy asks.

150　　"Don't be funny."

The cemetery, a green slope dotted with white markers, looks like a subdivision site. Leroy is trying to comprehend that his marriage is breaking up, but for some reason he is wondering about white slabs in a graveyard.

"Everything was fine till Mama caught me smoking," says Norma Jean, standing up. "That set something off."

"What are you talking about?"

"She won't leave me alone—*you* won't leave me alone." Norma Jean seems to be crying, but she is looking away from him. "I feel eighteen again. I can't face that all over again." She starts walking away. "No, it *wasn't* fine. I don't know what I'm saying. Forget it."

155　　Leroy takes a lungful of smoke and closes his eyes as Norma Jean's words sink in. He tries to focus on the fact that thirty-five hundred soldiers died on the grounds around him. He can only think of that war as a board game with plastic soldiers. Leroy almost smiles, as he compares the Confederates' daring attack on the Union camps and Virgil Mathis's raid on the bowling alley. General Grant, drunk and furious, shoved the Southerners back to Corinth, where Mabel and Jet Beasley were married years later, when Mabel was still thin and good-looking. The next day, Mabel and Jet visited the battleground, and then Norma Jean was born, and then she married Leroy and they had a baby, which they lost, and now Leroy and Norma Jean are here at the same battleground. Leroy knows he is leaving out a lot. He is leaving out the insides of history. History was always just names and dates to him. It occurs to him that building a house of logs is similarly empty—too simple. And the real inner workings of a marriage, like most of history, have escaped him. Now he sees that building a log house is the dumbest idea he could have had. It was clumsy of him to think Norma Jean would want a log house. It was a crazy idea. He'll have to think of something else, quickly. He will wad the blueprints into tight balls and fling them into the lake. Then he'll get moving again. He opens his eyes. Norma Jean has moved away and is walking through the cemetery, following a serpentine brick path.

Leroy gets up to follow his wife, but his good leg is asleep and his bad leg still hurts him. Norma Jean is far away, walking rapidly toward the bluff by the river, and he tries to hobble toward her. Some children run past him, screaming noisily. Norma Jean has reached the bluff, and she is looking out over the Tennessee River. Now she turns toward Leroy and waves her arms. Is she beckoning to him? She seems to be doing an exercise for her chest muscles. The sky is unusually pale—the color of the dust ruffle Mabel made for their bed.

# GUY DE MAUPASSANT

*Guy de Maupassant (1850–1893) was born in Dieppe, France. (When referring to him by his last name only, the name is Maupassant, not de Maupassant.) He studied law briefly, served in the Franco-Prussian War (1870–1871), and then lived in Paris, where he met such distinguished writers as Émile Zola and Gustave Flaubert. Maupassant for a time worked as a civil servant, but he resigned his job in 1880 when he published (in an anthology edited by Zola) the first of his two hundred or so stories. He had meanwhile contracted syphilis, which in later years affected his mind. He attempted suicide in 1891 and was confined to an asylum, where he died two years later.*

## *The Necklace*                                                [1885]

*Translated by Marjorie Laurie*

She was one of those pretty and charming girls who are sometimes, as if by a mistake of destiny, born in a family of clerks. She had no dowry, no expectations, no means of being known, understood, loved, wedded by any rich and distinguished man; and she let herself be married to a little clerk at the Ministry of Public Instruction.

She dressed plainly because she could not dress well, but she was as unhappy as though she had really fallen from her proper station, since with women there is neither caste nor rank: and beauty, grace and charm act instead of family and birth. Natural fineness, instinct for what is elegant, suppleness of wit, are the sole hierarchy, and make from women of the people the equals of the very greatest ladies.

She suffered ceaselessly, feeling herself born for all the delicacies and all the luxuries. She suffered from the poverty of her dwelling, from the wretched look of the walls, from the worn-out chairs, from the ugliness of the curtains. All those things, of which another woman of her rank would never even have been conscious, tortured her and made her angry. The sight of the little Breton peasant who did her humble housework aroused in her regrets which were despairing, and distracted dreams. She thought of the silent antechambers hung with Oriental tapestry, lit by tall bronze candelabra, and of the two great footmen in knee breeches who sleep in the big armchairs, made drowsy by the heavy warmth of the hot-air stove. She thought of the long *salons*[1] fitted up with ancient silk, of the delicate furniture carrying priceless curiosities, and of the coquettish perfumed boudoirs made for talks at five o'clock with intimate friends, with men famous and sought after, whom all women envy and whose attention they all desire.

When she sat down to dinner, before the round table covered with a table-cloth three days old, opposite her husband, who uncovered the soup tureen and declared with an enchanted air, "Ah, the good *pot-au-feu!*[2] I don't know anything better than that," she thought of dainty dinners, of shining silverware, of tapestry which peopled the walls with ancient personages and with strange birds flying in the midst of a fairy forest; and she thought of delicious dishes served on marvelous plates, and of the whispered gallantries which you listen to with a sphinxlike smile, while you are eating the pink flesh of a trout or the wings of a quail.

5      She had no dresses, no jewels, nothing. And she loved nothing but that; she felt made for that. She would so have liked to please, to be envied, to be charming, to be sought after.

She had a friend, a former schoolmate at the convent, who was rich, and whom she did not like to go and see any more, because she suffered so much when she came back.

But one evening, her husband returned home with a triumphant air, and holding a large envelope in his hand.

"There," said he. "Here is something for you."

She tore the paper sharply, and drew out a printed card which bore these words:

10      "The Minister of Public Instruction and Mme. Georges Ramponneau
request the honor of M. and Mme. Loisel's company at the palace of
the Ministry on Monday evening, January eighteenth."

Instead of being delighted, as her husband hoped, she threw the invitation on the table with disdain, murmuring:

"What do you want me to do with that?"

"But, my dear, I thought you would be glad. You never go out, and this is such a fine opportunity. I had awful trouble to get it. Everyone wants to go; it is very select, and they are not giving many invitations to clerks. The whole official world will be there."

She looked at him with an irritated glance, and said, impatiently:

15      "And what do you want me to put on my back?"

---

[1]**salons** drawing rooms.     [2]**pot-au-feu** stew.

He had not thought of that; he stammered:

"Why, the dress you go to the theater in. It looks very well, to me."

He stopped, distracted, seeing his wife was crying. Two great tears descended slowly from the corners of her eyes toward the corners of her mouth. He stuttered:

"What's the matter? What's the matter?"

20      But, by violent effort, she had conquered her grief, and she replied, with a calm voice, while she wiped her wet cheeks:

"Nothing. Only I have no dress and therefore I can't go to this ball. Give your card to some colleague whose wife is better equipped than I."

He was in despair. He resumed:

"Come, let us see, Mathilde. How much would it cost, a suitable dress, which you could use on other occasions, something very simple?"

She reflected several seconds, making her calculations and wondering also what sum she could ask without drawing on herself an immediate refusal and a frightened exclamation from the economical clerk.

25      Finally, she replied, hesitatingly:

"I don't know exactly, but I think I could manage it with four hundred francs."

He had grown a little pale, because he was laying aside just that amount to buy a gun and treat himself to a little shooting next summer on the plain of Nanterre, with several friends who went to shoot larks down there, of a Sunday.

But he said:

"All right. I will give you four hundred francs. And try to have a pretty dress."

30      The day of the ball drew near, and Mme. Loisel seemed sad, uneasy, anxious. Her dress was ready, however. Her husband said to her one evening:

"What is the matter? Come, you've been so queer these last three days."

And she answered:

"It annoys me not to have a single jewel, not a single stone, nothing to put on. I shall look like distress. I should almost rather not go at all."

He resumed:

35      "You might wear natural flowers. It's very stylish at this time of the year. For ten francs you can get two or three magnificent roses."

She was not convinced.

"No; there's nothing more humiliating than to look poor among other women who are rich."

But her husband cried:

"How stupid you are! Go look up your friend Mme. Forestier, and ask her to lend you some jewels. You're quite thick enough with her to do that."

40      She uttered a cry of joy:

"It's true. I never thought of it."

The next day she went to her friend and told of her distress.

Mme. Forestier went to a wardrobe with a glass door, took out a large jewel-box, brought it back, opened it, and said to Mme. Loisel:

"Choose, my dear."

45      She saw first of all some bracelets, then a pearl necklace, then a Venetian cross, gold and precious stones of admirable workmanship. She tried on the ornaments before the glass, hesitated, could not make up her mind to part with them, to give them back. She kept asking:

"Haven't you any more?"

"Why, yes. Look. I don't know what you like."

All of a sudden she discovered, in a black satin box, a superb necklace of diamonds, and her heart began to beat with an immoderate desire. Her hands trembled as she took it. She fastened it around her throat, outside her high-necked dress, and remained lost in ecstasy at the sight of herself.

Then she asked, hesitating, filled with anguish:

50    "Can you lend me that, only that?"

"Why, yes, certainly."

She sprang upon the neck of her friend, kissed her passionately, then fled with her treasure.

The day of the ball arrived. Mme. Loisel made a great success. She was prettier than them all, elegant, gracious, smiling, and crazy with joy. All the men looked at her, asked her name, endeavored to be introduced. All the attachés of the Cabinet wanted to waltz with her. She was remarked by the minister himself.

She danced with intoxication, with passion, made drunk by pleasure, forgetting all, in the triumph of her beauty, in the glory of her success, in a sort of cloud of happiness composed of all this homage, of all this admiration, of all these awakened desires, and of that sense of complete victory which is so sweet to a woman's heart.

55    She went away about four o'clock in the morning. Her husband had been sleeping since midnight, in a little deserted anteroom, with three other gentlemen whose wives were having a very good time. He threw over her shoulders the wraps which he had brought, modest wraps of common life, whose poverty contrasted with the elegance of the ball dress. She felt this, and wanted to escape so as not to be remarked by the other women, who were enveloping themselves in costly furs.

Loisel held her back.

"Wait a bit. You will catch cold outside. I will go and call a cab."

But she did not listen to him, and rapidly descended the stairs. When they were in the street they did not find a carriage; and they began to look for one, shouting after the cabmen whom they saw passing by at a distance.

They went down toward the Seine, in despair, shivering with cold. At last they found on the quay one of those ancient noctambulant coupés which, exactly as if they were ashamed to show their misery during the day, are never seen round Paris until after nightfall.

60    It took them to their door in the Rue des Martyrs, and once more, sadly, they climbed up homeward. All was ended, for her. And as to him, he reflected that he must be at the Ministry at ten o'clock.

She removed the wraps which covered her shoulders, before the glass, so as once more to see herself in all her glory. But suddenly she uttered a cry. She no longer had the necklace around her neck!

Her husband, already half undressed, demanded:

"What is the matter with you?"

She turned madly toward him:

65    "I have—I have—I've lost Mme. Forestier's necklace."

He stood up, distracted.

"What!—how?—impossible!"

And they looked in the folds of her dress, in the folds of her cloak, in her pockets, everywhere. They did not find it.

He asked:

70 "You're sure you had it on when you left the ball?"

"Yes, I felt it in the vestibule of the palace."

"But if you had lost it in the street we should have heard it fall. It must be in the cab."

"Yes. Probably. Did you take his number?"

"No. And you, didn't you notice it?"

75 "No."

They looked, thunderstruck, at one another. At last Loisel put on his clothes.

"I shall go back on foot," said he, "over the whole route which we have taken to see if I can find it."

And he went out. She sat waiting on a chair in her ball dress, without strength to go to bed, overwhelmed, without fire, without a thought.

Her husband came back about seven o'clock. He had found nothing.

80 He went to Police Headquarters, to the newspaper offices, to offer a reward: he went to the cab companies—everywhere, in fact, whither he was urged by the least suspicion of hope.

She waited all day, in the same condition of mad fear before this terrible calamity.

Loisel returned at night with a hollow, pale face; he had discovered nothing.

"You must write to your friend," said he, "that you have broken the clasp of her necklace and that you are having it mended. That will give us time to turn round."

She wrote at his dictation.

85 At the end of a week they had lost all hope.

And Loisel, who had aged five years, declared:

"We must consider how to replace that ornament."

The next day they took the box which had contained it, and they went to the jeweler whose name was found within. He consulted his books.

"It was not I, madame, who sold that necklace; I must simply have furnished the case."

90 Then they went from jeweler to jeweler, searching for a necklace like the other, consulting their memories, sick both of them with chagrin and anguish.

They found, in a shop at the Palais Royal, a string of diamonds which seemed to them exactly like the one they looked for. It was worth forty thousand francs. They could have it for thirty-six.

So they begged the jeweler not to sell it for three days yet. And they made a bargain that he should buy it back for thirty-four thousand francs, in case they found the other one before the end of February.

Loisel possessed eighteen thousand francs which his father had left him. He would borrow the rest.

He did borrow, asking a thousand francs of one, five hundred of another, five louis[3] here, three louis there. He gave notes, took up ruinous obligations, dealt with usurers and all the race of lenders. He compromised all the rest of his life, risked his signature without even knowing if he could

---

[3] **louis** a gold coin worth 20 francs.

meet it; and, frightened by the pains yet to come, by the black misery which was about to fall upon him, by the prospect of all the physical privation and of all the moral tortures which he was to suffer, he went to get the new necklace, putting down upon the merchant's counter thirty-six thousand francs.

95     When Mme. Loisel took back the necklace, Mme. Forestier said to her, with a chilly manner:

"You should have returned it sooner; I might have needed it."

She did not open the case, as her friend had so much feared. If she had detected the substitution, what would she have thought, what would she have said? Would she not have taken Mme. Loisel for a thief?

Mme. Loisel now knew the horrible existence of the needy. She took her part, moreover, all of a sudden, with heroism. That dreadful debt must be paid. She would pay it. They dismissed their servant; they changed their lodgings; they rented a garret under the roof.

She came to know what heavy housework meant and the odious cares of the kitchen. She washed the dishes, using her rosy nails on the greasy pots and pans. She washed the dirty linen, the shirts, and the dishcloths, which she dried upon a line; she carried the slops down to the street every morning, and carried up the water, stopping for breath at every landing. And, dressed like a woman of the people, she went to the fruiterer, the grocer, the butcher, her basket on her arm, bargaining, insulted, defending her miserable money sou by sou.

100     Each month they had to meet some notes, renew others, obtain more time.

Her husband worked in the evening making a fair copy of some tradesman's accounts, and late at night he often copied manuscript for five sous a page.

And this life lasted for ten years.

At the end of ten years, they had paid everything, everything, with the rates of usury, and the accumulations of the compound interest.

Mme. Loisel looked old now. She had become the woman of impoverished households—strong and hard and rough. With frowsy hair, skirts askew, and red hands, she talked loud while washing the floor with great swishes of water. But sometimes, when her husband was at the office, she sat down near the window, and she thought of that gay evening of long ago, of the ball where she had been so beautiful and so fêted.

105     What would have happened if she had not lost that necklace? Who knows? Who knows? How life is strange and changeful! How little a thing is needed for us to be lost or to be saved!

But, one Sunday, having gone to take a walk in the Champs Elysées to refresh herself from the labor of the week, she suddenly perceived a woman who was leading a child. It was Mme. Forestier, still young, still beautiful, still charming.

Mme. Loisel felt moved. Was she going to speak to her? Yes, certainly. And now that she had paid, she was going to tell her all about it. Why not?

She went up.

"Good day, Jeanne."

110     The other, astonished to be familiarly addressed by this plain goodwife, did not recognize her at all, and stammered:

"But—madam!—I do not know—You must be mistaken."

"No. I am Mathilde Loisel."

Her friend uttered a cry.

"Oh, my poor Mathilde! How you are changed!"

115     "Yes, I have had days hard enough, since I have seen you, days wretched enough—and that because of you!"

"Of me! How so?"

"Do you remember that diamond necklace which you lent me to wear at the ministerial ball?"

"Yes. Well?"

"Well, I lost it."

120     "What do you mean? You brought it back."

"I brought you back another just like it. And for this we have been ten years paying. You can understand that it was not easy for us, us who had nothing. At last it is ended, and I am very glad."

Mme. Forestier had stopped.

"You say that you bought a necklace of diamonds to replace mine?"

"Yes. You never noticed it, then! They were very like."

125     And she smiled with a joy which was proud and naïve at once.

Mme. Forestier, strongly moved, took her two hands.

"Oh, my poor Mathilde! Why, my necklace was paste. It was worth at most five hundred francs!"

# LORRIE MOORE

Lorrie Moore, born Marie Lorena Moore in 1957 in Glen Falls, New York, did her undergraduate work at St. Lawrence University and received an MFA, from Cornell University. While still an undergraduate she won first prize in the nationwide Seventeen magazine short story contest (1976), and she has won numerous prizes in recent years. She is the author of stories, novels, and essays. Recent books include The Collected Stories (2008) and the novel A Gate at the Stairs (2009). We reprint a story from her first collection, Self-Help (1985). This story, like most of the stories in Self-Help, is written in what Moore in an interview (in Contemporary Authors: New Revision Series, No. 39, 1992) called "The second person, mock-imperative narrative." She went on to explain:

Let's see what happens when one eliminates the subject, leaves the verb shivering at the start of a clause; what happens when one appropriates the "how-to" form for a fiction, for an irony, for a "how-not-to." I was interested in whatever tensions resulted when a writer foisted fictional experience off of the "I" of the first person and onto the more generalized "you" of the second—the vernacular "one."

The second person stories begin, ostensibly, to tell the generic tale, give the categorical advice, but become so entrenched in their own individuated details that they succeed in telling only their own specific story, suggesting that although life is certainly not jokeless, it probably is remediless.

## How to Become a Writer                                    [1985]

First, try to be something, anything, else. A movie star/astronaut. A movie star/missionary. A movie star/kindergarten teacher. President of the World. Fail miserably. It is best if you fail at an early age—say, fourteen. Early, critical disillusionment is necessary so that at fifteen you can write long haiku sequences about thwarted desire. It is a pond, a cherry blossom, a wind brushing against sparrow wing leaving for mountain. Count the syllables. Show it to your mom. She is tough and practical. She has a son in Vietnam and a husband who may be having an affair. She believes in wearing brown because it hides spots. She'll look briefly at your writing, then back up at you with a face blank as a donut. She'll say: "How about emptying the dishwasher?" Look away. Shove the forks in the fork drawer. Accidentally break one of the freebie gas station glasses. This is the required pain and suffering. This is only for starters.

In your high school English class look at Mr. Killian's face. Decide faces are important. Write a villanelle about pores. Struggle. Write a sonnet. Count the syllables: nine, ten, eleven, thirteen. Decide to experiment with fiction. Here you don't have to count syllables. Write a short story about an elderly man and woman who accidentally shoot each other in the head, the result of an inexplicable malfunction of a shotgun which appears mysteriously in their living room one night. Give it to Mr. Killian as your final project. When you get it back, he has written on it: "Some of your images are quite nice, but you have no sense of plot." When you are home, in the privacy of your own room, faintly scrawl in pencil beneath his black-inked comments: "Plots are for dead people, pore-face."

Take all the babysitting jobs you can get. You are great with kids. They love you. You tell them stories about old people who die idiot deaths. You sing them songs like "Blue Bells of Scotland," which is their favorite. And when they are in their pajamas and have finally stopped pinching each other, when they are fast asleep, you read every sex manual in the house, and wonder how on earth anyone could ever do those things with someone they truly loved. Fall asleep in a chair reading Mr. McMurphy's *Playboy*. When the McMurphys come home, they will tap you on the shoulder, look at the magazine in your lap, and grin. You will want to die. They will ask you if Tracey took her medicine all right. Explain, yes, she did, that you promised her a story if she would take it like a big girl and that seemed to work out just fine. "Oh, marvelous," they will exclaim.

Try to smile proudly.

5    Apply to college as a child psychology major.

As a child psychology major, you have some electives. You've always liked birds. Sign up for something called "The Ornithological Field Trip." It meets Tuesdays and Thursdays at two. When you arrive at Room 134 on the first day of class, everyone is sitting around a seminar table talking about metaphors. You've heard of these. After a short, excruciating while, raise your hand and say diffidently, "Excuse me, isn't this Birdwatching One-oh-one?" The class stops and turns to look at you. They seem to all have one face—giant and blank as a vandalized clock. Someone with a beard booms out, "No, this is Creative Writing." Say: "Oh—right," as if perhaps you knew all along. Look down at your schedule. Wonder how the hell you ended up here. The computer, apparently, has made an error. You start to get up to leave and then don't. The lines at the registrar this week are huge. Perhaps you should stick with this mistake. Perhaps your creative writing isn't all that bad. Perhaps it is fate. Perhaps this is what your dad meant when he said, "It's the age of computers, Francie, it's the age of computers."

Decide that you like college life. In your dorm, you meet many nice people. Some are smarter than you. And some, you notice, are dumber than you. You will continue, unfortunately, to view the world in exactly these terms for the rest of your life.

The assignment this week in creative writing is to narrate a violent happening. Turn in a story about driving with your Uncle Gordon and another one about two old people who are accidentally electrocuted when they go to turn on a badly wired desk lamp. The teacher will hand them back to you with comments: "Much of your writing is smooth and energetic. You have, however, a ludicrous notion of plot." Write another story about a man and a woman who, in the very first paragraph, have their lower torsos accidentally blitzed away by dynamite. In the second paragraph, with the insurance money, they buy a frozen yogurt stand together. There are six more paragraphs. You read the whole thing out loud in class. No one likes it. They say your sense of plot is outrageous and incompetent. After class someone asks you if you are crazy.

Decide that perhaps you should stick to comedies. Start dating someone who is funny, someone who has what in high school you called a "really great sense of humor" and what now your creative writing class calls "self-contempt giving rise to comic form." Write down all of his jokes, but don't tell him you are doing this. Make up anagrams of his old girlfriend's name and name all of your socially handicapped characters with them. Tell him his old girlfriend is in all of your stories and then watch how funny he can be, see what a really great sense of humor he can have.

10    Your child psychology advisor tells you you are neglecting courses in your major. What you spend the most time on should be what you're majoring in. Say yes, you understand.

In creative writing seminars over the next two years, everyone continues to smoke cigarettes and ask the same things: "But does it work?" "Why should we care about this character?" "Have you earned this cliché?" These seem like important questions.

On days when it is your turn, you look at the class hopefully as they scour your mimeographs for a plot. They look back up at you, drag deeply, and then smile in a sweet sort of way.

You spend too much time slouched and demoralized. Your boyfriend suggests bicycling. Your roommate suggests a new boyfriend. You are said to be self-mutilating and losing weight, but you continue writing. The only happiness you have is writing something new, in the middle of the night, armpits damp, heart pounding, something no one has yet seen. You have only those brief, fragile, untested moments of exhilaration when you know:

you are a genius. Understand what you must do. Switch majors. The kids in your nursery project will be disappointed, but you have a calling, an urge, a delusion, an unfortunate habit. You have, as your mother would say, fallen in with a bad crowd.

Why write? Where does writing come from? These are questions to ask yourself. They are like: Where does dust come from? Or: Why is there war? Or: If there's a God, then why is my brother now a cripple?

15    These are questions that you keep in your wallet, like calling cards. These are questions, your creative writing teacher says, that are good to address in your journals but rarely in your fiction.

The writing professor this fall is stressing the Power of the Imagination. Which means he doesn't want long descriptive stories about your camping trip last July. He wants you to start in a realistic context but then to alter it. Like recombinant DNA. He wants you to let your imagination sail, to let it grow big-bellied in the wind. This is a quote from Shakespeare.

Tell your roommate your great idea, your great exercise of imaginative power: a transformation of Melville to contemporary life. It will be about mono-mania and the fish-eat-fish world of life insurance in Rochester, New York. The first line will be "Call me Fishmeal," and it will feature a menopausal suburban husband named Richard, who because he is so depressed all the time is called "Mopey Dick" by his witty wife Elaine. Say to your roommate: "Mopey Dick, get it?" Your roommate looks at you, her face blank as a large Kleenex. She comes up to you, like a buddy, and puts an arm around your burdened shoulders. "Listen, Francie," she says, slow as speech therapy. "Let's go out and get a big beer."

The seminar doesn't like this one either. You suspect they are beginning to feel sorry for you. They say: "You have to think about what is happening. Where is the story here?"

The next semester the writing professor is obsessed with writing from personal experience. You must write from what you know, from what has happened to you. He wants deaths, he wants camping trips. Think about what has happened to you. In three years there have been three things: you lost your virginity; your parents got divorced; and your brother came home from a forest ten miles from the Cambodian border with only half a thigh, a permanent smirk nestled into one corner of his mouth.

20    About the first you write: "It created a new space, which hurt and cried in a voice that wasn't mine, 'I'm not the same anymore, but I'll be okay.'"

About the second you write an elaborate story of an old married couple who stumble upon an unknown land mine in their kitchen and accidentally blow themselves up. You call it: "For Better or for Liverwurst."

About the last you write nothing. There are no words for this. Your typewriter hums. You can find no words.

At undergraduate cocktail parties, people say, "Oh, you write? What do you write about?" Your roommate, who has consumed too much wine, too little cheese, and no crackers at all, blurts: "Oh, my god, she always writes about her dumb boyfriend."

Later on in life you will learn that writers are merely open, helpless texts with no real understanding of what they have written and therefore must half-believe anything and everything that is said of them. You, however, have not yet reached this stage of literary criticism. You stiffen and say, "I do not," the same way you said it when someone in the fourth grade accused you of really liking oboe lessons and your parents really weren't just making you take them.

25    Insist you are not very interested in any one subject at all, that you are interested in the music of language, that you are interested in—in—syllables, because they are the atoms of poetry, the cells of the mind, the breath of the soul. Begin to feel woozy. Stare into your plastic wine cup.

"Syllables?" you will hear someone ask, voice trailing off, as they glide slowly toward the reassuring white of the dip.

Begin to wonder what you do write about. Or if you have anything to say. Or if there even is such a thing as a thing to say. Limit these thoughts to no more than ten minutes a day; like sit-ups, they can make you thin.

You will read somewhere that all writing has to do with one's genitals. Don't dwell on this. It will make you nervous.

Your mother will come visit you. She will look at the circles under your eyes and hand you a brown book with a brown briefcase on the cover. It is entitled: *How to Become a Business Executive.* She has also brought the *Names for Baby* encyclopedia you asked for; one of your characters, the aging clown–school teacher, needs a new name. Your mother will shake her head and say: "Francie, Francie, remember when you were going to be a child psychology major?"

30    Say: "Mom, I like to write."

She'll say: "Sure you like to write. Of course. Sure you like to write."

Write a story about a confused music student and title it: "Schubert Was the One with the Glasses, Right?" It's not a big hit, although your roommate likes the part where the two violinists accidentally blow themselves up in a recital room. "I went out with a violinist once," she says, snapping her gum.

Thank god you are taking other courses. You can find sanctuary in nineteenth-century ontological snags and invertebrate courting rituals. Certain globular mollusks have what is called "Sex by the Arm." The male octopus, for instance, loses the end of one arm when placing it inside the female body during intercourse. Marine biologists call it "Seven Heaven." Be glad you know these things. Be glad you are not just a writer. Apply to law school.

From here on in, many things can happen. But the main one will be this: you decide not to go to law school after all, and, instead, you spend a good, big chunk of your adult life telling people how you decided not to go to law school after all. Somehow you end up writing again. Perhaps you go to graduate school. Perhaps you work odd jobs and take writing courses at night. Perhaps you are working on a novel and writing down all the clever remarks and intimate personal confessions you hear during the day. Perhaps you are losing your pals, your acquaintances, your balance.

35    You have broken up with your boyfriend. You now go out with men who, instead of whispering "I love you," shout: "Do it to me, baby." This is good for your writing.

Sooner or later you have a finished manuscript more or less. People look at it in a vaguely troubled sort of way and say, "I'll bet becoming a writer was always a fantasy of yours, wasn't it?" Your lips dry to salt. Say that of all the fantasies possible in the world, you can't imagine being a writer even making the top twenty. Tell them you were going to be a child psychology major. "I bet," they always sigh, "you'd be great with kids." Scowl fiercely. Tell them you're a walking blade.

Quit classes. Quit jobs. Cash in old savings bonds. Now you have time like warts on your hands. Slowly copy all of your friends' addresses into a new address book.

Vacuum. Chew cough drops. Keep a folder full of fragments.

*An eyelid darkening sideways.*
40    *World as conspiracy.*
*Possible plot? A woman gets on a bus.*
*Suppose you threw a love affair and nobody came.*

At home drink a lot of coffee. At Howard Johnson's order the cole slaw. Consider how it looks like the soggy confetti of a map: where you've been, where you're going—"You Are Here," says the red star on the back of the menu.

Occasionally a date with a face blank as a sheet of paper asks you whether writers often become discouraged. Say that sometimes they do and sometimes they do. Say it's a lot like having polio.

45    "Interesting," smiles your date, and then he looks down at his arm hairs and starts to smooth them, all, always, in the same direction.

# ALICE MUNRO

*Alice Munro was born in 1931 in Wingham, Ontario, a relatively rural community and the sort of place in which she sets much of her fiction. She began publishing stories when she was an undergraduate at the University of Western Ontario. She left Western after two years, worked in a library and in a bookstore, then married, moved to Victoria, British Columbia, and founded a bookstore there. She continued to write while raising three children. She divorced and remarried; much of her fiction concerns marriage or divorce, which is to say it concerns shifting relationships in a baffling world. Munro's recent books in-* clude two collections of short stories, The View from Castle Rock *(2006) and* Too Much Happiness *(2009).*

## *Boys and Girls*                                                    [1968]

My father was a fox farmer. That is, he raised silver foxes, in pens; and in the fall and early winter, when their fur was prime, he killed them and skinned them and sold their pelts to the Hudson's Bay Company or the Montreal Fur Traders. These companies supplied us with heroic calendars to hang, one on each side of the kitchen door. Against a background of cold blue sky and black pine forests and treacherous northern rivers, plumed adventurers planted the flags of England or of France; magnificent savages bent their backs to the portage.

For several weeks before Christmas, my father worked after supper in the cellar of our house. The cellar was whitewashed, and lit by a hundred-watt bulb over the worktable. My brother Laird and I sat on the top step and watched. My father removed the pelt inside-out from the body of the fox, which looked surprisingly small, mean and rat-like, deprived of its arrogant weight of fur. The naked, slippery bodies were collected in a sack and buried at the dump. One time the hired man, Henry Bailey, had taken a swipe at me with this sack, saying, "Christmas present!" My mother thought that was not funny. In fact she disliked the whole pelting operation—that was what the killing, skinning, and preparation of the furs was called—and wished it did not have to take place in the house. There was the smell. After the pelt had been stretched inside-out on a long board my father scraped away delicately, removing the little clotted webs of blood vessels, the bubbles of fat; the smell of blood and animal fat, with the strong primitive odour of the fox itself, penetrated all parts of the house. I found it reassuringly seasonal, like the smell of oranges and pine needles.

Henry Bailey suffered from bronchial troubles. He would cough and cough until his narrow face turned scarlet, and his light blue, derisive eyes filled up with tears; then he took the lid off the stove, and, standing well back, shot out a great clot of phlegm—hsss—straight into the heart of the flames. We admired him for this performance and for his ability to make his stomach growl at will, and for his laughter, which was full of high whistlings and gurglings and involved the whole faulty machinery of his chest. It was sometimes hard to tell what he was laughing at, and always possible that it might be us.

After we had been sent to bed we could still smell fox and still hear Henry's laugh, but these things, reminders of the warm, safe, brightly lit downstairs world, seemed lost and diminished, floating on the stale cold air upstairs. We were afraid at night in the winter. We were not afraid of *outside* though this was the time of year when snowdrifts curled around our house like sleeping whales and the wind harassed us all night, coming up from the buried fields, the frozen swamp, with its old bugbear chorus of threats and misery. We were afraid of *inside*, the room where we slept. At this time the upstairs of our house was not finished. A brick chimney went up one wall. In the middle of the floor was a square hole, with a wooden railing around it; that was where the stairs came up. On the other side of the stairwell were the things that nobody had any use for anymore—a soldiery roll of linoleum, standing on end, a wicker baby carriage, a fern basket, china jugs and basins with cracks in them, a picture of the Battle of Balaclava,[1] very sad to look at. I had told Laird, as soon as he was old enough to understand such things, that bats and skeletons lived over there; whenever a man escaped from the county jail, twenty miles away, I imagined that he had somehow let himself in the window and was hiding behind the linoleum. But we had rules to

---

[1]**Battle of Balaclava** A major battle, fought in October 1854, during the Crimean War. It culminated in the tragic Charge of the Light Brigade.

keep us safe. When the light was on, we were safe as long as we did not step off the square of worn carpet which defined our bedroom-space; when the light was off no place was safe but the beds themselves. I had to turn out the light kneeling on the end of my bed, and stretching as far as I could to reach the cord.

5        In the dark we lay on our beds, our narrow life rafts, and fixed our eyes on the faint light coming up the stairwell, and sang songs. Laird sang "Jingle Bells," which he would sing any time, whether it was Christmas or not, and I sang "Danny Boy." I loved the sound of my own voice, frail and supplicating, rising in the dark. We could make out the tall frosted shapes of the windows now, gloomy and white. When I came to the part, *When I am dead, as dead I well may be*—a fit of shivering caused not by the cold sheets but by plea-surable emotion almost silenced me. *You'll kneel and say, an Ave there above me*—What was an Ave? Every day I forgot to find out.

Laird went straight from singing to sleep. I could hear his long, satisfied, bubbly breaths. Now for the time that remained to me, the most perfectly private and perhaps the best time of the whole day, I arranged myself tightly under the covers and went on with one of the stories I was telling myself from night to night. These stories were about myself, when I had grown a lit-tle older; they took place in a world that was recognizably mine, yet one that presented opportunities for courage, boldness and self-sacrifice, as mine never did. I rescued people from a bombed building (it discouraged me that the real war had gone on so far away from Jubilee). I shot two rabid wolves who were menacing the schoolyard (the teachers cowered terrified at my back). I rode a fine horse spiritedly down the main street of Jubilee, ac-knowledging the townspeople's gratitude for some yet-to-be-worked-out piece of heroism (nobody ever rode a horse there, except King Billy in the Orangemen's Day[2] parade). There was always riding and shooting in these stories, though I had only been on a horse twice—bareback because we did not own a saddle—and the second time I had slid right around and dropped under the horse's feet; it had stepped placidly over me. I really was learning to shoot, but I could not hit anything yet, not even tin cans on fence posts.

Alive, the foxes inhabited a world my father made for them. It was sur-rounded by a high guard fence, like a medieval town, with a gate that was padlocked at night. Along the streets of this town were ranged large, sturdy pens. Each of them had a real door that a man could go through, a wooden ramp along the wire, for the foxes to run up and down on, and a kennel—something like a clothes chest with airholes—where they slept and stayed in winter and had their young. There were feeding and watering dishes at-tached to the wire in such a way that they could be emptied and cleaned from the outside. The dishes were made of old tin cans, and the ramps and kennels of odds and ends of old lumber. Everything was tidy and ingenious; my father was tirelessly inventive and his favourite book in the world was *Robinson Crusoe*. He had fitted a tin drum on a wheelbarrow, for bringing water down to the pens. This was my job in summer, when the foxes had to

---

[2]**Orangemen's Day** The Orange Society is named for William of Orange, who, as King William III of England, defeated James II of England at the Battle of the Boyne on 12 July 1690. It sponsors an annual procession on 12 July.

have water twice a day. Between nine and ten o'clock in the morning, and again after supper, I filled the drum at the pump and trundled it down through the barnyard to the pens, where I parked it, and filled my watering can and went along the streets. Laird came too, with his little cream and green gardening can, filled too full and knocking against his legs and slopping water on his canvas shoes. I had the real watering can, my father's, though I could only carry it three-quarters full.

The foxes all had names, which were printed on a tin plate and hung beside their doors. They were not named when they were born, but when they survived the first year's pelting and were added to the breeding stock. Those my father had named were called names like Prince, Bob, Wally and Betty. Those I had named were called Star or Turk, or Maureen or Diana. Laird named one Maud after a hired girl we had when he was little, one Harold after a boy at school, and one Mexico, he did not say why.

Naming them did not make pets out of them, or anything like it. Nobody but my father ever went into the pens, and he had twice had blood-poisoning from bites. When I was bringing them their water they prowled up and down on the paths they had made inside their pens, barking seldom—they saved that for nighttime, when they might get up a chorus of community frenzy—but always watching me, their eyes burning, clear gold, in their pointed, malevolent faces. They were beautiful for their delicate legs and heavy, aristocratic tails and the bright fur sprinkled on dark down their backs—which gave them their name—but especially for their faces, drawn exquisitely sharp in pure hostility, and their golden eyes.

10     Besides carrying water I helped my father when he cut the long grass, and the lamb's quarter and flowering money-musk, that grew between the pens. He cut with the scythe and I raked into piles. Then he took a pitchfork and threw fresh-cut grass all over the top of the pens, to keep the foxes cooler and shade their coats, which were browned by too much sun. My father did not talk to me unless it was about the job we were doing. In this he was quite different from my mother, who, if she was feeling cheerful, would tell me all sorts of things—the name of a dog she had had when she was a little girl, the names of boys she had gone out with later on when she was grown up, and what certain dresses of hers had looked like—she could not imagine now what had become of them. Whatever thoughts and stories my father had were private, and I was shy of him and would never ask him questions. Nevertheless I worked willingly under his eyes, and with a feeling of pride. One time a feed salesman came down into the pens to talk to him and my father said, "Like to have you meet my new hired man." I turned away and raked furiously, red in the face with pleasure.

"Could of fooled me," said the salesman. "I thought it was only a girl."

After the grass was cut, it seemed suddenly much later in the year. I walked on stubble in the earlier evening, aware of the reddening skies, the entering silences, of fall. When I wheeled the tank out of the gate and put the padlock on, it was almost dark. One night at this time I saw my mother and father standing on the little rise of ground we called the gangway, in front of the barn. My father had just come from the meathouse; he had his stiff bloody apron on, and a pail of cut-up meat in his hand.

It was an odd thing to see my mother down at the barn. She did not often come out of the house unless it was to do something—hang out the wash or dig potatoes in the garden. She looked out of place, with her bare lumpy legs, not touched by the sun, her apron still on and damp across the stomach from the supper dishes. Her hair was tied up in a kerchief, wisps of it falling out. She would tie her hair up like this in the morning, saying she did not have time to do it properly, and it would stay tied up all day. It was true, too; she really did not have time. These days our back porch was piled with baskets of peaches and grapes and pears, bought in town, and onions and tomatoes and cucumbers grown at home, all waiting to be made into jelly and jam and preserves, pickles and chili sauce. In the kitchen there was a fire in the stove all day, jars clinked in boiling water, sometimes a cheese-cloth bag was strung on a pole between two chairs straining blue-black grape pulp for jelly. I was given jobs to do and I would sit at the table peel-ing peaches that had been soaked in the hot water, or cutting up onions, my eyes smarting and streaming. As soon as I was done I ran out of the house, trying to get out of earshot before my mother thought of what she wanted me to do next. I hated the hot dark kitchen in summer, the green blinds and the flypapers, the same old oilcloth table and wavy mirror and bumpy linoleum. My mother was too tired and preoccupied to talk to me, she had no heart to tell about the Normal School Graduation Dance; sweat trickled over her face and she was always counting under her breath, pointing at jars, dumping cups of sugar. It seemed to me that work in the house was endless, dreary and peculiarly depressing; work done out of doors, and in my father's service, was ritualistically important.

I wheeled the tank up to the barn, where it was kept, and I heard my mother saying, "Wait till Laird gets a little bigger, then you'll have a real help."

15    What my father said I did not hear. I was pleased by the way he stood listening, politely as he would to a salesman or a stranger, but with an air of wanting to get on with his real work. I felt my mother had no business down here and I wanted him to feel the same way. What did she mean about Laird? He was no help to anybody. Where was he now? Swinging himself sick on the swing, going around in circles, or trying to catch caterpillars. He never once stayed with me till I was finished.

"And then I can use her more in the house," I heard my mother say. She had a dead-quiet, regretful way of talking about me that always made me un-easy. "I just get my back turned and she runs off. It's not like I had a girl in the family at all."

I went and sat on a feed bag in the corner of the barn, not wanting to appear when this conversation was going on. My mother, I felt, was not to be trusted. She was kinder than my father and more easily fooled, but you could not depend on her, and the real reasons for the things she said and did were not to be known. She loved me, and she sat up late at night making a dress of the difficult style I wanted, for me to wear when school started, but she was also my enemy. She was always plotting. She was plotting now to get me to stay in the house more, although she knew I hated it (*because* she knew I hated it) and keep me from working for my father. It seemed to me she would do this simply out of perversity, and to try her power. It did not occur to me that she could be lonely, or jealous. No grown-up could be; they were too fortunate. I sat and kicked my heels monotonously against a feedbag, raising dust, and did not come out till she was gone.

At any rate, I did not expect my father to pay any attention to what she said. Who could imagine Laird doing my work—Laird remembering the pad-lock and cleaning out the watering-dishes with a leaf on the end of a stick, or even wheeling the tank without it tumbling over? It showed how little my mother knew about the way things really were.

I have forgotten to say what the foxes were fed. My father's bloody apron reminded me. They were fed horsemeat. At this time most farmers still kept horses, and when a horse got too old to work, or broke a leg or got down and would not get up, as they sometimes did, the owner would call my father, and he and Henry went out to the farm in the truck. Usually they shot and butchered the horse there, paying the farmer from five to twelve dollars. If they had already too much meat on hand, they would bring the horse back alive, and keep it for a few days or weeks in our stable, until the meat was needed. After the war the farmers were buying tractors and gradually getting rid of horses altogether, so it sometimes happened that we got a good healthy horse, that there was just no use for any more. If this happened in the winter we might keep the horse in our stable till spring, for we had plenty of hay and if there was a lot of snow—and the plow did not always get our road cleared—it was convenient to be able to go to town with a horse and cutter.[3]

20    The winter I was eleven years old we had two horses in the stable. We did not know what names they had had before, so we called them Mack and Flora. Mack was an old black workhorse, sooty and indifferent. Flora was a sorrel mare, a driver. We took them both out in the cutter. Mack was slow and easy to handle. Flora was given to fits of violent alarm, veering at cars and even at other horses, but we loved her speed and high-stepping, her general air of gallantry and abandon. On Saturdays we went down to the stable and as soon as we opened the door on its cosy, animal-smelling darkness Flora threw up her head, rolled her eyes, whinnied despairingly and pulled herself through a crisis of nerves on the spot. It was not safe to go into her stall; she would kick.

This winter also I began to hear a great deal more on the theme my mother had sounded when she had been talking in front of the barn. I no longer felt safe. It seemed that in the minds of the people around me there was a steady undercurrent of thought, not to be deflected, on this one subject. The word *girl* had formerly seemed to me innocent and unburdened, like the word *child;* now it appeared that it was no such thing. A girl was not, as I had supposed, simply what I was; it was what I had to become. It was a definition, always touched with emphasis, with reproach and disappointment. Also it was a joke on me. Once Laird and I were fighting, and for the first time ever I had to use all my strength against him; even so, he caught and pinned my arm for a moment, really hurting me. Henry saw this, and laughed, saying, "Oh, that there Laird's gonna show you, one of these days!" Laird was getting a lot bigger. But I was getting bigger too.

My grandmother came to stay with us for a few weeks and I heard other things. "Girls don't slam doors like that." "Girls keep their knees together when they sit down." And worse still, when I asked some questions, "That's none of girls' business." I continued to slam the doors and sit as awkwardly as possible, thinking by such measures I kept myself free.

---

[3]**cutter** a small sleigh.

When spring came, the horses were let out in the barnyard. Mack stood against the barn wall trying to scratch his neck and haunches, but Flora trotted up and down and reared at the fences, clattering her hooves against the rails. Snow drifts dwindled quickly, revealing the hard gray and brown earth, the familiar rise and fall of the ground, plain and bare after the fantastic landscape of winter. There was a great feeling of opening-out, of release. We just wore rubbers now, over our shoes; our feet felt ridiculously light. One Saturday we went out to the stable and found all the doors open, letting in the unaccustomed sunlight and fresh air. Henry was there, just idling around looking at his collection of calendars which were tacked up behind the stalls in a part of the stable my mother had probably never seen.

"Come to say goodbye to your old friend Mack?" Henry said. "Here, you give him a taste of oats." He poured some oats in Laird's cupped hands and Laird went to feed Mack. Mack's teeth were in bad shape. He ate very slowly, patiently shifting the oats around in his mouth, trying to find a stump of a molar to grind it on. "Poor old Mack," said Henry mournfully. "When a horse's teeth's gone, he's gone. That's about the way."

25      "Are you going to shoot him today?" I said. Mack and Flora had been in the stable so long I had almost forgotten they were going to be shot.

Henry didn't answer me. Instead he started to sing in a high, trembly, mocking-sorrowful voice. *Oh, there's no more work, for poor Uncle Ned, he's gone where the good darkies go.* Mack's thick, blackish tongue worked diligently at Laird's hand. I went out before the song was ended and sat down on the gangway.

I had never seen them shoot a horse, but I knew where it was done. Last summer Laird and I had come upon a horse's entrails before they were buried. We had thought it was a big black snake, coiled up in the sun. That was around in the field that ran up beside the barn. I thought that if we went inside the barn, and found a wide crack or a knothole to look through, we would be able to see them do it. It was not something I wanted to see; just the same, if a thing really happened, it was better to see it, and know.

My father came down from the house, carrying the gun.

"What are you doing here?" he said.

30      "Nothing."

"Go on up and play around the house."

He sent Laird out of the stable. I said to Laird, "Do you want to see them shoot Mack?" and without waiting for an answer led him around to the front door of the barn, opened it carefully, and went in. "Be quiet or they'll hear us," I said. We could hear Henry and my father talking in the stable, then the heavy, shuffling steps of Mack being backed out of his stall.

In the loft it was cold and dark. Thin, crisscrossed beams of sunlight fell through the cracks. The hay was low. It was a rolling country, hills and hollows, slipping under our feet. About four feet up was a beam going around the walls. We piled hay up in one corner and I boosted Laird up and hoisted myself. The beam was not very wide; we crept along it with our hands flat on the barn walls. There were plenty of knotholes, and I found one that gave me the view I wanted—a corner of the barnyard, the gate, part of the field. Laird did not have a knothole and began to complain.

I showed him a widened crack between two boards. "Be quiet and wait. If they hear you you'll get us in trouble."

35      My father came in sight carrying the gun. Henry was leading Mack by the halter. He dropped it and took out his cigarette papers and tobacco; he rolled cigarettes for my father and himself. While this was going on Mack nosed around in the old, dead grass along the fence. Then my father opened the gate and they took Mack through. Henry led Mack away from the path to a patch of ground and they talked together, not loud enough for us to hear. Mack again began searching for a mouthful of fresh grass, which was not to be found. My father walked away in a straight line, and stopped short at a distance which seemed to suit him. Henry was walking away from Mack too, but sideways, still negligently holding on to the halter. My father raised the gun and Mack looked up as if he had noticed something and my father shot him.

Mack did not collapse at once but swayed, lurched sideways and fell, first on his side; then he rolled over on his back and, amazingly, kicked his legs for a few seconds in the air. At this Henry laughed, as if Mack had done a trick for him. Laird, who had drawn a long, groaning breath of surprise when the shot was fired, said out loud, "He's not dead." And it seemed to me it might be true. But his legs stopped, he rolled on his side again, his muscles quivered and sank. The two men walked over and looked at him in a businesslike way; they bent down and examined his forehead where the bullet had gone in, and now I saw his blood on the brown grass.

"Now they just skin him and cut him up," I said. "Let's go." My legs were a little shaky and I jumped gratefully down into the hay. "Now you've seen how they shoot a horse," I said in a congratulatory way, as if I had seen it many times before. "Let's see if any barn cats had kittens in the hay." Laird jumped. He seemed young and obedient again. Suddenly I remembered how, when he was little, I had brought him into the barn and told him to climb the ladder to the top beam. That was in the spring, too, when the hay was low. I had done it out of a need for excitement, a desire for something to happen so that I could tell about it. He was wearing a little bulky brown and white checked coat, made down from one of mine. He went all the way up just as I told him, and sat down on the top beam with the hay far below him on one side, and the barn floor and some old machinery on the other. Then I ran screaming to my father. "Laird's up on the top beam!" My father came, my mother came, my father went up the ladder talking very quietly and brought Laird down under his arm, at which my mother leaned against the ladder and began to cry. They said to me, "Why weren't you watching him?" but nobody ever knew the truth. Laird did not know enough to tell. But whenever I saw the brown and white checked coat hanging in the closet, or at the bottom of the rag bag, which was where it ended up, I felt a weight in my stomach, the sadness of unexorcised guilt.

I looked at Laird who did not even remember this, and I did not like the look on his thin, winter-paled face. His expression was not frightened or upset, but remote, concentrating. "Listen," I said, in an unusually bright and friendly voice, "you aren't going to tell, are you?"

"No," he said absently.

40      "Promise."

"Promise," he said. I grabbed the hand behind his back to make sure he was not crossing his fingers. Even so, he might have a nightmare; it might come out that way. I decided I had better work hard to get all thoughts of what he had seen out of his mind—which, it seemed to me, could not hold very many things at a time. I got some money I had saved and that afternoon we went into Jubilee and saw a show, with Judy Canova,[4] at which we both laughed a great deal. After that I thought it would be all right.

Two weeks later I knew they were going to shoot Flora. I knew from the night before, when I heard my mother ask if the hay was holding out all right, and my father said, "Well, after to-morrow there'll just be the cow, and we should be able to put her out to grass in another week." So I knew it was Flora's turn in the morning.

This time I didn't think of watching it. That was something to see just one time. I had not thought about it very often since, but sometimes when I was busy, working at school, or standing in front of the mirror combing my hair and wondering if I would be pretty when I grew up, the whole scene would flash into my mind: I would see the easy, practised way my father raised the gun, and hear Henry laughing when Mack kicked his legs in the air. I did not have any great feeling of horror and opposition, such as a city child might have had; I was too used to seeing the death of animals as a necessity by which we lived. Yet I felt a little ashamed, and there was a new wariness, a sense of holding-off, in my attitude to my father and his work.

It was a fine day, and we were going around the yard picking up tree branches that had been torn off in winter storms. This was something we had been told to do, and also we wanted to use them to make a teepee. We heard Flora whinny, and then my father's voice and Henry's shouting, and we ran down to the barnyard to see what was going on.

45      The stable door was open. Henry had just brought Flora out, and she had broken away from him. She was running free in the barnyard, from one end to the other. We climbed up on the fence. It was exciting to see her running, whinnying, going up on her hind legs, prancing and threatening like a horse in a Western movie, an unbroken ranch horse, though she was just an old driver, an old sorrel mare. My father and Henry ran after her and tried to grab the dangling halter. They tried to work her into a corner, and they had almost succeeded when she made a run between them, wild-eyed, and disappeared around the corner of the barn. We heard the rails clatter down as she got over the fence, and Henry yelled, "She's into the field now!"

That meant she was in the long L-shaped field that ran up by the house. If she got around the center, heading towards the lane, the gate was open; the truck had been driven into the field this morning. My father shouted to me, because I was on the other side of the fence, nearest the lane, "Go shut the gate!"

I could run very fast. I ran across the garden, past the tree where our swing was hung, and jumped across a ditch into the lane. There was the open gate. She had not got out, I could not see her up the road; she must have run to the other end of the field. The gate was heavy. I lifted it out of the gravel and carried it across the roadway. I had it half-way across when she came in sight, galloping straight towards me. There was just time to get the chain on. Laird came scrambling through the ditch to help me.

Instead of shutting the gate, I opened it as wide as I could. I did not make any decision to do this, it was just what I did. Flora never slowed down; she galloped straight past me, and Laird jumped up and down,

---

[4] **Judy Canova** American comedian, popular in films in the 1940s.

yelling, "Shut it, shut it!" even after it was too late. My father and Henry appeared in the field a moment too late to see what I had done. They only saw Flora heading for the township road. They would think I had not got there in time.

They did not waste any time asking about it. They went back to the barn and got the gun and the knives they used, and put these in the truck; then they turned the truck around and came bouncing up the field towards us. Laird called to them, "Let me go too, let me go too!" and Henry stopped the truck and they took him in. I shut the gate after they were all gone.

50      I supposed Laird would tell. I wondered what would happen to me. I had never disobeyed my father before, and I could not understand why I had done it. Flora would not really get away. They would catch up with her in the truck. Or if they did not catch her this morning somebody would see her and telephone us this afternoon or tomorrow. There was no wild country here for her to run to, only farms. What was more, my father had paid for her, we needed the meat to feed the foxes, we needed the foxes to make our living. All I had done was make more work for my father who worked hard enough already. And when my father found out about it he was not going to trust me any more; he would know that I was not entirely on his side. I was on Flora's side, and that made me no use to anybody, not even to her. Just the same, I did not regret it; when she came running at me and I held the gate open, that was the only thing I could do.

I went back to the house, and my mother said, "What's all the commotion?" I told her that Flora had kicked down the fence and got away. "Your poor father," she said, "now he'll have to go chasing over the countryside. Well, there isn't any use planning dinner before one." She put up the ironing board. I wanted to tell her, but thought better of it and went upstairs and sat on my bed.

Lately I had been trying to make my part of the room fancy, spreading the bed with old lace curtains, and fixing myself a dressing-table with some leftovers of cretonne for a skirt. I planned to put up some kind of barricade between my bed and Laird's, to keep my section separate from his. In the sunlight, the lace curtains were just dusty rags. We did not sing at night any more. One night when I was singing Laird said, "You sound silly," and I went right on but the next night I did not start. There was not so much need to anyway, we were no longer afraid. We knew it was just old furniture over there, old jumble and confusion. We did not keep to the rules. I still stayed awake after Laird was asleep and told myself stories, but even in these stories something different was happening, mysterious alterations took place. A story might start off in the old way, with a spectacular danger, a fire or wild animals, and for a while I might rescue people; then things would change around, and instead, somebody would be rescuing me. It might be a boy from our class at school, or even Mr. Campbell, our teacher, who tickled girls under the arms. And at this point the story concerned itself at great length with what I looked like—how long my hair was, and what kind of dress I had on; by the time I had these details worked out the real excitement of the story was lost.

It was later than one o'clock when the truck came back. The tarpaulin was over the back, which meant there was meat in it. My mother had to heat dinner up all over again. Henry and my father had changed from their bloody overalls into ordinary working overalls in the barn, and they washed their arms and necks and faces at the sink, and splashed water on their hair and combed it. Laird lifted his arm to show off a streak of blood. "We shot old Flora," he said, "and cut her up in fifty pieces."

"Well I don't want to hear about it," my mother said. "And don't come to my table like that."

55    My father made him go and wash the blood off.

We sat down and my father said grace and Henry pasted his chewing-gum on the end of his fork, the way he always did; when he took it off he would have us admire the pattern. We began to pass the bowls of steaming, overcooked vegetables. Laird looked across the table at me and said proudly, distinctly, "Anyway it was her fault Flora got away."

"What?" my father said.

"She could of shut the gate and she didn't. She just open' it up and Flora run out."

"Is that right?" my father said.

60    Everybody at the table was looking at me. I nodded, swallowing food with great difficulty. To my shame, tears flooded my eyes.

My father made a curt sound of disgust. "What did you do that for?"

I did not answer. I put down my fork and waited to be sent from the table, still not looking up.

But this did not happen. For some time nobody said anything, then Laird said matter-of-factly, "She's crying."

"Never mind," my father said. He spoke with resignation, even good humour, the words which absolved and dismissed me for good. "She's only a girl," he said.

65    I didn't protest that, even in my heart. Maybe it was true.

# GLORIA NAYLOR

*Gloria Naylor (b. 1950), a native of New York City, holds a bachelor's degree from Brooklyn College and a master's degree in Afro-American studies from Yale University. "The Two" comes from* The Women of Brewster Place *(1982), a "novel in seven stories" that won the American Book Award for First Fiction. Naylor's books include the novels* Linden Hills *(1985) and* Mama Days *(1988).*

## The Two
[1982]

At first they seemed like such nice girls. No one could remember exactly when they had moved into Brewster. It was earlier in the year before Ben[1] was killed—of course, it had to be before Ben's death. But no one remembered if it was in the winter or spring of that year that the two had come. People often came and went on Brewster Place like a restless night's dream, moving in and out in the dark to avoid eviction notices or neighborhood bulletins about the dilapidated condition of their furnishings. So it wasn't until the two were clocked leaving in the mornings and returning in the evenings at regular intervals that it was quietly absorbed that they now

---

[1]**Ben** the custodian of Brewster Place.

claimed Brewster as home. And Brewster waited, cautiously prepared to claim them, because you never knew about young women, and obviously single at that. But when no wild music or drunken friends careened out of the corner building on weekends, and especially, when no slightly eager husbands were encouraged to linger around that first-floor apartment and run errands for them, a suspended sigh of relief floated around the two when they dumped their garbage, did their shopping, and headed for the morning bus.

The women of Brewster had readily accepted the lighter, skinny one. There wasn't much threat in her timid mincing walk and the slightly protruding teeth she seemed so eager to show everyone in her bell-like good mornings and evenings. Breaths were held a little longer in the direction of the short dark one—too pretty, and too much behind. And she insisted on wearing those thin Qiana dresses that the summer breeze molded against the maddening rhythm of the twenty pounds of rounded flesh that she swung steadily down the street. Through slitted eyes, the women watched their men watching her pass, knowing the bastards were praying for a wind. But since she seemed oblivious to whether these supplications went answered, their sighs settled around her shoulders too. Nice girls.

And so no one even cared to remember exactly when they had moved into Brewster Place, until the rumor started. It had first spread through the block like a sour odor that's only faintly perceptible and easily ignored until it starts growing in strength from the dozen mouths it had been lying in, among clammy gums and scum-coated teeth. And then it was everywhere— lining the mouths and whitening the lips of everyone as they wrinkled up their noses at its pervading smell, unable to pinpoint the source or time of its initial arrival. Sophie could—she had been there.

It wasn't that the rumor had actually begun with Sophie. A rumor needs no true parent. It only needs a willing carrier, and it found one in Sophie. She had been there—on one of those August evenings when the sun's absence is a mockery because the heat leaves the air so heavy it presses the naked skin down on your body, to the point that a sheet becomes unbearable and sleep impossible. So most of Brewster was outside that night when the two had come in together, probably from one of those air-conditioned movies downtown, and had greeted the ones who were loitering around their building. And they had started up the steps when the skinny one tripped over a child's ball and the darker one had grabbed her by the arm and around the waist to break her fall. "Careful, don't wanna lose you now." And the two of them had laughed into each other's eyes and went into the building.

5        The smell had begun there. It outlined the image of the stumbling woman and the one who had broken her fall. Sophie and a few other women sniffed at the spot and then, perplexed, silently looked at each other. Where had they seen that before? They had often laughed and touched each other—held each other in joy or its dark twin—but where had they seen *that* before? It came to them as the scent drifted down the steps and entered their nostrils on the way to their inner mouths. They had seen that—done that—with their men. That shared moment of invisible communion reserved for two and hidden from the rest of the world behind laughter or tears or a touch. In the days before babies, miscarriages, and other broken dreams, after stolen caresses in barn stalls and cotton houses, after intimate walks from church and secret kisses with boys who were now long

forgotten or permanently fixed in their lives—that was where. They could almost feel the odor moving about in their mouths, and they slowly knitted themselves together and let it out into the air like a yellow mist that began to cling to the bricks on Brewster.

So it got around that the two in 312 were *that* way. And they had seemed like such nice girls. Their regular exits and entrances to the block were viewed with a jaundiced eye. The quiet that rested around their door on the weekends hinted of all sorts of secret rituals, and their friendly indifference to the men on the street was an insult to the women as a brazen flaunting of unnatural ways.

Since Sophie's apartment windows faced theirs from across the air shaft, she became the official watchman for the block, and her opinions were deferred to whenever the two came up in conversation. Sophie took her position seriously and was constantly alert for any telltale signs that might creep out around their drawn shades, across from which she kept a religious vigil. An entire week of drawn shades was evidence enough to send her flying around with reports that as soon as it got dark they pulled their shades down and put on the lights. Heads nodded in knowing unison—a definite sign. If doubt was voiced with a "But I pull my shades down at night too," a whispered "Yeah, but you're not *that* way" was argument enough to win them over.

Sophie watched the lighter one dumping their garbage, and she went outside and opened the lid. Her eyes darted over the crushed tin cans, vegetable peelings, and empty chocolate chip cookie boxes. What do they do with all them chocolate chip cookies? It was surely a sign, but it would take some time to figure that one out. She saw Ben go into their apartment, and she waited and blocked his path as he came out, carrying his toolbox.

"What ya see?" She grabbed his arm and whispered wetly in his face.

10    Ben stared at her squinted eyes and drooping lips and shook his head slowly. "Uh, uh, uh, it was terrible."

"Yeah?" She moved in a little closer.

"Worst busted faucet I seen in my whole life." He shook her hand off his arm and left her standing in the middle of the block.

"You old sop bucket," she muttered, as she went back up on her stoop. A broken faucet, huh? Why did they need to use so much water?

Sophie had plenty to report that day. Ben had said it was terrible in there. No, she didn't know exactly what he had seen, but you can imagine—and they did. Confronted with the difference that had been thrust into their predictable world, they reached into their imaginations and, using an ancient pattern, weaved themselves a reason for its existence. Out of necessity they stitched all of their secret fears and lingering childhood nightmares into this existence, because even though it was deceptive enough to try and look as they looked, talk as they talked, and do as they did, it had to have some hidden stain to invalidate it—it was impossible for them both to be right. So they leaned back, supported by the sheer weight of their numbers and comforted by the woven barrier that kept them protected from the yellow mist that enshrouded the two as they came and went on Brewster Place.

15    Lorraine was the first to notice the change in the people on Brewster Place. She was a shy but naturally friendly woman who got up early, and had

read the morning paper and done fifty sit-ups before it was time to leave for work. She came out of her apartment eager to start her day by greeting any of her neighbors who were outside. But she noticed that some of the people who had spoken to her before made a point of having something else to do with their eyes when she passed, although she could almost feel them staring at her back as she moved on. The ones who still spoke only did so after an uncomfortable pause, in which they seemed to be peering through her before they begrudged her a good morning or evening. She wondered if it was all in her mind and she thought about mentioning it to Theresa, but she didn't want to be accused of being too sensitive again. And how would Tee even notice anything like that anyway? She had a lousy attitude and hardly ever spoke to people. She stayed in that bed until the last moment and rushed out of the house fogged-up and grumpy, and she was used to being stared at—by men at least—because of her body.

Lorraine thought about these things as she came up the block from work, carrying a large paper bag. The group of women on her stoop parted silently and let her pass.

"Good evening," she said, as she climbed the steps.

Sophie was standing on the top step and tried to peek into the bag. "You been shopping, huh? What ya buy?" It was almost an accusation.

"Groceries." Lorraine shielded the top of the bag from view and squeezed past her with a confused frown. She saw Sophie throw a knowing glance to the others at the bottom of the stoop. What was wrong with this old woman? Was she crazy or something?

20      Lorraine went into her apartment. Theresa was sitting by the window, reading a copy of *Mademoiselle*. She glanced up from her magazine. "Did you get my chocolate chip cookies?"

"Why good evening to you, too, Tee. And how was my day? Just wonderful." She sat the bag down on the couch. "The little Baxter boy brought in a puppy for show-and-tell, and the damn thing pissed all over the floor and then proceeded to chew the heel off my shoe, but, yes, I managed to hobble to the store and bring you your chocolate chip cookies."

Oh, Jesus, Theresa thought, she's got a bug up her ass tonight.

"Well, you should speak to Mrs. Baxter. She ought to train her kid better than that." She didn't wait for Lorraine to stop laughing before she tried to stretch her good mood. "Here, I'll put those things away. Want me to make dinner so you can rest? I only worked half a day, and the most tragic thing that went down was a broken fingernail and that got caught in my typewriter."

Lorraine followed Theresa into the kitchen. "No, I'm not really tired, and fair's fair, you cooked last night. I didn't mean to tick off like that; it's just that . . . well, Tee, have you noticed that people aren't as nice as they used to be?"

25      Theresa stiffened. Oh, God, here she goes again. "What people, Lorraine? Nice in what way?"

"Well, the people in this building and on the street. No one hardly speaks anymore. I mean, I'll come in and say good evening—and just silence. It wasn't like that when we first moved in. I don't know, it just makes you wonder; that's all. What are they thinking?"

"I personally don't give a shit what they're thinking. And their good evenings don't put any bread on my table."

"Yeah, but you didn't see the way that woman looked at me out there. They must feel something or know something. They probably—"

"They, they, they!" Theresa exploded. "You know, I'm not starting up with this again, Lorraine. Who in the hell are they? And where in the hell are we? Living in some dump of a building in this God-forsaken part of town around a bunch of ignorant niggers with the cotton still under their finger-nails because of you and your theys. They knew something in Linden Hills, so I gave up an apartment for you that I'd been in for the last four years. And then they knew in Park Heights, and you made me so miserable there we had to leave. Now these mysterious theys are on Brewster Place. Well, look out that window, kid. There's a big wall down that block, and this is the end of the line for me. I'm not moving anymore, so if that's what you're working yourself up to—save it!"

30     When Theresa became angry she was like a lump of smoldering coal, and her fierce bursts of temper always unsettled Lorraine.

"You see, that's why I didn't want to mention it." Lorraine began to pull at her fingers nervously. "You're always flying up and jumping to con-clusions—no one said anything about moving. And I didn't know your life has been so miserable since you met me. I'm sorry about that," she fin-ished tearfully.

Theresa looked at Lorraine, standing in the kitchen door like a wilted leaf, and she wanted to throw something at her. Why didn't she ever fight back? The very softness that had first attracted her to Lorraine was now a frequent cause for irritation. Smoked honey. That's what Lorraine had re-minded her of, sitting in her office clutching that application. Dry autumn days in Georgia woods, thick bloated smoke under a beehive, and the first glimpse of amber honey just faintly darkened about the edges by the burning twigs. She had flowed just that heavily into Theresa's mind and had stuck there with a persistent sweetness.

But Theresa hadn't known then that this softness filled Lorraine up to the very middle and that she would bend at the slightest pressure, would be constantly seeking to surround herself with the comfort of everyone's good-will, and would shrivel up at the least touch of disapproval. It was becoming a drain to be continually called upon for this nurturing and support that she just didn't understand. She had supplied it at first out of love for Lorraine, hoping that she would harden eventually, even as honey does when ex-posed to the cold. Theresa was growing tired of being clung to—of being the one who was leaned on. She didn't want a child—she wanted someone who could stand toe to toe with her and be willing to slug it out at times. If they practiced that way with each other, then they could turn back to back and beat the hell out of the world for trying to invade their territory. But she had found no such sparring partner in Lorraine, and the strain of fighting alone was beginning to show on her.

"Well, if it was that miserable, I would have been gone a long time ago," she said, watching her words refresh Lorraine like a gentle shower.

35     "I guess you think I'm some sort of a sick paranoid, but I can't afford to have people calling my job or writing letters to my principal. You know I've al-ready lost a position like that in Detroit. And teaching is my whole life, Tee."

"I know," she sighed, not really knowing at all. There was no danger of that ever happening on Brewster Place. Lorraine taught too far from this neighborhood for anyone here to recognize her in that school. No, it wasn't her job she feared losing this time, but their approval. She wanted to stand out there and chat and trade makeup secrets and cake recipes. She wanted to be secretary of their block association and be asked to mind their kids while they ran to the store. And none of that was going to happen if they couldn't even bring themselves to accept her good evenings.

Theresa silently finished unpacking the groceries. "Why did you buy cottage cheese? Who eats that stuff?"

"Well, I thought we should go on a diet."

"If *we* go on a diet, then you'll disappear. You've got nothing to lose but your hair."

40      "Oh, I don't know. I thought that we might want to try and reduce our hips or something." Lorraine shrugged playfully.

"No, thank you. We are very happy with our hips the way they are," Theresa said, as she shoved the cottage cheese to the back of the refrigerator. "And even when I lose weight, it never comes off there. My chest and arms just get smaller, and I start looking like a bottle of salad dressing."

The two women laughed, and Theresa sat down to watch Lorraine fix dinner. "You know, this behind has always been my downfall. When I was coming up in Georgia with my grandmother, the boys used to promise me penny candy if I would let them pat my behind. And I used to love those jawbreakers—you know, the kind that lasted all day and kept changing colors in your mouth. So I was glad to oblige them, because in one afternoon I could collect a whole week's worth of jawbreakers."

"Really. That's funny to you? Having some boy feeling all over you."

Theresa sucked her teeth. "We were only kids, Lorraine. You know, you remind me of my grandmother. That was one straight-laced old lady. She had a fit when my brother told her what I was doing. She called me into the smokehouse and told me in this real scary whisper that I could get pregnant from letting little boys pat my butt and that I'd end up like my cousin Willa. But Willa and I had been thick as fleas, and she had already given me a step-by-step summary of how she'd gotten into her predicament. But I sneaked around to her house that night just to double-check her story, since that old lady had seemed so earnest. 'Willa, are you sure?' I whispered through her bedroom window. 'I'm tellin' ya, Tee,' she said. 'Just keep both feet on the ground and you home free.' Much later I learned that advice wasn't too biologically sound, but it worked in Georgia because those country boys didn't have much imagination."

45      Theresa's laughter bounced off of Lorraine's silent, rigid back and died in her throat. She angrily tore open a pack of the chocolate chip cookies. "Yeah," she said, staring at Lorraine's back and biting down hard into the cookie, "it wasn't until I came up north to college that I found out there's a whole lot of things that a dude with a little imagination can do to you even with both feet on the ground. You see, Willa forgot to tell me not to bend over or squat or—"

"Must you!" Lorraine turned around from the stove with her teeth clenched tightly together.

"Must I what, Lorraine? Must I talk about things that are as much a part of life as eating or breathing or growing old? Why are you always so uptight about sex or men?"

"I'm not uptight about anything. I just think it's disgusting when you go on and on about—"

"There's nothing disgusting about it, Lorraine. You've never been with a man, but I've been with quite a few—some better than others. There were a couple who I still hope to this day will die a slow, painful death, but then there were some who were good to me—in and out of bed."

50      "If they were so great, then why are you with me?" Lorraine's lips were trembling.

"Because—" Theresa looked steadily into her eyes and then down at the cookie she was twirling on the table. "Because," she continued slowly, "you can take a chocolate chip cookie and put holes in it and attach it to your ears and call it an earring, or hang it around your neck on a silver chain and pretend it's a necklace—but it's still a cookie. See—you can toss it in the air and call it a Frisbee or even a flying saucer, if the mood hits you, and it's still just a cookie. Send it spinning on a table—like this—until it's a wonderful blur of amber and brown light that you can imagine to be a topaz or rusted gold or old crystal, but the law of gravity has got to come into play, some-time, and it's got to come to rest—sometime. Then all the spinning and pre-tending and hoopla is over with. And you know what you got?"

"A chocolate chip cookie," Lorraine said.

"Uh-uh." Theresa put the cookie in her mouth and winked. "A lesbian." She got up from the table. "Call me when dinner's ready, I'm going back to read." She stopped at the kitchen door. "Now, why are you putting gravy on that chicken, Lorraine? You know it's fattening."

# JOYCE CAROL OATES

*Joyce Carol Oates was born in 1938 in Millerport, New York. She won a schol-arship to Syracuse University, from which she graduated (Phi Beta Kappa and valedictorian) in 1960. She then did graduate work in English, first at the University of Wisconsin and then at Rice University, but she withdrew from Rice to devote more time to writing. Her first collection of stories,* By the North Gate, *was published in 1963; since then she has published many stories, po-ems, essays, and novels. She has received many awards, has been elected to the American Academy and Institute of Arts and Letters, and now teaches creative writing at Princeton University.*

## *Where Are You Going, Where Have You Been?*    [1966]

*To Bob Dylan*

Her name was Connie. She was fifteen and she had a quick nervous giggling habit of craning her neck to glance into mirrors or checking other people's faces to make sure her own was all right. Her mother, who noticed every-thing and knew everything and who hadn't much reason any longer to look at her own face, always scolded Connie about it. "Stop gawking at yourself, who are you? You think you're so pretty?" she would say. Connie would raise her eyebrows at these familiar complaints and look right through her mother, into a shadowy vision of herself as she was right at that moment: she knew she was pretty and that was everything. Her mother had been pretty once too, if you could believe those old snapshots in the album, but now her looks were gone and that was why she was always after Connie.

"Why don't you keep your room clean like your sister? How've you got your hair fixed—what the hell stinks? Hair spray? You don't see your sister using that junk."

Her sister June was twenty-four and still lived at home. She was a secretary in the high school Connie attended, and if that wasn't bad enough—with her in the same building—she was so plain and chunky and steady that Connie had to hear her praised all the time by her mother and her mother's sisters. June did this, June did that, she saved money and helped clean the house and cooked and Connie couldn't do a thing, her mind was all filled with trashy daydreams. Their father was away at work most of the time and when he came home he wanted supper and he read the newspaper at supper and after supper he went to bed. He didn't bother talking much to them, but around his bent head Connie's mother kept picking at her until Connie wished her mother was dead and she herself was dead and it was all over. "She makes me want to throw up sometimes," she complained to her friends. She had a high, breathless, amused voice which made everything she said sound a little forced, whether it was sincere or not.

There was one good thing: June went places with girl friends of hers, girls who were just as plain and steady as she, and so when Connie wanted to do that her mother had no objections. The father of Connie's best girl friend drove the girls the three miles to town and left them off at a shopping plaza, so that they could walk through the stores or go to a movie, and when he came to pick them up again at eleven he never bothered to ask what they had done.

5          They must have been familiar sights, walking around that shopping plaza in their shorts and flat ballerina slippers that always scuffed the sidewalk, with charm bracelets jingling on their thin wrists; they would lean together to whisper and laugh secretly if someone passed by who amused or interested them. Connie had long dark blond hair that drew anyone's eye to it, and she wore part of it pulled up on her head and puffed out and the rest of it she let fall down her back. She wore a pull-over jersey blouse that looked one way when she was at home and another way when she was away from home. Everything about her had two sides to it, one for home and one for anywhere that was not home: her walk that could be childlike and bobbing, or languid enough to make anyone think she was hearing music in her head, her mouth which was pale and smirking most of the time, but bright and pink on these evenings out, her laugh which was cynical and drawling at home—"Ha, ha, very funny"—but high-pitched and nervous anywhere else, like the jingling of the charms on her bracelet.

Sometimes they did go shopping or to a movie, but sometimes they went across the highway, ducking fast across the busy road, to a drive-in restaurant where older kids hung out. The restaurant was shaped like a big bottle, though squatter than a real bottle, and on its cap was a revolving figure of a grinning boy who held a hamburger aloft. One night in midsummer they ran across, breathless with daring, and right away someone leaned out a car window and invited them over, but it was just a boy from high school they didn't like. It made them feel good to be able to ignore him. They went up through the maze of parked and cruising cars to the bright-lit, fly-infested restaurant, their faces pleased and expectant as if they were entering a sacred building that loomed out of the night to give them what haven and what blessing they yearned for. They sat at the counter and crossed their legs at the ankles, their thin shoulders rigid with excitement, and listened to the music that made everything so good: the music was always in the background like music at a church service, it was something to depend upon.

A boy named Eddie came in to talk with them. He sat backward on his stool, turning himself jerkily around in semicircles and then stopping and turning again, and after a while he asked Connie if she would like something to eat. She said she did and so she tapped her friend's arm on her way out— her friend pulled her face up into a brave droll look—and Connie said she would meet her at eleven, across the way. "I just hate to leave her like that," Connie said earnestly, but the boy said that she wouldn't be alone for long. So they went out to his car and on the way Connie couldn't help but let her eyes wander over the windshields and faces all around her, her face gleaming with a joy that had nothing to do with Eddie or even this place; it might have been the music. She drew her shoulders up and sucked in her breath with the pure pleasure of being alive, and just at that moment she happened to glance at a face just a few feet from hers. It was a boy with shaggy black hair, in a convertible jalopy painted gold. He stared at her and then his lips widened into a grin. Connie slit her eyes at him and turned away, but she couldn't help glancing back and there he was still watching her. He wagged a finger and laughed and said, "Gonna get you, baby," and Connie turned away again without Eddie noticing anything.

She spent three hours with him, at the restaurant where they ate hamburgers and drank Cokes in wax cups that were always sweating, and then down an alley a mile or so away, and when he left her off at five to eleven only the movie house was still open at the plaza. Her girl friend was there, talking with a boy. When Connie came up the two girls smiled at each other and Connie said, "How was the movie?" and the girl said, "*You* should know." They rode off with the girl's father, sleepy and pleased, and Connie couldn't help but look at the darkened shopping plaza with its big empty parking lot and its signs that were faded and ghostly now, and over at the drive-in restaurant where cars were still circling tirelessly. She couldn't hear the music at this distance.

Next morning June asked her how the movie was and Connie said, "So-so."

10    She and that girl and occasionally another girl went out several times a week that way, and the rest of the time Connie spent around the house—it was summer vacation—getting in her mother's way and thinking, dreaming, about the boys she met. But all the boys fell back and dissolved into a single face that was not even a face, but an idea, a feeling, mixed up with the urgent insistent pounding of the music and the humid night air of July. Connie's mother kept dragging her back to the daylight by finding things for her to do or saying, suddenly, "What's this about the Pettinger girl?"

And Connie would say nervously, "Oh, her. That dope." She always drew thick clear lines between herself and such girls, and her mother was simple and kindly enough to believe her. Her mother was so simple, Connie thought, that it was maybe cruel to fool her so much. Her mother went scuffling around the house in old bedroom slippers and complained over the telephone to one sister about the other, then the other called up and the two of them complained about the third one. If June's name was mentioned her mother's tone was approving, and if Connie's name was mentioned it was disapproving. This did not really mean she disliked Connie and actually Connie thought that her mother preferred her to June because she was prettier, but the two of them kept up a pretense of exasperation, a sense that they were tugging and struggling over something of little value to either of them. Sometimes, over coffee, they were almost friends, but something would come up—some vexation that was like a fly buzzing suddenly around their heads—and their faces went hard with contempt.

One Sunday Connie got up at eleven—none of them bothered with church—and washed her hair so that it could dry all day long, in the sun. Her parents and sister were going to a barbecue at an aunt's house and Connie said no, she wasn't interested, rolling her eyes to let her mother know just what she thought of it. "Stay home alone then," her mother said sharply. Connie sat out back in a lawn chair and watched them drive away, her father quiet and bald, hunched around so that he could back the car out, her mother with a look that was still angry and not at all softened through the windshield, and in the back seat poor old June all dressed up as if she didn't know what a barbecue was, with all the running yelling kids and the flies. Connie sat with her eyes closed in the sun, dreaming and dazed with the warmth about her as if this were a kind of love, the caresses of love, and her mind slipped over onto thoughts of the boy she had been with the night before and how nice he had been, how sweet it always was, not the way someone like June would suppose but sweet, gentle, the way it was in movies and promised in songs; and when she opened her eyes she hardly knew where she was, the back yard ran off into weeds and a fence line of trees and behind it the sky was perfectly blue and still. The asbestos "ranch house" that was now three years old startled her—it looked small. She shook her head as if to get awake.

It was too hot. She went inside the house and turned on the radio to drown out the quiet. She sat on the edge of her bed, barefoot, and listened for an hour and a half to a program called XYZ Sunday Jamboree, record after record of hard, fast, shrieking songs she sang along with, interspersed by exclamations from "Bobby King": "An' look here you girls at Napoleon's—Son and Charley want you to pay real close attention to this song coming up!"

And Connie paid close attention herself, bathed in a glow of slow-pulsed joy that seemed to rise mysteriously out of the music itself and lay languidly about the airless little room, breathed in and breathed out with each gentle rise and fall of her chest.

15    After a while she heard a car coming up the drive. She sat up at once, startled, because it couldn't be her father so soon. The gravel kept crunching all the way in from the road—the driveway was long—and Connie ran to the window. It was a car she didn't know. It was an open jalopy, painted a bright gold that caught the sunlight opaquely. Her heart began to pound and her fingers snatched at her hair, checking it, and she whispered "Christ, Christ," wondering how bad she looked. The car came to a stop at the side door and the horn sounded four short taps as if this were a signal Connie knew.

She went into the kitchen and approached the door slowly, then hung out the screen door, her bare toes curling down off the step. There were two boys in the car and now she recognized the driver: he had shaggy, shabby black hair that looked crazy as a wig and he was grinning at her.

"I ain't late, am I?" he said.

"Who the hell do you think you are?" Connie said.

"Toldja I'd be out, didn't I?"

20    "I don't even know who you are."

She spoke sullenly, careful to show no interest or pleasure, and he spoke in a fast bright monotone. Connie looked past him to the other boy, taking her time. He had fair brown hair, with a lock that fell onto his forehead. His sideburns gave him a fierce, embarrassed look, but so far he hadn't even bothered to glance at her. Both boys wore sunglasses. The driver's glasses were metallic and mirrored everything in miniature.

"You wanta come for a ride?" he said.

Connie smirked and let her hair fall loose over one shoulder.

"Don'tcha like my car? New paint job," he said. "Hey."

25    "What?"

"You're cute."

She pretended to fidget, chasing flies away from the door.

"Don'tcha believe me, or what?" he said.

"Look, I don't even know who you are," Connie said in disgust.

30    "Hey, Ellie's got a radio, see. Mine's broke down." He lifted his friend's arm and showed her the little transistor the boy was holding, and now Connie began to hear the music. It was the same program that was playing inside the house.

"Bobby King?" she said.

"I listen to him all the time. I think he's great."

"He's kind of great," Connie said reluctantly.

"Listen, that guy's *great*. He knows where the action is."

35    Connie blushed a little, because the glasses made it impossible for her to see just what this boy was looking at. She couldn't decide if she liked him or if he was just a jerk, and so she dawdled in the doorway and wouldn't come down or go back inside. She said, "What's all that stuff painted on your car?"

"Can'tcha read it?" He opened the door very carefully, as if he was afraid it might fall off. He slid out just as carefully, planting his feet firmly on the ground, the tiny metallic world in his glasses slowing down like gelatine hardening and in the midst of it Connie's bright green blouse. "This here is my name, to begin with," he said. ARNOLD FRIEND was written in tarlike black letters on the side, with a drawing of a round grinning face that reminded Connie of a pumpkin, except it wore sunglasses. "I wanta introduce myself, I'm Arnold Friend and that's my real name and I'm gonna be your friend, honey, and inside the car's Ellie Oscar, he's kinda shy." Ellie brought his transistor radio up to his shoulder and balanced it there. "Now these numbers are a secret code, honey," Arnold Friend explained. He read off the numbers 33, 19, 17 and raised his eyebrows at her to see what she thought of that, but she didn't think much of it. The left rear fender had been smashed and around it was written, on the gleaming gold background: DONE BY CRAZY WOMAN DRIVER. Connie had to laugh at that. Arnold Friend was pleased at her laughter and looked up at her. "Around the other side's a lot more—you wanta come and see them?"

"No."

"Why not?"

"Why should I?"

40      "Don'tcha wanta see what's on the car? Don'tcha wanta go for a ride?"

"I don't know."

"Why not?"

"I got things to do."

"Like what?"

45      "Things."

He laughed as if she had said something funny. He slapped his thighs. He was standing in a strange way, leaning back against the car as if he were balancing himself. He wasn't tall, only an inch or so taller than she would be if she came down to him. Connie liked the way he was dressed, which was the way all of them dressed: tight faded jeans stuffed into black, scuffed boots, a belt that pulled his waist in and showed how lean he was, and a white pullover shirt that was a little soiled and showed the hard small muscles of his arms and shoulders. He looked as if he probably did hard work, lifting and carrying things. Even his neck looked muscular. And his face was a familiar face, somehow: the jaw and chin and cheeks slightly darkened, because he hadn't shaved for a day or two, and the nose long and hawklike, sniffing as if she were a treat he was going to gobble up and it was all a joke.

"Connie, you ain't telling the truth. This is your day set aside for a ride with me and you know it," he said, still laughing. The way he straightened and recovered from his fit of laughing showed that it had been all fake.

"How do you know what my name is?" she said suspiciously.

"It's Connie."

50      "Maybe and maybe not."

"I know my Connie," he said, wagging his finger. Now she remembered him even better, back at the restaurant, and her cheeks warmed at the thought of how she sucked in her breath just at the moment she passed him—how she must have looked to him. And he had remembered her. "Ellie and I come out here especially for you," he said. "Ellie can sit in back. How about it?"

"Where?"

"Where what?"

"Where're we going?"

55      He looked at her. He took off the sunglasses and she saw how pale the skin around his eyes was, like holes that were not in shadow but instead in light. His eyes were like chips of broken glass that catch the light in an amiable way. He smiled. It was as if the idea of going for a ride somewhere, to some place, was a new idea to him.

"Just for a ride, Connie sweetheart."

"I never said my name was Connie," she said.

"But I know what it is. I know your name and all about you, lots of things," Arnold Friend said. He had not moved yet but stood still leaning back against the side of his jalopy. "I took a special interest in you, such a pretty girl, and found out all about you like I know your parents and sister are gone somewheres and I know where and how long they're going to be gone, and I know who you were with last night, and your best girl friend's name is Betty. Right?"

He spoke in a simple lilting voice, exactly as if he were reciting the words to a song. His smile assured her that everything was fine. In the car Ellie turned up the volume on his radio and did not bother to look around at them.

60        "Ellie can sit in the back seat," Arnold Friend said. He indicated his friend with a casual jerk of his chin, as if Ellie did not count and she should not bother with him.

"How'd you find out all that stuff?" Connie said.

"Listen: Betty Schultz and Tony Fitch and Jimmy Pettinger and Nancy Pettinger," he said, in a chant. "Raymond Stanley and Bob Hutter—"

"Do you know all those kids?"

"I know everybody."

65        "Look, you're kidding. You're not from around here."

"Sure."

"But—how come we never saw you before?"

"Sure you saw me before," he said. He looked down at his boots, as if he were a little offended. "You just don't remember."

"I guess I'd remember you," Connie said.

70        "Yeah?" He looked up at this, beaming. He was pleased. He began to mark time with the music from Ellie's radio, tapping his fists lightly together. Connie looked away from his smile to the car, which was painted so bright it almost hurt her eyes to look at it. She looked at that name, ARNOLD FRIEND. And up at the front fender was an expression that was familiar—MAN THE FLYING SAUCERS. It was an expression kids had used the year before, but didn't use this year. She looked at it for a while as if the words meant something to her that she did not yet know.

"What're you thinking about? Huh?" Arnold Friend demanded. "Not worried about your hair blowing around in the car, are you?"

"No."

"Think I maybe can't drive good?"

"How do I know?"

75        "You're a hard girl to handle. How come?" he said. "Don't you know I'm your friend? Didn't you see me put my sign in the air when you walked by?"

"What sign?"

"My sign." And he drew an X in the air, leaning out toward her. They were maybe ten feet apart. After his hand fell back to his side the X was still in the air, almost visible. Connie let the screen door close and stood perfectly still inside it, listening to the music from her radio and the boy's blend together. She stared at Arnold Friend. He stood there so stiffly relaxed, pretending to be relaxed, with one hand idly on the door handle as if he were keeping himself up that way and had no intention of ever moving again. She recognized most things about him, the tight jeans that showed his thighs and buttocks and the greasy leather boots and the tight shirt, and even that slippery friendly smile of his, that sleepy dreamy smile that all the boys used to get across ideas they didn't want to put into words. She recognized all this and also the singsong way he talked, slightly mocking, kidding, but serious and a little melancholy, and she recognized the way he tapped one fist against the other in homage to the perpetual music behind him. But all these things did not come together.

She said suddenly, "Hey, how old are you?"

His smile faded. She could see then that he wasn't a kid, he was much older—thirty, maybe more. At this knowledge her heart began to pound faster.

80        "That's a crazy thing to ask. Can'tcha see I'm your own age?"

"Like hell you are."

"Or maybe a coupla years older, I'm eighteen."

"Eighteen?" she said doubtfully.

He grinned to reassure her and lines appeared at the corners of his mouth. His teeth were big and white. He grinned so broadly his eyes became slits and she saw how thick the lashes were, thick and black as if painted with a black tarlike material. Then he seemed to become embarrassed, abruptly, and looked over his shoulder at Ellie. "*Him,* he's crazy," he said. "Ain't he a riot, he's a nut, a real character." Ellie was still listening to the music. His sunglasses told nothing about what he was thinking. He wore a bright orange shirt unbuttoned halfway to show his chest, which was a pale, bluish chest and not muscular like Arnold Friend's. His shirt collar was turned up all around and the very tips of the collar pointed out past his chin as if they were protecting him. He was pressing the transistor radio up against his ear and sat there in a kind of daze, right in the sun.

85        "He's kinda strange," Connie said.

"Hey, she says you're kinda strange! Kinda strange!" Arnold Friend cried. He pounded on the car to get Ellie's attention. Ellie turned for the first time and Connie saw with shock that he wasn't a kid either—he had a fair, hairless face, cheeks reddened slightly as if the veins grew too close to the surface of his skin, the face of a forty-year-old baby. Connie felt a wave of dizziness rise in her at this sight and she stared at him as if waiting for something to change the shock of the moment, make it all right again. Ellie's lips kept shaping words, mumbling along, with the words blasting in his ear.

"Maybe you two better go away," Connie said faintly.

"What? How come?" Arnold Friend cried. "We come out here to take you for a ride. It's Sunday." He had the voice of the man on the radio now. It was the same voice, Connie thought. "Don'tcha know it's Sunday all day and honey, no matter who you were with last night today you're with Arnold Friend and don't you forget it!—Maybe you better step out here," he said, and this last was in a different voice. It was a little flatter, as if the heat was finally getting to him.

"No. I got things to do."

90        "Hey."

"You two better leave."

"We ain't leaving until you come with us."

"Like hell I am—"

"Connie, don't fool around with me. I mean, I mean, don't fool *around,*" he said, shaking his head. He laughed incredulously. He placed his sunglasses on top of his head, carefully, as if he were indeed wearing a wig, and brought the stems down behind his ears. Connie stared at him, another wave of dizziness and fear rising in her so that for a moment he wasn't even in focus but was just a blur, standing there against his gold car, and she had the idea that he had driven up the driveway all right but had come from nowhere before that and belonged nowhere and that everything about him and even about the music that was so familiar to her was only half real.

95        "If my father comes and sees you—"

"He ain't coming. He's at a barbecue."

"How do you know that?"

"Aunt Tillie's. Right now they're—uh—they're drinking. Sitting around," he said vaguely, squinting as if he were staring all the way to town and over to Aunt Tillie's backyard. Then the vision seemed to get clear and he nodded energetically. "Yeah. Sitting around. There's your sister in a blue dress, huh? And high heels, the poor sad bitch—nothing like you, sweetheart! And your mother's helping some fat woman with the corn, they're cleaning the corn—husking the corn—"

"What fat woman?" Connie cried.

100    "How do I know what fat woman. I don't know every goddam fat woman in the world!" Arnold Friend laughed.

"Oh, that's Mrs. Hornby. . . . Who invited her?" Connie said. She felt a little light-headed. Her breath was coming quickly.

"She's too fat. I don't like them fat. I like them the way you are, honey," he said, smiling sleepily at her. They stared at each other for a while, through the screen door. He said softly, "Now what you're going to do is this: you're going to come out that door. You're going to sit up front with me and Ellie's going to sit in the back, the hell with Ellie, right? This isn't Ellie's date. You're my date. I'm your lover, honey."

"What? You're crazy—"

"Yes, I'm your lover. You don't know what that is but you will," he said. "I know that too. I know all about you. But look: it's real nice and you couldn't ask for nobody better than me, or more polite. I always keep my word. I'll tell you how it is, I'm always nice at first, the first time. I'll hold you so tight you won't think you have to try to get away or pretend anything because you'll know you can't. And I'll come inside you where it's all secret and you'll give in to me and you'll love me—"

105    "Shut up! You're crazy!" Connie said. She backed away from the door. She put her hands against her ears as if she'd heard something terrible, something not meant for her. "People don't talk like that, you're crazy," she muttered. Her heart was almost too big now for her chest and its pumping made sweat break out all over her. She looked out to see Arnold Friend pause and then take a step toward the porch lurching. He almost fell. But, like a clever drunken man, he managed to catch his balance. He wobbled in his high boots and grabbed hold of one of the porch posts.

"Honey?" he said. "You still listening?"

"Get the hell out of here!"

"Be nice, honey. Listen."

"I'm going to call the police—"

110    He wobbled again and out of the side of his mouth came a fast spat curse, an aside not meant for her to hear. But even this "Christ!" sounded forced. Then he began to smile again. She watched this smile come, awkward as if he were smiling from inside a mask. His whole face was a mask, she thought wildly, tanned down onto his throat but then running out as if he had plastered makeup on his face but had forgotten about his throat.

"Honey—? Listen, here's how it is. I always tell the truth and I promise you this: I ain't coming in that house after you."

"You better not! I'm going to call the police if you—if you don't—"

"Honey," he said, talking right through her voice, "honey, I'm not coming in there but you are coming out here. You know why?"

She was panting. The kitchen looked like a place she had never seen before, some room she had run inside but which wasn't good enough, wasn't going to help her. The kitchen window had never had a curtain, after three years, and there were dishes in the sink for her to do—probably—and if you ran your hand across the table you'd probably feel something sticky there.

115    "You listening, honey? Hey?"

"—going to call the police—"

"Soon as you touch the phone I don't need to keep my promise and can come inside. You won't want that."

She rushed forward and tried to lock the door. Her fingers were shaking. "But why lock it," Arnold Friend said gently, talking right into her face. "It's just a screen door. It's just nothing." One of his boots was at a strange angle, as if his foot wasn't in it. It pointed out to the left, bent at the ankle. "I mean, anybody can break through a screen door and glass and wood and iron or anything else if he needs to, anybody at all and specially Arnold Friend. If the place got lit up with a fire honey you'd come runnin' out into my arms, right into my arms an' safe at home—like you knew I was your lover and'd stopped fooling around. I don't mind a nice shy girl but I don't like no fooling around." Part of those words were spoken with a slight rhythmic lilt, and Connie somehow recognized them—the echo of a song from last year, about a girl rushing into her boyfriend's arms and coming home again—

Connie stood barefoot on the linoleum floor, staring at him. "What do you want?" she whispered.

120    "I want you," he said.

"What?"

"Seen you that night and thought, that's the one, yes sir. I never needed to look any more."

"But my father's coming back. He's coming to get me. I had to wash my hair first—" She spoke in a dry, rapid voice, hardly raising it for him to hear.

"No, your Daddy is not coming and yes, you had to wash your hair and you washed it for me. It's nice and shining and all for me, I thank you, sweetheart," he said, with a mock bow, but again he almost lost his balance. He had to bend and adjust his boots. Evidently his feet did not go all the way down; the boots must have been stuffed with something so that he would seem taller. Connie stared out at him and behind him Ellie in the car, who seemed to be looking off toward Connie's right, into nothing. This Ellie said, pulling the words out of the air one after another as if he were just discovering them, "You want me to pull out the phone?"

125    "Shut your mouth and keep it shut," Arnold Friend said, his face red from bending over or maybe from embarrassment because Connie had seen his boots. "This ain't none of your business."

"What—what are you doing? What do you want?" Connie said. "If I call the police they'll get you, they'll arrest you—"

"Promise was not to come in unless you touch that phone, and I'll keep that promise," he said. He resumed his erect position and tried to force his shoulders back. He sounded like a hero in a movie, declaring something important. He spoke too loudly and it was as if he were speaking to someone behind Connie. "I ain't made plans for coming in that house where I don't belong but just for you to come out to me, the way you should. Don't you know who I am?"

"You're crazy," she whispered. She backed away from the door but did not want to go into another part of the house, as if this would give him permission to come through the door. "What do you . . . You're crazy, you . . ."

"Huh? What're you saying, honey?"

130    Her eyes darted everywhere in the kitchen. She could not remember what it was, this room.

"This is how it is, honey: you come out and we'll drive away, have a nice ride. But if you don't come out we're gonna wait till your people come home and then they're all going to get it."

"You want that telephone pulled out?" Ellie said. He held the radio away from his ear and grimaced, as if without the radio the air was too much for him.

"I toldja shut up, Ellie," Arnold Friend said, "you're deaf, get a hearing aid, right? Fix yourself up. This little girl's no trouble and's gonna be nice to me, so Ellie keep to yourself, this ain't your date—right? Don't hem in on me. Don't hog. Don't crush. Don't bird dog. Don't trail me," he said in a rapid meaningless voice, as if he were running through all the expressions he'd learned but was no longer sure which one of them was in style, then rushing on to new ones, making them up with his eyes closed, "Don't crawl under my fence, don't squeeze in my chipmunk hole, don't sniff my glue, suck my popsicle, keep your own greasy fingers on yourself!" He shaded his eyes and peered in at Connie, who was backed against the kitchen table. "Don't mind him honey he's just a creep. He's a dope. Right? I'm the boy for you and like I said you come out here nice like a lady and give me your hand, and nobody else gets hurt, I mean, your nice old bald-headed daddy and your mummy and your sister in her high heels. Because listen: why bring them in this?"

"Leave me alone," Connie whispered.

135    "Hey, you know that old woman down the road, the one with the chickens and stuff—you know her?"

"She's dead!"

"Dead? What? You know her?" Arnold Friend said.

"She's dead—"

"Don't you like her?"

140    "She's dead—she's—she isn't here any more—"

"But don't you like her, I mean, you got something against her? Some grudge or something?" Then his voice dipped as if he were conscious of a rudeness. He touched the sunglasses perched on top of his head as if to make sure they were still there. "Now you be a good girl."

"What are you going to do?"

"Just two things, or maybe three," Arnold Friend said. "But I promise it won't last long and you'll like me the way you get to like people you're close to. You will. It's all over for you here, so come on out. You don't want your people in any trouble, do you?"

She turned and bumped against a chair or something, hurting her leg, but she ran into the back room and picked up the telephone. Something roared in her ear, a tiny roaring, and she was so sick with fear that she could do nothing but listen to it—the telephone was clammy and very heavy and her fingers groped down to the dial but were too weak to touch it. She began to scream into the phone, into the roaring. She cried out, she cried for her mother, she felt her breath start jerking back and forth in her lungs as if it were something Arnold Friend were stabbing her with again and again with no tenderness. A noisy sorrowful wailing rose all about her and she was locked inside it the way she was locked inside the house.

145    After a while she could hear again. She was sitting on the floor with her wet back against the wall.

Arnold Friend was saying from the door, "That's a good girl. Put the phone back."

She kicked the phone away from her.

"No, honey. Pick it up. Put it back right."

She picked it up and put it back. The dial tone stopped.

150     "That's a good girl. Now come outside."

She was hollow with what had been fear, but what was now just an emptiness. All that screaming had blasted it out of her. She sat, one leg cramped under her, and deep inside her brain was something like a pinpoint of light that kept going and would not let her relax. She thought, I'm not going to see my mother again. She thought, I'm not going to sleep in my bed again. Her bright green blouse was all wet.

Arnold Friend said, in a gentle-loud voice that was like a stage voice, "The place where you came from ain't there any more, and where you had in mind to go is canceled out. This place you are now—inside your daddy's house—is nothing but a cardboard box I can knock down any time. You know that and always did know it. You hear me?"

She thought, I have got to think. I have to know what to do.

"We'll go out to a nice field, out in the country here where it smells so nice and it's sunny," Arnold Friend said. "I'll have my arms tight around you so you won't need to try to get away and I'll show you what love is like, what it does. The hell with this house! It looks solid all right," he said. He ran a fingernail down the screen and the noise did not make Connie shiver, as it would have the day before. "Now put your hand on your heart, honey. Feel that? That feels solid too but we know better, be nice to me, be sweet like you can because what else is there for a girl like you but to be sweet and pretty and give in?—and get away before her people come back?"

155     She felt her pounding heart. Her hand seemed to enclose it. She thought for the first time in her life that it was nothing that was hers, that belonged to her, but just a pounding, living thing inside this body that wasn't really hers either.

"You don't want them to get hurt," Arnold Friend went on. "Now get up, honey. Get up all by yourself."

She stood up.

"Now turn this way. That's right. Come over here to me—Ellie, put that away, didn't I tell you? You dope. You miserable creepy dope," Arnold Friend said. His words were not angry but only part of an incantation. The incantation was kindly. "Now come out through the kitchen to me honey, and let's see a smile, try it, you're a brave sweet little girl and now they're eating corn and hot dogs cooked to bursting over an outdoor fire, and they don't know one thing about you and never did and honey you're better than them because not a one of them would have done this for you."

Connie felt the linoleum under her feet; it was cool. She brushed her hair back out of her eyes. Arnold Friend let go of the post tentatively and opened his arms for her, his elbows pointing in toward each other and his wrists limp, to show that this was an embarrassed embrace and a little mocking, he didn't want to make her self-conscious.

160     She put out her hand against the screen. She watched herself push the door slowly open as if she were safe back somewhere in the other doorway, watching this body and this head of long hair moving out into the sunlight where Arnold Friend waited.

"My sweet little blue-eyed girl," he said, in a half-sung sigh that had nothing to do with her brown eyes but was taken up just the same by the vast sunlit reaches of the land behind him and on all sides of him, so much land that Connie had never seen before and did not recognize except to know that she was going to it.

# TIM O'BRIEN

*Tim O'Brien, born in 1947 in Austin, Minnesota, was drafted into the army in 1968 and served as an infantryman in Vietnam. Drawing on this experience he wrote a memoir,* If I Die in a Combat Zone *(1973), in which he explains that he did not believe in the Vietnam War, considered dodging the draft, but, lacking the courage to do so, he served, largely out of fear and embarrassment. A later book, a novel titled* Going after Cacciato, *won the National Book Award in 1979. O'Brien's recent books include the novels* Tomcat in Love *(1998) and* July, July *(2002).*

*"The Things They Carried," first published in 1986, in 1990 was republished as one of a series of interlocking stories in a book titled* The Things They Carried. *In one of the stories, "How To Tell a True War Story," O'Brien writes,*

> *A true war story is never moral. It does not instruct, nor encourage virtue, nor suggest models of proper human behavior. . . . If a story seems moral, do not believe it. If at the end of a war story you feel uplifted, or if you feel that some small bit of rectitude has been salvaged from the larger waste, then you have been made the victim of a very old and terrible lie. There is no rectitude whatsoever. There is no virtue. As a first rule of thumb, therefore, you can tell a true war story by its absolute and uncompromising allegiance to obscenity and evil.*

## *The Things They Carried*                           [1986]

First Lieutenant Jimmy Cross carried letters from a girl named Martha, a junior at Mount Sebastian College in New Jersey. They were not love letters, but Lieutenant Cross was hoping, so he kept them folded in plastic at the bottom of his rucksack. In the late afternoon, after a day's march, he would dig his foxhole, wash his hands under a canteen, unwrap the letters, hold them with the tips of his fingers, and spend the last hour of light pretending. He would imagine romantic camping trips into the White Mountains in New Hampshire. He would sometimes taste the envelope flaps, knowing her tongue had been there. More than anything, he wanted Martha to love him as he loved her, but the letters were mostly chatty, elusive on the matter of love. She was a virgin, he was almost sure. She was an English major at Mount Sebastian, and she wrote beautifully about her professors and roommates and midterm exams, about her respect for Chaucer and her great affection for Virginia Woolf. She often quoted lines of poetry; she never mentioned the war, except to say, Jimmy, take care of yourself. The letters weighed 10 ounces. They were signed Love, Martha, but Lieutenant Cross understood that Love was only a way of signing and did not mean what he sometimes pretended it meant. At dusk, he would carefully return the letters to his rucksack. Slowly, a bit distracted, he would get up and move among his men, checking the perimeter, then at full dark he would return to his hole and watch the night and wonder if Martha was a virgin.

The things they carried were largely determined by necessity. Among the necessities or near-necessities were P-38 can openers, pocket knives, heat tabs, wrist watches, dog tags, mosquito repellent, chewing gum, candy, cigarettes, salt tablets, packets of Kool-Aid, lighters, matches, sewing kits, Military Payment Certificates, C rations, and two or three canteens of water. Together, these items weighed between 15 and 20 pounds, depending upon a man's habits or rate of metabolism. Henry Dobbins, who was a big man, carried extra rations; he was especially fond of canned peaches in heavy syrup over pound cake. Dave Jensen, who practiced field hygiene, carried a toothbrush, dental floss, and several hotel-sized bars of soap he'd stolen on R&R[1] in Sydney, Australia. Ted Lavender, who was scared, carried tranquilizers until he was shot in the head outside the village of Than Khe in mid-April. By necessity, and because it was SOP,[2] they all carried steel helmets that weighed 5 pounds including the liner and camouflage cover. They carried the standard fatigue jackets and trousers. Very few carried underwear. On their feet they carried jungle boots—2.1 pounds—and Dave Jensen carried three pairs of socks and a can of Dr. Scholl's foot powder as a precaution against trench foot. Until he was shot, Ted Lavender carried 6 or 7 ounces of premium dope, which for him was a necessity. Mitchell Sanders, the RTO,[3] carried condoms. Norman Bowker carried a diary. Rat Kiley carried comic books. Kiowa, a devout Baptist, carried an illustrated New Testament that had been presented to him by his father, who taught Sunday school in Oklahoma City, Oklahoma. As a hedge against bad times, however, Kiowa also carried his grandmother's distrust of the white man, his grandfather's old hunting hatchet. Necessity dictated. Because the land was mined and booby-trapped, it was SOP for each man to carry a steel-centered, nylon-covered flak jacket, which weighed 6.7 pounds, but which on hot days seemed much heavier. Because you could die so quickly, each man carried at least one large compress bandage, usually in the helmet band for easy access. Because the nights were cold, and because the monsoons were wet, each carried a green plastic poncho that could be used as a raincoat or groundsheet or makeshift tent. With its quilted liner, the poncho weighed almost 2 pounds, but it was worth every ounce. In April, for instance, when Ted Lavender was shot, they used his poncho to wrap him up, then to carry him across the paddy, then to lift him into the chopper that took him away.

They were called legs or grunts.

To carry something was to hump it, as when Lieutenant Jimmy Cross humped his love for Martha up the hills and through the swamps. In its intransitive form, to hump meant to walk, or to march, but it implied burdens far beyond the intransitive.

5      Almost everyone humped photographs. In his wallet, Lieutenant Cross carried two photographs of Martha. The first was a Kodacolor snapshot

---

[1]**R&R** rest and recreation leave.   [2]**SOP** standard operating procedure.   [3]**RTO** radio and telephone operator.

signed Love, though he knew better. She stood against a brick wall. Her eyes were gray and neutral, her lips slightly open as she stared straight-on at the camera. At night, sometimes, Lieutenant Cross wondered who had taken the picture, because he knew she had boyfriends, because he loved her so much, and because he could see the shadow of the picture taker spreading out against the brick wall. The second photograph had been clipped from the 1968 Mount Sebastian yearbook. It was an action shot—women's volley-ball—and Martha was bent horizontal to the floor, reaching, the palms of her hands in sharp focus, the tongue taut, the expression frank and competitive. There was no visible sweat. She wore white gym shorts. Her legs, he thought, were almost certainly the legs of a virgin, dry and without hair, the left knee cocked and carrying her entire weight, which was just over 100 pounds. Lieutenant Cross remembered touching that left knee. A dark theater, he remembered, and the movie was *Bonnie and Clyde,* and Martha wore a tweed skirt, and during the final scene, when he touched her knee, she turned and looked at him in a sad, sober way that made him pull his hand back, but he would always remember the feel of the tweed skirt and the knee beneath it and the sound of the gunfire that killed Bonnie and Clyde, how embarrassing it was, how slow and oppressive. He remembered kissing her goodnight at the dorm door. Right then, he thought, he should've done something brave. He should've carried her up the stairs to her room and tied her to the bed and touched that left knee all night long. He should've risked it. Whenever he looked at the photographs, he thought of new things he should've done.

What they carried was partly a function of rank, partly of field specialty.

As a first lieutenant and platoon leader, Jimmy Cross carried a compass, maps, code books, binoculars, and a .45-caliber pistol that weighed 2.9 pounds fully loaded. He carried a strobe light and the responsibility for the lives of his men.

As an RTO, Mitchell Sanders carried the PRC-25 radio, a killer, 26 pounds with its battery.

As a medic, Rat Kiley carried a canvas satchel filled with morphine and plasma and malaria tablets and surgical tape and comic books and all the things a medic must carry, including M&M's[4] for especially bad wounds, for a total weight of nearly 20 pounds.

10    As a big man, therefore a machine gunner, Henry Dobbins carried the M-60, which weighed 23 pounds unloaded, but which was almost always loaded. In addition, Dobbins carried between 10 and 15 pounds of ammunition draped in belts across his chest and shoulders.

As PFCs or Spec 4s, most of them were common grunts and carried the standard M-16 gas-operated assault rifle. The weapon weighed 7.5 pounds unloaded, 8.2 pounds with its full 20-round magazine. Depending on numerous factors, such as topography and psychology, the riflemen carried anywhere from 12 to 20 magazines, usually in cloth bandoliers, adding on another 8.4 pounds at minimum, 14 pounds at maximum. When it was available, they also carried M-16 maintenance gear—rods and steel brushes and swabs and tubes of LSA oil—all of which weighed about a pound.

---

[4]**M&M** joking term for medical supplies.

Among the grunts, some carried the M-79 grenade launcher, 5.9 pounds unloaded, a reasonably light weapon except for the ammunition, which was
heavy. A single round weighed 10 ounces. The typical load was 25 rounds.
But Ted Lavender, who was scared, carried 34 rounds when he was shot and
killed outside Than Khe, and he went down under an exceptional burden,
more than 20 pounds of ammunition, plus the flak jacket and helmet and rations and water and toilet paper and tranquilizers and all the rest, plus the
unweighed fear. He was dead weight. There was no twitching or flopping.
Kiowa, who saw it happen, said it was like watching a rock fall, or a big sand-
bag or something—just boom, then down—not like the movies where the
dead guy rolls around and does fancy spins and goes ass over teakettle—not
like that, Kiowa said, the poor bastard just flat-fuck fell. Boom. Down. Nothing else. It was a bright morning in mid-April. Lieutenant Cross felt the pain.
He blamed himself. They stripped off Lavender's canteens and ammo, all the
heavy things, and Rat Kiley said the obvious, the guy's dead, and Mitchell
Sanders used his radio to report one U.S. KIA[5] and to request a chopper.
Then they wrapped Lavender in his poncho. They carried him out to a dry
paddy, established security, and sat smoking the dead man's dope until the
chopper came. Lieutenant Cross kept to himself. He pictured Martha's
smooth young face, thinking he loved her more than anything, more than his
men, and now Ted Lavender was dead because he loved her so much and
could not stop thinking about her. When the dustoff arrived, they carried
Lavender aboard. Afterward they burned Than Khe. They marched until
dusk, then dug their holes, and that night Kiowa kept explaining how you
had to be there, how fast it was, how the poor guy just dropped like so
much concrete. Boom-down, he said. Like cement.

In addition to the three standard weapons—the M-60, M-16, and M-79—
they carried whatever presented itself, or whatever seemed appropriate as a
means of killing or staying alive. They carried catch-as-catch-can. At various
times, in various situations, they carried M-14s and CAR-15s and Swedish Ks
and grease guns and captured AK-47s and Chi-Coms and RPGs and Simonov
carbines and black market Uzis and .38-caliber Smith & Wesson handguns
and 66 mm LAWs and shotguns and silencers and blackjacks and bayonets
and C-4 plastic explosives. Lee Strunk carried a slingshot; a weapon of last
resort, he called it. Mitchell Sanders carried brass knuckles. Kiowa carried
his grandfather's feathered hatchet. Every third or fourth man carried a Clay-
more antipersonnel mine—3.5 pounds with its firing device. They all carried fragmentation grenades—14 ounces each. They all carried at least one
M-18 colored smoke grenade—24 ounces. Some carried CS or tear gas
grenades. Some carried white phosphorus grenades. They carried all they
could bear, and then some, including a silent awe for the terrible power of
the things they carried.

In the first week of April, before Lavender died, Lieutenant Jimmy Cross
received a good-luck charm from Martha. It was a simple pebble, an ounce at
most. Smooth to the touch, it was a milky white color with flecks of orange
and violet, oval-shaped, like a miniature egg. In the accompanying letter,

---

[5]**KIA** killed in action.

Martha wrote that she had found the pebble on the Jersey shoreline, precisely where the land touched water at high tide, where things came together but also separated. It was this separate-but-together quality, she wrote, that had inspired her to pick up the pebble and to carry it in her breast pocket for several days, where it seemed weightless, and then to send it through the mail, by air, as a token of her truest feelings for him. Lieutenant Cross found this romantic. But he wondered what her truest feelings were, exactly, and what she meant by separate-but-together. He wondered how the tides and waves had come into play on that afternoon along the Jersey shoreline when Martha saw the pebble and bent down to rescue it from geology. He imagined bare feet. Martha was a poet, with the poet's sensibilities, and her feet would be brown and bare, the toenails unpainted, the eyes chilly and somber like the ocean in March, and though it was painful, he wondered who had been with her that afternoon. He imagined a pair of shadows moving along the strip of sand where things came together but also separated. It was phantom jealousy, he knew, but he couldn't help himself. He loved her so much. On the march, through the hot days of early April, he carried the pebble in his mouth, turning it with his tongue, tasting sea salt and moisture. His mind wandered. He had difficulty keeping his attention on the war. On occasion he would yell at his men to spread out the column, to keep their eyes open, but then he would slip away into daydreams, just pretending, walking barefoot along the Jersey shore, with Martha, carrying nothing. He would feel himself rising. Sun and waves and gentle winds, all love and lightness.

     What they carried varied by mission.

15     When a mission took them to the mountains, they carried mosquito netting, machetes, canvas tarps, and extra bug juice.

     If a mission seemed especially hazardous, or if it involved a place they knew to be bad, they carried everything they could. In certain heavily mined AOs,[6] where the land was dense with Toe Poppers and Bouncing Betties, they took turns humping a 28-pound mine detector. With its headphones and big sensing plate, the equipment was a stress on the lower back and shoulders, awkward to handle, often useless because of the shrapnel in the earth, but they carried it anyway, partly for safety, partly for the illusion of safety.

     On ambush, or other night missions, they carried peculiar little odds and ends. Kiowa always took along his New Testament and a pair of moccasins for silence. Dave Jensen carried night-sight vitamins high in carotene. Lee Strunk carried his slingshot; ammo, he claimed, would never be a problem. Rat Kiley carried brandy and M&M's candy. Until he was shot, Ted Lavender carried the starlight scope, which weighed 6.3 pounds with its aluminum carrying case. Henry Dobbins carried his girlfriend's pantyhose wrapped around his neck as a comforter. They all carried ghosts. When dark came, they would move out single file across the meadows and paddies to their ambush coordinates, where they would quietly set up the Claymores and lie down and spend the night waiting.

---

[6]**AOs** areas of operation.

Other missions were more complicated and required special equipment. In mid-April, it was their mission to search out and destroy the elaborate tunnel complexes in the Than Khe area south of Chu Lai. To blow the
tunnels, they carried one-pound blocks of pentrite high explosives, four
blocks to a man, 68 pounds in all. They carried wiring, detonators, and
battery-powdered clackers. Dave Jensen carried earplugs. Most often, before blowing the tunnels, they were ordered by higher command to search
them, which was considered bad news, but by and large they just shrugged
and carried out orders. Because he was a big man, Henry Dobbins was excused from tunnel duty. The others would draw numbers. Before Lavender
died there were 17 men in the platoon, and whoever drew the number 17
would strip off his gear and crawl in headfirst with a flashlight and Lieutenant Cross's .45-caliber pistol. The rest of them would fan out as security.
They would sit down or kneel, not facing the hole, listening to the ground
beneath them, imagining cobwebs and ghosts, whatever was down there—
the tunnel walls squeezing in—how the flashlight seemed impossibly
heavy in the hand and how it was tunnel vision in the very strictest sense,
compression in all ways, even time, and how you had to wiggle in—ass and
elbows—a swallowed-up feeling—and how you found yourself worrying
about odd things: Will your flashlight go dead? Do rats carry rabies? If you
screamed, how far would the sound carry? Would your buddies hear it?
Would they have the courage to drag you out? In some respects, though not
many, the waiting was worse than the tunnel itself. Imagination was a killer.

On April 16, when Lee Strunk drew the number 17, he laughed and muttered something and went down quickly. The morning was hot and very
still. Not good, Kiowa said. He looked at the tunnel opening, then out across
a dry paddy toward the village of Than Khe. Nothing moved. No clouds or
birds or people. As they waited, the men smoked and drank Kool-Aid, not
talking much, feeling sympathy for Lee Strunk but also feeling the luck of
the draw. You win some, you lose some, said Mitchell Sanders, and sometimes you settle for a rain check. It was a tired line and no one laughed.

20    Henry Dobbins ate a tropical chocolate bar. Ted Lavender popped a
tranquilizer and went off to pee.

After five minutes, Lieutenant Jimmy Cross moved to the tunnel, leaned
down, and examined the darkness. Trouble, he thought—a cave-in maybe.
And then suddenly, without willing it, he was thinking about Martha. The
stresses and fractures, the quick collapse, the two of them buried alive under
all that weight. Dense, crushing love. Kneeling, watching the hole, he tried to
concentrate on Lee Strunk and the war, all the dangers, but his love was too
much for him, he felt paralyzed, he wanted to sleep inside her lungs and
breathe her blood and be smothered. He wanted her to be a virgin and not a
virgin, all at once. He wanted to know her. Intimate secrets: Why poetry?
Why so sad? Why that grayness in her eyes? Why so alone? Not lonely, just
alone—riding her bike across campus or sitting off by herself in the cafete-
ria—even dancing, she danced alone—and it was the aloneness that filled
him with love. He remembered telling her that one evening. How she nodded and looked away. And how, later, when he kissed her, she received the
kiss without returning it, her eyes wide open, not afraid, not a virgin's eyes,
just flat and uninvolved.

Lieutenant Cross gazed at the tunnel. But he was not there. He was
buried with Martha under the white sand at the Jersey shore. They were

pressed together, and the pebble in his mouth was her tongue. He was smiling. Vaguely, he was aware of how quiet the day was, the sullen paddies, yet
he could not bring himself to worry about matters of security. He was beyond that. He was just a kid at war, in love. He was twenty-four years old. He
couldn't help it.

A few moments later Lee Strunk crawled out of the tunnel. He came up
grinning, filthy but alive. Lieutenant Cross nodded and closed his eyes while
the others clapped Strunk on the back and made jokes about rising from the
dead.

Worms, Rat Kiley said. Right out of the grave. Fuckin' zombie.

25    The men laughed. They all felt great relief.

Spook city, said Mitchell Sanders.

Lee Strunk made a funny ghost sound, a kind of moaning, yet very
happy, and right then, when Strunk made that high happy moaning sound,
when he went *Ahhooooo,* right then Ted Lavender was shot in the head
on his way back from peeing. He lay with his mouth open. The teeth were
broken. There was a swollen black bruise under his left eye. The cheekbone
was gone. Oh shit, Rat Kiley said, the guy's dead. The guy's dead, he kept saying, which seemed profound—the guy's dead. I mean really.

The things they carried were determined to some extent by superstition. Lieutenant Cross carried his good-luck pebble. Dave Jensen carried a
rabbit's foot. Norman Bowker, otherwise a very gentle person, carried a
thumb that had been presented to him as a gift by Mitchell Sanders. The
thumb was dark brown, rubbery to the touch, and weighed 4 ounces at
most. It had been cut from a VC corpse, a boy of fifteen or sixteen. They'd
found him at the bottom of an irrigation ditch, badly burned, flies in his
mouth and eyes. The boy wore black shorts and sandals. At the time of his
death he had been carrying a pouch of rice, a rifle, and three magazines of
ammunition.

You want my opinion, Mitchell Sanders said, there's a definite moral
here.

30    He put his hand on the dead boy's wrist. He was quiet for a time, as if
counting a pulse, then he patted the stomach, almost affectionately, and used
Kiowa's hunting hatchet to remove the thumb.

Henry Dobbins asked what the moral was.

Moral?

You know. *Moral.*

Sanders wrapped the thumb in toilet paper and handed it across to Norman Bowker. There was no blood. Smiling, he kicked the boy's head,
watched the flies scatter, and said, It's like with that old TV show—Paladin.
Have gun, will travel.

35    Henry Dobbins thought about it.

Yeah, well, he finally said. I don't see no moral.

There it *is,* man.

Fuck off.

They carried USO stationery and pencils and pens. They carried
Sterno, safety pins, trip flares, signal flares, spools of wire, razor blades,
chewing tobacco, liberated joss sticks and statuettes of the smiling Buddha,
candles, grease pencils, *The Stars and Stripes,* fingernail clippers, Psy Ops

leaflets, bush hats, bolos, and much more. Twice a week, when the resupply choppers came in, they carried hot chow in green Mermite cans and large canvas bags filled with iced beer and soda pop. They carried plastic water containers, each with a 2-gallon capacity. Mitchell Sanders carried a set of starched tiger fatigues for special occasions. Henry Dobbins carried Black Flag insecticide. Dave Jensen carried empty sandbags that could be filled at night for added protection. Lee Strunk carried tanning lotion. Some things they carried in common. Taking turns, they carried the big PRC-77 scrambler radio, which weighed 30 pounds with its battery. They shared the weight of memory. They took up what others could no longer bear. Often, they carried each other, the wounded or weak. They carried infections. They carried chess sets, basketballs, Vietnamese-English dictionaries, insignia of rank, Bronze Stars and Purple Hearts, plastic cards imprinted with the Code of Conduct. They carried diseases, among them malaria and dysentery. They carried lice and ringworm and leeches and paddy algae and various rots and molds. They carried the land itself—Vietnam, the place, the soil—a powdery orange-red dust that covered their boots and fatigues and faces. They carried the sky. The whole atmosphere, they carried it, the humidity, the monsoons, the stink of fungus and decay, all of it, they carried gravity. They moved like mules. By daylight they took sniper fire, at night they were mortared, but it was not battle, it was just the endless march, village to village, without purpose, nothing won or lost. They marched for the sake of the march. They plodded along slowly, dumbly, leaning forward against the heat, unthinking, all blood and bone, simple grunts, soldiering with their legs, toiling up the hills and down into the paddies and across the rivers and up again and down, just humping, one step and then the next and then another, but no volition, no will, because it was automatic, it was anatomy, and the war was entirely a matter of posture and carriage, the hump was everything, a kind of inertia, a kind of emptiness, a dullness of desire and intellect and conscience and hope and human sensibility. Their principles were in their feet. Their calculations were biological. They had no sense of strategy or mission. They searched the villages without knowing what to look for, nor caring, kicking over jars of rice, frisking children and old men, blowing tunnels, sometimes setting fires and sometimes not, then forming up and moving on to the next village, then other villages, where it would always be the same. They carried their own lives. The pressures were enormous. In the heat of early afternoon, they would remove their helmets and flak jackets, walking bare, which was dangerous but which helped ease the strain. They would often discard things along the route of march. Purely for comfort, they would throw away rations, blow their Claymores and grenades, no matter, because by nightfall the resupply choppers would arrive with more of the same, then a day or two later still more, fresh watermelons and crates of ammunition and sunglasses and woolen sweaters—the resources were stunning—sparklers for the Fourth of July, colored eggs for Easter—it was the great American war chest—the fruits of science, the smoke stacks, the canneries, the arsenals at Hartford, the Minnesota forests, the machine shops, the vast fields of corn and wheat—they carried like freight trains; they carried it on their backs and shoulders—and for all the ambiguities of Vietnam, all the mysteries and unknowns, there was at least the single abiding certainty that they would never be at a loss for things to carry.

* * *

40        After the chopper took Lavender away, Lieutenant Jimmy Cross led his men into the village of Than Khe. They burned everything. They shot chickens and dogs, they trashed the village well, they called in artillery and watched the wreckage, then they marched for several hours through the hot afternoon, and then at dusk, while Kiowa explained how Lavender died, Lieutenant Cross found himself trembling.

He tried not to cry. With his entrenching tool, which weighed 5 pounds, he began digging a hole in the earth.

He felt shame. He hated himself. He had loved Martha more than his men, and as a consequence Lavender was now dead, and this was something he would have to carry like a stone in his stomach for the rest of the war.

All he could do was dig. He used his entrenching tool like an ax, slashing, feeling both love and hate, and then later, when it was full dark, he sat at the bottom of his foxhole and wept. It went on for a long while. In part, he was grieving for Ted Lavender, but mostly it was for Martha, and for himself, because she belonged to another world, which was not quite real, and because she was a junior at Mount Sebastian College in New Jersey, a poet and a virgin and uninvolved, and because he realized she did not love him and never would.

Like cement, Kiowa whispered in the dark. I swear to God—boom, down. Not a word.

45        I've heard this, said Norman Bowker.

A pisser, you know? Still zipping himself up. Zapped while zipping.

All right, fine. That's enough.

Yeah, but you had to see it, the guy just—

I *heard,* man. Cement. So why not shut the fuck *up?*

50        Kiowa shook his head sadly and glanced over at the hole where Lieutenant Jimmy Cross sat watching the night. The air was thick and wet. A warm dense fog had settled over the paddies and there was the stillness that precedes rain.

After a time Kiowa sighed.

One thing for sure, he said. The lieutenant's in some deep hurt. I mean that crying jag—the way he was carrying on—it wasn't fake or anything, it was real heavy-duty hurt. The man cares.

Sure, Norman Bowker said.

Say what you want, the man does care.

55        We all got problems.

Not Lavender.

No, I guess not, Bowker said. Do me a favor, though.

Shut up?

That's a smart Indian. Shut up.

60        Shrugging, Kiowa pulled off his boots. He wanted to say more, just to lighten up his sleep, but instead he opened his New Testament and arranged it beneath his head as a pillow. The fog made things seem hollow and unattached. He tried not to think about Ted Lavender, but then he was thinking how fast it was, no drama, down and dead, and how it was hard to feel anything except surprise. It seemed unchristian. He wished he could find some great sadness, or even anger, but the emotion wasn't there and he couldn't make it happen. Mostly he felt pleased to be alive. He liked the smell of the

New Testament under his cheek, the leather and ink and paper and glue, whatever the chemicals were. He liked hearing the sounds of night. Even his fatigue, it felt fine, the stiff muscles and the prickly awareness of his own body, a floating feeling. He enjoyed not being dead. Lying there, Kiowa admired Lieutenant Jimmy Cross's capacity for grief. He wanted to share the man's pain, he wanted to care as Jimmy Cross cared. And yet when he closed his eyes, all he could think was Boom-down, and all he could feel was the pleasure of having his boots off and the fog curling in around him and the damp soil and the Bible smells and the plush comfort of night.

After a moment Norman Bowker sat up in the dark.

What the hell, he said. You want to talk, *talk*. Tell it to me.

Forget it.

No, man, go on. One thing I hate, it's a silent Indian.

65    For the most part they carried themselves with poise, a kind of dignity. Now and then, however, there were times of panic, when they squealed or wanted to squeal but couldn't, when they twitched and made moaning sounds and covered their heads and said Dear Jesus and flopped around on the earth and fired their weapons blindly and cringed and sobbed and begged for the noise to stop and went wild and made stupid promises to themselves and to God and to their mothers and fathers, hoping not to die. In different ways, it happened to all of them. Afterward, when the firing ended, they would blink and peek up. They would touch their bodies, feeling shame, then quickly hiding it. They would force themselves to stand. As if in slow motion, frame by frame, the world would take on the old logic—absolute silence, then the wind, then sunlight, then voices. It was the burden of being alive. Awkwardly, the men would reassemble themselves, first in private, then in groups, becoming soldiers again. They would repair the leaks in their eyes. They would check for casualties, call in dustoffs, light cigarettes, try to smile, clear their throats and spit and begin cleaning their weapons. After a time someone would shake his head and say, No lie, I almost shit my pants, and someone else would laugh, which meant it was bad, yes, but the guy had obviously not shit his pants, it wasn't that bad, and in any case nobody would ever do such a thing and then go ahead and talk about it. They would squint into the dense, oppressive sunlight. For a few moments, perhaps, they would fall silent, lighting a joint and tracking its passage from man to man, inhaling, holding in the humiliation. Scary stuff, one of them might say. But then someone else would grin or flick his eyebrows and say, Roger-dodger, almost cut me a new asshole, *almost*.

There were numerous such poses. Some carried themselves with a sort of wistful resignation, others with pride or stiff soldierly discipline or good humor or macho zeal. They were afraid of dying but they were even more afraid to show it.

They found jokes to tell.

They used a hard vocabulary to contain the terrible softness. *Greased*, they'd say. *Offed, lit up, zapped while zipping.* It wasn't cruelty, just stage presence. They were actors. When someone died, it wasn't quite dying, because in a curious way it seemed scripted, and because they had their lines mostly memorized, irony mixed with tragedy, and because they called it by other names, as if to encyst and destroy the reality of death itself. They kicked corpses. They cut off thumbs. They talked grunt lingo. They told stories about Ted Lavender's supply of tranquilizers, how the poor guy didn't feel a thing, how incredibly tranquil he was.

There's a moral here, said Mitchell Sanders.

70      They were waiting for Lavender's chopper, smoking the dead man's dope.

The moral's pretty obvious, Sanders said, and winked. Stay away from drugs. No joke, they'll ruin your day every time.

Cute, said Henry Dobbins.

Mind-blower, get it? Talk about wiggy. Nothing left, just blood and brains.

They made themselves laugh.

75      There it is, they'd say. Over and over—there it is, my friend, there it is— as if the repetition itself were an act of poise, a balance between crazy and almost crazy, knowing without going, there it is, which meant be cool, let it ride, because Oh yeah, man, you can't change what can't be changed, there it is, there it absolutely and positively and fucking well *is*.

They were tough.

They carried all the emotional baggage of men who might die. Grief, ter-ror, love, longing—these were intangibles, but the intangibles had their own mass and specific gravity, they had tangible weight. They carried shameful memories. They carried the common secret of cowardice barely restrained, the instinct to run or freeze or hide, and in many respects this was the heav-iest burden of all, for it could never be put down, it required perfect balance and perfect posture. They carried their reputations. They carried the soldier's greatest fear, which was the fear of blushing. Men killed, and died, because they were embarrassed not to. It was what had brought them to the war in the first place, nothing positive, no dreams of glory or honor, just to avoid the blush of dishonor. They died so as not to die of embarrassment. They crawled into tunnels and walked point and advanced under fire. Each morning, despite the unknowns, they made their legs move. They endured. They kept humping. They did not submit to the obvious alternative, which was simply to close the eyes and fall. So easy, really. Go limp and tumble to the ground and let the muscles unwind and not speak and not budge until your buddies picked you up and lifted you into the chopper that would roar and dip its nose and carry you off to the world. A mere matter of falling, yet no one ever fell. It was not courage, exactly; the object was not valor. Rather, they were too frightened to be cowards.

By and large they carried these things inside, maintaining the masks of composure. They sneered at sick call. They spoke bitterly about guys who had found release by shooting off their own toes or fingers. Pussies, they'd say. Candy-asses. It was fierce, mocking talk, with only a trace of envy or awe, but even so the image played itself out behind their eyes.

They imagined the muzzle against flesh. So easy: squeeze the trigger and blow away a toe. They imagined it. They imagined the quick, sweet pain, then the evacuation to Japan, then a hospital with warm beds and cute geisha nurses.

80      And they dreamed of freedom birds.

At night, on guard, staring into the dark, they were carried away by jumbo jets. They felt the rush of takeoff. *Gone!* they yelled. And then velocity—wings and engines—a smiling stewardess—but it was more than a plane, it was a real bird, a big sleek silver bird with feathers and talons and high screeching. They were flying. The weights fell off; there was nothing to bear. They laughed and held on tight, feeling the cold slap of wind and altitude, soaring, thinking *It's over, I'm gone!*—they were naked, they were light and free—it was all lightness, bright and fast and buoyant, light as light, a helium buzz in the brain, a giddy bubbling in the lungs as they were taken up over the clouds and the war, beyond duty, beyond gravity and mortification and global entanglements—*Sin loi!*[7] they yelled, *I'm sorry, motherfuckers, but I'm out of it, I'm goofed, I'm on a space cruise, I'm gone!*—and it was a restful, unencumbered sensation, just riding the light waves, sailing that big silver freedom bird over the mountains and oceans, over America, over the farms and great sleeping cities and cemeteries and highways and the golden arches of McDonald's, it was flight, a kind of fleeing, a kind of falling, falling higher and higher, spinning off the edge of the earth and beyond the sun and through the vast, silent vacuum where there were no burdens and where everything weighed exactly nothing—*Gone!* they screamed. *I'm sorry but I'm gone!*—and so at night, not quite dreaming, they gave themselves over to lightness, they were carried, they were purely borne.

On the morning after Ted Lavender died, First Lieutenant Jimmy Cross crouched at the bottom of his foxhole and burned Martha's letters. Then he burned the two photographs. There was a steady rain falling, which made it difficult, but he used heat tabs and Sterno to build a small fire, screening it with his body, holding the photographs over the tight blue flame with the tips of his fingers.

He realized it was only a gesture. Stupid, he thought. Sentimental, too, but mostly just stupid.

Lavender was dead. You couldn't burn the blame.

85    Besides, the letters were in his head. And even now, without photographs, Lieutenant Cross could see Martha playing volleyball in her white gym shorts and yellow T-shirt. He could see her moving in the rain.

When the fire died out, Lieutenant Cross pulled his poncho over his shoulders and ate breakfast from a can.

There was no great mystery, he decided.

In those burned letters Martha had never mentioned the war, except to say, Jimmy, take care of yourself. She wasn't involved. She signed the letters Love, but it wasn't love, and all the fine lines and technicalities did not matter. Virginity was no longer an issue. He hated her. Yes, he did. He hated her. Love, too, but it was a hard, hating kind of love.

The morning came up wet and blurry. Everything seemed part of everything else, the fog and Martha and the deepening rain.

90    He was a soldier, after all.

Half smiling, Lieutenant Jimmy Cross took out his maps. He shook his head hard, as if to clear it, then bent forward and began planning the day's march. In ten minutes, or maybe twenty, he would rouse the men and they would pack up and head west, where the maps showed the country to be green and inviting. They would do what they had always done. The rain might add some weight, but otherwise it would be one more day layered upon all the other days.

---

[7]**Sin loi** Sorry.

He was realistic about it. There was that new hardness in his stomach. He loved her but he hated her.

No more fantasies, he told himself.

Henceforth, when he thought about Martha, it would be only to think that she belonged elsewhere. He would shut down the daydreams. This was not Mount Sebastian, it was another world, where there were no pretty poems or midterm exams, a place where men died because of carelessness and gross stupidity. Kiowa was right. Boom-down, and you were dead, never partly dead.

95       Briefly, in the rain, Lieutenant Cross saw Martha's gray eyes gazing back at him.

He understood.

It was very sad, he thought. The things men carried inside. The things men did or felt they had to do.

He almost nodded at her, but didn't.

Instead he went back to his maps. He was now determined to perform his duties firmly and without negligence. It wouldn't help Lavender, he knew that, but from this point on he would comport himself as an officer. He would dispose of his good-luck pebble. Swallow it, maybe, or use Lee Strunk's slingshot, or just drop it along the trail. On the march he would impose strict field discipline. He would be careful to send out flank security, to prevent straggling or bunching up, to keep his troops moving at the proper pace and at the proper interval. He would insist on clean weapons. He would confiscate the remainder of Lavender's dope. Later in the day, perhaps, he would call the men together and speak to them plainly. He would accept the blame for what had happened to Ted Lavender. He would be a man about it. He would look them in the eyes, keeping his chin level, and he would issue the new SOPs in a calm, impersonal tone of voice, a lieutenant's voice, leaving no room for argument or discussion. Commencing immediately, he'd tell them, they would no longer abandon equipment along the route of march. They would police up their acts. They would get their shit together, and keep it together, and maintain it neatly and in good working order.

100      He would not tolerate laxity. He would show strength, distancing himself.

Among the men there would be grumbling, of course, and maybe worse, because their days would seem longer and their loads heavier, but Lieutenant Jimmy Cross reminded himself that his obligation was not to be loved but to lead. He would dispense with love; it was not now a factor. And if anyone quarreled or complained, he would simply tighten his lips and arrange his shoulders in the correct command posture. He might give a curt little nod. Or he might not. He might just shrug and say, Carry on, then they would saddle up and form into a column and move out toward the villages west of Than Khe.

# DANIEL OROZCO

*Daniel Orozco, born in San Francisco in 1957, is chiefly known for his short stories. A professor of creative writing at the University of Idaho, Orozco has received several important awards, including a grant from the National Endowment for the Arts.*

## *Orientation*                                                                [1994]

Those are the offices and these are the cubicles. That's my cubicle there, and this is your cubicle. This is your phone. Never answer your phone. Let the Voicemail System answer it. This is your Voicemail System Manual. There are no personal phone calls allowed. We do, however, allow for emergencies. If you must make an emergency phone call, ask your supervisor first. If you can't find your supervisor, ask Phillip Spiers, who sits over there. He'll check with Clarissa Nicks, who sits over there. If you make an emergency phone call without asking, you may be let go.

These are your IN and OUT boxes. All the forms in your IN box must be logged in by the date shown in the upper left-hand corner, initialed by you in the upper right-hand corner, and distributed to the Processing Analyst whose name is numerically coded in the lower left-hand corner. The lower right-hand corner is left blank. Here's your Processing Analyst Numerical Code Index. And here's your Forms Processing Procedures Manual.

You must pace your work. What do I mean? I'm glad you asked that. We pace our work according to the eight-hour workday. If you have twelve hours of work in your IN box, for example, you must compress that work into the eight-hour day. If you have one hour of work in your IN box, you must expand that work to fill the eight-hour day. That was a good question. Feel free to ask questions. Ask too many questions, however, and you may be let go.

That is our receptionist. She is a temp. We go through receptionists here. They quit with alarming frequency. Be polite and civil to the temps. Learn their names, and invite them to lunch occasionally. But don't get close to them, as it only makes it more difficult when they leave. And they always leave. You can be sure of that.

5          The men's room is over there. The women's room is over there. John LaFountaine, who sits over there, uses the women's room occasionally. He says it is accidental. We know better, but we let it pass. John LaFountaine is harmless, his forays into the forbidden territory of the women's room simply a benign thrill, a faint blip on the dull flat line of his life.

Russell Nash, who sits in the cubicle to your left, is in love with Amanda Pierce, who sits in the cubicle to your right. They ride the same bus together after work. For Amanda Pierce, it is just a tedious bus ride made less tedious by the idle nattering of Russell Nash. But for Russell Nash, it is the highlight of his day. It is the highlight of his life. Russell Nash has put on forty pounds; and grows fatter with each passing month, nibbling on chips and cookies while peeking glumly over the partitions at Amanda Pierce, and gorging himself at home on cold pizza and ice cream while watching adult videos on TV.

Amanda Pierce, in the cubicle to your right, has a six-year-old son named Jamie, who is autistic. Her cubicle is plastered from top to bottom with the boy's crayon artwork—sheet after sheet of precisely drawn concentric circles and ellipses, in black and yellow. She rotates them every other Friday. Be sure to comment on them. Amanda Pierce also has a husband, who is a lawyer. He subjects her to an escalating array of painful and humiliating sex games, to which Amanda Pierce reluctantly submits. She comes to work exhausted and freshly wounded each morning, wincing from the abrasions on her breasts, or the bruises on her abdomen, or the second-degree burns on the backs of her thighs.

But we're not supposed to know any of this. Do not let on. If you let on, you may be let go.

Amanda Pierce, who tolerates Russell Nash, is in love with Albert Bosch, whose office is over there. Albert Bosch, who only dimly registers Amanda Pierce's existence, has eyes only for Ellie Tapper, who sits over there. Ellie Tapper, who hates Albert Bosch, would walk through fire for Curtis Lance. But Curtis Lance hates Ellie Tapper. Isn't the world a funny place? Not in the ha-ha sense, of course.

10       Anika Bloom sits in that cubicle. Last year, while reviewing quarterly reports in a meeting with Barry Hacker, Anika Bloom's left palm began to bleed. She fell into a trance, stared into her hand, and told Barry Hacker when and how his wife would die. We laughed it off. She was, after all, a new employee. But Barry Hacker's wife is dead. So unless you want to know exactly when and how you'll die, never talk to Anika Bloom.

Colin Heavey sits in that cubicle over there. He was new once, just like you. We warned him about Anika Bloom. But at last year's Christmas Potluck, he felt sorry for her when he saw that no one was talking to her. Colin Heavey brought her a drink. He hasn't been himself since. Colin Heavey is doomed. There's nothing he can do about it, and we are powerless to help him. Stay away from Colin Heavey. Never give any of your work to him. If he asks to do something, tell him you have to check with me. If he asks again, tell him I haven't gotten back to you.

This is the Fire Exit. There are several on this floor, and they are marked accordingly. We have a Floor Evacuation Review every three months, and an Escape Route Quiz once a month. We have our Biannual Fire Drill twice a year, and our Annual Earthquake Drill once a year. These are precautions only. These things never happen.

For your information, we have a comprehensive health plan. Any catastrophic illness, any unforeseen tragedy is completely covered. All dependents are completely covered. Larry Bagdikian, who sits over there, has six daughters. If anything were to happen to any of his girls, or to all of them, if all six were to simultaneously fall victim to illness or injury—stricken with a hideous degenerative muscle disease or some rare toxic blood disorder, sprayed with semiautomatic gunfire while on a class field trip, or attacked in their bunk beds by some prowling nocturnal lunatic—if any of this were to pass, Larry's girls would all be taken care of. Larry Bagdikian would not have to pay one dime. He would have nothing to worry about.

We also have a generous vacation and sick leave policy. We have an excellent disability insurance plan. We have a stable and profitable pension fund. We get group discounts for the symphony, and block seating at the ballpark. We get commuter ticket books for the bridge. We have Direct Deposit. We are all members of Costco.

15       This is our kitchenette. And this, this is our Mr. Coffee. We have a coffee pool, into which we each pay two dollars a week for coffee, filters, sugar, and CoffeeMate. If you prefer Cremora or half-and-half to CoffeeMate, there is a special pool for three dollars a week. If you prefer Sweet 'n Low to sugar, there is a special pool for two-fifty a week. We do not do decaf. You are allowed to join the coffee pool of your choice, but you are not allowed to touch the Mr. Coffee.

This is the microwave oven. You are allowed to *heat* food in the microwave oven. You are not, however, allowed to *cook* food in the microwave oven.

We get one hour for lunch. We also get one fifteen-minute break in the morning, and one fifteen-minute break in the afternoon. Always take your breaks. If you skip a break, it is gone forever. For your information, your break is a privilege, not a right. If you abuse the break policy, we are authorized to rescind your breaks. Lunch, however, is a right, not a privilege. If you abuse the lunch policy, our hands will be tied, and we will be forced to look the other way. We will not enjoy that.

This is the refrigerator. You may put your lunch in it. Barry Hacker, who sits over there, steals food from this refrigerator. His petty theft is an outlet for his grief. Last New Year's Eve, while kissing his wife, a blood-vessel burst in her brain. Barry Hacker's wife was two months pregnant at the time, and lingered in a coma for half a year before dying. It was a tragic loss for Barry Hacker. He hasn't been himself since. Barry Hacker's wife was a beautiful woman. She was also completely covered. Barry Hacker did not have to pay one dime. But his dead wife haunts him. She haunts all of us. We have seen her, reflected in the monitors of our computers, moving past our cubicles. We have seen the dim shadow of her face in our photocopies. She pencils herself in in the receptionist's appointment book, with the notation: To see Barry Hacker. She has left messages in the receptionist's Voicemail box, messages garbled by the electronic chirrups and buzzes in the phone line, her voice echoing from an immense distance within the ambient hum. But the voice is hers. And beneath her voice, beneath the tidal *whoosh* of static and hiss, the gurgling and crying of a baby can be heard.

In any case, if you bring a lunch, put a little something extra in the bag for Barry Hacker. We have four Barrys in this office. Isn't that a coincidence?

20    This is Matthew Payne's office. He is our Unit Manager, and his door is always closed. We have never seen him, and you will never see him. But he is here. You can be sure of that. He is all around us.

This is the Custodian's Closet. You have no business in the Custodian's Closet.

And this, this is our Supplies Cabinet. If you need supplies, see Curtis Lance. He will log you in on the Supplies Cabinet Authorization Log, then give you a Supplies Authorization Slip. Present your pink copy of the Supplies Authorization Slip to Ellie Tapper. She will log you in on the Supplies Cabinet Key Log, then give you the key. Because the Supplies Cabinet is located outside the Unit Manager's office, you must be very quiet. Gather your supplies quietly. The Supplies Cabinet is divided into four sections. Section One contains letterhead stationary, blank paper and envelopes, memo and note pads, and so on. Section Two contains pens and pencils and typewriter and printer ribbons, and the like. In Section Three we have erasers, correction fluids, transparent tapes, glue sticks, et cetera. And in Section Four we have paper clips and push pins and scissors and razor blades. And here are the spare blades for the shredder. Do not touch the shredder, which is located over there. The shredder is of no concern to you.

Gwendolyn Stich sits in that office there. She is crazy about penguins, and collects penguin knickknacks: penguin posters and coffee mugs and stationery, penguin stuffed animals, penguin jewelry, penguin sweaters and T-shirts and socks. She has a pair of penguin fuzzy slippers she wears when working late at the office. She has a tape cassette of penguin sounds which she listens to for relaxation. Her favorite colors are black and white. She has personalized license plates that read PEN GWEN. Every morning, she passes through all the cubicles to wish each of us a *good* morning. She brings Danish on Wednesdays for Hump Day morning break, and doughnuts on Fridays for TGIF afternoon break. She organizes the Annual Christmas Potluck, and is in charge of the Birthday List. Gwendolyn Stich's door is always open to all of us. She will always lend an ear, and put in a good word for you; she will always give you a hand, or the shirt off her back, or a shoulder to cry on. Because her door is always open, she hides and cries in a stall in the women's room. And John LaFountaine—who, enthralled when a woman enters, sits quietly in his stall with his knees to his chest—John LaFountaine has heard her vomiting in there. We have come upon Gwendolyn Stich huddled in the stairwell, shivering in the updraft, sipping a Diet Mr. Pibb and hugging her knees. She does not let any of this interfere with her work. If it interfered with her work, she might have to be let go.

Kevin Howard sits in that cubicle over there. He is a serial killer, the one they call the Carpet Cutter, responsible for the mutilations across town. We're not supposed to know that, so do not let on. Don't worry. His compulsion inflicts itself on strangers only, and the routine established is elaborate and unwavering. The victim must be a white male, a young adult no older than thirty, heavyset, with dark hair and eyes, and the like. The victim must be chosen at random, before sunset, from a public place; the victim is followed home, and must put up a struggle, et cetera. The carnage inflicted is precise: the angle and direction of the incisions; the layering of skin and muscle tissue; the rearrangement of the visceral organs, and so on. Kevin Howard does not let any of this interfere with his work. He is, in fact, our fastest typist. He types as if he were on fire. He has a secret crush on Gwendolyn Stich, and leaves a red-foil-wrapped Hershey's Kiss on her desk every afternoon. But he hates Anika Bloom, and keeps well away from her. In his presence, she has uncontrollable fits of shaking and trembling. Her left palm does not stop bleeding.

25        In any case, when Kevin Howard gets caught, act surprised. Say that he seemed like a nice person, a bit of a loner, perhaps, but always quiet and polite.

This is the photocopier room. And this, this is our view. It faces southwest. West is down there, toward the water. North is back there. Because we are on the seventeenth floor, we are afforded a magnificent view. Isn't it beautiful? It overlooks the park, where the tops of those trees are. You can see a segment of the bay between those two buildings there. You can see the sun set in the gap between those two buildings over there. You can see this building reflected in the glass panels of that building across the way. There. See? That's you, waving. And look there. There's Anika Bloom in the kitchenette, waving back.

Enjoy this view while photocopying. If you have problems with the photocopier, see Russell Nash. If you have any questions, ask your supervisor. If you can't find your supervisor, ask Phillip Spiers. He sits over there. He'll check with Clarissa Nicks. She sits over there. If you can't find them, feel free to ask me. That's my cubicle. I sit in there.

# EDGAR ALLAN POE

*Edgar Allan Poe (1809–1849) born in Boston, was the son of traveling actors. His father abandoned the family almost immediately after Poe was born, and his mother died when he was two. The child was adopted—though never legally—by a prosperous merchant and his wife in Richmond, Virginia. The tensions were great, aggravated by Poe's drinking and heavy gambling, and in 1827 Poe left Richmond for Boston. He wrote, served briefly in the army, attended West Point but left within a year, and became an editor for the remaining eighteen years of his life. It was during these years, too, that he wrote the poems, essays, and fiction—especially detective stories and horror stories— that have made him famous.*

## The Cask of Amontillado                      [1846]

The thousand injuries of Fortunato I had borne as I best could; but when he ventured upon insult, I vowed revenge. You, who so well know the nature of my soul, will not suppose, however, that I gave utterance to a threat. *At length* I would be avenged; this was a point definitely settled—but the very definitiveness with which it was resolved, precluded the idea of risk. I must not only punish, but punish with impunity. A wrong is unredressed when retribution overtakes its redresser. It is equally unredressed when the avenger fails to make himself felt as such to him who has done the wrong.

It must be understood, that neither by word nor deed had I given Fortunato cause to doubt my good will. I continued, as was my wont, to smile in his face, and he did not perceive that my smile *now* was at the thought of his immolation.

He had a weak point—this Fortunato—although in other regards he was a man to be respected and even feared. He prided himself on his connoisseurship in wine. Few Italians have the true virtuoso spirit. For the most part their enthusiasm is adopted to suit the time and opportunity—to practise imposture upon the British and Austrian *millionaires*. In painting and gemmary Fortunato, like his countrymen, was a quack—but in the matter of old wines he was sincere. In this respect I did not differ from him materially: I was skilful in the Italian vintages myself, and bought largely whenever I could.

It was about dusk, one evening during the supreme madness of the carnival season, that I encountered my friend. He accosted me with excessive warmth, for he had been drinking much. The man wore motley. He had on a tight-fitting parti-striped dress, and his head was surmounted by the conical cap and bells. I was so pleased to see him, that I thought I should never have done wringing his hand.

5      I said to him—"My dear Fortunato, you are luckily met. How remarkably well you are looking to-day! But I have received a pipe[1] of what passes for Amontillado, and I have my doubts."

"How?" said he. "Amontillado? A pipe? Impossible! And in the middle of the carnival?"

"I have my doubts," I replied; "and I was silly enough to pay the full Amontillado price without consulting you in the matter. You were not to be found, and I was fearful of losing a bargain."

"Amontillado!"

"I have my doubts."

10     "Amontillado!"

---

[1]**pipe** wine cask.

"And I must satisfy them."

"Amontillado!"

"As you are engaged, I am on my way to Luchesi. If any one has a critical turn, it is he. He will tell me——"

"Luchesi cannot tell Amontillado from Sherry."

15   "And yet some fools will have it that his taste is a match for your own."

"Come, let us go."

"Whither?"

"To your vaults."

"My friend, no; I will not impose upon your good nature. I perceive you have an engagement. Luchesi——"

20   "I have no engagement;—come."

"My friend, no. It is not the engagement, but the severe cold with which I perceive you are afflicted. The vaults are insufferably damp. They are encrusted with nitre."

"Let us go, nevertheless. The cold is merely nothing. Amontillado! You have been imposed upon. And as for Luchesi, he cannot distinguish Sherry from Amontillado."

Thus speaking, Fortunato possessed himself of my arm. Putting on a mask of black silk, and drawing a *roquelaire*[2] closely about my person, I suffered him to hurry me to my palazzo.

There were no attendants at home; they had absconded to make merry in honor of the time. I had told them that I should not return until the morning, and had given them explicit orders not to stir from the house. These orders were sufficient, I well knew, to insure their immediate disappearance, one and all, as soon as my back was turned.

25   I took from their sconces two flambeaux, and giving one to Fortunato, bowed him through several suites of rooms to the archway that led into the vaults. I passed down a long and winding staircase, requesting him to be cautious as he followed. We came at length to the foot of the descent, and stood together on the damp ground of the catacombs of the Montresors.

The gait of my friend was unsteady, and the bells upon his cap jingled as he strode.

"The pipe," said he.

"It is farther on," said I; "but observe the white web-work which gleams from these cavern walls."

He turned towards me, and looked into my eyes with two filmy orbs that distilled the rheum of intoxication.

30   "Nitre?" he asked, at length.

"Nitre," I replied. "How long have you had that cough?"

"Ugh! ugh! ugh!—ugh! ugh! ugh!—ugh! ugh! ugh!—ugh! ugh! ugh!— ugh! ugh! ugh!"

My poor friend found it impossible to reply for many minutes.

"It is nothing," he said, at last.

35   "Come," I said, with decision, "we will go back; your health is precious. You are rich, respected, admired, beloved; you are happy, as once I was. You are a man to be missed. For me it is no matter. We will go back; you will be ill, and I cannot be responsible. Besides, there is Luchesi——"

---

[2]**roquelaire** short cloak.

"Enough," he said; "the cough is a mere nothing; it will not kill me. I shall not die of a cough."

"True—true," I replied; "and, indeed, I had no intention of alarming you unnecessarily—but you should use all proper caution. A draught of this Medoc will defend us from the damps."

Here I knocked off the neck of a bottle which I drew from a long row of its fellows that lay upon the mould.

"Drink," I said, presenting him the wine.

40      He raised it to his lips with a leer. He paused and nodded to me familiarly, while his bells jingled.

"I drink," he said, "to the buried that repose around us."

"And I to your long life."

He again took my arm, and we proceeded.

"These vaults," he said, "are extensive."

45      "The Montresors," I replied, "were a great and numerous family."

"I forget your arms."

"A huge human foot d'or, in a field azure; the foot crushes a serpent rampant whose fangs are imbedded in the heel."

"And the motto?"

*Nemo me impune lacessit.*[3]

50      "Good!" he said.

The wine sparkled in his eyes and the bells jingled. My own fancy grew warm with the Medoc. We had passed through walls of piled bones, with casks and puncheons intermingling, into the inmost recesses of the catacombs. I paused again, and this time I made bold to seize Fortunato by an arm above the elbow.

"The nitre!" I said; "see, it increases. It hangs like moss upon the vaults. We are below the river's bed. The drops of moisture trickle among the bones. Come, we will go back ere it is too late. Your cough——"

"It is nothing," he said; "let us go on. But first, another draught of the Medoc."

I broke and reached him a flaçon of De Grâve. He emptied it at a breath. His eyes flashed with a fierce light. He laughed and threw the bottle upwards with a gesticulation I did not understand.

55      I looked at him in surprise. He repeated the movement—a grotesque one.

"You do not comprehend?" he said.

"Not I," I replied.

"Then you are not of the brotherhood."

"How?"

60      "You are not of the masons."

"Yes, yes," I said, "yes, yes."

"You? Impossible! A mason?"

"A mason," I replied.

"A sign," he said.

65      "It is this," I answered, producing a trowel from beneath the folds of my *roquelaire.*

---

[3]**Nemo me impune lacessit.** No one dare attack me with impunity (the motto of Scotland).

"You jest," he exclaimed, recoiling a few paces. "But let us proceed to the Amontillado."

"Be it so," I said, replacing the tool beneath the cloak, and again offering him my arm. He leaned upon it heavily. We continued our route in search of the Amontillado. We passed through a range of low arches, descended, passed on, and descending again, arrived at a deep crypt, in which the foulness of the air caused our flambeaux rather to glow than flame.

At the most remote end of the crypt there appeared another less spacious. Its walls had been lined with human remains, piled to the vault overhead, in the fashion of the great catacombs of Paris. Three sides of this interior crypt were still ornamented in this manner. From the fourth the bones had been thrown down, and lay promiscuously upon the earth, forming at one point a mound of some size. Within the wall thus exposed by the displacing of the bones, we perceived a still interior recess, in depth about four feet, in width three, in height six or seven. It seemed to have been constructed for no especial use within itself, but formed merely the interval between two of the colossal supports of the roof of the catacombs, and was backed by one of their circumscribing walls of solid granite.

It was in vain that Fortunato, uplifting his dull torch, endeavored to pry into the depth of the recess. Its termination the feeble light did not enable us to see.

70    "Proceed," I said; "herein is the Amontillado. As for Luchesi——"

"He is an ignoramus," interrupted my friend, as he stepped unsteadily forward, while I followed immediately at his heels. In an instant he had reached the extremity of the niche, and finding his progress arrested by the rock, stood stupidly bewildered. A moment more and I had fettered him to the granite. In its surface were two iron staples, distant from each other about two feet, horizontally. From one of these depended a short chain, from the other a padlock. Throwing the links about his waist, it was but the work of a few seconds to secure it. He was too much astounded to resist. Withdrawing the key I stepped back from the recess.

"Pass your hand," I said, "over the wall; you cannot help feeling the nitre. Indeed it is *very* damp. Once more let me *implore* you to return. No? Then I must positively leave you. But I must first render you all the little attentions in my power."

"The Amontillado!" ejaculated my friend, not yet recovered from his astonishment.

"True," I replied; "the Amontillado."

75    As I said these words I busied myself among the pile of bones of which I have before spoken. Throwing them aside, I soon uncovered a quantity of building stone and mortar. With these materials and with the aid of my trowel, I began vigorously to wall up the entrance of the niche.

I had scarcely laid the first tier of the masonry when I discovered that the intoxication of Fortunato had in a great measure worn off. The earliest indication I had of this was a low moaning cry from the depth of the recess. It was *not* the cry of a drunken man. There was then a long and obstinate silence. I laid the second tier, and the third, and the fourth; and then I heard the furious vibrations of the chain. The noise lasted for several minutes, during which, that I might hearken to it with the more satisfaction, I ceased my labors and sat down upon the bones. When at last the clanking subsided, I resumed the trowel, and finished without interruption the fifth, the sixth, and the seventh tier. The wall was now nearly upon a level with my breast. I again paused, and holding the flambeaux over the mason-work, threw a few feeble rays upon the figure within.

A succession of loud and shrill screams, bursting suddenly from the throat of the chained form, seemed to thrust me violently back. For a brief moment I hesitated—I trembled. Unsheathing my rapier, I began to grope with it about the recess: but the thought of an instant reassured me. I placed my hand upon the solid fabric of the catacombs, and felt satisfied. I reapproached the wall. I replied to the yells of him who clamored. I re-echoed—I aided—I surpassed them in volume and in strength. I did this, and the clamorer grew still.

It was now midnight, and my task was drawing to a close. I had completed the eighth, the ninth, and the tenth tier. I had finished a portion of the last and the eleventh; there remained but a single stone to be fitted and plastered in. I struggled with its weight; I placed it partially in its destined position. But now there came from out the niche a low laugh that erected the hairs upon my head. It was succeeded by a sad voice, which I had difficulty in recognising as that of the noble Fortunato. The voice said—

"Ha! ha! ha!—he! he!—a very good joke indeed—an excellent jest. We will have many a rich laugh about it at the palazzo—he! he! he!—over our wine—he! he! he!"

80     "The Amontillado!" I said.

"He! he! he!—he! he! he!—yes, the Amontillado. But is it not getting late? Will not they be awaiting us at the palazzo, the Lady Fortunato and the rest? Let us be gone."

"Yes," I said, "let us be gone."

*"For the love of God, Montresor!"*

"Yes," I said, "for the love of God!"

85     But to these words I hearkened in vain for a reply. I grew impatient. I called aloud—

"Fortunato!"

No answer. I called again—

"Fortunato!"

No answer still. I thrust a torch through the remaining aperture and let it fall within. There came forth in return only a jingling of the bells. My heart grew sick—on account of the dampness of the catacombs. I hastened to make an end of my labor. I forced the last stone into its position; I plastered it up. Against the new masonry I re-erected the old rampart of bones. For the half of a century no mortal has disturbed them. *In pace requiescat!*[4]

---

[4]*In pace requiescat!* May he rest in peace!

# MICHELE SERROS

*Michele Serros, born in Oxnard, California, in 1966, published her first book of poems and stories,* Chicana Falsa and Other Stories of Death, Identity and Oxnard, *while she was still a student at Santa Monica City College. We reprint a story from her second book,* How to Be a Chicana Role Model *(2000), which achieved national attention.*

## Senior Picture Day     [2000]

Sometimes I put two different earrings in the same ear. And that's on a day I'm feeling preppy, not really new wave or anything. One time, during a track meet over at Camarillo High, I discovered way too late that I'd forgot to put on deodorant and that was the worst 'cause everyone knows how snooty those girls at Camarillo can be. Hmmm. Actually the worst thing I've ever forgotten to do was take my pill. That happened three mornings in a row and you can bet I was praying for weeks after that.

So many things to remember when you're seventeen years old and your days start at six a.m. and sometimes don't end until five in the afternoon. But today of all days there's one thing I have to remember to do and that's to squeeze my nose. I've been doing it since the seventh grade. Every morning with my thumb and forefinger I squeeze the sides of it, firmly pressing my nostrils as close as they possibly can get near the base. Sometimes while I'm waiting for the tortilla to heat up, or just when I'm brushing my teeth, I squeeze. Nobody ever notices. Nobody ever asks. With all the other shit seniors in high school go through, squeezing my nose is nothing. It's just like some regular early-morning routine, like yawning or wiping the egg from my eyes. Okay, so you might think it's just a total waste of time, but to tell you the truth, I do see the difference. Just last week I lined up all my class pictures and could definitely see the progress. My nose has actually become smaller, narrower. It looks less Indian. *I* look less Indian and you can bet that's the main goal here. Today, when I take my graduation pictures, my nose will look just like Terri's and then I'll have the best picture in the yearbook. I think about this as Mrs. Milne's Duster comes honking in the driveway to take me to school.

Terri was my best friend in seventh grade. She came from Washington to Rio Del Valle Junior High halfway through October. She was the first girl I knew who had contact lenses and *four* pairs of Chemin de Fers. Can you believe that? She told everyone that her daddy was gonna build 'em a swimming pool for the summer. She told me that I could go over to swim anytime I wanted. But until then, she told me, I could go over and we could play on her dad's CB.[1]

"Your dad's really got a CB?" I asked her.

5       "Oh, yeah," she answered, jiggling her locker door. "You can come over and we can make up handles for ourselves and meet lots of guys. Cute ones."

"Whaddaya mean, handles?" I asked.

"Like names, little nicknames. I never use my real name. I'm 'G.G.' when I get on. That stands for Golden Girl. Oh, and you gotta make sure you end every sentence with 'over.' You're like a total nerd if you don't finish with 'over.' I never talk to anyone who doesn't say 'over.' They're the worst."

Nobody's really into citizen band radios anymore. I now see 'em all lined up in pawnshops over on Oxnard Boulevard. But back in the seventh grade, everyone was getting them. They were way better than using a phone 'cause, first of all, there was no phone bill to bust you for talking to boys who lived

---

[1]**CB** Citizens Band (a radio frequency used by the general public to talk to one another over a short distance).

past The Grade and second, you didn't have your stupid sister yelling at you for tying up the phone line. Most people had CBs in their cars, but Terri's dad had his in the den.

When I showed up at Terri's to check out the CB, her mama was in the front yard planting some purple flowers.

10     "Go on in already." She waved me in. "She's in her father's den."

I found Terri just like her mama said. She was already on the CB, looking flustered and sorta excited.

"Hey," I called out to her, and plopped my tote bag on her dad's desk.

She didn't answer but rather motioned to me with her hands to hurry up. Her mouth formed an exaggerated, "Oh, *my* God!" She held out a glass bowl of Pringles and pointed to a glass of Dr Pepper on the desk.

It turned out Terri had found a boy on the CB. An older *interested* one. He was fifteen, a skateboarder, and his handle was Lightning Bolt.

15     "Lightning Bolt," he bragged to Terri. "Like, you know, powerful and fast. That's the way I skate. So," he continued, "where you guys live? Over."

"We live near Malibu," Terri answered. "Between Malibu and Santa Barbara. Over."

"Oh, excuse me, fan-ceee. Over."

"That's right." Terri giggled. "Over."

We actually lived in Oxnard. Really, in El Rio, a flat patch of houses, churches, and schools surrounded by lots of strawberry fields and some new snooty stucco homes surrounded by chainlink. But man, did Terri have this way of making things sound better. I mean, it *was* the truth, geographically, and besides it sounded way more glamorous.

20     I took some Pringles from the bowl and thought we were gonna have this wonderful afternoon of talking and flirting with Lightning Bolt until Terri's dad happened to come home early and found us gabbing in his den.

"What the . . . !" he yelled as soon as he walked in and saw us hunched over his CB. "What do you think this is? Party Central? Get off that thing!" He grabbed the receiver from Terri's hand. "This isn't a toy! It's a tool. A tool for communication, you don't use it just to meet boys!"

"Damn, Dad," Terri complained as she slid off her father's desk. "Don't have a cow." She took my hand and led me to her room. "Come on, let's pick you out a handle."

When we were in her room, I told her I had decided on Cali Girl as my handle.

"You mean, like California?" she asked.

25     "Yeah, sorta."

"But you're Mexican."

"So?"

"So, you look like you're more from Mexico than California."

"What do you mean?"

30     "I mean, California is like, blond girls, you know."

"Yeah, but I *am* Californian. I mean, real Californian. Even my great-grandma was born here."

"It's just that you don't look like you're from California."

"And you're not exactly golden," I snapped.

* * *

We decided to talk to Lightning Bolt the next day, Friday, right after school. Terri's dad always came home real late on Fridays, sometimes even early the next Saturday morning. It would be perfect. When I got to her house the garage door was wide open and I went in through the side door. I almost bumped into Terri's mama. She was spraying the house with Pine Scent and offered me some Hi-C.

35     "Help yourself to a Pudding Pop, too," she said before heading into the living room through a mist of aerosol. "They're in the freezer."

Man, Terri's mama made their whole life like an afternoon commercial. Hi-C, Pringles in a bowl, the whole house smelling like a pine forest. Was Terri lucky or what? I grabbed a Pudding Pop out of the freezer and was about to join her when I picked up on her laugh. She was already talking to Lightning Bolt. Dang, she didn't waste time!

"Well, maybe we don't ever want to meet you," I heard Terri flirt with Lightning Bolt. "How do you know we don't already have boyfriends? Over."

"Well, you both sound like foxes. So, uh, what *do* you look like? Over."

"I'm about five-four and have green eyes and ginger-colored hair. Over."

40     Green? Ginger? I always took Terri for having brown eyes and brown hair.

"What about your friend? Over."

"What about her? Over."

Oh, this was about me! I *had* to hear this. Terri knew how to pump up things good.

"I mean, what does she look like?" Lightning Bolt asked. "She sounds cute. Over."

45     "Well . . ." I overheard Terri hesitate. "Well, she's real skinny and, uh . . ."

"I like skinny girls!"

"You didn't let me finish!" Terri interrupted. "And you didn't say 'over.' Over."

"Sorry," Lightning Bolt said. "Go ahead and finish. Over."

I tore the wrapper off the Pudding Pop and continued to listen.

50     "Well," Terri continued. "She's also sorta flat-chested, I guess. Over."

*What?* How could Terri say that?

"Flat-chested? Oh yeah? Over." Lightning Bolt answered.

"Yeah. Over."

Terri paused uncomfortably. It was as if she knew what she was saying was wrong and bad and she should've stopped but couldn't. She was saying things about a friend, things a real friend shouldn't be saying about another friend, but now there was a boy involved and he was interested in that other friend, in me, and her side was losing momentum. She would have to continue to stay ahead.

55     "Yeah, and she also has this, this nose, a nose like . . . like an *Indian*. Over."

"An, Indian?" Lightning Bolt asked. "What do ya mean an Indian? Over."

"You know, *Indian*. Like powwow Indian."

"Really?" Lightning Bolt laughed on the other end. "Like Woo-Woo-Woo Indian?" He clapped his palm over his mouth and wailed. A sound I knew all too well.

"Yeah, just like that!" Terri laughed. "In fact, I think she's gonna pick 'Li'l Squaw' as her handle!"

60          I shut the refrigerator door quietly. I touched the ridge of my nose. I felt
the bump my mother had promised me would be less noticeable once my
face "filled out." The base of my nose was far from feminine and was broad,
like, well, like Uncle Rudy's nose, Grandpa Rudy's nose, and yeah, a little bit
of Uncle Vincente's nose, too. Men in my family who looked like Indians and
here their Indian noses were lumped together on me, on my face. My nose
made me look like I didn't belong, made me look less Californian than my
blond counterparts. After hearing Terri and Lightning Bolt laugh, more than
anything I hated the men in my family who had given me such a hideous
nose.

          I grabbed my tote bag and started to leave out through the garage door
when Terri's mama called out from the living room. "You're leaving already?"
she asked. "I know Terri would love to have you for dinner. Her daddy's
working late again."

          I didn't answer and I didn't turn around. I just walked out and went
home.

          And so that's how the squeezing began. I eventually stopped hanging
out with Terri and never got a chance to use my handle on her dad's CB. I
know it's been almost four years since she said all that stuff about me, about
my nose, but man, it still stings.

          During freshman year I heard that Terri's dad met some lady on the CB
and left her mama for this other woman. Can you believe that? Who'd wanna
leave a house that smelled like a pine forest and always had Pudding Pops in
the freezer?

65          As Mrs. Milne honks from the driveway impatiently, I grab my books and
run down the driveway, squeezing my nose just a little bit more. I do it because
today is Senior Picture Day and because I do notice the difference. I might be
too skinny. My chest might be too flat. But God forbid I look too Indian.

# LESLIE MARMON SILKO

*Leslie Marmon Silko was born in 1948 in Albuquerque, New Mexico, and
grew up on the Laguna Pueblo Reservation some fifty miles to the west. Of her
family she says,*

> *We are mixed blood—Laguna, Mexican, white. . . . All those languages,
> all those ways of living are combined, and we live somewhere on the
> fringes of all three. But I don't apologize for this any more—not to
> whites, not to full bloods—our origin is unlike any other. My poetry,
> my storytelling rise out of this source.*

*After graduating from the University of New Mexico in 1969, Silko en-
tered law school but soon left to become a writer. She taught for two years at
Navajo Community College at Many Farms, Arizona, and then went to
Alaska for two years where she studied Eskimo-Aleut culture and worked on
a novel,* Ceremony. *After returning to the Southwest, she taught at the University of Arizona and then at the University of New Mexico. Silko's recent
books include the novels* Almanac of the Dead *(1991) and* Gardens in the
Dunes *(2000).*

*In addition to writing stories, a novel, and poems, Silko has written the
screenplay for Marlon Brando's film,* Black Elk. *In 1981 she was awarded one
of the so-called genius grants from the MacArthur Foundation, which supports "exceptionally talented individuals."*

## The Man to Send Rain Clouds                                    [1969]

They found him under a big cottonwood tree. His Levi jacket and pants
were faded light blue so that he had been easy to find. The big cottonwood
tree stood apart from a small grove of winterbare cottonwoods which grew
in the wide, sandy arroyo. He had been dead for a day or more, and the
sheep had wandered and scattered up and down the arroyo. Leon and his
brother-in-law, Ken, gathered the sheep and left them in the pen at the sheep
camp before they returned to the cottonwood tree. Leon waited under the
tree while Ken drove the truck through the deep sand to the edge of the
arroyo. He squinted up at the sun and unzipped his jacket—it sure was hot
for this time of year. But high and northwest the blue mountains were still in
snow. Ken came sliding down the low, crumbling bank about fifty yards
down, and he was bringing the red blanket.

Before they wrapped the old man, Leon took a piece of string out of his
pocket and tied a small gray feather in the old man's long white hair. Ken
gave him the paint. Across the brown wrinkled forehead he drew a streak of
white and along the high cheekbones he drew a strip of blue paint. He
paused and watched Ken throw pinches of corn meal and pollen into the
wind that fluttered the small gray feather. Then Leon painted with yellow
under the old man's broad nose, and finally, when he had painted green
across the chin, he smiled.

"Send us rain clouds, Grandfather." They laid the bundle in the back of
the pickup and covered it with a heavy tarp before they started back to the
pueblo.

They turned off the highway onto the sandy pueblo road. Not long after
they passed the store and post office they saw Father Paul's car coming toward them. When he recognized their faces he slowed his car and waved for
them to stop. The young priest rolled down the car window.

5        "Did you find old Teofilo?" he asked loudly.

Leon stopped the truck. "Good morning, Father. We were just out to the
sheep camp. Everything is O.K. now."

"Thank God for that. Teofilo is a very old man. You really shouldn't allow
him to stay at the sheep camp alone."

"No, he won't do that any more now."

"Well, I'm glad you understand. I hope I'll be seeing you at Mass this
week—we missed you last Sunday. See if you can get old Teofilo to come
with you." The priest smiled and waved at them as they drove away.

10       Louise and Teresa were waiting. The table was set for lunch, and the coffee
was boiling on the black iron stove. Leon looked at Louise and then at Teresa.

"We found him under a cottonwood tree in the big arroyo near sheep
camp. I guess he sat down to rest in the shade and never got up again." Leon
walked toward the old man's bed. The red plaid shawl had been shaken and
spread carefully over the bed, and a new brown flannel shirt and pair of stiff

new Levi's were arranged neatly beside the pillow. Louise held the screen door open while Leon and Ken carried in the red blanket. He looked small and shriveled, and after they dressed him in the new shirt and pants he seemed more shrunken.

It was noontime now because the church bells rang the Angelus.[1] They ate the beans with hot bread, and nobody said anything until after Teresa poured the coffee.

Ken stood up and put on his jacket. "I'll see about the gravediggers. Only the top layer of soil is frozen. I think it can be ready before dark."

Leon nodded his head and finished his coffee. After Ken had been gone for a while, the neighbors and clanspeople came quietly to embrace Teofilo's family and to leave food on the table because the gravediggers would come to eat when they were finished.

15      The sky in the west was full of pale yellow light. Louise stood outside with her hands in the pockets of Leon's green army jacket that was too big for her. The funeral was over, and the old men had taken their candles and medicine bags and were gone. She waited until the body was laid into the pickup before she said anything to Leon. She touched his arm, and he noticed that her hands were still dusty from the corn meal that she had sprinkled around the old man. When she spoke, Leon could not hear her.

"What did you say? I didn't hear you."

"I said that I had been thinking about something."

"About what?"

"About the priest sprinkling holy water for Grandpa. So he won't be thirsty."

20      Leon stared at the new moccasins that Teofilo had made for the ceremonial dances in the summer. They were nearly hidden by the red blanket. It was getting colder, and the wind pushed gray dust down the narrow pueblo road. The sun was approaching the long mesa where it disappeared during the winter. Louise stood there shivering and watching his face. Then he zipped up his jacket and opened the truck door. "I'll see if he's there."

Ken stopped the pickup at the church, and Leon got out; and then Ken drove down the hill to the graveyard where people were waiting. Leon knocked at the old carved door with its symbols of the Lamb. While he waited he looked up at the twin bells from the king of Spain with the last sunlight pouring around them in their tower.

The priest opened the door and smiled when he saw who it was. "Come in! What brings you here this evening?"

The priest walked toward the kitchen, and Leon stood with his cap in his hand, playing with the earflaps and examining the living room—the brown sofa, the green armchair, and the brass lamp that hung down from the ceiling by links of chain. The priest dragged a chair out of the kitchen and offered it to Leon.

"No thank you, Father. I only came to ask you if you would bring your holy water to the graveyard."

---

[1] **Angelus** a devotional prayer commemorating the Annunciation (the angel Gabriel's announcement of the Incarnation of God in the human form of Jesus).

25        The priest turned away from Leon and looked out the window at the patio full of shadows and the dining-room windows of the nuns' cloister across the patio. The curtains were heavy, and the light from within faintly penetrated; it was impossible to see the nuns inside eating supper. "Why didn't you tell me he was dead? I could have brought the Last Rites anyway."

Leon smiled. "It wasn't necessary, Father."

The priest stared down at his scuffed brown loafers and the worn hem of his cassock. "For a Christian burial it was necessary."

His voice was distant, and Leon thought that his blue eyes looked tired.

"It's O.K., Father, we just want him to have plenty of water."

30        The priest sank down into the green chair and picked up a glossy missionary magazine. He turned the colored pages full of lepers and pagans without looking at them.

"You know I can't do that, Leon. There should have been the Last Rites and a funeral Mass at the very least."

Leon put on his green cap and pulled the flaps down over his ears. "It's getting late, Father. I've got to go."

When Leon opened the door Father Paul stood up and said, "Wait." He left the room and came back wearing a long brown overcoat. He followed Leon out the door and across the dim churchyard to the adobe steps in front of the church. They both stooped to fit through the low adobe entrance. And when they started down the hill to the graveyard only half of the sun was visible above the mesa.

The priest approached the grave slowly, wondering how they had managed to dig into the frozen ground; and then he remembered that this was New Mexico, and saw the pile of cold loose sand beside the hole. The people stood close to each other with little clouds of steam puffing from their faces. The priest looked at them and saw a pile of jackets, gloves, and scarves in the yellow, dry tumbleweeds that grew in the graveyard. He looked at the red blanket, not sure that Teofilo was so small, wondering if it wasn't some perverse Indian trick—something they did in March to ensure a good harvest—wondering if maybe old Teofilo was actually at sheep camp corraling the sheep for the night. But there he was, facing into a cold dry wind and squinting at the last sunlight, ready to bury a red wool blanket while the faces of his parishioners were in shadow with the last warmth of the sun on their backs.

35        His fingers were stiff, and it took him a long time to twist the lid off the holy water. Drops of water fell on the red blanket and soaked into dark icy spots. He sprinkled the grave and the water disappeared almost before it touched the dim, cold sand; it reminded him of something—he tried to remember what it was, because he thought if he could remember he might understand this. He sprinkled more water; he shook the container until it was empty, and the water fell through the light from sundown like August rain that fell while the sun was still shining, almost evaporating before it touched the wilted squash flowers.

The wind pulled at the priest's brown Franciscan robe and swirled away the corn meal and pollen that had been sprinkled on the blanket. They lowered the bundle into the ground, and they didn't bother to untie the stiff pieces of new rope that were tied around the ends of the blanket. The sun was gone, and over on the highway the eastbound lane was full of headlights. The priest walked away slowly. Leon watched him climb the hill, and when he had disappeared within the tall, thick walls, Leon turned to look up at the high blue mountains in the deep snow that reflected a faint red light from the west. He felt good because it was finished, and he was happy about the sprinkling of the holy water; now the old man could send them big thunderclouds for sure.

# AMY TAN

*Amy Tan was born in 1952 in Oakland, California, two and a half years after her parents had emigrated from China. She entered Linfield College in Oregon but then followed a boyfriend to California State University at San Jose, where she shifted her major from premedical studies to English. After earning a master's degree in linguistics from San Jose, Tan worked as a language consultant and then, under the name of May Brown, as a freelance business writer.*

*In 1985, having decided to try her hand at fiction, she joined the Squaw Valley Community of Writers, a fiction workshop. In 1987 she visited China with her mother; on her return to the United States she learned that her agent had sold her first book,* The Joy Luck Club, *a collection of 16 interwoven stories (including "Two Kinds") about four Chinese mothers and their four American daughters. She is also author of* The Kitchen God's Wife *(1991),* The Hundred Secret Senses *(1995), and* The Bonesetter's Daughter *(2001).*

## *Two Kinds*

[1989]

My mother believed you could be anything you wanted to be in America. You could open a restaurant. You could work for the government and get good retirement. You could buy a house with almost no money down. You could become rich. You could become instantly famous.

"Of course you can be prodigy, too," my mother told me when I was nine. "You can be best anything. What does Auntie Lindo know? Her daughter, she is only best tricky."

America was where all my mother's hopes lay. She had come here in 1949 after losing everything in China: her mother and father, her family home, her first husband, and two daughters, twin baby girls. But she never looked back with regret. There were so many ways for things to get better.

We didn't immediately pick the right kind of prodigy. At first my mother thought I could be a Chinese Shirley Temple. We'd watch Shirley's old movies on TV as though they were training films. My mother would poke my arm and say, "*Ni kan*"—You watch. And I would see Shirley tapping her feet, or singing a sailor song, or pursing her lips into a very round O while saying, "Oh my goodness."

5    "*Ni kan,*" said my mother as Shirley's eyes flooded with tears. "You already know how. Don't need talent for crying!"

Soon after my mother got this idea about Shirley Temple, she took me to a beauty training school in the Mission district and put me in the hands of a student who could barely hold the scissors without shaking. Instead of getting big fat curls, I emerged with an uneven mass of crinkly black fuzz. My mother dragged me off to the bathroom and tried to wet down my hair.

"You look like Negro Chinese," she lamented, as if I had done this on purpose.

The instructor of the beauty training school had to lop off these soggy clumps to make my hair even again. "Peter Pan is very popular these days," the instructor assured my mother. I now had hair the length of a boy's, with straight-across bangs that hung at a slant two inches above my eyebrows. I liked the haircut and it made me actually look forward to my future fame.

In fact, in the beginning, I was just as excited as my mother, maybe even more so. I pictured this prodigy part of me as many different images, trying each one on for size. I was a dainty ballerina girl standing by the curtains, waiting to hear the right music that would send me floating on my tiptoes. I was like the Christ child lifted out of the straw manger, crying with holy indignity. I was Cinderella stepping from her pumpkin carriage with sparkly cartoon music filling the air.

10    In all of my imaginings, I was filled with a sense that I would soon become *perfect*. My mother and father would adore me. I would be beyond reproach. I would never feel the need to sulk for anything.

But sometimes the prodigy in me became impatient. "If you don't hurry up and get me out of here, I'm disappearing for good," it warned. "And then you'll always be nothing."

Every night after dinner, my mother and I would sit at the Formica kitchen table. She would present new tests, taking her examples from stories of amazing children she had read in *Ripley's Believe It or Not,* or *Good Housekeeping, Reader's Digest,* and a dozen other magazines she kept in a pile in our bathroom. My mother got these magazines from people whose houses she cleaned. And since she cleaned many houses each week, we had a great assortment. She would look through them all, searching for stories about remarkable children.

The first night she brought out a story about a three-year-old boy who knew the capitals of all the states and even most of the European countries. A teacher was quoted as saying the little boy could also pronounce the names of the foreign cities correctly.

"What's the capital of Finland?" my mother asked me, looking at the magazine story.

15    All I knew was the capital of California, because Sacramento was the name of the street we lived on in Chinatown. "Nairobi!" I guessed, saying the most foreign word I could think of. She checked to see if that was possibly one way to pronounce "Helsinki" before showing me the answer.

The tests got harder—multiplying numbers in my head, finding the queen of hearts in a deck of cards, trying to stand on my head without using my hands, predicting the daily temperatures in Los Angeles, New York, and London.

One night I had to look at a page from the Bible for three minutes and then report everything I could remember. "Now Jehoshaphat had riches and honor in abundance and . . . that's all I remember, Ma," I said.

And after seeing my mother's disappointed face once again, something inside of me began to die. I hated the tests, the raised hopes and failed expectations. Before going to bed that night, I looked in the mirror above the bathroom sink and when I saw only my face staring back—and that it would always be this ordinary face—I began to cry. Such a sad, ugly girl! I made high-pitched noises like a crazed animal, trying to scratch out the face in the mirror.

And then I saw what seemed to be the prodigy side of me—because I had never seen that face before. I looked at my reflection, blinking so I could see more clearly. The girl staring back at me was angry, powerful. This girl and I were the same. I had new thoughts, willful thoughts, or rather thoughts filled with lots of won'ts. I won't let her change me, I promised myself. I won't be what I'm not.

20        So now on nights when my mother presented her tests, I performed listlessly, my head propped on one arm. I pretended to be bored. And I was. I got so bored I started counting the bellows of the foghorns out on the bay while my mother drilled me in other areas. The sound was comforting and reminded me of the cow jumping over the moon. And the next day, I played a game with myself, seeing if my mother would give up on me before eight bellows. After a while I usually counted only one, maybe two bellows at most. At last she was beginning to give up hope.

Two or three months had gone by without any mention of my being a prodigy again. And then one day my mother was watching *The Ed Sullivan Show* on TV. The TV was old and the sound kept shorting out. Every time my mother got halfway up from the sofa to adjust the set, the sound would go back on and Ed would be talking. As soon as she sat down, Ed would go silent again. She got up, the TV broke into loud piano music. She sat down. Silence. Up and down, back and forth, quiet and loud. It was like a stiff embraceless dance between her and the TV set. Finally she stood by the set with her hand on the sound dial.

She seemed entranced by the music, a little frenzied piano piece with this mesmerizing quality, quick sort of passages and then teasing lilting ones before it returned to the quick playful parts.

"*Ni kan,*" my mother said, calling me over with hurried hand gestures, "Look here."

I could see why my mother was fascinated by the music. It was being pounded out by a little Chinese girl, about nine years old, with a Peter Pan haircut. The girl had the sauciness of a Shirley Temple. She was proudly modest like a proper Chinese child. And she also did this fancy sweep of a curtsy, so that the fluffy skirt of her white dress cascaded slowly to the floor like the petals of a large carnation.

25        In spite of these warning signs, I wasn't worried. Our family had no piano and we couldn't afford to buy one, let alone reams of sheet music and piano lessons. So I could be generous in my comments when my mother bad-mouthed the little girl on TV.

"Play note right, but doesn't sound good! No singing sound," complained my mother.

"What are you picking on her for?" I said carelessly. "She's pretty good. Maybe she's not the best, but she's trying hard." I knew almost immediately I would be sorry I said that.

"Just like you," she said. "Not the best. Because you not trying." She gave a little huff as she let go of the sound dial and sat down on the sofa.

The little Chinese girl sat down also to play an encore of "Anitra's Dance" by Grieg.[1] I remember the song, because later on I had to learn how to play it.

---

[1] **"Anitra's Dance"** a section from the incidental music that Edvard Grieg (1843–1907) wrote for *Peer Gynt,* a play by Henrik Ibsen.

30        Three days after watching *The Ed Sullivan Show,* my mother told me what my schedule would be for piano lessons and piano practice. She had talked to Mr. Chong, who lived on the first floor of our apartment building. Mr. Chong was a retired piano teacher and my mother had traded house-cleaning services for weekly lessons and a piano for me to practice on every day, two hours a day, from four until six.

When my mother told me this, I felt as though I had been sent to hell. I whined and then kicked my foot a little when I couldn't stand it anymore.

"Why don't you like me the way I am? I'm not a genius! I can't play the piano. And even if I could, I wouldn't go on TV if you paid me a million dollars!" I cried.

My mother slapped me. "Who ask you be genius?" she shouted. "Only ask you be your best. For you sake. You think I want you be genius? Hnnh! What for! Who ask you!"

"So ungrateful," I heard her mutter in Chinese. "If she had as much talent as she has temper, she would be famous now."

35        Mr. Chong, whom I secretly nicknamed Old Chong, was very strange, always tapping his fingers to the silent music of an invisible orchestra. He looked ancient in my eyes. He had lost most of the hair on top of his head and he wore thick glasses and had eyes that always looked tired and sleepy. But he must have been younger than I thought, since he lived with his mother and was not yet married.

I met Old Lady Chong once and that was enough. She had this peculiar smell like a baby that had done something in its pants. And her fingers felt like a dead person's, like an old peach I once found in the back of the refrigerator; the skin just slid off the meat when I picked it up.

I soon found out why Old Chong had retired from teaching piano. He was deaf. "Like Beethoven!" he shouted to me. "We're both listening only in our head!" And he would start to conduct his frantic silent sonatas.

Our lessons went like this. He would open the book and point to different things, explaining their purpose: "Key! Treble! Bass! No sharps or flats! So this is C major! Listen now and play after me!"

And then he would play the C scale a few times, a simple chord, and then, as if inspired by an old, unreachable itch, he gradually added more notes and running trills and a pounding bass until the music was really something quite grand.

40        I would play after him, the simple scale, the simple chord, and then I just played some nonsense that sounded like a cat running up and down on top of garbage cans. Old Chong smiled and applauded and then said, "Very good! But now you must learn to keep time!"

So that's how I discovered that Old Chong's eyes were too slow to keep up with the wrong notes I was playing. He went through the motions in half-time. To help me keep rhythm, he stood behind me, pushing down on my right shoulder for every beat. He balanced pennies on top of my wrists so I would keep them still as I slowly played scales and arpeggios. He had me curve my hand around an apple and keep that shape when playing chords. He marched stiffly to show me how to make each finger dance up and down, staccato like an obedient little soldier.

He taught me all these things, and that was how I also learned I could be lazy and get away with mistakes, lots of mistakes. If I hit the wrong notes because I hadn't practiced enough, I never corrected myself. I just kept playing in rhythm. And Old Chong kept conducting his own private reverie.

So maybe I never really gave myself a fair chance. I did pick up the basics pretty quickly, and I might have become a good pianist at that young age. But I was so determined not to try, not to be anybody different that I learned to play only the most ear-splitting preludes, the most discordant hymns.

Over the next year, I practiced like this, dutifully in my own way. And then one day I heard my mother and her friend Lindo Jong both talking in a loud bragging tone of voice so others could hear. It was after church, and I was leaning against the brick wall wearing a dress with stiff white petticoats. Auntie Lindo's daughter, Waverly, who was about my age, was standing farther down the wall about five feet away. We had grown up together and shared all the closeness of two sisters squabbling over crayons and dolls. In other words, for the most part, we hated each other. I thought she was snotty. Waverly Jong had gained a certain amount of fame as "Chinatown's Littlest Chinese Chess Champion."

45    "She bring home too many trophy," Auntie Lindo lamented that Sunday. "All day she play chess. All day I have no time do nothing but dust off her winnings." She threw a scolding look at Waverly, who pretended not to see her.

"You lucky you don't have this problem," said Auntie Lindo with a sigh to my mother.

And my mother squared her shoulders and bragged: "Our problem worser than yours. If we ask Jing-mei wash dish, she hear nothing but music. It's like you can't stop this natural talent."

And right then, I was determined to put a stop to her foolish pride.

A few weeks later, Old Chong and my mother conspired to have me play in a talent show which would be held in the church hall. By then, my parents had saved up enough to buy me a secondhand piano, a black Wurlitzer spinet with a scarred bench. It was the showpiece of our living room.

50    For the talent show, I was to play a piece called "Pleading Child" from Schumann's *Scenes from Childhood*.[2] It was a simple, moody piece that sounded more difficult than it was. I was supposed to memorize the whole thing, playing the repeat parts twice to make the piece sound longer. But I dawdled over it, playing a few bars and then cheating, looking up to see what notes followed. I never really listened to what I was playing. I daydreamed about being somewhere else, about being someone else.

The part I liked to practice best was the fancy curtsy: right foot out, touch the rose on the carpet with a pointed foot, sweep to the side, left leg bends, look up and smile.

My parents invited all the couples from the Joy Luck Club to witness my debut. Auntie Lindo and Uncle Tin were there. Waverly and her two older brothers had also come. The first two rows were filled with children both younger and older than I was. The littlest ones got to go first. They recited simple nursery rhymes, squawked out tunes on miniature violins, twirled Hula Hoops, pranced in pink ballet tutus, and when they bowed or curtsied, the audience would sigh in unison, "Awww," and then clap enthusiastically.

---

[2]**Scenes from Childhood** a piano work by Robert Schumann (1810–1856) with twelve titled sections and an epilogue.

When my turn came, I was very confident. I remember my childish excitement. It was as if I knew, without a doubt, that the prodigy side of me really did exist. I had no fear whatsoever, no nervousness. I remember thinking to myself, This is it! This is it! I looked out over the audience, at my mother's blank face, my father's yawn, Auntie Lindo's stiff-lipped smile, Waverly's sulky expression. I had on a white dress layered with sheets of lace, and a pink bow in my Peter Pan haircut. As I sat down I envisioned people jumping to their feet and Ed Sullivan rushing up to introduce me to everyone on TV.

And I started to play. It was so beautiful. I was so caught up in how lovely I looked that at first I didn't worry how I would sound. So it was a surprise to me when I hit the first wrong note and I realized something didn't sound quite right. And then I hit another and another followed that. A chill started at the top of my head and began to trickle down. Yet I couldn't stop playing, as though my hands were bewitched. I kept thinking my fingers would adjust themselves back, like a train switching to the right track. I played this strange jumble through two repeats, the sour notes staying with me all the way to the end.

55     When I stood up, I discovered my legs were shaking. Maybe I had just been nervous and the audience, like Old Chong, had seen me go through the right motions and had not heard anything wrong at all. I swept my right foot out, went down on my knee, looked up and smiled. The room was quiet, except for Old Chong, who was beaming and shouting, "Bravo! Bravo! Well done!" But then I saw my mother's face, her stricken face. The audience clapped weakly, and as I walked back to my chair, with my whole face quivering as I tried not to cry, I heard a little boy whisper loudly to his mother, "That was awful," and the mother whispered back, "Well, she certainly tried."

And now I realized how many people were in the audience, the whole world it seemed. I was aware of eyes burning into my back. I felt the shame of my mother and father as they sat stiffly throughout the rest of the show.

We could have escaped during intermission. Pride and some strange sense of honor must have anchored my parents to their chairs. And so we watched it all: the eighteen-year-old boy with a fake mustache who did a magic show and juggled flaming hoops while riding a unicycle. The breasted girl with white makeup who sang from *Madama Butterfly* and got honorable mention. And the eleven-year-old boy who won first prize playing a tricky violin song that sounded like a busy bee.

After the show, the Hsus, the Jongs, and the St. Clairs from the Joy Luck Club came up to my mother and father.

"Lots of talented kids," Auntie Lindo said vaguely, smiling broadly.

60     "That was somethin' else," said my father, and I wondered if he was referring to me in a humorous way, or whether he even remembered what I had done.

Waverly looked at me and shrugged her shoulders. "You aren't a genius like me," she said matter-of-factly. And if I hadn't felt so bad, I would have pulled her braids and punched her stomach.

But my mother's expression was what devastated me: a quiet, blank look that said she had lost everything. I felt the same way, and it seemed as if everybody were now coming up, like gawkers at the scene of an accident, to see what parts were actually missing. When we got on the bus to go home, my father was humming the busy-bee tune and my mother was silent. I kept thinking she wanted to wait until we got home before shouting at me. But when my father unlocked the door to our apartment, my mother walked in and then went to the back, into the bedroom. No accusations. No blame. And in a way, I felt disappointed. I had been waiting for her to start shouting, so I could shout back and cry and blame her for all my misery.

I assumed my talent-show fiasco meant I never had to play the piano again. But two days later, after school, my mother came out of the kitchen and saw me watching TV.

"Four clock," she reminded me as if it were any other day. I was stunned, as though she were asking me to go through the talent-show torture again. I wedged myself more tightly in front of the TV.

65 "Turn off TV," she called from the kitchen five minutes later.

I didn't budge. And then I decided. I didn't have to do what my mother said anymore. I wasn't her slave. This wasn't China. I had listened to her before and look what happened. She was the stupid one.

She came out from the kitchen and stood in the arched entryway of the living room. "Four clock," she said once again, louder.

"I'm not going to play anymore," I said nonchalantly. "Why should I? I'm not a genius."

She walked over and stood in front of the TV. I saw her chest was heaving up and down in an angry way.

70 "No!" I said, and I now felt stronger, as if my true self had finally emerged. So this was what had been inside me all along.

"No! I won't!" I screamed.

She yanked me by the arm, pulled me off the floor, snapped off the TV. She was frighteningly strong, half pulling, half carrying me toward the piano as I kicked the throw rugs under my feet. She lifted me up and onto the hard bench. I was sobbing by now, looking at her bitterly. Her chest was heaving even more and her mouth was open, smiling crazily as if she were pleased I was crying.

"You want me to be someone that I'm not!" I sobbed. "I'll never be the kind of daughter you want me to be!"

"Only two kinds of daughters," she shouted in Chinese. "Those who are obedient and those who follow their own mind! Only one kind of daughter can live in this house. Obedient daughter!"

75 "Then I wish I wasn't your daughter. I wish you weren't my mother," I shouted. As I said these things I got scared. I felt like worms and toads and slimy things were crawling out of my chest, but it also felt good, as if this awful side of me had surfaced, at last.

"Too late change this," said my mother shrilly.

And I could sense her anger rising to its breaking point. I wanted to see it spill over. And that's when I remembered the babies she had lost in China, the ones we never talked about. "Then I wish I'd never been born!" I shouted. "I wish I were dead! Like them."

It was as if I had said the magic words. Alakazam!—and her face went blank, her mouth closed, her arms went slack, and she backed out of the room, stunned, as if she were blowing away like a small brown leaf, thin, brittle, lifeless.

It was not the only disappointment my mother felt in me. In the years that followed, I failed her so many times, each time asserting my own will, my right to fall short of expectations. I didn't get straight As. I didn't become class president. I didn't get into Stanford. I dropped out of college.

80      For unlike my mother, I did not believe I could be anything I wanted to be. I could only be me.

And for all those years, we never talked about the disaster at the recital or my terrible accusations afterward at the piano bench. All that remained unchecked, like a betrayal that was now unspeakable. So I never found a way to ask her why she had hoped for something so large that failure was inevitable.

And even worse, I never asked her what frightened me the most: Why had she given up hope?

For after our struggle at the piano, she never mentioned my playing again. The lessons stopped. The lid to the piano was closed, shutting out the dust, my misery, and her dreams.

So she surprised me. A few years ago, she offered to give me the piano, for my thirtieth birthday. I had not played in all those years. I saw the offer as a sign of forgiveness, a tremendous burden removed.

85      "Are you sure?" I asked shyly. "I mean, won't you and Dad miss it?"

"No, this your piano," she said firmly. "Always your piano. You only one can play."

"Well, I probably can't play anymore," I said. "It's been years."

"You pick up fast," said my mother, as if she knew this was certain. "You have natural talent. You could been genius if you want to."

"No I couldn't."

90      "You just not trying," said my mother. And she was neither angry nor sad. She said it as if to announce a fact that could never be disproved. "Take it," she said.

But I didn't at first. It was enough that she had offered it to me. And after that, every time I saw it in my parents' living room, standing in front of the bay windows, it made me feel proud, as if it were a shiny trophy I had won back.

Last week I sent a tuner over to my parents' apartment and had the piano reconditioned, for purely sentimental reasons. My mother had died a few months before and I had been getting things in order for my father, a little bit at a time. I put the jewelry in special silk pouches. The sweaters she had knitted in yellow, pink, bright orange—all the colors I hated—I put those in moth-proof boxes. I found some old Chinese silk dresses, the kind with little slits up the sides. I rubbed the old silk against my skin, then wrapped them in tissue and decided to take them home with me.

After I had the piano tuned, I opened the lid and touched the keys. It sounded even richer than I remembered. Really, it was a very good piano. Inside the bench were the same exercise notes with handwritten scales, the same secondhand music books with their covers held together with yellow tape.

I opened up the Schumann book to the dark little piece I had played at the recital. It was on the left-hand page, "Pleading Child." It looked more difficult than I remembered. I played a few bars, surprised at how easily the notes came back to me.

95      And for the first time, or so it seemed, I noticed the piece on the right-hand side. It was called "Perfectly Contented." I tried to play this one as well.

It had a lighter melody but the same flowing rhythm and turned out to be quite easy. "Pleading Child" was shorter but slower; "Perfectly Contented" was longer but faster. And after I played them both a few times, I realized they were two halves of the same song.

# JAMES THURBER

*James Thurber (1894-1961) was born in Columbus, Ohio. He attended Ohio State University, where he edited the college humor magazine, but he left without a degree. During World War I, ineligible for military service because of an eye injury, he worked for the State Department in Washington and in Paris. He then returned to Columbus, where he worked as a reporter for the* Columbus Dispatch *and began writing and directing musical comedies for a theatrical group at Ohio State University. Thurber then went to New York as a journalist; in 1927 he accepted Harold Ross's invitation to join the staff of the* New Yorker—*an association that lasted for thirty years and is remembered in Thurber's book,* The Years with Ross.

*Thurber wrote, or drew (he was a cartoonist as well as a writer), more than twenty books of essays, stories, autobiographical sketches, and memoirs. T. S. Eliot said of Thurber's work:*

> *It is a form of humour which is also a way of saying something serious. Unlike so much humour it is not merely a criticism of manners—that is, of the superficial aspects of society at a given moment—but something more profound. His writing and also his illustrations are capable of surviving the immediate environment and time out of which they spring. To some extent they will be a document of the age they belong to.*

> *When asked to define humour, Thurber quoted someone whose name he had forgotten: He said that "the English treat the commonplace as if it were remarkable and the Americans treat the remarkable as if it were commonplace. . . . In 'The Secret Life of Walter Mitty' I tried to treat the remarkable as commonplace."*

## The Secret Life of Walter Mitty                                    [1939]

"We're going through!" The Commander's voice was like thin ice breaking. He wore his full-dress uniform, with the heavily braided white cap pulled down rakishly over one cold gray eye. "We can't make it, sir. It's spoiling for a hurricane, if you ask me." "I'm not asking you, Lieutenant Berg," said the Commander. "Throw on the power lights! Rev her up to 8,500! We're going through!" The pounding of the cylinders increased: ta-pocketa-pocketa-pock-eta-*pocketa-pocketa.* The Commander stared at the ice forming on the pilot window. He walked over and twisted a row of complicated dials. "Switch on No. 8 auxiliary!" he shouted. "Switch on No. 8 auxiliary!" repeated Lieutenant Berg. "Full strength in No. 3 turret!" shouted the Commander. "Full strength in No. 3 turret!" The crew, bending to their various tasks in the huge, hurtling eight-engined Navy hydroplane, looked at each other and grinned. "The Old Man'll get us through," they said to one another. "The Old Man ain't afraid of Hell!" . . .

"Not so fast! You're driving too fast!" said Mrs. Mitty. "What are you driving so fast for?"

"Hmm?" said Walter Mitty. He looked at his wife, in the seat beside him, with shocked astonishment. She seemed grossly unfamiliar, like a strange woman who had yelled at him in a crowd. "You were up to fifty-five," she said. "You know I don't like to go more than forty. You were up to fifty-five." Walter Mitty drove on toward Waterbury in silence, the roaring of the SN202 through the worst storm in twenty years of Navy flying fading in the remote, intimate airways of his mind. "You're tensed up again," said Mrs. Mitty. "It's one of your days. I wish you'd let Dr. Renshaw look you over."

Walter Mitty stopped the car in front of the building where his wife went to have her hair done. "Remember to get those overshoes while I'm having my hair done," she said. "I don't need overshoes," said Mitty. She put her mirror back into her bag. "We've been all through that," she said, getting out of the car. "You're not a young man any longer." He raced the engine a little. "Why don't you wear your gloves? Have you lost your gloves?" Walter Mitty reached in a pocket and brought out the gloves. He put them on, but after she had turned and gone into the building and he had driven on to a red light, he took them off again. "Pick it up, brother!" snapped a cop as the light changed, and Mitty hastily pulled on his gloves and lurched ahead. He drove around the streets aimlessly for a time, and then he drove past the hospital on his way to the parking lot.

5 . . . . "It's the millionaire banker, Wellington McMillan," said the pretty nurse. "Yes?" said Walter Mitty, removing his gloves slowly. "Who has the case?" "Dr. Renshaw and Mr. Benbow, but there are two specialists here, Dr. Remington from New York and Mr. Pritchard-Mitford from London. He flew over." A door opened down a long, cool corridor and Dr. Renshaw came out. He looked distraught and haggard. "Hello, Mitty," he said. "We're having the devil's own time with McMillan, the millionaire banker and close personal friend of Roosevelt. Obstreosis of the ductal tract. Tertiary. Wish you'd take a look at him." "Glad to," said Mitty.

In the operating room there were whispered introductions: "Dr. Remington, Dr. Mitty. Mr. Pritchard-Mitford, Dr. Mitty." "I've read your book on streptothricosis," said Pritchard-Mitford, shaking hands. "A brilliant performance, sir." "Thank you," said Walter Mitty. "Didn't know you were in the States, Mitty," grumbled Remington. "Coals to Newcastle, bringing Mitford and me up here for a tertiary." "You are very kind," said Mitty. A huge, complicated machine, connected to the operating table, with many tubes and wires, began at this moment to go pocketa-pocketa-pocketa. "The new anesthetizer is giving way!" shouted an interne. "There is no one in the East who knows how to fix it!" "Quiet, man!" said Mitty, in a low, cool voice. He sprang to the machine, which was now going pocketa-pocketa-queep-pocketa-queep. He began fingering delicately a row of glistening dials. "Give me a fountain pen!" he snapped. Someone handed him a fountain pen. He pulled a faulty piston out of the machine and inserted the pen in its place. "That will hold for ten minutes," he said. "Get on with the operation." A nurse hurried over and whispered to Renshaw, and Mitty saw the man turn pale. "Coreopsis has set in," said Renshaw nervously. "If you would take over, Mitty?" Mitty looked at him and at the craven figure of Benbow, who drank, and at the grave, uncertain faces of the two great specialists. "If you wish," he said. They slipped a white gown on him; he adjusted a mask and drew on thin gloves; nurses handed him shining . . .

"Back it up, Mac! Look out for that Buick!" Walter Mitty jammed on the brakes. "Wrong lane, Mac," said the parking-lot attendant, looking at Mitty closely. "Gee. Yeh," muttered Mitty. He began cautiously to back out of the lane marked "Exit Only." "Leave her sit there," said the attendant. "I'll put her away." Mitty got out of the car. "Hey, better leave the key." "Oh," said Mitty, handing the man the ignition key. The attendant vaulted into the car, backed it up with insolent skill, and put it where it belonged.

They're so damn cocky, thought Walter Mitty, walking along Main Street; they think they know everything. Once he had tried to take his chains off, outside New Milford, and he had got them wound around the axles. A man had had to come out in a wrecking car and unwind them, a young, grinning garageman. Since then Mrs. Mitty always made him drive to a garage to have the chains taken off. The next time, he thought, I'll wear my right arm in a sling; they won't grin at me then. I'll have my right arm in a sling and they'll see I couldn't possibly take the chains off myself. He kicked at the slush on the sidewalk. "Overshoes," he said to himself, and he began looking for a shoe store.

When he came out into the street again, with the overshoes in a box under his arm, Walter Mitty began to wonder what the other thing was his wife had told him to get. She had told him, twice, before they set out from their house for Waterbury. In a way he hated these weekly trips to town—he was always getting something wrong. Kleenex, he thought, Squibb's, razor blades? No. Toothpaste, toothbrush, bicarbonate, carborundum, initiative and referendum? He gave it up. But she would remember it. "Where's the what's-its-name?" she would ask. "Don't tell me you forgot the what's-its-name." A newsboy went by shouting something about the Waterbury trial.

10      . . . "Perhaps this will refresh your memory." The District Attorney suddenly thrust a heavy automatic at the quiet figure on the witness stand. "Have you ever seen this before?" Walter Mitty took the gun and examined it expertly. "This is my Webley-Vickers 50.80," he said calmly. An excited buzz ran around the courtroom. The Judge rapped for order. "You are a crack shot with any sort of firearms, I believe?" said the District Attorney, insinuatingly. "Objection!" shouted Mitty's attorney. "We have shown that the defendant could not have fired the shot. We have shown that he wore his right arm in a sling on the night of the fourteenth of July." Walter Mitty raised his hand briefly and the bickering attorneys were stilled. "With any known make of gun," he said evenly, "I could have killed Gregory Fitzhurst at three hundred feet *with my left hand*." Pandemonium broke loose in the courtroom. A woman's scream rose above the bedlam and suddenly a lovely, dark-haired girl was in Walter Mitty's arms. The District Attorney struck at her savagely. Without rising from his chair, Mitty let the man have it on the point of the chin. "You miserable cur!". . .

"Puppy biscuit," said Walter Mitty. He stopped walking and the buildings of Waterbury rose up out of the misty courtroom and surrounded him again. A woman who was passing laughed. "He said 'Puppy biscuit,'" she said to her companion. "That man said 'Puppy biscuit' to himself." Walter Mitty hurried on. He went into an A. & P., not the first one he came to but a smaller one farther up the street. "I want some biscuit for small, young dogs," he said to the clerk. "Any special brand, sir?" The greatest pistol shot in the world thought a moment. "It says 'Puppies Bark for It' on the box," said Walter Mitty.

His wife would be through at the hairdresser's in fifteen minutes, Mitty saw in looking at his watch, unless they had trouble drying it; sometimes they had trouble drying it. She didn't like to get to the hotel first; she would want him to be there waiting for her as usual. He found a big leather chair in the lobby, facing a window, and he put the overshoes and the puppy biscuit on the floor beside it. He picked up an old copy of *Liberty* and sank down into the chair. "Can Germany Conquer the World Through the Air?" Walter Mitty looked at the pictures of bombing planes and of ruined streets.

. . . "The cannonading has got the wind up in young Raleigh, sir," said the sergeant. Captain Mitty looked up at him through tousled hair. "Get him to bed," he said wearily. "With the others. I'll fly alone." "But you can't, sir," said the sergeant anxiously. "It takes two men to handle that bomber and the Archies are pounding hell out of the air. Von Richtman's circus is between here and Saulier." "Somebody's got to get that ammunition dump," said Mitty. "I'm going over. Spot of brandy?" He poured a drink for the sergeant and one for himself. War thundered and whined around the dugout and battered at the door. There was a rending of wood and splinters flew through the room. "A bit of a near thing," said Captain Mitty carelessly. "The box barrage is closing in," said the sergeant. "We only live once, Sergeant," said Mitty, with his faint, fleeting smile. "Or do we?" He poured another brandy and tossed it off. "I never see a man could hold his brandy like you, sir," said the sergeant. "Begging your pardon, sir." Captain Mitty stood up and strapped on his huge Webley-Vickers automatic. "It's forty kilometers through hell, sir," said the sergeant. Mitty finished one last brandy. "After all," he said softly, "what isn't?" The pounding of the cannon increased; there was the rat-tat-tatting of machine guns, and from somewhere came the menacing pocket-pocketa-pocketa of the new flame-throwers. Walter Mitty walked to the door of the dugout humming "Auprès de Ma Blonde." He turned and waved to the sergeant. "Cheerio!" he said. . . .

Something struck his shoulder. "I've been looking all over this hotel for you," said Mrs. Mitty. "Why do you have to hide in this old chair? How did you expect me to find you?" "Things close in," said Walter Mitty vaguely. "What?" Mrs. Mitty said. "Did you get the what's-its-name? The puppy biscuit? What's in that box?" "Overshoes," said Mitty. "Couldn't you have put them on in the store?" "I was thinking," said Walter Mitty. "Does it ever occur to you that I am sometimes thinking?" She looked at him. "I'm going to take your temperature when I get you home," she said.

15      They went out through the revolving doors that made a faintly derisive whistling sound when you pushed them. It was two blocks to the parking lot. At the drugstore on the corner she said, "Wait here for me. I forgot something. I won't be a minute." She was more than a minute. Walter Mitty lighted a cigarette. It began to rain, rain with sleet in it. He stood up against the wall of the drugstore, smoking. . . . He put his shoulders back and his heels together. "To hell with the handkerchief," said Walter Mitty scornfully. He took one last drag on his cigarette and snapped it away. Then, with that faint, fleeting smile playing about his lips, he faced the firing squad; erect and motionless, proud and disdainful, Walter Mitty the Undefeated, inscrutable to the last.

# HELENA MARIA VIRAMONTES

*Helena Maria Viramontes was born in East Los Angeles in 1954. After completing her undergraduate studies at Immaculate Heart College, she did graduate work at California State University, Los Angeles, and further work between 1979 and 1981 in the MFA Creative Writing Program at the University of California, Irvine. Viramontes has won first prize in several fiction contests, including the Irvine Chicano Literary Contest. In 1989, the year in which she was awarded a Creative Writing Fellowship from the National Endowment for the Arts, she participated in a "Storytelling for Film" workshop at the Sundance Film Institute.*

*Viramontes writes chiefly about women whose lives are circumscribed by a patriarchal Latino society. Eight of her stories have been collected in "The Moths" and Other Stories (1985).*

## The Moths                                           [1982]

I was fourteen years old when Abuelita[1] requested my help. And it seemed only fair. Abuelita had pulled me through the rages of scarlet fever by placing, removing and replacing potato slices on the temples of my forehead; she had seen me through several whippings, an arm broken by a dare jump off Tío Enrique's toolshed, puberty, and my first lie. Really, I told Amá, it was only fair.

Not that I was her favorite granddaughter or anything special. I wasn't even pretty or nice like my older sisters and I just couldn't do the girl things they could do. My hands were too big to handle the fineries of crocheting or embroidery and I always pricked my fingers or knotted my colored threads time and time again while my sisters laughed and called me bull hands with their cute waterlike voices. So I began keeping a piece of jagged brick in my sock to bash my sisters or anyone who called me bull hands. Once, while we all sat in the bedroom, I hit Teresa on the forehead, right above her eyebrow and she ran to Amá with her mouth open, her hand over her eye while blood seeped between her fingers. I was used to the whippings by then.

I wasn't respectful either. I even went so far as to doubt the power of Abuelita's slices, the slices she said absorbed my fever. "You're still alive, aren't you?" Abuelita snapped back, her pasty gray eye beaming at me and burning holes in my suspicions. Regretful that I had let secret questions drop out of my mouth, I couldn't look into her eyes. My hands began to fan out, grow like a liar's nose until they hung by my side like low weights. Abuelita made a balm out of dried moth wings and Vicks and rubbed my hands, shaped them back to size and it was the strangest feeling. Like bones melting. Like sun shining through the darkness of your eyelids. I didn't mind helping Abuelita after that, so Amá would always send me over to her.

In the early afternoon Amá would push her hair back, hand me my sweater and shoes, and tell me to go to Mama Luna's. This was to avoid another fight and another whipping, I knew. I would deliver one last direct shot on Marisela's arm and jump out of our house, the slam of the screen door burying her cries of anger, and I'd gladly go help Abuelita plant her wild lilies or jasmine or heliotrope or cilantro or hierbabuena in red Hills

---

[1]**Abuelita** Grandma (Spanish); other Spanish words for relatives mentioned in the story are *Tío,* Uncle, *Amá,* Mother, and *Apá,* Dad.

Brothers coffee cans. Abuelita would wait for me at the top step of her porch holding a hammer and nail and empty coffee cans. And although we hardly spoke, hardly looked at each other as we worked over root transplants, I always felt her gray eye on me. It made me feel, in a strange sort of way, safe and guarded and not alone. Like God was supposed to make you feel.

5    On Abuelita's porch, I would puncture holes in the bottom of the coffee cans with a nail and a precise hit of a hammer. This completed, my job was to fill them with red clay mud from beneath her rose bushes, packing it softly, then making a perfect hole, four fingers round, to nest a sprouting avocado pit, or the spidery sweet potatoes that Abuelita rooted in mayonnaise jars with toothpicks and daily water, or prickly chayotes[2] that produced vines that twisted and wound all over her porch pillars, crawling to the roof, up and over the roof, and down the other side, making her small brick house look like it was cradled within the vines that grew pear-shaped squashes ready for the pick, ready to be steamed with onions and cheese and butter. The roots would burst out of the rusted coffee cans and search for a place to connect. I would then feed the seedlings with water.

But this was a different kind of help, Amá said, because Abuelita was dying. Looking into her gray eye, then into her brown one, the doctor said it was just a matter of days. And so it seemed only fair that these hands she had melted and formed found use in rubbing her caving body with alcohol and marihuana, rubbing her arms and legs, turning her face to the window so that she could watch the Bird of Paradise blooming or smell the scent of clove in the air. I toweled her face frequently and held her hand for hours. Her gray wiry hair hung over the mattress. Since I could remember, she'd kept her long hair in braids. Her mouth was vacant and when she slept, her eyelids never closed all the way. Up close, you could see her gray eye beaming out the window, staring hard as if to remember everything. I never kissed her. I left the window open when I went to the market.

Across the street from Jay's Market there was a chapel. I never knew its denomination, but I went in just the same to search for candles. I sat down on one of the pews because there were none. After I cleaned my fingernails, I looked up at the high ceiling. I had forgotten the vastness of these places, the coolness of the marble pillars and the frozen statues with blank eyes. I was alone. I knew why I had never returned.

That was one of Apá's biggest complaints. He would pound his hands on the table, rocking the sugar dish or spilling a cup of coffee and scream that if I didn't go to mass every Sunday to save my goddamn sinning soul, then I had no reason to go out of the house, period. Punto final.[3] He would grab my arm and dig his nails into me to make sure I understood the importance of catechism. Did he make himself clear? Then he strategically directed his anger at Amá for her lousy ways of bringing up daughters, being disrespectful and unbelieving, and my older sisters would pull me aside and tell me if I didn't get to mass right this minute, they were all going to kick the holy shit out of me. Why am I so selfish? Can't you see what it's

---

[2]**chayotes** squashlike fruit.    [3]**Punto final** period.

doing to Amá, you idiot? So I would wash my feet and stuff them in my black Easter shoes that shone with Vaseline, grab a missal and veil, and wave good-bye to Amá.

I would walk slowly down Lorena to First to Evergreen, counting the cracks on the cement. On Evergreen I would turn left and walk to Abuelita's. I liked her porch because it was shielded by the vines of the chayotes and I could get a good look at the people and car traffic on Evergreen without them knowing. I would jump up the porch steps, knock on the screen door as I wiped my feet and call Abuelita? mi Abuelita? As I opened the door and stuck my head in, I would catch the gagging scent of toasting chile on the placa.[4] When I entered the sala,[5] she would greet me from the kitchen, wringing her hands in her apron. I'd sit at the corner of the table to keep from being in her way. The chiles made my eyes water. Am I crying? No, Mama Luna, I'm sure not crying. I don't like going to mass, but my eyes watered anyway, the tears dropping on the tablecloth like candle wax. Abuelita lifted the burnt chiles from the fire and sprinkled water on them until the skins began to separate. Placing them in front of me, she turned to check the menudo.[6] I peeled the skins off and put the flimsy, limp looking green and yellow chiles in the molcajete[7] and began to crush and crush and twist and crush the heart out of the tomato, the clove of garlic, the stupid chiles that made me cry, crushed them until they turned into liquid under my bull hand. With a wooden spoon, I scraped hard to destroy the guilt, and my tears were gone. I put the bowl of chile next to a vase filled with freshly cut roses. Abuelita touched my hand and pointed to the bowl of menudo that steamed in front of me. I spooned some chile into the menudo and rolled a corn tortilla thin with the palms of my hands. As I ate, a fine Sunday breeze entered the kitchen and a rose petal calmly feathered down to the table.

10      I left the chapel without blessing myself and walked to Jay's. Most of the time Jay didn't have much of anything. The tomatoes were always soft and the cans of Campbell soups had rusted spots on them. There was dust on the tops of cereal boxes. I picked up what I needed: rubbing alcohol, five cans of chicken broth, a big bottle of Pine Sol. At first Jay got mad because I thought I had forgotten the money. But it was there all the time, in my back pocket.

When I returned from the market, I heard Amá crying in Abuelita's kitchen. She looked up at me with puffy eyes. I placed the bags of groceries on the table and began putting the cans of soup away. Amá sobbed quietly. I never kissed her. After a while, I patted her on the back for comfort. Finally: "¿Y mi Amá?"[8] she asked in a whisper, then choked again and cried into her apron.

Abuelita fell off the bed twice yesterday, I said, knowing that I shouldn't have said it and wondering why I wanted to say it because it only made Amá cry harder. I guess I became angry and just so tired of the quarrels and beatings and unanswered prayers and my hands just there hanging helplessly by my side. Amá looked at me again, confused, angry, and her

---

[4]**placa** round cast-iron griddle.    [5]**sala** living room.    [6]**menudo** tripe soup.
[7]**molcajete** mixing vessel, mortar.    [8]**¿Y mi Amá?** And my Mother?

eyes were filled with sorrow. I went outside and sat on the porch swing and watched the people pass. I sat there until she left. I dozed off repeating the words to myself like rosary prayers: when do you stop giving when do you start giving when do you . . . and when my hands fell from my lap, I awoke to catch them. The sun was setting, an orange glow, and I knew Abuelita was hungry.

There comes a time when the sun is defiant. Just about the time when moods change, inevitable seasons of a day, transitions from one color to another, that hour or minute or second when the sun is finally defeated, finally sinks into the realization that it cannot with all its power to heal or burn, exist forever, there comes an illumination where the sun and earth meet, a final burst of burning red orange fury reminding us that although endings are inevitable, they are necessary for rebirths, and when that time came, just when I switched on the light in the kitchen to open Abuelita's can of soup, it was probably then that she died.

The room smelled of Pine Sol and vomit and Abuelita had defecated the remains of her cancerous stomach. She had turned to the window and tried to speak, but her mouth remained open and speechless. I heard you, Abuelita, I said, stroking her cheek, I heard you. I opened the windows of the house and let the soup simmer and overboil on the stove. I turned the stove off and poured the soup down the sink. From the cabinet I got a tin basin, filled it with lukewarm water and carried it carefully to the room. I went to the linen closet and took out some modest bleached white towels. With the sacredness of a priest preparing his vestments, I unfolded the towels one by one on my shoulders. I removed the sheets and blankets from her bed and peeled off her thick flannel nightgown. I toweled her puzzled face, stretching out the wrinkles, removing the coils of her neck, toweled her shoulders and breasts. Then I changed the water. I returned to towel the creases of her stretch-marked stomach, her sporadic vaginal hairs, and her sagging thighs. I removed the lint from between her toes and noticed a mapped birthmark on the fold of her buttock. The scars on her back which were as thin as the life lines on the palms of her hands made me realize how little I really knew of Abuelita. I covered her with a thin blanket and went into the bathroom. I washed my hands, and turned on the tub faucets and watched the water pour into the tub with vitality and steam. When it was full, I turned off the water and undressed. Then, I went to get Abuelita.

15      She was not as heavy as I thought and when I carried her in my arms, her body fell into a V, and yet my legs were tired, shaky, and I felt as if the distance between the bedroom and bathroom was miles and years away. Amá, where are you?

I stepped into the bathtub one leg first, then the other. I bent my knees slowly to descend into the water slowly so I wouldn't scald her skin. There, there, Abuelita, I said, cradling her, smoothing her as we descended, I heard you. Her hair fell back and spread across the water like eagle's wings. The water in the tub overflowed and poured onto the tile of the floor. Then the moths came. Small, gray ones that came from her soul and out through her mouth fluttering to light, circling the single dull light bulb of the bathroom. Dying is lonely and I wanted to go to where the moths were, stay with her and plant chayotes whose vines would crawl up her fingers and into the clouds; I wanted to rest my head on her chest with her stroking my hair, telling me about the moths that lay within the soul and slowly eat the spirit up; I wanted to return to the waters of the womb with her so that we would never be alone again. I wanted. I wanted my Amá. I removed a few strands of hair from Abuelita's face and held her small light head within the hollow of my neck. The bathroom was filled with moths, and for the first time in a long time I cried, rocking us, crying for her, for me, for Amá, the sobs emerging from the depths of anguish, the misery of feeling half born, sobbing until finally the sobs rippled into circles and circles of sadness and relief. There, there, I said to Abuelita, rocking us gently, there, there.

# PART

# III

# Poetry

The original caption for this photograph of poet Gwendolyn Brooks, taken in 1950, ran as follows:

> A 32-year-old housewife and part-time secretary has won the Pulitzer Prize in poetry for *Annie Allen,* a ballad of Chicago Negro life. The first woman to capture one of the famed awards, she is the mother of a 9-year-old boy and the wife of Henry Blakely, partner in an auto repair shop.

These sentences are informative and accurate, and perhaps that is enough to ask of them, but we can't help remarking that if you want to know what poetry is *not,* you have only to read those sentences again. Despite the metaphor in "capture," the language is unexciting, even trite ("famed awards"). We are not talking about the lack of rhyme or of meter, qualities that of course are not found in prose (though they are not essential to poetry either). We might compare the caption with the prose that begins Brooks's most famous poem, "We Real Cool" (page 594), which starts thus: "The Pool Players. / Seven at the Golden Shovel." "Seven" has a mystical hint (it is widely regarded as a lucky number, there are seven days in the week, Seven Deadly Sins, Seven Wonders of the World, Seven Seas, and a host of other sevens) and "Golden Shovel"—presumably the name of a pool parlor—has

539

an interesting paradoxical quality: "Golden" suggests great wealth, "Shovel" suggests the humble soil, and in the context of the poem it suggests death.

As you will see when you come to read Brooks's poems (and the poems of others in this section of the book), poets do not use language the way journalists (including the writer of the caption for the photograph) use language. It is not, we hasten to add, that poets do not write about life. They certainly do: Brooks herself said "Poetry is life distilled," and "I wrote about what I saw and heard on the street." But for poets, words are sensuous materials, like colors for a painter or stones for a sculptor, and when words are combined they make not only good sense but also an almost physical thing that the reader feels as he or she recites the poem aloud or silently. We urge you to turn to page 594 and to read Brooks's "We Real Cool."

# 16

# Approaching Poetry: Responding in Writing

The title of this chapter is a bit misleading, since we have already spent a few pages discussing poems in Chapter 2, "Reading and Responding to Literature." But here we will begin again, taking a different approach.

First, some brief advice about how to approach a poem:

1. Read the poem aloud; or, if you can't bring yourself to read aloud, at least sound the poem in your mind's ear. Try to catch the speaker's tone of voice.
2. Pay attention not only to the black marks on the white paper but also to the white spaces between groups of lines. If a space follows some lines, pause briefly, and take the preceding lines as a unit of thought.
3. Read the poem a second and a third time. Now that you know how it ends, you'll be able to see the connections between the beginning and what follows.

## LANGSTON HUGHES

*Langston Hughes (1902-1967), an African American writer born in Joplin, Missouri, lived part of his youth in Mexico, spent a year at Columbia University, served as a merchant seaman, and worked in a Paris nightclub. There, he showed some of his poems to Alain Locke, an African American patron of the arts and a strong advocate of African American literature. Encouraged by Locke, Hughes continued to write when he returned to the United States, publishing fiction, plays, essays, and biographies; he also founded theaters and gave public readings. The poem that we reprint, "Harlem" (1951), provided Lorraine Hansberry with the title of her well-known play* A Raisin in the Sun *(1958). For a generous selection of poems by Langston Hughes, see Chapter 27.*

### *Harlem* [1951]

What happens to a dream deferred?

Does it dry up
like a raisin in the sun?

Or fester like a sore—
And then run?                                                        5
Does it stink like rotten meat?
Or crust and sugar over—
like a syrupy sweet?

Maybe it just sags
like a heavy load.                                                   10

*Or does it explode?*

Read the poem at least twice, and then think about its effect on you.

1. Do you find the poem interesting? Why or why not?
2. Do some things in it interest you more than others? If so, why?
3. Does anything in it puzzle you? If so, what?

Before reading any further, you might jot down your responses to some of these questions. And, whatever your responses, can you point to features of the poem to account for them?

Of course, different readers will respond at least somewhat differently to any work. On the other hand, since writers want to communicate, they try to control their readers' responses, and they count on their readers to understand the meanings of words as the writers understand them. Thus, Hughes assumed his readers knew that Harlem was the site of a large African American community in New York City.

Let's assume that the reader understands Hughes is talking about Harlem, New York, and, further, that the reader understands the "dream deferred" to refer to the unfulfilled hopes of African Americans who live in a society dominated by whites. But Hughes does not say "hopes," he says "dream," and he does not say "unfulfilled," he says "deferred." You might ask yourself exactly what differences there are between these words. Next, when you have read the poem several times, you might think about which expression is better in the context, "unfulfilled hopes" or "dream deferred," and why.

## Thinking About "Harlem"

Let's turn to an analysis of the poem, an examination of how the parts fit. As you look at the poem, think about the parts, and jot down whatever notes come to mind. After you have written your own notes, consider the annotations of one student.

These annotations chiefly get at the structure of the poem, the relationship of the parts. The student notices that the poem begins with a line set off by itself and ends with a line set off by itself, and he also notices that each of these lines is a question. Further, he indicates that each of these two lines is emphasized in other ways. The first begins further to the left than any of the other lines—as though the other lines are subheadings or are in some way subordinate—and the last is italicized. In short, he comments on the structure of the poem.

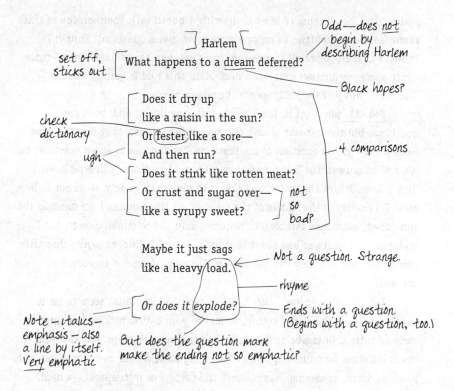

The annotated poem (with handwritten notes):

*set off,*
*sticks out*

**Harlem** — *Odd—does not begin by describing Harlem*

What happens to a <u>dream</u> deferred? — *Black hopes?*

*check dictionary* —
Does it dry up
like a raisin in the sun?

*ugh* —
Or (fester) like a sore—
And then run?

*4 comparisons*

Does it stink like rotten meat?
Or crust and sugar over— *not so bad?*
like a syrupy sweet?

Maybe it just sags
like a heavy/load. — *Not a question. Strange.*

— *rhyme*

*Note—italics— emphasis—also a line by itself. Very emphatic*

Or does it (explode)? — *Ends with a question. (Begins with a question, too.)*

*But does the question mark make the ending not so emphatic?*

## Some Journal Entries

The student who made these annotations later wrote an entry in his journal:

    <u>Feb. 18.</u>  Since the title is "Harlem," it's obvious that the "dream" is by African American people. Also, obvious that Hughes thinks that if the "dream" doesn't become real there may be riots ("explode"). I like "raisin in the sun" (maybe because I like the play), and I like the business about "a syrupy sweet"—much more pleasant than the festering sore and the rotten meat. But if the dream becomes "sweet," what's wrong with that? Why should something "sweet" explode?

    <u>Feb. 21.</u> Prof. Stahl said to think of structure or form of a poem as a sort of architecture, a building with a foundation, floors, etc., topped by a roof—but since we read a poem from top to bottom, it's like a building upside down. Title or first line is foundation (even though it's at top); last line is roof, capping the whole. As you read, you add layers. Foundation of "Harlem" is a question (first line). Then, set back a bit from foundation, or built on it by

white space, a tall room (7 lines high, with 4 questions); then, on top of this room, another room (two lines, one statement, not a question). Funny; I thought that in poems all stanzas are the same number of lines. Then—more white space, so another unit—the roof. Man, this roof is going to fall in— "explode." Not just the roof, maybe the whole house.

**Feb. 21, pm.** I get it; one line at start, one line at end; both are questions, but the last sort of says (because it is in italics) that it is the *most likely* answer to the question of the first line. The last line is also a question, but it's still an answer. The big stanza (7 lines) has 4 questions: 2 lines, 2 lines, 1 line, 2 lines. Maybe the switch to 1 line is to give some variety, so as not to be dull? It's exactly in the middle of the poem. I get the progress from raisin in the sun (dried, but not so terrible), to festering sore and to stinking meat, but I still don't see what's so bad about "a syrupy sweet." Is Hughes saying that after things are very bad they will get better? But why, then, the explosion at the end?

**Feb. 23.** "Heavy load" and "sags" in next-to-last stanza seem to me to suggest slaves with bales of cotton, or maybe poor cotton pickers dragging big sacks of cotton. Or maybe people doing heavy labor in Harlem. Anyway, very tired. Different from running sore and stinking meat earlier; not disgusting, but pressing down, deadening. Maybe *worse* than a sore or rotten meat—a hard, hopeless life. And then the last line. Just one line, no fancy (and disgusting) simile. Boom! Not just pressed down and tired, like maybe some racist whites think (hope?) blacks will be? Bang! Will there be survivors?

Drawing chiefly on these notes, the student jotted down some key ideas to guide him through a draft of an analysis of the poem. (The organization of the draft posed no problem; the student simply followed the organization of the poem.)

```
11 lines; short, but powerful; explosive
Question (first line)
Answers (set off by space & also indented)
"raisin in the sun": shrinking     ⎫
"sore"                              ⎬  disgusting
"rotten meat"                       ⎭
"syrupy sweet": relief from disgusting comparisons
final question (last line): explosion?
    explosive (powerful) because:
        short, condensed, packed
        in italics
        stands by itself—like first line
        no fancy comparison; very direct
```

Here is the student's final draft of his essay.

Michael Locke
Professor Stahl
English 2B
10 June 2010

Langston Hughes's "Harlem"

"Harlem" is a poem that is only eleven lines long, but it is charged with power. It explodes. Hughes sets the stage, so to speak, by telling us in the title that he is talking about Harlem, and then he begins by asking, "What happens to a dream deferred?" The rest of the poem is set off by being indented, as though it is the answer to his question. This answer is in three parts (three stanzas, of different lengths).

In a way, it's wrong to speak of the answer, since the rest of the poem consists of questions, but I think Hughes means that each question (for instance, does a "deferred" hope "dry up / like a raisin in the sun?") really is an answer, something that really has happened and that will happen again. The first question, "Does it dry up / like a raisin in the sun?," is a famous line. To compare hope to a raisin dried in the sun is to suggest a terrible shrinking. The next two comparisons are to a "sore" and to "rotten meat." These comparisons are less clever, but they are very effective because they are disgusting. Then, maybe because of the disgusting comparisons, he gives a comparison that is not at all disgusting. In this comparison he says that maybe the "dream deferred" will "crust and sugar over— / like a syrupy sweet."

The seven lines with four comparisons are followed by a stanza of two lines with just one comparison:

> Maybe it just sags
> like a heavy load.

So if we thought that this postponed dream might finally turn into something "sweet," we were kidding ourselves. Hughes comes down to earth, in a short stanza, with an image of a heavy load, which probably also calls to mind images of people bent under heavy loads, maybe of cotton, or maybe just any sort of heavy load carried by African Americans in Harlem and elsewhere.

Locke 2

The opening question ("What happens to a dream deferred?") was followed by four questions in seven lines, but now, with "Maybe it just sags / like a heavy load," we get a statement, as though the poet at last has found an answer. But at the end we get one more question, set off by itself and in italics: *Or does it explode?* This line itself is explosive for three reasons: it is short, it is italicized, and it is a stanza in itself. It's also interesting that this line, unlike the earlier lines, does *not* use a simile. It's almost as though Hughes is saying, "OK, we've had enough fancy ways of talking about this terrible situation; here it is, straight."

Locke 3

Work Cited

Hughes, Langston. "Harlem." *An Introduction to Literature*. Ed. Sylvan Barnet, William Burto, and William E. Cain. 16th ed. New York: Longman, 2011. 541–42. Print.

### YOUR TURN

1. The student's analysis suggests that the comparison with "a syrupy sweet" is a deliberately misleading happy ending that serves to make the real ending even more powerful. In class another student suggested that Hughes may be referring to African Americans who play the Uncle Tom, people who adopt a smiling manner in order to cope with an oppressive society. Which explanation do you prefer, and why? What do you think of combining the two? Or can you offer a different explanation?
2. Do you suppose that virtually all African Americans respond to this poem in a way that is substantially different from the way virtually all Caucasians or Asian Americans respond? Explain your position.
3. When Hughes reprinted this poem in 1959, he retitled it "Dream Deferred." Your response?

Let's now look at another poem, and at the responses of another student. Here is a seventeenth-century poem—actually a song—that makes use of the idea that the eyes of the beloved woman can dart fire, and that she can kill (or at least severely wound) the sighing, helpless male lover. The male speaker describes the appearance of Cupid, the tyrannic god of love, who (he claims) is equipped with darts and death-dealing fire taken from the eyes of the proud, cruel woman whom the speaker loves.

# APHRA BEHN

*Aphra Behn (1640-1689) is regarded as the first English woman to have made a living by writing. Not much is known of her life, but she seems to have married a London merchant of Dutch descent, and after his death to have served as a spy in the Dutch Wars (1665-1667). After her return to England she took up playwriting, and she gained fame with* The Rover *(1677). Behn also wrote novels, the most important of which is* Oroonoko, or The Royal Slave *(1688), which is among the first works in English to express sympathy for enslaved Africans.*

*In the following poem, Cupid represents love. The poem was written by a woman but the imagined speaker is a male, who laments that the woman whom he loves is indifferent to him.*

## Song: Love Armed                                                            [1676]

Love in fantastic triumph sate,
   Whilst bleeding hearts around him flowed,
For whom fresh pains he did create,
   And strange tyrannic power he showed:
From thy bright eyes he took his fire,                                          5
   Which round about in sport he hurled;
But 'twas from mine he took desire,
   Enough to undo the amorous world.

From me he took his sighs and tears:
   From thee, his pride and cruelty;                                  10
From me, his languishments and fears;
   And every killing dart from thee.
Thus thou and I the god have armed
   And set him up a deity;
But my poor heart alone is harmed,                                             15
   Whilst thine the victor is, and free.

### YOUR TURN

1. The speaker talks of the suffering he is undergoing (Behn is using the poetic convention of the passionate man who addresses a disdainful woman). Can we nevertheless feel that he enjoys his plight? *Why*, by the way, do we (as readers, singers, or listeners) often enjoy songs of unhappy love?
2. The woman ("thee") is said to exhibit "pride and cruelty" (line 10). Is the poem sexist? Is it therefore offensive?
3. Do you suppose that men can enjoy the poem more than women? Explain.

# Some Journal Entries

The subject is Aphra Behn's "Song." We begin with two entries in a journal, kept by a first-year student, Geoffrey Sullivan, and we follow these entries with Sullivan's completed essay.

**October 10.** The title "Love Armed" puzzled me at first; funny, I somehow was thinking of the expression "strong-armed" and at first I didn't understand that "Love" in this poem is a human—no, not a human, but the god Cupid, who has a human form—and that he is shown as armed, with darts and so forth.

**October 13.** This god of "Love" is Cupid, and so he is something like what is on a valentine card—Cupid with his bow and arrow. But valentine cards just show cute little Cupids, and in this poem Cupid is a real menace. He causes lots of pain ("bleeding hearts," "tears," "killing dart," etc.). So what is Aphra Behn telling us about the god of love, or love? That love hurts? And she is *singing* about it! But we *do* sing songs about how hard life is. But do we sing them when we are really hurting, or only when we are pretty well off and just thinking about being hurt?

When you love someone and they don't return your love, it hurts, but even when love isn't returned it still gives some intense pleasure. Strange, but I think true. I wouldn't say that love always has this two-sided nature, but I do see the idea that love *can* have two sides, pleasure and pain. And love takes two kinds of people, male and female. Well, for most people, anyway. Maybe there's also something to the idea that "opposites attract." Anyway, Aphra Behn seems to be talking about men vs. women, pain vs. pleasure, power vs. weakness, etc. Pairs, opposites. And in two stanzas (a pair of stanzas?).

The final essay makes use of some, but not all, of the preliminary jottings. It includes much that Sullivan did not think of until he reread his jottings, reread the poem, and began drafting the essay.

---

Sullivan 1

Geoffrey Sullivan
Professor Diaz
English 2G
15 June 2010

The Double Nature of Love

Aphra Behn's "Love Armed" is in two stanzas, and it is about two people, "me" and "thee"—that is, you and I, the lover and the woman he loves. I think the speaker is a man, since according to the usual code men are supposed to be the active lovers and women are the (relatively) passive people who are loved. In this poem, the beloved—the woman, I think—has "bright eyes" (line 5) that provide the God of Love with fire, and she also provides the god with "pride and cruelty" (10). This of course is the way the man sees it if a woman doesn't respond to him; if she doesn't love him in return, she is (he thinks) arrogant and cruel.

Sullivan 2

What does the man give to Love? He provides "desire" (7), "sighs and tears" (9), "languishments and fears" (11). None of this sounds very manly, but the joke is that the God of Love—which means love—can turn a strong man into a crybaby when a woman does not respond to him.

Although both stanzas are clever *descriptions* of the God of Love, the poem is not just a description. Of course there is not a plot in the way that a short story has a plot, but there is a sort of a switch at the end, giving the poem something of a plot. The poem is, say, ninety percent expression of feeling and description of love, but during the course of expressing feelings and describing love something happens, so there is a tiny *story*. The first stanza sets the scene ("Love in fantastic triumph sate" [1]) and tells of some of the things that the speaker and the woman contributed to the God of Love. The woman's eyes provided Love with fire, and the man's feelings provided Love with "desire" (7). The second stanza goes on to mention other things that Love got from the speaker ("sighs and tears," etc. [9]), and other things that Love got from the beloved ("pride and cruelty," etc. [10]), and in line 13 the poet says, "Thus thou and I the god have armed," so the two humans share something. They have both given Love his weapons. But—and this is the story I spoke of—the poem ends by emphasizing their difference: Only the man is "harmed," and the woman is the "victor" because her heart is not captured, as the man's heart is. In the battle that Love presides over, the woman is the winner; the man's heart has fallen for the woman, but, according to the last line, the woman's heart remains "free."

We have all seen the God of Love on valentine cards, a cute little Cupid armed with a bow and arrow. But despite the bow and arrow that the Valentine's Day Cupid carries, I think that until I read Aphra Behn's "Love Armed" I had never really thought about Cupid as *powerful* and as capable of causing real pain. On valentine cards, he is just cute, but when I think about it, I realize the truth of Aphra Behn's concept of love. Love *is* (or can be) two-sided, whereas the valentine cards show only the sweet side.

I think it is interesting to notice that although the poem is about the destructive power of love, it is fun to read. I am not bothered by the fact that the lover is miserable. Why? I think I enjoy the poem, rather than am bothered by it, because *he is enjoying his misery*. After all, he is singing about it, sort of singing in the rain, telling anyone who will listen about how miserable he is, and he is having a very good time doing it.

Sullivan 3

Work Cited

Behn, Aphra. "Love Armed." *An Introduction to Literature.* Ed. Sylvan
    Barnet, William Burto, and William E. Cain. 16th ed. New York:
    Longman, 2011. 547. Print.

## DAVID MURA

*David Mura (b. 1952) is a* sansei, *a third-generation Japanese American.
Mura's publications include novels, books of poetry, and two memoirs. He has
received several awards, including a US/Japan Creative Artist Fellowship, and
an NEA Literature Fellowship.*

## *An Argument: On 1942*                                    [1989]

*For my mother*

Near Rose's Chop Suey and Jinosuke's grocery,
the temple where incense hovered and inspired
dense evening chants (prayers for Buddha's mercy,
colorless and deep), that day he was fired . . .                      4

—No, no, no, she tells me. Why bring it back?
The camps are over. (Also overly dramatic.)
Forget *shoyu*-stained *furoshiki,°* *mochi°* on a stick:
You're like a terrier, David, gnawing a bone, an old, old trick . . .    8

Mostly we were bored. Women cooked and sewed,
men played blackjack, dug gardens, a *benjo.°*
Who noticed barbed wire, guards in the towers?
We were children, hunting stones, birds, wild flowers.                 12

Yes, Mother hid tins of *tsukemono°* and eel
beneath the bed. And when the last was peeled,
clamped tight her lips, growing thinner and thinner.
But cancer not the camps made her throat blacker                       16

. . . And she didn't die then . . . after the war, in St. Paul,
you weren't even born. Oh I know, I know, it's all
part of your job, your way, but why can't you glean
how far we've come, how much I can't recall—                           20

David, it was so long ago—how useless it seems . . .

---

**7 shoyu-stained furoshiki** a soy-sauce-stained scarf that is used to carry things.
**mochi** rice cakes.    **10 benjo** toilet.    **13 tsukemono** Japanese pickles [Author's notes].

Finally, a word about some of the most popular professional folksingers today. They have aptly been called "folksongers" because unlike illiterate or scarcely literate folksingers—who intend only to sing the traditional songs in the traditional way for themselves or their neighbors—these professionals are vocal artists who make commercial and political use (not bad things in themselves) of traditional folk songs, deliberately adapting old songs and inventing new songs that only loosely resemble the old ones. These contemporary ballads tend to be more personal than traditional ballads and they tend to have a social consciousness that is alien to traditional balladry. Many of the songs of Pete Seeger and Bob Dylan, for instance, are conspicuous examples of art in the service of morality or politics; they call attention to injustice and they seek to move the hearers to action. That traditional ballads have assisted in this task is not the least of their value; the influence of a work of art is never finished, and the old ballads can rightly claim to share in the lives of their modern descendants.

We print a popular traditional English ballad here ("Sir Patrick Spence"), followed (page 560) by a poem that is indebted to traditional ballads (John Keats's "La Belle Dame sans Merci"). We also present several short narrative poems—poems that tell a story—that are *not* in the ballad tradition. (For additional ballads, see "The Three Ravens," "The Twa Corbies," and "John Henry" in Chapter 28; for a literary ballad by an African American author, see Langston Hughes's "Ballad of the Landlord," page 765.)

## ANONYMOUS BRITISH BALLAD

### *Sir Patrick Spence*

The king sits in Dumferling toune,
    Drinking the blude-reid wine:
"O whar will I get guid sailor,
    To sail this schip of mine?"                                    4

Up and spak an eldern knicht,
    Sat at the kings richt kne:
"Sir Patrick Spence is the best sailor,
    That sails upon the se."                                        8

Itch of haydust in the
      sweaty shirt and shoes.
At lunchtime under Black oak         15
Out in the hot corral,
—The old mare nosing lunchpails,
Grasshoppers crackling in the weeds—
"I'm sixty-eight" he said,
"I first bucked hay when I was seventeen.      20
I thought, that day I started,
I sure would hate to do this all my life.
And dammit, that's just what
I've gone and done."

### YOUR TURN

1. The speaker does not explicitly offer his opinion of the man who "had driven half the night" but do the first two sentences (lines 1–14) communicate at least a hint of an attitude?
2. The old man who speaks lines 19–24 sums up his life. He seems to regard it as wasted, but as we hear his words do we hear bitterness? Self-pity? What is our attitude toward him, and how does it compare with that of the speaker of the poem?

# PHILLIS WHEATLEY

*Kidnapped in Africa when she was a child of about age seven, and brought to Boston on the schooner* Phillis, *Phillis Wheatley (1753–1784) owed her first name to the ship and her second to the family name of the merchant who bought her to attend on his wife. She was educated in English, Latin, history, and geography, and especially in the Bible, and within a few years she was writing poetry in the approved manner—that is, the manner of eighteenth-century England. In 1773, the year she was granted freedom, she published a book of her poems in England.*

    *Despite her education and the style of writing that she adopted, Wheatley of course did not move freely in the white world. But neither did she move freely in the black world, since her educators kept her away from other persons of African origin. Perhaps the best single sentence ever written about Phillis Wheatley is Richard Wright's:"Before the webs of slavery had so tightened as to snare nearly all Negroes in our land, one was freed by accident to give in clear, bell-like limpid cadence the hope of freedom in the New World." One other sentence about Wheatley, by another African American writer, should also be quoted here. Alice Walker, commenting on Wheatley's much criticized assumption of white values, says, in an address to Wheatley, "It is not so much what you sang, as that you kept alive, in so many of our ancestors, the notion of song."*

    *"On Being Brought from Africa to America" alludes to the story of Cain and Abel (Genesis 4.15), which reports that Cain killed Abel, and that "the Lord set a mark upon Cain." The biblical text explicitly says that the mark was to protect Cain from someone who might take vengeance on him, but it does*

Phillis Wheatley was probably brought to America on a slave ship such as this one showing how the slaves were packed. The English abolitionist Thomas Clarkson (1760–1846) distributed this drawing with his *Essay on the Slavery and Commerce of the Human Species* (1786; rpt. 1804).

*not say what the mark was. Nevertheless, some Christians developed the idea that the color of Africans was the mark of Cain.*

### On Being Brought from Africa to America    [1772]

'Twas mercy brought me from my pagan land,
Taught my benighted soul to understand
That there's a God, that there's a Savior too:
Once I redemption neither sought nor knew.
Some view our sable race with scornful eye,                    5
"Their color is a diabolic dye."
Remember, Christians; Negroes, black as Cain,
May be refined, and join the angelic train.

## JOHN KEATS

*John Keats (1795–1821), son of a London stable keeper, was taken out of school at age fifteen and apprenticed to a surgeon and apothecary. In 1816 he was licensed to practice as an apothecary-surgeon, but he almost immediately abandoned medicine and decided to make a career as a poet. His progress was amazing; he published books of poems—to mixed reviews—in 1817, 1818, and 1820, before dying of tuberculosis at the age of twenty-five. Today he is esteemed as one of England's greatest poets.*

*Additional poems by Keats appear on pages 587, 622, and 810.*

## *La Belle Dame sans Merci*\*                              [1819]

O what can ail thee, knight-at-arms,
　　Alone and palely loitering?
The sedge has withered from the lake,
　　And no birds sing.                                        4

O what can ail thee, knight-at-arms,
　　So haggard and so woe-begone?
The squirrel's granary is full,
　　And the harvest's done.                                   8

I see a lily on thy brow,
　　With anguish moist and fever dew,
And on thy cheeks a fading rose
　　Fast withereth too.                                       12

"I met a lady in the meads,
　　Full beautiful—a faery's child,
Her hair was long, her foot was light,
　　And her eyes were wild.                                   16

"I made a garland for her head,
　　And bracelets too, and fragrant zone;°
She looked at me as she did love,
　　And made sweet moan.                                      20

"I sct her on my pacing steed,
　　And nothing else saw all day long,
For sidelong would she bend and sing
　　A faery's song.                                           24

"She found me roots of relish sweet,
　　And honey wild, and manna dew,
And sure in language strange she said
　　'I love thee true.'                                       28

"She took me to her elfin grot,
　　And there she wept and sighed full sore,
And there I shut her wild wild eyes
　　With kisses four.                                         32

"And there she lullèd me asleep,
　　And there I dreamed—Ah! woe betide!
The latest dream I ever dreamed
　　On the cold hill side.                                    36

"I saw pale kings and princes too,
　　Pale warriors, death-pale were they all;
They cried, 'La Belle Dame sans Merci
　　Hath thee in thrall!'                                     40

---

\**La Belle Dame sans Merci* the beautiful lady without pity.   **18 fragrant zone** belt of flowers.

"I saw their starved lips in the gloam
  With horrid warning gapèd wide,
And I awoke, and found me here,
  On the cold hill's side.                                    44

"And this is why I sojourn here,
  Alone and palely loitering,
Though the sedge has withered from the lake,
  And no birds sing."                                         48

---

**YOUR TURN**

1. In the first three stanzas the speaker describes the knight as pale, haggard, and so forth. In the rest of the poem the knight recounts his experience. In a few sentences summarize the knight's experience, and indicate why it has caused him to appear as he now does.
2. The *femme fatale*—the dangerously seductive woman—appears often
   in literature. If you are familiar with one such work, compare it with
   Keats's poem.
3. What characteristics of the popular ballad (see page 554) do you find in
   this poem? What characteristic does it *not* share with popular ballads?
   Set forth your response in an essay of 500 words.
4. Is this poem about love, or death, or both? Please explain, making references to details in the text.
5. What is your response to this poem? Do you feel a connection to the
   characters? What kind of connection?
6. Keats said that "La Belle Dame sans Merci" was not one of his best or
   most serious poems, yet later generations of readers have valued it
   highly. How do you explain this discrepancy? Are poets reliable judges
   of the merits of their own poems?

# SIEGFRIED SASSOON

*Siegfried Sassoon (1886-1967), a wealthy Englishman, served with such dis-*
*tinction in World War I—in 1915 under heavy fire he helped a wounded sol-*
*dier to safety—that he was awarded the Military Cross. Later, wounded by a*
*bullet in the chest, he was sent from France back to England, where, upon re-*
*flection, he concluded that the war was not a war of defense but of aggres-*
*sion. Military officials shrewdly chose not to dispute him, but merely asserted*
*that he was shell-shocked. When Sassoon recovered from the bullet wound, he*
*was again sent into combat, and was again wounded and hospitalized.*

   *Sassoon expressed his views in* Memoirs of a Fox-Hunting Man *(1928) and*
Memoirs of an Infantry Officer *(1930), as well as in* Collected Poems,
1908-1956 *(1961).*

## The General                                               [1917]

"Good-morning, good-morning!" the General said
When we met him last week on our way to the line.
Now the soldiers he smiled at are most of 'em dead,

And we're cursing his staff for incompetent swine.
"He's a cheery old card," grunted Harry to Jack
As they slogged up to Arras with rifle and pack.

But he did for them both by his plan of attack.

### YOUR TURN

1. Who is the storyteller, and what is the story he tells?
2. Why do you suppose Sassoon put an extra space between the next-to-last line and the last line? Speaking of the last line, notice that it rhymes with the two preceding lines—i.e., the last three lines end with identical sounds, whereas in the preceding four lines, no two adjacent lines rhyme. Why do you suppose Sassoon changed the rhyme-scheme for the final lines?
3. How would you characterize the General? How would you characterize Harry? How would you characterize the storyteller?

## COUNTEE CULLEN

*Countee Cullen (1903–1946) was born Countee Porter in New York City, raised by his grandmother, and then adopted by the Reverend Frederick A. Cullen, a Methodist minister in Harlem. Cullen received a bachelor's degree from New York University (Phi Beta Kappa) and a master's degree from Harvard. He earned his living as a high school teacher of French, but his literary gifts were recognized in his own day, and he went on to become a leading African American poet of the modern period.*

### *Incident*    [1925]

*(For Eric Walrond)*

Once riding in old Baltimore,
  Heart-filled, head-filled with glee,
I saw a Baltimorean
  Keep looking straight at me.                              4

Now I was eight and very small,
  And he was no whit bigger,
And so I smiled, but he poked out
  His tongue, and called me, "Nigger."                      8

I saw the whole of Baltimore
  From May until December;
Of all the things that happened there
  That's all that I remember.                               12

### YOUR TURN

1. How would you define an "incident"? A serious occurrence? A minor occurrence, or what? Think about the word, and then think about Cullen's use of it as a title for the event recorded in this poem. Test out

one or two other possible titles as a way of helping yourself to see the strengths or weaknesses of Cullen's title.

2. The dedicatee, Eric Walrond (1898–1966) was an African American essayist and writer of fiction, who in an essay, "On Being Black," had described his experiences of racial prejudice. How does the presence of the dedication bear on our response to Cullen's account of the "incident"?

3. What is the tone of the poem? Indifferent? Angry? Or what? What do you think is the speaker's attitude toward the "incident"? What is your attitude?

4. Ezra Pound, poet and critic, once defined literature as "news that *stays* news." What do you think he meant by this? Do you think that the definition fits Cullen's poem?

# EDWIN ARLINGTON ROBINSON

*Edwin Arlington Robinson (1869–1935) grew up in Gardiner, Maine, spent two years at Harvard, and then returned to Maine, where he published his first book of poetry in 1896. Though he received encouragement from neighbors, his finances were precarious, even after President Theodore Roosevelt, having been made aware of the book, secured for him an appointment as customs inspector in New York from 1905 to 1909. Additional books won fame for Robinson, and in 1922 he was awarded the first of the three Pulitzer Prizes for poetry that he would win.*

## Richard Cory

[1897]

Whenever Richard Cory went down town,
We people on the pavement looked at him:
He was a gentleman from sole to crown,
Clean favored, and imperially slim.                                    4

And he was always quietly arrayed,
And he was always human when he talked;
But still he fluttered pulses when he said,
"Good-morning," and he glittered when he walked.                       8

And he was rich—yes, richer than a king—
And admirably schooled in every grace:
In fine,° we thought that he was everything
To make us wish that we were in his place.                            12

So on we worked, and waited for the light,
And went without the meat, and cursed the bread;
And Richard Cory, one calm summer night,
Went home and put a bullet through his head.                          16

---

**11 In fine** in short.

"Tell them I came, and no one answered,
  That I kept my word," he said.
Never the least stir made the listeners,
  Though every word he spake                                    30
Fell echoing through the shadowiness of the still house
  From the one man left awake:
Aye, they heard his foot upon the stirrup,
  And the sound of iron on stone,
And how the silence surged softly backward,                    35
  When the plunging hoofs were gone.

---

**YOUR TURN**

1. Walter de la Mare is reported to have said that the Traveler is a ghost. He is also reported to have said on another occasion that the poem records a class reunion at which he found himself the only one present. Is either of these explanations convincing? Is there anything in the poem to refute the first explanation?
2. Is the poem a narrative of a man who fulfilled a promise, though the ones to whom the promise was made are dead? Is it a narrative of a man who fulfilled a promise in the face of evil forces? Of a frustrated, heroic search for the meaning of life? Of our mysterious separation from the dead? In 100 to 150 words, evaluate one of these interpretations.
3. Why are the actions of the horse described (lines 3, 23)?
4. Why did de la Mare call the poem "The Listeners" rather than "The Traveler"?

# JOHN LENNON AND PAUL McCARTNEY

*John Lennon (1940–1980) and Paul McCartney (b. 1942) were original members of the Beatles.*

## *Eleanor Rigby*                                            [1966]

Ah, look at all the lonely people!
Ah, look at all the lonely people!

Eleanor Rigby
Picks up the rice in the church where a wedding has been,
Lives in a dream.                                              5
Waits at the window
Wearing the face that she keeps in a jar by the door.
Who is it for?

All the lonely people,
Where do they all come from?                                   10
All the lonely people,
Where do they all belong?

Father McKenzie,
Writing the words of a sermon that no one will hear,
No one comes near.                                    15
Look at him working,
Darning his socks in the night when there's nobody there.
What does he care?

All the lonely people,
Where do they all come from?                          20
All the lonely people,
Where do they all belong?

Ah, look at all the lonely people!
Ah, look at all the lonely people!
Eleanor Rigby                                         25
Died in the church and was buried along with her name,
Nobody came.
Father McKenzie,
Wiping the dirt from his hands as he walks from the grave,
No one was saved.                                     30

All the lonely people,
Where do they all come from?
All the lonely people,
Where do they all belong?

Ah, look at all the lonely people!                    35
Ah, look at all the lonely people!

### YOUR TURN

Is the poem chiefly about Eleanor Rigby? What is Father McKenzie doing
in the poem?

# E. E. CUMMINGS

*e. e. cummings was the pen name of Edward Estlin Cummings (1894-1962),
who grew up in Cambridge, Massachusetts, and graduated from Harvard,
where he became interested in modern literature and art, especially in the
movements called cubism and futurism. His father, a conservative clergyman
and a professor at Harvard, seems to have been baffled by the youth's interests, but cummings's mother encouraged his artistic activities, including his
use of unconventional punctuation and capitalization.*

*Politically liberal in his youth, cummings became more conservative after
a visit to Russia in 1931, but early and late his work emphasizes individuality and freedom of expression.*

## *anyone lived in a pretty how town*                [1940]

anyone lived in a pretty how town
(with up so floating many bells down)
spring summer autumn winter
he sang his didn't he danced his did.                 4

Women and men(both little and small)
cared for anyone not at all
they sowed their isn't they reaped their same
sun moon stars rain                                    8

children guessed(but only a few
and down they forgot as up they grew
autumn winter spring summer)
that noone loved him more by more           12

when by now and tree by leaf
she laughed his joy she cried his grief
bird by snow and stir by still
anyone's any was all to her                       16

someones married their everyones
laughed their cryings and did their dance
(sleep wake hope and then)they
said their nevers they slept their dream     20

stars rain sun moon
(and only the snow can begin to explain
how children are apt to forget to remember
with up so floating many bells down)          24

one day anyone died i guess
(and noone stooped to kiss his face)
busy folk buried them side by side
little by little and was by was                     28

all by all and deep by deep
and more by more they dream their sleep
noone and anyone earth by april
wish by spirit and if by yes.                         32

Women and men(both dong and ding)
summer autumn winter spring
reaped their sowing and went their came
sun moon stars rain                                    36

### YOUR TURN

1. Put into normal order (as far as possible) the words of the first two stanzas, and then compare your version with cummings's. What does cummings gain—or lose?
2. Characterize the "anyone" who "sang his didn't" and "danced his did." In your opinion, how does he differ from the people who "sowed their isn't they reaped their same"?
3. Some readers interpret "anyone died" (line 25) to mean that the child matured and became as dead as the other adults. How might you support or refute this interpretation?

# 18

# Lyric Poetry

For the ancient Greeks, a **lyric** was a song accompanied by a lyre. It was short, and it usually expressed a single emotion, such as joy or sorrow. The word is now used more broadly, referring to a poem that, neither narrative (telling a story) nor strictly dramatic (performed by actors), is an emotional or reflective soliloquy. Still, it is rarely very far from a singing voice. In *A Portrait of the Artist as a Young Man* (1916), James Joyce describes the lyric as the "verbal vesture of an instant of emotion, a rhythmical cry such as ages ago cheered on the man who pulled at the oar." Such lyrics, too, were sung more recently than "ages ago." Here is a song that American slaves sang when rowing heavy loads.

## ANONYMOUS

### Michael Row the Boat Ashore

Michael row the boat ashore, Hallelujah!
Michael's boat's a freedom boat, Hallelujah!
Sister, help to trim the sail, Hallelujah!
Jordan stream is wide and deep, Hallelujah!
Freedom stands on the other side, Hallelujah!                    5

We might pause for a moment to comment on why people sing at work. There are at least three reasons: (1) work done rhythmically goes more efficiently; (2) the songs relieve the boredom of the work; and (3) the songs—whether narrative or lyrical—provide something of an outlet for the workers' frustrations.

Speaking roughly, we can say that whereas a narrative (whether in prose or poetry) is set in the past, telling what happened, a lyric is set in the present, catching a speaker in a moment of expression. But a lyric can, of course, glance backward or forward, as in this folk song, usually called "Careless Love."

## ANONYMOUS

### Careless Love

Love, O love, O careless love,
You see what careless love can do.

When I wore my apron low,
Couldn't keep you from my do,°
   Fare you well, fare you well.                               5
Now I wear my apron high,
Scarce see you passin' by,
   Fare you well, fare you well.

---

**4 do** door.

Notice, too, that a lyric, like a narrative, can have a plot: "Michael" moves toward the idea of freedom, and "Careless Love" implies a story of desertion—something has happened between the time that the singer could not keep the man from her door and now, when she "scarce" sees him passing by—but, again, the emphasis is on a present state of mind.

Lyrics are sometimes differentiated among themselves. For example, if a lyric is melancholy or mournfully contemplative, especially if it laments a death, it may be called an **elegy.** If a lyric is rather long, elaborate, and on a lofty theme such as immortality or a hero's victory, it may be called an **ode** or a **hymn.** Distinctions among lyrics are often vague, and one person's ode may be another's elegy. Still, when writers use one of these words in their titles, they are inviting the reader to recall the tradition in which they are working. Of the poet's link to tradition T. S. Eliot said:

> No poet, no artist of any art, has his complete meaning alone. His significance, his appreciation is the appreciation of his relation to the dead poets and artists. You cannot value him alone; you must set him, for contrast and comparison, among the dead.

Although the lyric is often ostensibly addressed to someone (the "you" in "Careless Love"), the reader usually feels that the speaker is really talking to himself or herself. In "Careless Love," the speaker need not be in the presence of her man; rather, her heart is overflowing (the reader senses) and she pretends to address him.

A comment by the nineteenth-century english philosopher John Stuart Mill on poetry is especially true of the lyric:

> Eloquence is *heard*, poetry is *over*heard. Eloquence supposes an audience; the peculiarity of poetry appears to us to lie in the poet's utter unconsciousness of a listener. Poetry is feeling confessing itself to itself, in moments of solitude.

This is particularly true in work songs such as "Michael Row the Boat Ashore," where there is no audience: the singers sing for themselves, participating rather than performing. As one prisoner in Texas said: "They really be singing about the way they feel inside. Since they can't say it to nobody, they sing a song about it." The sense of "feeling confessing itself to itself, in moments of solitude" or of "singing about the way they feel inside" is strong and clear in this short cowboy song.

# ANONYMOUS

## *The Colorado Trail*

Eyes like the morning star,
Cheeks like a rose,
Laura was a pretty girl
God Almighty knows.                                              4

Weep all ye little rains,
Wail winds wail,
All along, along, along
The Colorado trail.                                              8

When we read a lyric poem, no matter who the speaker is, for a moment—
while we recite or hear the words—we become the speaker. That is, we get into
the speaker's mind, or, perhaps more accurately, the speaker takes charge of our
mind, and we undergo (comfortably seated in a chair or sprawled on a bed) the
mental experience that is embodied in the words.

Next, another anonymous poem, this one written in England, probably in
the early sixteenth century. Aside from modern reprintings, it survives in only
one manuscript, a song book, the relevant portion of which we reproduce here.
But first, here is the poem in modern typography.

# ANONYMOUS

## *Western Wind*

Westron wind, when will thou blow?
The small rain down can rain.
Christ, that my love were in my arms,
And I in my bed again.

*Westron wynde when wilt thou blow.* Musical setting in a tenor part-book; early sixteenth
century. (Reproduced by permission of the British Library Royal Appendix 58 f.5. ©
British Library Board. All rights reserved.)

The angular handwriting is in a style quite different from modern writing, but when you are told that the first three words are "Westron [i.e., western] wynde when," you can probably see some connections. And you can probably make out the last handwritten word on the second line ("And"), and all of the third line: "I yn my bed A gayne" ("I in my bed again").

Incidentally—we hope we are not boring you with trifles—some controversy surrounds the transcription of one of the words—the fifth word in the second line of writing, the word that looks like a *y* followed by an *f* (just after "Chryst" and just before "my"). The issue is this: Is the letter a *y*, in which case the word is "if," or is it a letter we no longer have, a letter called *thorn*, which was pronounced "th," as in either "thin" or "this"? If indeed it is a thorn, the next letter is a *t*, not an *f*, and the word therefore is not "if" but "that." (Incidentally, signs that say "Ye Olde Antique Shoppe" make no sense; "Ye" was never used as a definite article. What these signs are reproducing is a thorn, and the word really is "The," not "Ye.")

**YOUR TURN**

1. In "Western Wind," what do you think is the tone of the speaker's voice in the first two lines? Angry? Impatient? Supplicating? Be as precise as possible. What is the tone in the next two lines?
2. In England the west wind, warmed by the Gulf Stream, rises in the spring. What associations link the wind and rain of lines 1 and 2 with lines 3 and 4?
3. Should we have been told why the lovers are separated? Explain.

Love poems are by no means all the same—to take an obvious point, some are happy and some are sad—but those that are about the loss of a beloved or about the pains of love seem to be especially popular.

# JULIA WARD HOWE

*Julia Ward Howe (1819–1910) was born in New York City. A social reformer, her work for the emancipation of African Americans and the right of women to vote is notable. She was the first woman to be elected to the American Academy of Arts and Letters. Howe is the author of many poems, including "The Battle Hymn of the Republic," set to already-existing music composed by William Steffe. The poem was first published in* The Atlantic Monthly *in 1862. It soon became one of the most popular songs of the Union during the Civil War.*

## Battle Hymn of the Republic

[1861]

Mine eyes have seen the glory of the coming of the Lord:
He is trampling out the vintage where the grapes of wrath are stored;
He hath loosed the fateful lightning of his terrible swift sword;
    His truth is marching on.                                    4

*Chorus*
    Glory! glory! Hallelujah!
    Glory! glory! Hallelujah!
    Glory! glory! Hallelujah!
        His truth is marching on!                                8

I have seen him in the watch-fires of a hundred circling camps;
They have builded him an altar in the evening dews and damps;
I can read his righteous sentence by the dim and flaring lamps;
    His day is marching on.                                          12

I have read a fiery gospel, writ in burnished rows of steel:
"As ye deal with my contemners, so with you my grace shall deal;
Let the Hero, born of woman, crush the serpent with his heel,
    Since God is marching on."                                       16

He has sounded forth the trumpet that shall never call retreat;
He is sifting out the hearts of men before his judgment seat;
Oh, be swift, my soul, to answer him! be jubilant, my feet!
    Our God is marching on.                                          20

In the beauty of the lilies Christ was born across the sea,
With a glory in his bosom that transfigures you and me:
As he died to make men holy, let us die to make men free,
    While God is marching on.                                        24

> **YOUR TURN**

1. This poem of the Civil War, draws some of its militant imagery from the Bible, especially from Isaiah 63.1–6 and Revelation 19.11–15. Do you think the lines about Christ are inappropriate here? Explain.
2. If you know the tune to which "Battle Hymn of the Republic" is sung, think about the interplay between the music and the words. Do you think people have a different response to Howe's words when they read her text as a poem, rather than experience it as a song?

# WILLIAM SHAKESPEARE

*William Shakespeare (1564–1616) is best known as the writer of sonnets and of plays, but he also wrote lyrics for songs in some of the plays. The following two lyrics are sung at the end of an early comedy,* Love's Labor's Lost. *Conflict is essential in drama, and in these two poems we get a sort of melodious conflict, a song in praise of spring, juxtaposed against a song in praise of winter. But notice that within each song there are elements of conflict. For other works by Shakespeare* (Hamlet, a Midsummer Night's Dream, *and several sonnets), consult the index.*

## *Spring*                                                          [c. 1595]

When daisies pied and violets blue
    And lady-smocks° all silver-white
And cuckoo-buds° of yellow hue
    Do paint the meadows with delight,
The cuckoo then, on every tree,                                      5
Mocks married men; for thus sings he,
                        "Cuckoo,
Cuckoo, cuckoo!" O word of fear,

---

**2 lady-smocks** also called cuckooflowers.    **3 cuckoo-buds** buttercups.

Unpleasing to a married ear!
When shepherds pipe on oaten straws,°                              10
   And merry larks are ploughmen's clocks,
When turtles tread,° and rooks, and daws,
   And maidens bleach their summer smocks,
The cuckoo then, on every tree,
Mocks married men; for thus sings he,                              15
                "Cuckoo,
Cuckoo, cuckoo!" O word of fear,
Unpleasing to a married ear!

---

**10 oaten straws** musical instruments.    **12 turtles tread** turtledoves mate.

## Winter
[c. 1595]

When icicles hang by the wall,
   And Dick the shepherd blows his nail,°
And Tom bears logs into the hall,
   And milk comes frozen home in pail,
When blood is nipped, and ways° be foul,                          5
Then nightly sings the staring owl,
        "Tu-whit, tu-who!"
A merry note,
While greasy Joan doth keel° the pot.
When all aloud the wind doth blow,                                10
   And coughing drowns the parson's saw,°
And birds sit brooding in the snow,
   And Marian's nose looks red and raw,
When roasted crabs° hiss in the bowl,
Then nightly sings the staring owl,                               15
        "Tu-whit, tu-who!"
A merry note,
While greasy Joan doth keel the pot.

---

**2 blows his nail** breathes on his fingernails to warm them.    **5 ways** roads.    **9 keel** cool, by skimming.    **11 coughing . . . saw** wise saying.    **14 crabs** crab apples.

   **YOUR TURN**

1. Why is the cuckoo appropriate to spring? The owl to winter?
2. Did you expect a poem on spring to bring in infidelity? Is the poem bitter? Explain. (If in doubt, check the word "cuckold" in a dictionary.)
3. Does "Winter" describe only the hardships of the season, or does it communicate also the joys?

Here is another song from one of Shakespeare's plays, a comedy called *Much Ado about Nothing* (1598–99). The song (2.3.62–79) is about male infidelity, and it seems to be addressed to women ("Sigh no more, ladies, sigh no more") but in fact it is sung by a male singer and, in the play, his listeners are all males.

## *Sigh no more, ladies, sigh no more*

Sigh no more, ladies, sigh no more;
  Men were deceivers ever;
One foot in sea and one on shore,
  To one thing constant never;
    Then sigh not so,              5
    But let them go,
And be you blithe and bonny;°
Converting all your sounds of woe
  Into Hey nonny, nonny.

Sing no more ditties, sing no mo,°           10
  Of dumps° so dull and heavy;
The fraud of men was ever so,
  Since summer first was leavy.°
    Then sigh not so,
    But let them go,              15
And be you blithe and bonny,
Converting all your sounds of woe
  Into Hey, nonny, nonny.

---

**7 bonny** carefree.   **10 mo** more.   **11 dumps** mournful songs.   **13 leavy** leafy.

---

**YOUR TURN**

1. Is the song offensive? Trivial? Engaging? Probably true in its assertion about males?
2. Given that the subject of this lyric is "the fraud of men," and the advice to women is "sigh not so / But let them go, / And be you blithe and bonny," do you think that the female response to the lyric is very different from the male response? Please explain.
3. The two stanzas are pretty similar—in fact, each stanza ends with the same four lines—but do you agree that there is, in a very quiet way, a sort of plot, or narrative? Our thought is that although the first stanza says that "Men were deceivers ever," in the next stanza the word "fraud" goes a step further, thereby justifying the advice to "let them go." Do you agree that if the stanzas were reversed, the poem would not be equally satisfactory?

In a later chapter you will find an even shorter poem on this topic, Dorothy Parker's "General Review of the Sex Situation." (Skipping ahead is permissible; the poem appears on page 651. You may want to compare the *tone—the* attitude of each speaker as you detect it from the printed words.)

# W. H. AUDEN

*Wystan Hugh Auden (1907–1973) was born in York, England, and educated at Oxford. In the 1930s his left-wing poetry earned him wide acclaim as the leading poet of his generation. In 1939 Auden came to the United States, and in 1946 he became an American citizen, though he spent his last years in*

*England. In addition to being a prolific poet, Auden also wrote many essays on literature and other subjects.*

## Funeral Blues                                                    [1936]

Stop all the clocks, cut off the telephone,
Prevent the dog from barking with a juicy bone,
Silence the pianos and with muffled drum
Bring out the coffin, let the mourners come.                          4

Let aeroplanes circle moaning overhead
Scribbling on the sky the message He Is Dead,
Put crêpe bows round the white necks of the public doves,
Let the traffic policemen wear black cotton gloves.                   8

He was my North, my South, my East and West,
My working week and my Sunday rest,
My noon, my midnight, my talk, my song;
I thought that love would last for ever: I was wrong.               12

The stars are not wanted now: put out every one;
Pack up the moon and dismantle the sun;
Pour away the ocean and sweep up the wood.
For nothing now can ever come to any good.                         16

### YOUR TURN

1. Let's assume that poems are rooted in real-life situations—that is, they take their origin from responses to experience, whether the experience is falling in love or losing a loved one, or praising God or losing one's faith, or celebrating a war (as in "Battle Hymn of the Republic") or lamenting the tragic destruction of war. But of course the poet then shapes the experience into a memorable statement and somehow makes a distinctive work on a traditional theme. Cite some phrases in Auden's poem that you would *not* expect to find in a poem on the death of the beloved. (For example, would you expect to find a reference to a dog eating "a juicy bone" in a poem on this theme?) Do you think these passages are effective, or do you think they are just silly? Explain.
2. Perhaps another way of getting at the question we have just asked is this: Can you imagine reading this at the funeral of someone you love? Or would you want a lover to read it at your funeral? Why?
3. The words of the last line of the poem are simple, almost a cliché. Yet we find them very powerful, and we wonder if you agree. What is the relationship of this line to the preceding lines of the stanza, with its images of mighty actions and cosmic gestures, and to the poem as a whole?

# EMILY BRONTË

*Emily Brontë (1818–1848) spent most of her short life (she died of tuberculosis) in an English village on the Yorkshire moors. The sister of Charlotte Brontë (author of* Jane Eyre, *1847) and of Anne Brontë (author of* Agnes Grey, *1847), Emily is best known for her novel* Wuthering Heights *(1847), but she was a considerable poet, and her first significant publication (1846) was in a volume of poems by the three sisters.*

## Spellbound

[1837]

The night is darkening round me,
The wild winds coldly blow;
But a tyrant spell has bound me
And I cannot, cannot go.                          4

The giant trees are bending
Their bare boughs weighed with snow.
And the storm is fast descending,
And yet I cannot go.                              8

Clouds beyond clouds above me,
Wastes beyond wastes below;
But nothing drear can move me;
I will not, cannot go.                            12

### YOUR TURN

1. What exactly is a "spell," and what does it mean to be "spellbound"?
2. What difference, if any, would it make if the first line said "has darkened" instead of "is darkening"?
3. What difference would it make, if any, if lines 4 and 12 were switched?
4. What does "drear" (line 11) mean? Is this word too unusual? Should the poet have used a more familiar word?
5. Describe the speaker's state of mind. Have you ever experienced anything like this yourself? What was the situation and how did you move beyond it?

# Spirituals, or Sorrow Songs

We have already mentioned that the lyric can range from expressions of emotion focused on personal matters to expressions of emotion focused on public matters, and the latter are sometimes characterized as odes or hymns. Among the most memorable hymns produced in the United States are the spirituals, or Sorrow Songs, created by black slaves in the United States, chiefly in the first half of the nineteenth century. The origins of the spirituals are still a matter of some dispute, but most specialists agree that the songs represent a distinctive fusion of African rhythms with European hymns.

Many of the texts derive ultimately from biblical sources: One of the chief themes, the desire for release, is sometimes presented with imagery drawn from ancient Israel. Examples include references to crossing the river Jordan (which runs from north of the Sea of Galilee to the Dead Sea), the release of the Israelites from slavery in Egypt (Exodus), Jonah's release from the whale (Book of Jonah), and Daniel's deliverance from a fiery furnace and from the lions' den (Book of Daniel, chapters 3 and 6).

Texts were collected and published during the 1860s in such books as *Slave Songs of the United States* (1867).

# ANONYMOUS AFRICAN AMERICAN SPIRITUAL

## *Go Down, Moses*

22                     JUBILEE SONGS.

### Go down, Moses.

1. When Is-rael was in E-gypt's land: Let my peo-ple go,

Op-pressed so hard they could not stand, Let my peo-ple go.

Go down, Mo-ses, way down in E-gypt land,

Tell ole Pha-roh, Let my peo-ple go.

2 Thus saith the Lord, bold Moses said,
        Let my people go ;
   If not I'll smite your first-born dead,
        Let my people go.
   Go down, Moses, etc.

3 No more shall they in bondage toil,
        Let my people go ;
   Let them come out with Egypt's spoil,
        Let my people go.
   Go down, Moses, etc.

4 When Israel out of Egypt came,
        Let my people go ;
   And left the proud oppressive land,
        Let my people go.
   Go down, Moses, etc.

Two pages from *Jubilee Songs* (1872), an early printed collection of spirituals.

*(continued)*

**5.**
0, 'twas a dark and dismal night,
  Let my people go;
When Moses led the Israelites,
  Let my people go.

**6.**
'Twas good old Moses and Aaron, too,
  Let my people go;
'Twas they that led the armies through,
  Let my people go.

**7.**
The Lord told Moses what to do,
  Let my people go;
To lead the children of Israel through,
  Let my people go.

**8.**
0 come along Moses, you'll not get lost,
  Let my people go;
Stretch out your rod and come across,
  Let my people go.

**9.**
As Israel stood by the water side,
  Let my people go;
At the command of God it did divide,
  Let my people go.

**10.**
When they had reached the other shore,
  Let my people go;
They sang a song of triumph o'er,
  Let my people go.

**11.**
Pharaoh said he would go across,
  Let my people go;
But Pharaoh and his host were lost,
  Let my people go.

**12.**
0 Moses the cloud shall cleave the way,
  Let my people go;
A fire by night, a shade by day,
  Let my people go.

**13.**
You'll not get lost in the wilderness,
  Let my people go;
With a lighted candle in your breast,
  Let my people go.

**14.**
Jordan shall stand up like a wall,
  Let my people go;
And the walls of Jericho shall fall
  Let my people go.

**15.**
Your foes shall not before you stand,
  Let my people go;
And you'll possess fair Canaan's land,
  Let my people go.

**16.**
'Twas just about in harvest time,
  Let my people go;
When Joshua led his host divine,
  Let my people go.

**17.**
0 let us all from bondage flee,
  Let my people go;
And let us all in Christ be free,
  Let my people go

**18.**
We need not always weep and moan,
  Let my people go;
And wear these slavery chains forlorn,
  Let my people go.

**19.**
This world's a wilderness of woe,
  Let my people go ;
0, let us on to Canaan go,
  Let my people go.

**20.**
What a beautiful morning that will be,
  Let my people go ;
When time breaks up in eternity,
  Let my people go.

**21.**
The Devil he thought he had me fast,
  Let my people go;
But I thought I'd break his chains at
  Let my people go.          [last,

**22.**
0 take yer shoes from off yer feet,
  Let my people go;
And walk into the golden street,
  Let my people go.

**23.**
I'll tell you what I likes de best,
  Let my people go ;
It is the shouting Methodist,
  Let my people go.

**24.**
I do believe without a doubt,
  Let my people go;
That a Christian has the right to shout,
  Let my people go.

# ANONYMOUS

## *Swing Low, Sweet Chariot*

*We reprint here a song from J. B. T. March's* The Story of the Jubilee Singers *(1881).*

From J. B. T. March, *The Story of the Jubilee Singers,* 1881.

*"Swing Low, Sweet Chariot" derives its basic images from the geography of ancient Israel (the Jordan River flows north from the Sea of Galilee to the*

*Dead Sea) and from a book in the Hebrew Bible (2 Kings 2.11 reports that Eli-jah and his friend Elisha were walking by the Jordan, when "there appeared a chariot of fire, and horses of fire, and parted them both asunder, and Elijah went up by a whirlwind into heaven"). There may also be some influence of the New Testament, Luke 16.22, which reports that a rich man named Dives and a poor man were "carried by the angels into Abraham's bosom." Further, the line "I'm sometimes up and sometimes down," from a secular song, "No-body Knows the Trouble I've Seen," often found its way into "Swing Low," as in this version, where the fourth verse goes:*

> *I'm sometimes up and sometimes down.*
> *But still my soul feels heavenly bound.*

# LANGSTON HUGHES

*For a biographical note, see page 761.*

## Evenin' Air Blues

[1942]

Folks, I come up North
Cause they told me de North was fine.
I come up North
Cause they told me de North was fine.
Been up here six months—                                    5
I'm about to lose my mind.

This mornin' for breakfast
I chawed de mornin' air.
This mornin' for breakfast
Chawed de mornin' air.                                       10
But this evenin' for supper,
I got evenin' air to spare.

Believe I'll do a little dancin'
Just to drive my blues away—
A little dancin'                                             15
To drive my blues away,
Cause when I'm dancin'
De blues forgets to stay.

But if you was to ask me
How de blues they come to be,                               20
Says if you was to ask me
How de blues they come to be—
You wouldn't need to ask me:
Just look at me and see!

### YOUR TURN

In what ways (subject, language) does this poem resemble blues you may have heard? Does it differ in any way? If so, how?

# LI-YOUNG LEE

*Li-Young Lee was born in 1957 in Jakarta, Indonesia, of Chinese parents. In 1964 his family brought him to the United States. He was educated at the University of Pittsburgh, the University of Arizona, and the State University of New York, Brockport. He now lives in Chicago. Lee's books of poetry include* Book of My Nights *(2001) and* Behind My Eyes *(2008).*

## I Ask My Mother to Sing

[1986]

She begins, and my grandmother joins her.
Mother and daughter sing like young girls.
If my father were alive, he would play
his accordion and sway like a boat.                                    4

I've never been in Peking, or the Summer Palace,
nor stood on the great Stone Boat to watch
the rain begin on Kuen Ming Lake, the picnickers
running away in the grass.                                             8

But I love to hear it sung;
how the waterlilies fill with rain until
they overturn, spilling water into water,
then rock back, and fill with more.                                   12

Both women have begun to cry.
But neither stops her song.

### YOUR TURN

1. Why might the speaker ask the women to sing?
2. Why do the women cry? Why do they continue to sing?

# EDNA ST. VINCENT MILLAY

*Edna St. Vincent Millay (1892–1950) was born in Rockland, Maine. Even as a child she wrote poetry, and by the time she graduated from Vassar College (1917) she had achieved some notice as a poet. Millay settled for a while in Greenwich Village, a center of Bohemian activity in New York City, where she wrote, performed in plays, and engaged in feminist causes. In 1923, the year she married, she became the first woman to win the Pulitzer Prize for Poetry. Numerous other awards followed. Though she is best known as a lyric poet—especially as a writer of sonnets—she also wrote memorable political poetry and nature poetry as well as short stories, plays, and a libretto for an opera.*

## The Spring and the Fall

[1923]

In the spring of the year, in the spring of the year,
I walked the road beside my dear.
The trees were black where the bark was wet.
I see them yet, in the spring of the year.
He broke me a bough of the blossoming peach               5
That was out of the way and hard to reach.

In the fall of the year, in the fall of the year,
I walked the road beside my dear.
The rooks went up with a raucous trill.
I hear them still, in the fall of the year.                    10
He laughed at all I dared to praise,
And broke my heart, in little ways.

Year be springing or year be falling,
The bark will drip and the birds be calling.
There's much that's fine to see and hear                       15
In the spring of a year, in the fall of a year.
'Tis not love's going hurts my days,
But that it went in little ways.


YOUR TURN

1. The first stanza describes the generally happy beginning of a love story. Where do you find the first hint of an unhappy ending?
2. Describe the rhyme scheme of the first stanza, including internal rhymes. Do the second and third stanzas repeat the pattern, or are there some variations? What repetition of sounds other than rhyme do you note?
3. Put the last two lines into your own words. How do you react to them; that is, do you find the conclusion surprising, satisfying, recognizable from your own experience, anticlimactic, or what?
4. In two or three paragraphs, explain how the imagery of the poem (drawn from the seasons of the year) contributes to its meaning.


# WILFRED OWEN

*Wilfred Owen (1893–1918) was born in Shropshire, in England, and studied at London University. He enlisted in the army at the outbreak of World War I and fought in the Battle of the Somme in July–December 1916, in which 1.5 million men were killed or wounded, until he was hospitalized with shell shock. After his recuperation in England, he returned to the front, only to be killed in action one week before the end of the war. His collected poems were published posthumously.*

*For another poem by Owen, see page 606.*

## Anthem for Doomed Youth                                      [1920]

What passing-bells for these who die as cattle?
Only the monstrous anger of the guns.
Only the stuttering rifles' rapid rattle
Can patter out their hasty orisons.
No mockeries for them from prayers or bells,                    5
Nor any voice of mourning save the choirs—
The shrill, demented choirs of wailing shells;
And bugles calling for them from sad shires.

What candles may be held to speed° them all?
Not in the hands of boys, but in their eyes                              10
Shall shine the holy glimmers of good-byes.
The pallor of girls' brows shall be their pall;
Their flowers the tenderness of patient minds,
And each slow dusk a drawing-down of blinds.

---

**9 speed** aid.

### YOUR TURN

1. What is an anthem? What are some of the words or phrases in this poem that might be found in a traditional anthem? What are some of the words or phrases that you would not expect in an anthem?
2. How would you characterize the speaker's state of mind? (Your response probably will require more than one word.)

# WALT WHITMAN

*Walt Whitman (1819–1892) was born on Long Island, the son of a farmer. The young Whitman taught school and worked as a carpenter, a printer, a newspaper editor, and, during the Civil War, as a volunteer nurse on the Union side. In Whitman's own day his poetry was highly controversial because of its unusual form (formlessness, many people said) and (though not in the following poem) its abundant erotic implications. Whitman's important book* Leaves of Grass, *was first published in 1855 and then revised and greatly expanded it in a number of editions until his death.*

*Other poems by Whitman appear on pages 633, 687, 721, and 828.*

## *A Noiseless Patient Spider*                                    [1862–1863]

A noiseless patient spider,
I mark'd where on a little promontory it stood isolated,
Mark'd how to explore the vacant vast surrounding,
It launch'd forth filament, filament, filament, out of itself,
Ever unreeling them, ever tirelessly speeding them.                      5

And you O my soul where you stand,
Surrounded, detached, in measureless oceans of space,
Ceaselessly musing, venturing, throwing, seeking the spheres to
      connect them,
Till the bridge you will need be form'd, till the ductile anchor hold,
Till the gossamer thread you fling catch somewhere, O my soul.           10

### YOUR TURN

1. How are the suggestions in "launch'd" (line 4) and "unreeling" (line 5) continued in the second stanza?
2. How are the varying lengths of lines 1, 4, and 8 relevant to their ideas?
3. The second stanza is not a complete sentence. Why? The poem is unrhymed. What effect does the near-rhyme (*hold: soul*) in the last two lines have on you?

# DYLAN THOMAS

*Dylan Thomas (1914–1953) was born and grew up in Swansea, in Wales. His first volume of poetry, published in 1934, immediately made him famous. Endowed with a highly melodious voice, on three tours of the United States he was immensely successful as a reader of both his own and other poets' work. He died in New York City.*

## Fern Hill                                                                 [1946]

Now as I was young and easy under the apple boughs
About the lilting house and happy as the grass was green,
    The night above the dingle starry,
        Time let me hail and climb
      Golden in the heydays of his eyes,                                    5
And honored among wagons I was prince of the apple towns
And once below a time I lordly had the trees and leaves
        Trail with daisies and barley
      Down the rivers of the windfall light.

And as I was green and carefree, famous among the barns               10
About the happy yard and singing as the farm was home,
    In the sun that is young once only,
        Time let me play and be
      Golden in the mercy of his means,
And green and golden I was huntsman and herdsman,
      the calves                                                                15
Sang to my horn, the foxes on the hills barked clear and cold,
        And the sabbath rang slowly
      In the pebbles of the holy streams.

All the sun long it was running, it was lovely, the hay
Fields high as the house, the tunes from the chimneys,
      it was air                                                                  20
        And playing, lovely and watery
          And fire green as grass.
And nightly under the simple stars
As I rode to sleep the owls were bearing the farm away,
All the moon long I heard, blessed among stables, the night-
      jars                                                                         25
        Flying with the ricks, and the horses
          Flashing into the dark.
And then to awake, and the farm, like a wanderer white
With the dew, come back, the cock on his shoulder: it was all
      Shining, it was Adam and maiden,                                      30
        The sky gathered again
        And the sun grew round that very day.
So it must have been after the birth of the simple light
In the first, spinning place, the spellbound horses walking warm
      Out of the whinnying green stable                                   35
        On to the fields of praise.

And honored among foxes and pheasants by the gay house
Under the new made clouds and happy as the heart was long,
    In the sun born over and over,
        I ran my heedless ways,          40
    My wishes raced through the house high hay
And nothing I cared, at my sky blue trades, that time allows
In all his tuneful turning so few and such morning songs
    Before the children green and golden
        Follow him out of grace,        45

Nothing I cared, in the lamb white days, that time would take me
Up to the swallow thronged loft by the shadow of my hand,
    In the moon that is always rising,
        Nor that riding to sleep
    I should hear him fly with the high fields    50
And wake to the farm forever fled from the childless land.
Oh as I was young and easy in the mercy of his means,
        Time held me green and dying
    Though I sang in my chains like the sea.

**YOUR TURN**

Evaluate the thesis that Thomas's poem is about nature deceiving the speaker by furnishing him with an unrealistic attitude toward reality.

# JOHN KEATS

*For a biographical note, see page 559.*

## Ode on a Grecian Urn    [1820]

### I

Thou still unravished bride of quietness,
    Thou foster-child of silence and slow time,
Sylvan historian, who canst thus express
    A flowery tale more sweetly than our rhyme:
What leaf-fringed legend haunts about thy shape    5
    Of deities or mortals, or of both,
        In Tempe or the dales of Arcady?
    What men or gods are these? What maidens loth?
What mad pursuit? What struggle to escape?
    What pipes and timbrels? What wild ecstasy?    10

### II

Heard melodies are sweet, but those unheard
    Are sweeter; therefore, ye soft pipes, play on;
Not to the sensual° ear, but, more endeared,

---

**13 sensual** sensuous.

*seem, they describe all the worlds that are and were and some others besides."*
*The recipient of many honors and awards, and a former poet laureate of the*
*United States, Collins was born in New York City in 1941. He has taught at*
*both the City University of New York and Sarah Lawrence College.*

*Collins wrote the following poem on the first anniversary of the attack on*
*the United States that took place on September 11, 2001, when al-Qaeda ter-*
*rorists hijacked four commercial passenger jet airliners, crashing two of them*
*into the Twin Towers of the World Trade Center in New York City. (For another*
*poem by Collins, see page 680.)*

## The Names
[2002]

Yesterday, I lay awake in the palm of the night.
A soft rain stole in, unhelped by any breeze,
And when I saw the silver glaze on the windows,
I started with A, with Ackerman, as it happened,
Then Baxter and Calabro,
Davis and Eberling, names falling into place                          5
As droplets fell through the dark.

Names printed on the ceiling of the night.
Names slipping around a watery bend.
Twenty-six willows on the banks of a stream.                          10

In the morning, I walked out barefoot
Among thousands of flowers
Heavy with dew like the eyes of tears,
And each had a name—
Fiori inscribed on a yellow petal                                     15
Then Gonzalez and Han, Ishikawa and Jenkins.

Names written in the air
And stitched into the cloth of the day.
A name under a photograph taped to a mailbox.
Monogram on a torn shirt,                                             20
I see you spelled out on storefront windows
And on the bright unfurled awnings of this city.
I say the syllables as I turn a corner—
Kelly and Lee,
Medina, Nardella, and O'Connor.                                       25

When I peer into the woods,
I see a thick tangle where letters are hidden
As in a puzzle concocted for children.
Parker and Quigley in the twigs of an ash,
Rizzo, Schubert, Torres, and Upton,                                   30
Secrets in the boughs of an ancient maple.

Names written in the pale sky.
Names rising in the updraft amid buildings.
Names silent in stone
Or cried out behind a door.                                           35
Names blown over the earth and out to sea.

In the evening—weakening light, the last swallows.
A boy on a lake lifts his oars.
A woman by a window puts a match to a candle,
And the names are outlined on the rose clouds—                    40
Vanacore and Wallace,
(let X stand, if it can, for the ones unfound)
Then Young and Ziminsky, the final jolt of Z.

Names etched on the head of a pin.
One name spanning a bridge, another undergoing a tunnel.          45
A blue name needled into the skin.
Names of citizens, workers, mothers and fathers,
The bright-eyed daughter, the quick son.
Alphabet of names in a green field.
Names in the small tracks of birds.                              50
Names lifted from a hat
Or balanced on the tip of the tongue.
Names wheeled into the dim warehouse of memory.
So many names, there is barely room on the walls of the heart.

### YOUR TURN

1. In an interview that appeared several years before "The Names" was published, Collins says of his intention as a poet: "By the end of the poem, the reader should be in a different place from where he started." When you finished reading "The Names," did you find yourself in a "different place"? How would you describe this place?

2. Collins has also observed, again in an interview before he wrote "The Names": "Poetry is clearly very serious for me, but without heaviness or a glib sense of spirituality." Do you perceive a "spiritual" dimension to this poem—one that is not "glib"? What does it mean to say that a poem is "spiritual," that it creates a spiritual effect? Is this the same thing as saying that a poem is "religious," or is it something different?

3. Many readers have expressed their high regard for "The Names," referring to it as a "great poem." Do you agree? What defines a great poem? Do you think a poet does or does not face a special challenge in trying to write a poem, great or simply good, about the tragedy of September 11, 2001? Please explain.

4. One critic, who otherwise admires Collins's work, has objected to "The Names" for being "too sentimental." How would you define "sentimentality"? (Clarify your definition with an example.) Can you locate evidence in the text that might support the judgment that Collins's poem is sentimental? Are there other passages you could cite and analyze in order to argue against it? And what's the matter with sentimentality? Is sentimentality something that poets should always avoid?

5. How do you feel about your own name? Is it something you give much thought to? Any thought? Why is that? Now that you have read Collins's poem, has your relationship to your own name changed in any way?

# 19

# The Speaking Tone of Voice

Everything is as good as it is dramatic. . . . [A poem is] heard as sung or spoken by a person in a scene—in character, in a setting. By whom, where and when is the question. By the dreamer of a better world out in a storm in Autumn; by a lover under a window at night.

—Robert Frost, Preface, *A Way Out*

If we fall into the habit of saying, "Julia Ward Howe says that her 'eyes have seen the glory of the coming of the Lord,'" or "Robert Frost says that he thinks he knows 'Whose woods these are,'" we neglect the important truth in Frost's comment about poetry as drama: A poem is written by an author (Howe, Frost), but it is spoken by an invented speaker. The author counterfeits the speech of a person in a particular situation.

The anonymous author of "Western Wind" (page 571), for instance, invents the speech of an unhappy lover who longs for the spring ("Westron wind, when will thou blow?"); Julia Ward Howe invents the speech of someone who has seen God working in this world; Robert Frost, in "Stopping by Woods on a Snowy Evening" (page 755), invents a speaker who, sitting in a horse-drawn sleigh, watches the woods fill up with snow.

The speaker's voice often has the ring of the author's own voice—certainly Robert Frost did a great deal to cultivate the idea that he was a farmer-poet—but even when the resemblance seems close, we should recall that in the poem we get a particular speaker in a particular situation. That is, we get, for instance, not the whole of Frost (the father, the competitive poet, the public lecturer, and so on), but only a man in a horse-drawn sleigh watching the woods fill up with snow. It is customary, then, in writing about the voice one hears in a poem, to write not about the author but about the **speaker,** or **voice,** or **mask,** or **persona** (Latin for "mask") that speaks the poem.

In reading a poem, the first and most important question to ask yourself is this: *Who is speaking?* If an audience and a setting are suggested, keep them in mind, too. Consider, for example, the following poem.

# EMILY DICKINSON

*Emily Dickinson (1830–1886) was born into a proper New England family in Amherst, Massachusetts. Because she never married, and because in her last twenty years she may never have left her house, she has sometimes been pitied. But as the critic Allen Tate said, "All pity for Miss Dickinson's 'starved life' is misdirected. Her life was one of the richest and deepest ever lived on this continent." Her brother was probably right in saying that, having seen something of the rest of the world, "she could not resist the feeling that it was painfully hollow. It was to her so thin and unsatisfying in the face of the Great Realities of Life." For a more complete biographical account, and for a selection of Dickinson's poems and letters, see Chapter 27.*

## I'm Nobody! Who are you?

[1861?]

I'm Nobody! Who are you?
Are you—Nobody—too?
Then there's a pair of us!
Don't tell! they'd banish us—you know!                          4

How dreary—to be—Somebody!
How public—like a Frog—
To tell your name—the livelong June—
To an admiring Bog!                                             8

Let's consider the sort of person we hear in "I'm Nobody! Who are you?" (Read it aloud, to see if you agree. In fact, you should test each of our assertions by reading the poem aloud.) The voice in line 1 is rather like that of a child playing a game with a friend. In lines 2 and 3 the speaker sees the reader as a fellow spirit ("Are you—Nobody—too?") and invites the reader to join her ("Then there's a pair of us!") in forming a sort of conspiracy of silence against outsiders ("Don't tell!"). In "they'd banish us," however, we hear a word that a child would not be likely to use, and we probably feel that the speaker is a shy but (with the right companion) playful adult, who here is speaking to an intimate friend. And since we hear this voice—we are reading the poem—we are or we become the friend. Because "banish" is a word that brings to mind images of a king's court, the speaker almost comically inflates and thereby makes fun of the "they" who are opposed to "us."

In the second stanza, or we might better say in the space between the two stanzas, the speaker puts aside the childlike manner. In "How dreary," the first words of the second stanza, we hear a sophisticated voice, one might even say a world-weary voice, or a voice with perhaps more than a touch of condescension. But since by now we are paired with the speaker in a conspiracy against outsiders, we enjoy the contrast that the speaker makes between the Nobodies and the Somebodies. Who are these Somebodies, these people who would imperiously "banish" the speaker and the friend? What are the Somebodies like?

How dreary—to be—Somebody!
How public—like a Frog—
To tell your name—the livelong June—
To an admiring Bog!

The last two lines do at least two things: They amusingly explain to the speaker's new friend (the reader) in what way a Somebody is public (it proclaims its presence all day). They also indicate the absurdity of the Somebody-Frog's behavior (the audience is "an admiring Bog"). By the end of the poem we are quite convinced that it is better to be a Nobody (like Dickinson's speaker, and the reader?) than a Somebody (a loudmouth, like a croaking frog).

Though why should I whine,
Whine that the crime was other than mine?—
Since anyhow you are dead.
Or rather, or instead,                                          25
You were never made.
But that too, I am afraid,
Is faulty: oh, what shall I say, how is the truth to be said?
You were born, you had body, you died.
It is just that you never giggled or planned or cried.          30

Believe me, I loved you all.
Believe me, I knew you, though faintly, and I loved, I loved you
All.

### YOUR TURN

1. Who is being addressed?
2. The first ten lines sound like a chant. What gives them that quality? What makes them nonetheless serious?
3. In lines 20–23 the mother attempts to deny the "crime" but cannot. What is her reasoning here?
4. Do you find the last lines convincing? Explain.
5. The poem was first published in 1945. Do you think that the abundant debate about abortion in recent years has somehow made the poem seem dated, or more timely than ever? Explain.

# LINDA PASTAN

*For a biographical note, see page 589.*

## Marks                                                        [1978]

My husband gives me an A
for last night's supper,
an incomplete for my ironing,

a B plus in bed.
My son says I am average,                                       5
an average mother, but if
I put my mind to it
I could improve.

My daughter believes
in Pass/Fail and tells me                                       10
I pass. Wait 'til they learn
I'm dropping out.

### YOUR TURN

1. In addition to the A and B that are mentioned, where else in the poem does Pastan use the language of the world of the school? The speaker of the poem receives grades, but does she also give a grade, or imply one?
2. What would be gained or lost if Pastan's first sentence came last?

# The Reader as the Speaker

We have been arguing that the speaker of the poem usually is not the author but a dramatized form of the author, and that we overhear this speaker in some situation. But with poems of the sort that we have been looking at, we can also say that *the reader* is the speaker. That is, as we read the poem, at least to some degree *we* utter the thoughts, and *we* experience the sensations or emotions that the writer sets forth. Probably this is what Robert Frost was getting at, in a remark we quoted in Chapter 2, when he said that a poem "is the *act* of having an idea and how it feels to have an idea." Thus, when we read "Stopping by Woods on a Snowy Evening" (page 755), *we* are acting, *we* are having the ideas presented in the poem.

Similarly, when we read Emily Dickinson's "I'm Nobody! Who are you?" (page 593) we set forth feelings about what it is to be Nobody in a world where others are Somebody (and Dickinson has also helped us to say that the Somebody is a noisy frog); with Gwendolyn Brooks (page 594) we hear or overhear thoughts and feelings that perhaps strike us as more relevant and more profound and more moving than most of what we hear on television or read in the newspapers about urban violence.

In the following poem you will hear at least three voices—the voice of the person who begins the poem by telling us about a dead man ("Nobody heard him, the dead man"), the voice of the dead man ("I was much further out than you thought / And not waving but drowning"), and the collective voice of the dead man's friends ("Poor chap, he always loved larking"). But see if you don't find that all of the voices together say things that you have said (or almost said).

## STEVIE SMITH

*Stevie Smith (1902–1971), christened Florence Margaret Smith, was born in England, in Hull. In addition to writing poems, (see her* Collected Poems, *1983) she wrote stories, essays, and three novels. She is the subject of* Stevie *(1978), a film in which the acclaimed English actress Glenda Jackson plays Smith.*

### *Not Waving but Drowning*                          [1957]

Nobody heard him, the dead man,
But still he lay moaning:
I was much further out than you thought
And not waving but drowning.                          4

Poor chap, he always loved larking
And now he's dead
It must have been too cold for him his heart gave way,
They said.                                            8

Oh, no no no, it was too cold always
(Still the dead one lay moaning)
I was much too far out all my life
And not waving but drowning.                          12

> **YOUR TURN**
>
> 1. Identify the speaker of each line.
> 2. What sort of man did the friends of the dead man think he was? What type of man do you think he was?
> 3. The first line, "Nobody heard him, the dead man," is literally true. Dead men do not speak. In what other ways is it true?

# WISLAWA SZYMBORSKA

*Born in 1923, Wislawa Szymborska (pronounced "Vislawa Zimborska"), a native of Poland, is a renowned poet, essayist and translater. In 1996 she received the Nobel Prize for her poetry.*

## *The Terrorist, He Watches*

[1981]

*Translated by Robert A. Maguire and Magnus Jan Krynski*

The bomb will go off in the bar at one twenty p.m.
Now it's only one sixteen p.m.
Some will still have time to get in,
some to get out.

The terrorist has already crossed to the other side of the street.    5
The distance protects him from any danger,
and what a sight for sore eyes:

A woman in a yellow jacket, she goes in.
A man in dark glasses, he comes out.

Guys in jeans, they are talking.    10
One seventeen and four seconds.
That shorter guy's really got it made, and gets on a scooter,
and that taller one, he goes in.

One seventeen and forty seconds.
That girl there, she's got a green ribbon in her hair.    15
Too bad that bus just cut her off.
One eighteen p.m.
The girl's not there any more.
Was she dumb enough to go in, or wasn't she?
That we'll see when they carry them out.    20

One nineteen p.m.
No one seems to be going in.
Instead a fat baldy's coming out.
Like he's looking for something in his pockets and
at one nineteen and fifty seconds    25
he goes back for those lousy gloves of his.

It's one twenty p.m.
The time, how it drags.
Should be any moment now.
Not yet.                                                    30
Yes, this is it.
The bomb, it goes off.

---

**YOUR TURN**

1. Who speaks the poem? The terrorist? Or someone watching the terrorist? Or a sort of combination? Or what?
2. Characterize the speaker.

# JOHN UPDIKE

*John Updike (1932–2009) was best known as a writer of fiction—short sto-
ries and novels—but throughout his professional career he also wrote essays
and poems. (For a more complete biographical note, see page 191.)*

## Icarus                                                  [2001]

O.K., you are sitting in an airplane and
the person in the seat next to you is a sweaty, swarthy gentleman of
    Middle Eastern origin
whose carry-on luggage consists of a bulky black briefcase he
    stashes,
in compliance with airline regulations,
underneath the seat ahead.                                  5
He keeps looking at his watch and closing his eyes in prayer,
resting his profusely dank forehead against the seatback ahead of him
just above the black briefcase,
which if you listen through the droning of the engines seems to be
    ticking, ticking
softly, softer than your heartbeat in your ears.            10

Who wants to have all their careful packing—the travellers' checks,
    the folded underwear—
end as floating sea-wrack five miles below,
drifting in a rainbow scum of jet fuel,
and their docile hopes of a plastic-wrapped meal
dashed in a concussion whiter than the sun?                 15

I say to my companion, "Smooth flight so far."
"So far."
"That's quite a briefcase you've got there."
He shrugs and says, "It contains my life's work."
"And what is it, exactly, that you do?"                     20
"You could say I am a lobbyist."

He does not want to talk.
He wants to keep praying.
His hands, with their silky beige backs and their nails cut close like
   a technician's,
tremble and jump in handling the plastic glass of Sprite when it
   comes with its exploding bubbles.       25

Ah, but one gets swept up
in the airport throng, all those workaday faces,
faintly pampered and spoiled in the boomer style,
and those elders dressed like children for flying
in hi-tech sneakers and polychrome catsuits,     30
and those gum-chewing attendants taking tickets
while keeping up a running flirtation with a uniformed bystander,
   a stoic blond pilot—
all so normal, who could resist
this vault into the impossible?

Your sweat has slowly dried. Your praying neighbor    35
has fallen asleep, emitting an odor of cardamom.
His briefcase seems to have deflated.
Perhaps not this time, then.
But the possibility of impossibility will keep drawing us back
to this scrape against the numbed sky,    40
to this sleek sheathed tangle of color-coded wires, these million rivets,
   this wing
like a frozen lake at your elbow.

**YOUR TURN**

1. Take a moment to look up the Icarus myth in a classical dictionary or encyclopedia. Do you see connections between the myth and the story that Updike tells in this poem?
2. Who is the "you" in the first line?
3. What kinds of assumptions does the poem make about the "gentleman of Middle Eastern origin"? Are these assumptions challenged? Point to specific details in the language to explain your responses.
4. What kind of conclusion does the poem reach?
5. Does "Icarus" disturb you? If so, why?
6. Which poem do you think is more effective: Updike's "Icarus" or Syzmborska's "The Terrorist"? What, more generally, does it mean to say that one poem is more effective than another?

# AURORA LEVINS MORALES

*Aurora Levins Morales, born in Puerto Rico in 1954, came to the United States with her family in 1967. She has lived in Chicago and New Hampshire and now lives in the San Francisco Bay area. A member of the Latina Feminist Group, Levins Morales has published stories, essays, prose poems, and poems.*

## *Child of the Americas* [1986]

I am a child of the Americas,
a light-skinned mestiza of the Caribbean,
a child of many diaspora,° born into this continent at a crossroads.

I am a U.S. Puerto Rican Jew,
a product of the ghettos of New York I have never known.                    5
An immigrant and the daughter and granddaughter of immigrants.
I speak English with passion: it's the tongue of my consciousness,
a flashing knife blade of crystal, my tool, my craft.

I am Caribeña,° island grown. Spanish is in my flesh,
ripples from my tongue, lodges in my hips:                                   10
the language of garlic and mangoes,
the singing in my poetry, the flying gestures of my hands.

I am of Latinoamerica, rooted in the history of my continent:
I speak from that body.

I am not african. Africa is in me, but I cannot return.                     15
I am not taína.° Taíno is in me, but there is no way back.
I am not european. Europe lives in me, but I have no home there.

I am new. History made me. My first language was spanglish.°
I was born at the crossroads
and I am whole.                                                              20

---

**3 diaspora** literally, "scattering"; the term is used especially to refer to the dispersion of
the Jews outside of Israel from the sixth century BCE, when they were exiled to Babylo-
nia, to the present time.   **9 Caribeña** Caribbean woman.   **16 taína** the Taínos were the
Indian tribe native to Puerto Rico.   **18 spanglish** a mixture of Spanish and English.

# JOSEPH BRUCHAC III

*Joseph Bruchac III (the name is pronounced "Brew-shack") was born in Saratoga Springs, New York, in 1942, and educated at Cornell University, Syracuse University, and Union Graduate School. Like many other Americans, he has a multicultural ethnic heritage, and he includes Native Americans as well as Slovaks among his ancestors. Bruchac is a widely published writer, editor, teacher, and storyteller. He lives in Greenfield Center, New York, in the Adirondack mountain region.*

*"Much of my writing and my life," Bruchac says, "relates to the problem of being an American.... While in college I was active in Civil Rights work and in the antiwar movement.... I went to Africa to teach—but more than that to be taught. It showed me many things. How much we have as Americans and take for granted. How much our eyes refuse to see because they are blinded to everything in a man's face except his color."*

Never to stoop. Oh, Sir, she smiled, no doubt,
Whene'er I passed her; but who passed without
Much the same smile? This grew; I gave commands;                    45
Then all smiles stopped together. There she stands
As if alive. Will't please you rise? We'll meet
The company below, then. I repeat,
The Count your master's known munificence
Is ample warrant that no just pretense                              50
Of mine for dowry will be disallowed;
Though his fair daughter's self, as I avowed
At starting, is my object. Nay, we'll go
Together down, Sir. Notice Neptune, though,
Taming a sea-horse, thought a rarity,                               55
Which Claus of Innsbruck° cast in bronze for me!

---

56 **Claus of Innsbruck** a fictitious sculptor.

**YOUR TURN**

1. What is the occasion for the meeting?
2. What words or lines do you think especially convey the speaker's arrogance? What is your attitude toward the speaker? Loathing? Fascination? Respect? Explain.
3. The time and place are Renaissance Italy; how do they affect your attitude toward the duke? What would be the effect if the poem were set
   in the early twenty-first century?
4. Years after writing this poem, Browning explained that the duke's "commands" (line 45) were "that she should be put to death, or he might
   have had her shut up in a convent." Do you think the poem should have
   been more explicit? Does Browning's later uncertainty indicate that the
   poem is badly thought out? Suppose we did not have Browning's comment on line 45. Do you think the line then could mean only that he
   commanded her to stop smiling and that she obeyed? Explain.

# Diction and Tone

From the whole of language, one consciously or unconsciously selects certain
words and grammatical constructions; this selection constitutes one's **diction**. It
is partly by the diction that we come to know the speaker of a poem. Stevie
Smith's speaker (page 597) used words such as "chap" and "larking," which are
scarcely imaginable in the mouth of Browning's Renaissance duke. But of course
some words are used in both poems: "I," "you," "thought," "the," and so on. The fact
remains, however, that although a large part of language is shared by all speakers,
certain parts of language are used only by certain speakers.

Like some words, some grammatical constructions are used only by certain
kinds of speakers. Consider these two passages:

In Adam's fall
We sinned all.

—Anonymous, *The New England Primer*

Of Man's first disobedience, and the fruit
Of that forbidden tree whose mortal taste
Brought death into the World, and all our woe,
With loss of Eden, till one greater Man
Restore us, and regain the blissful seat,
Sing, Heavenly Muse, that, on the secret top
Of Oreb, or of Sinai, didst inspire
That shepherd who first taught the chosen seed
In the beginning how the heavens and earth
Rose out of Chaos. . . .

—John Milton, *Paradise Lost*

There is an enormous difference in the diction of these two passages. Milton, speaking as an inspired poet, appropriately uses words and grammatical constructions somewhat removed from common life. Hence, while the anonymous author of the primer speaks directly of "Adam's fall," Milton speaks allusively of the fall, calling it "Man's first disobedience." Milton's sentence is nothing that any Englishman ever said in conversation; its genitive beginning ("Of Man's first disobedience"), its length (the sentence continues for six lines beyond the quoted passage), and its postponement of the main verb ("Sing") until the sixth line mark it as the utterance of a poet working in the tradition of Latin poetry. The primer's statement, by its choice of words as well as by its brevity, suggests a far less sophisticated speaker.

Speakers have attitudes toward themselves, their subjects, and their audiences, and (consciously or unconsciously) they choose their words, pitch, and modulation accordingly; all these add up to the **tone.** In written literature, tone must be detected without the aid of the ear; the reader must understand by the selection and sequence of words the way in which they are meant to be heard (that is, playfully, angrily, confidentially, sarcastically, etc.). The reader must catch what Frost calls "the speaking tone of voice somehow entangled in the words and fastened to the page of the ear of the imagination."

Finally, we should mention that although this discussion concentrates on the speaker's tone, we can also talk of the author's tone—that is, of the author's attitude toward the invented speaker. The speaker's tone might, for example, be angry, but the author's tone (as detected by the reader) might be humorous.

# ROBERT HERRICK

*Robert Herrick (1591–1674) was born in London, the son of a goldsmith. After taking an MA at Cambridge, he was ordained in the Church of England. Later, he was sent to the country parish of Dean Prior in Devonshire, where he wrote most of his poetry. A loyal supporter of the king, in 1647 he was expelled from his parish by the Puritans, though in 1662 he was restored to Dean Prior.*

## To the Virgins, to Make Much of Time    [1648]

Gather ye rosebuds while ye may,
    Old Time is still a-flying;
And this same flower that smiles today,
    Tomorrow will be dying.

4

The glorious lamp of heaven, the sun,
   The higher he's a-getting,
The sooner will his race be run,
   And nearer he's to setting.        8

That age is best which is the first,
   When youth and blood are warmer;
But being spent, the worse, and worst
   Times still succeed the former.       12

Then be not coy, but use your time;
   And while ye may, go marry:
For having lost but once your prime,
   You may for ever tarry.       16

*Carpe diem* (Latin:"seize the day") is the theme. But if we want to get the full force of the poem, we must understand who is talking to whom. Look, for example, at "Old Time" in line 2. Time is "old" in the sense of having been around a long while, but doesn't "old" in this context suggest also that the speaker regards Time with easy familiarity, almost affection? We visit the old school, and our friend is old George. Time is destructive, yes, and the speaker urges the young maidens to make the most of their spring. But the speaker is neither bitter nor importunate; rather, he seems to be the wise old man, the counselor, the man who has made his peace with Time and is giving advice to the young. Time moves rapidly in the poem (the rosebud of line 1 is already a flower in line 3), but the speaker is unhurried; in line 5 he has leisure to explain that the glorious lamp of heaven is the sun.

    In "To the Virgins," the pauses, indicated by punctuation at the ends of the lines (except in line 11, where we tumble without stopping from "worst" to "Times"), slow the reader down. But even if there is no punctuation at the end of a line of poetry, the reader probably pauses slightly or gives the final word an additional bit of emphasis. Similarly, the space between stanzas slows a reader down, increasing the emphasis on the last word of one stanza and the first word of the next.

# WILFRED OWEN

*For a biographical note, see page 584.*

## Dulce et Decorum Est*                     [1917]

Bent double, like old beggars under sacks,
Knock-kneed, coughing like hags, we cursed through sludge,
Till on the haunting flares we turned our backs
And towards our distant rest began to trudge.
Men marched asleep. Many had lost their boots       5
But limped on, blood-shod. All went lame; all blind;
Drunk with fatigue; deaf even to the hoots
Of tired, outstripped Five-Nines° that dropped behind.

---

***Dulce et Decorum Est** From the Latin poet Horace's *Odes* (3:2.13): *Dulce et decorum est pro patria mori*—"It is sweet and honorable to die for your country."   **8 Five-Nines** shells containing poison gas.

Gas! Gas! Quick, boys!—An ecstasy of fumbling,
Fitting the clumsy helmets just in time;                                    10
But someone still was yelling out and stumbling
And flound'ring like a man in fire or lime . . .
Dim, through the misty panes and thick green light,
As under a green sea, I saw him drowning.

In all my dreams, before my helpless sight,                                 15
He plunges at me, guttering, choking, drowning.
If in some smothering dreams you too could pace
Behind the wagon that we flung him in,
And watch the white eyes writhing in his face,
His hanging face, like a devil's sick of sin;                               20
If you could hear, at every jolt, the blood
Come gargling from the froth-corrupted lungs,
Obscene as cancer, bitter as the cud
Of vile, incurable sores on innocent tongues,—
My friend,° you would not tell with such high zest                         25
To children ardent for some desperate glory,
The old Lie: Dulce et decorum est
Pro patria mori.

---

**25 My friend** Early drafts of "Dulce et Decorum Est" are dedicated to Jessie Pope, author
of children's books and conventional patriotic verse.

> **YOUR TURN**

1. Owen uses two similes in the first two lines. Please explain the meaning of each one.
2. Describe in your own words what is happening in the second stanza.
3. Please focus on the word "guttering" in line 16. In one of the drafts of
   this poem, Owen first wrote "gargling" here but then he crossed it out
   and wrote "gurgling" instead. He crossed out that word too and wrote
   "goggling," which he also crossed out, before finally settling on "guttering." Do you think he made the right choice, or do you prefer one of
   the other three words?
4. What might have led Owen to decide to present the poem in a first-
   person voice? What is a relationship of this speaker to the reader?
5. One scholar has highly praised Owen's poem but also has said of it,
   "The poem is almost too disturbing." Do you agree? Provide evidence
   from the text to explain and support your response.

# THOMAS HARDY

*Thomas Hardy (1840–1928) was born in Dorset, England, the son of a stone-
mason. Despite great obstacles he studied the classics and architecture, and in
1862 he moved to London to study and practice as an architect. Ill health
forced him to return to Dorset, where he continued to work as an architect
and to write. Best known for his novels, Hardy ceased writing fiction after the*

*hostile reception of* Jude the Obscure *in 1896—it was attacked as indecent— and turned to writing lyric poetry.*

## The Man He Killed                                    [1902]

"Had he and I but met
By some old ancient inn,
We should have sat us down to wet
Right many a nipperkin!°                                    4

"But ranged as infantry,
And staring face to face,
I shot at him as he at me,
And killed him in his place.                                8

"I shot him dead because—
Because he was my foe,
Just so: my foe of course he was;
That's clear enough; although                              12

"He thought he'd 'list, perhaps,
Off-hand like—just as I—
Was out of work—had sold his traps°—
No other reason why.                                       16

"Yes; quaint and curious war is!
You shoot a fellow down
You'd treat if met where any bar is,
Or help to half-a-crown."                                  20

---

**4 nipperkin** cup.    **15 traps** personal belongings.

### YOUR TURN

1. What do we learn about the speaker's life before he enlisted in the infantry? How does his diction characterize him?
2. What is the effect of the series of monosyllables in lines 7 and 8?
3. Consider the punctuation of the third and fourth stanzas. Why are the heavy, frequent pauses appropriate? What question is the speaker trying to answer?
4. In the last stanza, what attitudes toward war does the speaker express? What, from the evidence of this poem, would you infer Hardy's attitude toward war to be?

## The Ruined Maid                                     [1902]

"O 'Melia, my dear, this does everything crown!°
Who could have supposed I should meet you in Town?
And whence such fair garments, such prosperi-ty?"—
"O didn't you know I'd been ruined?" said she.            4

---

**1 O 'Melia . . . crown** O Amelia, this crowns (i.e., tops) everything.

—"You left us in tatters, without shoes or socks,
Tired of digging potatoes, and spudding up docks;°
And now you've gay bracelets and bright feathers three!"—
"Yes: that's how we dress when we're ruined," said she.                    8

—"At home in the barton° you said 'thee' and 'thou,'
And 'thik oon,' and 'theäs oon,' and 't'other';° but now
Your talking quite fits ee° for high compa-ny!"—
"Some polish is gained with one's ruin," said she.                    12

—"Your hands were like paws then, your face blue and bleak
But now I'm bewitched by your delicate cheek,
And your little gloves fit as on any la-dy!"—
"We never do work when we're ruined," said she.                    16

—"You used to call home-life a hag-ridden dream,
And you'd sigh, and you'd sock;° but at present you seem
To know not of megrims° or melancho-ly!"—
"True. One's pretty lively when ruined," said she.                    20

—"I wish I had feathers, a fine sweeping gown,
And a delicate face, and could strut about Town!"—
"My dear—a raw country girl, such as you be,
Cannot quite expect that. You ain't ruined," said she.                    24

---

**6 spudding up docks** digging up weeds.    **9 in the barton** on the farm.    **9–10 thee . . .
t' other** rural words for "you," "that one," "this one," and "the other."    **11 'ee** rural word for
"you."    **18 sock** groan.    **19 megrims** migraine headaches.

**YOUR TURN**

1. Thomas Hardy wrote the poem more than a hundred years ago. What
   did it mean for a woman to be "ruined"? Who are the two speakers?
   What is the attitude of each speaker toward the other?
2. Amelia's clothing and her citified speech (she no longer uses "thee"
   and "thou," and so forth) imply sophistication. What does the final line
   of the poem tell us about the degree of her sophistication? What do
   you suppose the author's attitude is toward Amelia?

# COUNTEE CULLEN

*For a biographical note, see page 562.*

### For a Lady I Know                    [1925]

She even thinks that up in heaven
    Her class lies late and snores,
While poor black cherubs rise at seven
    To do celestial chores.

**YOUR TURN**

1. What is the gist of what Cullen is saying?
2. How would you characterize the tone? Furious? Indifferent?

# ANNE BRADSTREET

*Anne Bradstreet (1612–1678) was born in Northampton, England; her father was Thomas Dudley, who later served several terms as governor of the Massachusetts Bay Colony. She married at age sixteen, and two years later she and her husband, Simon Bradstreet, along with her father, made the long, arduous voyage to Massachusetts. She settled in North Andover, and she lived there until her death. Bradstreet was a devoted wife, the mother of eight children, and a gifted poet.*

## To My Dear and Loving Husband                                [1678]

If ever two were one, then surely we.
If ever man were lov'd by wife, then thee;
If ever wife was happy in a man,
Compare with me ye women if you can.
I prize thy love more than whole Mines of gold,          5
Or all the riches that the East doth hold.
My love is such that Rivers cannot quench,
Nor ought but love from thee, give recompence.
Thy love is such I can no way repay,
The heavens reward thee manifold I pray.                 10
Then while we live, in love let's so persever,
That when we live no more, we may live ever.

### YOUR TURN

1. Each of the first three lines begins with "if." What is the effect of this repetition on your response as a reader?
2. The title suggests that Bradstreet is addressing her husband. But if this is the case, how do we explain line 4?
3. Please explain the comparison between love and wealth that Bradstreet gives in lines 5 and 6.
4. What does the word "quench" in line 7 imply? What are the implications of the references to reward and repayment in lines 8–10?
5. Please explain the paradox that Bradstreet describes in the final two lines. *Note:* Each line in the poem has ten syllables, except for these final two lines, which have an extra syllable. Also, the word "persevere" should be pronounced to rhyme with "ever," as in the word "sever."
6. What is your response to this poem as a whole? Do you find it simple, or complicated?
7. Could you try your hand at a poem written in reply to this one? Imagine that you are Bradstreet's husband, and that your poem is titled "My Dear and Loving Wife."

# LYN LIFSHIN

*Born in Burlington, Vermont, in 1944 and educated at Syracuse University and the University of Vermont, Lyn Lifshin has written many books of poetry on a range of topics, from Shaker communities of early America to Eskimo culture in the Arctic. Much of her work shows a strong feminist concern.*

## My Mother and the Bed

[1999]

No, not that way she'd
say when I was 7, pulling
the bottom sheet smooth,
you've got to        saying
hospital corners                                                    5

I wet the bed much later
than I should, until
just writing this I
hadn't thought of
the connection                                                     10

My mother would never
sleep on sheets someone
else had        I never
saw any stains on hers
tho her bedroom was                                                15

a maze of powder        hair
pins        black dresses
Sometimes she brings her
own sheets to my house,
carries toilet seat covers                                         20

Did anybody sleep
in my        she always asks
Her sheets        her hair
she says the rooms here
smell funny                                                        25

We drive at 3 am
slowly into Boston and
strip what looks like
two clean beds as the
sky gets light        I                                            30

smooth on the form
fitted flower bottom,
she redoes it

She thinks of my life
as a bed only she                                                  35
can make right

### YOUR TURN

1. What do you make of the extra spaces—for instance, the space between "to" and "saying" in line 4? In reading the poem aloud, how do
   you "read" the spaces?
2. Would you agree that the poem is humorous and, on the whole, ge-
   nial? Or do you think that bitterness overshadows the humor? Explain.
3. One student made the suggestion that the final stanza, perhaps because it seems to "explain" the poem to the reader, is the least

effective part of the poem. Do you agree? If you do, write a new final stanza.

# MITSUYE YAMADA

*Mitsuye Yamada, the daughter of Japanese immigrants to the United States, was born in Japan in 1923, during her mother's return visit to her native land. Yamada was raised in Seattle, but in 1942 she and her family were incarcerated and then relocated in a camp in Idaho, when Executive Order 9066 gave military authorities the right to remove any and all persons from "military areas." In 1954 she became an American citizen.*

## To the Lady                                          [1976]

The one in San Francisco who asked:
Why did the Japanese Americans let
the government put them in
those camps without protest?

Come to think of it I                                      5
    should've run off to Canada
    should've hijacked a plane to Algeria
    should've pulled myself up from my
    bra straps
    and kicked'm in the groin                              10
    should've bombed a bank
    should've tried self-immolation
    should've holed myself up in a
    woodframe house
    and let you watch me                                   15
    burn up on the six o'clock news
    should've run howling down the street
    naked and assaulted you at breakfast
    by AP wirephoto
    should've screamed bloody murder                       20
    like Kitty Genovese°

    Then
YOU would've
    come to my aid in shining armor
    laid yourself across the railroad track                25
    marched on Washington
    tatooed a Star of David on your arm
    written six million enraged
    letters to Congress

    But we didn't draw the line                            30

---

**21 Kitty Genovese** In 1964 Kitty Genovese of Kew Gardens, New York, was stabbed to death when she left her car and walked toward her home. Thirty-eight persons heard her screams, but no one came to her assistance.

anywhere
law and order Executive Order 9066°
social order moral order internal order

YOU let'm
I let'm                                                                        35
All are punished.

---

**32 Executive Order 9066** an authorization, signed in 1941 by President Franklin D.
Roosevelt, allowing military authorities to relocate Japanese and Japanese-Americans who
resided on the Pacific Coast of the United States.

> **YOUR TURN**
>
> 1. Has the lady's question (lines 2–4) ever crossed your mind? If so, what
>    answers did you think of?
> 2. What, in effect, is the speaker really saying in lines 5–21? And in lines
>    24–29?
> 3. Explain the last line.

# The Voice of the Satirist

The writer of **satire,** in one way or another, ridicules an aspect or several aspects of human behavior, seeking to arouse in the reader some degree of amused
contempt for the object. However urbane in tone, the satirist is always critical. By
cleverly holding up foibles or vices for the world's derision, satire (Alexander
Pope claimed) "heals with morals what it hurts with wit." The laughter of comedy is an end in itself; the laughter of satire is a weapon against the world: "The
intellectual dagger," Frank O'Connor called satire, "opposing the real dagger."
Jonathan Swift, of whom O'Connor is speaking, insisted that his satires were not
malice but medicine:

> His satire points at no defect
> But what all mortals may correct. . . .
> He spared a hump or crooked nose,
> Whose owners set not up for beaux.

But Swift, although he claimed that satire is therapeutic, also saw its futility:
"Satire is a sort of glass [i.e., mirror] wherein beholders do generally discover
everybody's face but their own."

Sometimes the satirist speaks out directly as defender of public morals, abu-
sively but wittily chopping off heads. Byron, for example, wrote:

> Prepare for rhyme—I'll publish, right or wrong:
> Fools are my theme, let Satire be my song.

But sometimes the satirist chooses to invent a speaker far removed from himself
or herself, just as Browning chose to invent a Renaissance duke. The satirist may
invent a callous brigadier general or a pompous judge who unconsciously annihi-
lates himself. Consider this satirical poem by e. e. cummings.

# E. E. CUMMINGS

*For a biographical note, see page 567.*

### next to of course god america i                                    [1926]

"next to of course god america i
love you land of the pilgrims' and so forth oh
say can you see by the dawn's early my
country 'tis of centuries come and go
and are no more what of it we should worry          5
in every language even deaf and dumb
thy sons acclaim your glorious name by gorry
by jingo by gee by gosh by gum
why talk of beauty what could be more beautiful than these heroic happy dead                   10
who rushed like lions to the roaring slaughter
they did not stop to think they died instead
then shall the voice of liberty be mute?"

He spoke. And drank rapidly a glass of water

Cummings might have written, in the voice of a solid citizen or a good poet, a direct attack on chauvinistic windbags; instead, he chose to invent a windbag whose rhetoric punctures itself. Yet the last line tells that we are really hearing someone who is recounting what the windbag said; that is, the speaker of all the lines but the last is a combination of the chauvinist *and* the satiric observer of the chauvinist. (When cummings himself recited these lines, there was mockery in his voice.)

Only in the final line of the poem does the author seem to speak entirely on his own, and even here he adopts a matter-of-fact pose that is far more potent than **invective** (direct abuse) would be. Yet the last line is not totally free of explicit hostility.

# MARGE PIERCY

*Marge Piercy, born in Detroit in 1936, was the first member of her family to attend college. After earning a bachelor's degree from the University of Michigan in 1957 and a master's degree from Northwestern University in 1958, she moved to Chicago. There she worked at odd jobs while writing novels (unpublished) and engaging in action on behalf of women and blacks and against the war in Vietnam. In 1970 she moved to Wellfleet, Massachusetts, where she still lives. She is the author of many novels as well as short stories, poems, and essays.*

### Barbie Doll                                                          [1969]

This girlchild was born as usual
and presented dolls that did pee-pee
and miniature GE stoves and irons
and wee lipsticks the color of cherry candy.
Then in the magic of puberty, a classmate said:       5
You have a great big nose and fat legs.

She was healthy, tested intelligent,
possessed strong arms and back,
abundant sexual drive and manual dexterity.
She went to and fro apologizing.                         10
Everyone saw a fat nose on thick legs.

She was advised to play coy,
exhorted to come on hearty,
exercise, diet, smile and wheedle.
Her good nature wore out                                 15
like a fan belt.
So she cut off her nose and her legs
and offered them up.

In the casket displayed on satin she lay
with the undertaker's cosmetics painted on,              20
a turned-up putty nose,
dressed in a pink and white nightie.
Doesn't she look pretty? everyone said.
Consummation at last.
To every woman a happy ending.                           25

### YOUR TURN

1. Why is the poem called "Barbie Doll"?
2. What voice do you hear in lines 1–4? Line 6 is, we are told, the voice of "a classmate." How do these voices differ? What voice do you hear in the first three lines of the second stanza?
3. Explain in your own words what Piercy is saying about women in this poem. Does her view seem to you fair, slightly exaggerated, or greatly exaggerated?

# LOUISE ERDRICH

*Louise Erdrich, born in 1954 in Little Falls, Minnesota, grew up in North Dakota, a member of the Turtle Mountain Band of Chippewa. Her father had been born in Germany; her mother was a Chippewa; both parents taught at the Bureau of Indian Affairs School. After graduating from Dartmouth College (major in anthropology) in 1976, Erdrich returned briefly to North Dakota to teach in the Poetry in the Schools Program, and went to Johns Hopkins University, where she earned a master's degree in creative writing.*

*Erdrich has published several collections of poems and many novels, one of which,* Love Medicine *(1986), won the National Book Critics Circle Award.*

## Dear John Wayne                                        [1984]

August and the drive-in picture is packed.
We lounge on the hood of the Pontiac
surrounded by the slow-burning spirals they sell
at the window, to vanquish the hordes of mosquitoes.
Nothing works. They break through the smoke screen for blood.    5

Always the lookout spots the Indians first,
spread north to south, barring progress.
The Sioux or some other Plains bunch
in spectacular columns, ICBM missiles,
feathers bristling in the meaningful sunset.                         10
The drum breaks. There will be no parlance.
Only the arrows whining, a death-cloud of nerves
swarming down on the settlers
who die beautifully, tumbling like dust weeds
into the history that brought us all here                            15
together: this wide screen beneath the sign of the bear.

The sky fills, acres of blue squint and eye
that the crowd cheers. His face moves over us,
a thick cloud of vengeance, pitted
like the land that was once flesh. Each rut,                         20
each scar makes a promise: *It is*
*not over, this fight, not as long as you resist.*
*Everything we see belongs to us.*

A few laughing Indians fall over the hood
slipping in the hot spilled butter.                                  25
*The eye sees a lot, John, but the heart is so blind.*
*Death makes us owners of nothing.*
He smiles, a horizon of teeth
the credits reel over, and then the white fields
again blowing in the true-to-life dark.                             30
The dark films over everything.
We get into the car
scratching our mosquito bites, speechless and small
as people are when the movie is done.
We are back in our skins.                                            35
How can we help but keep hearing his voice,
the flip side of the sound track, still playing:
*Come on, boys, we got them*
*where we want them, drunk, running.*
*They'll give us what we want, what we need.*                        40

Even his disease was the idea of taking everything.
Those cells, burning, doubling, splitting out of their skins.

---

### YOUR TURN

1. Who is the speaker of most of the poem? Who speaks the italicized lines?
2. There are curious shifts in the diction, for instance from "some other Plains bunch" (line 8) to "parlance" (line 11). Whose voice do we hear in "some. . . bunch"? Consider, too, the diction in "to vanquish the hordes of mosquitoes" (line 4). If you were talking about mosquitoes, you probably would not use the word "vanquish." What do you think Erdrich is up to?
3. What do you make of lines 24–25, talking of Indians "slipping in the hot spilled butter"? What connection do these lines have with what presumably is going on in the film?

# STEPHEN DUCK

*Stephen Duck (1705?-1756), born in rural England of impoverished parents, left school at thirteen and became a farm laborer. He later wrote about such work, but he also wrote on other topics, as in the satiric piece that we reprint here.*

Note: *Pronunciation in eighteenth-century England was not identical with pronunciation today, and in any case Duck's pronunciation would not have been identical with the pronunciation of an educated Londoner. In line 2, "cheese" rhymes with "gaze" in line 1; in line 4, "live" rhymes with "perceive" in line 3; and in line 9 "cream" was probably pronounced "crem," rhyming with "them."*

## *On Mites*                                                           [1736]

### *To a Lady*

*"'Tis but by way of Simile."*

                    —Prior°

Dear Madam, did you never gaze,
Through optic-glass,° on rotten Cheese?
There, Madam, did you ne'er perceive
A crowd of dwarfish creatures live?
The little things, elate with pride,                                    5
Strut to and fro, from side to side:
In tiny pomp, and pertly vain,
Lords of their pleasing orb they reign;
And, filled with hardened curds and cream,
Think the whole dairy made for them.                                   10
So men, conceited lords of all,
Walk proudly o'er this pendent° Ball,
Fond of their little spot below,
Nor greater beings care to know;
But think those worlds which deck the skies,                           15
Were only formed to please their eyes.

---

**Prior** Matthew Prior (1664-1721), important English diplomat and minor poet.    **2 optic glass** microscope.    **12 pendent** floating in space.

---

**YOUR TURN**

Duck is pretty straightforward in his attack on human pride. Is he merely abusive, or does he also display some wit? To put the matter bluntly: Is there anything enjoyable about the poem? Or think about the poem from this angle: In Chapter 2 we discuss Robert Frost's opinion that literature is "a performance in words." Obviously Duck is giving a performance when he rhymes certain words, but are there other aspects to his performance?

# Figurative Language: Simile, Metaphor, Personification, Apostrophe

HIPPOLYTA.  'Tis strange, my Theseus, that these lovers speak of.
THESEUS.   More strange than true. I never may believe
    These antique fables, nor these fairy toys.
    Lovers and madmen have such seething brains,
    Such shaping fantasies, that apprehend
    More than cool reason ever comprehends.
    The lunatic, the lover, and the poet
    Are of imagination all compact.
    One sees more devils than vast hell can hold,
    That is the madman. The lover, all as frantic,
    Sees Helen's beauty in a brow of Egypt.
    The poet's eye, in a fine frenzy rolling,
    Doth glance from heaven to earth, from earth to heaven;
    And as imagination bodies forth
    The forms of things unknown, the poet's pen
    Turns them to shapes, and gives to airy nothing
    A local habitation and a name.
            —Shakespeare, *A Midsummer Night's Dream,* 5.1–17

Theseus was neither the first nor the last to suggest that poets, like lunatics and lovers, freely employ their imaginations. Terms such as *poetic license* and *poetic justice* imply that poets are free to depict a never-never land. One has only to leaf through any anthology of poetry to encounter numerous statements that are, from a logical point of view, lunacies. Here are two quotations:

Look like th' innocent flower,
But be the serpent under 't.

            —Shakespeare

Each outcry from the hunted hare
A fiber from the brain does tear.

            —William Blake

The first of these is spoken by Lady Macbeth, when she urges her husband to murder King Duncan. How can a human being "Look like th' innocent flower," and how can a human being "be the serpent"? But Macbeth knows, and we know, exactly what she means. We see and we feel her point, in a way that we would not if she had said, "Put on an innocent-looking face, but in fact kill the king."

And in the quotation from Blake, when we read that the hunted hare's plaintive cry serves to "tear" a "fiber" from our brain, we almost wince, even though we know that the statement is literally untrue.

On a literal level, then, such assertions are nonsense (so, too, is Theseus's notion that reason is cool). But of course they are not to be taken literally; rather, they employ **figures of speech**—departures from logical usage that are aimed at gaining special effects. Consider the lunacies that Robert Burns heaps up here.

# ROBERT BURNS

*Robert Burns (1759-1796) was born in Ayrshire in southwestern Scotland. Many of his best poems and songs were written in the Scots dialect, though he also wrote English as the English spoke it.*

## A Red, Red Rose                                          [1796]

O, my luve is like a red, red rose,
    That's newly sprung in June.
O, my luve is like the melodie,
    That's sweetly played in tune.                                    4

As fair art thou, my bonnie lass,
    So deep in luve am I,
And I will luve thee still, my dear,
    Till a'° the seas gang° dry.                                       8

Till a' the seas gang dry, my dear,
    And the rocks melt wi' the sun!
And I will luve thee still, my dear,
    While the sands o' life shall run.                                12

And fare thee weel, my only luve,
    And fare thee weel awhile!
And I will come again, my luve,
    Though it were ten thousand mile!                                 16

---

8 a' all. **gang** go.

To the charge that these lines are lunacies or untruths, at least two replies can be made. First, it might be said that the speaker is not really making assertions about a woman; he is saying he feels a certain way. His words, it can be argued, are not assertions about external reality but expressions of his state of mind, just as a tune one whistles asserts nothing about external reality but expresses the whistler's state of mind. In this view, the nonlogical language of poetry (like a groan of pain or an exclamation of joy) is an expression of emotion; its further aim, if it has one, is to induce in the hearer an emotion.

Second, and more to the point here, it can be said that nonlogical language does indeed make assertions about external reality, and even gives the reader an insight into this reality that logical language cannot. The opening comparison in Burns's poem ("my luve is like a red, red rose") brings before our eyes the lady's beauty in a way that the reasonable assertion "She is beautiful" does not. By comparing the woman to a rose, the poet invites us to see the woman through a special sort of lens: she is fragrant; her lips (and perhaps her cheeks) are like a rose in texture and color; she will not keep her beauty long. Also, "my love is like a red, red rose" says something different from "like a red, red beet," or "a red, red cabbage."

The poet, then, has not only communicated a state of mind but also discovered, through the lens of imagination, some things (both in the beloved and in the lover's own feelings) that interest us. The discovery is not world-shaking; it is less important than the discovery of America or the discovery that the meek are blessed, but it *is* a discovery and it leaves the reader with the feeling, "Yes, that's right. I hadn't quite thought of it that way, but that's right."

A poem, Robert Frost said, "assumes direction with the first line laid down, . . . runs a course of lucky events, and ends in a clarification of life—not necessarily a great clarification, such as sects and cults are founded on, but in a momentary stay against confusion." What is clarified? In another sentence Frost gives an answer: "For me the initial delight is in the surprise of remembering something I didn't know I knew." John Keats made a similar statement: "Poetry . . . should strike the Reader as a wording of his own highest thoughts, and appear almost a Remembrance."

Some figures of speech are, in effect, riddling ways of speech. To call fishermen "farmers of the sea"—a metaphor—is to give a sort of veiled description of fishermen, bringing out, when the term is properly understood, certain aspects of a fisherman's activities. And a riddle, after all, is a veiled description—though intentionally obscure or deceptive—calling attention to characteristics, especially similarities, not usually noticed. (*Riddle*, like *read*, is from Old English *redan*, "to guess," "to interpret," and thus its solution provides knowledge.) "Two sisters upstairs, often looking but never seeing each other" is (after the riddle is explained) a way of calling attention to the curious fact that the eye, the instrument of vision, never sees its mate.

# SYLVIA PLATH

*Sylvia Plath (1932–1963) was born in Boston, the daughter of German immigrants. While still an undergraduate at Smith College, she published in* Seventeen *and* Mademoiselle; *but her years at college, like her later years, were marked by manic-depressive periods. After graduating from college, she went to England to study at Cambridge University, where she met the English poet Ted Hughes, whom she married in 1956. The marriage was unsuccessful, and they separated. One day she committed suicide by turning on the kitchen gas.*

## Metaphors

[1960]

I'm a riddle in nine syllables,
An elephant, a ponderous house,
A melon strolling on two tendrils.

O red fruit, ivory, fine timbers!
This loaf's big with its yeasty rising.                                                5
Money's new-minted in this fat purse.
I'm a means, a stage, a cow in calf.
I've eaten a bag of green apples,
Boarded the train there's no getting off.

### YOUR TURN

The riddling speaker says that she is, among other things, "a ponderous house" and "a cow in calf." What is she?

# Simile

In a **simile,** items from different classes are explicitly compared by a connective such as *like, as,* or *than* or by a verb such as *appears* or *seems.* (If the objects compared are from the same class—for example, "New York is like Chicago"—no simile is present.)

Sometimes I feel like a motherless child.

—Anonymous

It is a beauteous evening, calm and free.
The holy time is quiet as a Nun,
Breathless with adoration.

—Wordsworth

How sharper than a serpent's tooth it is
To have a thankless child.

—Shakespeare

Seems he a dove? His feathers are but borrowed.

—Shakespeare

Again, although the comparison is explicit (*like, as*) there is something uncanny in it, in a way that there is not in, say, "John's hair is like Jane's."

# Metaphor

A **metaphor** asserts the identity, without a connective such as *like* or a verb such as *appears,* of terms that are literally incompatible.

She is the rose, the glory of the day.

—Spenser

O western orb sailing the heaven.

—Whitman

Notice how in the second example only one of the terms ("orb") is stated; the other ("ship") is implied in "sailing."

# JOHN KEATS

*For a biographical note, see page 559.*

## On First Looking into Chapman's Homer*    [1816]

Much have I traveled in the realms of gold,
  And many goodly states and kingdoms seen;
  Round many western islands have I been
Which bards in fealty to Apollo° hold.
Oft of one wide expanse had I been told                          5
  That deep-browed Homer ruled as his demesne;°
  Yet did I never breathe its pure serene°
Till I heard Chapman speak out loud and bold:
Then felt I like some watcher of the skies
  When a new planet swims into his ken;                          10
Or like stout Cortez when with eagle eyes
  He stared at the Pacific—and all his men
Looked at each other with a wild surmise—
  Silent, upon a peak in Darien.

---

*George Chapman (1559–1634?), Shakespeare's contemporary, is chiefly known for his translations (from the Greek) of Homer's *Odyssey* and *Iliad*. In lines 11–14 Keats mistakenly says that Cortés was the first European to see the Pacific, from the heights of Darien, in Panama. In fact, Balboa was the first.   **4 Apollo** god of poetry.   **6 demesne** domain.
**7 serene** open space.

> **YOUR TURN**
>
> 1. In line 1, what do you think "realms of gold" stands for? Chapman lived during the late sixteenth and the early seventeenth centuries; how does this fact add relevance to the metaphor in the first line?
> 2. Does line 9 introduce a totally new idea, or can you somehow connect it to the opening metaphor?

Two types of metaphor deserve special mention. In **metonymy,** something is named that replaces something closely related to it; "City Hall," for example, sometimes is used to stand for municipal authority. In the following passage James Shirley names certain objects (scepter and crown; scythe and spade), using them to replace social classes (royalty; agricultural labor) to which they are related:

Scepter and crown must tumble down
And in the dust be equal made
With the poor crooked scythe and spade.

In **synecdoche,** the whole is replaced by the part, or the part by the whole. For example, *bread* in "Give us this day our daily bread" replaces the whole class of edibles. Similarly, an automobile can be "wheels," and workers are "hands." Robert Frost was fond of calling himself "a Synecdochist" because he believed that it is the nature of poetry to "have intimations of something more than itself. It almost always comes under the head of synecdoche, a part, a hem of the garment for the whole garment."

Sometimes a poet will describe and explore the nature of a person, place, or thing through a metaphor, or, as in this poem, through a series of metaphors.

# KAY RYAN

*Kay Ryan, born in San Jose, California, in 1945, holds a bachelor's and a master's degree in English from the University of California, Los Angeles. She has published a number of books of poetry, and in 2009 she was appointed the sixteenth Poet Laureate Consultant in Poetry to the Library of Congress.*

## Turtle                                                                        [1994]

Who would be a turtle who could help it?
A barely mobile hard roll, a four-oared helmet,
She can ill afford the chances she must take
In rowing toward the grasses that she eats.
Her track is graceless, like dragging                                            5
A packing-case places, and almost any slope
Defeats her modest hopes. Even being practical,
She's often stuck up to the axle on her way
To something edible. With everything optimal,
She skirts the ditch which would convert                                        10
Her shell into a serving dish. She lives
Below luck-level, never imagining some lottery
Will change her load of pottery to wings.
Her only levity is patience,
The sport of truly chastened things.                                            15

Notice that Ryan begins with a question, and her poem might be understood as an answer, or set of answers, to this question, unfolding through witty, vivid, playful metaphors. The turtle is a "roll"—and a hard one at that. Then, it is a helmet, but a curious kind of helmet that also has four oars (the turtle's four feet), a metaphor that Ryan extends by saying that the turtle rows toward the grass that it eats. But then, in line 6, she depicts the turtle as a heavy packing case that is hard to move. And so on, to the ending—an ending that implies the way in which the turtle is itself a metaphor, suggesting the important lesson of patience for all of us.

Perhaps the turtle, then, for all of its limitations that Ryan illustrates through engaging metaphors, possesses a virtue that many of us do not. Turtles and human beings might (or could) have something in common after all—something we come to see and think about through the metaphors that Ryan presents in her poem.

Incidentally, although metaphor is essential to "Turtle," and metaphor is our chief topic here, we cannot resist pointing out that Ryan is also exploiting other aspects of the poet's craft, notably rhyme. Notice that some rhymes occur at the ends of lines—"wings" in 13 and "things" in 15—but some rhymes, or near-rhymes (also called "off-rhymes"), occur within lines: "oared" in line 2 and "afford" in line 3; "graceless" in 5, "packing-case places" in 6; "practical" in 7 and "axle" in 8; "slope" in 6, "hopes" in 7; "ditch" and "which" in 10; "lottery" in 12 and "pottery" in 13. The effect, we think, is to communicate something of the lumbering quality of this beast whose patience Ryan is celebrating largely through metaphors.

# MARGE PIERCY

*For a biographical note, see page 614.*

### A Work of Artifice                                                [1973]

The bonsai tree
in the attractive pot
could have grown eighty feet tall
on the side of a mountain
till split by lightning.                                                    5
But a gardener
carefully pruned it.
It is nine inches high.
Every day as he
whittles back the branches                                              10
the gardener croons,
It is your nature
to be small and cozy,
domestic and weak;
how lucky, little tree,                                                    15
to have a pot to grow in.
With living creatures
one must begin very early
to dwarf their growth:
the bound feet,                                                            20
the crippled brain,
the hair in curlers,
the hands you
love to touch.

---

**YOUR TURN**

1. Piercy uses a bonsai tree as a metaphor—but a metaphor for what? (If
   you have never seen a bonsai tree, try to visit a florist or a nursery to
   take a close look at one. You can find a picture of a bonsai by looking
   online.)
2. The gardener "croons" (line 11) a song to the bonsai tree. If the tree
   could respond, what might it say?
3. Explain lines 17–24 to someone who doesn't get the point. In your response, explain how these lines are connected with "hair in curlers."
   Explain, too, what "the hands you / love to touch" has to do with the
   rest of the poem. What tone of voice do you hear in "the hands you /
   love to touch"?
4. How does the form of the poem suggest its subject?

# Personification

The attribution of human feelings or characteristics to abstractions or to inanimate objects is called **personification**.

But Time did beckon to the flowers, and they
By noon most cunningly did steal away.

                                        —Herbert

Herbert attributes a human gesture to Time and shrewdness to flowers. Of all figures, personification most surely gives to airy nothings a local habitation and a name:

There's Wrath who has learnt every trick of guerrilla warfare,
The shamming dead, the night-raid, the feinted retreat.

                                        —Auden

Hope, thou bold taster of delight.

                                        —Crashaw

The alarm clock meddling in somebody's sleep.

                                        —Brooks

. . . neon script leering from the shuddering asphalt.

                                        —Dove

In the next poem, the speaker, addressing a former mistress ("come let us kiss and part"), seems to grant that their love is over—is dying—and he personifies this love, this passion, as a person on his deathbed ("Now at last gasp of Love's latest breath"). Further, he surrounds the dying Love with two mourners, Faith, who is kneeling by Love's bed, and Innocence, who is closing Love's eyes. But notice that the poem takes a sudden twist at the end where, it seems, Love may not have to die.

# MICHAEL DRAYTON

*Michael Drayton (1563–1631) was born in Warwickshire in England a year before Shakespeare, and like Shakespeare he wrote sonnets. Among his other works is a long poem,* Poly-Olbion *(1612/13, 1622), on the geography and local lore of England.*

## Since There's No Help                          [1619]

Since there's no help, come let us kiss and part;
Nay, I have done, you get no more of me,
And I am glad, yea glad with all my heart
That thus so cleanly I myself can free;
Shake hands for ever, cancel all our vows,                     5
And when we meet at any time again,
Be it not seen in either of our brows
That we one jot of former love retain.
Now at the last gasp of Love's latest breath,
When, his pulse failing, Passion speechless lies,              10
When Faith is kneeling by his bed of death,
And Innocence is closing up his eyes,
    Now if thou wouldst, when all have given him over,
    From death to life you mightst him yet recover.

**YOUR TURN**

1. What do you think is the tone of lines 1–8? What words especially establish this tone? What do you think is the tone of lines 9–14?

2. Some readers find the personifications in lines 9–14 a sign that the speaker is not deeply moved, and perhaps is putting on an act. Do you agree or not? Please explain.

# Apostrophe

Crashaw's personification, "Hope, thou bold taster of delight," quoted a moment ago, is also an example of the figure of speech called **apostrophe,** an address to a person or thing not literally listening. Wordsworth begins a sonnet by apostrophizing John Milton:

Milton, thou shouldst be living at this hour,

And Shelley begins an ode by apostrophizing a skylark:

Hail to thee, blithe Spirit!

The following poem is largely built on apostrophe.

## EDMUND WALLER

*Edmund Waller (1606–1687), born into a wealthy country family in Buckinghamshire in England, attended Eton and Cambridge before spending most of his life as a member of Parliament. When the Puritans came to power, he was imprisoned and eventually banished to France, although he was soon allowed to return to England. When the monarchy was restored to the throne, he returned to Parliament.*

   *Esteemed for his poetry and wit, Waller circulated many of his poems in manuscript before eventually publishing them in books. John Dryden, Alexander Pope, and other writers greatly admired Waller, especially for his skillful use of the heroic couplet (pairs of rhyming lines of iambic pentameter).*

### Song                                              [1645]

    Go, lovely rose,
Tell her that wastes her time and me,
    That now she knows,
When I resemble her to thee,
    How sweet and fair she seems to be.            5

    Tell her that's young,
And shuns to have her graces spied,
    That hadst thou sprung
In deserts where no men abide,
    Thou must have uncommended died.             10
    Small is the worth
Of beauty from the light retired:
    Bid her come forth,
Suffer her self to be desired,
    And not blush so to be admired.              15

> Then die, that she
> The common fate of all things rare
>   May read in thee,
> How small a part of time they share,
> That are so wondrous sweet and fair.    20

What conclusions, then, can we draw about **figurative language?** First, such language, with its literally incompatible terms, forces the reader to attend to the **connotations** (suggestions, associations) rather than to the **denotations** (dictionary definitions) of a term.

Second, although figurative language is said to differ from ordinary discourse, it is found in ordinary discourse as well as in literature. "It rained cats and dogs," "War is hell," "Don't be a pig," and other tired figures are part of our daily utterances. But through repeated use, these (and most of the figures we use) have lost whatever impact they once had and are only a shade removed from expressions that, though once figurative, have become literal: the *eye* of a needle, a *branch* office, the *face* of a clock.

Third, good figurative language is usually

1. concrete,
2. condensed, and
3. interesting.

The concreteness lends precision and vividness; when Keats writes that he felt

> like some watcher of the skies / When a new planet swims into his ken,

he more sharply characterizes his feelings than if he had said, "I felt excited." His simile isolates for us a precise kind of excitement, and the metaphoric "swims" vividly brings up the oceanic aspect of the sky. The second of these three qualities, condensation, can be seen by attempting to paraphrase some of the figures. A paraphrase or rewording will commonly use more words than the original and will have less impact—as the gradual coming of night usually has less impact on us than a sudden darkening of the sky, or as a prolonged push has less impact than a sudden blow. The third quality, interest, largely depends on the previous two: the successful figure often makes us open our eyes wider and take notice. Keats's "deep-browed Homer" arouses our interest in Homer as "thoughtful Homer" or "meditative Homer" does not. Similarly, when W. B. Yeats says (page 834):

> An aged man is but a paltry thing,
> A tattered coat upon a stick, unless
> Soul clap its hands and sing, and louder sing
> For every tatter in its mortal dress,

the metaphoric identification of an old man with a scarecrow jolts us out of all our usual unthinking attitudes about old men as kind, happy folk content to have passed from youth to senior citizenship.

Finally, the point must be made that although figurative language is one of the poet's chief tools, a poem does not have to contain figures. Here is a poem by William Carlos Williams. Does it contain any figures of speech?

1. The poem ends with the speaker saying that he will "dig" with his pen. Given all the preceding lines, what will he dig?
2. The first lines compare the pen with a gun. What implications are suggested by this comparison?

# LINDA PASTAN

*For a biographical note, see page 589.*

## Baseball    [1995]

When you tried to tell me
baseball was a metaphor

for life: the long, dusty travail
around the bases, for instance,

to try to go home again;                                    5
the Sacrifice for which you win

approval but not applause;
the way the light closes down

in the last days of the season—
I didn't believe you.                                      10

It's just a way of passing
the time, I said.

And you said: that's it.
Yes.

1. What does it mean to say that baseball is "a metaphor for life"? Does the speaker agree? She seems not to at first, but perhaps by the end she changes her mind. Or is that a misreading of the poem?
2. Take a step back: What is the story that this poem is telling? How does it begin? What takes place in the middle? How does it conclude?
3. Do you understand this poem? How would you explain its meaning to someone who found it perplexing?
4. Why is the word "Sacrifice" capitalized?
5. "Baseball" consists of seven short two-line stanzas. Why did Pastan structure it this way? Would her poem have been more effective if she had presented it as a single stanza?

# WILLIAM SHAKESPEARE

*You will encounter Shakespeare (1564–1616) several times in this book—for instance, as the author of songs (Chapter 18), sonnets (Chapter 23), a tragedy (Chapter 30), and a comedy (Chapter 31).*

*Here we give one of his sonnets (probably written in the mid-1590s), in which he playfully rejects similes and other figures of speech. His contemporaries often compared a woman's hair to fine-spun gold, her lips to coral or to cherries, her cheeks to roses, her white breast to snow; when such a woman walked, she seemed to walk on air (the grass did not bend beneath her), and when she spoke, her voice was music. Shakespeare himself uses such figures in some of his poems and plays, but in this sonnet he praises his beloved by saying she does not need such figures.*

## Sonnet 130

My mistress' eyes are nothing like the sun;
Coral is far more red than her lips' red;
If snow be white, why then her breasts are dun;
If hairs be wires, black wires grow on her head.
I have seen roses damasked, red and white,                5
But no such roses see I in her cheeks;
And in some perfumes is there more delight
Than in the breath that from my mistress reeks.
I love to hear her speak, yet well I know
That music hath a far more pleasing sound;              10
I grant I never saw a goddess go;°
My mistress, when she walks, treads on the ground.
   And yet, by heaven, I think my love as rare°
   As any she belied° with false compare.

---

11 **go** walk.    13 **rare** exceptional.    14 **any she belied** any woman misrepresented.

# Imagery and Symbolism

When we read the word "rose"—or, for that matter, "finger" or "thumb"—we may more or less call to mind a picture, an image. The term **imagery** is used to refer to whatever in a poem appeals to any of our sensations, including sensations of pressure and heat as well as of sight, smell, taste, touch, and sound.

Consider the opening lines of Seamus Heaney's "Digging" (page 629):

> Between my finger and my thumb
> The squat pen rests; snug as a gun.

We may in our mind's eye see a finger, thumb, and pen; and perhaps, stimulated by "squat," we may almost feel the pen. Notice, too, that in Heaney's line the pen is compared to a gun, so there is yet another image in the line. In short, images are the sensory content of the work, whether literal (the finger, thumb, and pen) or figurative (the gun, to which the pen is compared). Edmund Waller's rose in "Go, lovely rose" (page 626) is an image that happens to be compared in the first stanza to a woman ("I resemble her to thee"); later in the poem this image comes to stand for "all things rare." Yet we never forget that the rose is a rose, and that the poem is chiefly a revelation of the poet's attitude toward his beloved.

If a poet says "my rose" and is speaking about a rose, we have an image, even though we do not have a figure of speech. If a poet says "my rose" and, we gather, is speaking not really or chiefly about a rose but about something else—let's say the transience of beauty—we can say that the poet is using the rose as a symbol.

Some symbols are **natural symbols,** recognized as standing for something in particular even by people from different cultures. Rain, for instance, usually stands for fertility or the renewal of life. A forest often stands for mental darkness or chaos, a mountain for stability, a valley for a place of security, and so on. There are many exceptions, but by and large these meanings prevail.

Other symbols, however, are **conventional symbols,** which people have agreed to accept as standing for something other than themselves: A poem about the cross would probably be about Christianity. Similarly, the rose has long been a symbol for love. In Virginia Woolf's novel *Mrs. Dalloway* (1925), the husband communicates his love by proffering this conventional symbol: "He was holding out flowers—roses, red and white roses. (But he could not bring himself to say he loved her; not in so many words.)" Objects that are not conventional symbols, however, also may give rise to rich, multiple, indefinable associations. The following poem uses the symbol of the rose, but uses it in a nontraditional way.

# WILLIAM BLAKE

*A biography of Blake, followed by five additional poems, appears on page 784.*

## The Sick Rose [1794]

O rose, thou are sick!
The invisible worm
That flies in the night
In the howling storm 4

Has found out thy bed
Of crimson joy,
And his dark secret love
Does thy life destroy. 8

One might argue that the worm is "invisible" (line 2) merely because it is hidden within the rose, but an "invisible worm / That flies in the night" is more than a long, slender, soft-bodied creeping animal; and a rose that has, or is, a "bed/ Of crimson joy" is more than a gardener's rose.

Blake's worm and rose suggest things beyond themselves—a stranger, more vibrant world than the world we are usually aware of. Many readers find themselves half-thinking, for example, that the worm is male, the rose female, and that the poem is about the violation of virginity. Or that the poem is about the destruction of beauty: woman's beauty, rooted in joy, is destroyed by a power that feeds on her. But these interpretations are not fully satisfying: the poem presents a worm and a rose, and yet it is not merely about a worm and a rose. These objects resonate, stimulating our thoughts toward something else, but the something else is elusive, whereas it is not elusive in Burns's "A Red, Red Rose" (page 619).

A **symbol,** then, is an image so loaded with significance that it is not simply literal, and it does not simply stand for something else; it is both itself *and* something else that it richly suggests, a manifestation of something too complex or too elusive to be otherwise revealed. Blake's poem is about a blighted rose and at the same time about much more. In a symbol, as Thomas Carlyle wrote in *Sartor Resartus* (1836), "the Infinite is made to blend with the Finite, to stand visible, and as it were, attainable there." Probably it is not fanciful to say that the American slaves who sang "Joshua fought the battle of Jericho, / And the walls came tumbling down" were singing both about an ancient occurrence *and* about a new embodiment of the ancient, the imminent collapse of slavery in the nineteenth century. Not one or the other, but both: the present partook of the past, and the past partook of the present.

# WALT WHITMAN

*Walt Whitman (1819–1892) was born in a farmhouse in rural Long Island, New York, but was brought up in Brooklyn, then an independent city in New York. He attended public school for a few years (1825–1830), apprenticed as a printer in the 1830s, and then worked as a typesetter, journalist, and newspaper editor. In 1855 he published the first edition of a collection of his poems,*

## *I Saw in Louisiana a Live-Oak Growing*                    [1867]

I saw in Louisiana a live-oak growing,
All alone stood it and the moss hung down from the branches,
Without any companion it grew there uttering joyous leaves
    of dark green,
And its look, rude, unbending, lusty, made me think of myself,
But I wonder'd how it could utter joyous leaves standing alone there
    without its friend near, for I knew I could not,                    5
And I broke off a twig with a certain number of leaves upon it,
    and twined around it a little moss,
And brought it away, and I have placed it in sight in my room,
It is not needed to remind me as of my own dear friends,
(For I believe lately I think of little else than of them,)
Yet it remains to me a curious token, it makes me think of manly love;                    10
For all that, and though the live-oak glistens there in Louisiana solitary
    in a wide flat space,
Uttering joyous leaves all its life without a friend a lover near,
I know very well I could not.

---

### YOUR TURN

Compare the final version (1867) of the poem with the manuscript version
of 1860. Which version do you prefer? Why?

## SAMUEL TAYLOR COLERIDGE

*Samuel Taylor Coleridge (1772–1834) was born in Devonshire in England, the
son of a clergyman. He attended Christ's Hospital school in London and Cambridge University, which he left without receiving a degree. With his friend
William Wordsworth he published anonymously in 1798 a volume of poetry,*
Lyrical Ballads, *which became the manifesto of the Romantic movement.*

## *Kubla Khan*                    [1798]

*Or, A Vision in a Dream. A Fragment.*

In Xanadu did Kubla Khan
A stately pleasure-dome decree:
Where Alph, the sacred river, ran
Through caverns measureless to man
    Down to a sunless sea.                    5
So twice five miles of fertile ground
With walls and towers were girdled round:
And here were gardens bright with sinuous rills,
Where blossomed many an incense-bearing tree;
And here were forests ancient as the hills,                    10
Enfolding sunny spots of greenery.

But oh! that deep romantic chasm which slanted
Down the green hill athwart a cedarn cover!

A savage place! as holy and enchanted
As e'er beneath a waning moon was haunted          15
By woman wailing for her demon-lover!
And from this chasm, with ceaseless turmoil seething,
As if this earth in fast thick pants were breathing
A mighty fountain momently was forced;
Amid whose swift half-intermitted burst            20
Huge fragments vaulted like rebounding hail,
Or chaffy grain beneath the thresher's flail:
And 'mid these dancing rocks at once and ever
It flung up momently the sacred river.
Five miles meandering with a mazy motion           25
Through wood and dale the sacred river ran,
Then reached the caverns measureless to man,
And sank in tumult to a lifeless ocean:
And 'mid this tumult Kubla heard from far
Ancestral voices prophesying war!                  30
    The shadow of the dome of pleasure
    Floated midway on the waves;
    Where was heard the mingled measure
    From the fountain and the caves.
It was a miracle of rare device,                   35
A sunny pleasure-dome with caves of ice!

    A damsel with a dulcimer
    In a vision once I saw:
    It was an Abyssinian° maid,
    And on her dulcimer she played,                40
    Singing of Mount Abora.
    Could I revive within me
    Her symphony and song,
    To such a deep delight 'twould win me,
That with music loud and long,                     45
I would build that dome in air,
That sunny dome! those caves of ice!
And all who heard should see them there,
And all should cry, Beware! Beware!
His flashing eyes, his floating hair!              50
Weave a circle round him thrice,
And close your eyes with holy dread,
For he on honey-dew hath fed,
And drunk the milk of Paradise.

When Coleridge published "Kubla Khan" in 1816, he prefaced it with this explanatory note:

> The following fragment is here published at the request of a poet of great and deserved celebrity, and, as far as the author's own opinions are concerned, rather as a psychological curiosity, than on the ground of any supposed *poetic* merits.

---

**39 Abyssinian** Abyssinia was the Ethiopian Empire, in East Africa.

In the summer of the year 1797, the author, then in ill health, had retired to a lonely farmhouse between Porlock and Linton, on the Exmoor
confines of Somerset and Devonshire. In consequence of a slight indispo-
sition, an anodyne had been prescribed, from the effects of which he fell
asleep in his chair at the moment that he was reading the following sentence, or words of the same substance, in *Purchas' Pilgrimage*: "Here
the Khan Kubla commanded a palace to be built, and a stately garden
thereunto. And thus ten miles of fertile ground were inclosed with a
wall." The author continued for about three hours in a profound sleep,
at least of the external senses, during which time he has the most vivid
confidence that he could not have composed less than from two to three
hundred lines; if that indeed can be called composition in which all
the images rose up before him as *things*, with a parallel production of the
correspondent expressions, without any sensation or consciousness of
effort. On awaking he appeared to himself to have a distinct recollection
of the whole, and taking his pen, ink, and paper, instantly and eagerly
wrote down the lines that are here preserved. At this moment he was
unfortunately called out by a person on business from Porlock, and detained by him above an hour, and on his return to his room, found, to
his no small surprise and mortification, that though he still retained
some vague and dim recollection of the general purport of the vision,
yet, with the exception of some eight or ten scattered lines and images, all the rest had passed away like the images on the surface of a
stream into which a stone has been cast, but, alas! without the after
restoration of the latter!

> Then all the charm
> Is broken—all that phantom world so fair
> Vanishes, and a thousand circlets spread,
> And each misshape[s] the other. Stay awhile,
> Poor youth! who scarcely dar'st lift up thine eyes—
> The stream will soon renew its smoothness, soon
> The visions will return! And lo, he stays,
> And soon the fragments dim of lovely forms
> Come trembling back, unite, and now once more
> The pool becomes a mirror.
> —Coleridge, *The Picture; or, the Lover's Resolution,* lines 91–100

Yet from the still surviving recollections in his mind, the author has
frequently purposed to finish for himself what had been originally, as
it were, given to him. Σαμερον αδιον ασω [today I shall sing more
sweetly]: "But the tomorrow is yet to come."

### YOUR TURN

1. Coleridge changed the "palace" of his source into a "dome" (line 2).
   What do you think are the relevant associations of "dome"?
2. What pairs of contrasts (e.g., underground river, fountain) do you find?
   What do you think they contribute to the poem?
3. If Coleridge had not said that the poem is a fragment, might you take it
   as a complete poem, the first thirty-six lines describing the creative
   imagination, and the remainder lamenting the loss of poetic power?

# EMMA LAZARUS

*Emma Lazarus (1849–1887) was of German-Jewish descent on her mother's side, and of Sephardic descent on her father's side. (Sephardic Jews trace their ancestry back to Spain under Moslem rule, before the Jews were expelled by the Christians in 1492.)*

*In 1883 a committee was formed to raise funds for a pedestal for the largest statue in the world,* Liberty Enlightening the People, *to be installed on a small island in New York Harbor. Authors were asked to donate manuscripts which then were auctioned to raise money. Emma Lazarus, keenly aware of ancient persecutions and of contemporary Jewish refugees fleeing Russian persecutions, contributed the following poem. It was read when the statue was unveiled in 1886, and the words of Liberty, spoken in the last five lines, were embossed on a plaque inside the pedestal.*

*For the ancients, a colossus was a statue larger than life. "The brazen giant of Greek fame," mentioned in Lazarus's first line, was a statue of the sun god, erected in the harbor of the Greek island of Rhodes, celebrating the island's success in resisting the Macedonians in 305–304 BCE. More than 100 feet tall, it stood in the harbor until it toppled during an earthquake in 225 BCE. In later years its size became mythical; it was said to have straddled the harbor (Lazarus speaks of "limbs astride from land to land"), so that ships supposedly entered the harbor by sailing between its legs.*

*In Lazarus's poem, the "imprisoned lightning" (line 5) in the torch is electricity. The harbor is said to be "air-bridged" because in 1883, the year of the poem, the Brooklyn Bridge was completed, connecting Brooklyn with New York. (These are the "twin cities" of the poem.)*

## The New Colossus                                              [1883]

Not like the brazen giant of Greek fame,
With conquering limbs astride from land to land;
Here at our sea-washed, sunset gates shall stand
A mighty woman with a torch, whose flame
Is the imprisoned lightning, and her name                        5
Mother of Exiles. From her beacon-hand
Glows world-wide welcome; her mild eyes command
The air-bridged harbor that twin cities frame.
"Keep, ancient lands, your storied pomp!" cries she
With silent lips. "Give me your tired, your poor,               10
Your huddled masses yearning to breathe free,
The wretched refuse of your teeming shore.
Send these, the homeless, tempest-tost to me,
I lift my lamp beside the golden door!"

> **YOUR TURN**

Why should a woman be a symbol of liberty? and why should she hold a torch? Why "golden door"?

# NILA NORTHSUN

*Nila northSun was born in 1951 in Schurz, Nevada, of Shoshone-Chippewa stock. She studied at the California State University campuses at Hayward and Humboldt and the University of Montana at Missoula, beginning as a psychology major but switching to art history, specializing in American Indian art. She is a photographer, a teacher, and the author of a number of books of poetry.*

## Moving Camp Too Far                                                [1977]

   i can't speak of
      many moons
      moving camp on travois°
   i can't tell of
      the last great battle                                    5
      counting coup° or
      taking scalp
   i don't know what it
      was to hunt buffalo
      or do the ghost dance                                    10

---

**3 travois** a frame slung between trailing poles that are pulled by a horse. Plains Indians used the device to transport their goods.   **6 counting coup** recounting one's exploits in battle

Blackfoot travois. (Photograph by Edward S. Curtis. Vol. 18, No. 637, *The North American Indian.* Courtesy of Laboratory of Anthropology/Museum of Indian Arts & Culture)

but
i can see an eagle
    almost extinct
    on slurpee plastic cups
i can travel to powwows                                    15
    in campers & winnebagos
i can eat buffalo meat
    at the tourist burger stand
i can dance to indian music
    rock-n-roll hey-a-hey-o                          20
i can
    & unfortunately
    i do

# ADRIENNE RICH

*Adrienne Rich's most recent books of poetry are* Telephone Ringing in the Labyrinth: Poems 2004–2006 *and* The School Among the Ruins: 2000–2004. *A selection of her essays,* Arts of the Possible: Essays and Conversations, *appeared in 2003. She edited Muriel Rukeyser's* Selected Poems *for the Library of America.* A Human Eye: Essays on Art in Society, *appeared in April 2009. She is a recipient of the National Book Foundation's 2006 Medal for Distinguished Contribution to American Letters, among other honors. She lives in California.*

## *Aunt Jennifer's Tigers*                              [1951]

Aunt Jennifer's tigers prance across a screen,
Bright topaz denizens of a world of green.
They do not fear the men beneath the tree;
They pace in sleek chivalric certainty.                    4

Aunt Jennifer's fingers fluttering through her wool
Find even the ivory needle hard to pull.
The massive weight of Uncle's wedding band
Sits heavily upon Aunt Jennifer's hand.                    8

When Aunt is dead, her terrified hands will lie
Still ringed with ordeals she was mastered by.
The tigers in the panel that she made
Will go on prancing, proud and unafraid.                   12

## *Diving into the Wreck*                              [1973]

First having read the book of myths,
and loaded the camera,
and checked the edge of the knife-blade,
I put on
the body-armor of black rubber                             5

the absurd flippers
the grave and awkward mask.
I am having to do this
not like Cousteau° with his
assiduous team                                        10
aboard the sun-flooded schooner
but here alone.

There is a ladder.
The ladder is always there
hanging innocently                                    15
close to the side of the schooner.
We know what it is for,
we who have used it.
Otherwise
it's a piece of maritime floss                        20
some sundry equipment.

I go down.
Rung after rung and still
the oxygen immerses me
the blue light                                        25
the clear atoms
of our human air.
I go down.
My flippers cripple me,
I crawl like an insect down the ladder                30
and there is no one
to tell me when the ocean
will begin.

First the air is blue and then
it is bluer and then green and then                   35
black I am blacking out and yet
my mask is powerful
it pumps my blood with power
the sea is another story
the sea is not a question of power                    40
I have to learn alone
to turn my body without force
in the deep element.

And now: it is easy to forget
what I came for                                       45
among so many who have always
lived here
swaying their crenellated fans
between the reefs
and besides                                           50
you breathe differently down here.

---

**9 Cousteau** Jacques Cousteau (1910–1997), French underwater explorer.

\* \* \*

I came to explore the wreck.
The words are purposes.
The words are maps.
I came to see the damage that was done                                55
and the treasures that prevail.
I stroke the beam of my lamp
slowly along the flank
of something more permanent
than fish or weed                                                      60

the thing I came for:
the wreck and not the story of the wreck
the thing itself and not the myth
the drowned face always staring
toward the sun                                                         65
the evidence of damage
worn by salt and sway into this threadbare beauty
the ribs of the disaster
curving their assertion
among the tentative haunters.                                          70

This is the place.
And I am here, the mermaid whose dark hair
streams black, the merman in his armored body
We circle silently
about the wreck                                                        75
we dive into the hold.
I am she: I am he

whose drowned face sleeps with open eyes
whose breasts still bear the stress
whose silver, copper, vermeil cargo lies                               80
obscurely inside barrels
half-wedged and left to rot
we are the half-destroyed instruments
that once held to a course
the water-eaten log                                                    85
the fouled compass

We are, I am, you are
by cowardice or courage
the one who find our way
back to this scene                                                     90
carrying a knife, a camera
a book of myths
in which
our names do not appear.

# CHRISTINA ROSSETTI

*Christina Rossetti (1830–1894) was the daughter of an exiled Italian patriot who lived in London and the sister of the poet and painter Dante Gabriel Rossetti. After her father became an invalid, she led an extremely ascetic life, devoting most of her life to doing charitable work. Her first and best-known volume of poetry,* Goblin Market and Other Poems, *was published in 1862.*

## Uphill                                                              [1858]

Does the road wind uphill all the way?
  Yes, to the very end.
Will the day's journey take the whole long day?
  From morn to night, my friend.                                   4

But is there for the night a resting-place?
  A roof for when the slow dark hours begin.
May not the darkness hide it from my face?
  You cannot miss that inn.                                         8

Shall I meet other wayfarers at night?
  Those who have gone before.
Then must I knock, or call when just in sight?
  They will not keep you standing at that door.                    12

Shall I find comfort, travel-sore and weak?
  Of labor you shall find the sum.
Will there be beds for me and all who seek?
  Yea, beds for all who come.                                       16

### YOUR TURN

1. Suppose that someone told you this poem is about a person preparing to go on a hike. The person is supposedly making inquiries about the road and the possible hotel arrangements. What would you reply?
2. Who is the questioner? A woman? A man? All human beings collectively? "Uphill" does not use quotation marks to distinguish between two speakers. Can one say that in "Uphill" the questioner and the answerer are the same person?
3. Are the answers unambiguously comforting? Or can it, for instance, be argued that the "roof" is (perhaps among other things) the lid of a coffin—hence the questioner will certainly not be kept "standing at that door"? If the poem can be read along these lines, is it chilling rather than comforting?

# WALLACE STEVENS

*Wallace Stevens (1879-1955), educated at Harvard and at New York Law School, earned his living as a lawyer and an insurance executive; at his death he was a vice president of the Hartford Accident and Indemnity Company. While pursuing this career, however, he also achieved distinction as a poet, and today he is widely regarded as among the most important American poets of the twentieth century.*

## The Emperor of Ice-Cream                                            [1923]

Call the roller of big cigars,
The muscular one, and bid him whip

In kitchen cups concupiscent curds.
Let the wenches dawdle in such dress
As they are used to wear, and let the boys                    5
Bring flowers in last month's newspapers.
Let be be finale of seem.
The only emperor is the emperor of ice-cream.

Take from the dresser of deal,°
Lacking the three glass knobs, that sheet                    10
On which she embroidered fantails once
And spread it so as to cover her face.
If her horny feet protrude, they come
To show how cold she is, and dumb.
Let the lamp affix its beam.                                 15
The only emperor is the emperor of ice-cream.

---

**9 deal** fir or pine wood.

### YOUR TURN

What associations does the word "emperor" have for you? The word "ice-cream"? What, then, do you make of "the emperor of ice-cream"? The poem describes the preparations for a wake, and in line 15 ("Let the lamp affix its beam") it insists on facing the reality of death. In this context, then, what do you make of the last line of each stanza?

# EDGAR ALLAN POE

*For a biographical note, see page 509.*

## To Helen*                                                 [1831–1843]

Helen, thy beauty is to me
    Like those Nicean° barks of yore,
That gently, o'er a perfumed sea,
    The weary, way-worn wanderer bore
    To his own native shore.                                 5

On desperate seas long wont to roam,
    Thy hyacinth hair,° thy classic face
Thy Naiad° airs have brought me home
    To the glory that was Greece
And the grandeur that was Rome.                              10

---

***Helen** Helen of Troy, considered the most beautiful woman of ancient times.  **2 Nicean** perhaps referring to Nicea, an ancient city associated with the god Dionysus, or perhaps meaning "victorious," from Nike, Greek goddess of Victory.  **7 hyacinth hair** naturally curling hair, like that of Hyacinthus, beautiful Greek youth beloved by Apollo.  **8 Naiad** a nymph associated with lakes and streams.

Lo! in yon brilliant window-niche
How statue-like I see thee stand,
The agate lamp within thy hand!
Ah, Psyche,° from the regions which
Are Holy-Land!°                                                        15

---

**14 Psyche** Greek for "soul."    **15 Holy-Land** ancient Rome or Athens, i.e., a sacred realm of art.

**YOUR TURN**

1. In the first stanza, to what is Helen's beauty compared? To whom does the speaker apparently compare himself? What does "way-worn" in line 4 suggest to you? To what in the speaker's experience might the "native shore" in line 5 correspond?
2. What do you take "desperate seas" to mean in line 6, and who has been traveling them? To what are they contrasted in line 8? How does "home" seem to be defined in this stanza (stanza 2)?
3. What further light is shed on the speaker's home or destination in stanza 3?
4. Do you think that "To Helen" can be a love poem and also a poem about spiritual beauty or about the love of art? Why or why not?

# A Note on Haiku

One form of poetry that puts a great emphasis on sharp images is the **haiku,** a Japanese poem of seventeen syllables, arranged in three lines of five, seven, and five syllables. Japanese poetry is unrhymed, but English versions sometimes rhyme the first and third lines. The subject matter can be high or low—the Milky Way or the screech of automobile brakes—but usually it is connected with the seasons, and it is described objectively and sharply. Most haiku set forth a sense of *where, what,* and *when*—but the when may be implicit, as in the first haiku.

## MORITAKE (1452–1540)

### Fallen petals rise

*Translated by Harold G. Henderson*

Fallen petals rise
back to the branch—I watch
oh . . . butterflies!

Concentrating his attention on the phenomenon (butterflies moving upward), the poet nevertheless conveys an emotion through the images (wonder, and then the recognition of the familiar), stirring the reader's imagination to supply the emotion that completes the experience.

# SÔKAN (1465–1553)

## *If only we could*

*Translated by Kenneth Yasuda*

If only we could
Add a handle to the moon
It would make a good fan.

# SHIKI (1867–1902)

## *River in summer*

River in summer
there is a bridge, but my horse
walks through the water.

# Writing a Haiku

Although the haiku originated in Japan, it is now written throughout the world.

To start writing your own haiku, you may want to take some ordinary experience—tying your shoelaces, seeing a cat at the foot of the stairs, glancing out of a window and seeing unexpected snowflakes, hearing the alarm clock—and present it interestingly. One way to make it interesting is to construct the poem in two parts—the first line balanced against the next two lines, or the first two lines balanced against the last line. If you construct a poem on this principle, the two sections should be related to each other, but they should also in some degree make a contrast with each other. For instance, in the following poem by Taigi, there is a contrast between pleasant sociability (the first two lines) and loneliness (the last line).

# TAIGI (1723–1776)

## *Look, O look, there go*

*Translated by Kenneth Yasuda*

"Look, O look, there go
Fireflies," I would like to say—
But I am alone.

Basho said, "He who creates three to five haiku during a lifetime is a haiku poet. He who attains to ten is a master."

irony here, it should be mentioned, is often called **sarcasm,** but a distinction can be made: sarcasm is notably contemptuous and crude or heavy-handed ("You're a great guy, a real friend," said to a friend who won't lend you ten dollars). Sarcasm is only one kind of irony, and a kind almost never found in literature.

**Overstatement (hyperbole),** like understatement, is ironic when it contains a contradictory suggestion:

> For Brutus is an honorable man;
> So are they all, all honorable men.

—Shakespeare

The sense of contradiction that is inherent in verbal irony is also inherent in a paradox. **Paradox** has several meanings for philosophers, but we need only be concerned with its meaning of an apparent contradiction. Examples of paradox follow:

> The child is father of the man;

—Wordsworth

and (on the soldiers who died to preserve the British Empire)

> The saviors come not home tonight;
> Themselves they could not save;

—Housman

and

> One short sleep past, we wake eternally,
> And Death shall be no more; Death, thou shalt die.

—Donne

Donne's lines are a reminder that paradox is not only an instrument of the poet. Christianity embodies several paradoxes: God became a human being; through the death on the cross, human beings can obtain eternal life; human beings do not live fully until they die.

Some critics have put a high premium on ironic and paradoxical poetry. Briefly, their argument runs that great poetry recognizes the complexity of experience, and that irony and paradox are ways of doing justice to this complexity. I. A. Richards uses "irony" to denote "The bringing in of the opposite, the complementary impulses," and suggests in *The Principles of Literary Criticism* (1924/25) that irony in this sense is a characteristic of poetry of "the highest order." It is dubious that all poets must always bring in the opposite, but it is certain that much poetry is ironic and paradoxical.

# DOROTHY PARKER

*Dorothy Parker (1893–1967), born in West End, New Jersey, but brought up in New York City, from 1917 to 1920 served as drama critic for the magazine* Vanity Fair, *where her witty, satiric reviews gained her the reputation of being hard to please. She distinguished between wit and wisecracking: "Wit has truth in it; wisecracking is simply calisthenics with words." In addition to writing essays and stories, Parker also wrote light verse, especially about love.*

## General Review of the Sex Situation [1926]

Woman wants monogamy;
Man delights in novelty.
Love is woman's moon and sun;
Man has other forms of fun.                                    4

Woman lives but in her lord;
Count to ten, and man is bored.
With this the gist and sum of it,
What earthly good can come of it?                             8

**YOUR TURN**

1. How would you characterize Parker's message? (For instance, is it sad, happy, pitiful, or what?) How would you characterize her tone—her attitude, as you perceive it?
2. Take note of and describe Parker's use of language—for example, the contrast she makes between "monogamy" and "novelty," and the image she gives in line 3, "Love is woman's moon and sun." Where else in this short poem do you see evidence of careful handling of language?
3. How much truth do you think there is in Parker's lines? (Remember: No poem, or, for that matter, no novel—however long—can tell the whole truth about life.) As for truth, how would you compare it with the following passage, from Barbara Dafoe Whitehead's review (*The Times Literary Supplement,* 9 June 1995) of two sociological studies, *The Social Organization of Sexuality: Sexual Practice in the U.S.* and *Sex in America?*

> Men and women have different sexual interests, stakes and appetites, with men more oriented to the sex act and women more interested in sex as an expression of affiliative and romantic love.

4. Compare the tone of Parker's poem with the tone of Shakespeare's "Sigh no more, ladies" (page 576).

# PERCY BYSSHE SHELLEY

*Percy Bysshe Shelley (1792–1822) was born in Sussex in England, the son of a prosperous country squire. Educated at Eton, he went on to Oxford but was expelled for having written a pamphlet supporting a belief in atheism. Like John Keats he was a member of the second generation of English Romantic poets. (The first generation included Wordsworth and Coleridge.) And like Keats, Shelley died young; he was drowned during a violent storm off the coast of Italy while sailing with a friend.*

## Ozymandias* [1817]

I met a traveler from an antique land
Who said: Two vast and trunkless legs of stone

---

*Ozymandias is another name for Ramesses the Great, Pharaoh of the nineteenth dynasty of ancient Egypt. He is believed to have taken the throne in his early twenties and to have ruled Egypt from 1279 BCE to 1213 BCE.

Stand in the desert . . . Near them, on the sand,
Half sunk, a shattered visage lies, whose frown,
And wrinkled lip, and sneer of cold command,                         5
Tell that its sculptor well those passions read
Which yet survive, stamped on these lifeless things,
The hand that mocked them, and the heart that fed:
And on the pedestal these words appear:
"My name is Ozymandias, king of kings:                               10
Look on my works, ye Mighty, and despair!"
Nothing beside remains. Round the decay
Of that colossal wreck, boundless and bare
The lone and level sands stretch far away.

---

Lines 4–8 are somewhat obscure, but the gist is that the passions—still evident in the "shattered visage"—survive the sculptor's hand that "mocked"—that is, (1) imitated or copied, (2) derided—them, and the passions also survive the king's heart that had nourished them.

> **YOUR TURN**
>
> There is an irony of plot here: Ozymandias believed that he created enduring works, but his intentions came to nothing. However, another irony is also present: How are his words, in a way he did not intend, true?

# ANDREW MARVELL

*Born near Hull in England, Andrew Marvell (1621–1678) attended Trinity College, Cambridge, and graduated in 1638. During the English Civil War, he was tutor to the daughter of Sir Thomas Fairfax in Yorkshire at Nun Appleton House, where most of his best-known poems were written. In 1657 he was appointed assistant to John Milton, the Latin Secretary for the Commonwealth. After the Restoration of the monarchy in 1660, Marvell represented Hull as a member of Parliament until his death. Most of his poems were not published until after his death.*

## *To His Coy Mistress*                                            [1681]

Had we but world enough, and time,
This coyness, lady, were no crime.
We would sit down, and think which way
To walk, and pass our long love's day.
Thou by the Indian Ganges° side                                     5
Should'st rubies find: I by the tide
Of Humber° would complain.° I would
Love you ten years before the Flood,
And you should, if you please, refuse

---

**5 Indian Ganges** the Ganges is the major river of India, running for 1,560 miles from the Himalayas to the Bay of Bengal.    **7 Humber** the Humber is a large tidal estuary on the east coast of Northern England.    **complain** write love poems.

Till the conversion of the Jews.    10
My vegetable° love should grow
Vaster than empires, and more slow.
An hundred years should go to praise
Thine eyes, and on thy forehead gaze:
Two hundred to adore each breast:    15
But thirty thousand to the rest.
An age at least to every part,
And the last age should show your heart.
For, lady, you deserve this state,
Nor would I love at lower rate.    20
    But at my back I always hear
Time's wing'ed chariot hurrying near;
And yonder all before us lie
Deserts of vast eternity.
Thy beauty shall no more be found,    25
Nor in thy marble vault shall sound
My echoing song; then worms shall try
That long preserved virginity,
And your quaint honor turn to dust,
And into ashes all my lust.    30
The grave's a fine and private place,
But none, I think, do there embrace.
    Now therefore, while the youthful hue
Sits on thy skin like morning dew,
And while thy willing soul transpires    35
At every pore with instant fires,
Now let us sport us while we may;
And now, like am'rous birds of prey,
Rather at once our time devour,
Than languish in his slow-chapt° power,    40
Let us roll all our strength, and all
Our sweetness, up into one ball;
And tear our pleasures with rough strife
Thorough° the iron gates of life.
Thus, though we cannot make our sun    45
Stand still, yet we will make him run.

---

**11 vegetable** i.e., unconsciously growing.    **40 slow-chapt** slowly devouring.
**44 Thorough** through.

### YOUR TURN

1. Do you find the assertions in lines 1–20 so inflated that you detect behind them a playfully ironic tone? Explain. Why does the speaker say, in line 8, that he would love "ten years before the Flood," rather than merely "since the Flood"?
2. Explain lines 21–24. Why is time behind the speaker, and eternity in front of him? Is this "eternity" the same as the period discussed in lines 1–20? What do you make of the change in the speaker's tone after line 20?

3. Do you agree with the comment on page 649 about the understatement in lines 31–32? What more can you say about these lines, in context?
4. Why "am'rous birds of prey" (line 38) rather than the conventional doves? Is the idea of preying continued in the poem?
5. Try to explain the last two lines, and characterize the speaker's tone. Do you find these lines anticlimactic?
6. The poem is organized in the form of an argument. Trace the steps.

# JOHN DONNE

*John Donne (1572–1631) was born into a Roman Catholic family in England, but in the 1590s he abandoned that faith. In 1615 he became an Anglican priest and soon was known as a great preacher. Of his sermons, 160 survive, including one with the famous line, "No man is an island, entire of itself; every man is a piece of the continent, a part of the main; if a clod be washed away by the sea, Europe is the less . . . ; and therefore never send to know for whom the bell tolls; it tolls for thee." From 1621 until his death, Donne was dean of St. Paul's Cathedral in London. His love poems (often bawdy and cynical) are said to be his early work, and his "Holy Sonnets" (among the greatest religious poems written in English) his later work.*

## Holy Sonnet 14                                             [1633]

Batter my heart, three-personed God; for you
As yet but knock, breathe, shine, and seek to mend;
That I may rise and stand, o'erthrow me, and bend
Your force, to break, blow, burn, and make me new.
I, like an usurped town, to another due,                              5
Labor to admit you, but oh, to no end,
Reason, your viceroy in me, me should defend,
But is captived, and proves weak or untrue.
Yet dearly I love you, and would be loved fain,
But am betrothed unto your enemy:                                    10
Divorce me, untie, or break that knot again,
Take me to you, imprison me, for I
Except you enthrall me, never shall be free,
Nor ever chaste, except you ravish me.

**YOUR TURN**

1. Explain the paradoxes in lines 1, 3, 13, and 14. Explain the double meanings of "enthrall" (line 13) and "ravish" (line 14).
2. In lines 1–4, what is God implicitly compared to (considering especially lines 2 and 4)? How does this comparison lead into the comparison that dominates lines 5–8? What words in lines 9–12 are especially related to the earlier lines?

3. What do you think is gained by piling up verbs in lines 2–4?
4. Do you find sexual references irreverent in a religious poem? (As already mentioned, Donne was an Anglican priest.)

# LANGSTON HUGHES

*A biographical note and other poems by Langston Hughes appear on pages 761–768 in Chapter 27.*

## Dream Boogie [1951]

Good morning, daddy!
Ain't you heard
The boogie-woogie rumble
Of a dream deferred?

Listen closely:                                     5
You'll hear their feet
Beating out and beating out a—

*You think
It's a happy beat?*

Listen to it closely:                               10
Ain't you heard
something underneath
like a—

*What did I say?*

Sure,                                               15
I'm happy!
Take it away!

*Hey, pop!
Re-bop!
Mop!*                                               20

*Y-e-a-h!*

1. What is boogie, or boogie-woogie?
2. Why did many whites assume that boogie was "a happy beat" (line 9)? In fact, what was boogie chiefly an expression of?

# MARTÍN ESPADA

*Martín Espada was born in Brooklyn in 1957. He received a bachelor's degree from the University of Wisconsin and a law degree from Northeastern University. A poet who publishes regularly, Espada teaches creative writing at the University of Massachusetts-Amherst.*

## Tony Went to the Bodega*
## but He Didn't Buy Anything

[1987]

*para Angel Guadalupe*

Tony's father left the family
and the Long Island city projects,
leaving a mongrel-skinny puertorriqueño boy
nine years old
who had to find work.                                             5

Makengo the Cuban
let him work at the bodega.
In grocery aisles
he learned the steps of the dry-mop mambo,
banging the cash register                                        10
like piano percussion
in the spotlight of Machito's orchestra,
polite with the abuelas° who bought on credit,
practicing the grin on customers
he'd seen Makengo grin                                           15
with his bad yellow teeth.

Tony left the projects too,
with a scholarship for law school.
But he cursed the cold primavera°
in Boston;                                                       20
the cooking of his neighbors
left no smell in the hallway
and no one spoke Spanish
(not even the radio).

So Tony walked without a map                                     25
through the city,
a landscape of hostile condominiums
and the darkness of white faces,
sidewalk-searcher lost
till he discovered the projects.                                 30

Tony went to the bodega
but he didn't buy anything:
he sat by the doorway satisfied
to watch la gente° (people
island-brown as him)                                             35
crowd in and out,
hablando español,°
thought: this is beautiful,
and grinned
his bodega grin.                                                 40

---

*\*Bodega* grocery and liquor store; in the dedication, after the title, *para* means "for."
**13 abuelas** grandmothers.    **19 primavera** spring season.    **34 la gente** the people.
**37 hablando español** speaking Spanish.

This is a rice and beans
success story:
today Tony lives on Tremont Street,
above the bodega.

**YOUR TURN**

1. Why do you suppose Espada included the information about Tony's father? The information about young Tony "practicing" a grin?
2. Why does Tony leave?
3. How would you characterize Tony?

# EDNA ST. VINCENT MILLAY

*For a biographical note, see page 583.*

## *Love Is Not All: It Is Not Meat nor Drink*    [1931]

Love is not all: it is not meat nor drink
Nor slumber nor a roof against the rain;
Nor yet a floating spar to men that sink
And rise and sink and rise and sink again;
Love can not fill the thickened lung with breath,      5
Nor clean the blood, nor set the fractured bone;
Yet many a man is making friends with death
Even as I speak, for lack of love alone.
It well may be that in a difficult hour,
Pinned down by pain and moaning for release,      10
Or nagged by want past resolution's power,
I might be driven to sell your love for peace,
Or trade the memory of this night for food.
It well may be. I do not think I would.

**YOUR TURN**

1. "Love Is Not All" is a sonnet. Using your own words, briefly summarize the argument of the octet (the first 8 lines). Next, paraphrase the sestet (the six lines from line 9 through line 14), line by line. On the whole, does the sestet repeat the idea of the octet, or does it add a new idea? Whom did you imagine to be speaking the octet? What does the sestet add to your knowledge of the speaker and the occasion? (And how did you paraphrase line 11?)
2. The first and last lines of the poem consist of words of one syllable, and both lines have a distinct pause in the middle. Do you imagine the lines to be spoken in the same tone of voice? If not, can you describe the difference and account for it?
3. Lines 7 and 8 appear to mean that the absence of love can be a cause of death. To what degree do you believe that to be true?
4. Would you call "Love Is Not All" a love poem? Why or why not? Describe the kind of person who might include the poem in a love letter or valentine, or who would be happy to receive it. (One of our friends recited it at her wedding. What do you think of that idea?)

# SHERMAN ALEXIE

*The short-story writer, essayist, poet, and film director Sherman J. Alexie Jr. was born in October 1966 and was raised on the Spokane Indian Reservation in Wellpinit, Washington, located fifty miles northwest of Spokane. He went to high school off reservation in the small town of Reardan, Washington, where he was an excellent student and played on the basketball team. He attended Gonzaga University in Spokane for two years and then transferred to Washington State University in Pullman. There, he began writing poetry, graduating with a degree in American Studies. His books include* The Business of Fancydancing: Stories and Poems *(1992),* The Lone Ranger and Tonto Fistfight in Heaven *(1994), and* Reservation Blues *(1995).*

*For another poem by Alexie, see page 777.*

## Evolution [1992]

Buffalo Bill opens a pawn shop on the reservation
right across the border from the liquor store
and he stays open 24 hours a day, 7 days a week

and the Indians come running in with jewelry
television sets, a VCR, a full-length beaded buckskin outfit        5
it took Inez Muse 12 years to finish. Buffalo Bill

takes everything the Indians have to offer, keeps it
all catalogued and filed in a storage room. The Indians
pawn their hands, saving the thumbs for last, they pawn

their skeletons, falling endlessly from the skin        10
and when the last Indian has pawned everything
but his heart, Buffalo Bill takes that for twenty bucks

closes up the pawn shop, paints a new sign over the old
calls his venture THE MUSEUM OF NATIVE AMERICAN CULTURES
charges the Indians five bucks a head to enter.        15

# HENRY REED

*Born in Birmingham, England, Henry Reed (1914–1986) served in the British army during World War II. Later, in civilian life he had a distinguished career as a journalist, a translator of French and Italian literature, a writer of radio plays, and a poet. "Naming of Parts" draws on his experience as a military recruit.*

## Naming of Parts [1946]

Today we have naming of parts. Yesterday,
We had daily cleaning. And tomorrow morning,
We shall have what to do after firing. But today,
Today we have naming of parts. Japonica°
Glistens like coral in all of the neighboring gardens,        5
　　　　And today we have naming of parts.

---

4 **Japonica** shrub with glossy green leaves and showy fragrant rose-like flowers.

This is the lower sling swivel. And this
Is the upper sling swivel, whose use you will see,
When you are given your slings. And this is the piling swivel,
Which in your case you have not got. The branches                10
Hold in the gardens their silent, eloquent gestures,
        Which in our case we have not got.

This is the safety-catch, which is always released
With an easy flick of the thumb. And please do not let me
See anyone using his finger. You can do it quite easy            15
If you have any strength in your thumb. The blossoms
Are fragile and motionless, never letting anyone see
        Any of them using their finger.

And this you can see is the bolt. The purpose of this
Is to open the breech, as you see. We can slide it               20
Rapidly backwards and forwards: we call this
Easing the spring. And rapidly backwards and forwards
The early bees are assaulting and fumbling the flowers:
        They call it easing the Spring.

They call it easing the Spring: it is perfectly easy             25
If you have any strength in your thumb: like the bolt,
And the breech, and the cocking-piece, and the point of balance,
Which in our case we have not got; and the almond-blossom
Silent in all of the gardens and the bees going backwards and forwards,
        For today we have naming of parts.              30

**YOUR TURN**

   1. How many speakers do you hear in the poem? How would you char-
      acterize each of them?
   2. Why do we include this poem in a chapter on "irony"?

In much poetry, rhythm is only half-heard, but its omnipresence is suggested by the fact that when poetry is printed it is customary to begin each line with a capital letter. Prose (from Latin *prorsus,* "forward," "straight on") keeps running across the paper until the right-hand margin is reached, and then, merely because the paper has given out, the writer or printer starts again at the left, with a small letter. But verse (Latin *versus,* "a turning") often ends well short of the right-hand margin, and the next line begins at the left—usually with a capital—not because paper has run out but because the rhythmic pattern begins again. Lines of poetry are continually reminding us that they have a pattern.

Before turning to some other highly rhythmical pieces, a word of caution: a mechanical, unvarying rhythm may be good to put the baby to sleep, but it can be deadly to readers who wish to keep awake. Poets vary their rhythm according to their purpose; a poet ought not to be so regular that he or she is (in W. H. Auden's words) an "accentual pest." In competent hands, rhythm contributes to meaning; it says something. The rhythm in the lines from *Macbeth,* for example, helps suggest the strong binding power of magic. Again Ezra Pound has a relevant comment: "Rhythm *must* have meaning. It can't be merely a careless dash off, with no grip and no real hold to the words and sense, a tumty tum tumty tum tum ta." Some examples will be useful.

Consider this description of Hell from John Milton's *Paradise Lost* (the relatively unstressed syllables are marked by a symbol called *breve,* whereas heavier stresses are marked by ´, an acute accent, thus):

> Rŏcks, caˊves, lakes, feñs, bŏgs, deñs, añd shaˊdes oˇ deaˊth.

Such a succession of stresses is highly unusual. Elsewhere in the poem Milton chiefly uses iambic feet—alternating unstressed and stressed syllables—but here he immediately follows one heavy stress with another, thereby helping to communicate the "meaning"—the impressive monotony of Hell. As a second example, consider the function of the rhythm in two lines by Alexander Pope:

> Whĕn Ájăx strˊives sŏme rocˊk's vaˊst weˊight tŏ thrˊow,
> Thĕ liˊne toˊo lábŏrs, añd thĕ wordˊs móve slóˊw.

The heavier stresses (again, marked by ´) do not merely alternate with the lighter ones (marked ˘); rather, the great weight of the rock is suggested by three consecutive stressed words, "rock's vast weight," and the great effort involved in moving it is suggested by another three consecutive stresses, "line too labors," and by yet another three, "words move slow." Note, also, the abundant pauses within the lines. In the first line, unless one's speech is slovenly, one must pause at least slightly after "Ajax," "strives," "rock's," "vast," "weight," and "throw." The grating sounds in "Ajax" and "rock's" do their work, too, and so do the explosive *t*'s. When—in the second line, below—Pope wishes to suggest lightness, he reverses his procedure and he groups *un*stressed syllables:

> Not so, when swift Camilla scours the plain,
> Fliés o'ĕr th'uñbéndĭng córn, añd skíms ălŏng thĕ máin.

This last line has twelve syllables and is thus longer than the line about Ajax, but the addition of "along" helps to communicate lightness and swiftness because in this line (it can be argued) neither syllable of "along" is strongly stressed. If "along" is omitted, the line still makes grammatical sense and becomes more "regular," but it also becomes less imitative of lightness.

The very regularity of a line may be meaningful too. Shakespeare begins a sonnet thus:

Whĕn Í dŏ coúnt thĕ cloćk thăt télls thĕ timé.

This line about a mechanism runs with appropriate regularity. (It is worth noting, too, that "count the clock" and "tells the time" emphasize the regularity by the repetition of sounds and syntax.) But notice what Shakespeare does in the middle of the next line:

Aňd sée thĕ bráve dáy suńk iň hídeŏus níght.

What has he done? And what is the effect?

Here is another poem that refers to a clock. In England, until capital punishment was abolished, executions regularly took place at 8:00 AM.

# A. E. HOUSMAN

*A. E. Housman (1859–1936) was one of the most distinguished classical scholars of his time. Though he left Oxford without a degree (having failed his examinations), through hard work, discipline, and rigorous study he earned an appointment in 1892 as professor of Latin at University College, London, and in 1911 as professor of Latin at Cambridge and fellow of Trinity College. Only two volumes of Housman's poems appeared during his lifetime:* A Shropshire Lad *(1896) and* Last Poems *(1922).*

## Eight O'Clock                                        [1922]

He stood, and heard the steeple
  Sprinkle the quarters on the morning town.
One, two, three, four, to market-place and people
  It tossed them down.                                          4

Strapped, noosed, nighing his hour,
  He stood and counted them and cursed his luck;
And then the clock collected in the tower
  Its strength, and struck.                                       8

The chief (but not unvarying) pattern is iambic; that is, the odd syllables are less emphatic than the even ones, as in

Hĕ stóod, aňd heárd thĕ stéeplĕ

Try to mark the syllables, stressed and unstressed, in the rest of the poem. Be guided by your ear, not by a mechanical principle, and don't worry too much about difficult or uncertain parts; different readers may reasonably come up with different results.

### YOUR TURN

1. Where do you find two or more consecutive stresses? What explanations (related to meaning) can be offered?
2. What do you think is the effect of the short line at the end of each stanza? And what significance can you attach to the fact that these lines (unlike the first and third lines in each stanza) end with a stress?

Following are some poems in which the strongly felt pulsations are highly important.

# WILLIAM CARLOS WILLIAMS

*A poem by William Carlos Williams (1883–1963), along with a brief biography, appears on page 628. The Breughel (also spelled Brueghel) painting described in "The Dance" is shown below.*

## The Dance
[1944]

In Breughel's great picture, The Kermess,°
the dancers go round, they go round and
around, the squeal and the blare and the
tweedle of bagpipes, a bugle and fiddles
tipping their bellies (round as the thick-                5
sided glasses whose wash they impound)
their hips and their bellies off balance
to turn them. Kicking and rolling about
the Fair Grounds, swinging their butts, those
shanks must be sound to bear up under such          10
rollicking measures, prance as they dance
in Breughel's great picture, The Kermess.

---

**1 Kermess** in the Netherlands, Belgium, etc., an outdoor fair or carnival, originally the feast day of the local patron saint, hence a fair or carnival held on that day.

Pieter Breughel the Eider. *Peasant Dance*, c 1568, oil on wood, 114 × 164 cm. (Kunsthistorisches Museum, Vienna.)

**YOUR TURN**

1. Read Williams's poem aloud several times, and decide where the heavy stresses fall. Mark the heavily stressed syllables ´, the lightly stressed ones ∧, and the unstressed ones ˘. Are all the lines identical? What effect is thus gained, especially when the poem is read aloud? What does the parenthetical statement (lines 5–6) do to the rhythm? Does a final syllable often receive a heavy stress here? Are there noticeable pauses at the ends of the lines? What is the consequence? Are the dancers waltzing?

2. What syllables rhyme or are repeated (e.g., "round" in lines 2 and 5, and "–pound" in line 6; "–ing" in lines 5, 8, 9, and 11)? What effect do they have?

3. What do you think the absence at the beginning of each line of the customary capital contributes to the meaning? Why is the last line the same as the first?

# Versification: A Glossary for Reference

The technical vocabulary of **prosody** (the study of the principles of verse structure, including meter, rhyme, and other sound effects, and stanzaic patterns) is large. An understanding of these terms will not turn anyone into a poet, but it will enable one to discuss some aspects of poetry more efficiently. A knowledge of them, like a knowledge of most other technical terms (e.g., "misplaced modifier," "woofer," "automatic transmission"), allows for quick and accurate communication. The following are the chief terms of prosody.

## Meter

Most English poetry has a pattern of **stressed (accented)** sounds, and this pattern is the **meter** (from the Greek word for "measure"). Although in Old English poetry (poetry written in England before the Norman-French Conquest in 1066) a line may have any number of unstressed syllables in addition to four stressed syllables, most poetry written in England since the Conquest not only has a fixed number of stresses in a line but also has a fixed number of unstressed syllables before or after each stressed one. (One really ought not to talk of "unstressed" or "unaccented" syllables, since to utter a syllable—however lightly—is to give it some stress. It is really a matter of *relative* stress, but the fact is that "unstressed" and "unaccented" are parts of the established terminology of versification.)

In a line of poetry, the **foot** is the basic unit of measurement. On rare occasions it is a single stressed syllable, but generally a foot consists of two or three syllables, one of which is stressed. (Stress is indicated by the acute symbol ´, lack of stress by the breve symbol ˘.) The repetition of feet, then, produces a pattern of stresses throughout the poem.

Two cautions:

1. A poem will seldom contain only one kind of foot throughout; significant variations usually occur, but one kind of foot is dominant.

2. In reading a poem pay attention to the sense as well as to the metrical pattern. By paying attention to the sense, you will often find that the stress falls on a word that according to the metrical pattern would be unstressed. Or a word that according to the pattern would be stressed may be seen to be unstressed. Furthermore, by reading for sense, you will find that not all stresses are equally heavy; some are almost as light as unstressed syllables, and sometimes there is a **hovering stress;** that is, the stress is equally distributed over two adjacent syllables. To repeat: *read for sense,* allowing the meaning to help indicate the stresses.

## Metrical Feet

The most common feet in English poetry are the following six:

1. **Iamb** (adjective: **iambic**): one unstressed syllable followed by one stressed syllable. The iamb, said to be the most common pattern in English speech, is surely the most common in English poetry. The following example has four iambic feet:

    Mў héart ĭs líke ă síngiňg bírd.

    —Christina Rossetti

2. **Trochee (trochaic)**: one stressed syllable followed by one unstressed.

    Wé weře véřy tíreŏ, wé wěre véřy mérřy

    —Edna St. Vincent Millay

3. **Anapest (anapestic)**: two unstressed syllables followed by one stressed.

    Thěre aře mánў whŏ sáy thăt ă dóg hăs hĭ s dáy

    —Dylan Thomas

4. **Dactyl (dactylic)**: one stressed syllable followed by two unstressed. This tri-syllabic foot, like the anapest, is common in light verse or verse suggesting joy, but its use is not limited to such material, as Longfellow's *Evangeline* shows. Thomas Hood's sentimental "The Bridge of Sighs" begins:

    Táke hěr ủp téndĕrlў.

5. **Spondee (spondaic)**: two stressed syllables; most often used as a substitute for an iamb or trochee.

    Smárt lád, tŏ slíp bĕtímes ăwáy.

    —A. E. Housman

6. **Pyrrhic**: two unstressed syllables; it is often not considered a legitimate foot in English.

## Metrical Lines

A metrical line consists of one or more feet and is named for the number of feet in it. The following names are used:

| | |
|---|---|
| **monometer:** one foot | **pentameter:** five feet |
| **dimeter:** two feet | **hexameter:** six feet |
| **trimeter:** three feet | **heptameter:** seven feet |
| **tetrameter:** four feet | **octameter:** eight feet |

A line is scanned for the kind and number of feet in it, and the **scansion** tells you if it is, say, anapestic trimeter (three anapests):

Ăs Ĭ cáme tŏ thē édge ŏf thē wóods.

—Robert Frost

Or, in another example, iambic pentameter:

Thē súmmĕr thúndĕr, líke ă wóodĕn béll

—Louise Bogan

A line ending with a stress has a **masculine ending;** a line ending with an extra unstressed syllable has a **feminine ending.** The **caesura** (usually indicated by the symbol //) is a slight pause within the line. It need not be indicated by punctuation (notice the fourth and fifth lines in the following quotation), and it does not affect the metrical count:

Awake, my St. John! // leave all meaner things
To low ambition, // and the pride of kings.
Let us // (since life can little more supply
Than just to look about us // and to die)
Expatiate free // o'er all this scene of Man;
A mighty maze! // but not without a plan;
A wild, // where weeds and flowers promiscuous shoot;
Or garden, // tempting with forbidden fruit.

—Alexander Pope

The varying position of the caesura helps to give Pope's lines an informality that plays against the formality of the pairs of rhyming lines.

An **end-stopped line** concludes with a distinct syntactical pause, but a **run-on line** has its sense carried over into the next line without syntactical pause. (The running on of a line is called **enjambment.**) In the following passage, only the first is a run-on line:

Yet if we look more closely we shall find
Most have the seeds of judgment in their mind:
Nature affords at least a glimmering light;
The lines, though touched but faintly, are drawn right.

—Alexander Pope

Meter produces **rhythm,** recurrences at equal intervals; but rhythm (from a Greek word meaning "flow") is usually applied to larger units than feet. Often it depends most obviously on pauses. Thus, a poem with run-on lines will have a different rhythm from a poem with end-stopped lines, even though both are in the same meter. And prose, though it is unmetrical, can have rhythm, too.

In addition to being affected by syntactical pauses, rhythm is affected by pauses attributable to consonant clusters and to the length of words. Words of several syllables establish a different rhythm from words of one syllable, even in metrically identical lines. One can say, then, that rhythm is altered by shifts in meter, syntax, and the length and ease of pronunciation. But even with no such shift, even if a line is repeated word for word, a reader may sense a change in rhythm. The rhythm of the final line of a poem, for example, may well differ from that of the line before, even though in all other respects the lines are identical, as in Frost's "Stopping by Woods on a Snowy Evening" (page 755), which concludes by repeating "And miles to go before I sleep." One may simply sense that the final line ought to be spoken, say, more slowly and with more stress on "miles."

# Patterns of Sound

Though rhythm is basic to poetry, **rhyme**—the repetition of the identical or similar stressed sound or sounds—is not. Rhyme is, presumably, pleasant in itself; it suggests order; and it may also be related to meaning, for it brings two words sharply together, often implying a relationship, as in the now trite *dove* and *love,* or in the more imaginative *throne* and *alone.*

> **Perfect, or exact, rhyme:** Differing consonant sounds are followed by identical stressed vowel sounds, and the following sounds, if any, are identical *(foe—toe; meet—fleet; buffer—rougher).* Notice that perfect rhyme involves identity of sound, not of spelling. *Fix* and *sticks,* like *buffer* and *rougher,* are perfect rhymes.
>
> **Half-rhyme** (or **off-rhyme**): Only the final consonant sounds of the words are identical; the stressed vowel sounds as well as the initial consonant sounds, if any, differ *(soul—oil; mirth—forth; trolley—bully).*
>
> **Eye-rhyme:** The sounds do not in fact rhyme, but the words look as though they would rhyme *(cough—bough).*
>
> **Masculine rhyme**: The final syllables are stressed and, after their differing initial consonant sounds, are identical in sound *(stark—mark; support—retort).*
>
> **Feminine rhyme** (or **double rhyme**): Stressed rhyming syllables are followed by identical unstressed syllables *(revival—arrival; flatter—batter).*
>
> **Triple rhyme** is a kind of feminine rhyme in which identical stressed vowel sounds are followed by two identical unstressed syllables *(machinery—scenery; tenderly—slenderly).*
>
> **End rhyme** (or **terminal rhyme**): The rhyming words occur at the ends of the lines.
>
> **Internal rhyme**: At least one of the rhyming words occurs within the line (Oscar Wilde's "Each narrow *cell* in which we *dwell*").

Other patterns of sound are:

> **Alliteration**: Sometimes defined as the repetition of initial sounds ("*A*ll the *a*wful *a*uguries," or "*B*ring me my *b*ow of *b*urning gold"), and sometimes as the prominent repetition of a consonant ("a*f*ter li*f*e's *f*it*f*ul *f*ever").
>
> **Assonance**: The repetition, in words of proximity, of identical vowel sounds preceded and followed by differing consonant sounds. Whereas *tide* and *hide* are rhymes, *tide* and *mine* are assonantal.
>
> **Consonance**: The repetition of identical consonant sounds and differing vowel sounds in words in proximity *(fail—feel; rough—roof; pitter—patter).* Sometimes consonance is more loosely defined merely as the repetition of a consonant *(fail—peel).*
>
> **Onomatopoeia**: The use of words that imitate sounds, such as *hiss* and *buzz.* There is a mistaken tendency to see onomatopoeia everywhere—for example in *thunder* and *horror.* Many words sometimes thought to be onomatopoeic are not clearly imitative of the thing they refer to; they

merely contain some sounds that, when we know what the word means, seem to have some resemblance to the thing they denote. Tennyson's lines from "Come down, O maid" are usually cited as an example of onomatopoeia:

> The moan of doves in immemorial elms
> And murmuring of innumerable bees.

If you have read the preceding—and, admittedly, not entirely engaging— paragraphs, you may have found yourself mentally repeating some catchy sounds, let's say our example of internal rhyme ("Each narrow cell in which we dwell") or our example of alliteration ("Bring me my bow of burning gold"). As the creators of advertising slogans know, all of us—not just poets—can be hooked by the sounds of words, but probably poets are especially fond of savoring words. Consider the following poem.

## GALWAY KINNELL

*Born in 1927 in Providence, Rhode Island, Galway Kinnell was educated at Princeton and the University of Rochester. He is the author of many books of poems, a novel, and translations of French and German literature. Among Kinnell's many awards are the Pulitzer Prize for Poetry and the National Book Award for* Selected Poems *(1980).*

### Blackberry Eating                                                   [1980]

I love to go out in late September
among the fat, overripe, icy, black blackberries
to eat blackberries for breakfast,
the stalks very prickly, a penalty
they earn for knowing the black art                                         5
of blackberry-making: and as I stand among them
lifting the stalks to my mouth, the ripest berries
fall almost unbidden to my tongue,
as words sometimes do, certain peculiar words
like *strengths* or *squinched,*                                          10
many-lettered, one-syllabled lumps,
which I squeeze, squinch open, and splurge well
in the silent, startled, icy, black language
of blackberry-eating in late September.

Kinnell does not use rhyme, but he uses other kinds of aural repetition. For instance, in the first line we get "*l*ove" and "*l*ate," and the *l* sound (already present in the title of the poem) is picked up in the second line, in "black blackberries." The *k* sound is then continued in the next line, in "stalks" and the *l* and *k* in "prickly," and "prickly" contains not only the *k* and the *l* of "blackberry" but also the *r.*

In lines 7–9 Kinnell compares eating blackberries—an action involving the tongue and the lips, and the mind also, if one is savoring the berries—to speaking "certain peculiar words." There is no need for us to point out additional connections between words in the poem, but we do want to mention that the last line ends with the same three words as the first, providing closure, which is one of the things rhyme normally does.

> ### YOUR TURN
>
> 1. Specify three words that you like to "squinch," and explain why.
> 2. Specify one poem, other than a poem in this chapter (the poem need not be in this book), in which you think the repetitions of sounds are especially important, and explain why you hold this view.

# WILLIAM CARLOS WILLIAMS

*For a biographical note, see page 628.*

### *The Artist*                                                    [1954]

```
Mr. T.
          bareheaded
                    in a soiled undershirt
his hair standing out
          on all sides                                             5
                    stood on his toes
heels together
          arms gracefully
                    for the moment
curled above his head.                                             10
                    Then he whirled about
                              bounded
into the air
          and with an *entrechat*°
                    perfectly achieved                             15
completed the figure.
                    My mother
                              taken by surprise
where she sat
          in her invalid's chair                                   20
                    was left speechless.
Bravo! she cried at last
          and clapped her hands.
                    The man's wife
came from the kitchen:                                             25
          What goes on here? she said.
                    But the show was over.
```

---

**14 entrechat** a leap, in ballet.

**YOUR TURN**

1. Why does Williams tell us that Mr. T.'s hair was untidy and that he wore "a soiled undershirt"?
2. Suppose the poem ended with line 23, "and clapped her hands." Would it be just as good, better, or less good? Why?

# LAWRENCE FERLINGHETTI

*Lawrence Ferlinghetti (b. 1919) has been much concerned with bringing poetry to the people. To this end he has not only written poetry but has also been the editor and publisher of City Lights Books in San Francisco and (since 1953) has operated a bookstore, the City Lights Bookshop, the first all-paperback bookstore in the United States. In 1956 Ferlinghetti achieved national fame when, as the publisher of Allen Ginsberg's* Howl, *he was arrested (and later acquitted) on an obscenity charge.*

## Constantly Risking Absurdity [1958]

Constantly risking absurdity
                    and death
        whenever he performs
                    above the heads
                            of his audience              5
the poet like an acrobat
                climbs on rime
                    to a high wire of his own making
and balancing on eyebeams
                    above a sea of faces               10
            paces his way
                    to the other side of day
performing entrechats°
                    and sleight-of-foot tricks
and other high theatrics                               15
            and all without mistaking
        any thing
                for what it may not be

For he's the super realist
            who must perforce perceive                 20
        taut truth
                before the taking of each stance or step
in his supposed advance
                toward that still higher perch
where Beauty stands and waits                          25
                with gravity
                to start her death-defying leap

---
**13 entrechats** a leap in ballet.

And he
    a little charleychaplin man
           who may or may not catch          30
her fair eternal form
        spreadeagled in the empty air
  of existence

### YOUR TURN

1. In this poem, which compares a poet to an acrobat, is Ferlinghetti "constantly risking absurdity"?
2. What examples of wordplay do you find, in addition to "above the heads / of his audience"?

## A Note About Poetic Forms

"Art is nothing without form," the French author Gustave Flaubert maintained, and it is true that works of art have a carefully designed shape. Most obviously, for instance, a good story has an ending that satisfies the reader or hearer. In real life, things keep going, but when a good story ends, the audience feels that there is nothing more to say, at least nothing more of interest to say.

With poems that rhyme, the rhyme-scheme provides a pattern, a shape, a structure that seems inseparable from the content. If you recite a limerick, you will immediately see how the shape is inseparable from the content:

There was a young fellow from Lynn
Who was so exceedingly thin
    That when he essayed
    To drink lemonade
He slipped through the straw and fell in.

If you put the words in a different order, and you ignore meter and rhyme—that is, if you destroy the form and turn the passage into something like "A young man, so thin that he fell through a straw into a glass of lemonade, lived in Lynn"—you can instantly see the importance of form.

Let's briefly look again at a more serious example—Housman's "Eight O'Clock" (page 663), a poem whose title corresponds to the hour at which executions used to take place in England.

He stood, and heard the steeple
    Sprinkle the quarters on the morning town.
One, two, three, four, to market-place and people
    It tossed them down.

Strapped, noosed, nighing his hour,
    He stood and counted them and cursed his luck;
And then the clock collected in the tower
    Its strength, and struck.

The rhyme of "struck" with "luck" (in this instance, bad luck) is conclusive. We don't ask if the body was removed from the gallows and buried, or if the condemned man's wife (if he had one) grieved, or if his children (if he had any) turned out well or badly. None of these things is of any relevance. There is nothing more to say. The form and the content perfectly go together. In this example, the lines, each of which rhymes with another line—we might say that each line is tied to another line—seem especially appropriate for a man who is "strapped" and "noosed."

But why do poets use forms established by rhyme? In an essay called "The Constant Symbol," Robert Frost says that a poet regards rhymes as "stepping stones. . . .The way will be zigzag, but it will be a straight crookedness like the walking stick he cuts in the bushes for an emblem." Housman's stepping stones in the second stanza took Housman (and take the reader) from *hour* to *luck,* then to *tower* and then with great finality to the end of the walk, *struck.* We think this stanza is inspired, and we imagine that Housman's inspiration was mightily helped by his need for rhymes—his need to get "stepping stones" that would allow him to continue the "straight crookedness" of his walk with this condemned man. His walk-with-words, or rather his walk with words-that-set-forth-ideas, produced "luck" and "struck," and enabled him to give to his readers the memorable image of the clock as a machine that executes the man.

When you read Housman's or Frost's actual lines—or better, when you read them aloud and hear and feel the effect of these rhymes—you can understand why Frost more than once said he would as soon write unrhymed poetry as he would "play tennis with the net down." The rules governing the game of tennis or the game of writing do not interfere with the game; rather, the rules allow the players to play the game. The rules allow poets to write poems; the rules—the restraints—provide the structure that allows poets to accomplish something.

Poets are somewhat like Houdini, who accepted shackles so that he could triumph over them. Without the handcuffs and other restraints, he could accomplish nothing. Or consider the string on a kite; far from impeding the kite's flight, the string allows the kite to fly. Speaking in less high-flying terms, we can quote from a talk that Frost gave to college students in 1937, "The Poet's Next of Kin in College." He told them—and he was speaking not only to young poets but to all students—that in their endeavors, of whatever sort, they "must have form—performance. The thing itself is indescribable, but it is felt like athletic form. To have form, feel form in sports—and by analogy feel form in verse."

Poets have testified that they use rhyme partly because, far from impeding them, it helps them to say interesting things in a memorable way. True, some rhymes have been used so often that although they were once rich in meaning—for instance—"love" and "dove" or "moon" and "June"—they have become clichés, their use indicating not an imaginative leap but a reliance on what has been said too often. But other rhymes—let's say "earth" and "birth" or "law" and "flaw"—can lead poets to say interesting things that they might otherwise not have thought of.

In his "Letter of Advice to a Young Poet," Jonathan Swift (whom you may know as the author of *Gulliver's Travels,* 1726), said: "Verse without rhyme is a body without a soul." A striking, and indeed surprising, comment: Swift dares to propose that the soul of a poem depends not on the content but, rather, on a crucial element of its form, the presence of rhyme. In part he is reminding us here of the importance of craft in the writing of a poem, of the sheer skill and deliberation that make the literary work feel exactly right, as though it *had* to be this way.

## Stanzaic Patterns

Lines of poetry are commonly arranged in a rhythmical unit called a **stanza** (from an Italian word meaning "room" or "stopping-place"). Usually all the stanzas in a poem have the same rhyme pattern. A stanza is sometimes called a **verse,** though *verse* may also mean a single line of poetry. (In discussing stanzas, rhymes are indicated by identical letters. Thus, *abab* indicates that the first and third lines rhyme with each other, while the second and fourth lines are linked by a different rhyme. An unrhymed line is denoted by *x*.) Common stanzaic forms in English poetry are the following:

1. **Couplet**: a stanza of two lines, usually but not necessarily with end rhymes. *Couplet* is also used for a pair of rhyming lines. The **octosyllabic couplet** is iambic or trochaic tetrameter:

   > Had we but world enough and time,
   > This coyness, lady, were no crime.
   >
   > —Andrew Marvell

2. **Heroic couplet**: a rhyming couplet of iambic pentameter, often "closed—" that is, containing a complete thought, with a fairly heavy pause at the end of the first line and a still heavier one at the end of the second. Commonly, there is a parallel or an *antithesis* (contrast) within a line or between the two lines. It is called heroic because in England, especially in the eighteenth century, it was much used for heroic (epic) poems.

   > Some foreign writers, some our own despise;
   > The ancients only, or the moderns, prize.
   >
   > —Alexander Pope

3. **Triplet** (or **tercet**): a three-line stanza, usually with one rhyme.

   > Whenas in silks my Julia goes
   > Then, then (methinks) how sweetly flows
   > That liquefaction of her clothes.
   >
   > —Robert Herrick

4. **Quatrain**: a four-line stanza, rhymed or unrhymed. The **heroic** (or **elegiac) quatrain** is iambic pentameter, rhyming *abab*. That is, the first and third lines rhyme (so they are designated *a*), and the second and fourth lines rhyme (so they are designated *b*).

# Three Complex Forms: The Sonnet, the Villanelle, and the Sestina

## The Sonnet

A sonnet is a fourteen-line poem, predominantly in iambic pentameter. The rhyme is usually according to one of two schemes. The **Italian** or **Petrarchan sonnet,** named for the Italian poet Petrarch (1304–1374), has two divisions: The first eight lines (rhyming *abba abba*) are the octave, and the last six (rhyming *cd cd cd,* or a variant) are the **sestet.** Gerard Manley Hopkins's "God's Grandeur" (page 807) is an Italian sonnet. The second kind of sonnet, the **English** or **Shakespearean sonnet,** is usually arranged into three quatrains and a couplet, rhyming *abab cdcd efef gg.* (For examples see the next two poems.)

In many sonnets there is a marked correspondence between the rhyme scheme and the development of the thought. Thus an Italian sonnet may state a generalization in the octave and a specific example in the sestet. Or an English sonnet may give three examples—one in each quatrain—and draw a conclusion in the couplet.

Why poets choose to imprison themselves in fourteen tightly rhymed lines is something of a mystery. Tradition has a great deal to do with it: the form, having been handled successfully by major poets, stands as a challenge. In writing a sonnet a poet gains a little of the authority of Petrarch, Shakespeare, Milton, Wordsworth, and other masters who showed that the sonnet is not merely a trick. A second reason perhaps resides in the very tightness of the rhymes, which can help as well as hinder. Many poets have felt, along with Richard Wilbur (in *Mid-Century American Poets,* ed. John Ciardi), that the need for a rhyme has suggested

> . . . arbitrary connections of which the mind may take advantage if it likes. For example, if one has to rhyme with *tide,* a great number of rhyme-words at once come to mind (ride, bide, shied, confide, Akenside, etc.). Most of these, in combination with *tide,* will probably suggest nothing apropos, but one of them may reveal precisely what one wanted to say. If none of them does, *tide* must be dispensed with. Rhyme, austerely used, may be a stimulus to discovery and a stretcher of the attention.

# WILLIAM SHAKESPEARE

*William Shakespeare (1564–1616), born in Stratford-upon-Avon in England, is chiefly known as a dramatic poet, but he also wrote nondramatic poetry. In 1609 a volume of 154 of his sonnets was published, apparently without his permission. Probably he chose to keep his sonnets unpublished not because he thought that they were of little value, but because it was more prestigious to be an amateur (unpublished) poet than a professional (published) one. Although the sonnets were published in 1609, they were probably written in the mid-1590s, when there was a vogue for sonneteering. A contemporary writer in 1598 said that Shakespeare's "sugred Sonnets [circulate] among his private friends."*

*Other sonnets by Shakespeare are on pages 822–23.*

## Sonnet 73

That time of year thou mayst in me behold
When yellow leaves, or none, or few, do hang
Upon those boughs which shake against the cold,
Bare ruined choirs° where late the sweet birds sang.
In me thou see'st the twilight of such day                    5
As after sunset fadeth in the west,

---

**4 choir** the part of the church where services were sung.

Which by-and-by black night doth take away,
Death's second self that seals up all in rest.
In me thou see'st the glowing of such fire
That on the ashes of his youth doth lie,                                                    10
As the deathbed whereon it must expire,
Consumed with that which it was nourished by.
  This thou perceiv'st, which makes thy love more strong,
  To love that well which thou must leave ere long.

### YOUR TURN

1. In the first quatrain (the first four lines) to what "time of year" does Shakespeare compare himself? In the second quatrain (lines 5–8) to what does he compare himself? In the third? If the sequence of the three quatrains were reversed, what would be gained or lost?
2. In line 8, what is "Death's second self"? What implications do you perceive in "seals up all in rest," as opposed, for instance, to "brings most welcome rest"?
3. In line 13, exactly what is "This"?
4. In line 14, suppose in place of "To love that well which thou must leave ere long," Shakespeare had written "To love me well whom thou must leave ere long." What, if anything, would have been gained or lost?
5. What is your personal response to this sonnet? Do you feel that its lessons apply to you? Please explain.
6. Did you find this sonnet hard to understand when you read it for the first time? After you reread and studied it, did it become more difficult, or less so? Do you like to read difficult poems?

## *Sonnet 146*

Poor soul, the center of my sinful earth,
My sinful earth° these rebel pow'rs that thee array,
Why doest thou pine within and suffer dearth,
Painting thy outward walls so costly gay?
Why so large cost,° having so short a lease,                                               5
Dost thou upon thy fading mansion spend?
Shall worms, inheritors of this excess,
Eat up thy charge? Is this thy body's end?
Then, soul, live thou upon thy servant's loss,
And let that pine to aggravate thy store;                                                  10
Buy terms divine° in selling hours of dross;
Within be fed, without be rich no more.
  So shalt thou feed on Death, that feeds on men,
  And death once dead, there's no more dying then.

---

**2 My sinful earth** see the comment beneath the facsimile on page 677.   **5 cost** expense.   **11 Buy terms divine** buy ages of immortality.

POore foule the center of my finfull earth,
My finfull earth thefe rebbell powres that thee array
Why doft thou pine within and fuffer dearth}
Painting thy outward walls fo coftlie gay?
Why fo large coft hauing fo fhort a leafe,
Doft thou vpon thy fading manfion fpend?
Shall wormes inheritors of this exceffe
Eate vp thy charge?is this thy bodies end?
Then foule liue thou vpon thy feruants loffe,
And let that pine to aggrauat thy ftore;
Buy tearmes diuine in felling houres of droffe:
Within be fed, without be rich no more,
So fhalt thou feed on death,that feeds on men,
And death once dead,ther's no more dying then.

Sonnet 146 as it appears in the first publication of Shakespeare's sonnets, 1609. Notice that the first line ends with the words "my sinful earth," and the second line begins with the same words. Virtually all readers agree that the printer mistakenly repeated the words. First of all, the line makes almost no sense; secondly, it has 12 syllables ("powres" is monosyllabic) where 10 syllables are normal. Among attractive suggested emendations—usually two syllables instead of the four of "My sinful earth"—are those that pick up imagery of conflict explicit in "rebbell powres," such as "Prey to," "Thrall to," "Foiled by," and "Vexed by," and emendations that pick up imagery of hunger explicit in "Eate" and "fed," such as "Feeding" and "Starved by." But there are plenty of other candidates, such as "Fooled by," "Rebuke these," and "Leagued with."

### YOUR TURN

1. As we indicate in our comment on the facsimile of this poem, the first three words of the second line probably should be replaced with other words. What words would you suggest? (We give some of the most widely accepted suggestions, but feel free to offer your own.)
2. In what tone of voice would you speak the first line? The last line? Trace the speaker's shifts in emotion throughout the poem.
3. What is your personal response to this poem? Do you feel that its lessons apply to you? Do you find this sonnet more meaningful, or less meaningful, to you than Sonnet 73 (page 675)? Please explain.
4. Did you find this poem hard to understand when you read it for the first time? After you reread and studied it, did the poem become more difficult, or less so? Is this sonnet more difficult than Sonnet 73? What is the difference between a poem that is challenging, a poem that is difficult, and a poem that is obscure?

# JOHN MILTON

*John Milton (1608–1674) was born into a well-to-do family in London, where from childhood he was a student of languages, mastering at an early age Latin, Greek, Hebrew, and a number of modern languages. Instead of becoming a minister in the Anglican Church, he resolved to become a poet and spent five years at his family's country home, reading. His attacks against the monarchy secured him a position in Oliver Cromwell's Puritan government as Latin secretary for foreign affairs. He became totally blind, but he continued his work through secretaries, one of whom was Andrew Marvell, author of "To His Coy Mistress" (page 652). With the restoration of the monarchy in 1660, Milton was for a time confined but was later pardoned in the general amnesty. Until his death he continued to work on many subjects, including his greatest poem, the epic* Paradise Lost.

## When I Consider How My Light Is Spent                    [1655]

When I consider how my light is spent
  Ere half my days, in this dark world and wide,
  And that one talent which is death to hide°
  Lodged with me useless,° though my soul more bent
To serve therewith my Maker, and present                                      5
  My true account, lest he returning chide;
  "Doth God exact day-labor, light denied?"
  I fondly° ask; but Patience to prevent°
That murmur, soon replies, "God doth not need
  Either man's work or his own gifts; who best                            10
  Bear his mild yoke, they serve him best. His state
Is kingly. Thousands at his bidding speed
  And post o'er land and ocean without rest:
  They also serve who only stand and wait."

---

**3** There is a pun in *talent*, relating Milton's literary talent to Christ's Parable of the Talents (Matthew 25.14 ff.), in which a servant is rebuked for not putting his talent (a unit of money) to use.    **4 useless** a pun on *use*, i.e., usury, interest.    **8 fondly** foolishly. **prevent** forestall.

### YOUR TURN

1. This sonnet is sometimes called "On His Blindness," though Milton never gave it a title. Do you think this title gets toward the heart of the poem? Explain. If you were to give it a title, what would the title be?
2. Read the parable in Matthew 25.14–30, and then consider how close the parable is to Milton's life as Milton describes it in this poem.
3. Where is the turn? What characteristics are attributed to God after the turn?
4. Compare the tone of the first and the last sentences. How does the length of each of these sentences contribute to the tone?
5. Could you imagine someone saying, "This poem changed my life"? What kind of change in a person's life might this sonnet produce?

6. What is your own experience of blindness? Have you ever lost your eyesight? For a long or a short period? Do you know a blind person? What is the nature of your interaction with him or her?

## X. J. KENNEDY

*X. J. Kennedy was born in New Jersey in 1929. He has taught at Tufts University and is the author of many books of poems, books for children, and college textbooks.*

*Kennedy alludes (line 4) to Milton's* Paradise Lost, *VII, 205-207: "Heaven opened wide / Her ever-during gates, harmonious sound / On golden hinges moving. . . ." For an account of the slaughter of the innocents (line 5), see Matthew 2.16. The Venerable Bede (675-735), in line 6, was an English theologian and historian.*

### *Nothing in Heaven Functions as It Ought*                [1965]

Nothing in Heaven functions as it ought:
Peter's bifocals, blindly sat on, crack;
His gates lurch wide with the cackle of a cock,
Not turn with a hush of gold as Milton had thought;
Gangs of the slaughtered innocents keep huffing          5
The nimbus off the Venerable Bede
Like that of an old dandelion gone to seed;
And the beatific choir keep breaking up, coughing.

But Hell, sleek Hell hath no freewheeling part:
None takes his own sweet time, none quickens pace.          10
Ask anyone, How come you here, poor heart?—
And he will slot a quarter through his face,
You'll hear an instant click, a tear will start
Imprinted with an abstract of his case.

### YOUR TURN

In the octave Kennedy uses off-rhymes *(crack, cock; huffing, coughing)*, but in the sestet all the rhymes are exact. How do the rhymes help to convey the meaning? (Notice, too, that lines, 3, 4, 5, 7, and 8 all have more than the usual ten syllables. Again, why?)

## BILLY COLLINS

*For a bibliograpical note, see page 589.*

The following sonnet uses the Petrarchan form of an octave and a sestet (see page 674). Petrarch is additionally present in the poem by the allusion in line 3 to "a little ship on love's storm-tossed seas," because Petrarch compared the hapless lover, denied the favor of his mistress, to a ship in a storm: The lover cannot guide his ship because the North Star is hidden (Petrarch's beloved Laura averts her eyes), and the sails of the ship are agitated by the lover's pitiful sighs. As you will see, Petrarch and Laura explicitly enter the poem in the last three lines.

In line 8 Collins refers to the stations of the cross. In Roman Catholicism, one of the devotions consists of prayers and meditations before each of fourteen crosses or images set up along a path that commemorates the fourteen places at which Jesus halted when, just before the Crucifixion, he was making his way in Jerusalem to Golgotha.

### *Sonnet* [2001]

All we need is fourteen lines, well, thirteen now,
and after this next one just a dozen
to launch a little ship on love's storm-tossed seas,
then only ten more left like rows of beans.
How easily it goes unless you get Elizabethan                    5
and insist the iambic bongos must be played
and rhymes positioned at the ends of lines,
one for every station of the cross.
But hang on here while we make the turn
into the final six where all will be resolved,                   10
where longing and heartache will find an end,
where Laura will tell Petrarch to put down his pen,
take off those crazy medieval tights,
blow out the lights, and come at last to bed.

### YOUR TURN

1. The headnote explains the stations of the cross (line 8), but what is the point of introducing this image into a sonnet?
2. Normally the "turn" (*volta*) in an Italian sonnet occurs at the beginning of the ninth line; the first eight lines (the octave) establish some sort of problem, and the final six lines (the sestet) respond, for instance by answering a question, or by introducing a contrasting emotion. In your view, how satisfactorily does Collins handle this form?
3. Does this sonnet interest you? Do you find it clever? Is that a good thing or a bad thing?
4. Do you think that you could have written this sonnet? Could you have written Shakespeare's sonnets 73 and 146 (pages 675–76)? What do your responses to these questions suggest to you about the writing of poetry?

## The Villanelle

The name comes from an Italian words, *villanella*, meaning "country song" or "peasant song," and originally, in the sixteenth century, the subject was the supposedly simple life of the shepherd, but in France in the seventeenth century elaborate rules were developed. Variations occur, but usually a **villanelle** has the following characteristics:

- Five stanzas with three lines each (tercets), rhyming *aba,* and a final stanza with four lines (a quatrain).

**YOUR TURN**

1. What was your response to the title when you first read it? Did your re-sponse change after you read the poem and studied it further?
2. Is the form connected to the poem's theme? If so, in what way?
3. Linger over line 1: Why is "losing" an "art"? And why does Bishop echo the phrasing of the first line in lines later in the poem? Does the echo make the poem feel repetitive?
4. Follow Bishop's uses of the words "lose," "losing," and "loss" from one to the next. Do you find her reliance on these very closely related words to be important for the poem's meaning, or does it strike you as a lot or a little confusing? Can a poem be a lot or a little confusing and yet still be a good poem?
5. Can we tell what kind of loss Bishop is exploring? If we can, where does this kind of loss become clear?
6. Whom is Bishop addressing when she says (note the exclamation point) "*Write* it!"? Why is this command in the poem, and why is it in parentheses?
7. Has this poem helped you to understand a loss or losses that you have experienced yourself? Something, perhaps, that you did not understand before about what "losing" someone or something important means? Do you have an insight of your own into losing and loss that Bishop has not considered, at least not in this poem? Is this an insight that you would want to share with others—in a poem, for example—or keep to yourself?

# The Sestina

This fiendishly elaborate form developed in twelfth-century Europe, especially in southern France, among the troubadours, court poets who sang for nobles. (The name comes from the Italian *sesto,* "sixth," because there are six stanzas of six lines each—but then, to complicate matters, there is a seventh stanza, a three-line "envoy" or "envoi," a summing up that uses key words of the first six stanzas.)

More precisely—this is mind-boggling—the six words that end the six lines of the first stanza are used at the ends of all the following lines but in a different though fixed order in each stanza. (Rhyme is *not* used in this form.) This fixed or-der has been characterized as a sort of bottoms-up pattern, a term that will be-come clear as we describe the stanzas. In the second stanza the *first* line ends with the *last* word of the *last* line (the bottom) of the first stanza; the second line of the second stanza ends with the first line of the first; the third line ends with the last word of the fifth line of the first stanza—i.e., with the next-to-bottom line of the first stanza. The fourth line of the second stanza ends with the second line of the first, the fifth with the fourth line of the first, and the sixth with the third line of the first.

Thus, if we designate the final words of the first stanza, line by line, as 1, 2, 3, 4, 5, 6,

> the final words of the second stanza are 6, 1, 5, 2, 4, 3;
> the third stanza: 3, 6, 4, 1, 2, 5
> the fourth stanza: 5, 3, 2, 6, 1, 4
> the fifth stanza: 4, 5, 1, 3, 6, 2
> the sixth stanza: 2, 4, 6, 5, 3, 1

The envoy of three lines must use these six words, but there are various possible patterns—for instance, 5, 3, 1 at the ends of the three lines, and 2, 4, 6 in the middle of the lines.

If you are going to write a sestina, two tips:

- Once you have settled on your topic—let's say "loss" or "a restless spirit of adventure"—jot down six words that you think are relevant, and get going.
- You need not end each line with a pause, and in fact most good sestinas use considerable enjambment—i.e., the sense of the line runs over into the next line.

## ELIZABETH BISHOP

*For a biographical note, see page 682.*

### Sestina                                                                    [1965]

September rain falls on the house.
In the failing light, the old grandmother
sits in the kitchen with the child
beside the Little Marvel Stove,
reading the jokes from the almanac,                                            5
laughing and talking to hide her tears.

She thinks that her equinoctial tears
and the rain that beats on the roof of the house
were both foretold by the almanac,
but only known to a grandmother.                                               10
The iron kettle sings on the stove.
She cuts some bread and says to the child,

*It's time for tea now;* but the child
is watching the teakettle's small hard tears
dance like mad on the hot black stove,                                         15
the way the rain must dance on the house.
Tidying up, the old grandmother
hangs up the clever almanac

on its string. Birdlike, the almanac
hovers half open above the child,                                              20
hovers above the old grandmother
and her teacup full of dark brown tears.
She shivers and says she thinks the house
feels chilly, and puts more wood in the stove.

*It was to be,* says the Marvel° Stove.                                        25
*I know what I know,* says the almanac.
With crayons the child draws a rigid house
and a winding pathway. Then the child
puts in a man with buttons like tears
and shows it proudly to the grandmother.                                       30

---

25 **Marvel** a brand of stoves and appliances.

But secretly, while the grandmother
busies herself about the stove,
the little moons fall down like tears
from between the pages of the almanac
into the flower bed the child                                    35
has carefully placed in the front of the house.

*Time to plant tears,* says the almanac.
The grandmother sings to the marvelous stove
and the child draws another inscrutable house.

**YOUR TURN**

1. Does Bishop's choice of title seem strange to you? Why would she use
the name of the poetic form for her title? Do you think that a different
title might be more effective? Please give examples, and explain why
they would or would not be better.
2. As carefully as you can, describe the effect of line 1.
3. In the first stanza, why is the grandmother crying? How are her tears in
lines 6 and 7 related to the "small hard tears" of the teakettle in line 14?
Note, too, the later references to tears. Please comment on these as
well.
4. Several of the lines in this poem are italicized. Do the italics make the
lines more forceful? Should Bishop have made the force of the lines
clear without changing the "look" of the lines on the page?
5. What is an almanac? Have you ever seen one? Why would someone
want an almanac? What is the significance of the almanac in this
poem?
6. What is your response to the fact that this poem is a sestina? Do you
think you could write a poem in this form? What would be the benefit
to you of such an assignment?

# Shaped Poetry or Pattern Poetry

We have been talking about shapes or patterns determined by rhymes, but some
poems—admittedly few—take their shape from the length of the lines, which
form a simple image, such as a sphere, an egg, a vase, or a wing.

Here is a famous example of shaped poetry, a pair of wings. We print it
sideways, as it was printed in the earliest edition, in 1633, though in that edition the first stanza was printed on the left-hand page, the second on the right-
hand page.

## GEORGE HERBERT

*George Herbert (1593–1633), born into a distinguished Welsh family, studied
at the University of Cambridge (England) and became a clergyman. By all accounts he lived an admirable life and was deservedly known in his community as "Holy Mr. Herbert."*

Note: *In line 1,* store *means "abundance," "plenty." In line 10,* the fall *refers to the loss of innocence that resulted when Adam ate the forbidden fruit in the garden of Eden. In the next-to-last line,* imp, *a term from falconry, means "to graft, to insert feathers into a wing."*
*We print the poem in the way that it was originally printed.*

### Easter-Wings

[1633]

Lord, who createdst man in wealth and store,
  Though foolishly he lost the same,
    Decaying more and more,
      Till he became
        Most poor:
        With thee
      O let me rise
    As larks, harmoniously,
  And sing this day thy victories:
Then shall the fall further the flight in me.

My tender age in sorrow did begin:
  And still with sicknesses and shame
    Thou didst so punish sin,
      That I became
        Most thin.
        With thee
      Let me combine,
    And feel this day thy victory:
  For, if I imp my wing on thine,
Affliction shall advance the flight in me.

5

10

15

20

---

**YOUR TURN**

1. Why are wings especially relevant to a poem about Easter?
2. We don't think one can argue that the length of every line is exactly suited to the meaning of the line, but we do think that some of the lengths are parallel or reinforce some of the ideas within those lines. For instance, the first line, speaking of a man's original "wealth and store," is a long line. Why is this length more appropriate to the meaning than it would be to, say, "Lord, who created a man who soon would fall"? And note especially the fifth and sixth lines of each stanza: Would you agree that their length suits their meaning?
3. Do you think this poem is a mere novelty, or do you think it deserves close attention and indeed is memorable? Please explain.

## Blank Verse and Free Verse

A good deal of English poetry is unrhymed, much of it in **blank verse**—that is, unrhymed iambic pentameter. Introduced into English poetry by Henry Howard, the Earl of Surrey, in the middle of the sixteenth century, late in the century it became the standard medium (especially in the hands of Marlowe and Shakespeare) of English drama. In the seventeenth century, Milton used it for *Paradise Lost,* and it has continued to be used in both dramatic and nondramatic literature. For an example see the first scene of *Hamlet* (page 1001). A passage of blank verse that has a rhetorical unity is sometimes called a **verse paragraph.**

The second kind of unrhymed poetry fairly common in English, especially in the twentieth century, is **free verse** (or **vers libre**): rhythmical lines varying in length, adhering to no fixed metrical pattern and usually unrhymed. Such poetry may seem formless; Robert Frost, who strongly preferred regular meter and rhyme, said that he would not consider writing free verse any more than he would consider playing tennis without a net. But free verse does have a form or pattern, often largely based on repetition and parallel grammatical structure. Whitman's "A Noiseless Patient Spider" (page 585) is an example; Arnold's "Dover Beach" (page 778) is another example, though less typical because it uses rhyme. Thoroughly typical is Whitman's "When I Heard the Learn'd Astronomer."

# WALT WHITMAN

*For a biographical note, see page 633.*

## *When I Heard the Learn'd Astronomer*      [1865]

When I heard the learn'd astronomer,
When the proofs, the figures, were ranged in columns before me,
When I was shown the charts and diagrams, to add, divide, and measure
  them,
When I sitting heard the astronomer where he lectured with much
  applause in the lecture-room,
How soon unaccountable I became tired and sick,                    5
Till rising and gliding out I wander'd off by myself,
In the mystical moist night-air, and from time to time,
Look'd up in perfect silence at the stars.

What can be said about the rhythmic structure of this poem? Rhymes are absent, and the lines vary greatly in the number of syllables, ranging from 9 (the first line) to 23 (the fourth line), but when we read the poem we sense a rhythmic structure. The first four lines obviously hang together, each beginning with "When"; indeed, three of these four lines begin "When I." We may notice, too, that each of these four lines has more syllables than its predecessor (the numbers are 9, 14, 18, and 23); this increase in length, like the initial repetition, is a kind of pattern. But then, with the fifth line, which speaks of fatigue and surfeit, there is a shrinkage to 14 syllables, offering an enormous relief from the previous swollen line with its 23 syllables. The second half of the poem—the pattern established by "When" in the first four lines is dropped, and in effect we get a new stanza, also of four lines—does not relentlessly diminish the number of syllables in each succeeding line, but it *almost* does so: 14, 14, 13, 10.

The second half of the poem thus has a pattern too, and this pattern is more or less the reverse of the first half of the poem. We may notice too that the last line (in which the poet, now released from the oppressive lecture hall, is in communion with nature) is very close to an iambic pentameter line; that is, the poem concludes with a metrical form said to be the most natural in English. The effect of naturalness or ease in this final line, moreover, is increased by the absence of repetitions (e.g., not only of "When I," but even of such syntactic repetitions as "charts and diagrams," "tired and sick," "rising and gliding") that characterize most of the previous lines. This final effect of naturalness is part of a carefully constructed pattern in which rhythmic structure is part of meaning. Though at first glance free verse may appear unrestrained, as T. S. Eliot (a practitioner) said, "No *vers* is *libre* for the man who wants to do a good job"—or for the woman who wants to do a good job.

# The Prose Poem

The term *prose poem* is sometimes applied to a short work that looks like prose but that is highly rhythmical or rich in images, or both. Here is a modern example.

## CAROLYN FORCHÉ

*Carolyn Forché was born in Detroit in 1950. After earning a bachelor's degree from Michigan State University and a master's degree from Bowling Green State University, she traveled widely in the Southwest, living among Pueblo Indians. Between 1978 and 1986 she made several visits to El Salvador, documenting human rights violations for Amnesty International. Her first book of poems,* Gathering the Tribes, *won the Yale Younger Poets award in 1975. Forché is the Director of the Lannan Center for Poetry and Poetics and holds the Lannan Chair in Poetry at Georgetown University in Washington D.C.*

### *The Colonel*                                                        [1978, publ. 1981]

What you have heard is true. I was in his house. His wife carried a tray of coffee and sugar. His daughter filed her nails, his son went out for the night. There were daily papers, pet dogs, a pistol on the cushion beside him. The moon swung bare on its black cord over the house. On the television was a cop show. It was in English. Broken bottles were embedded in the walls around the house to scoop the kneecaps from a man's legs or cut his hands to lace. On the windows there were gratings like those in liquor stores. We had dinner, rack of lamb, good wine, a gold bell was on the table for calling the maid. The maid brought green mangoes, salt, a type of bread. I was asked how I enjoyed the country. There was a brief commercial in Spanish. His wife took everything away. There was some talk then of how difficult it had become to govern. The parrot said hello on the terrace. The colonel told it to shut up, and pushed himself from the table. My friend said to me with his eyes: say nothing. The colonel returned with a sack used to bring groceries home. He spilled many human ears on the table. They were like dried peach halves. There is no other way to say this. He took one of them in his hands, shook it in our faces, dropped it into a water glass. It came alive there. I am tired of fooling around he said. As for the rights of anyone, tell your people they can go fuck themselves. He swept the ears to the floor with his arm and held the last of his wine in the air. Something for your poetry, no? he said. Some of the ears on the floor caught this scrap of his voice. Some of the ears on the floor were pressed to the ground.

*May 1978*

## YOUR TURN

1. How would you characterize the colonel in a few sentences?
2. We are told that the colonel spoke of "how difficult it had become to govern." What do you suppose the colonel assumes is the purpose of government? What do you assume its purpose is?
3. How much do we know about the narrator? Can we guess the narrator's purpose in visiting the colonel? How would you characterize the narrator's tone? Do you believe the narrator?
4. What is your response to the last sentence?
5. What, if anything, is gained by calling this work a "prose poem" rather than a short story?

# Students Writing About Poems

If you are going to write about a fairly short poem (say, under 30 lines), it's not a bad idea to copy out the poem, writing or typing it double-spaced. By writing it out you will be forced to notice details, down to the punctuation. After you have copied the poem, proofread it carefully against the original. Catching an error—even the addition or omission of a comma—may help you to notice a detail in the original that you might otherwise have overlooked. And now that you have the poem with ample space between the lines, you have a worksheet with room for jottings.

A good essay is based on a genuine response to a poem; a response may be stimulated in part by first reading the poem aloud and then considering the questions that follow in the sections below.

Remember, even an explication—an unfolding of the implications of the poem—is an argument. In the example on page 545, the student begins by asserting a thesis, a claim: "'Harlem' is only eleven lines long, but it is charged with power." The thesis, the arguable claim, of course is not that "the poem is only eleven lines long" but that "it is charged with power," and the rest of the explication is devoted to supporting this claim, to pointing out almost word by word the sources of the power.

## First Response

1. What was your response to the poem on first reading?
2. Did some parts of the poem especially please or displease you, or puzzle you?
3. After some study—perhaps checking the meanings of some of the words in a dictionary and reading the poem several times—did you modify your initial response to the parts and to the whole?

## Speaker and Tone

1. Who is the speaker? (Consider age, sex, personality, frame of mind, and tone of voice.) Is the speaker defined fairly precisely (for instance, an older woman speaking to a child), or is the speaker simply a voice meditating? (Jot down your first impressions, then reread the poem and make further jottings, if necessary.)

2. Do you think the speaker is fully aware of what he or she is saying, or does the speaker unconsciously reveal his or her personality and values? What is your attitude toward this speaker?

3. Is the speaker narrating or reflecting on an earlier experience or attitude? If so, does he or she convey a sense of new awareness, such as regret for innocence lost?

# Audience

1. To whom is the speaker speaking?

2. What is the situation (including time and place)? In some poems a listener is strongly implied, but in others, especially those in which the speaker is meditating, there may be no audience other than the reader, who "overhears" the speaker.

# Structure and Form

1. Does the poem proceed in a straightforward way, or at some point or points does the speaker reverse course, altering his or her tone or perception? If there is a shift, what do you make of it?

2. Is the poem organized into sections? If so, what are these sections—stanzas, for instance—and how does each section (characterized, perhaps, by a certain tone of voice, or a group of rhymes) grow out of what precedes it?

3. What is the effect on you of the form—say, quatrains (stanzas of four lines) or blank verse (unrhymed lines of ten syllables of iambic pentameter)? If the sense overflows the form, running without pause from (for example) one quatrain into the next, what effect is created?

# Center of Interest and Theme

1. What is the poem about? Is the interest chiefly in a distinctive character, or is it in meditation? That is, is the poem chiefly psychological or chiefly philosophical?

2. Is the theme stated explicitly (directly) or implicitly? How might you state the theme in a sentence? What is lost by reducing the poem to a statement of a theme?

# Diction

1. How would you characterize the language? Colloquial, elevated, or what?

2. Do certain words have rich and relevant associations that relate to other words and help to define the speaker or the theme or both?

3. What is the role of figurative language, if any? Does it help to define the speaker or the theme?

4. What do you think is to be taken figuratively or symbolically, and what literally?

# Sound Effects

1. What is the role of sound effects, including repetitions of sound (for instance, alliteration) and of entire words, and shifts in versification?
2. If there are off-rhymes (for instance, *dizzy* and *easy,* or *home* and *come*), what effect do they have on you? Do they, for instance, add a note of tentativeness or uncertainty?
3. If there are unexpected stresses or pauses, what do they communicate about the speaker's experience? How do they affect you?

# A Note on Explication

On pages 80–81 we discuss the form known as *explication,* a line-by-line commentary seeking to make explicit or to explain the meaning that is implicit or hidden within the words. (*Explication* comes from the Latin *explicare,* meaning "to unfold," from *ex* = out + *plicare* = to fold.) The implication of such an activity is that writers "fold" a meaning into their words, and the reader perceives or unfolds the message. (*Implication,* also from the Latin word for "fold," means something entangled or involved in something else.)

Think about someone who says, "Shut the door" rather than "Would you mind shutting the door, please?" Obviously, the message in "Shut the door" is *not* exactly the same as the message in "Would you mind shutting the door, please?" An explication would point out that the first sentence contains an authoritative tone that is not found in the second. In effect, the first sentence "says" (in addition to the point about the door) that the speaker may give orders to the hearer; or, to put it the other way around, folded into the second sentence (but not the first) is the speaker's awareness that the person receiving the words is the speaker's social equal.

A slightly more complicated and much more interesting example is Julius Caesar's "I came, I saw, I conquered" (Latin: *veni, vidi, vici*). An explication would point out that in addition to the explicit meaning there are implicit meanings, for example that a man like Caesar does not waste words, that he is highly disciplined (the pattern of words suggests that he is a master of language), and that he is the sort of person who, on seeing something, immediately gets it under control by taking the appropriate action.

Because explication is chiefly concerned with making explicit what is implicit in a text, it is not concerned with such matters as the poet's place in history or the poet's biography, nor is it concerned with the reader's response to the poem—except to the degree that the reader's explication really may *not* be an objective decoding of the poem but may depend in large part on the reader's private associations. (Some literary critics would argue that the underlying premise of explication—that a writer puts a specific meaning into a work and that a reader can objectively recover that meaning—is based on the mistaken belief that readers can be objective.) If you look at the sample explication on page 82, you can decide for yourself whether the student unfolded implicit meanings that the author (William Butler Yeats) had tucked into the words of his poem or whether the explication really is a personal response to the poem.

# Seven Students Write About Poems

The first student essay in this chapter is not only an explication but also, first, a more personal response to a poem by Louise Glück. Like an explication, it is concerned with the author's meaning; but unlike an explication, it does not hesitate to go beyond the poem and into "the real world" that the writer of the paper lives in. The essay is not so personal that the poem disappears (as it might in an essay that says something like "This poem reminds me of the time that I . . ."), but it does not claim merely to unfold meanings that Glück has embodied or entangled in her words.

First read the following biographical note and the poem.

## LOUISE GLÜCK

*One of the leading contemporary poets, Louise Glück (pronounced "glick") was born in New York City in 1943, grew up on Long Island, and attended Sarah Lawrence College and Columbia University. She has taught at a number of colleges and universities, including the University of Iowa and Williams College.* Firstborn, *her first book of poems, was published in 1968. Her later books include* The House on Marshland *(1975), from which the following poem is taken;* The Triumph of Achilles *(1985);* The Wild Iris *(1992);* Vita Nova *(1999) and* Averno *(2006).*

*Glück's poetry has been widely anthologized and trans-lated.* Proofs and Theories: Essays on Poetry *(1995) is a collection of her literary criticism on Stanley Kunitz, T. S. Eliot, and other authors.*

### Gretel in Darkness                                    [1975]

This is the world we wanted.
All who would have seen us dead
are dead. I hear the witch's cry
break in the moonlight through a sheet
of sugar: God rewards.                                         5
Her tongue shrivels into gas . . . .

Now, far from women's arms
and memory of women, in our father's hut
we sleep, are never hungry.
Why do I not forget?                                          10
My father bars the door, bars harm
from this house, and it is years.

No one remembers. Even you, my brother,
summer afternoons you look at me as though
you meant to leave,                                           15
as though it never happened.
But I killed for you. I see armed firs,
the spires of that gleaming kiln—

Nights I turn to you to hold me
but you are not there.
Am I alone? Spies                                                    20
hiss in the stillness, Hansel,
we are there still and it is real, real,
that black forest and the fire in earnest.

Jennifer Anderson was assigned to write about this poem in an introduction
to literature course. Anderson started her work by copying the poem on a sheet
of paper and annotating it.

*Speaker?????*    (Gretel) in Darkness    — *Gretel and*
                                            *her brother*

This is the world (we) wanted.
All who would have seen us (dead) are (dead.)
I hear the witch's cry break in the moonlight
through a sheet of sugar: <u>God</u> rewards.  *Christian theme?*
Her tongue shrivels into gas. . . .
*Why*
*this space?*    Now, far from women's arms    —— *Women*
                                                  *(mother)*
and memory of women, in our father's hut        *vs.*
we sleep, are never hungry.                   —— *Father*

[Why do I not forget?]—————— *the Key Question*
My father (bars) the door, (bars) harm
                                        from this house, and it is years.
*The*
*speaker*    <u>No one remembers.</u> Even you, my brother,
*does*       summer afternoons <u>you look at me as though</u>
             <u>you meant to leave</u>, as though it never happened.
*intense,*   But I <u>killed</u> for you. I see armed firs,   *oven, furnace*
*direct*     the spires of that gleaming (kiln—)
*word*                                          *Hansel's separation /*
*choice*     Nights I turn to you to hold me      *distance from Gretel*
             but you are not there.—
                                   *compare with opening lines—*
*"S"*        Am I alone? Spies               *everything's not dead*
*sounds*     hiss in the stillness, Hansel,
             (we are there) still and it is (real,) (real,)
             that black forest and the fire in <u>earnest.</u>  *serious +*
                                                              *intense*

To follow up on these annotations and develop them, Anderson turned next
to her writing journal. She jotted down responses and ideas and her questions
about aspects of the poem and details of the language that intrigued and puzzled
her.

Here are the pages from Anderson's journal:

Great poem! Haunting, eerie. My favorite so far in the course.

Story of Hansel and Gretel—Look this up. Should I summarize the story in the paper?

Speaker—Gretel. Why *her*, and not Hansel? Not both of them as speakers?

"in darkness"—really in darkness, or is darkness a metaphor?

*Repetition* in the poem: dead/dead, bar/bar, real/real.

The tone of the opening stanza—scary, ominous. Darkness, dead.

The reference to the witch. "Shrivels into gas"—creepy detail.

But the witch has been defeated. Through the power of God? *Why is God mentioned* in this line?—not mentioned elsewhere.

Women (not mothers) seem the enemy in stanza two. (Odd that the second stanza is indented.) The *father* provides safety. But safety is not enough. Gretel cannot forget the past: the real enemy is not the witch or the mothers, but her memory.

She has to talk about her memory, her experiences. "No one remembers," but she *does*.

I think that this is a poem about Memory: "Why do I not forget?"

Gretel doesn't want her brother to forget. She reminds him.

"Killed"—such a strong word, very direct. *Gretel is angry with her brother;* she feels him pulling away from her.

Something disturbed, unnatural about the poem?—the detail about Gretel looking for her brother to hold her. But he is absent. Where is he?

Who are the "Spies"? Lots of "s" sounds in these lines—spies, hiss, stillness, Hansel, still.

She addresses him *by name*.

She cannot escape, maybe she doesn't want to escape. Note that Gretel is *describing her memories of what happened*—not a poem that *tells the story* of Hansel and Gretel. Glück is interested in how Gretel *remembers,* how she feels about remembering.

Anderson knew the main features of the Hansel and Gretel story—the brother and sister, their abandonment, their capture by a witch, and their escape. But she wanted to remind herself about the details, as her note to herself in her journal indicates.

As an experiment, Anderson went to Google and searched for "hansel and gretel." A number of the results looked promising, and she linked to this one:

Grimm's Fairy Tales—Hansel and Gretel
http://www.mordent.com/folktales/grimms/hng/hng.html

Anderson had not reread "Hansel and Gretel" since she was a child. Rereading it now was very helpful, for it clarified a number of important details in Glück's poem. It explained, for example, "the witch's cry" in the first stanza, which alludes to the witch's "horrible howl" when Gretel pushes her into the oven. It also fills out the reference to the "women" in the second stanza, who in the story include the children's cruel stepmother as well as the evil witch. Anderson could have prepared and written her paper without taking the time to check on the story, but it was better that she did.

Here is the essay that Jennifer Anderson wrote.

---

Anderson 1

Jennifer Anderson
Professor Washington
English 102
12 June 2010

A Memory Poem:<br>Louise Glück's "Gretel in Darkness"

Everyone knows the story of Hansel and Gretel, one of the best-known of Grimm's fairy tales. In her poem "Gretel in Darkness," Louise Glück takes for granted that we know the story—the brother and sister who are mistreated by their father and, especially, by their stepmother; their abandonment in a forest; their capture by a witch who lives in a house made of cakes and candy; the witch's plan to fatten them up (Hansel first) and then eat them; Gretel's killing of the witch by pushing her into an oven; and, finally, the children's discovery of the witch's jewels that makes them and their father (the stepmother has died) rich and happy at last. Glück's subject is not the story itself but, instead, Gretel's memories. "Gretel in Darkness" is a haunting poem about horrors that Gretel, Glück's speaker, cannot forget.

The poem takes place after the witch has been killed and Hansel and Gretel have returned to the safety of their father's cottage. Everything now should be fine, Gretel says: "This is the world we wanted." "God rewards": God has heard their prayers and saved them. But as if it were still present, Gretel hears "the witch's cry," the witch whom Gretel killed. And the image about the witch's death that she uses is graphic and disturbing: "Her tongue shrivels into gas. . . ." The witch was horrible, but this image is horrifying; it sticks in Gretel's mind, and the reader's too, like a shocking detail from a nightmare.

In a way the entire poem reports on a nightmare that Gretel is doomed to live in forever. "Why do I not forget?"—the key line in the poem, I think—really means that she knows she will always remember what happened to her and her brother. For Gretel this fairy tale does not have a happy ending.

Yet it does for her brother, or so it seems to Gretel. She resents Hansel's failure to remember as she does, and, with a vivid, direct choice of verb, she reminds him: "I killed for you." The nightmarish quality of Gretel's thoughts and feelings is shown again in the next lines, which once more make clear how much her past dominates the present:

> . . . I see armed firs,
>
>   the spires of that gleaming kiln—

Gretel is safe but threatened, sheltered at home but still in danger. She is caught by a terrifying and terrible past she cannot break free from. The repetitions—dead/dead, bars/bar, real/real—imply that she is trapped, not able to re-enter the present and look forward to the future. She turns to her brother for help, yet without finding the support she seeks:

> Nights I turn to you to hold me
>
>   but you are not there.

Hansel (who is only named once) is not there for Gretel, and at first I felt her hurt. But Glück is not meaning to criticize Hansel for his distance, his separation from his sister. Or if Glück is, she is balancing that against Gretel's absorption in the terror of her experiences. She feels that she and her brother are still in the middle of them.

As I thought further about this poem, I wondered: Strange as it sounds, maybe Gretel prefers the past to the present because the past was so real. Life is all too safe and comfortable now, while *then* everything, like the fire in the oven, was so earnest, that is, so serious and intense. It was not the world she wanted—who would want to be in that house of horrors! Even now her life is menaced, as those snaky "s" sounds in the middle of the final stanza suggest. But perhaps the frightful feelings, in their intensity, were (and still are) keener and deeper than anything that Gretel knew before, or knows now, in the secure world she lives in with her father and brother. She and her brother then were so absolutely close, as they are not now. Gretel cannot let go of her past, and she does not want to.

Anderson 3

Work Cited

Glück, Louise. "Gretel in Darkness." *An Introduction to Literature*. Ed.
Sylvan Barnet, William Burto, and William E. Cain. 16th ed.
New York: Longman, 2011. 693. Print.

**YOUR TURN**

1. Jennifer Anderson's instructor told the class that the essay should be "about 500 words." Anderson's paper is more than that—about 650 words. Do you think that she uses her space well? Could she have shortened the essay to bring it closer to the assigned length? If you had to suggest cuts, where would you propose to make them?

2. Does Anderson omit important details in the poem that you think she should have included in the paper? Explain why these elements should be part of her response.

3. Give Anderson's paper a grade, and in a paragraph written to her, highlight the strengths and limitations of this paper. Provide her, too, with one or two specific suggestions for improving her writing in the next paper.

# Annotation and Essay on Adrienne Rich's "Aunt Jennifer's Tigers"

Maria Fuentes, a first-year student, produced the following jottings, annotations, and essay concerning a poem that we print on page 641.

*odd–arouses interest*

### Aunt Jennifer's Tigers

Aunt Jennifer's tigers prance across a screen, Bright
topaz denizens of a world of green. They do not fear the men
beneath the tree; They pace in sleek chivalric certainty.??

*her work
embroidery?*

Aunt Jennifer's fingers fluttering through her wool Find
even the ivory needle hard to pull. The massive weight of Uncle's
wedding band Sits heavily upon Aunt Jennifer's hand.

*he tyrannized
over her*

When Aunt is dead, her terrified hands will
lie Still ringed with ordeals she was mastered by.
The tigers in the panel that she made
will go on prancing, proud and unafraid. *uncle?*

*contrast to
the prancing
tigers she
created*

*we are told
only that she
was oppressed
& that she
created a
lively work of
art That's
about all we
know of her.*

*in contrast to "terrified"
Aunt J. BUT She created these
"proud and unafraid" tigers.
Her vision of a better life?*

Maria Fuentes
Professor Johnston
English 1202
8 April 2010

Aunt Jennifer's Screen and Adrienne Rich's Poem

What especially pleases me in Adrienne Rich's "Aunt Jennifer's Tigers" is the combination of neat, tight, highly disciplined stanzas of four rhyming lines (like marching squadrons) with the explosive rebellious content of the poem. Somehow the message seems especially powerful *because* it is so tightly packed, because the form is so restrained.

The poem is, on the surface at least, about what the title says it is about, "Aunt Jennifer's Tigers." Aunt Jennifer has made a screen, in embroidery or needlepoint, showing tigers that "prance." Presumably Aunt Jennifer was a sweet old lady, but she has created a picture of enormous energy, expressing, through her work of art, her own repressed energy.

We learn in the second stanza that she was repressed by the man she was married to:

> The massive weight of Uncle's wedding band
> Sits heavily upon Aunt Jennifer's hand.

The wedding band for her, as for many women in the present as well as in the past, is like a heavy chain. Rich tells us that Aunt Jennifer was "terrified" and was "mastered," obviously by Uncle. Rich makes a pun on the word "ringed," but the joke is very bitter:

> When Aunt is dead, her terrified hands will lie
> Still ringed with ordeals she was mastered by.

And yet, Rich points out, this "terrified" woman created something beautiful, a picture of tigers who "go on prancing, proud and unafraid." Apparently Aunt Jennifer was able, despite being oppressed by Uncle, to make something that gives pleasure to a later generation—just as the poet, however unhappy she may be, produces a work of art that gives pleasure to those who later read it.

Aunt Jennifer's work of art shows, in the prancing tigers, an energy that she apparently felt and understood, but because of her husband and perhaps because of the period in which she lived, she could express herself only in a "ladylike" activity such as embroidering. Aunt Jennifer

was "mastered" (line 10), but she had nevertheless "made"
(line 11) something depicting creatures who are "proud and unafraid."
She was "terrified" (line 9), as many women were terrified by the
patriarchal society in which they lived (and still live), but in her art she
created an image of energy. Adrienne Rich, too, makes a work of art—a
highly patterned poem consisting of three rhymed quatrains—that is as
elegantly crafted as a work of embroidery. Rich speaks matter-of-factly
and in a disciplined way in her quatrains about Aunt Jennifer and her
tigers, but in this elegant poem she conveys energy and outrage on behalf
of her terrified aunt who could not openly protest against the role that
society had assigned to her.

Work Cited

Rich, Adrienne. "Aunt Jennifer's Tigers." *An Introduction to Literature*.
    Ed. Sylvan Barnet, William Burto, and William E. Cain. 16th ed.
    New York: Longman, 2011. 641. Print.

# An Essay on a Theme in Several Poems by One Poet

For a collection of poems by Emily Dickinson including the ones discussed in
the following essay, see pages 736–47.

Peter Gottsegen
Professor Laurey
English 150G
12 April 2010

### Religion and Religious Imagery in Emily Dickinson

Emily Dickinson was not a preacher but a poet, so if we read her
poetry about God we should not be surprised if we do not find a simple,

Gottsegen 2

consistent view or even a clear development from one view—for instance, belief—to another—for instance, loss of faith. Rather, judging from some examples of her poetry, she explored various views, and we should not try to convert this variety into unity.

We can begin by looking at extreme views, first two poems of faith, and then a poem of doubt. One of the poems of faith, "Papa above!" (737), begins with a childlike or almost playful version of the Lord's Prayer. (In Matthew 6.9 Jesus begins a prayer by saying, "Our father who art in heaven.") I think this poem says that God will see to it that even a mouse or rat will get into heaven and will remain there for eternity. But Dickinson's God is not always concerned for all of the creatures of the world. In another poem that expresses belief in the existence of God, "Apparently with no surprise" (744), Dickinson describes the frost as beheading a flower—that is, beauty perishes—and she goes on to make the point that this occurs under the eyes of "an Approving God." Here she seems to be saying that evil takes place, and God approves of it. It is important to realize that in this poem Dickinson still says that God exists, even if he is indifferent to suffering.

In another poem, "Those—dying, then" (743), Dickinson expresses doubt that God exists. In olden days, she says, people mistakenly thought that God would protect them, but now, she says, "God cannot be found." She uses a particularly terrifying image to convey the loss of God. In the past, Dickinson says, the faithful went to "God's Right Hand," but, she goes on to say, "The Hand is amputated now. . . ." The faith in God that earlier people had was an illusion, but it was something, and it was "better" than the nothingness we now experience. This nothingness, or something not much more than nothingness, is the subject of "I heard a Fly buzz—when I died" (739). In this poem, the speaker expects "the King" (God) to appear to her as she dies, but all she sees is a fly, and then she hears its buzz. God ("the King") never appears.

Even these few poems show that Dickinson held a variety of views about God and religion, and it is difficult or perhaps impossible for us to say exactly what her religious beliefs were. But what is certain is that religious ideas were so important to her, so much a part of her mind, that even when she was not explicitly writing about the existence of a benevolent God or the absence of God, she used religious imagery—for instance, to describe impressive things in the natural world around her.

In "These are the days when Birds come back" (736), she talks about what we call Indian summer, fall days that are like summer days. But the poem is filled with religious words: "belief," "Sacrament," "Communion," "consecrated bread," "immoral wine." The fifth stanza goes like this:

> Oh Sacrament of summer days,
>
> Oh Last Communion in the Haze—
>
> Permit a child to join.

I don't think Dickinson is really talking about traditional religion here. Instead, she is using religious imagery to talk about a particular precious moment in the seasons. As a second example of her use of religious imagery in a poem that is about nature and not about God, we might look at "There's a certain Slant of light" (737). In this poem she says that on "Winter Afternoons" this particular light has "the Heft / Of Cathedral Tunes." That is, the wintry light has the solidity, the feel, the "heft" of religious music. When we see this light, Dickinson says, we are moved in a way that we are moved by music in church. She is not saying anything here about whether God is benevolent or not, or whether he exists or not. Rather, she is drawing on experiences in church—probably experiences shared by many people even today—to help us to see nature more effectively.

Speaking as someone who was brought up with traditional religious beliefs but who does not go to church now, I can say that Dickinson effectively represents the ideas of a believer and also of a non-believer. But what I think is especially impressive is that she sees that someone who no longer is a believer can't help but still think in religious terms when he or she sees something exceptionally beautiful, for instance on a winter day "a certain Slant of light."

## Works Cited

Barnet, Sylvan, William Burto, and William E. Cain, eds. *An Introduction to Literature*. 16th ed. New York: Longman, 2011. Print.

Dickinson, Emily. "Apparently with no surprise." Barnet, Burto, and Cain 744.

Gottsegen 5

---. "I heard a Fly buzz—when I died." Barnet, Burto, and Cain 739.

---. "Papa above!" Barnet, Burto, and Cain 737.

---. "There's a certain Slant of light." Barnet, Burto, and Cain 737.

---. "These are the days when Birds come back." Barnet, Burto, and Cain 736.

---. "Those—dying, then." Barnet, Burto, and Cain 743.

**YOUR TURN**

1. In this essay Gottsegen comments on the poems "Papa above!," "Apparently with no surprise," "Those—dying, then," "I heard a Fly buzz—when I died," "These are the days when Birds come back," and "There's a certain Slant of light." Read or reread each of these poems to see if you agree with Gottsegen's interpretations.
2. Are there other poems by Dickinson that you think Gottsegen could have used with better effect than poems he did use? Explain.
3. Reread the concluding paragraph. Do you think it is effective? Explain.

## An Essay on the Structure of a Poem

The arrangement of its parts, the organization of an entire poem, is its **structure.** Sometimes a poem is divided into blocks of, say, four lines each, but even when the poem is printed as a solid block, it probably has some principle of organization—for example, from sorrow in the first two lines to joy in the next two, or from a question in the first three lines to an answer in the last line.

Consider this short poem by an English poet of the seventeenth century.

## ROBERT HERRICK

*For a biographical note, see page 605.*

### *Upon Julia's Clothes*

Whenas in silks my Julia goes,
Then, then, methinks, how sweetly flows
That liquefaction of her clothes.

Next, when I cast mine eyes, and see
That brave° vibration, each way free,                              5
O how that glittering taketh me!

David Thurston, a student, began thinking about this poem by copying it, double-spaced, and by making the following notes on his copy.

---

5 **Brave** splendid.

Upon Julia's Clothes

Whenas in silks (my Julia) goes, ——————————— *cool tone?*

3 { Then, then, methinks, how sweetly flows

That liquefaction of her clothes. ——————— *"Then, then"—more excited? almost at a loss for words?*

Next, when I cast mine eyes, and see

3 { That brave vibration, each way free, ——————— *free to do what? free from what?*

O how that glittering taketh me!

*emotional?*

Thurston got further ideas by thinking about several of the questions that we have given earlier in this chapter, such as:

Does the poem proceed in a straightforward way, or at some point or points does the speaker reverse course, altering his or her tone or perception?

With various questions in mind, Thurston was stimulated to see if Herrick's poem has a reversal or change and, if so, how it is related to the structure. After rereading the poem several times, thinking about it in the light of these questions and perhaps others, he produced the following notes:

Two stanzas, each of three lines, with the same structure

Basic structure of 1st stanza: When X (one line), then Y (Two lines)

Basic structure of second stanza: Next (one line), then Z (two lines)

When he marked the text after reading the poem a few times, he noticed that the last line—an exclamation of delight ("O, how that glittering taketh me")—is much more personal than the rest of the poem. A little further thought enabled him to refine this last perception:

Although the pattern of stanzas is repeated, the somewhat analytic, detached tone of the beginning ("Whenas," "Then," "Next") changes to an open, enthusiastic confession of delight in what the poet sees.

Further thinking led to this:

Although the title is "Upon Julia's Clothes," and the first five lines describe Julia's silken dress, the poem finally is not only about Julia's clothing but about the effect of Julia (moving in silk that liquefies or seems to become a liquid) on the poet.

This is a nice observation, but when Thurston looked again at the poem the next day and started to write about it, he found that he was able to refine his observation.

Even at the beginning, the speaker is not entirely detached, for he speaks of "*my* Julia."

In writing about Herrick's "Upon Julia's Clothes," Thurston reported, the thoughts did not come quickly or neatly. After two or three thoughts, he started to write. Only after drafting a paragraph and rereading the poem did he notice that the personal element appears not only in the last line ("taketh *me*") but even in the first line ("*my* Julia"). In short, for almost all of us, the only way to get to a good final essay is to read, to think, to jot down ideas, to write a draft, and to revise and revise again. Having gone through such processes, David Thurston came up with the following excellent essay.

By the way, Thurston did not hit on the final version of his title until shortly before he typed his final version. His preliminary title was

Structure and Personality in

Herrick's "Upon Julia's Clothes"

That's a bit heavy-handed, but at least it is focused, as opposed to such an uninformative title as "On a poem." He soon revised his tentative title to

Julia, Julia's Clothing, and Julia's Poet

That's a good title: It is neat, and it is appropriate; it moves (as the poem and the essay do) from Julia and her clothing to the poet. It doesn't tell the reader exactly what the essay will be about, and three uses of Julia may be one too many, but it does stimulate the reader's interest. The essayist's final title, however, is even better:

Herrick's Julia, Julia's Herrick

Again, it is neat (the balanced structure, and structure is part of the essay's topic), less repetitive, and it moves (as the poem itself moves) from Julia to the poet.

---

Thurston 1

David Thurston

Professor James

English 102

31 May 2010

Herrick's Julia, Julia's Herrick

Robert Herrick's "Upon Julia's Clothes" begins as a description of Julia's clothing and ends as an expression of the poet's response not just to Julia's clothing but to Julia herself. Despite the apparently objective or detached tone of the first stanza and the first two lines of the second stanza, the poem finally conveys a strong sense of the speaker's excitement.

The first stanza seems to say, "Whenas" X (one line), "Then" Y (two lines). The second stanza repeats this basic structure of one line of assertion and two lines describing the consequence: "Next" (one line), "then" (two lines). But the logic or coolness of "Whenas," "Then," and "Next," and of such rather scientific language as *liquefaction* (a more technical-sounding word than "melting") and *vibration* is undercut by the breathlessness or excitement of "Then, then" (that is very different from a simple "Then"). It is also worth mentioning that although there is a personal rather than a fully detached note even in the first line, in *"my Julia,"* this expression scarcely reveals much feeling. In fact, it reveals a touch of male chauvinism, a suggestion that the woman is a possession of the speaker's. Not until the last line does the speaker reveal that, far from Julia's being his possession, he is possessed by Julia: "O how that glittering taketh me!" If he begins coolly, objectively, and somewhat complacently and uses a structure that suggests a somewhat detached mind, in the exclamatory "O" he nevertheless at last confesses (to our delight) that he is enraptured by Julia.

### Work Cited

Herrick, Robert. "Upon Julia's Clothes." *An Introduction to Literature*. Ed. Sylvan Barnet, William Burto, and William E. Cain. 16th ed. New York: Longman, 2011. 703. Print.

Other things might be said about this poem. For instance, the writer says nothing about the changes in the meter and their possible value in the poem. Nor does he say anything about the sounds of any of the words (he might have commented on the long vowels in "sweetly flows" and shown how the effect would have been different if instead of "sweetly flows" Herrick had written "swiftly flits"). But such topics might be material for another essay. Furthermore, another reader might have found the poem less charming—even offensive in its exclusive concern with Julia's appearance and its utter neglect of her mind. Still, this essay is, in itself, an interesting and perceptive discussion of the way the poet used a repeated structure to set forth a miniature drama in which observation is, at the end, replaced by emotion.

## An Essay on Metrics

Here is an excellent analysis by a student, Julia Jeffords, of a poem by A. E. Housman that appears on page 663. Notice that she quotes the poem and indicates the metrical pattern and that she proceeds chiefly by explaining the effect of the variations or departures from the norm in the order in which they occur.

Notice, too, that although it is a good idea to announce your thesis early— that is, in the first paragraph—this writer does *not* say, "This paper will show that Housman effectively uses rhythm to support his ideas" or some such thing. It's sufficient that the writer announces her topic in the title and again, in slightly different words, in the first sentence (the paper will "analyze the effects of sounds and rhythms in Housman's 'Eight O'Clock'"). We know where we will be going, and we read even with a bit of suspense, looking to see what the analysis will produce.

---

Jeffords 1

Julia Jeffords

Professor Rozan

English 2

15 March 2010

Sound and Sense in A. E. Housman's "Eight O'Clock"

Before trying to analyze the effects of sounds and rhythms in A. E. Housman's "Eight O'Clock" (1922) it will be useful to quote the poem and to indicate which syllables are stressed and which are unstressed. It must be understood, however, that the following scansion is relatively crude, because it falsely suggests that all stressed syllables (marked /) are equally stressed, but of course they are not: In reading the poem aloud, one would stress some of them relatively heavily, and one would stress others only a trifle more than the unstressed syllables. It should be understood, too, that in the discussion that follows the poem some other possible scansions will be proposed.

He stood,|and heard|the steeple

Sprinkle|the quar|ters on|the mor|ning town.

One, two,|three, four,|to mar|ket-place| and people

It tossed|them down.

Strapped, noosed,|nighing|his hour.

He stood|and coun|ted them|and cursed|his luck;
And then|the clock|collec|ted in|the tower
Its strength,|and struck.

As the first line of the second stanza makes especially clear, the
poem is about a hanging at eight o'clock, according to the title.
Housman could have written about the man's thoughts on the justice
or injustice of his fate, or about the reasons for the execution, but he
did not. Except for the second line of the second stanza—"He stood
and counted them and cursed his luck"—he seems to tell us little
about the man's thoughts. But the poem is not merely a narrative
of an event; the sound effects in the poem help to convey an idea as
well as a story.

The first line establishes an iambic pattern. The second line begins
with a trochee ("Sprinkle"), not an iamb, and later in the line possibly
"on" should not be stressed even though I marked it with a stress and
made it part of an iambic foot, but still the line is mainly iambic. The
poem so far is a fairly jingling description of someone's hearing the
church clock chiming at each quarter of the hour. Certainly, even though
the second line begins with a stress, there is nothing threatening in
"Sprinkle," a word in which we almost hear a tinkle.

But the second half of the first stanza surprises us and maybe even
jolts us. In "One, two, three, four" we get four consecutive heavy stresses.
These stresses are especially emphatic because there is a pause, indicated
by a comma, after each of them. Time is not just passing to the chimes of
a clock: This is a countdown, and we sense that it may lead to something
significant. Moreover, the third line, which is longer than the two
previous lines, does not end with a pause. This long line (eleven syllables)
runs on into the next line, almost as though once the countdown has
begun there is no stopping it. But then we do stop suddenly, because the
last line of the stanza has only four syllables—far fewer than we would
have expected. In other words, this line stops unexpectedly because it has
only two feet. The first line had three feet, and the second and third lines
had five feet. Furthermore, this short, final line of the stanza ends with a
heavy stress in contrast to the previous line, which ends with an
unstressed syllable, "people." As we will see, the sudden stopping at the
end is a sort of preview of a life cut short. Perhaps it is also a preview of a

man dropping through a trapdoor and then suddenly stopping when the slack in the hangman's rope has been taken up.

In the first line of the second stanza the situation is made clear, and it is also made emphatic by three consecutive stresses: "Strápped, noósed, nig̈hiṅg his hŏur." The pauses before the first three stresses make the words especially emphatic. And though I have marked the first two words of the next line "Hĕ stoód," possibly "He" should be stressed too. In any case even if "He" is not heavily stressed, it is certainly stressed more than the other unstressed syllables, "and," "-ed" (in "counted"), and "his." Similarly in the third line of the stanza an effective reading might even stress the first word as well as the second, thus: "Aṅd thén." And although normal speech would stress only the second syllable in "coĺlécted̆," in this poem the word appears after "clock," and so one must pause after the *k* sound in "clock" (one simply can't say "clock collected" without pausing briefly between the two words), and the effect is to put more than usual stress on the first syllable, almost turning it into "cóllected̆." And so this line can reasonably be scanned like this:

> Aṅd thén thĕ cloćk coĺlécted̆ iṅ thĕ tóweř

And again the third line of the stanza runs over into the fourth, propelling us onward. The final line surely begins with a stress, even though "Its" is not a word usually stressed, and so in the final line we begin with two strong stresses, "Itś stréngth." This line, like the last line of the first stanza, is unusually short, and it, too, ends with a heavy stress. The total effect, then, of the last two lines of this stanza is of a clock striking, not just sprinkling music but forcefully and emphatically and decisively striking. The pause after "strength" is almost like the suspenseful pause of a man's collecting his strength before he strikes a blow, and that is what the clock does:

> Aṅd thén thĕ cloćk coĺlécted̆ iṅ thĕ tóweř
> Itś streṅgth aṅd strúck.

If "clock collected" has in its *k* sounds a sort of ticktock effect, the clock at the end shows its force, for when it strikes the hour, the man dies.

I said near the beginning of this essay that Housman did not write about the man's thoughts about the justice or injustice of the sentence, and I think this is more or less true, but if we take into

Jeffords 4

account the sound effects in the poem we can see that in part the poem is about the man's thoughts: He sees himself as the victim not only of his "luck" but of this machine, this ticking, unstoppable contraption that strikes not only the hours but a man's life.

---

Jeffords 5

Work Cited

Housman, A. E. "Eight O'Clock." *An Introduction to Literature*. Ed. Sylvan Barnet, William Burto, and William E. Cain. 16th ed. New York: Longman, 2011. 663. Print.

## A Brief Overview of the Essay

- The *title* suggests the writer's topic, and the first sentence of the *opening paragraph* establishes it without doubt: "the effects of sounds and rhythms" in a particular poem. This paragraph also includes some sentences whereby the author quite reasonably indicates her awareness that not everyone will scan the poem exactly as she does. Willingness to concede differences of opinion is a good argumentative strategy; it establishes the reader as a person who is open-minded.
- Jeffords provides the reader with the *text of the poem,* marked with her sense of the stresses. Don't expect your reader to read your paper and also to be thumbing through a book to find the poem.
- The *organization* is simple but adequate. Jeffords begins at the beginning and moves through the poem to its end.
- In her *final paragraph* Jeffords interestingly modifies an assertion she made earlier, that Housman "did not write about the man's thoughts about the justice or injustice of the sentence." She now shows that, in a way, the metrical effects—her chief topic—do tell us something about the victim's thoughts. This modification is not a contradiction. If indeed she now sees that Housman did write about these topics, she of course should have revised the earlier passage. But the earlier passage remains true, at least in a broad sense. Housman did not write about the victim's thoughts about justice. What Jeffords is saying, at the end of her essay, is that the metrical effects *do* in some degree get us into the mind of the victim, helping us to see him as someone struck down by an implacable machine.

# Two Essays, for Evaluation, on Robert Frost's "Stopping by Woods on a Snowy Evening"

Here are the annotations that a student, Darrel MacDonald, jotted down, followed by the final version of the essay that he developed from the annotations.

Whose woods these are I think I know.
His house is in the village, though;

*afraid of being seen? Why? Because on private property? Or because not going about his business?*

He will not see me stopping here
To watch his woods fill up with snow.

My little horse must think it queer   *odd? gay?*
To stop without a farmhouse near
Between the woods and frozen lake
The darkest evening of the year.

He gives his harness bells a shake    *What is the*
To ask if there is some mistake.      *mistake? Is it a*
The only other sound's the sweep      *mistake to enjoy*
Of easy wind and downy flake.         *nature?*

The woods are lovely dark and deep,   *a women's*
But I have promises to keep,          *word? But isn't the*

*Why twice? Is he emphatically telling himself to get moving?*

And miles to go before I sleep,       *speaker a man? May*
And miles to go before I sleep.       *be a woman?*

*apparently he does not stay to see the "woods fill up with snow."*

Now for the essay that MacDonald developed out of these annotations.

Darrel MacDonald

Professor Lui

English 102

5 May 2010

Stopping by Woods—and Going On

Robert Frost's "Stopping by Woods on a Snowy Evening" is about what the title says it is. It is also about something more than the title says.

When I say it is about what the title says, I mean that the poem really does give us the thoughts of a person who pauses (that is, a person who is "stopping") by woods on a snowy evening. (This person probably is a man, since Robert Frost wrote the poem and nothing in the poem clearly indicates that the speaker is not a man. But, and this point will be important, the speaker perhaps feels that he is not a very masculine man. As we will see, the word "queer" appears in the poem, and, also, the speaker uses the word "lovely," which sounds more like the word a woman would use than a man.) In line 3 the speaker says he is "stopping here," and it is clear that "here" is by woods, since "woods" is mentioned not only in the title but also in the first line of the poem, and again in the second stanza, and still again in the last stanza. It is equally clear that, as the title says, there is snow, and that the time is evening. The speaker mentions "snow" and "downy flake," and he says this is "The darkest evening of the year."

But in what sense is the poem about *more* than the title? The title does not tell us anything about the man who is "stopping by woods," but the poem—the man's meditation—tells us a lot about him. In the first stanza he reveals that he is uneasy at the thought that the owner of the woods may see him stopping by the woods. Maybe he is uneasy because he is trespassing, but the poem does not actually say that he has illegally entered someone else's property. More likely, he feels uneasy, almost ashamed, of watching the "woods fill up with snow." That is, he would not want anyone to see that he is enjoying a beautiful aspect of nature and is not hurrying about whatever his real business is in thrifty Yankee style.

The second stanza gives more evidence that he feels guilty about enjoying beauty. He feels so guilty that he even thinks the horse thinks there is something odd about him. In fact, he says that the horse thinks he is "queer," which of course may just mean odd, but also (as is shown by *The American Heritage Dictionary*) it can mean "gay," "homosexual." A real man, he sort of suggests, wouldn't spend time looking at snow in the woods.

So far, then, the speaker in two ways has indicated that he feels insecure, though perhaps he does not realize that he has given himself away. First, he expresses uneasiness that someone might see him watching the woods fill up with snow. Second, he expresses uneasiness when he suggests that even the horse thinks he is strange, maybe even "queer" or unmanly, or at least unbusinesslike. And so in the last stanza, even though he finds the woods beautiful, he decides *not* to stop and to see the woods fill up with snow. And his description of the woods as "lovely"—a woman's word—sounds as though he may be something less than a he-man. He seems to feel ashamed of himself for enjoying the sight of the snowy woods and for seeing them as "lovely," and so he tells himself that he has spent enough time looking at the woods and that he must go on about his business. In fact, he tells himself *twice* that he has business to attend to. Why? Perhaps he is insisting too much. Just as we saw that he was excessively nervous in the first stanza, afraid that someone might see him trespassing and enjoying the beautiful spectacle, now at the end he is again afraid that someone might see him loitering, and so he very firmly, using repetition as a form of emphasis, tries to reassure himself that he is not too much attracted by beauty and is a man of business who keeps his promises.

Frost gives us, then, a man who indeed is seen "stopping by woods on a snowy evening," but a man who, afraid of what society will think of him, is also afraid to "stop" long enough to fully enjoy the sight that attracts him because he is driven by a sense that he may be seen to be trespassing and also may be thought to be unmanly. So after only a brief stop in the woods he forces himself to go on, a victim (though he probably doesn't know it) of the work ethic and of an over-simple idea of manliness.

MacDonald 3

Work Cited

Frost, Robert. "Stopping by Woods on a Snowy Evening." *An Introduction to Literature*. Ed. Sylvan Barnet, William Burto, and William E. Cain. 16th ed. New York: Longman, 2011. 755. Print.

**YOUR TURN**

1. In a sentence or two state the thesis of the essay.
2. Is the thesis adequately supported? Explain, pointing out strengths, if any, and weaknesses, if any.
3. Do you find the organization satisfactory? Why, or why not?
4. Do you find the title and the opening paragraph of interest? If not, how might you improve them?
5. Given the thesis and the development of it, is the final paragraph satisfactory? Why, or why not?
6. If you think that, on the whole, the essay is effectively written, take two or three sentences and explain what their strengths are. If you think that, on the whole, the writing could be more effective, take two or three sentences and revise them into more effective sentences. (It's not a matter of agreeing or of disagreeing with the argument; we are talking chiefly about style.)

The second student, Sara Fong, kept a journal. We give an entry from her journal concerning Frost's poem and then the final version of her essay.

> I think that when the class talked about "the death wish" in "Stopping by Woods," they were on to something, but they went too far. It's not really a "death wish." The poet wants to lose himself, so to speak, by merging himself with the woods ("the woods are lovely, dark and deep"), or maybe with the soft white snow ("downy flake"), but that's not really the same as saying he wishes for death. Still, the beauty of the woods—we might say the world of peaceful solitude—is set against the world of the living, the world of "promises" to other humans.
>
> We have already studied short stories this term, and I think it is a good idea to see this poem as a very short short story. As I see it, the plot has three stages: (1) the character (the poet) has fairly ordinary thoughts as he looks at the wood (he thinks of the person who owns it and of the owner's house in the village), but soon he begins to feel that there is something special, something odd ("queer") in looking at the woods on what is, in fact, a special day ("The darkest evening of the year"). Then (2) he seems to get almost fully caught up

with (or drawn in by) the beauty of the scene ("easy wind and downy flake," "The woods are lovely, dark and deep"), and then, finally, (3) he shakes off the pull of nature, the appeal of nature that has almost made him forget everything else.

I'm not so sure, come to think of it, that at the very end he does completely reject the impulse to give himself up to nature. He repeats the last line ("And miles to go before I sleep, / And miles to go before I sleep"), and it seems to me that maybe this repetition is sort of hypnotic, almost as though he is drowsing off. I *feel* this, and when I read the lines aloud I can make them sound almost as though the speaker is drowsing off, but I'm not really sure that I'm right. After all, I can also read them aloud so they sound sort of perky or chipper, with a sense of "Well, I've put that behind me." I wonder if there is any way of deciding exactly how the last two lines should be read.

Now for Sara Fong's essay. You'll notice that it draws heavily on her journal, but it differs in two important ways. First, whereas in the journal she saw the story as having three stages, in the final essay she sees four stages. (What in the journal is said to be the first stage of the poem, in the essay becomes two stages.) Second, you'll notice that the point made in the last paragraph of the journal is not included in the essay. Why? Here are three possibilities: (1) Fong came to feel that the point was not sound; (2) she came to feel that the point was sound but not worth making; (3) she came to feel that the point, though interesting and sound and worth making, required more space than was available. It was, so to speak, the material for a different paper. Doubtless you can think of other reasons why Fong omitted the point in the final paper.

---

Fong 1

Sara Fong

Professor Nagle

English 1204

5 April 2010

"Stopping by Woods on a Snowy Evening"

as a Short Story

Robert Frost's "Stopping by Woods on a Snowy Evening" can be read as a poem about a man who pauses to observe the beauty of nature, and it can also be read as a poem about a man with a death wish, a man who seems to long to give himself up completely to nature and thus escape his responsibilities as a citizen. Much depends, apparently, on what a reader wants to emphasize. For instance, a reader can emphasize especially appealing lines about the beauty of nature: "The only other

## Work Cited

Frost, Robert. "Stopping by Woods on a Snowy Evening." *An Introduction to Literature.* Ed. Sylvan Barnet, William Burto, and William E. Cain. 16th ed. New York: Longman, 2011. 755. Print.

**YOUR TURN**

We can ask of this essay the same questions we asked of the previous essay.

1. In a sentence or two state the thesis of the essay.
2. Is the thesis adequately supported? Explain, pointing out strengths, if any, and weaknesses, if any.
3. Do you find the organization satisfactory? Why, or why not?
4. Do you find the title and the opening paragraph of interest? If not, how might you improve them?
5. Given the thesis and the development of it, is the final paragraph satisfactory? Why, or why not?

# 25

# Poets at Work

When we read a poem aloud, whether an anonymous nursery rhyme such as "Jack and Jill went up the hill" or a work by one of the great names, the words seem so right, so inevitable, that it is hard to believe they did not flow easily. Reading, say, Keats's "On First Looking into Chapman's Homer" (page 622), we may think that he must have sat down and simply let the words stream from his pen. And certainly Keats himself emphasized spontaneity: In a letter he says, "If poetry comes not as naturally as leaves to a tree it had better not come at all." Yet Keats's manuscripts indicated that he revised his work heavily, so heavily that some of the manuscripts are almost indecipherable. Probably William Butler Yeats was speaking for all poets when he said (in a poem called "Adam's Curse") that a poem must seem spontaneous but is the result of hard work:

> A line will take us hours maybe;
> Yet if it does not seem a moment's thought,
> Our stitching and unstitching has been naught.

In this chapter we give the following material:

1. Two versions of a poem by Walt Whitman.
2. Two versions of a poem by Cathy Song, introduced by her comments.
3. Three versions of a poem by Yeats.

## WALT WHITMAN

*For a biographical note, see page 633.*

In the third edition of *Leaves of Grass* (1860) Whitman added two groups of poems, one called "Children of Adam" and the other (named for an aromatic grass that grows near ponds and swamps) called "Calamus." "Children of Adam" celebrates heterosexual relations, whereas "Calamus" celebrates what Whitman called "manly love." Although many of the "Calamus" poems seem clearly homosexual, perhaps the very fact that Whitman published them made them seem relatively innocent; in any case, those nineteenth-century critics who condemned Whitman for the sexuality of his writing concentrated on the poems in "Children of Adam."

Manuscript of Walt Whitman's "Once I Passed Through a Populous City" in *Leaves of Grass*, Walt Whitman, MSS 3829, Clifton Waller Barrett Library of American Literature, Special Collections, University of Virginia Library. Used by permission.

   We give here the 1860 manuscript of the poem "Once I Passed Through a Populous City," included in the "Enfans d'Adam" (Children of Adam) section of *Leaves of Grass* (1860 ed.). The extensive markings on this page, some of them in dark ink and others in light pencil, show that Whitman revised this poem carefully. Notice, for example, that Whitman wrote and crossed out both "great" and "populous" and then seemed to settle on the word "celebrated," only to write (barely visible in the upper right corner) "populous" again, which became his final choice for the phrase "a populous city." Note, too, the changes in gender from "only a man" and "that youth" (crossed out) and "one rude and ignorant man" to—in the published poem—"that woman" and "she holds me."

## Enfans d'Adam, number 9 [1860]

[*Leaves of Grass*, 1860 edition]

Once, I passed through a populous city, imprinting my brain, for
　　future use, with its shows, architecture, customs, and traditions;
Yet now, of all that city, I remember only a woman I casually met
　　there, who detained me for love of me,
Day by day and night by night we were together,—
　　All else has long been forgotten by me,
I remember, I say only that woman who passionately clung to me,
Again we wander—we love—we separate again,
Again she holds me by the hand—I must not go!
I see her close beside me, with silent lips, sad and tremulous.

# CATHY SONG

*Cathy Song, born in Honolulu in 1955 of a Chinese-American mother and a Korean-American father, holds a bachelor's degree from Wellesley College and a master's degree in creative writing from Boston University. The author of three books of poems, she won the Yale Series of Younger Poets award for* Picture Bride *(1983), her first book. She has also won the Hawaii Award for Literature and the Shelley Memorial Award from the Poetry Society of America. Song's recent books include* The Land of Bliss *(2001) and* Cloud Moving Hands *(2007).*

Here we print a draft of an untitled poem and the final version, now titled "Out of Our Hands." Ms. Song's comment on the origins of the poem follow:

　　"Out of Our Hands" was written for the poet Wing Tek Lum. Long before Wing Tek and I became friends, I had already encountered his work. The poem is informed by our friendship; my abiding respect for the poet is deepened by my affection for the man. Knowing the reality of his warm humanity allowed me to imagine the poem in a larger context—what I had felt in his poems was present and true—and in a sense, when I first encountered his work, I was ready to receive the "seeds of a language / I needed to know." I was ready for this poet who had something to teach me.

　　The sense of magic and transformation is alive and well in the poem because his poems, his presence allowed that to happen with me. The images of birds and flight, children and language have everything to do with the way gifts are given and received—serendipitous and yet, there are no coincidences. When a poem is written there is someone out there waiting to read it, to have the gift descend, touch you like a leaf, a feather, a letter written just for you.

Cathy Song's draft for "Out of Our Hands." ("Out of Our Hands" by Cathy Song. Draft is reprinted with permission of the author.)

## *Out of Our Hands*                                        [1994]

### *—for Wing Tek Lum*

Out of a hat
on a piece of paper
someone once gave me your name.

Your name flew
out of my hand,                                                    5
the black letters
dismantling the air
above the school.
I watched the letters

form the bird                                                      10
seeds of a language
I needed to know,

a language borrowed
from the children I taught
who shivered in borrowed coats.                                    15

Toward evening they scattered
outside the school,
red-bricked and torn

on the edge of Chinatown.
I watched them disappear          20
into their lives,

undisciplined like starlings,
they disappeared
in the broken shoes of the wind.

One day your name                 25
came back
in a poem you were

writing in another city,
a poem you were determined
to write for the rest of your life.   30

The poem a subversive act.
The poem about being Chinese,
skin the glorious color of chicken fat.

# WILLIAM BUTLER YEATS

## *"Leda and the Swan" (Three Versions)*

*William Butler Yeats (1865–1939) was born in Dublin, Ireland. The young Yeats was much interested in highly lyrical, romantic poetry, often drawing on Irish mythology. The later poems, from about 1910 (and especially after Yeats met Ezra Pound in 1911), are often more colloquial. Although these later poems often employ mythological references, too, they seem more down-to-earth. Yeats was awarded the Nobel Prize in Literature in 1923.*

According to Greek mythology, Zeus fell in love with Leda, disguised himself as a swan, and ravished her. Among the offspring of this union were Helen and Clytemnestra. Paris abducted Helen, causing the Greeks to raze Troy; Clytemnestra, wife of Agamemnon, murdered her husband on his triumphant return to Greece. Yeats saw political significance in the myth of beauty and war engendered by a god; but, as he tells us, when he was composing "Leda and the Swan" the political significance evaporated:

> After the individualistic, demagogic movements, founded by Hobbes and popularized by the Encyclopaedists and the French Revolution, we have a soil so exhausted that it cannot grow that crop again for centuries. Then I thought "Nothing is now possible but some movement, or birth from above, preceded by some violent annunciation." My fancy began to play with "Leda and the Swan" for metaphor, and I began this

poem, but as I wrote, bird and lady took such possession of the scene that all politics went out of it.

The first version of the poem, titled "Annunciation," is from a manuscript dated 18 September 1923—"annunciation" is the act of announcing or of being announced, and, more specifically, it refers to the angel Gabriel's announcement of the Incarnation to the Virgin Mary, in Luke 1.26–38; the second version was printed in a magazine in June 1924; the third version, first published in his *Collected Poems* of 1933, is Yeats's final one. But this third version had been almost fully achieved by 1925; the 1933 version differs from the 1925 version only in two punctuation marks: The question marks at the ends of lines 6 and 8 in the latest version were, in 1925, respectively, a comma and a semicolon.

## *Annunciation*

[1923]

Now can the swooping Godhead have his will
Yet hovers, though her helpless thighs are pressed
By the webbed toes; and that all powerful bill
Has suddenly bowed her face upon his breast,
How can those terrified vague fingers push                    5
The feathered glory from her loosening thighs?

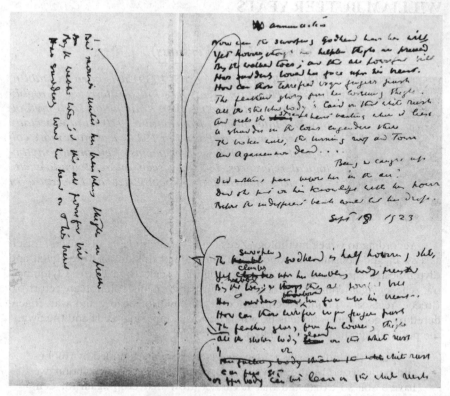

William Butler Yeats's first drafts of "Leda and the Swan," 1923.

All the stretched body's laid on that white rush
And feels the strange heart beating where it lies
A shudder in the loins engenders there
The broken wall, the burning roof and tower                    10
And Agamemnon dead . . .
                Being so caught up
Did nothing pass before her in the air?
Did she put on his knowledge with his power
Before the indifferent beak could let her drop.                15

## Leda and the Swan                                        [1924]

A rush, a sudden wheel, and hovering still
The bird descends, and her frail thighs are pressed
By the webbed toes, and that all-powerful bill
Has laid her helpless face upon his breast.
How can those terrified vague fingers push                     5
The feathered glory from her loosening thighs!
All the stretched body's laid on the white rush
And feels the strange heart beating where it lies;
A shudder in the loins engenders there
The broken wall, the burning roof and tower                    10
And Agamemnon dead.
                Being so caught up,
So mastered by the brute blood of the air,
Did she put on his knowledge with his power
Before the indifferent beak could let her drop?               15

## Leda and the Swan                                        [1933]

A sudden blow: the great wings beating still
Above the staggering girl, her thighs caressed
By the dark webs, her nape caught in his bill,
He holds her helpless breast upon his breast.

How can those terrified vague fingers push                     5
The feathered glory from her loosening thighs?
And how can body, laid in that white rush,
But feel the strange heart beating where it lies?

A shudder in the loins engenders there
The broken wall, the burning roof and tower                    10
And Agamemnon dead.
                Being so caught up,
So mastered by the brute blood of the air,
Did she put on his knowledge with his power
Before the indifferent beak could let her drop?               15

# 26

# Variations on Themes:
# Poems and Paintings

## Writing About Poems and Paintings

Are there, one may ask, significant correspondences among the arts? If we talk about *rhythm* in a painting, are we talking about a quality similar to *rhythm* in a poem? Are the painter's colors comparable to the poet's images? Does it make sense to say, as the German writer Johann Wolfgang von Goethe (1749–1832) said, that architecture is frozen music? Or to call architecture "music in space"? Many artists of one sort have felt that their abilities *ought* to enable them to move into a "sister art," and they have tried their hand at something outside their specialty, usually with no great success. (William Blake, represented in this book by several poems, is often said to be the only figure in English arts who is significant both as a poet and as a painter.) For instance, the painter Edgar Degas (1834–1917) tried to write sonnets, but could not satisfy even himself. When he complained to his friend, the poet Stéphane Mallarmé, that he couldn't write poems even though he had plenty of ideas, Mallarmé replied, "You don't write poems with ideas; you write them with words."

Painters have been moved, for many centuries, to illustrate texts. More than two thousand years ago the painters of Greek vases illustrated the Greek myths, and from the Middle Ages onward artists have illustrated the Bible. Conversely, poets have been moved to write about paintings or sculptures. In this chapter we reprint three poems about paintings by Brueghel, van Gogh, and Demuth.

Despite Mallarmé's witty remark that poems are made not with ideas but with words (and despite Archibald MacLeish's assertion, on page 814, that "A poem should not mean / But be"), poems use ideas, and they have meanings. When you read the poems that we include here along with paintings, you might think about some of the following questions:

- What is your own first response to the painting? (Using Google, find the images online.) In interpreting the painting, consider the subject matter, the composition (for instance, balanced masses, as opposed to an apparent lack of equilibrium), the technique (for instance, vigorous brushstrokes of thick